Praise for

"A PROBLEM FROM HELL"

Awards and Accolades

Winner of the Pulitzer Prize for the Best Book in Nonfiction

Winner of the Robert F. Kennedy Book Award

Winner of the National Book Critics Circle Award for General Nonfiction

Winner of the National Magazine Award for her *Atlantic Monthly* article "Bystanders to Genocide"

Winner of the Raphael Lemkin Award
(Institute for the Study of Genocide)

Winner of the J. Anthony Lukas Book Prize for the Best Book on American Political or Social Concern That Exemplifies Literary Grace and Commitment to Serious Research

Winner of the Anisfield-Wolf Book Award for Nonfiction
for Contributing to Our Understanding of Racism and Our Appreciation of the Rich Diversity of Human Culture

Short-listed for the *Los Angeles Times* Book Prize for the Best Book in Current Interest

Short-listed for the Arthur Ross Book Award for the
Best Book in International Affairs
(Council on Foreign Relations)

Short-listed for the Lionel Gelber Prize for the
Best Book in International Relations
(Munk Center for International Studies, Canada)

Best-of-the-Year and Notable Lists

New York Times Book Review
The Atlantic Monthly
San Francisco Chronicle
Washington Post
Chicago Tribune
Los Angeles Times
St. Louis Post-Dispatch
The Chronicle of Higher Education
Book magazine
Ms. magazine
Raleigh News & Observer
Kirkus Reviews (starred review)
The Globe and Mail (Toronto)
Publishers Weekly (starred review)

"Forceful. . . . Power tells this long, sorry history with great clarity and vividness. She is particularly good at bringing alive various people who were eyewitnesses to these catastrophes as they were happening and who tried to make Americans share their outrage." —Adam Hochschild, *Washington Post*

"Anyone who wants to understand why America has permanently entered a new era in international relations must read *'A Problem from Hell.'* . . . Vividly written and thoroughly researched." —Jacob Heilbrun, *Los Angeles Times*

"Power expertly documents American passivity. . . . This vivid and gripping work of American history . . . gives us a Washington that is vibrant, complex, and refreshingly human." —Laura Secor, *New York Times Book Review*

"Nothing less than a masterwork of contemporary journalism. . . . Extraordinary. . . . Everybody in the foreign policy apparatus of the American government must read it. . . . An angry, brilliant, fiercely useful, absolutely essential book." —*The New Republic*

"Agonizingly persuasive. . . . The main part of Samantha Power's extremely important and highly readable book is devoted to the century's subsequent history of almost unchecked genocide, and the lack of practical response to it, especially in the United States." —Brian Urquhart, *New York Review of Books*

"Disturbing. . . . Power's book will likely become the standard text on genocide prevention because it thoroughly debunks the usual excuses for past failures, while offering a persuasive framework that can help predict future outcomes and suggest policy responses. It is also engaging and well written. . . . This should be enough to guarantee that it will be widely read by both students and policy makers." —Chaim Kaufman, *Foreign Affairs*

"[A] magisterial chronicle. . . . Though clearly imbued with a sense of outrage, Power is judicious in her portraits of those who opposed intervention, and keenly aware of the perils and costs of military action. Her indictment of U.S. policy is therefore all the more damning." —*The New Yorker*

"It's one of those rare books that can change one's thinking. I think it's going to have a lasting impact. It's very painful reading, but it has to be read." —Richard Holbrooke, former U.S. ambassador to the United Nations

"[Power] asks us to consider what the obligations of a democratic world power, empire or no, should be. . . . A gripping work of historical analysis written with much care . . . that will move and outrage any reader."

—Matthew Price, *Chicago Tribune*

"Does a masterful job of conveying important, clear, and faultlessly non-hysterical information and interpretation on so many dark episodes in recent human history. . . . Power does not preach, and she does not pontificate. What she does, gently but insistently, is to prod."   —Steve Kettmann, *San Francisco Chronicle*

"Her book is one of those rare volumes that makes news, that is so original on a topic of such importance that it must be read. . . . Power is such a skillful author— she has produced a book brilliantly conceived, superbly researched, mixing passion and erudition—it must be placed in the 'must read' category for both misanthropes and lovers of humanity, for isolationists and internationalists alike."

—Steve Weinberg, *Denver Post*

"By building [the cases] into a larger story shaped by a compelling argument, she takes her book beyond journalism to something approaching moral and political philosophy. . . . Ms. Power sets this expanded American story within a still larger, more than American story of the advance of international law. It is here that her book achieves both its greatest intellectual depth and its most powerful forward momentum."   —Jack Miles, *New York Observer*

"Samantha Power's groundbreaking book explores the essential question of why the United States has so often been slow to respond to clear evidence of genocide. Power . . . elegantly makes her case that U.S. government officials not only knew of the genocides occurring in Cambodia, Iraq, Bosnia, and Rwanda but in some cases took steps to cover it up, while other heroic individuals were risking their careers and lives to stop it."   —Nan Goldberg, *Newark Star-Ledger*

"A superb analysis of the U.S. government's evident unwillingness to intervene in ethnic slaughter. . . . A well-reasoned argument for the moral necessity of halting genocide wherever it occurs, and an unpleasant reminder of our role in enabling it, however unwittingly."   —*Kirkus Reviews* (starred review)

"The emotional force of Power's argument is carried by moving, sometimes almost unbearable stories of the victims and survivors of brutality. . . . This is a well-researched and powerful study that is both a history and a call to action."

—*Publishers Weekly* (starred review)

"A towering history of the inadequacy of American responses to genocide. . . . The challenge is to make genocide real for the American public. Power's own work is an important contribution to that effort, and deserves a wide reading."
—Siddharth Mohandas, *American Prospect*

"Some books elegantly record history; some books make history. This book does both. Power brings a storyteller's gift for gripping narrative together with a reporter's hunger for the inside story. Drawing on newly declassified documents and scores of exclusive interviews, she has produced an unforgettable history of Americans who stood up and stood by in the face of genocide. It is a history of our country that has never before been told, and it should change the way we see America and its role in the world."
—Doris Kearns Goodwin, author of *No Ordinary Time: Franklin and Eleanor Roosevelt: The Home Front in World War II*

"This is a serious and compelling work, and should be read by policy makers everywhere, before they confront the genocides that are waiting in the wings."
—Paul M. Kennedy, Dilworth Professor of History and Director, International Security Studies, Yale University

"Samantha Power has written one of those rare books that is truly as important as its subject. With great narrative verve, and a sober and subtle intelligence, she carries us deep behind the scenes of history-in-the-making to map the gray zones of diplomatic politics where the rhetoric of best intentions founders against inertia and inaction."
—Philip Gourevitch, author of *We Wish to Inform You That Tomorrow We Will Be Killed with Our Families: Stories from Rwanda*

"American officials have been highly inventive in finding arguments not to breach sovereignty and engage in common action to stop genocide. Timidity and tradition have resulted in endless horror and terror. Samantha Power writes with an admirable mix of erudition and passion, she focuses fiercely on the human costs of indifference and passivity, and she instills shame and dismay in the reader."
—Stanley Hoffmann, Buttenwieser University Professor, Harvard University

"Power gives us the behind-the-scenes story of how and why policy makers made the decisions they did, and she offers recommendations for improving our individual and collective response. This is a moving account of how millions of lives were lost."
—former Senate majority leader George J. Mitchell (D.-Maine)

"Samantha Power has written a much-needed and powerful book exposing our unreadiness to fulfill the commitment implied by 'never again.' Her research is pathbreaking; and her writing is lucid, nuanced, and compelling. This is a work of landmark significance."

—Aryeh Neier, president of the Open Society Institute and author of
War Crimes: Brutality, Genocide, Terror, and the Struggle for Justice

"Power . . . writes compellingly of the major and lesser massacres of our time. . . . This is a powerful book, and is so skillfully written that at more than 600 pages it still manages to be a compelling read."   —John Leonard, *New York Newsday*

"A marvelous book. . . . She brings to her narrative the conviction and drive of investigative reporting at its best. . . . She also brings to it the rigour of a scholar trained in law. Many academics have forgotten how to research and tell a story so as actually to engage the reader. Power meets this challenge magnificently. This is one of the few key books of the decade so far, required reading for any student of history, law, philosophy, or foreign policy."

—David M. Malone, president of the International Peace Academy,
The Globe and Mail (Toronto)

"Make[s] important contributions to our understanding of today's international turbulence and uncertainty. . . . Fascinating and disturbing."

—Stephen Holmes, *London Review of Books*

"Samantha Power has written one of those rare books that will not only endure as an authoritative history but is a timely and important contribution to a critical policy debate."   —Derek Chollet, *Policy Review*

"Regardless of what one believes about what the United States could have and should have done to stop the killings, Power's book raises vital questions. It deserves the most serious possible response."   —Charles Peña, *Reason*

"Power's critique of American policy is devastating and fully substantiated by the evidence she brings to bear."

—Warren I. Cohen, *Times Literary Supplement*

"Samantha Power has written a profoundly important book. She revives enduring and troubling questions about government policy toward genocide. We are in her debt."   —Emran Qureshi, *National Post*

"Power wrote the book to find out why America didn't respond. And her book is a remarkable effort to answer that question."
—Pat Reed, *Santa Fe New Mexican*

"Superb. . . . A stunning history of modern genocide that should be read by anyone who makes foreign policy or cares about America's role in the world."
—Philip Seib, *Dallas Morning News*

"*'A Problem from Hell'* forces us to come to terms with the difficult recognition that in many important ways we have all been bystanders to genocide."
—*Ethics and International Affairs*

"A persuasive and credible history of genocide, accompanied by an eloquent call to action . . . with an impressive touch of sensitivity."
—Dennis Lythgoe, *Deseret News*

"A magisterial history of genocide. . . . [Power] has found new and fascinatingly detailed ways to tell these tragic stories."   —Salon.com

"A damning indictment of American passivity in the face of some of history's worst crimes. Power builds her case carefully, sifting through reams of media accounts, interviews, and newly declassified government documents."
—Jonathan Tepperman, *Newsweek International*

"The myriad horror stories of this age of genocide have many ugly characters, several of whom Power profiles in her well-written and extensively documented book."   —Joseph Nevins, *The Nation*

"Historical reckoning takes time. . . . Power has pushed that process through sheer personal engagement and intellectual ferocity. Whatever has been written and released, she has read. Whoever might speak, she has spoken to. However we might evade the facts, she has gathered and explained them here. . . . Power's book should be read cover to cover, literally."
—Jennifer Leaning, *Harvard Magazine*

"Bracing . . . one of the decade's most important books on U.S. foreign policy. . . . Power [is] the new conscience of the U.S. foreign-policy establishment."
—Romesh Ratnesar, *Time*

"Magisterial." —*The New Yorker*

"Disturbing . . . engaging and well written . . . will likely become the standard text on genocide prevention."—*Foreign Affairs*

"An angry, brilliant, fiercely useful, absolutely essential book."—*The New Republic*

"Forceful. . . . Power tells this long, sorry history with great clarity and vividness." —*Washington Post*

"Agonizingly persuasive." —*New York Review of Books*

"Avoids partisan finger-pointing [and] is a clarion call for America to remain an engaged moral power." —*Weekly Standard*

"Bracing. . . . Power [is] the new conscience of the U.S. foreign-policy establishment." —*Time*

"A damning indictment of American passivity in the face of some of history's worse crimes." —*Newsweek International*

"A superb piece of reporting which cumulatively grows into a major political work, part polemic, part moral philosophy . . . Power's book makes a major contribution to that debate and is required reading for anyone inclined to take part." —*The Guardian*

"Substantial and highly impressive." —*The Sunday Telegraph*

"Brilliant and angry . . . It makes for shocking, dreadful, compelling reading . . . In short, Power's work is a master-class of history, law and politics and is a required read for anyone concerned with the prevention of grave human rights abuse." —Amnesty International UK

"Stunning narrative . . . Samantha Power has written one of those rare books that will not only endure as an authoritative history, but is a timely and important contribution to a critical policy debate. Washington officials would be wise to heed its lessons." —Hoover Institution

"Groundbreaking. . . . Power elegantly makes her case." —*Newark Star-Ledger*

"Compelling. . . . Power leads her readers on a long and often gut-wrenching journey. . . . Power's book raises vital questions." —*Reason*

"Brilliantly conceived, superbly researched, mixing passion and erudition—it must be placed in the 'must read' category." —*Denver Post*

"The emotional force of Power's argument is carried by moving, sometimes almost unbearable stories of the victims and survivors."
—*Publishers Weekly*, starred review

"A superb analysis of the US government's evident unwillingness to intervene in ethnic slaughter" —*Kirkus*, starred review

"[*A Problem from Hell*] challenges our conscience and should influence what we do in the future."—Lawrence H. Summers, President Emeritus, Harvard University

"[Power] is one of the most striking talents to emerge in the human rights field in a long time." —Aryeh Neier, founder of Human Rights Watch

"One of those rare books that can change one's thinking . . . very painful reading, but it has to be read." —Former UN Ambassador Richard Holbrooke

"This is a moving account of how millions of lives were lost."
—Former Senate Majority Leader George J. Mitchell

"A serious and compelling work . . . should be read by policy makers everywhere."
—Paul M. Kennedy, author of *The Rise and Fall of the Great Powers*

"Power writes with an admirable mix of erudition and passion . . . [and] focuses fiercely on the human costs of indifference and passivity."
—Stanley Hoffmann, Buttenwieser University Professor, Harvard University

"Samantha Power has written one of those rare books that is truly as important as its subject." —Philip Gourevitch, author of *We Wish To Inform You That Tomorrow We Will Be Killed With Our Families*

"Avoids partisan finger-pointing [and] is a clarion call for America to remain an engaged moral power." —*Weekly Standard*

"A PROBLEM FROM HELL"

America and the Age of Genocide

Samantha Power

BASIC BOOKS
A Member of the Perseus Books Group
New York

Copyright © 2002, 2003, 2007, 2013 by Samantha Power

Published in 2013 by Basic Books,
A Member of the Perseus Books Group
Previously published in paperback by HarperCollins in 2003 and 2007.

Books published by Basic Books are available at special discounts for bulk purchases in the United States by corporations, institutions, and other organizations. For more information, please contact the Special Markets Department at the Perseus Books Group, 2300 Chestnut Street, Suite 200, Philadelphia, PA 19103, or call (800) 810-4145, ext. 5000, or e-mail special.markets@perseusbooks.com.

A CIP catalog record for this book is available from the Library of Congress.
ISBN: 978-0-465-06150-1 (hardcover)
ISBN: 978-0-465-06151-8 (paperback)
ISBN: 978-0-465-05089-5 (e-book)

10 9 8 7 6 5

For Mum and Eddie

"We—even we here—hold the power, and bear the responsibility."

—ABRAHAM LINCOLN

Contents

Preface

My introduction to Sidbela Zimic, a nine-year-old Sarajevan, came unexpectedly one Sunday in June 1995. Several hours after hearing the familiar whistle and crash of a nearby shell, I traveled a few blocks to one of the neighborhood's once-formidable apartment houses. Its battered façade bore the signature pockmarks left from three years of shrapnel spray and gunfire. The building lacked windows, electricity, gas, and water. It was uninhabitable to all but Sarajevo's proud residents, who had no place else to go.

Sidbela's teenage sister was standing not far from the entrance to the apartment, dazed. A shallow pool of crimson lay beside her on the playground, where one blue slipper, two red slippers, and a jump rope with ice-cream-cone handles had been cast down. Bosnian police had covered the reddened spot of pavement with plastic wrapping that bore the cheery baby blue and white emblem of the United Nations.

Sidbela had been known in the neighborhood for her bookishness and her many "Miss" pageants. She and her playmates made the best of a childhood that constrained movement, crowning "Miss Apartment Building," "Miss Street Corner," and "Miss Neighborhood." On that still morning, Sidbela had begged her mother for five minutes of fresh air.

Mrs. Zimic was torn. A year and a half before, in February 1994, just two blocks from the family's home, a shell had landed in the main downtown market, tearing sixty-eight shoppers and vendors to bits. The graphic images from this massacre generated widespread American sympathy and galvanized President Bill Clinton and his NATO allies. They issued an unprecedented ultimatum, in which they threatened massive air strikes against the Bosnian Serbs if they resumed their bombardment of Sarajevo or continued what Clinton described as the "murder of innocents."

"No one should doubt NATO's resolve," Clinton warned. "Anyone," he said, repeating the word for effect, "*anyone* shelling Sarajevo must . . . be prepared to deal with the consequences."[1] In response to America's perceived commitment, Sarajevo's 280,000 residents gradually adjusted to life under NATO's imperfect but protective umbrella. After a few cautious months, they began trickling outside, strolling along the Miljacka River and rebuilding cafes with outdoor terraces. Young boys and girls bounded out of dank cellars and out of their parents' lines of vision to rediscover outdoor sports. Tasting childhood, they became greedy for sunlight and play. Their parents thanked the United States and heaped praise upon Americans who visited the Bosnian capital.

But American resolve soon wilted. Saving Bosnian lives was not deemed worth risking U.S. soldiers or challenging America's European allies who wanted to remain neutral. Clinton and his team shifted from the language of genocide to that of "tragedy" and "civil war," downplaying public expectations that there was anything the United States could do. Secretary of State Warren Christopher had never been enthusiastic about U.S. involvement in the Balkans. He had long appealed to context to ease the moral discomfort that arose from America's nonintervention. "It's really a tragic problem," Christopher said. "The hatred between all three groups—the Bosnians and the Serbs and the Croatians—is almost unbelievable. It's almost terrifying, and it's centuries old. That really is a problem from hell."[2] Within months of the market massacre, Clinton had adopted this mindset, treating Bosnia as *his* problem from hell—a problem he hoped would burn itself out, disappear from the front pages, and leave his presidency alone.

Serb nationalists took their cue. They understood that they were free to resume shelling Sarajevo and other Bosnian towns crammed with civilians. Parents were left battling their children and groping for inducements that might keep them indoors. Sidbela's father remembered, "I converted the washroom into a playroom. I bought the children Barbie dolls, Barbie cars, everything, just to keep them inside." But his precocious daughter had her way, pressing, "Daddy, please let me live my life. I can't stay at home all the time."

America's promises, which Serb gunners took seriously at first, bought Sarajevans a brief reprieve. But they also raised expectations among Bosnians that they were safe to live again. As it turned out, the brutality of Serb political, military, and paramilitary leaders would be met with condemnation but not with the promised military intervention.

On June 25, 1995, minutes after Sidbela kissed her mother on the cheek and flashed a triumphant smile, a Serb shell crashed into the playground where she, eleven-year-old Amina Pajevic, twelve-year-old Liljana Janjic, and five-year-old Maja Skoric were jumping rope. All were killed, raising the total number of children slaughtered in Bosnian territory during the war from 16,767 to 16,771.

*   *   *

If any event could have prepared a person to imagine evil, it should have been this one. I had been reporting from Bosnia for nearly two years at the time of the playground massacre. I had long since given up hope that the NATO jets that roared overhead every day would bomb the Serbs into ceasing their artillery assault on the besieged capital. And I had come to expect only the worst for Muslim civilians scattered throughout the country.

Yet when Bosnian Serb forces began attacking the so-called "safe area" of Srebrenica on July 6, 1995, ten days after I visited the grieving Zimic family, I was not especially alarmed. I thought that even the Bosnian Serbs would not dare to seize a patch of land under UN guard. On the evening of July 10, I casually dropped by the Associated Press house, which had become my adopted home for the summer because of its spirited reporters and its functional generator. When I arrived that night, I received a jolt. There was complete chaos around the phones. The Serb attack on Srebrenica that had been "deteriorating" for several days had suddenly "gone to hell." The Serbs were poised to take the town, and they had issued an ultimatum, demanding that the UN peacekeepers there surrender their weapons and equipment or face a barrage of shelling. Some 40,000 Muslim men, women, and children were in grave danger.

Although I had been slow to grasp the magnitude of the offensive, it was not too late to meet my American deadlines. A morning story in the *Washington Post* might shame U.S. policymakers into responding. So frantic were the other correspondents that it took me fifteen minutes to secure a free phone line. When I did, I reached Ed Cody, the *Post*'s deputy foreign editor. I knew American readers had tired of bad news from the Balkans, but the stakes of this particular attack seemed colossal. Bosnian Serb general Ratko Mladic was not dabbling or using a petty landgrab to send a political signal; he was taking a huge chunk of internationally "protected" territory and challenging the world to stop him. I began spewing the facts to Cody as I understood them: "The Serbs are closing in on the Srebrenica safe area. The UN says tens of thousands of Muslim refugees have already poured into their base north of the town center. It's only a matter of hours before the Serbs take the whole pocket. This is a catastrophe in the making. A United Nations safe area is going to fall."

A new contributor to the *Post,* I had been advised that Cody, a veteran of carnage in the Middle East, would not be one to get easily rattled. In this instance he heard me out and then posed a few incisive questions—questions that led me to believe he had understood the severity of the crisis unfolding. Then he stunned me: "Well, from what you are telling me, even if things proceed, the Serbs are not going to take the town tonight." I grimaced in anticipation of his next sentence, which duly followed. "It sounds like *when* Srebrenica falls, we'll have a story."

I protested, but not strenuously. I was half sure the Serbs would back down and was reluctant to cry wolf. By the following afternoon, however, Srebrenica had fallen, and the petrified inhabitants of the enclave were in the hands of General Mladic, a suspected war criminal known to have orchestrated the savage siege of Sarajevo.

I had worked in Sarajevo, where Serb snipers took target practice on bundled old ladies hauling canisters of filthy water across town and where picturesque parks had been transformed into cemeteries to accommodate the deluge of young arrivals. I had interviewed emaciated men who had dropped forty and fifty pounds and who bore permanent scars from their time in Serb concentration camps. And I had only recently covered the massacre of four schoolgirls. Yet despite my experiences, or perhaps because of them, I could only imagine what I had already witnessed. It never dawned on me that General Mladic would or could systematically execute every last Muslim man and boy in his custody.

A few days after Srebrenica fell, a colleague of mine telephoned from New York and said the Bosnian ambassador to the UN was claiming that the Bosnian Serbs had murdered more than 1,000 Muslim men from Srebrenica in a football stadium. It was not possible. "No," I said simply. My friend repeated the charge. "No," I said again, determined.

I was right. Mladic did not execute 1,000 men. He killed more than 7,000.

*   *   *

When I returned to the United States, Sidbela and Srebrenica stayed with me. I was chilled by the promise of protection that had drawn a child out of a basement and onto an exposed Sarajevan playground. I was haunted by the murder of Srebrenica's Muslim men and boys, my own failure to sound a proper early warning, and the outside world's refusal to intervene even once the men's peril had become obvious. I found myself flashing back to the many debates I had had with my colleagues about intervention. We had wondered aloud—at press briefings, on road trips, and in interviews with senior Bosnian and American officials—how the United States and its allies might have responded if the same crimes had been committed in a different place (the Balkans evoke age-old animosities and combustible tinderboxes), against different victims (most of the atrocities were committed against individuals of Muslim faith), or at a different time (the Soviet Union had just collapsed, no new world vision had yet replaced the old world order, and the United Nations had not oiled its rusty parts or rid itself of its anachronistic practices and assumptions). In 1996, with some distance from the field, I began exploring America's responses to previous cases of mass slaughter. It did not take long to discover that the American response to the Bosnia genocide was in fact the most robust of the century. The United States had never in its history intervened to stop genocide and had in fact rarely even made a point of condemning it as it occurred.

As I surveyed the major genocides of the twentieth century, a few stood out. In addition to the Bosnian Serbs' eradication of non-Serbs, I examined the Ottoman slaughter of the Armenians, the Nazi Holocaust, Pol Pot's terror in Cambodia, Saddam Hussein's destruction of Kurds in northern Iraq, and the Rwandan Hutus' systematic extermination of the Tutsi minority. Although the cases varied in scope and not all involved the intent to exterminate every last member of a group, each met the terms of the 1948 genocide convention and presented the United States with options for meaningful diplomatic, economic, legal, or military intervention. The crimes occurred in Europe, Asia, the Middle East, and Africa. The victims covered a spectrum of races and religions—they were Asian, African, Caucasian, Christian, Jewish, Buddhist, and Muslim. The perpetrators operated at different stages of American might: The Armenian genocide (1915–1916) was committed during World War I, before the United States had become a world leader. The Holocaust (1939–1945) took place just as the United States was moving into that role. The Cambodian (1975–1979) and Iraqi (1987–1988) genocides were perpetrated after the Holocaust but during the Cold War and after Vietnam. Bosnia (1992–1995) and Rwanda (1994) happened after the Cold War and while American supremacy and awareness of the "lessons" of the Holocaust were at their height. U.S. decisionmakers also brought a wide variety of backgrounds and foreign policy ideologies to the table. Every American president in office in the last three decades of the twentieth century—Nixon, Ford, Carter, Reagan, Bush, and Clinton—made decisions related to the prevention and suppression of genocide. Yet notwithstanding all the variety among cases and within U.S. administrations, the U.S. policy responses to genocide were astonishingly similar across time, geography, ideology, and geopolitical balance.

In order to understand U.S. responses to genocide, I interviewed more than 300 Americans who had a hand in shaping or influencing U.S. policy.* Most were officials of varying ranks at the White House, State Department, Pentagon, and Central Intelligence Agency (CIA). Some were lawmakers and staff members on Capitol Hill. Others were journalists who covered the carnage or nongovernmental advocates who attempted to ameliorate it. A grant from the Open Society Institute enabled me to travel to Bosnia, Cambodia, Kosovo, and Rwanda, where I spoke with victims, perpetrators, and bystanders. I also visited the international war crimes tribunal for the former Yugoslavia at The Hague in the Netherlands, as well the UN court for Rwanda, located in Arusha, Tanzania. Thanks to the National Security Archive, a nonprofit organization that uses the Freedom of Information Act to secure the release of classified U.S. documents, I was able to draw on hundreds of pages of newly available government records. This material provides a clearer picture than was previously discernible of the interplay among people, motives, and genocidal events.

People have explained U.S. failures to respond to specific genocides by claiming that the United States didn't know what was happening, that it knew but didn't care, or that regardless of what it knew, there was nothing useful to be done. I have found that in fact U.S. policymakers knew a great deal about the crimes being perpetrated. Some Americans cared and fought for action, making considerable personal and professional sacrifices. And the United States did have countless opportunities to mitigate and prevent slaughter. But time and again, decent men and women chose to look away. We have all been bystanders to genocide. The crucial question is why.

---

*Quotes that are not sourced in the notes are taken from these exclusive interviews, conducted between July 1993 and November 2001. I have introduced these quotations using the present tense (e.g., "Senator McGovern recalls . . . ").

The answers seemed to lie in the critical decisions—and decisions not to decide—made before, during, and after the various genocides. In exploring a century of U.S. reactions to genocide, I asked: Were there early warnings that mass killing was set to commence? How seriously were the warnings taken? By whom? Was there any reason to believe the violence expected would be qualitatively or quantitatively different from the "run-of-the-mill" killings that were sadly typical of local warfare? Once the violence began, what classified or open intelligence was available? What constraints operated to impede diagnosis? How and when did U.S. officials recognize that genocide was under way? Who inside or outside the U.S. government wanted to do what? What were the risks or costs? Who opposed them? Who prevailed? How did public opinion and elite opinion diverge? And finally, how were the U.S. responses, the genocides, and the Americans who urged intervention remembered later? In reconstructing a narrative of events, I have divided most of the cases into warning, recognition, response, and aftermath sections.

Contrary to any assumption I may have harbored while I traveled around the former Yugoslavia, the Bush and Clinton administrations' responses to atrocities in Bosnia were consistent with prior American responses to genocide. Early warnings of massive bloodshed proliferated. The spewing of inflammatory propaganda escalated. The massacres and deportations started. U.S. policymakers struggled to wrap their minds around the horrors. Refugee stories and press reports of atrocities became too numerous to deny. Few Americans at home pressed for intervention. A hopeful but passive and ultimately deadly American waiting game commenced. And genocide proceeded unimpeded by U.S. action and often emboldened by U.S. inaction.

The book's major findings can be summarized as follows:

- Despite graphic media coverage, American policymakers, journalists, and citizens are extremely slow to muster the imagination needed to reckon with evil. Ahead of the killings, they assume rational actors will not inflict seemingly gratuitous violence. They trust in good-faith negotiations and traditional diplomacy. Once the killings start, they assume that civilians who keep their heads down will be left alone. They urge ceasefires and donate humanitarian aid.

- It is in the realm of domestic politics that the battle to stop genocide is lost. American political leaders interpret society-wide silence as an indicator of public indifference. They reason that they will incur no costs if the United States remains uninvolved but will face steep risks if they engage. Potential sources of influence—lawmakers on Capitol Hill, editorial boards, non-governmental groups, and ordinary constituents—do not generate political pressure sufficient to change the calculus of America's leaders.

- The U.S. government not only abstains from sending its troops, but it takes very few steps along a continuum of intervention to deter genocide.

- U.S. officials spin themselves (as well as the American public) about the nature of the violence in question and the likely impact of an American intervention. They render the bloodshed two-sided and inevitable, not genocidal. They insist that any proposed U.S. response will be futile. Indeed, it may even do more harm than good, bringing perverse consequences to the victims and jeopardizing other precious American moral or strategic interests.★ They brand as "emotional" those U.S. officials who urge intervention and who make moral arguments in a system that speaks principally in the cold language of interests. They avoid use of the word "genocide." Thus, they can in good conscience favor stopping genocide in the abstract, while simultaneously opposing American involvement in the moment.

The sharpest challenge to the world of bystanders is posed by those who have refused to remain silent in the age of genocide. In each case a few Americans stood out by standing up. They did not lose sight of right and wrong, even as they were repeatedly steered to a "context" that others said precluded action. They refused to accept either that they could not influence U.S. policy or that the United States could not influence the killers. These individuals were not alone in their struggles, but they were not in crowded company either. By seeing what they tried to get done, we see what America

---

★I borrow the categories of justification—futility, perversity, and jeopardy—from Albert O. Hirschman's *Rhetoric of Reaction: Perversity, Futility, Jeopardy* (Cambridge, Mass.: Belknap Press, 1991). Hirschman shows how those who oppose action tend to take issue not with the goals of the proposed measure but with its likely "unintended consequences."

could have done. We also see what we might ourselves have attempted. By seeing how and why they failed, we see what we as a nation let happen.

In 1915 Henry Morgenthau Sr., the U.S. ambassador in Constantinople, responded to Turkey's deportation and slaughter of its Armenian minority by urging Washington to condemn Turkey and pressure its wartime ally Germany. Morgenthau also defied diplomatic convention by personally protesting the atrocities, denouncing the regime, and raising money for humanitarian relief. He was joined by former president Theodore Roosevelt, who went a step further, calling on the administration of Woodrow Wilson to enter World War I and forcibly stop the slaughter. But the United States clung to its neutrality and insisted that Turkey's internal affairs were not its business. An estimated 1 million Armenians were murdered or died of disease and starvation during the genocide.

Raphael Lemkin, a Polish Jew and international lawyer, warned about Hitler's designs in the 1930s but was scoffed at. After finding refuge in the United States in 1941, he failed to win support for any measure to protect imperiled Jews. The Allies resisted denouncing Hitler's atrocities, granting refuge to Europe's Jewry, and bombing the railroad tracks to the Nazi concentration camps. Undaunted, Lemkin invented the word "genocide" and secured the passage of the first-ever United Nations human rights treaty, which was devoted to banning the new crime. Sadly, he lived to see the genocide convention rebuffed by the U.S. Senate. William Proxmire, the quixotic U.S. senator from Wisconsin, picked up where Lemkin left off and delivered 3,211 speeches on the Senate floor urging ratification of the UN treaty. After nineteen years of daily soliloquies, Proxmire did manage to get the Senate to accept the genocide convention, but the U.S. ratification was so laden with caveats that it carried next to no force.

A handful of U.S. diplomats and journalists in Cambodia warned of the depravity of a sinister band of Communist rebels known as the Khmer Rouge. They were derided by the American left for falling for anti-Communist propaganda, and they failed to influence a U.S. policy that could not contemplate engagement of any kind in Southeast Asia after Vietnam. Pol Pot's four-year reign left some 2 million Cambodians dead, but the massacres elicited barely a whimper from Washington, which maintained diplomatic recognition of the genocidal regime even after it had been overthrown.

Peter Galbraith, a staff member of the Senate Foreign Relations Committee, drafted punishing legislation for his boss, Senator Claiborne

Pell, that would have cut off U.S. agricultural and manufacturing credits to Saddam Hussein in retaliation for his 1987–1988 attempt to wipe out Iraq's rural Kurds. The sanctions package was defeated by a determined White House, State Department, and U.S. farm lobby, which were eager to maintain friendly ties and sell rice and wheat to Iraq. And so Hussein's regime received generous American financial support while it gassed and executed some 100,000 Kurds.

Romeo Dallaire, a Canadian major general who commanded UN peacekeeping forces in Rwanda in 1994, appealed for permission to disarm militias and to prevent the extermination of Rwanda's Tutsi three months before the genocide began. Denied this by his political masters at the United Nations, he watched corpses pile up around him as Washington led a successful effort to remove most of the peacekeepers under his command and then aggressively worked to block authorization of UN reinforcements. The United States refused to use its technology to jam radio broadcasts that were a crucial instrument in the coordination and perpetuation of the genocide. And even as, on average, 8,000 Rwandans were being butchered each day, the issue never became a priority for senior U.S. officials. Some 800,000 Rwandans were killed in 100 days.

A few diplomats at the State Department and several lawmakers on Capitol Hill relentlessly tried to convince an intransigent bureaucracy to bomb Serb ethnic cleansers in Bosnia. These men watched the sanitization of cables, the repackaging of the conflict as "intractable" and "ancient," and the maintenance of an arms embargo against Bosnia's outgunned Muslims. Several foreign service officers who quit the department in disgust then watched, from a no less frustrating perch outside the U.S. government, the fall of the Srebrenica safe area and the largest massacre in Europe in fifty years. Between 1992 and 1995, while the nightly news broadcast the Serb onslaught, some 200,000 Bosnians were killed. Only when U.S. military intervention came to feel unavoidable and Bob Dole, the Kansas Republican and Senate majority leader, had persuaded Congress to lift the arms embargo did U.S. policy change. By bringing the war in Bosnia home, Dole helped spur President Clinton to begin NATO bombing. By then, however, Bosnia's genocide had been largely completed, and a multiethnic state had been destroyed.

This book deliberately spotlights the response of *American* policymakers and citizens for several reasons. First, the United States' decisions to act or not to act have had a greater impact on the victims' fortunes than those of any other major power. Second, since World War II, the United States has had a tremendous capacity to curb genocide. It could have used its vast resources to do so without undermining U.S. security. Third, the United States has made an unusually pronounced commitment to Holocaust commemoration and education. The Holocaust Memorial Museum, which stands baldly on the Mall alongside the Lincoln Monument and the Jefferson Memorial and just yards from the Vietnam Veterans Memorial, draws 5,500 visitors a day, or 2 million per year, almost double the number of visitors tallied annually by the White House. Fourth, in recent years American leaders, steeped in a new culture of Holocaust awareness, have repeatedly committed themselves to preventing the recurrence of genocide. In 1979 President Jimmy Carter declared that out of the memory of the Holocaust, "we must forge an unshakable oath with all civilized people that never again will the world stand silent, never again will the world fail to act in time to prevent this terrible crime of genocide."[3] Five years later, President Ronald Reagan, too, declared. "Like you, I say in a forthright voice, 'Never again!'"[4] President George Bush Sr. joined the chorus in 1991. Speaking "as a World War II veteran, as an American, and now as President of the United States," Bush said his visit to Auschwitz had left him with "the determination, not just to remember, but also to act."[5] Before becoming president, candidate Clinton chided Bush over Bosnia. "If the horrors of the Holocaust taught us anything," Clinton said, "it is the high cost of remaining silent and paralyzed in the face of genocide."[6] Once in office, at the opening of the Holocaust Museum, Clinton faulted America's inaction during World War II. "Even as our fragmentary awareness of crimes grew into indisputable facts, far too little was done," he said. "We must not permit that to happen again."[7] But the forward-looking, consoling refrain of "never again," a testament to America's can-do spirit, never grappled with the fact that the country had done nothing, practically or politically, to prepare itself to respond to genocide. The commitment proved hollow in the face of actual slaughter.

Before I began exploring America's relationship with genocide, I used to refer to U.S. policy toward Bosnia as a "failure." I have changed my mind. It is daunting to acknowledge, but this country's consistent policy of nonintervention in the face of genocide offers sad testimony not to a broken American political system but to one that is ruthlessly effective. The system, as it stands now, *is working*.[8] No U.S. president has ever made genocide prevention a priority, and no U.S. president has ever suffered politically for his indifference to its occurrence. It is thus no coincidence that genocide rages on.

"A PROBLEM FROM HELL"

Chapter 1

"Race
Murder"

Trial by Fire

On March 14, 1921, on a damp day in the Charlottenburg district of Berlin, a twenty-four-year-old Armenian crept up behind a man in a heavy gray overcoat swinging his cane. The Armenian, Soghomon Tehlirian, placed a revolver at the back of the man's head and pulled the trigger, shouting, "This is to avenge the death of my family!" The burly target crumpled. If you had heard the shot and spotted the rage distorting the face of the young offender, you might have suspected that you were witnessing a murder to avenge a very different kind of crime. But back then you would not have known to call the crime in question "genocide." The word did not yet exist.

Tehlirian, the Armenian assassin, was quickly tackled. As pedestrians beat him with their fists and house keys, he shouted in broken German, "I foreigner, he foreigner, this not hurt Germany. . . . It's nothing to do with you."[1] It was national justice carried out in an international setting. Tehlirian had just murdered Mehmed Talaat, the former Turkish interior minister who had set out to rid Turkey of its Armenian "problem." In 1915 Talaat had presided over the killing by firing squad, bayoneting, bludgeoning, and starvation of nearly 1 million Armenians.[2]

The outside world had known that the Armenians were at grave risk well before Talaat and the Young Turk leadership ordered their deportation.

When Turkey entered World War I on the side of Germany against Britain, France, and Russia, Talaat made it clear that the empire would target its Christian subjects. In January 1915, in remarks reported by the *New York Times,* Talaat said that there was no room for Christians in Turkey and that their supporters should advise them to clear out.[3] By late March Turkey had begun disarming Armenian men serving in the Ottoman army. On April 25, 1915, the day the Allies invaded Turkey, Talaat ordered the roundup and execution of some 250 leading Armenian intellectuals in Constantinople. In each of Turkey's six eastern provinces, local Armenian notables met roughly the same fate. Armenian men in rural areas were initially enlisted as pack animals to transport Turkish supplies to the front, but soon even this was deemed too dignified an existence for the traitorous Christians. Churches were desecrated. Armenian schools were closed, and those teachers who refused to convert to Islam were killed. All over Anatolia the authorities posted deportation orders requiring the Armenians to relocate to camps prepared in the deserts of Syria. In fact, the Turkish authorities knew that no facilities had been prepared, and more than half of the deported Armenians died on the way. "By continuing the deportation of the orphans to their destinations during the intense cold," Talaat wrote, "we are ensuring their eternal rest."[4]

"Official proclamations," like this one from June 1915, cropped up around town:

> Our Armenian fellow countrymen, . . . because . . . they have . . . attempted to destroy the peace and security of the Ottoman state, . . . have to be sent away to places which have been prepared in the interior. . . and a literal obedience to the following orders, in a categorical manner, is accordingly enjoined upon all Ottomans:
>
> 1. With the exception of the sick, all Armenians are obliged to leave within five days from the date of this proclamation. . . .
> 2. Although they are free to carry with them on their journey the articles of their movable property which they desire, they are forbidden to sell their land and their extra effects, or to leave them here and there with other people. . . .[5]

The Young Turks—Talaat; Enver Pasha, the minister of war; and Djemal Pasha, the minister of public works—justified the wholesale deportation of the Armenians by claiming that it was necessary to suppress Armenian revolts.[6]

Haitenik Archives

Soghomon Tehlirian

When Russia had declared war on Turkey the previous year, it had invited Armenians living within Turkey to rise up against Ottoman rule, which a small minority did. Although two prominent Ottoman Armenians led a pair of czarist volunteer corps to fight Turkey, most expressed loyalty to Constantinople. But this did not stop the Turkish leadership from using the pretext of an Armenian "revolutionary uprising" and the cover of war to eradicate the Armenian presence in Turkey. Very few of those killed were plotting anything other than survival. The atrocities were carried out against women, children, and unarmed men. They were not incidental "by-products" of war but in fact resulted from carefully crafted decisions made by Turkey's leaders.

In June 1915 Erzindjan, the hometown of Talaat's eventual assassin, was emptied. Soghomon Tehlirian, then nineteen, marched in a column of some 20,000 people, with his mother and siblings—two sisters of fifteen and sixteen, another of twenty-six who carried a two-and-a-half-year-old child, and two brothers of twenty-two and twenty-six. The journey was harrowing. The gendarmes said to be protecting the convoy first dragged Tehlirian's sisters off behind the bushes to rape them. Next he watched a man split his twenty-two-year-old brother's head open with an ax. Finally,

Project SAVE Armenian Photograph Archives, courtesy of John Mirak

Armenian children at the Apostolic Church School in the village of Arapgir in the Ottoman Empire. Only four of the children survived the Turkish slaughter.

the soldiers shot his mother and struck Tehlirian unconscious with a blow to the head. He was left for dead and awoke hours later in a field of corpses. He spotted the mangled body of a sister and the shattered skull of his brother. His other relatives had disappeared. He guessed he was the sole survivor of the caravan.[7]

Recognition

The "international community," such as it was, did little to contest the Turkish horrors, which began nine months into World War I. Germany was aligned with the brutal regime and thus was best positioned to influence it. Instead, German officials generally covered up Talaat's campaign, ridiculing the Allied accounts of the terror as "pure inventions" and "gross exaggerations." The Germans echoed the Turks' claims that any harsh policies were a measured response to Armenian treason during wartime.[8] The German

chancellor met in person with German Christian missionaries who presented eyewitness testimony about the slaughter. But he rejected their
appeals. Berlin would not offend its Turkish ally.

Britain and France were at war with the Ottoman Empire and publicized the atrocities. The British Foreign Office dug up photographs of the
massacre victims and the Armenian refugees in flight. An aggressive,
London-based, pro-Armenian lobby helped spur the British press to cover
the savagery.[9] But some had trouble believing the tales. British foreign secretary Sir Edward Grey, for one, cautioned that Britain lacked "direct
knowledge" of massacres. He urged that "the massacres were not all on one
side" and warned that denunciation would likely be futile. Indeed, when
Russia's foreign minister drafted a public threat that he hoped the Allies
could issue jointly, Grey said he doubted that the message would influence
Turkish behavior and might even cause Turkey to adopt more serious
measures against the Armenians.[10] Since Britain was already at war with
Turkey, other British officials argued that the most expedient way to end
the killings would be to defeat the German-Austrian-Turkish alliance. On
May 24, 1915, the Allied governments did deliver a joint declaration that
took the unprecedented step of condemning "crimes against humanity and
civilization." The declaration warned the members of the Turkish government that they and their "agents" would be held "personally responsible"
for the massacres.[11] Generally, though, the Allies were busy trying to win
the war. At the same time the Turks were waging their campaign against
the Armenian minority, the German army was using poison gas against the
Allies in Belgium. In May 1915 the German army had torpedoed the
Lusitania passenger liner, killing 1,200 (including 190 Americans). The
Germans had also just begun zeppelin attacks against London.[12]

The United States, determined to maintain its neutrality in the war,
refused to join the Allied declaration. President Woodrow Wilson chose not
to pressure either the Turks or their German backers. It was better not to
draw attention to the atrocities, lest U.S. public opinion get stirred up and
begin demanding U.S. involvement. Because the Turks had not violated the
rights of Americans, Wilson did not formally protest.

But in Turkey itself America's role as bystander was contested. Henry
Morgenthau Sr., a German-born Jew who had come to the United States
as a ten-year-old boy and had been appointed ambassador to the Ottoman
Empire by President Wilson in 1913, agitated for U.S. diplomatic intervention. In January and February 1915, Morgenthau had begun receiving

graphic but fragmentary intelligence from his ten American consuls posted throughout the Ottoman Empire. At first he did not recognize that the atrocities against the Armenians were of a different nature than the wartime violence. He was taken in by Talaat's assurances that uncontrolled elements had simply embarked upon "mob violence" that would soon be contained.[13] In April, when the massacres began in earnest, the Turkish authorities severed Morgenthau's communication with his consuls and censored their letters. Morgenthau was reluctant to file reports back to Washington based on rumors, and the Turks were making it impossible for him to fact-check.

Although he was initially incredulous, by July 1915 the ambassador had come around. He had received too many visits from desperate Armenians and trusted missionary sources to remain skeptical. They had sat in his office with tears streaming down their faces, regaling him with terrifying tales. When he compared this testimony to the strikingly similar horrors relayed in the rerouted consular cables, Morgenthau came to an astonishing conclusion. What he called "race murder" was under way. On July 10, 1915, he cabled Washington with a description of the Turkish campaign:

> Persecution of Armenians assuming unprecedented proportions. Reports from widely scattered districts indicate systematic attempt to uproot peaceful Armenian populations and through arbitrary arrests, terrible tortures, whole-sale expulsions and deportations from one end of the Empire to the other accompanied by frequent instances of rape, pillage, and murder, turning into massacre, to bring destruction and destitution on them. These measures are not in response to popular or fanatical demand but are purely arbitrary and directed from Constantinople in the name of military necessity, often in districts where no military operations are likely to take place.

Response

Morgenthau was constrained by two background conditions that seemed immutable. First, the Wilson administration was resolved to stay out of World War I. Picking fights with Turkey did not seem a good way to advance that objective. And second, diplomatic protocol demanded that ambassadors act respectfully toward their host governments. U.S. diplomats were expected to

Henry Morgenthau III

U.S. ambassador Henry Morgenthau Sr.

stay out of business that did not concern U.S. national interests. "Turkish authorities have definitely informed me that I have no right to interfere with their internal affairs," Morgenthau wrote. Still, he warned Washington, "there seems to be a systematic plan to crush the Armenian race."[14]

Local witnesses urged him to invoke the moral power of the United States. Otherwise, he was told, "the whole Armenian nation would disappear."[15] The ambassador did what he could, continuing to send blistering cables back to Washington and raising the matter at virtually every meeting he held with Talaat. He found his exchanges with the interior minister infuriating. Once, when the ambassador introduced eyewitness reports of slaughter, Talaat snapped back: "Why are you so interested in the Armenians anyway? You are a Jew, these people are Christians. . . . What have you to complain of? Why can't you let us do with these Christians as we please?" Morgenthau replied, "You don't seem to realize that I am not here as a Jew but as the American Ambassador. . . . I do not appeal to you in the name of any race or religion but merely as a human being." Talaat looked confused. "We treat the Americans all right, too," he said. "I don't see why you should complain."[16]

But Morgenthau continued to complain, warning that Talaat and other senior officials would eventually be held responsible before the court of public opinion, particularly in the United States. Talaat had a ready response: "We don't give a rap for the future!" he exclaimed. "We live only in the present!" Talaat believed in collective guilt. It was legitimate to punish all Armenians even if only a few refused to disarm or harbored seditious thoughts. "We have been reproached for making no distinction between the innocent Armenians and the guilty," Talaat told a German reporter. "But that was utterly impossible, in view of the fact that those who were innocent today might be guilty tomorrow."[17]

Instead of hiding his achievements, as later perpetrators would do, Talaat boasted of them. According to Morgenthau, he liked to tell friends, "I have accomplished more toward solving the Armenian problem in three months than Abdul Hamid accomplished in thirty years!"[18] (The Turkish sultan Abdul Hamid had killed some 200,000 Armenians in 1895–1896.) Talaat once asked Morgenthau whether the United States could get the New York Life Insurance Company and Equitable Life of New York, which for years had done business with the Armenians, to send a complete list of the Armenian policyholders to the Turkish authorities. "They are practically all dead now and have left no heirs," Talaat said. "The Government is the beneficiary now."[19]

Morgenthau was incensed at the request and stormed out of Talaat's office. He again cabled back to Washington, imploring his higher-ups to take heed:

> I earnestly beg the Department to give this matter urgent and exhaustive consideration with a view to reaching a conclusion which may possibly have the effect of checking [Turkey's] Government and certainly provide opportunity for efficient relief which now is not permitted. It is difficult for me to restrain myself from doing something to stop this attempt to exterminate a race, but I realize that I am here as Ambassador and must abide by the principles of non-interference with the internal affairs of another country.[20]

Morgenthau had to remind himself that one of the prerogatives of sovereignty was that states and statesmen could do as they pleased within their own borders. "Technically," he noted to himself, "I had no right to interfere. According to the cold-blooded legalities of the situation, the treatment of Turkish subjects by the Turkish Government was purely a domestic affair; unless it directly affected American lives and American interests, it was outside the concern of the American Government."[21] The ambassador found this maddening.

The *New York Times* gave the Turkish horrors steady coverage, publishing 145 stories in 1915. It helped that Morgenthau and *Times* publisher Adolph Ochs were old friends. Beginning in March 1915, the paper spoke of Turkish "massacres," "slaughter," and "atrocities" against the Armenians, relaying accounts by missionaries, Red Cross officials, local religious authorities, and survivors of mass executions. "It is safe to say," a correspondent noted in July, "that unless Turkey is beaten to its knees very speedily there will soon be no more Christians in the Ottoman Empire."[22] By July 1915 the paper's headlines had begun crying out about the danger of the Armenians' "extinction." Viscount Bryce, former British ambassador to the United States, pleaded that the United States use its influence with Germany. "If anything can stop the destroying hand of the Turkish Government," Bryce argued, as did the missionaries who had appealed to Morgenthau, "it will be an expression of the opinion of neutral nations, chiefly the judgment of humane America."[23] On October 7, 1915, a *Times* headline blared, "800,000 ARMENIANS COUNTED DESTROYED." The article reported Bryce's testimony before the House of Lords in which he urged the United States to demonstrate that there were "some crimes which, even now in the convulsion of a great war, the public opinion of the world will not tolerate."[24] By December the paper's headline read, "MILLION ARMENIANS KILLED OR IN EXILE."[25] The number of victims were estimates, as the bodies were impossible to count. Nevertheless, governmental and nongovernmental officials were sure that the atrocities were "unparalleled in modern times" and that the Turks had set out to achieve "nothing more or less than the annihilation of a whole people."[26]

Witnesses to the terror knew that American readers would have difficulty processing such gruesome horrors, so they scoured history for parallels to events that they believed had already been processed in the public mind. One report said, "The nature and scale of the atrocities dwarf anything perpetrated. . . under Abdul Hamid, whose exploits in this direction now assume an aspect of moderation compared with those of the present Governors of Turkey." Before Adolf Hitler, the standard for European brutality had been set by Abdul Hamid and the Belgian king Leopold, who pillaged the Congo for rubber in the late nineteenth and early twentieth centuries.[27]

Because the Turks continued to block access to the caravans, reporters often speculated on whether their sources were reliable. "The Turkish Government has succeeded in throwing an impenetrable veil over its actions toward all Armenians," a frustrated Associated Press correspondent noted. "Constantinople has for weeks had its daily crop of Armenian rumors. . . . What has happened . . . is still an unwritten chapter. No newspapermen are allowed to visit the affected districts and reports from these are altogether unreliable. The reticence of the Turkish Government cannot be looked upon as a good sign, however."[28] Turkish representatives in the United States predictably blurred the picture with denials and defenses. The Turkish consul, Djelal Munif Bey, told the *New York Times*, "All those who have been killed were of that rebellious element who were caught red-handed or while otherwise committing traitorous acts against the Turkish Government, and not women and children, as some of these fabricated reports would have the Americans believe." But the same representative added that if innocent lives had in fact been lost, that was because in wartime "discrimination is utterly impossible, and it is not alone the offender who suffers the penalty of his act, but also the innocent whom he drags with him. . . . The Armenians have only themselves to blame."[29]

The Turks, who had attempted to conduct the massacres secretly, were unhappy about the attention they were getting. In November 1915 Talaat advised the authorities in Aleppo that Morgenthau knew far too much. "It is important that foreigners who are in those parts shall be persuaded that the expulsion of the Armenians is in truth only deportation," Talaat wrote. "It is important that, to save appearances, a show of gentle dealing shall be made for a time, and the usual measures be taken in suitable places." A month later, angry that foreigners had obtained photographs of corpses along the road, Talaat recommended that these corpses be "buried at once," or at least hidden from view.[30]

Sensing Turkish sensitivity to the outside world's opinion, Morgenthau pleaded with his superiors to throw protocol and neutrality aside and to issue a direct government-to-government appeal "on behalf of humanity" to stop the killings. He also urged the United States to convince the German kaiser to stop the Turks'"annihilation of a Christian race." And he called on Washington to press the Turks to allow humanitarian aid deliveries to those Armenians already deported and in danger of starving to death in the desert.[31] But because Americans were not endangered by the Turkish horrors and because American neutrality in World War I remained fixed, Washington did not act on Morgenthau's recommendations. Officials urged him instead to seek aid from private sources.

Morgenthau did get help from outside the U.S. government. The Congregationalist, Baptist, and Roman Catholic churches made donations. The Rockefeller Foundation gave $290,000 in 1915 alone. And most notable, a number of distinguished Americans, none of Armenian descent, set up a new Committee on Armenian Atrocities.[32] The committee raised $100,000 for Armenian relief and staged high-profile rallies, gathering delegations from more than 1,000 churches and religious organizations in New York City to join in denouncing the Turkish crimes.

But in calling for "action," the committee was not urging U.S. military intervention. It was worried about the impact of an American declaration of war on American schools and churches in Turkey. In addition, the sentiment that made committee members empathize with their fellow Christians in Armenia also made some pacifists. In decrying the atrocities but opposing the war against Turkey, the committee earned the scorn of former president Theodore Roosevelt. In a letter to Samuel Dutton, the Armenia committee secretary, Roosevelt slammed the hypocrisy of the "peace-at-any-price type" who acted on the motto of "safety first," which, he wrote, "could be appropriately used by the men on a sinking steamer who jump into boats ahead of the women and children." He continued:

> Mass meetings on behalf of the Armenians amount to nothing whatever if they are mere methods of giving a sentimental but ineffective and safe outlet to the emotion of those engaged in them. Indeed they amount to less than nothing. . . . Until we put honor and duty first, and are willing to risk something in order to achieve righteousness both for ourselves and for others, we shall accomplish nothing; and we shall earn and deserve the contempt of the strong nations of mankind.[33]

Roosevelt wondered how anyone could possibly advise neutrality "between despairing and hunted people, people whose little children are murdered and their women raped, and the victorious and evil wrongdoers." He observed that such a position put "safety in the present above both duty in the present and safety in the future."[34] Roosevelt would grow even angrier later in the war, when the very relief campaign initiated to aid the Armenians would be invoked as reason not to make war on Turkey. In 1918 he wrote to Cleveland Dodge, the most influential member of the Armenia committee: "To allow the Turks to massacre the Armenians and then solicit permission to help the survivors and then to allege the fact that we are helping the survivors as a reason why we should not follow the only policy that will permanently put a stop to such massacres is both foolish and odious."[35]

Morgenthau tried to work around America's determined neutrality. In September 1915 he offered to raise $1 million to transport to the United States the Armenians who had escaped the massacres. "Since May," Morgenthau said, "350,000 Armenians have been slaughtered or have died of starvation. There are 550,000 Armenians who could now be sent to America, and we need help to save them." Turkey accepted the proposal, and Morgenthau called upon each of the states in the western United States to raise funds to equip a ship to transport and care for Armenian refugees. He appealed to American self-interest, arguing, "The Armenians are a moral, hard working race, and would make good citizens to settle the less thickly populated parts of the Western States."[36] He knew he had to preemptively rebut those who expected Armenian freeloaders. But the Turks, insincere even about helping Armenians leave, blocked the exit of refugees. Morgenthau's plan went nowhere.[37]

As American missionaries were driven out of Turkey, they returned to the United States with stories to tell. William A. Shedd, a Presbyterian missionary, chose to write directly to the new U.S. secretary of state, Robert Lansing:

> I am sure there are a great many thoughtful Americans who, like myself, feel that silence on the part of our Government is perilous and that for our Government to make no public protest against a crime of such magnitude perpetrated by a Government on noncombatants, the great majority of them helpless women and children, is to miss an unusual opportunity to serve humanity, if not to risk grave danger of dishonor on the name of America and of lessening our right to speak for humanity and justice. I am aware, of course, that it may seem presumptuous to suggest procedure in matters of diplomacy; but the need of these multitudes of people suffering in Turkey is desperate, and the only hope of influence is the Government of the United States.[38]

But Lansing had been advised by the Division of Near East Affairs at the State Department that "however much we may deplore the suffering of the

Armenians, we cannot take any active steps to come to their assistance at the present time."[39] Lansing instructed Morgenthau to continue telling the Turkish authorities that the atrocities would "jeopardize the good feeling of the people of the United States toward the people of Turkey."[40] Lansing also eventually asked Germany to try to restrain Turkey. But he expressed understanding for Turkey's security concerns. "I could see that [the Armenians'] well-known disloyalty to the Ottoman Government and the fact that the territory which they inhabited was within the zone of military operations constituted grounds more or less justifiable for compelling them to depart their homes," Secretary Lansing wrote in November 1916.[41] Morgenthau examined the facts and saw a cold-blooded campaign of annihilation; Lansing processed many of those same facts and saw an unfortunate but understandable effort to quell an internal security threat.

After twenty-six months in Constantinople, Morgenthau left in early 1916. He could no longer stand his impotence. "My failure to stop the destruction of the Armenians," he recalled, "had made Turkey for me a place of horror—I had reached the end of my resources."[42] More than 1 million Armenians had been killed on his watch. Morgenthau, who had earned a reputation as a loose cannon, did not receive another appointment in the Wilson administration. President Wilson, reflecting the overwhelming view of the American people, stayed on the sidelines of World War I as long as he could. And when the United States finally entered the conflict against Germany in April 1917, he refused to declare war on or even break off relations with the Ottoman Empire. "We shall go wherever the necessities of this war carry us," Wilson told Congress, "but it seems to me that we should go only where immediate and practical considerations lead us and not heed any others."[43] In the end it was Turkey that broke off ties with the United States.

America's nonresponse to the Turkish horrors established patterns that would be repeated. Time and again the U.S. government would be reluctant to cast aside its neutrality and formally denounce a fellow state for its atrocities. Time and again though U.S. officials would learn that huge numbers of civilians were being slaughtered, the impact of this knowledge would be blunted by their uncertainty about the facts and their rationalization that a firmer U.S. stand would make little difference. Time and again American assumptions and policies would be contested by Americans in the field closest to the slaughter, who would try to stir the imaginations of their political superiors. And time and again these advocates would fail to sway Washington. The United States would offer humanitarian aid to the survivors of "race murder" but would leave those committing it alone.

Aftermath

When the war ended in 1918, the question of war guilt loomed large at the Paris peace conference. Britain, France, and Russia urged that state authorities in Germany, Austria, and Turkey be held responsible for violations of the laws of war and the "laws of humanity." They began planning the century's first international war crimes tribunal, hoping to try the kaiser and his German underlings, as well as Talaat, Enver Pasha, and the other leading Turkish perpetrators. But Lansing dissented on behalf of the United States. In general the Wilson administration opposed the Allies' proposals to emasculate Germany. But it also rejected the notion that some allegedly "universal" principle of justice should allow punishment. The laws of humanity, Lansing argued, "vary with the individual." Reflecting the widespread view of the time, Lansing said that sovereign leaders should be immune from prosecution. "The essence of sovereignty," he said, was "the absence of responsibility."[44] The United States could judge only those violations that were committed upon American persons or American property.[45]

If such a tribunal were set up, then, the United States would not participate. In American thinking at that time, there was little question that the state's right to be left alone automatically trumped any individual right to justice. A growing postwar isolationism made the United States reluctant to entangle itself in affairs so clearly removed from America's narrow national interests.

Even without official U.S. support, it initially seemed that Britain's wartime pledge to try the Turkish leaders would be realized. In early 1919 the British, who still occupied Turkey with some 320,000 soldiers, pressured the cooperative sultan to arrest a number of Turkish executioners. Of the eight Ottoman leaders who led Turkey to war against the Allies, five were apprehended. In April 1919 the Turks set up a tribunal in Constantinople that convicted two senior district officials for deporting Armenians and acting "against humanity and civilization." The Turkish court found that women and children had been brutally forced into deportation caravans and the men murdered: "They were premeditatedly, with intent, murdered, after the men had had their hands tied behind their backs." The police commander Tevfik Bey was sentenced to fifteen years of hard labor, and Lieutenant Governor Kemal Bey was hanged. The court also convicted Talaat and his partners in crime in absentia for their command responsibility in the slaughter, finding a top-down, carefully executed plan: "The disaster visiting the Armenians was not a local or isolated event. It was the result of a premeditated decision taken by a central body;. . . and the immolations and excesses which took place were based on oral and written orders issued by that central body."[46]

Talaat, who was sentenced to death, was living peacefully as a private citizen in Germany, which rejected Allied demands for extradition. Conscious of his place in history, Talaat had begun writing his memoirs. In them he downplayed the scale of the violence and argued that any abuses (referred to mainly in the passive voice) were fairly typical if "regrettable" features of war, carried out by "uncontrolled elements." "I confess," he wrote, "that the deportation was not carried out lawfully everywhere. . . . Some of the officials abused their authority, and in many places people took the preventive measures into their own hands and innocent people were molested." Acknowledging it was the government's duty to prevent and punish "these abuses and atrocities," he explained that doing so would have aroused great popular "discontent," and Turkey could not afford to be divided during war. "We did all we could," he claimed, "but we preferred to postpone the solution of our internal difficulties until after the defeat of our external enemies." Although other countries at war also enacted harsh "preventive measures," he wrote, "the regrettable results were passed over in silence," whereas "the echo of our acts was heard the world over, because everybody's eyes were upon us." Even as Talaat attempted to burnish his image, he could not help but blame the Armenians for their own fate. "I admit that we deported many Armenians from our eastern provinces," he wrote, but "the responsibility for these acts falls first of all upon the deported people themselves."[47]

After a promising start, enthusiasm for trying Talaat and his henchmen faded and politics quickly intervened. With the Turkish nationalist leader Mustafa Kemal (later Atatürk) rapidly gaining popularity at home, the Ottoman regime began to fear a backlash if it was seen to be succumbing to British designs. In addition, the execution of Kemal Bey had made him a martyr to nationalists around the empire. To avoid further unrest, the Turkish authorities began releasing low-level suspects. The British had grown frustrated by the incompetence and politicization of what they called the "farcical" Turkish judicial system. Fearing none of the suspects in Turkish custody would ever be tried, the British occupation forces shipped many of the arrested war crimes suspects from Turkey to Malta and Mudros, a port on the Aegean island of Lemnos, for eventual international trials. But support for this, too, evaporated. By 1920 the condemnations and promises of 1915 were five years old. Kemal, who was rapidly consolidating his control over Turkey, had denounced as treasonous the 1920 Treaty of Sèvres, which committed the Ottomans to surrender war crimes suspects to an international tribunal. The British clung for a time to the idea that they might at least prosecute the eight Turks in custody who had committed crimes against Britons. But Winston Churchill gave up even this hope in 1920 when Kemal seized twenty-nine British soldiers whose immediate fates Britain privileged above all else.[48]

In November 1921 Kemal put an end to the promise of an international tribunal by negotiating a prisoner swap. The incarcerated Britons were traded for all the Turkish suspects in British custody. In 1923 the European powers replaced the Treaty of Sèvres with the Treaty of Lausanne, which dropped all mention of prosecution. Former British prime minister David Lloyd George called the treaty an "abject, cowardly, and infamous surrender."[49]

Chapter 2

"A Crime Without a Name"

Soghomon Tehlirian, the young Armenian survivor, knew little of international treaties or geopolitics. He knew only that his life had been empty since the war, that Talaat was responsible, and that the former minister of the interior would never stand trial. Since the massacre of his family and injury to his head, Tehlirian had been unable to sleep and had been overcome by frequent epileptic seizures. In 1920 he had found a cause, enlisting in Operation Nemesis, a Boston-based Armenian plot to assassinate the Turkish leaders involved in targeting the Armenians. He was assigned to murder Talaat, a crime that earned him everlasting glory in the Armenian community and brief global notoriety.

While Tehlirian awaited trial in Berlin, Raphael Lemkin, a twenty-one-year-old Polish Jew studying linguistics at the University of Lvov, came upon a short news item on Talaat's assassination in the local paper. Lemkin was intrigued and brought the case to the attention of one of his professors. Lemkin asked why the Armenians did not have Talaat arrested for the massacre. The professor said there was no law under which he could be arrested. "Consider the case of a farmer who owns a flock of chickens," he said. "He kills them and this is his business. If you interfere, you are trespassing."

"It is a crime for Tehlirian to kill a man, but it is not a crime for his oppressor to kill more than a million men?" Lemkin asked. "This is most inconsistent."[1]

Jewish boy being forced to write *Jude* on his father's store in Vienna, Austria, within days of Germany's Anschluss.

Lemkin was appalled that the banner of "state sovereignty" could shield men who tried to wipe out an entire minority. "Sovereignty," Lemkin argued to the professor, "implies conducting an independent foreign and internal policy, building of schools, construction of roads . . . all types of activity directed towards the welfare of people. Sovereignty cannot be conceived as the right to kill millions of innocent people."[2] But it was states, and particularly strong states, that made the rules.

Lemkin read about the abortive British effort to try the Turkish perpetrators and saw that states would rarely pursue justice out of a commitment to justice alone. They would do so only if they came under political pressure, if the trials served strategic interests, or if the crimes affected their citizens.

Lemkin was torn about how to judge Tehlirian's act. On the one hand, Lemkin credited the Armenian with upholding the "moral order of mankind" and drawing the world's attention to the Turkish slaughter. Tehlirian's case had quickly turned into an informal trial of the deceased Talaat for his crimes against the Armenians; the witnesses and written evidence introduced in Tehlirian's defense brought the Ottoman horrors to their fullest light to date. The *New York Times* wrote that the documents introduced in the trial "established once and for all the fact that the purpose of the Turkish authorities was not deportation but annihilation."[3] But Lemkin was uncomfortable that Tehlirian, who had been acquitted on the grounds of what today would be called "temporary insanity," had acted as the "self-appointed legal officer for the conscience of mankind."[4] Passion, he knew, would often make a travesty of justice. Impunity for mass murderers like Talaat had to end; retribution had to be legalized.

A decade later, in 1933, Lemkin, then a lawyer, made plans to speak before an international criminal law conference in Madrid before a distinguished gathering of elder colleagues.[5] Lemkin drafted a paper that drew attention both to Hitler's ascent and to the Ottoman slaughter of the Armenians, a crime that most Europeans either had ignored or had filed away as an "Eastern" phenomenon. If it happened once, the young lawyer urged, it would happen again. If it happened there, he argued, it could happen here. Lemkin offered up a radical proposal. If the international community ever hoped to prevent mass slaughter of the kind the Armenians had suffered, he insisted, the world's states would have to unite in a campaign to ban the practice. With that end in mind, Lemkin had prepared a law that would prohibit the destruction of nations, races, and religious groups. The law hinged on what he called "universal repression," a precursor to what today is called "universal jurisdiction": The instigators and per-petrators of these acts should be punished wherever they were caught, regardless of where the crime was committed, or the criminals' nationality or official status.[6] The attempt to wipe out national, ethnic, or religious groups like the Armenians would become an international crime that could be punished anywhere, like slavery and piracy. The threat of punish-ment, Lemkin argued, would yield a change in practice.

"Barbarity"

Raphael Lemkin had been oddly consumed by the subject of atrocity even before he heard Tehlirian's story. In 1913, when he was twelve, Lemkin had read Nobel Prize winner Henryk Sienkiewicz's *Quo Vadis?* which recounts the Roman emperor Nero's massacres of Christian converts in the first century. Lemkin grew up on a sprawling farm in eastern Poland near the town of Wolkowysk, some 50 miles from the city of Bialystok, which was then part of czarist Russia. Although Lemkin was Jewish, many of his neighbors were Christian. He was aghast that Nero could feed Christians to the lions and asked his mother, Bella, how the emperor could have elicited cheers from a mob of spectators. Bella, a painter, linguist, and stu-dent of philosophy who home-schooled her three sons, explained that once the state became determined to wipe out an ethnic or religious group, the police and the citizenry became the accomplices and not the guardians of human life.

As a boy, Lemkin often grilled his mother for details on historical cases of mass slaughter, learning about the sacking of Carthage, the Mongol invasions, and the targeting of the French Huguenots. A bibliophile, he raced through an unusually grim reading list and set out to play a role in ending the destruction of ethnic groups. "I was an impressionable young-ster, leaning to sentimentality," he wrote years later. "I was appalled by the frequency of the evil . . . and, above all, by the impunity coldly relied upon by the guilty."

The subject of slaughter had an unfortunate personal relevance for him growing up in the Bialystok region of Poland: In 1906 some seventy Jews were murdered and ninety gravely injured in local pogroms. Lemkin had heard that mobs opened the stomachs of their victims and stuffed them with feathers from pillows and comforters in grotesque mutilation rituals.

He feared that the myth that Jews liked to grind young Christian boys into matzoh would lead to more killings. Lemkin saw what he later described as "a line of blood" leading from the massacre of the Christians in Rome to the massacre of Jews nearby.[7]

During World War I, while the Armenians were suffering under Talaat's menacing rule, the battle between the Russians and the Germans descended upon the doorstep of the Lemkin family farm.[8] His mother and father buried the family's books and their few valuables and took the boys to hide out in the forest that enveloped their land. In the course of the fighting, artillery fire ripped their farmhouse apart. The Germans seized their crops, cattle, and horses. Samuel, one of Lemkin's two brothers, died in the woods of pneumonia and malnourishment.

The interwar period brought a brief respite for Lemkin and his fellow Poles. After the Russian-Polish war resulted in a rare Polish victory, Lemkin enrolled in the University of Lvov in 1920. His childhood Torah study had sparked a curiosity in the power of naming, and he had long been interested in the insight words supplied into culture. He had a knack for languages, and having already mastered Polish, German, Russian, French, Italian, Hebrew, and Yiddish, he began to study philology, the evolution of language. He planned next to learn Arabic and Sanskrit.

But in 1921, when Lemkin read the article about the assassination of Talaat, he veered away from philology and back toward his dark, childhood preoccupation. He transferred to the Lvov law school, where he scoured ancient and modern legal codes for laws prohibiting slaughter. He kept his eye trained on the local press, and his inquiry gained urgency as he got wind of pogroms being committed in the new Soviet state. He went to work as a local prosecutor and in 1929 began moonlighting on drafting an international law that would commit his government and others to stopping the targeted destruction of ethnic, national, and religious groups. It was this law that the cocksure Lemkin presented to his European legal colleagues in Madrid in 1933.

Lemkin felt that both the physical and the cultural existence of groups had to be preserved. And so he submitted to the Madrid conference a draft law banning two linked practices—"barbarity" and "vandalism." "Barbarity" he defined as "the premeditated destruction of national, racial, religious and social collectivities." "Vandalism" he classified as the "destruction of works of art and culture, being the expression of the particular genius of these collectivities."[9] Punishing these two practices—the destruc-

tion of groups and the demolition of their cultural and intellectual life—
would occupy him fully for the next three decades.

Lemkin met with two disappointments. First, the Polish foreign minister
Joseph Beck, who was attempting to endear himself to Hitler, refused to
permit Lemkin to travel to Madrid to present his ideas in person.[10]
Lemkin's draft had to be read out loud in his absence. Second, Lemkin
found few allies for his proposal. In an interwar Europe composed of isolationist, nationalistic, economically ailing nations, European jurists and liti-
gators were unmoved by Lemkin's talk of crimes that "shock the
conscience." The League of Nations was too divided to make joint law—
never mind joint law on behalf of imperiled minorities. The delegates
talked at length about "collective security," but they did not mean for the
phrase to include the security of collectives *within* states. Besides, in the
words of one delegate, this crime of barbarity took place "too seldom to
legislate." Most of the lawyers present (representing thirty-seven countries)
wondered how crimes committed a generation ago in the Ottoman
Empire concerned lawyers on the civilized Continent. Although the
German delegation had just walked out of the League of Nations and
thousands of Jewish families had already begun fleeing Nazi Germany, they
were also skeptical about apocalyptic references to Hitler. When Lemkin's
plan was presented, the president of the supreme court of Germany and the
president of Berlin University left the room in protest.[11] As Lemkin put it
later in his characteristically stiff style, "Cold water was poured on me."[12]

Lemkin had issued a moral challenge, and the lawyers at the conference did
not reject his proposal outright. They tabled it. Lemkin noted, "They would
not say 'yes,' and they *could not* say 'no.'" They were not prepared to agree to
intervene, even diplomatically, across borders. But neither were they prepared
to admit that they would stand by and allow innocent people to die.

Back in Poland, Lemkin was accused of trying to advance the status of
Jews with his proposal. Foreign minister Beck slammed him for "insulting
our German friends."[13] Soon after the conference, the anti-Semitic Warsaw
government fired him as deputy public prosecutor for refusing to curb his
criticisms of Hitler.[14]

Jobless and chastened by the reception of his draft law, Lemkin still did
not question the soundness of his strategy. History, he liked to say, was
"much wiser than lawyers and statesmen." The crime of barbarity repeated
itself with near "biological regularity."[15] But Lemkin saw that people living
in peacetime were clearly going to have difficulty hearing, never mind

heeding, warning pleas for early action. The prospect of atrocity seemed too remote, the notion of a plot to destroy a collective too inhuman, and the fate of vulnerable groups too removed from the core interests of outsiders. Yet by the time the crimes had been committed, it would be too late for concerned states to deter them. States would forever be stuck dealing with the consequences of genocide, unable to see or unwilling to act ahead of time to prevent it. But Lemkin did not give up. Over the next few years, at law conferences in Budapest, Copenhagen, Paris, Amsterdam, and Cairo, Lemkin rose in his crisply pressed suit and spoke in commanding French about the urgency of the proposal.

Lemkin was not the only European who had learned from the past. So, too, had Hitler. Six years after the Madrid conference, in August 1939, Hitler met with his military chiefs and delivered a notorious tutorial on a central lesson of the recent past: Victors write the history books. He declared:

> It was knowingly and lightheartedly that Genghis Khan sent thousands of women and children to their deaths. History sees in him only the founder of a state. . . . The aim of war is not to reach definite lines but to annihilate the enemy physically. It is by this means that we shall obtain the vital living space that we need. *Who today still speaks of the massacre of the Armenians?*[16]

A week later, on September 1, 1939, the Nazis invaded Poland. In 1942 Hitler restored Talaat's ashes to Turkey, where the Turkish government enshrined the fallen hero's remains in a mausoleum on the Hill of Liberty in Istanbul.[17]

Flight

If Lemkin had been in a position to utter a public "I told you so" in September 1939, he would have done so. But like all Jews scrambling to flee or to fight, Lemkin had only survival on his mind. Six days after the Wehrmacht's invasion of Poland, he heard a radio broadcast instructing able-bodied men to leave the capital. Lemkin rushed to the train station, carrying only a shaving kit and a summer coat. When the train was bombed and set aflame by the German Luftwaffe, Lemkin hid and hiked for days in the woods nearby, joining what he called a "community of nomads." He saw German bombers hit a train crammed with refugees and then a group of children huddling by the tracks. Three of his traveling companions were killed in an air raid. Hundreds of Poles marching with him collapsed of fatigue, starvation, and disease.

Under the terms of the secret Soviet-German deal known as the Molotov-Ribbentrop pact, the Soviets invaded Poland just after the Germans, and the country was divided into a Soviet and a German zone. Lemkin kept on the move until November 1939, when he wound up in a small town in Poland's Soviet-occupied half and persuaded a devout Jewish family to shelter him for a few days. There, despite the warmth and generosity of his hosts, Lemkin was frustrated by their passivity and wishful thinking in the face of Hitler's brutality.

"There is nothing new in the suffering of Jews, especially in time of war," the man of the house, a baker, insisted. "The main thing for a Jew is not to get excited and to outlast the enemies. A Jew must wait and pray. The Almighty will help. He always helps."

Lemkin asked the man if he had heard of *Mein Kampf*. The man said he had heard of it but that he did not believe Hitler would follow through on his threats.

"How can Hitler destroy the Jews, if he must trade with them?" the baker asked Lemkin. "I grant you some Jews will suffer under Hitler, but this is the lot of the Jews, to suffer and to wait."

Lemkin argued that this was not like other wars. The Germans were not interested only in grabbing territory. Hitler wanted to destroy the Jews completely.

"In the last war, 1915–1918, we lived three years under the Germans," the baker said. "It was never good, but somehow we survived. I sold bread to the Germans; we baked for them their flour. We Jews are an eternal people, we cannot be destroyed. We can only suffer."[18]

This disbelief, this faith in reason, in human contact, in commerce, convinced millions to remain in place and risk their fates. Only a small number of Jews had Lemkin's foresight. The vast majority expected persecution and maybe even the occasional pogrom, but not extermination.

Lemkin studied the man carefully and reflected:

> Many generations spoke through this man. He could not believe the reality of [Hitler's intent], because it was so much against nature,

against logic, against life itself, and against the warm smell of bread in his house, against his poor but comfortable bed. . . . There was not much sense in disturbing or confusing him with facts. He had already made up his mind.[19]

Lemkin took a train to eastern Poland, where his brother and parents lived. He begged them to join him in flight. "I have been living in retirement for more than ten years because of my sickness," his father said. "I am not a capitalist. The Russians will not bother me." His brother chimed in, "I gave up my store and registered as an employee before it was taken over by the new government. They will not touch me either." Lemkin later remembered: "I read in the eyes of all of them one plea: do not talk of our leaving this warm home, our beds, our stores of food, the security of our customs. . . . We will have to suffer, but we will survive somehow." He spent the next day feeling as if he was living their funerals while they were still alive. "The best of me was dying with the full cruelty of consciousness," he noted.[20]

Before Lemkin left Wolkowysk, his mother lectured him on the importance of rounding out his life. She reminded him that his goal of writing a book a year was not as important as developing "the life of the heart." Lemkin, who had not dated, joked that maybe he would have more luck in his new capacity as a nomad than he had had "as a member of a sedentary society." He told his parents that he planned to travel first to Sweden and then, he hoped, to the United States, because that was where decisions were made.

After waving good-bye to his parents with a determined casualness, Lemkin headed toward Vilnius, Lithuania, a town bustling with refugees. He spent what was left of his money on two telegrams. The first the fastidious scholar sent to Paris to inquire whether his publisher had received a manuscript that he had mailed a week before the war's outbreak. The second, a plea for refuge, he dispatched to a friend, the minister of justice in Sweden.[21] As he awaited notification from the Swedish consulate, he visited with various Jewish intellectuals around town. None planned to leave.

The life of the vagrant was not agreeing with Lemkin. Although his acquaintances were generous, he felt his personality "disintegrate" as apathy set in. "There were three things I wanted to avoid in my life: to wear eyeglasses, to lose my hair, and to become a refugee," he wrote. "Now all these three things have come to me in implacable succession."[22] He busied himself by buying a dictionary and learning Lithuanian from the daily newspaper. But only the arrival of a package from his publisher in France cheered him up. The publisher enclosed galleys of his latest book on international finance regulations, as well as copies of Lemkin's 1933 draft law banning acts of barbarity and vandalism. In his newfound free time, the lawyer immediately set out to improve them.

Lemkin's request for refuge was granted, and he traveled to neutral Sweden by ship in February 1940. He was able to lecture in Swedish after just five months, an achievement he credited with enabling him to "rise spiritually from the 'refugee' fall of modern man."[23] While lecturing on international law at the University of Stockholm, he began assembling the legal decrees the Nazis had issued in each of the countries they occupied. He relied upon a corporation whose legal affairs he had once managed from Warsaw—as well as Swedish embassies around Europe, Red Cross delegations, and German occupation radio—to gather the official gazettes from any branches that remained open in the occupied countries. In compiling these laws, Lemkin hoped he would be able to demonstrate the sinister ways in which law could be used to propagate hate and incite murder. He also hoped decrees and ordinances in the Nazis' own words would serve as "objective and irrefutable evidence" for the legions of disbelievers in what he called the "blind world."[24]

Lemkin was desperate to leave the libraries of neutral Stockholm and get to the United States, which he had idealized. Thanks to a professor at Duke University with whom he had once translated the Polish criminal code into English, Lemkin secured an appointment to the Duke faculty to teach international law. He flew to Moscow, took the Trans-Siberian railroad to Vladivostok, and then picked up a small boat, which he and the other refugees called the "floating coffin," to the Japanese port of Tsuruga. He then took a bigger boat from Yokohama to Vancouver and on to Seattle, the U.S. port of entry, where he landed on April 18, 1941.

A New Beginning, an Old Crusade

Lemkin traveled by train to North Carolina, marking the end of what had been a 14,000-mile journey. The evening he arrived, he was asked to deliver a speech at a dinner with the university president. Without preparation or a full command of English, Lemkin urged Americans to do as Ambassador Morgenthau had done for the Armenians. "If women, children, and old people would be murdered a hundred miles from here," Lemkin asked, "wouldn't you run to help? Then why do you stop this decision of your heart when the distance is 3,000 miles instead of a hundred?"[25] This was the first of hundreds of speeches Lemkin gave around the state. He bought himself a white suit, white shoes, white socks, and a dark silk tie for his appearances before chambers of commerce, women's groups, and colleges. Members of the audiences approached Lemkin after his talks and apologized for America's reluctance to join the fight against Hitler.

While at Duke, Lemkin received a letter from his parents on a scrap of paper a quarter the size of a regular sheet. "We are well," the letter read. "We hope you are happy. We are thinking of you." Several days later, on June 24, 1941, he heard a radio broadcaster announce that the German army had declared war on the Soviet Union, abrogating the Molotov-Ribbentrop pact that had divided the country into a German and a Soviet zone. Hitler's forces were now storming into eastern Poland. Colleagues on campus asked, "Have you heard the news about the Nazis?" Lemkin, dazed and sullen, looked down. "Sorry," they said, pulling away.[26]

Although Lemkin was panicked about the fate of his missing family, he busied himself by proselytizing about Hitler's crimes. The prevailing wisdom in the United States, as it had been in Lithuania, was that the Nazis were waging a war against Europe's armies. When Lemkin told U.S. government officials that Germany was also wiping out the Jews, he was greeted either with indifference or incredulity. But with Hitler's declaration of war against the United States, Lemkin, then fluent in nine languages, thought he might acquire more cachet. In June 1942 the Board of Economic Warfare and the Foreign Economic Administration in Washington, D.C., hired him as chief consultant, and in 1944 the U.S. War Department brought him on board as an international law expert. But his horror stories were not a U.S. governmental concern. "My companions were mildly and only politely interested," he remembered. "Their attention was rather absorbed by their own assignments. . . . They were masters in switching the discussion in their direction."[27]

Lemkin reached out to those at the top. He met with Henry Wallace, Roosevelt's vice president, and attempted to personalize his message. Ahead of the meeting, he had studied up on the Tennessee Valley Authority project on irrigation, which he knew would interest Wallace. Because the vice president had been raised in the cornfields of Iowa, Lemkin also slipped in references to his farm upbringing. Lemkin met with Wallace on several occasions and introduced his proposals to ban the destruction of peoples. "I looked hopefully for a reaction," Lemkin remembered. "There was none."[28]

Lemkin next tried to approach President Roosevelt directly. An aide urged him to summarize his proposal in a one-page memo. Lemkin was aghast that he had to "compress the pain of millions, the fear of nations, the hopes for salvation from death" in one page. But he managed, suggesting that the United States adopt a treaty banning barbarity and urging that the Allies declare the protection of Europe's minorities a central war aim. Several weeks later a courier relayed a message from the president. Roosevelt said he recognized the danger to groups but saw difficulties adopting such a law at the present. He assured Lemkin that the United States would issue a warning to the Nazis and urged patience. Lemkin was livid. "'Patience' is a good word to be used when one expects an appointment, a budgetary allocation or the building of a road," he noted. "But when the rope is already around the neck of the victim and strangulation is imminent, isn't the word 'patience' an insult to reason and nature?"[29] He believed a "double murder" was being committed—one by the Nazis against the Jews and the second by the Allies, who knew about Hitler's extermination campaign but refused to publicize or denounce it. After he received word of Roosevelt's brush-off, Lemkin left the department and walked slowly down Constitution Avenue, trying not to think about what it meant for his parents.

He was sure politicians would always put their own interests above the interests of others. To stand any chance of influencing U.S. policy, he would have to take his message to the general public, who in turn would pressure their leaders. "I realized that I was following the wrong path," he later wrote. "Statesmen are messing up the world, and [only] when it seems to them that they are drowning in the mud of their own making, [do] they rush to extricate themselves."[30] Those Americans who had been so responsive to Lemkin in person were not making their voices heard. And most Americans were uninterested. Lemkin told himself:

All over Europe the Nazis were writing the book of death with the blood of my brethren. Let me now tell this story to the American people, to the man in the street, in church, on the porches of their houses and in their kitchens and drawing rooms. I was sure they would understand me. . . . I will publish the decrees spreading death over Europe. . . . They will have no other choice but to believe. The

recognition of truth will cease to be a personal favor to me, but a logical necessity.[31]

As he lobbied for action in Washington and around the country in 1942
and 1943, he flashed back to a speech delivered by British prime minister
Winston Churchill in August 1941, broadcast on the BBC, which had
urged Allied resolve. "The whole of Europe has been wrecked and trampled down by the mechanical weapons and barbaric fury of the Nazis. . . .
As his armies advance, whole districts are exterminated," Churchill had
thundered. "We are in the presence of a crime without a name."[32]

Suddenly Lemkin's crusade took on a specific objective: the search for a
new word. He replayed in his mind the Churchill speech and the response
of the lawyers in Madrid to his proposal. Perhaps he had not adequately
distinguished the crime he was campaigning against from typical, wartime
violence. Maybe if he could capture the crime in a word that connoted
something truly unique and evil, people and politicians alike might get
more exercised about stopping it. Lemkin began to think about ways he
might combine his knowledge of international law, his aim of preventing
atrocity, and his long-standing interest in language. Convinced that it was
only the packaging of his legal and moral cause that needed refining, he
began to hunt for a term commensurate with the truth of his experience
and the experience of millions. He would be the one to give the ultimate
crime a name.

Raphael Lemkin

Chapter 3

The Crime
With a Name

"Believe the Unbelievable"

Although he did not realize it at the time, Lemkin belonged to a kind of virtual community of frustrated, grief-stricken witnesses. A continent away, Szmul Zygielbojm, a fellow Polish Jew, was making arguments similar to those Lemkin registered in the U.S. War Department. In late May 1942, when reports of Nazi terror were still branded "rumors," Zygielbojm, a member of the Polish National Council in London, released and publicized a report prepared by the underground Jewish Socialist Bund in Poland. For the previous two years, Zygielbojm had been traveling around Europe and the United States describing ghastly conditions in occupied Poland, but the Bund report offered the most complete, precise, and chilling picture of Hitler's extermination plot. The Nazis had dispatched *Einsatzgruppen,* or mobile killing units, to conquered territory in eastern Europe. In Lithuania and Poland in the summer of 1941, the Bund reported,

> men, fourteen to sixty years old, were driven to a single place, a square or a cemetery, where they were slaughtered or shot by machine guns or killed by hand grenades. They had to dig their own graves. Children in orphanages, inmates in old-age homes, the sick in hospital were shot, women were killed in the streets. In many towns the

Jews were carried off to "an unknown destination" and killed in adjacent woods.[1]

The Bund report introduced readers to the gas vans that roamed around the Polish town of Chelmno, gassing an average of 1,000 people every day (ninety per van) from the winter of 1941 to March 1942. The report revealed that Germany had set out to "exterminate all the Jews of Europe." More than 700,000 Jews had already been killed; millions more were endangered. Its authors called upon the Polish government-in-exile to press the Allies to retaliate against German citizens in their countries.[2] Others urged the Allies publicly to link their bombing of Germany to Nazi atrocities and to drop leaflets over German territory informing German citizens of the atrocities. Zygielbojm appeared on the BBC on June 26, 1942, to deliver the same message. Speaking in Yiddish, he read aloud a letter from a Jewish woman in one ghetto to her sister in another: "My hands are shaking. I cannot write. Our minutes are numbered. The Lord knows whether we shall see one another again. I write and weep. My children are whimpering. They want to live. We bless you. If you get no more letters from me you will know that we are no longer alive." The Bund report and the woman's letter, Zygielbojm said, were "a cry to the whole world."[3]

Earlier that year Jan Karski, a twenty-eight-year-old Polish diplomat and a Roman Catholic, had disguised himself as a Jew, donning an armband with the Star of David, and smuggled himself through a tunnel into the Warsaw ghetto. Posing as a Ukrainian militiaman, he also infiltrated Belzec, a Nazi death camp near the border between Poland and Ukraine. In late 1942 Karski escaped carrying hundreds of documents on miniature microfilm contained in the shaft of a key. He arranged to meet in London with Zygielbojm and his colleague, Ignacy Schwarzbart. On the eve of the meeting, Schwarzbart examined Karski's documents, and, aghast, cabled the World Jewish Congress in New York, describing the suffering of the Jews in Poland:

JEWS IN POLAND ALMOST COMPLETELY ANNIHILATED STOP READ
REPORTS DEPORTATION TEN THOUSAND JEWS FOR DEATH STOP IN
BELZEC FORCED TO DIG THEIR OWN GRAVE MASS SUICIDE HUNDREDS
CHILDREN THROWN ALIVE INTO GUTTERS DEATH CAMPS IN BELZEC
TREBLINKA DISTRICT MALKINIA THOUSANDS DEAD NOT BURIED IN
SOBIBOR DISTRICT WLODAWSKI MASS GRAVES MURDER PREGNANT

WOMEN STOP JEWS NAKED DRAGGED INTO DEATH CHAMBERS GESTAPO
MEN ASKED PAYMENT FOR QUICKER KILLING HUNTING FUGITIVES
STOP THOUSANDS DAILY VICTIMS THROUGHOUT POLAND STOP *BELIEVE
THE UNBELIEVABLE* STOP[4]

Karski met with Schwarzbart and Zygielbojm the next day in their office near Piccadilly Circus. He told them of naked corpses in the Warsaw ghetto, yellow stars, starving children, Jew hunts, and the smell of burning flesh. Karski relayed a personal message to Zygielbojm from Leon Feiner, the leader of the Bund trapped in Warsaw. Feiner had instructed Zygielbojm to stop with the empty protests and urge retaliatory bombing, leafleting, and the execution of Germans in Allied hands.[5] Karski said that when he had cautioned that the proposals were "bitter and unrealistic," Feiner had countered with: "We don't know what is realistic, or not realistic. We are dying here! Say it!"[6] Karski, who had a photographic memory, recited Feiner's parting appeal to Jewish leaders to do something dramatic to force people to believe the reports:

> We are all dying here; let [the Jews in Allied countries] die too. Let them crowd the offices of Churchill, of all the important English and American leaders and agencies. Let them proclaim a fast before the doors of the mightiest, not retreating until they will believe us, until they will undertake some action to rescue those of our people who are still alive. Let them die a slow death while the world is looking on. This may shake the conscience of the world.

Upon hearing Feiner's message, Zygielbojm leaped from his seat and began pacing back and forth across the room. "It is impossible," he said, "utterly impossible. You know what would happen. They would simply bring in two policemen and have me dragged away to an institution. . . . Do you think they will let me die a slow lingering death? Never. . . . They would never let me die."[7] As he continued questioning Karski, an agitated Zygielbojm pleaded with his messenger to believe he had done all he could. Two weeks later in a BBC broadcast Zygielbojm declared, "It will actually be a shame to go on living, to belong to the human race, if steps are not taken to halt the greatest crime in history."[8]

Karski traveled to the United States and met with Supreme Court justice Felix Frankfurter, who graciously heard him out and then responded,

"I don't believe you." When a stunned Karski protested, Frankfurter interrupted him and explained, "I do not mean that you are lying. I simply said
I cannot believe you."[9] Frankfurter literally could not conceive of the
atrocities Karski was describing. He was not alone. Isaiah Berlin, who
worked at the British embassy in Washington from 1942, saw only a massive pogrom. So, too, did Nahum Goldman, Chaim Weizmann, David Ben-
Gurion, and other leading Zionists.[10]

The Germans did their part, issuing ritual denials and cloaking the Final
Solution in the euphemisms of "resettlement." Joseph Goebbels, Hitler's
minister of propaganda and national enlightenment, met atrocity reports by
pointing to British abuses carried out in India and elsewhere, a tactic he
deemed "our best chance of getting away from the embarrassing subject of
the Jews."[11] The Swiss-based International Committee of the Red Cross
(ICRC), which documented the deportations, did not publicly protest
because, it concluded, "public protests are not only ineffectual but are apt
to produce a stiffening of the indicted country's attitude with regard to
Committee, even the rupture of relations with it."[12] Intervention would be
futile and would jeopardize the organization's ability to conduct prison
inspections, deliver humanitarian parcels, and transmit messages among
family members. Neutrality was paramount.

The Allies' suppression of the truth about Hitler's Final Solution has
been the subject of a great deal of historical scholarship.[13] Intelligence on
Hitler's extermination was plentiful in both classified and open sources.
The United States maintained embassies in Berlin until December 1941, in
Budapest and Bucharest until January 1942, and in Vichy France until late
1942.[14] The British used sophisticated decryption technology to intercept
German communications. The major Jewish organizations had representatives in Geneva who relayed vivid and numerous refugee reports through
Stephen Wise, the president of the World Jewish Congress (WJC), and others. In July 1942, Gerhard Riegner, the WJC Geneva representative,
informed the State Department of a well-placed German industrialist's
report that Hitler had ordered the extermination of European Jewry by
gassing. In November 1942, Rabbi Wise, who knew President Roosevelt
personally, told a Washington press conference that he and the State
Department had reliable information that some 2 million Jews had already
been murdered. The Polish government-in-exile was a goldmine of information. Already by the fall of 1942, for instance, Zygielbojm had begun
meeting regularly with Arthur J. Goldberg, General Bill Donovan's special

assistant at the Office of Strategic Services (OSS), to discuss the death camps.

But the intelligence was often played down. In June 1942, for instance, the London *Daily Telegraph* published the Bund report's claim that 700,000 Polish Jews and more than 1 million Jews throughout Europe had been killed. The *New York Times* picked up the *Telegraph*'s reports but buried them deep inside the paper.[15] When Riegner cabled word of Hitler's plot the following month, British and U.S. officials and journalists were skeptical about the veracity of "unsubstantiated information." In the words of one Swiss foreign editor, "We received no picture of photographic exactitude, only silhouettes."[16] In 1944, when John Pehle, the director of Roosevelt's War Refugee Board, wanted to publish the report of two Auschwitz escapees, Elmer Davis, the head of the U.S. Office of War Information, turned down his request. The American public would not believe such wild stories, he said, and Europeans would be so demoralized by them that their resistance would crumble. The U.S. ambassador to Sweden, Hershel Johnson, sent a cable in April 1943 detailing the extermination of Jews in Warsaw, but he ended his message by noting: "So fantastic is the story. . . that I hesitate to make it the subject of an official report."[17] In the November 1943 Stalin-Roosevelt-Churchill declaration, reference to the gas chambers was deleted because the evidence was deemed untrustworthy. To paraphrase Walter Laqueur, a pioneer in the study of the Allies' response to the Holocaust, although many people thought that the Jews were no longer alive, they did not necessarily believe they were dead.[18]

Why and how did people live in "a twilight between knowing and not knowing"?[19] For starters, the threat Hitler posed to all of civilization helped overshadow his specific targeting of the Jews. Widespread anti-Semitism also contributed. It was not that readers' prejudice against Jews necessarily made them happy to hear reports of Hitler's monstrosity. Rather, their indifference to the fate of Jews likely caused them to skim the stories and to focus on other aspects of the war. Others did not take the time to process the reports because they believed the Allies were doing all they could; there was no point in getting depressed about something they could not control. Such knowledge was inconvenient. Karski later recalled that Allied leaders "discarded their conscience" with the rationale that "the Jews were totally helpless. The war strategy was the military defeat of Germany."[20] Winning the war was the most efficient way to stop Hitler's murder of civilians. The Allied governments worked indirectly to help

Jewish victims by attempting to defeat him, but they rejected the Jewish leaders' request to declare as a war aim the rescue of Europe's Jews.

The vast majority of people simply did not believe what they read; the notion of getting attacked for being (rather than for doing) was too discomfiting and too foreign to process readily. A plot for outright annihilation had never been seen and therefore could not be imagined. The tales of German cremation factories and gas chambers sounded far-fetched. The deportations could be explained: Hitler needed Jewish slave labor for the war effort. During the Turkish campaign against the Armenians, this same propensity for incredulity was evident, but it was even more pronounced in the 1940s because of a backlash against the hyped-up "Belgian atrocities" of World War I.[21] During that war, journalists had faithfully relayed tales of bloodthirsty "Huns" mutilating and raping nuns and dismembering Belgian babies. Indeed, they reported claims that the Germans had erected a "corpse-conversion factory" where they boiled human fat and bones into lubricants and glycerine.[22] In the 1920s and 1930s, the press had debunked many of the Allies' wartime reports of German savagery, yielding a "hangover of skepticism." Although many of these stories were confirmed years later, they were still being discredited at the outbreak of World War II.[23] When tales of Nazi gas vans and extermination plots emerged, many people believed that such stories were being manufactured or embellished as part of an Allied propaganda effort. Just as military strategists are apt to "fight the last war"—to employ tactics tailored for prior battlefield foes—political leaders and ordinary citizens tend to overapply the "lessons of history" to new and distinct challenges.

In his campaign to convey the horror of Nazi atrocities, Zygielbojm tried to overcome people's instinctive mistrust of accounts of gratuitous violence. But he began to despair of doing so. In 1943 he learned that his wife and child had died in the Warsaw ghetto. In April 1943, at the Bermuda conference, after twelve days of secretive and ineffectual meetings, the Allies rejected most of the modest proposals to expand refugee admissions, continuing to severely limit the number of Jews who would be granted temporary refuge in the United States and unoccupied Europe.[24] On May 10, over dinner in London, Arthur Goldberg of the OSS informed Zygielbojm that the United States had rejected his requests to bomb Auschwitz and the Warsaw ghetto. "With understandable pain and anguish," Goldberg remembered later, "I told him that our government was not prepared to do what he requested because in the view of our high command, aircraft were not available for this purpose."[25]

Zygielbojm could take it no more. He typed up a letter, addressed it to the president and prime minister of the Polish government-in-exile, and explained his imminent act:

> The responsibility for this crime of murdering the entire Jewish population of Poland falls in the first instance on the perpetrators, but indirectly also it weighs on the whole of humanity, the peoples and governments of the Allied States, which so far have made no effort toward a concrete action for the purpose of curtailing this crime.
>
> By passive observation of this murder of defenseless millions and of the maltreatment of children, women, and old men, these countries have become the criminals' accomplices. . . .
>
> I can not be silent and I can not live while the remnants of the Jewish people of Poland, of whom I am a representative, are perishing. . . .
>
> By my death I wish to express my strongest protest against the inactivity with which the world is looking on and permitting the extermination of Jewish people. I know how little human life is worth, especially today. But as I was unable to do anything during my life, perhaps by my death I shall contribute to destroying the indifference of those who are able and should act.[26]

Szmul Zygielbojm took an overdose of sleeping pills in his Paddington flat on May 12, 1943. News that the Nazis had crushed the Warsaw ghetto uprising and liquidated its inhabitants reached London and Washington the day of his memorial service.[27]

The *New York Times* published Zygielbojm's suicide letter on June 4, 1943, under the headline "Pole's Suicide Note Pleads for Jews" with the further headline "He Denounced Apathy." The last line of the *Times* piece suggested that Zygielbojm "may have achieved more in his death than in his life." In fact, he failed to alter Allied policy in either state.[28]

In Their Own Words

Back in Washington, Raphael Lemkin, too, thought of taking his own life but concluded he was too "peculiarly placed" to bow out. After all, while others were mulling atrocity prevention for the first time, he had been

National Archives, courtesy of USHMM Photo Archives

Jews in the Warsaw ghetto being marched to the rail station for deportation, in 1943. Of the four members of the family shown at the head of the column, only the man survived.

thinking about it for more than a decade. He identified himself with the cause and quickly began to personify it. When he read the chilling reports from his homeland, he did what Zyegielbojm had done initially—he placed faith in information. Lemkin also played to his strengths: law and language.

In November 1944 the Carnegie Endowment for International Peace published Lemkin's *Axis Rule in Occupied Europe,* by then a 712-page book of the rules and decrees imposed by the Axis powers and their client states in nineteen Nazi-occupied countries and territories in Europe. Having begun gathering these laws while in Sweden, Lemkin had continued the compilation as part of his service to the U.S. government. Whatever Lemkin's stated aspirations to appeal to a popular audience, *Axis Rule* was a dry and staunchly legalistic reference book.[29] It included proposals for post-war restitution of property to the dispossessed and for the reimbursement of millions to foreign workers who had been forced into labor in Germany. It also restated his 1933 Madrid proposal to outlaw the targeted destruction of groups and urged the creation of an international treaty that could be used as a basis for trying and punishing perpetrators.

However useful the book's recommendations, Lemkin believed his real contribution lay in reproducing the stark collection of decrees (which accounted for some 360 of the book's pages). These, he was certain, would do wonders to combat widespread disbelief and despondency, especially in the Anglo-American reader, who, he wrote, "with his innate respect for human rights and human personality may be inclined to believe that the Axis regime could not possibly have been as cruel and ruthless as it has been hitherto described." By presenting documents authored by Hitler and his advisers, he was ensuring that nobody in the United States could say he was exaggerating or propagandizing.

A few scholars still rejected atrocity reports and tried to relativize German responsibility. The harshest review of *Axis Rule* appeared in the *American Journal of Sociology* in 1946. The reviewer, Melchior Palyi, blamed Lemkin for his failure to explore the "extenuating circumstances" for Nazi behavior. According to Palyi, Lemkin had written a "prosecutor's brief" rather than an "impartial" inquiry. The reviewer claimed that almost every one of the nine charges Lemkin made against the Nazis could be made against the Allies. "Of course," the reviewer wrote, "there is this substantial difference: that the Nazis shamelessly displayed their intentionally planned misdeeds, while the western Allies stumble into illegal practices and cover them with humanitarian or other formulas."[30]

But most reviews were favorable and did not dabble in such false equivalency. The *American Journal of International Law* described Lemkin's collection of Nazi legislation as a "tour de force."[31] Another reviewer wrote, "The terrorism of the German police is well enough known, but to see matters described in cold legal terminology creates in one perhaps an even greater sense of indignation."[32] At this time Lemkin was somewhat conflicted about the roots of responsibility and the relative role of individual and collective guilt, theories of accountability that continue to compete today. On the one hand, Lemkin urged the punishment of those *individuals* responsible for Nazi horrors. On the other, he espoused an early version of the theory, put forth again recently by Daniel Jonah Goldhagen in his book *Hitler's Willing Executioners,* that ascribed guilt not only to the perpetrators of the crimes but to their fellow citizens who failed to stop them and often appeared actively supportive.[33] In *Axis Rule* Lemkin wrote, "The present destruction of Europe would not be complete and thorough had the German people not accepted freely [the Nazi] plan, participated voluntarily in its execution, and up to this point profited greatly therefrom." He refused to accept the line that all but the most senior German authorities were just "obeying orders," insisting that "all important classes and groups of the population have voluntarily assisted Hitler in the scheme of world domination."[34]

In January 1945 the *New York Times Book Review* devoted its cover to *Axis Rule.* "Out of its dry legalism," the reviewer wrote, "there emerge the contours of the monster that now bestrides the earth." This monster "gorges itself on blood, bestializes its servants and perverts some of the noblest human emotions to base ends, all with the semblance of authority and spurious legality which leave the individual helpless." The reviewer credited Lemkin with capturing "what Axis rule in occupied Europe means and what it would have meant to us had it ever spread to our shores." But he faulted Lemkin's sweeping ascription of blame. By finding "innate viciousness" in the German people, Lemkin was feeding "nazism-in-reverse." "Surely," the reviewer wrote, "just because he is a Pole Dr. Lemkin would not want to be held personally responsible for all the acts of the Pilsudski regime."[35]

A Word Is a Word Is a Word

Axis Rule is not remembered for stirring this once and future debate about the nature of individual and collective guilt. Instead, it is known because it was in this rather arcane, legalistic tome that Lemkin followed through on his pledge to himself and to his imagined co-conspirator, Winston Churchill. Ever since Lemkin had heard Churchill's 1941 radio address, he had been determined to find a new word to replace "barbarity" and "vandalism," which had failed him at the 1933 Madrid conference. Lemkin had hunted for a term that would describe assaults on all aspects of nationhood—physical, biological, political, social, cultural, economic, and religious. He wanted to connote not only full-scale extermination but also Hitler's other means of destruction: mass deportation, the lowering of the birthrate by separating men from women, economic exploitation, progressive starvation, and the suppression of the intelligentsia who served as national leaders.

New York Times Book Review cover story on Raphael
Lemkin's *Axis Rule in Occupied Europe*.

Lemkin, the former philology student, knew that his word choice mattered a great deal. He weighed a number of candidates. "Mass murder" was inadequate because it failed to incorporate the singular motive behind the perpetration of the crime he had in mind. "Denationalization," a word that had been used to describe attempts to destroy a nation and wipe out its cultural personality, failed because it had come to mean depriving citizens of citizenship. And "Germanization," "Magyarization," and other specified words connoting forced assimilation of culture came up short because they could not be applied universally and because they did not convey biological destruction.[36]

Lemkin read widely in linguistic and semantic theory, modeling his own process on that of individuals responsible for coinages he admired. Of particular interest to Lemkin were the reflections of George Eastman, who said he had settled upon "Kodak" as the name for his new camera because: "First. It is short. Second. It is not capable of mispronunciation. Third. It

does not resemble anything in the art and cannot be associated with anything in the art except the Kodak."

Lemkin saw he needed a word that could not be used in other contexts
(as "barbarity" and "vandalism" could). He self-consciously sought one that
would bring with it "a color of freshness and novelty" while describing
something "as shortly and as poignantly as possible."[37]

But Lemkin's coinage had to achieve something Eastman's did not.
Somehow it had to chill listeners and invite immediate condemnation. On
an otherwise undecipherable page of one of his surviving notebooks,
Lemkin scribbled and circled "THE WORD" and drew a line connecting the
circle to the phrase, penned firmly, "MORAL JUDGEMENT." His word would
do it all. It would be the rare term that carried in it society's revulsion and
indignation. It would be what he called an "index of civilization."[38]

The word that Lemkin settled upon was a hybrid that combined the
Greek derivative *geno,* meaning "race" or "tribe," together with the Latin
derivative *cide,* from *caedere,* meaning "killing." "Genocide" was short, it was
novel, and it was not likely to be mispronounced. Because of the word's
lasting association with Hitler's horrors, it would also send shudders down
the spines of those who heard it.

Lemkin was unusual in the trust he placed in language. Many of his
Jewish contemporaries despaired of it, deeming silence preferable to the
necessarily inadequate verbal and written attempts to approximate the
Holocaust. Austrian writer and philosopher Jean Améry was one of many
Holocaust survivors estranged from words:

> Was it "like a red-hot iron in my shoulders" and was this "like a blunt
> wooden stake driven into the base of my head?"—a simile would
> only stand for something else, and in the end we would be led around
> by the nose in a hopeless carousel of comparisons. Pain was what it
> was. There's nothing further to say about it. Qualities of feeling are as
> incomparable as they are indescribable. They mark the limits of lan-
> guage's ability to communicate.[39]

The suffering inflicted by Hitler fell outside the realm of expression.

But Lemkin was prepared to reinvest in language. New to the United
States and wracked by anxiety about his family, he viewed the preparation of *Axis Rule* and the coinage of a new word as a constructive distrac-

tion. At the same time, he did not intend for "genocide" to capture or communicate Hitler's Final Solution. The word derived from Lemkin's original interpretations of barbarity and vandalism. In *Axis Rule* he wrote that "genocide" meant "a coordinated plan *of different* actions aiming at the destruction of essential foundations of the life of national groups, with the aim of annihilating the groups themselves."[40] The perpetrators of genocide would attempt to destroy the political and social institutions, the culture, language, national feelings, religion, and economic existence of national groups. They would hope to eradicate the personal security, liberty, health, dignity, and lives of individual members of the targeted group. He continued:

> Genocide has two phases: one, destruction of the national pattern of the oppressed group; the other, the imposition of the national pattern of the oppressor. This imposition, in turn, may be made upon the oppressed population which is allowed to remain, or upon the territory alone, after removal of the population and colonization of the area by the oppressor's own nationals.[41]

A group did not have to be physically exterminated to suffer genocide. They could be stripped of all cultural traces of their identity. "It takes centuries and sometimes thousands of years to create a natural culture," Lemkin wrote, "but Genocide can destroy a culture instantly, like fire can destroy a building in an hour."[42]

From the start, the meaning of "genocide" was controversial. Many people were receptive to the idea of coining a word that would connote a practice so horrid and so irreparable that the very utterance of the word would galvanize all who heard it. They also recognized that it would be unwise and undesirable to make Hitler's crimes the future standard for moving outsiders to act. Statesmen and citizens needed to learn from the past without letting it paralyze them. They had to respond to mass atrocity long before the carnage had reached the scale of the Holocaust. But the link between Hitler's Final Solution and Lemkin's hybrid term would cause endless confusion for policymakers and ordinary people who assumed that genocide occurred only where the perpetrator of atrocity could be shown, like Hitler, to possess an intent to exterminate every last member of an ethnic, national, or religious group.

Others were critical not so much of Lemkin's definition as his apparent naivete. His innovation was interesting, they said, but a word is a word is a word. Merely affixing the genocide label would not necessarily cause statesmen to put aside their other interests, fears, or constraints. Even if lawyers in Madrid had adopted Lemkin's proposal, they noted, neither the existence of the label nor the application of it would have affected Hitler's decisionmaking, his ideology, or the outside world's lethargic response to his crimes. Lemkin met these criticisms with defensive bombast. He told a North Carolina audience that the rejection of his Madrid proposal was "one of the thousand reasons why. . . your boys are fighting and dying in different parts of the world at this very moment."[43]

Yet for all of the criticisms, the word took hold. Lemkin proudly brandished the letter from the *Webster's New International Dictionary* that informed him that "genocide" had been admitted. Other lexicographers followed suit.[44] In the book he began writing immediately after *Axis Rule,* Lemkin noted that the "individual creator" of a word would see his word absorbed only "if, and in so far as, it meets popular needs and tastes." He insisted that the rapid acceptance of "genocide" by lexicographers and humanity served as "social testimony" to the world's readiness to confront the crime.[45]

Certainly, current events seemed to ratify Lemkin's assumption. The very week the Carnegie Endowment published his book, the Roosevelt administration's War Refugee Board for the first time officially backed up European charges of mass executions by the Germans.[46] "So revolting and diabolical are the German atrocities that the minds of civilized people find it difficult to believe that they have actually taken place," the board stated. "But the governments of the United States and other countries have evidence which clearly substantiates the facts." Many newspapers linked their coverage of the board report with Lemkin's term. On December 3, 1944, for instance, after Lemkin persuaded Eugene Meyer, the publisher of the *Washington Post,* the paper's editorial board hailed "genocide" as the only word befitting the revelation that between April 1942 and April 1944 some 1,765,000 Jews had been gassed and cremated at Auschwitz-Birkenau. "It is a mistake, perhaps, to call these killings 'atrocities,'" the editorial entitled "Genocide" read. "An atrocity is a wanton brutality. . . . But the point about these killings is that they were systematic and purposeful. The gas chambers and furnaces were not improvisations; they were scientifically designed instruments for the extermination of an entire ethnic group."[47]

Lemkin made little secret of his desire to see "genocide" gain international fame. As he proselytized on behalf of the new concept, he studied the lingual inventions of science and literary greats.[48] But fame for the word was just the beginning. The world had embraced the term "genocide." Lemkin assumed this meant the major powers were ready both to apply the word and oppose the deed.

Sergeant William Best greets nineteen-year-old Joseph Guttman, survivor of Buchenwald, whom he adopted. New York, December 24, 1948.

Chapter 4

Lemkin's Law

"Only man has law. . . . You must build the law!"
—Raphael Lemkin

The Nuremberg Beginning

With the end of war in Europe on May 8, 1945, and the Allied liberation of the Nazi death camps, the scale of Hitler's madness had been revealed. Practically all that had sounded far-fetched proved real. Some 6 million Jews and 5 million Poles, Roma, Communists, and other "undesirables" had been exterminated. American and European leaders saw that a state's treatment of its own citizens could be indicative of how it would behave toward its neighbors. And though sovereignty was still thought to be sacrosanct, a few scholars had begun gently urging that it not be defined so as to permit slaughter.[1]

Raphael Lemkin had never needed much encouragement, but Allied rhetoric made him believe that the world might be ready to listen. If genocide were to be prevented or punished, "genocide" would need more than a place in *Webster's*. Naming the crime was just a first step along the road to banning it. That road would prove a long one. Law had of course been one tool among many used and abused to facilitate the destruction of the Jews. Hans Frank, former German minister of justice, had summed up a core Nazi premise when he said, "Law is that which is useful and necessary for the German nation."[2] Nobody knew better than Lemkin the legal minutiae deployed by Germany to achieve its eliminationist ends. Yet for Lemkin this recent soiling of law only highlighted the need to restore its integrity through humane invention. A set of universal, higher norms, was needed as a backstop to national law. The "theory of master race had to be replaced," he said, by a "theory of master morality."[3]

It would be the new United Nations that would decide whether to criminalize genocide as states had already done with piracy; forgery; trade in women, slaves, and drugs; and as they would later do with terrorism. In a letter to the *New York Times,* Lemkin wrote:

> It seems inconsistent with our concepts of civilization that selling a drug to an individual is a matter of worldly concern, while gassing millions of human beings might be a problem of internal concern. It seems also inconsistent with our philosophy of life that abduction of one woman for prostitution is an international crime while sterilization of millions of women remains an internal affair of the state in question.[4]

If piracy was an international crime, he could not understand why genocide was not. "Certainly human beings and their cultures are more important than a ship and its cargo," he exclaimed at a postwar international law conference in Cambridge. "Surely Shakespeare is more precious than cotton."[5]

Lemkin was initially quite well received in the United States. After years of getting jeered or yawned out of international law conferences, he suddenly found himself with a measure of cachet in the U.S. capital and with a standing invitation to contribute to the country's major publications.

In Nuremberg, Germany, the three victors (and France) had set up an international military tribunal to try the leading Nazi perpetrators. The Nuremberg court was placing important dents in state armor. Indeed, it was amid considerable controversy that the Nuremberg charter prosecuted "crimes against humanity," the concept the Allies had introduced during World War I to condemn the Turks for their atrocities against the Armenians. With Nuremberg going so far as to try European officials for crimes committed against their own citizens, future perpetrators of atrocities—even those acting under explicit state authority—could no longer be confident that their governments or their borders would shelter them from trial.

Since Nuremberg was making this inroad into state sovereignty, one might have expected Lemkin to cheer from the sidelines. In fact, he was a fierce critic of the court. Nuremberg was prosecuting "crimes against humanity," but the Allies were not punishing slaughter whenever and wherever it occurred, as Lemkin would have wished. The court treated aggressive war ("crimes against peace"), or the violation of another state's sovereignty, as the cardinal sin and prosecuted only those crimes against humanity and war crimes committed *after* Hitler crossed an internationally recognized border.[6] Nazi defendants were thus tried for atrocities they committed during but not before World War II. By inference, if the Nazis had exterminated the entire German Jewish population but never invaded Poland, they would not have been liable at Nuremberg. States and individuals who did not cross an international frontier were still free under international law to commit genocide. Thus, although the court did a fine job building a case against Hitler and his associates, Lemkin felt it would do little to deter future Hitlers.

In May 1946 Lemkin turned up in the rubble of Nuremberg as a kind of semiofficial adviser (or lobbyist) so that he could proselytize in person. He knew the charter's terms were fixed, but he hoped to get "genocide" incorporated into the prosecutors' parlance and spotlighted on the Nuremberg stage. Even if genocide were not punished, at least the court could help popularize the new term. Lemkin had been teaching part time at Yale Law School. He convinced the dean, Wesley Sturges, to grant him leave on the grounds that it was better to develop international law than to teach it.

Lemkin had spent most of his time since the war's end tracking down his missing family members. In Nuremberg he met up with his older brother, Elias; Elias's wife; and their two sons. They told him that they were the family's sole survivors. At least forty-nine others, including his parents, aunts, uncles, and cousins, had perished in the Warsaw ghetto, in concentration camps, or on Nazi death marches.[7] In the words of one lawyer who remembers Lemkin roaming around the corridors at the Nuremberg Palace of Justice, he was "obviously a man in pain."

If Lemkin was relentless before, the loss of his parents pressed him into overdrive. He spent his days buttonholing lawyers in the halls of the Palace of Justice. Some were sympathetic to his graphic war stories. Others were irritated. Benjamin Ferencz was a young lawyer on Nuremberg prosecutor Telford Taylor's staff, which was building a case against the *Einsatzgruppen*, the mobile killing units that butchered Jews in Eastern Europe. He remembers Lemkin as a disheveled, disoriented refugee less concerned with hanging the Nazi war criminals than with getting genocide included in the tribunal's list of punishable crimes. Most of the prosecutors tried to avoid him, seeing him as a nag or, in Yiddish, a nudnik. "We were all extremely busy. This new idea of his was not something we had time to think about," Ferencz recalls. "We wanted him to just leave us alone so we could convict these guys of mass murder."

Lemkin did score an occasional victory. Because of his prior lobbying efforts, the third count of the October 1945 Nuremberg indictment had stated that all twenty-four defendants "conducted deliberate and systematic genocide, viz., the extermination of racial and national groups, against the civilian populations of certain occupied territories." This was the first official mention of genocide in an international legal setting. On June 26, 1946, British prosecutor David Maxwell Fyfe cheered Lemkin by telling Nazi suspect Constantin von Neurath, "Now, defendant, you know that in the indictment in this trial we are charging you and your fellow defendants, among other things, with genocide."[8] Lemkin wrote Fyfe that summer to thank him "for your great and so effective support which you lent to the concept of Genocide." He also urged Fyfe to get "genocide" included in the Nuremberg judgment.[9]

In late 1946 a weary Lemkin flew from Germany to a pair of peace conferences in England and France. His proposal was again rejected, here on the grounds that he was "trying to push international law into a field where it did not belong." "Afterward he was admitted to an American military hospital in Paris with high blood pressure.[10] No sooner did he land in the hospital ward than he caught two stories on the radio that convinced him he had to return to the United States immediately. First, on what he would later call the "the blackest day" of his life, he heard the pronouncement of the Nuremberg tribunal. Nineteen Nazi defendants were convicted of crimes against peace, war crimes, and crimes against humanity. No mention was made of genocide. But Lemkin heard a second item: The new UN General Assembly had begun deliberating the contents of its autumn agenda. Lemkin checked himself out of the hospital and flew to New York. On the plane he drafted a sample General Assembly resolution condemning genocide.

Closing the Loophole:
Moving from Word to Declaration

Lemkin's aim in New York was to establish an international law that did not link the destruction of groups to cross-border aggression, which accompanied genocide in the Nazi case but often would not. Nuremberg, he noted, had made "an advance of 10 or 20 percent" toward outlawing genocide.[12] It had left far too many loopholes through which killers could squirm. Statesmen were interested in preventing war, but they had less interest in genocide. "Genocide is not war!" he wrote, "It is more dangerous than war!"[13] War, of course, has killed more individuals in history than has genocide, and it too leaves its survivors permanently scarred. But Lemkin argued that when a group was targeted with genocide—and was effectively destroyed physically or culturally—the loss was permanent. Even those individuals who survived genocide would be forever shorn of an invaluable part of their identity.

On October 31, 1946, Lemkin arrived at the newly improvised UN headquarters, located in an abandoned Sperry Gyroscope war plant on Long Island.[14] The entrenched and somewhat impenetrable UN of today was then unimaginable. Security guards were willing to look the other way when the unaccredited, somewhat fanatical lawyer would turn any empty UN office into his home for the day—"like a hermit crab," a Hungarian friend said.[15] Lemkin spent endless hours haunting the drafty halls.

Kathleen Teltsch and A. M. Rosenthal were then cub reporters with the *New York Times*. Both were fond of Lemkin but recall the horror of many a correspondent and diplomat when the wild-eyed professor with steel-rimmed glasses and a relentless appetite for rejection began sprinting after them in the corridors, saying, "You and I, we must change the world." Teltsch remembers:

> He was always there like a shadow, a presence, floating through the halls and constantly pulling scraps of paper out of his pockets. He was not loved because he was known as a time consumer. If he managed to nab you, you were trapped. Correspondents on deadline used to run from him like mad. But he would run after them, tie flopping in the air, genocide story at the ready.

Rosenthal occupied the desk nearest the door of the *New York Times* office, where Lemkin popped his head in several times a day offering a new angle on the genocide story. "I don't remember how I met him," Rosenthal says, "but I remember I was *always* meeting him." Carrying his black briefcase, he would say, "Here is that pest, that Lemkin. . . . I have a genocide story for you."[16]

Most of the correspondents who bothered to notice Lemkin wondered how he made ends meet. He was learned enough to maintain a quiet dignity about him, but his collar and cuffs were frayed at the edges, his black shoes scuffed. The journalists frequently spotted him in the UN cafeteria cornering delegates, but they never saw him eat. In his rush to persuade delegates to support him, he frequently fainted from hunger. Completely alone in the world and perennially sleepless, he often wandered the streets at night.[17] A *New York Post* reporter described him as growing "paler, thinner and shabbier" as the months passed. He seemed determined to stay in perpetual motion.

However irritating the correspondents and delegates found Lemkin, his efforts in New York were well timed. The images of Allied camp liberations remained fresh in people's minds; the Nuremberg proceedings had fueled interest in international law; the United Nations had high hopes for itself as a collective security body; and powerful member states seemed prepared to invest clout and resources toward ensuring its success. Around the world, even in the United States, people believed in the UN's promise. The organization carried with it a grand air of possibility. When UN planners had met in San Francisco in 1945 to complete the UN charter, E. B. White summed up the hopes of many. "The delegates to San Francisco have the most astonishing job that has ever been dumped into the laps of a few individuals," White wrote. "On what sort of rabbit they pull from the hat hang the lives of most of us, and of our sons and daughters."[18]

The United Nations was new; it was newsworthy; and if you wanted something done, it was the place to bring your proposal.[19] Many advocates peddled schemes to the new body. But diplomats quietly learned to distinguish Lemkin (thanks to hefty packages that he thrust upon them containing his memos, letters, and his 712-page *Axis Rule*). He was the one who had foreseen the need to ban genocide ahead of World War II. Indeed, when the UN delegates in the new General Assembly began debating whether to pass a resolution on genocide, Lemkin beamed as Britain's UN delegate pointed out that the League of Nation's failure to accept Lemkin's Madrid proposal had allowed the Nazis to escape punishment at Nuremberg for the atrocities they committed before the war.

Ten years of lobbying had taught Lemkin to play up both the values at stake and the interests. He stressed the costs of genocide not only to victims, with whom few in New York would identify, but also to bystanders. The destruction of foreign national or ethnic identities would bring huge losses to the world's cultural heritage. All of humankind, even those who did not feel vulnerable to genocide, would suffer:

> We can best understand this when we realize how impoverished our culture would be if the peoples doomed by Germany, such as the Jews, had not been permitted to create the Bible, or to give birth to an Einstein, a Spinoza; if the Poles had not had the opportunity to give to the world a Copernicus, a Chopin, a Curie; the Czechs, a Huss, a Dvořák; the Greeks, a Plato and a Socrates; the Russians, a Tolstoy and a Shostakovich.[20]

With time running out in the General Assembly session, Lemkin homed in on the ambassadors from several developing countries and urged them to introduce a resolution on genocide. His logic—"large countries can defend themselves by arms; small countries need the protection of the law"—proved persuasive. After convincing the Panamanian, Cuban, and Indian representatives to sign a draft resolution, he rushed "like an intoxicated man" to the office of the secretary-general, where he deposited the proposed text.[21] Lemkin also got essential support from Adlai Stevenson, the U.S. representative on the UN Steering Committee. Hoping to neutralize anticipated Soviet opposition, he called upon Jan Masaryk of Czechoslovakia. Ahead of the meeting, Lemkin had hurriedly reviewed the works of Masaryk's father, Thomas Garrigue Masaryk, who had written extensively on the cultural personality of nations. Lemkin told Masaryk that if his father were alive, he would be lobbying for the passage of the genocide convention. Lemkin urged him to win over the Russian foreign minister, Andrei Vishinsky, saying that the Soviet Union had nothing to fear from the law, as "penicillin is not an intrigue against the Soviet Union." Masaryk pulled out his appointment calendar for the next day and jotted: "Vishinsky. Genocide. Penicillin." He called Lemkin within twenty-four hours to inform him that he had persuaded Vishinsky to support the measure.[22]

As the language for the genocide resolution was batted around the special committee, some proposed using the word "extermination" instead of "genocide." But Judge Abdul Monim Bey Riad of Saudi Arabia, whom

Lemkin considered the most sophisticated of all representatives, pleaded that "extermination" was a term that could also apply to insects and animals. He also warned that the word would limit the prohibited crime to circumstances where every member of the group was killed. Lemkin's broader concept, "genocide," was important because it signaled destruction apart from physical destruction and because it would require states to respond before all the damage had been done. The more expansive term "genocide" was preserved.

On December 11, 1946, one year after the final armistice, the General Assembly unanimously passed a resolution that condemned genocide as "the denial of the right of existence of entire human groups," which "shocks the conscience of mankind" and is "contrary to moral law and to the spirit and aims of the United Nations." More gratifying to Lemkin, who was no fan of declarations, the resolution tasked a UN committee with drafting a full-fledged UN treaty banning the crime. If that measure passed the General Assembly and was ratified by two-thirds of the UN member states, it would become international law.

A *New York Times* editorial proclaimed that the resolution and the ensuing law would mark a "revolutionary development" in international law. The editors wrote, "The right to exterminate entire groups which prevailed before the resolution was adopted is gone. From now on no government may kill off a large block of its own subjects or citizens of any country with impunity."[23] Lemkin returned to his run-down one-room apartment in Manhattan, pulled down the shades, and slept for two days.[24]

Closing the Loophole: Moving from Resolution to Law

At the behest of UN Secretary-General Trygve Lie, Lemkin helped prepare the first draft of the UN genocide convention.[25] When the official UN process kicked in, however, the Polish lawyer bowed out, knowing he could be more valuable on the outside. In 1947 Lemkin began work on a history of genocide and carried a thick file folder bulging with gruesome details on various cases. He took his cause and himself exceptionally seriously. Later, with full sincerity, he wrote that "of particular interest" to UN delegates were his "files on the destruction of the Maronites, the Herreros in Africa, the Huguenots in France, the Protestants in Bohemia after the

Battle of White Mountain, the Hottentots, the Armenians in 1915 and the Jews, gypsies and Slavs by the Nazis."[26] Many stuffy UN delegates would eventually agree to vote for the proposed convention simply in order to bring the daily litany of carnage to as rapid an end as possible.

This was a crucial phase. If he kept up the pressure, Lemkin believed the law would at last be born. Rosenthal often challenged Lemkin with the realist reproach: "Lemkin, what good will it do to write mass murder down as a crime; will a piece of paper stop a new Hitler or Stalin?" Lemkin, the believer, would stiffen and snap: "Only man has law. Law must be built, do you understand me? You must build the law!" As Rosenthal notes, "He was not naive. He didn't expect criminals to lay down and stop committing crimes. He simply believed that if the law was in place it would have an effect—sooner or later."[27]

For a legal dreamer, a man with no experience in Polish politics, and a newcomer to the American and UN political processes, Lemkin had surprisingly sharp political instincts. He had learned one lesson during the Holocaust, which was that if a UN genocide convention were ever to come to pass, he would have to appeal to the domestic political interests of UN delegates. He obtained lists of the most important organizations in each of the UN member states and assembled a committee that spoke for groups in twenty-eight countries and claimed a remarkable joint membership of more than 240 million people. The committee, which was more of a front for Lemkin, compiled and sent petitions to each UN delegate urging passage of the convention. UN diplomats who hesitated received telegrams—usually drafted by Lemkin—from organizations at home. He used the letters to make delegates feel as if "by working for the Genocide Convention," they were "representing the wishes of their own people."[28] Lemkin wrote personally to UN delegates and foreign ministers from most countries. In Catholic countries he preached to bishops and archbishops. In Scandinavia, where organized labor was active, he penned notes to the large labor groups. He cornered intellectuals like Pearl Buck, Bertrand Russell, Aldous Huxley, and Gabriela Mistral, who published an appeal in the New York Times on November 11, 1947. A Times editorial branded Lemkin "the man who speaks through sixty nations."

Although Lemkin was determined to see genocidal perpetrators prosecuted, he did not believe the genocide convention should itself create a permanent international criminal court. The world was "not ready," he said, as the court would mark too great an affront to state sovereignty. Instead, under the "universal repression" principle, genocidists should be treated as pirates had been in the past: Any country could try a genocide suspect, regardless of where the atrocities were committed.

In August 1948 Lemkin cobbled together the funds to fly to Geneva to lobby the UN subcommittee that was overseeing the drafting of the actual text of the genocide convention.[29] No longer working at the State Department or teaching, he lived off donations from religious groups and borrowed from a cousin who lived on Long Island. He found his stay in Geneva eerie, as it was the first visit he had paid to the former home of the League of Nations since 1938, when he had lobbied "paralyzed minds" to prohibit barbarity. With "the blood . . . not yet dried" in Europe, he hoped his plea would be heard differently this time. He also knew that he had a distinct advantage operating in Geneva rather than New York because the UN delegates, away from their headquarters, were likely to be lonelier and more prepared to endure him. Lemkin knew he grated on people's nerves. Often, before entering a room, he would pause outside and make a pledge to himself not to bring up genocide and instead allow the conversation to drift from art to philosophy to literature, subjects in which he was fluent. If he could bring himself to hold his tongue, he told himself, eventually his companion would be better disposed to his campaign. When he delivered formal lectures on genocide in Geneva, he was less shy. "I did not refrain from reading aloud from my historical files in considerable detail," he wrote.[30] Indeed, he rarely censored his graphic tales of torture and butchery.

Wherever the law went, Lemkin followed. He decided to prepare for the September 1948 General Assembly session with a short rest near Montreux, France. Lemkin recovered some of the strength sapped by years of unceasing commotion. While visiting a local casino, he even invited a young lady to dance a tango. He was captivated by her beauty and recalled, "Every word the girl said was intelligent and meaningful." She told him she was of Indian descent, born in Chile. Lemkin saw his opening: He informed her that his work on mass slaughter would be of particular interest to her because of the destruction of the Incas and the Aztecs.[31] This was one pickup line the young woman had probably never heard before. She soon departed.

When he returned to Geneva, Lemkin attended every single session of the Legal Committee. In between sessions he prepared memos for the delegates.[32] He felt it essential that they draw upon historic cases of mass atrocity so the law would capture a variety of techniques of destruction. He ritually reminded the representatives of the old maxim that the "legislator's imagination must be superior to the imagination of the criminal."[33] The convention's chief opponent in Britain was Hartley Shawcross, who had prosecuted the Nazi defendants at Nuremberg and considered the genocide law a waste of time. Shawcross ran into Lemkin in the hall in the fall of 1948 and remarked, "The Committee is becoming emotional, this is a bad sign." Lemkin, who was so tired that he could hardly stand up, was heartened.[34] The Legal Committee approved the draft and submitted it to the General Assembly, which scheduled a vote on the measure for December 9, 1948.

After a bruising year of drafting battles, the 1948 Convention on the Prevention and Punishment of the Crime of Genocide settled on a definition of genocide as

> any of the following acts committed with intent to destroy, in whole or in part, a national, ethnical, racial, or religious group, as such:
>   A. Killing members of the group;
>   B. Causing serious bodily or mental harm to members of the group;
>   C. Deliberately inflicting on the group the conditions of life calculated to bring about its physical destruction in whole or in part;
>   D. Imposing measures intended to prevent births within the group;
>   E. Forcibly transferring children of the group to another group.

For a party to be found guilty of perpetrating this new crime of genocide, it had to (1) carry out one of the aforementioned acts, (2) with the intent to destroy all or part of (3) one of the groups protected. The law did not require the extermination of an entire group, only acts committed with the intent to destroy a substantial part. If the perpetrator did not target a national, ethnic, or religious group *as such,* then killings would constitute mass homicide, not genocide.

Lemkin of course opposed all forms of state-sponsored murder, but his legal efforts were focused on the subset of state terror that he believed caused the largest number of deaths, was the most common, and did the most severe long-term damage—to the targeted groups themselves and to the rest of society. The perpetrator's particular motives for wanting to destroy the group were irrelevant. Thus, when Iraq sought in 1987–1988 to purge its Kurdish minority on the grounds that it inhabited a vital border area, it was still genocide. When the Rwandan government tried to exterminate the country's Tutsi minority in 1994, claiming that armed Tutsi rebels posed a military threat, it was still genocide. And when the Bosnian Serbs tried to wipe out the non-Serb presence in Bosnia after the Muslims and Croats had declared independence from Yugoslavia in 1992, it was still genocide. What mattered was that one set of individuals intended to destroy the members of a group not because of anything they did but because of who they were. If the General Assembly passed the convention, nobody would be immune from punishment—not leaders, public officials, nor private citizens. The treaty would enshrine a new reality: States would no longer have the legal right to be left alone. Interfering in a genocidal state's internal affairs as Morgenthau had tried to do was not only authorized but required by the convention. If a government committed or permitted genocide, signatories would have to take steps to prevent, suppress, and punish the crime, which no instrument had ever required before. States had considerable autonomy in deciding what steps to take, but they were expected to act. The convention could be read to permit military intervention. The law even implied its necessity by enshrining a legal duty to "suppress" the crime, but neither the law nor the law's drafters discussed the use of force. It was a large enough leap to convince a state's leaders to denounce or punish the crimes of a fellow state.

The genocide convention boldly closed many of Nuremberg's loopholes. It made states (and rebels) liable for genocide regardless of whether they committed aggression against another country or attacked only their internal "enemies." Peacetime or wartime, inside a country or outside, the 1948 treaty made no distinction.

The convention's enforcement mechanisms were more explicit about punishment than prevention. A state signatory would be bound to pass a domestic genocide law and to try any private citizen or public official for genocide committed on or outside its territory. Countries would try their own genocide suspects as well as those who wandered inside their borders. This left gaps. In the case of postwar Germany, for instance, it would have meant relying principally on former members of the Nazi Party to try Nazi criminals. Still, even if those responsible for genocide continued to hold power, they would be reluctant to leave their country and risk arrest. The basic idea, as the *Washington Post* noted in one editorial endorsing the criminalization of genocide, was that the law "would throw a sort of cordon sanitaire around the guilty nation." Genocide perpetrators would be trapped at home, and "the sort of persecution of helpless minorities which has hitherto gone unrebuked" would be stigmatized. "Genocide can never be the exclusive internal concern of any country," the editorial concluded. "Wherever it occurs, it must concern the entire civilized world."[35] If the convention were passed, genocide would become everybody's business.

Lemkin thought December 9, 1948, would never arrive. When it did, he stood in the press galley of the Palais de Chaillot in Paris and kept his eyes trained on the General Assembly debate, restraining himself from interjecting. Finally, the vote arrived. Fifty-five delegates voted yes to the pact. None voted no. Just four years after Lemkin had introduced "genocide" to the world, the General Assembly had unanimously passed a law banning it.[36] Lemkin remembered:

> There were many lights in the large hall. The galleries were full and the delegates appeared to have a solemn radiating look. Most of them had a good smile for me. John Foster Dulles told me in a somewhat businesslike manner that I had made a great contribution to international law. The Minister of Foreign Affairs of France, [Robert] Schumann, thanked me for my work and said he was glad that this great event took place in France. Sir Zafrullah Khan said this new law should be called the "Lemkin Convention." Then Dr. Evatt put the resolution on the Genocide Convention to a vote. Somebody requested a roll call. The first to vote was India. After her "yes" there was an endless number of "yeses." A storm of applause followed. I felt on my face the flashlight of cameras. . . . The world was smiling and approving and I had only one word in answer to all that, "thanks."[37]

The world's states committed themselves, in the words of the convention preamble, "to liberate mankind from such an odious scourge." After announcing the result of the roll call, General Assembly president Herbert V. Evatt of Australia, whom Lemkin had befriended in Geneva, proclaimed the passage "an epoch-making event in the development of international law." He urged that the convention be signed by all states and ratified by all parliaments at the earliest date. In a sweeping ode to the promise of the United Nations and international law, Evatt declared that the days of political intervention dressed up as humanitarianism were past:

Today we are establishing international collective safeguards for the very existence of such human groups. . . . Whoever will act in the name of the United Nations will do it on behalf of universal conscience as embodied in this great organization. Intervention of the United Nations and other organs which will have to supervise application of the convention will be made according to international law and not according to unilateral political considerations. In this field relating to the sacred right of existence of human groups we are proclaiming today the supremacy of international law once and forever.[38]

It marked the first time the United Nations had adopted a human rights treaty.

Nobody who was familiar with the genocide convention was unfamiliar with the man behind it. The *New York Times* praised the success of Lemkin's "15 year fight." When reporters looked for Lemkin after the vote to share his triumph, they could not find him. "Had he been in character," remembered John Hohenberg of the *New York Post,* "he should have been strutting proudly in the corridors, proclaiming his own merit and the virtues of the protocol that had been his dream."[39] But he had gone missing. That evening journalists finally tracked him down, alone in the darkened assembly hall, weeping, in Rosenthal's words, "as if his heart would break."[40] The man who for so long had insisted on imposing himself upon journalists now waved them off, pleading, "Let me sit here alone."[41] He had been victorious at last, and the relief and grief overwhelmed him. He described the pact as an "epitaph on his mother's grave" and as a recognition that "she and many millions did not die in vain."[42]

Lemkin was struck that night with a vicious fever. Two days later he was again admitted to a Paris hospital, where he remained confined for three weeks. Although the doctors thought he was suffering complications stemming from his high blood pressure, they struggled to make a firm diagnosis. Lemkin offered his own account of his ailment: *"Genociditis,"* he said, or "exhaustion from work on the Genocide Convention."[43]

Unfortunately, though Lemkin could not know it, the most difficult struggles lay ahead. Nearly four decades would pass before the United States would ratify the treaty, and fifty years would elapse before the international community would convict anyone for genocide.

Chapter 5

"A Most Lethal Pair of Foes"

Lemkin's Lobby

Never in history had states even resolved to prevent atrocities. But enforcement was another matter entirely. Lemkin needed to make two things happen. First, twenty UN member states that had voted for the ban in the General Assembly had to ratify it domestically in order for the treaty to become official international law. And second, the United States, the world's most powerful democracy, would have to take the lead in enforcing the genocide ban. In the absence of U.S. participation, the League of Nations had been impotent, and the sponsors of all new initiatives at the nascent UN were determined to involve the United States at every turn. "This treaty is like a ship carrying survivors," Lemkin wrote to himself. "It cannot be permitted to sink."[1]

When it came to tallying twenty domestic ratifications, Lemkin again became a one-man, one-globe, multilingual, single-issue lobbying machine. Sifting through Lemkin's papers, one is awed by the quantity of correspondence he maintained. He sent letters out in English, French, Spanish, Hebrew, Italian, and German. Long before computers or photocopiers, he handcrafted each letter to suit the appropriate individual,

Convention on the Prevention and Punishment of the Crime of Genocide

Approved and proposed for signature and ratification or accession by
General Assembly resolution 260 A (III) of 9 December 1948
Entry into Force 12 January 1951, in Accordance with Article XIII

The Contracting Parties,

Having considered the declaration made by the General Assembly of the United Nations in its resolution 96 (I) dated 11 December 1946 that genocide is a crime under international law, contrary to the spirit and aims of the United Nations and condemned by the civilized world,

Recognizing that at all periods of history genocide has inflicted great losses on humanity, and

Being convinced that, in order to liberate mankind from such an odious scourge, international co-operation is required,

Hereby agree as hereinafter provided:

Article 1
The Contracting Parties confirm that genocide, whether committed in time of peace or in time of war, is a crime under international law which they undertake to prevent and to punish.

Article 2
In the present Convention, genocide means any of the following acts committed with intent to destroy, in whole or in part, a national, ethnical, racial or religious group, as such:
  (a) Killing members of the group;
  (b) Causing serious bodily or mental harm to members of the group;
  (c) Deliberately inflicting on the group conditions of life calculated to bring about its physical destruction in whole or in part;
  (d) Imposing measures intended to prevent births within the group;
  (e) Forcibly transferring children of the group to another group.

Article 3
The following acts shall be punishable:
  (a) Genocide;
  (b) Conspiracy to commit genocide;
  (c) Direct and public incitement to commit genocide;
  (d) Attempt to commit genocide;
  (e) Complicity in genocide.

Article 4
Persons committing genocide or any of the other acts enumerated in article III shall be punished, whether they are constitutionally responsible rulers, public officials or private individuals.

Article 5
The Contracting Parties undertake to enact, in accordance with their respective Constitutions, the necessary legislation to give effect to the provisions of the present Convention, and, in particular, to provide effective penalties for persons guilty of genocide or any of the other acts enumerated in article III.

(continues)

Article 6

Persons charged with genocide or any of the other acts enumerated in article III shall be tried by a competent tribunal of the State in the territory of which the act was committed, or by such international penal tribunal as may have jurisdiction with respect to those Contracting Parties which shall have accepted its jurisdiction.

Article 7

Genocide and the other acts enumerated in article III shall not be considered as political crimes for the purpose of extradition.

The Contracting Parties pledge themselves in such cases to grant extradition in accordance with their laws and treaties in force.

Article 8

Any Contracting Party may call upon the competent organs of the United Nations to take such action under the Charter of the United Nations as they consider appropriate for the prevention and suppression of acts of genocide or any of the other acts enumerated in article III.

Article 9

Disputes between the Contracting Parties relating to the interpretation, application or fulfilment of the present Convention, including those relating to the responsibility of a State for genocide or for any of the other acts enumerated in article III, shall be submitted to the International Court of Justice at the request of any of the parties to the dispute.

Articles 1–9 of the UN Convention on the Prevention and Punishment of the Crime of Genocide.

organization, or country. Occasionally, Lemkin commandeered a student assistant from Yale Law School or a volunteer from one of the Jewish groups with which he periodically allied himself, but these helpers rarely lasted under the employ of such a stringent taskmaster. Lemkin used friends, friends of friends, and acquaintances of acquaintances to familiarize himself with a country. When he wanted to know which buttons to press in Uruguay, a country he had never visited, he sent an elaborate set of questions to a distant contact. He inquired into the status of its ratification drive and asked how it approved international treaties. He wrote to the leaders of the most influential political parties, the heads of the private women's or civic groups, and the editors of prominent newspapers. He usually asked his contact to gauge the influence of the local Jewish community. He varied his pitch. If a country had not yet ratified the convention, he appealed for haste in doing so and often attached sample legislation from Denmark, an early implementer. If a country had experienced genocide in the past, he reminded its citizens of the human costs of allowing it. But if a country had *committed* genocide in the past, as Turkey had done,

Lemkin was willing to keep the country's atrocities out of the discussion, so as not to scare off a possible signatory.

On October 16, 1950, thanks largely to this behind-the-scenes prodding, the twentieth country ratified the genocide convention.[2] Thus, seventeen years after Lemkin had first proposed it, the attempted destruction of national, ethnic, and religious groups became an international crime. He told reporters, "This is a day of triumph for mankind and the most beautiful day of my life."[3]

The tougher challenge was the more important one: securing ratification in the U.S. Senate and then enforcement by the United States. When the convention cleared the General Assembly in 1948, few doubted that the United States would be one of the first countries to ratify it. The UN passage had been an American effort in many respects. In 1946 Lemkin had teamed up with several State Department lawyers to prepare the first draft of the treaty. It had been U.S. delegate at the United Nations John Maktos who chaired the Ad Hoc Committee of the Economic and Social Council that assembled another version of the text in Geneva. The United States had been the first country to sign the pact at the General Assembly in 1948.

In June 1949 President Harry Truman heartily endorsed the genocide convention, calling on U.S. senators to ratify it because America had "long been a symbol of freedom and democratic progress to peoples less favored" and because it was time to outlaw the "world-shocking crime of genocide." Dean Rusk, then deputy undersecretary of state, stressed that ratification was needed to "demonstrate to the rest of the world that the United States is determined to maintain its moral leadership in international affairs." Securing the two-thirds Senate vote seemed a mere formality.

But American spokesmen for the convention had to look outside the realm of human rights to find examples of treaties that earned U.S. support. Rusk testified, "It should be noted that the Genocide Convention does not represent the first instance in which the United States has cooperated with other nations to suppress criminal or quasi-criminal conduct which has become a matter of international concern." He went on, anticlimactically, to list those instances of international cooperation: "The United States is party to the multilateral Convention for Protection of Submarine Cables of 1884. . . . The United States is party to a convention of 1911 with Great Britain, Russia, and Japan for the preservation and protection of fur seals in the North Pacific Ocean." Treaties that obliged signatories to punish those who injured submarine cables or pelagic seals did not exactly constitute the same challenge to international policymakers as the ban on genocide. Thus, there was something absurd if admirable in Rusk's attempt to build the case that genocide convention ratification constituted the natural culmination of previous campaigns. "The United States has cooperated in the past with other nations in the suppression of such lesser offenses as the killing of fur seals," Rusk noted. "It is natural that other nations look to the United States for cooperation in the suppression of the most heinous offense of all, the destruction of human groups."[4] Rusk would later admit in his testimony that there was no evidence the seal convention had ever been violated.

The Critics

The early U.S. leadership on the genocide treaty largely evaporated in the months and years that followed. Some of the opposition to U.S. ratification was rooted in legitimate grievances about the text of the law. The convention's plain wording was not terribly specific about the nature of the violence that needed to occur in order to trigger a global or national response. Lemkin had wanted to create a sacrosanct category of crime that the world would team up to prevent and punish. But the new convention did not clear up confusion about the meaning of "genocide." Far from constituting a high-bar trigger, critics claimed the genocide pact offered a low-bar trampoline.

"Genocide," as defined in the UN treaty, suffered then (as it suffers now) from several inherent definitional problems. One is what might be called a numbers problem. On the question of how many individuals have to be killed and/or expelled from their homes in order for mass murder or ethnic cleansing to amount to genocide, there is—and can be—no consensus. If the law were to require a pre-specified percentage of killings before outsiders responded, perpetrators would be granted a free reign up to a dastardly point. The law would be little use if it kicked in only when a group had been entirely or largely eliminated. By focusing on the perpetrators' intentions and whether they were attempting to destroy a collective, the law's drafters thought they might ensure that diagnosis of and action against genocide would not come too late. The broader, intent-based definition was essential if statesmen hoped to nip the crime in the bud.

But some U.S. senators feared the expansive language would be used to target Americans. The law's most potent foe in the United States was the

respected American Bar Association (ABA). Alfred T. Schweppe, chairman
of the ABA's Committee on Peace and Law Through the United Nations,
challenged the convention's definition of "genocide" before a U.S. Senate
subcommittee hearing in 1950:

> Certainly [the convention's definition] doesn't mean if I want to drive
> 5 Chinamen out of town, to use that invidious illustration, that I must
> have the intent to destroy all the 400,000,000 Chinese in the world or
> the 250,000 within the United States. It is part of a racial group, and if
> it is a group of 5, a group of 10, a group of 15, and I proceed after
> them with guns in some community to get rid of them solely because
> they belong to some racial group. . . . I think you have got a serious
> question. That is what bothers me.[5]

Senator Brien McMahon (D.–Conn.), the chairman of the first Senate
subcommittee, who himself supported ratification, wanted answers, and
this often resulted in a quest to pin down numbers. He asked, "Let us
assume there is a group of 200,000. Would that have to mean that you
would have to murder 100,001 before a major part would come under the
definition?" Lemkin stressed that partial destruction obviously had to be
"of such substantial nature that it affects the existence of the group as a
group" and wrote graphically that partial destruction meant that "by cutting out the brains of a nation, the entire body becomes paralyzed."[6] In the
end the McMahon subcommittee recommended including an "understanding" that the United States interpreted "in part" to mean "a substantial
portion of the group concerned." Even though this should have satisfied
the senators' need for reassurance, many ignored the proposed compromise
language and continued to complain.[7] Years later, when the Khmer Rouge,
the Iraqi government, and the Bosnian Serbs began eradicating minority
groups, those who opposed a U.S. response often ignored the genocide
convention's terms and denied genocide was under way, claiming the number of dead or the percentage of the group eliminated was too small.

The genocide convention also earned criticism for stipulating that a
perpetrator could attempt to obliterate a group not only by killing its
members but by causing serious bodily or mental harm, deliberately
inflicting damaging conditions of life, preventing births, or forcibly removing children. But in order to constitute acts of genocide, these crimes could

not be carried out in isolation. They had to be a piece of a plan to destroy all or part of the designated group. The aim of including acts besides murder was to ensure that the international community looked to—and reacted against—such "lesser" crimes as mini-massacres, population transfers, and sterilization because they were evils in their own right and because they fell on a continuum that often preceded the physical elimination of a people. In criminal law an intent to commit a crime is generally hard to prove, and intent to commit genocide even harder. Only rarely would those planning a genocide record their intentions on tape or in documents. Proving an intent to exterminate an entire people would usually be impossible until the bulk of the group had already been wiped out. The convention drafters believed it would be better to act too soon rather than too late. When one group started expelling another group from its midst, as the Turks had done in 1915 and the Serbs would do in Bosnia in 1992, it could signal a larger plan of destruction.

The law's opponents ignored the reasoning that lay behind the ban's provisions. Instead they zeroed in on the possibility of stretching the new law's language to apply to practices too mild to warrant interference in another state's domestic affairs. Some suggested that U.S. ratification would license critics of the United States to investigate the eradication of Native American tribes in the nineteenth century.[8] Southern senators feared that inventive lawyers might argue that segregation in the South inflicted "mental harm" and thus counted as genocide.[9] Legislators warned that the convention would empower politicized rabble-rousers to drag the United States or the senators themselves before an international court.

Reckoning with American brutality against native peoples was long overdue, but the convention, which was not retroactive, could not be used to press the matter. And although the United States' dismal record on race certainly exposed it to charges of racism and human rights abuse, only a wildly exaggerated reading of the genocide convention left the southern lawmakers vulnerable to genocide charges. Lemkin himself addressed the issue: "In the Negro problem the intent is to preserve the group on a different level of existence," he said, "but not to destroy it."[10] Eunice Carter, a spokeswoman for the National Council on Negro Women, agreed, testifying that "the lynching of an individual or of several individuals has no relation to the extinction of masses of peoples because of race, religion, or political belief." The council supported the convention because women

and children were often the first victims of genocide and because minorities would be safe nowhere if genocide went "unchecked or unpunished."[11]

Again, the 1950 Senate subcommittee had sought to soothe the senators'
fears by attaching an explicit, legal "understanding" that shielded the southern states by stating clearly, "Genocide does not apply to lynchings, race
riots or any form of segregation." The critics did not heed this (embarrassing) recommendation. Nor did they acknowledge that "trumped-up"
charges could be filed regardless of whether the United States ratified the
convention. The problem in the decades ahead would not be that too many
states would file genocide charges against fellow states at the International
Court of Justice (ICJ). Rather, too few would do so. And as of late 2001 no
state had yet dared to challenge the United States by filing genocide charges
against it in the ICJ. The southern opposition was driven mainly by xenophobia and an isolationism that led it to try to exempt the United States
from all international frameworks.

Lemkin himself became a target of xenophobic slurs. In 1950 Senate
Foreign Relations Committee member H. Alexander Smith (R.–N.J.)
was aggrieved that the "biggest propagandist" for the convention was "a
man who comes from a foreign country who . . . speaks broken English."
The senator claimed to know "many people . . . irritated no end by this
fellow running around." Senator Henry Cabot Lodge (R.-Mass.), who
supported ratification, suggested that somebody tell Lemkin he had
"done his own cause a great deal of harm." Much of the criticism was
rooted less in Lemkin's tirelessness than in his Jewishness. Smith said that
he himself was "sympathetic with the Jewish people," but "they ought
not to be the ones who are propagandizing [for the convention], and
they are."[12] Despite having invented the concept of genocide, Lemkin
was not invited by the Senate subcommittee to testify in the congressional hearings on ratification.

Lemkin reflected upon congressional opposition to his convention by
noting, "If somebody does not like mustard, he will always find a reason
why he doesn't like it, after you have convinced him that the previous reason has no validity." Critics complained that the treaty was both too broad
(and thus could implicate the United States) and not broad enough (and
thus might not implicate the Soviet Union). Although it protected
"national, ethnical or religious groups" that were targeted "as such," the law
did not protect political groups. The Soviet delegation and its supporters,

mainly Communist countries in Eastern Europe as well as some Latin American countries, had argued that including political groups in the convention would inhibit states that were attempting to suppress internal armed revolt.[13] Behind the Soviet position was the fear that the convention would invite outside powers to punish Stalin for wiping out national minorities throughout Central Asia, as well as his alleged counterrevolutionary "enemies." Stalin, it came as no surprise, was not interested in creating a right of international intervention (or what he considered a right of unwanted meddling) to stop such practices. Because Lemkin recognized that including political groups would split the Legal Committee and doom the law, he, too, had lobbied for their exclusion.[14] Instead of curing the law of its defects or supplementing it with other measures, American critics contended that a state had arguably committed genocide if it caused mental harm to five persons because of the color of their skin but had not committed genocide if it killed 100,000 people because of the color of their party membership card. The exclusion of political groups from the convention made it much harder in the late 1970s to demonstrate that the Khmer Rouge were committing genocide in Cambodia when they set out to wipe out whole classes of alleged "political enemies."

The core American objections to the treaty, of course, had little to do with the text, which was no vaguer than any other law that had not yet been interpreted in a courtroom. Rather, American opposition was rooted in a traditional hostility toward any infringement on U.S. sovereignty, which was only amplified by the red scare of the 1950s. If the United States ratified the pact, senators worried they would thus authorize outsiders to poke around in the internal affairs of the United States or embroil the country in an "entangling alliance." It was hard to see how it was in the U.S. interest to make a state's treatment of its own citizens the legitimate object of international scrutiny. Genocide prevention was a low priority in the United States, and international law offered few rewards to the most powerful nation on earth.

In May 1950 McMahon's Senate subcommittee reported favorably on the treaty, but the North Korean invasion of South Korea the following month caused the Foreign Relations Committee to postpone its vote. The war unleashed an anti-Communist panic. Republican senators Joseph McCarthy and John Bricker criticized the United Nations as a "world government" that had dragged the United States into war. They were champions of states' rights, which they said the federal government was trampling by joining international treaties. The genocide convention represented a stronger UN at the expense of American sovereignty and a stronger federal government at the expense of the states. Senator A. Willis Robertson, a conservative Democrat from Virginia and a Bricker supporter, wrote that he already had "enough trouble with do-gooders in our own country" who demanded a federal government role in regulating human rights. The American people certainly did not need the United Nations applying "that same type of pressure."[15] In 1952, hoping to limit the federal government's power and backed overwhelmingly by Senate Republicans, Bricker introduced an amendment to the U.S. Constitution that would have reduced the president's authority to approve foreign treaties.

When Eisenhower succeeded Truman in 1953, Lemkin viewed the former U.S. general as a natural ally. After his troops had liberated the Buchenwald concentration camp, Eisenhower had fired off a cable to Army Chief of Staff George Marshall denouncing the Nazi savagery: "We are told that the American soldier does not know what he is fighting for," Eisenhower said, reflecting on the piles of corpses. "Now, at least, he will know what he is fighting against." But generals are taught to choose their battles, and Eisenhower quickly dropped the fight for the genocide convention. In 1953, in the hopes of appeasing Bricker's supporters, the president disavowed this and all human rights treaties.[16] Secretary of State John Foster Dulles pledged that the administration would never "become a party to any covenant [on human rights] for consideration by the Senate." He also flatly abrogated the Nuremberg precedent, charging that the genocide convention exceeded the "traditional limits" of treaties by attempting to generate "internal social changes" in other countries. The United States would advance human rights through education, Dulles declared, not through law.

The genocide convention was far from perfect. But whatever its ambiguities, its ratification in the U.S. Senate would have signaled to the world and the American people that the United States believed genocide was an international crime that should be prevented and punished, wherever it occurred. It would have required the United States to prosecute genocide suspects who wandered onto American shores. And it would have empowered and obligated American policymakers "to undertake" to stop future genocide.

The Home Front

Just as he had earlier tried to drum up international support, Lemkin here tried to create a U.S. constituency for ratification with speaking tours, op-eds, and mass mailings. Hoping to get Eisenhower to reverse his position, Lemkin borrowed stationery from supportive community organizations, applied for grants to pay for postage, and sent thousands of letters to absolutely anybody whose moral heartstrings he felt he might tug or on whose connections he might prey to get the ear of a U.S. senator. Although most of his letters contained a mix of flattery and moral prodding, he sometimes slipped into bluntly bullying his contacts and demanding that they acquire a conscience. Thelma Stevens, a volunteer at the Methodist Women's Council, was probably startled one summer to read this portion of an otherwise grateful letter from Lemkin urging her to coordinate a campaign on behalf of Senate passage:

> This Convention is a matter of our conscience and is a test of our personal relationship to evil. I know it is very hot in July and August for work and planning, but without becoming sentimental or trying to use colorful speech, let us not forget that the heat of this month is less unbearable to us than the heat in the ovens of Auschwitz and Dachau and more lenient than the murderous heat in the desert of Aleppo which burned to death the bodies of hundreds of thousands of Christian Armenian victims of genocide in 1915.[17]

Humorless though he was, Lemkin knew it was essential for him to win over elite opinion. He struck up his most fruitful correspondence with Gertrude Samuels of the *New York Times* editorial board. Samuels's editorials, which appeared in the paper throughout the ratification fight, often seemed to flow right from Lemkin's pen. At first they echoed his conviction; later they reflected his frustration. One editorial termed the criminalization of genocide "one of the greatest civilizing ideas of our century" and lambasted the Senate for its "indifference and delay." Another used the same words that Lemkin had penned to Samuels in a letter dated June 6, 1950: "Humanity is our client," the editorial proclaimed. "Every day of delay is concession to crime."[18] Lemkin was eager to be plagiarized.

Lemkin also attempted to mobilize American grassroots groups. The international human rights organizations familiar to us today did not yet exist. Amnesty International was not founded until 1961, and Helsinki Watch, which later grew into Human Rights Watch, was set up only in 1978. But four decades ahead of the dramatic power shift toward non-governmental organizations that occurred in the 1990s, Lemkin enlisted a panoply of American civic organizations, churches, and synagogues.[19] The U.S. Committee for a United Nations Genocide Convention was formed, made up of representatives and leaders from a wide range of organizations, from the Federal Council of Churches of Christ and the American Association for the UN to the National Council of Women and the American Federation of Labor (AFL).[20] The American Jewish Committee, the American Zionist Council, and B'nai B'rith gave some financial support to Lemkin as he tried to chip away at U.S. opposition.

Lemkin was at a disadvantage in the immediate postwar period because the singular genocide so well known today was barely discussed.[21] American Jews who would later became a potent force in promoting Holocaust commemoration and education were reticent, eager to assimilate, leery of fueling further anti-Semitism, and determined not to be depicted as victims. Other Americans were uncomfortable with the topic of extermination.

In the rare instances when Hitler's genocide was mentioned, American television and film revealed a desire to inform viewers without alienating them. In one example, a May 1953 episode of *This Is Your Life* introduced many American television viewers to a Holocaust survivor for the first time. Host Ralph Edwards profiled Hanna Bloch Kohner, a woman in her thirties who had survived Auschwitz. "Looking at you it's hard to believe that during seven short years of a still short life, you lived a lifetime of fear, terror and tragedy," Edwards declared, telling her she looked "like a young American girl just out of college, not at all like a survivor of Hitler's cruel purge of German Jews." Never mentioning that 6 million Jews had been murdered, Edwards adopted a tone of renewal that characterized the optimistic age: "This is your life, Hanna Bloch Kohner. To you in your darkest hour, America held out a friendly hand. Your gratitude is reflected in your unwavering devotion and loyalty to the land of your adoption."[22]

The dramatization of the *Diary of Anne Frank,* which began running in 1955, garnered huge crowds, rave reviews, a Pulitzer Prize, and a Tony

Award for best play, but as both critics and fans of the play have noted, young Anne embodied the American mood by refusing to lose her faith in humanity.[23] The film version of the *Diary,* which premiered in 1959 and won three Academy Awards, largely omitted the Holocaust from the narrative. Director George Stevens, who had served in the U.S. Army and entered Dachau with the American liberators, screened an early version of the film in San Francisco. The last shot depicted Anne in a concentration camp uniform swaying in the fog, but after the preview he cut the scene because he thought it was "too tough in audience impact."[24] Instead, the film adopted the hopeful ending of the play, in which Anne declares, "In spite of everything, I still believe that people are really good at heart." Anne actually went on to write in her diary: "I simply can't build up my hopes on a foundation consisting of confusion, misery, and death." But this was omitted, as it was far too somber a tone for Stevens or play director Garson Kanin, who said that he did not consider the infliction of depression on an audience "a legitimate theatrical end."[25]

Hollywood eased into more realistic accounts of the horrors. The 1961 film *Judgment at Nuremberg,* starring Judy Garland and Spencer Tracy, jarred millions of viewers by including actual graphic footage from the camps, but the film contained few references to the specific victim groups.[26] When a major network sponsor, the American Gas Association, objected to the mention of gas chambers in the 1959 teleplay version of the film, CBS caved in to pressure and blanked out the references.[27] The word "holocaust" did not appear in the *New York Times* until 1959.[28]

Only in the late 1960s did people who had spoken of a holocaust and then *the* holocaust begin to use the capital letter to specify the German destruction of Europe's Jews. The references to the Holocaust had become sufficiently widespread that by 1968 the Library of Congress had to create a class of work called "Holocaust: Jewish 1939–1945."[29] The *Readers' Guide to Periodical Literature* did not include the subject heading until 1971. American memorials to Hitler's crimes against the Jews did not exist. Even such celebrated works as Elie Wiesel's *Night* and Primo Levi's *Survival in Auschwitz* had trouble finding publishers.[30] It was not really until the 1970s that Americans became prepared to discuss the horrors.

With America unwilling in the 1950s to confront Hitler's Final Solution, it is not surprising that Lemkin, with his briefcase bulging with gruesome parables and his indefatigable, in-your-face manner, earned few friends on Capitol Hill.

Picking Fights

Lemkin took out much of his mounting frustration on an unlikely target: spokespersons for the cause of human rights. At the 1945 conference in San Francisco where the UN charter was drafted, smaller nations of the United Nations, as well as American church, Jewish, labor, and women's groups, had helped secure seven references to human rights in the UN founding charter. Because the content of these rights and the enforcement mechanisms were left open, a Human Rights Commission chaired by Eleanor Roosevelt was formed to draw up an "international bill of rights" that would consist of a Universal Declaration of Human Rights (UDHR) as well as a pair of binding legal conventions.

Lemkin initially fumed less over the substance of the human rights agenda than over its timing. He had worked since 1944 to get his word embraced in official circles and since 1933 to get the crime banned. Lemkin was upset that the General Assembly had passed its historic universal declaration on December 10, 1948, the day after the genocide convention's passage. He felt the association of national celebrities like Eleanor Roosevelt with the UDHR had overshadowed the vote on the genocide convention.[31]

The UDHR was a nonbinding, thirty-article declaration of principles of civil, political, economic, and social justice.[32] This aspirational set of principles was only a "date," Lemkin said, whereas the convention, which required states to behave a certain way, was more like a "marriage."[33] He naively believed that unanimous passage of the convention meant that states intended to live up to their legal commitments. Thus, he feared respect for "his" law would be lessened by association with "her" declaration.

Yet it was when the human rights movement attempted to legalize this initial declaration of principles and turn it into a legal convention modeled on the genocide ban that Lemkin erupted.[34] He simply could not believe that diplomats, drafters, and concerned citizens would attempt to make low-level rights abuses the subject of international law, which he was convinced should be reserved for the most extreme crimes, which were most likely to elude national prosecution. Slavery and genocide were appropriate international crimes; abridgement of speech and press, which were patently unenforceable, were not. His more justified and far more urgent ends had to be distinguished from the human rights crowd's largely prosaic concerns.

In an unpublished op-ed entitled "The U.N. Is Killing Its Own Child," Lemkin warned against those articles in the proposed human rights covenant that "encroached" upon *his* convention: "The same provisions apply to mass beatings in a concentration camp and to the spanking of a child by its parents. In brief, the dividing line between the crime of Genocide, which changes the course of civilization on one hand, and uncivilized behavior of individuals on the other hand, disappears."[35] If every abuse were to become a subject of international concern, Lemkin worried, states would recoil against international law and would not respond to the greatest crime of all.

Lemkin also predicted (quite accurately) that some critics of the genocide convention would use the human rights law to kill his law in a different way, arguing that there was no need for a genocide pact because the human rights law was so expansive that it covered the crime of genocide.[36] Indeed, some began to claim that genocide simply constituted an egregious form of discrimination. Lemkin was understandably adamant that the destruction of groups not be absorbed under the heading of prejudice. In a 1953 memo he snapped: "Genocide implies destruction, death, annihilation, while discrimination is a regrettable denial of certain opportunities of life. To be unequal is not the same as to be dead."[37]

Foreshadowing some of the turf warfare that has plagued nongovernmental organizations since their formation, Lemkin began lobbying for the excision from the human rights law of those provisions that overlapped with his. Two clauses in particular gnawed at him: "Nobody shall be deprived of the right to life" and "No one shall be subjected to torture or to cruel, inhuman or degrading treatment or punishment." If these were included in the human rights law, genocide convention critics would claim that genocide had already been "covered." Lemkin urged dumbfounded U.S. officials to insist that the human rights law omit references to the right to life and the right to be free of inhuman treatment. He received a gracious letter back from Assistant Secretary of State John D. Hickerson, who observed, "Certainly it would be difficult to deny that these two rights are among the most basic of human rights generally recognized throughout the world."[38] Yet Lemkin thought international law should reserve itself for the base and not busy itself with the "basic."

As he attacked the human rights treaty and its sponsors, Lemkin found himself mouthing the same arguments as notorious human rights abusers.[39] In his fury, he ignored all he had in common with his human rights rivals. René Cassin, a French Jewish lawyer who took the lead on the Human Rights Commission in drafting the Universal Declaration and who in 1968 was awarded the Nobel Prize for his efforts, had lost twenty-nine members of his family, including his sister, in Nazi concentration camps. Cassin's response to Soviet critics who bristled at outside interference might well have been written by Lemkin. "The right of interference is here; it is here," Cassin noted. "Why? Because we do not want a repetition of what happened in 1933, where Germany began to massacre its own nationals, and everybody. . . bowed, saying 'Thou art sovereign and master in thine own house.'"[40]

Lemkin, Cassin, and Roosevelt also squared off against the same opponents. Senator Bricker teamed with Senator McCarthy to deride all UN instruments as vehicles of world government and socialism that would swallow U.S. sovereignty and aid in a Communist plot to rule (and internationalize) the world. The bedfellows who united in opposition to the genocide ban and the human rights law were not only fierce anti-Communists like Bricker but also devoted Communists from the Soviet Union and the Soviet bloc representing their countries at the United Nations.

But instead of seeing or seeking common ground, Lemkin chided human rights advocates for the very utopianism that his opponents ascribed to him. The draft human rights covenant naturally included a demand that signatories respect rights "without distinction of any kind, such as race, color, sex, language, religion, political or other opinion, national or social origin, property, birth or other status." Lemkin found this laughably unrealistic: "History has tried to achieve this task through a combined travail of revolution and evolution, but never before has a philosopher or lawyer dreamed of this unique opportunity of replacing a historical process by fiat of law. In short, it is merely a description of Utopia, but Utopia belongs to fiction and poetry and not to law."[41]

Back in the United States, the gatekeepers at the Senate Foreign Relations Committee quashed all prospective hearings on the genocide convention. After another wave of countries signed the convention in 1957, the New York Times again lauded Lemkin, calling him "that exceedingly patient and totally unofficial man."[42]

But Lemkin's patience was thinning and his health worsening. He took each year's delay personally, and the stress of the extended struggle took its toll. He began to disappear from sight for long stretches, cutting himself off from his few friends. A close friend, Maxwell Cohen, said Lemkin "was very warm to those close to him, but he antagonized so many people with his insistence and his impatience." Although Lemkin spent weekends and summers with Cohen's family, they always referred to him as "Dr. Lemkin." Lemkin could woo people with his Old World gentility, but he always kept them at a distance. According to Cohen, "Women were attracted to him. He was a very charming man with an extraordinary inner dignity." But Lemkin continued to make no time for them, telling Cohen, "I can't afford to fall in love."[43]

Lemkin's enemies and disappointments were piling up. He was nominated for the Nobel Peace Prize in 1950, 1951, 1952, 1958, and 1959.[44] But journalists had stopped calling. And the "multilateral moment" where the UN and international law held promise had passed. Lemkin lived off small donations from Jewish and Eastern European émigré groups. He had begun a four-volume history of genocide. The first volume, which he had nearly completed, would be entitled "An Introduction into the Study of Genocide"; the second would cover genocide in antiquity; the third would focus on genocide in the Middle Ages; and the fourth would take readers through genocide in modern times. But if Lemkin saw the indispensable service to humanity such a collection would supply, American publishers foresaw only dim sales. The president of the John Day Company informed him that the company had concluded they could not "successfully sell a book about the history of genocide, whether condensed or at length."[45] Charles Pearce of Duell, Sloan and Pearce replied to his inquiry by stating, "It would not be possible for us to find a large enough audience of buyers for a book of this nature," and a Simon and Schuster reviewer described it as a "very dubious commercial risk."[46] Lemkin next tried to market a full-length autobiography, claiming confidently in the introduction that "this book will be interesting because it shows how a private individual almost single handedly can succeed in imposing a moral law on the world and how he can stir world conscience to this end." But for this book, to be called "The Totally Unofficial Man," after the *New York Times* description, he received similarly dejecting feedback.

Accused of fighting the whole world, Lemkin used to insist, "I am not fighting the whole world. But only against an infinitely small part of the world, which arrogates to itself the right to speak for the whole world. What you call the whole world is really on my side." If American critics of the genocide convention actually believed they had the American people on their side, he argued, they would freely admit that they opposed the genocide treaty and permit the measure to come before the full Senate for debate.

On August 28, 1959, after a quarter-century battle to ban genocide, Lemkin collapsed and died of a heart attack in the public relations office of Milton H. Blow on Park Avenue, his blazer leaking papers at the seams. His one-room apartment on West 112th Street in Manhattan was left overflowing with memos prepared for foreign ministers and ambassadors, as well as some 500 books, each read, reread, and emphatically underlined. He had published eleven books, most of them on international law but one volume of art criticism and another on rose cultivation. At the time of his death, he was fifty-nine and penniless. A *New York Times* editorial two days later observed:

> Diplomats of this and other nations who used to feel a certain concern when they saw the slightly stooped figure of Dr. Raphael Lemkin approaching them in the corridors of the United Nations need not be uneasy anymore. They will not have to think up explanations for a failure to ratify the genocide convention for which Dr. Lemkin worked so patiently and so unselfishly for a decade and a half. . . . Death in action was his final argument—a final word to our own State Department, which has feared that an agreement not to kill would infringe upon our sovereignty.[47]

Lemkin had coined the word "genocide." He had helped draft a treaty designed to outlaw it. And he had seen the law rejected by the world's most powerful nation. Seven people attended Lemkin's funeral.[48]

"Successors"

After Lemkin's death, the genocide convention languished unattended in the United States until the mid-1960s. Bruno Bitker, a Milwaukee international lawyer, sparked a second wave of interest when he urged

William Proxmire, the wiry senator from Wisconsin, to take up the cause of the genocide ban. Nearly seventy countries had by then ratified the law, and Proxmire could not grasp what could be slowing the U.S. Senate.[49]

Unlike Lemkin, Proxmire had led a privileged life, graduating from Yale, receiving two master's degrees from Harvard, and marrying Elsie Rockefeller, a great-granddaughter of oil baron William A. Rockefeller, the brother and partner of John D. Rockefeller. But like Lemkin, Proxmire was a loner who had a habit of breaking with convention. Reared in a staunch Republican family in Illinois, he declared himself a Democrat in the late 1940s and moved to Wisconsin, home of the iconoclastic populist Robert La Follette and a state that columnist Mary McGrory likened to "a portly Teutonic old lady, full of beer and cheese, with a weakness for wild men and underdogs."[50]

When he lost the race for Wisconsin governor in 1952, 1954, and 1956, Proxmire turned up at Milwaukee factories the next morning to pass out "We lost, but . . ." cards to groggy workers.[51] In 1957, when he ran for the late Joseph McCarthy's Senate seat, instead of distancing himself from prior races, Proxmire embraced the "three-time loser" label. "Let my opponent have the support of the man who has never proposed to a girl and lost," Proxmire declared in one radio broadcast. "I'll take the losers. . . . If all those who have ever lost in business, love, sports or politics will vote for me as one who knows what it is to lose and fight back, I will be glad to give my opponent the support of all those lucky voters who have never lost anything."[52]

If Proxmire intended to pick a loser on the legislative front, he could not have done any better then the genocide convention. Ever since Eisenhower had struck his 1953 deal with Senator Bricker agreeing to drop the pact from consideration, nobody in the Senate had cared to reintroduce the measure. On January 11, 1967, Proxmire stood up on the Senate floor to deliver his first genocide speech. He casually announced his intention to begin a campaign that would not cease until the United States had ratified the pact. To a largely uninterested, deserted Senate chamber, he declared: "The Senate's failure to act has become a national shame. . . . I serve notice today that from now on I intend to speak day after day in this body to remind the Senate of our failure to act and of the necessity for prompt action."[53]

Senator William Proxmire
(D.–Wisc.)

Ellen Proxmire

Proxmire's speech-a-day approach to ratification was one of many rituals he observed in the Senate. He made a point (and a show) of never missing a roll call vote during his twenty-two years in the Senate, tallying more than 10,000 consecutively. A renowned skinflint, he became famous nationally for crusading against pork-barrel projects and passing out the monthly Golden Fleece Awards to government agencies for waste in spending. The first award in 1975 went to the National Science Foundation for funding a $84,000 study on "why people fall in love." Later recipients were "honored" for a $27,000 project to determine why inmates want to escape from prison; a $25,000 grant to learn why people cheat, lie, and act rudely on Virginia tennis courts; and a $500,000 grant to research why monkeys, rats, and humans clench their jaws. The award infuriated many of Proxmire's colleagues in the Senate, who deemed it a publicity stunt designed to earn Proxmire kudos at their expense.[54]

Although Proxmire alienated some colleagues by "fleecing" them, a few joined him in fighting for the genocide convention. Claiborne Pell, a fellow Democrat from Rhode Island, was one who endorsed Proxmire's pursuit.[55] Pell's father, Herbert C. Pell, had served during World War II as U.S. representative to the War Crimes Commission, which the Allies established in 1943 to investigate allegations of Nazi atrocities. The elder Pell had hardly been able to get senior officials in the Roosevelt administration to return his calls. In late 1944 he was informed that the war crimes office would close for budgetary reasons. The Roosevelt team rejected Pell's offer to pay his secretary and the office rent out of his own pocket, reversing the decision only when Pell publicized the office's closing. When the younger Pell spoke publicly on behalf of the genocide convention decades later, he recalled those years in which he watched his father come to terms with the outside world's disregard for Nazi brutality:

> I remember the shock and horror that my father suffered—he was a gentle man—at becoming aware of the horror and heinousness of what was going on. . . . I am convinced. . . that there was an unwritten gentleman's understanding to ignore the Jewish problem in Germany, and that we and the British would not intervene in any particular way. . . . We wrung our hands and did nothing.[56]

Backed by Pell, Proxmire pressed ahead in an effort to resurrect Lemkin's law. Proxmire's daily ritual became as regular and predictable as the bang of the gavel and the morning prayer. Yet it was also as varied as the weather. Each speech had to be an original. The senator put his interns to good use, trusting them, in weekly rotations, to prepare the genocide remarks. The office developed files like Lemkin's on each of the major genocides of the past millennium, and the interns tapped the files each day for a new theme. Anniversaries helped. The Turkish genocide against the Armenians and the Holocaust were often invoked.

But sadly, Proxmire's best source of material was the morning paper. In 1968 Nigeria responded to Biafra's attempted secession by waging war against the Christian Ibo resistance and by cutting off food supplies to the civilian population. "Mr. President, the need of the starving is obvious. Indeed, it cries to high heaven for action," Proxmire declared. "And to the degree that the nations of the world allow themselves to be lulled by the claim that the elimination of hundreds of thousands of their fellows is an internal affair, to that degree will our moral courage be bankrupt and our humane concern for others a thin veneer. Our responsibility grows awesomely with the death of each innocent man, woman and child."[57] But the United States stood behind Nigerian unity. Reeling from huge losses in

Vietnam as well as the assassinations of Martin Luther King Jr. and Robert Kennedy, the Johnson administration followed the lead of the State Department's Africa bureau and its British allies, both of which adamantly opposed Biafran secession. Citing fears of further Soviet incursions in Africa and eyeing potentially vast oil reserves in Iboland, U.S. officials stalled effective famine relief measures for much of the conflict. The United States insisted that food be delivered through Lagos, even though Nigerian commanders were open about their objectives. "Starvation is a legitimate weapon of war," one said.[58] In the end Nigeria crushed the Ibo resistance and killed and starved to death more than 1 million people

Beginning in March 1971, after Bengali nationalists in East Pakistan's Awami League won an overall majority in the proposed national assembly and made modest appeals for autonomy, Pakistani troops killed between 1 and 2 million Bengalis and raped some 200,000 girls and women. The Nixon administration, which was hostile to India and using Pakistan as an intermediary to China, did not protest. The U.S. consul general in Dacca, Archer Blood, cabled Washington on April 6, 1971, soon after the massacres began, charging:

> Our government has failed to denounce atrocities . . . while at the same time bending over backwards to placate the West Pak[istan] dominated government. . . . We have chosen not to intervene, even morally, on the grounds that the Awami conflict, in which unfortunately the overworked term genocide is applicable, is purely an internal matter of a sovereign state. Private Americans have expressed disgust. We, as professional civil servants, express our dissent.

The cable was signed by twenty U.S. diplomats in Bangladesh and nine South Asia hands back in the State Department.[59] "Thirty years separate the atrocities of Nazi Germany and the Asian sub-continent," Proxmire noted, "but the body counts are not so far apart. Those who felt that genocide was a crime of the past had a rude awakening during the Pakistani occupation of Bangladesh."[60] Only the Indian army's invasion, combined with Bengali resistance, halted Pakistan's genocide and gave rise to the establishment of an independent Bangladesh. Archer Blood was recalled from his post.

In Burundi in the spring and summer of 1972, after a violent Hutu-led rebellion, members of the ruling Tutsi minority hunted down and killed tens of thousands of Hutu.[61] The rate of slaughter reached 1,000 per day, and, in their cables back to Washington, U.S. ambassador Thomas Patrick Melady and his deputy, Michael Hoyt, routinely reported "extermination," a "vast bloodbath of Hutu," and "thousands" of executions (some by "sledgehammer"). Embassy officials also supplied a running tally of the burial pits being dug and filled nightly near the airport. In one confidential cable in May 1972, for instance, Hoyt noted:

> In Bujumbira we were able to see [when] shouting men surrounded Hutus and clubbed them to death in the streets. The army throughout the land and revolutionary youth groups arrested and executed educated Hutus, including secondary school students. After a month we can assume only a relative handful of educated Hutus . . . are still alive. The [killing] toll may be above tens of thousands. . . . Trucks ply the road to the airport every night with a fresh contribution to the mass grave.[62]

Despite these graphic reports, neither Ambassador Melady nor his superiors in Washington believed the United States should condemn the killings. And although the United States was the world's main purchaser of the country's coffee, which accounted for 65 percent of Burundi's commercial revenue, the State Department opposed any suspension of commerce.[63] Melady assured Washington that his response had been "to follow our strict policy of noninvolvement in the internal affairs and to associate ourselves with urgent relief efforts."[64] Secretary of State William Rogers cabled that embassy officials were right to "avoid any indication [the] USG [was] taking sides in [the] current tragic problem."[65] One State Department official met a junior official's appeal for action by asking, "Do you know of any official whose career has been advanced because he spoke out for human rights?"[66]

U.S. policymakers placed their hope in the Organization for African Unity (OAU) and the UN. "Our general prescription is that Africans should settle African problems,"[67] Melady wrote. But the OAU pledged "total solidarity" with the genocidal Burundian government; the UN mustered only an ineffectual fact-finding mission; and the killings continued unimpeded. "So far, we have been able to maintain our two primary interests, that of not becoming involved and in protecting our citizens," Melady reported, adding, "We cannot at this time say how many people have died ... but figures of 100,000 no longer make us incredulous."[68] In fact, somewhere between 100,000 and 150,000 Burundian Hutu were murdered between April and September 1972.

While the executive branch refrained from much public comment, Senator Proxmire criticized the OAU and the UN for failing to investigate and denounce the slaughter, and he called on the United States to do more to stop it. He noted that the genocide convention made clear that such a crime was not merely a matter of internal concern but a violation of international law that demanded international attention. "The United States has for too long blithely ignored the issues of genocide," Proxmire said. "Evidence that genocide is going on in the 1970s should shake our complacency."[69]

Proxmire had no shortage of grim news pegs on which to hang his appeal. His staff drew upon a range of sources, but their creative juices sometimes dried up. Even the lugubrious Lemkin with his file folders on medieval slaughter would have struggled to devise a novel speech each day. One evening an enterprising intern in Proxmire's office was struggling to prepare the next morning's speech when a pest control team arrived to sanitize the senator's quarters. The next morning Proxmire rose on the Senate floor and heard himself declare that the late-night visit of exterminators to his office "reminds me, once again, Mr. President, of the importance of ratifying the genocide convention." As taxing as it sometimes was to diversify the ratification pitch, nobody on Proxmire's staff considered slipping an old speech into Proxmire's floor folder in the hopes he would not remember having seen it before. "Prox had a hawk-like memory, the sharpest mind I ever came across," says Proxmire's convention expert Larry Patton, "I never had the guts to try."

Proxmire used his daily soliloquy to rebut common American misperceptions that had persisted since Lemkin's day. Powerful right-wing isolationist groups would never come around. But most Americans, the senator believed, did not really oppose ratification; they were just misinformed. "The true opponents to ratification in this case are not groups or individuals," Proxmire noted in one of 199 speeches he gave on the convention in 1967. "They are the most lethal pair of foes for human rights everywhere in the world—ignorance and indifference."[70] He used the speeches to educate. As critics picked apart the treaty and highlighted its shortcomings, he responded, "I do not dismiss this criticism or skepticism. But if the U.S.

Senate waited for the perfect law without any flaw. . . the legislative record of any Congress would be a total blank. I am amazed that men who daily see that the enactment of any legislation is the art of the possible can captiously nit pick an international covenant on the outlawing of genocide."[71]

Proxmire believed the United States could be doing far more in the court of public opinion to impact state and individual behavior. "The United States is the greatest country in the world," he said. "The pressures of the greatest country in the world could make a potential wrongdoer think before committing genocide."[72] But the United States neither ratified the UN genocide convention nor denounced regimes committing genocide. U.S. military intervention was not even considered.

Initially, Proxmire thought it might take a year or two at most to secure passage. "I couldn't think of a more outrageous crime than genocide," he recalls. "Of all the laws pending before Congress, this seemed a no-brainer." On the floor he listed other treaties that the Senate had endorsed in the period it had allowed the convention to languish:

> Included among the hundred-plus treaties are a Tuna Convention with Costa Rica, a bridge across the Rainy River, a Halibut Convention with Canada, a Road Traffic Convention allowing licensed American drivers to drive on European highways, a Shrimp Convention with Cuba . . . a treaty of amity with Muscat and Oman, and even a most colorful and appetizing treaty entitled the "Pink Salmon Protocol." I do not mean to suggest that any of these treaties should not have been ratified. . . . But every one . . . has as its objective the promotion of either profit or pleasure.[73]

The genocide convention, by contrast, dealt with people. Because it did not promote profit or pleasure for Americans, it did not easily garner active support. Opponents of the treaty were more numerous, more vocal, and in the end more successful than Proxmire could have dreamed. Undeterred by failure, Proxmire would continue his campaign into the next decade. Indeed, nineteen years and 3,211 speeches after casually pledging in 1967 to speak daily, Proxmire would still be rising in an empty Senate chamber, dressed in his trademark tweed blazers and his Ivy League ties, insisting that ratification would advance America's interests and its most cherished values.

Samantha Power

Photo of a Cambodian woman and her child, taken at the Tuol Sleng torture center, shortly before they were murdered.

Chapter 6

Cambodia: "Helpless Giant"

On April 17, 1975, eight years after Proxmire began his campaign to get the United States to commit itself to prevent genocide, the Khmer Rouge (KR) turned back Cambodian clocks to year zero. After a five-year civil war, the radical Communist revolutionaries entered the capital city of Phnom Penh, triumphant. They had just defeated the U.S.-backed Lon Nol government.

Still hoping for a "peaceful transition," the defeated government welcomed the Communist rebels by ordering the placement of white flags and banners on every building in the city. But it did not take long for all in the capital to gather that the Khmer Rouge had not come to talk. After several days of monotonous military music interspersed with such tunes as "Marching Through Georgia" and "Old Folks at Home," the old regime delivered its last broadcast at noontime on the 17th.[1] The government announcer said talks between the two sides had begun, but before he could finish, a KR official in the booth harshly interrupted him: "We enter Phnom Penh not for negotiation, but as conquerors."[2]

The sullen conquerors, dressed in their trademark black uniforms, with their red-and-white-checkered scarves and their Ho Chi Minh sandals cut out of old rubber tires, marched single file into the Cambodian capital. The soldiers had the look of a weary band that had fought a savage battle for control of the country and its people. They carried guns. They gathered material goods, like television sets, refriger-

ators, and cars, and piled them on top of one another in the center of the
street to create a pyre. Influenced by the thinking of Mao Zedong, the
Khmer Rouge leadership had recruited into their army those they
deemed, in Mao's words, "poor and blank," rather than those with
schooling. "A sheet of blank paper carries no burden," Mao had noted,
"and the most beautiful characters can be written on it, the most beautiful pictures painted."[3]

Upon arrival, the only burden the KR cadres carried was that of swiftly
executing orders from their higher-ups, who were removed from sight.
Over the radio and mobile megaphones, they began blasting their demand
that citizens leave the capital immediately. As a rationale, the militant new-
comers claimed that American B-52 bombers were about to "raze the
city." The KR insisted that only a citywide exodus would guarantee citizens' safety. Purposeful Communist soldiers filed into the city on one side
of Phnom Penh's leafy boulevards, while on the other side hundreds of
thousands of ashen-faced Cambodian civilians tripped over one another to
obey the KR's inflexible orders. Over the next few days, more than 2 million people were herded onto the road. KR soldiers slashed the tires of cars
around the capital, and citizens trundled along on foot, moving no quicker
than a half a mile an hour. In scenes reminiscent of the Turkish deportation
of the Armenians in 1915, unwieldy crowds clogged the roads, leaving in
their wake stray sandals, clothing, and in some cases expired bodies. The
first sign for most Cambodians and foreigners that this revolution would be
like no other was the sight of the city's main Calmette Hospital being
emptied at gunpoint. Scattered among the anxious citizenry were patients
dressed in wispy hospital gowns, wheeling their own IVs, carrying fellow
patients in their arms, or being pushed in their hospital beds by their trembling loved ones. The infirm collapsed for lack of water, babies were born
at the side of the road, heat-struck children squealed for maternal succor,
and fathers and husbands cowed before the guns in command. Some
Cambodians made their way to the French embassy and pleaded for asy-
lum, hurling themselves against the barbed wire that ringed the compound
and flinging their suitcases and even their children over the walls. But most
Cambodians meekly trudged away from their homes.

Although the symptoms of the Khmer Rouge evacuation of Phnom
Penh bore a superficial resemblance to the symptoms of what we now
know as "ethnic cleansing," the KR did not really discriminate on ethnic
grounds. The entire capital was to be emptied.

All but a few American citizens had already departed. One week before, on April 12, 1975, as the KR closed in on the capital, U.S. ambassador John Gunther Dean had led the evacuation of the embassy staff and American nationals. Lon Nol, the U.S.-backed head of state, fled with a tidy sum of U.S. money in his pocket for "retirement" and bought a home in an upper-middle-class suburb east of Honolulu. Prince Sirik Matak, a former Lon Nol ally and premier who had recently been placed under house arrest because of his criticisms of the corrupt Cambodian regime, was released and tapped to become the official head of state. At 7 a.m. on the morning of the evacuation, Ambassador Dean offered Matak a place on a departing U.S. helicopter. Matak, whose apartment was decorated with photographs of President Richard Nixon and Vice President Spiro Agnew, idolized the United States. At 9 a.m. Dean received a handwritten note from Cambodia's new leader, who thanked Dean for his offer of transport but said, "I cannot, alas, leave in such a cowardly fashion." The letter continued: "As for you and in particular for your great country, I never believed for a moment that you would [abandon] a people which has chosen liberty. You have refused us your protection and we can do nothing about it. . . . If I shall die here on this spot in my country that I love . . . I have only committed this mistake of believing in you, the Americans."[4] Dean, himself a childhood refugee from Hitler's Germany, boarded a helicopter carrying the U.S. flag folded under his arm. Matak took shelter at the French embassy, where foreigners had already begun to gather, and hoped for the best.

On April 20 and 21, 1975, as the final hours of the foreign presence in Cambodia ticked away, the Cambodians at the French embassy were turned out into the street. French vice-consul Jean Dyrac had fought in Spain in the International Brigade against Francisco Franco and in the French Resistance against the Nazis, who captured and tortured him. The KR now told him that the 1,300 people gathered in the compound would be deprived of food and water if the Cambodians among them did not leave. The departures were wrenching, as parents and children, husbands and wives, and close friends were separated. The Cambodians who had hoped for reprieve at the embassy no longer stood any chance of disappearing into the thicket of evacuees and burying their past identities. They were alone to meet fates worsened by the taint of their association with the capitalist West. Senior Cambodian government officials stood no chance, and vice-consul Dyrac accompanied several members of the toppled regime to the gate. Premier Sirik Matak walked out proudly, but former national assembly pres-

ident Hong Boun Hor, who carried a suitcase of U.S. dollars, was so agitated that he had to be sedated with an injection. As Dyrac turned the men
over to the Khmer Rouge, he leaned his head against a pillar and, with tears
streaming down his face, repeated again and again, "We are no longer men."[5]
The officials, including Sirik Matak, who had trusted earlier American
assurances, were taken away in the back of a sanitation truck and executed.

A Khmer curtain quickly descended. For the next three and a half years,
the Khmer Rouge rendered Cambodia a black hole that outsiders could
not enter and some 2 million Cambodians would not survive.

The U.S. response followed a familiar pattern. In advance of the KR
seizure of Phnom Penh, prolific early warnings of the organization's brutality were matched by boundless wishful thinking on the part of
American observers and Cambodian citizens. By sealing the country after
their victory, the KR delayed and initially muddied outside diagnosis of
the depths of their savagery. But even when the facts had emerged, the
American policy of nonengagement, noncondemnation, and noninterest
went virtually unchallenged. With the United States smothering under
the legacy of the Vietnam War, which had just ended, no Lemkin figure
emerged, no U.S. official owned the issue day in and day out, and no individual or organization convinced U.S. decisionmakers that the deaths of
Cambodians mattered enough to Americans to warrant their attention.
Thus, while analogies to the Holocaust were invoked and isolated appeals
made, in three years of systematic terror, a U.S. policy of silence was never
seriously contested. It would have been politically unthinkable to intervene militarily and emotionally unpleasant to pay close heed to the horrors unfolding, but it was cost-free to look away. And this was what two
U.S. presidents and most lawmakers, diplomats, journalists, and citizens
did, before, during, and after the Khmer Rouge's reign of terror.

Warning

Background: U.S. Policy Before Pol Pot

As Lemkin noted, war and genocide are almost always connected. The
Ottomans killed more than 1 million Armenians during World War I, and
the Germans exterminated 6 million Jews and 5 million Poles, Roma,

homosexuals, political opponents, and others during World War II. Iraq later targeted its Kurdish minority during the Iran-Iraq war; Bosnian Serbs set out to destroy Muslims and Croats during a Balkan civil war; and Rwandan Hutu nationalists exterminated some 800,000 Tutsi while the Rwandan army also fought a more conventional civil war against a Tutsi rebel force. History is replete with conflicts between regular armed forces that unleash and fuel the passions that give rise to campaigns to eliminate certain "undesirables." War legitimates such extreme violence that it can make aggrieved or opportunistic citizens feel licensed to target their neighbors. For outsiders, war between armies can also mask genocide, making it initially difficult to discern eliminationist campaigns against civilians and inviting customary diplomatic efforts. In Cambodia two wars preceded the genocide: the U.S. war in Vietnam and a civil war in Cambodia. These wars earned the Khmer Rouge converts to their cause, and they also helped obscure the savagery of the new Communist movement.

American reticence in the face of the Cambodian horrors between 1975 and 1979 is tightly intertwined with the U.S. role in the region in the previous decade. The American war in Vietnam was intended to prevent South Vietnam, another "domino," from becoming Communist. The U.S. troop presence in Vietnam peaked at 550,000 in early 1968. The same year the stunning Vietcong Tet offensive against all the main U.S. bases in South Vietnam left some 4,000 Americans dead and strengthened American domestic opposition to the war.[6] This restiveness on the home front only intensified with coverage of the 1968 My Lai massacre and the outrage over American use of defoliants and napalm.[7] American lives were being lost in Vietnam, American honor was being soiled, *and* North Vietnam was winning the war.

Richard Nixon became president in 1969. Although he had pledged to end the Vietnam War, Nixon in fact expanded it into Cambodia. Because North Vietnamese units were taking sanctuary in neighboring Cambodia, the country became a "sideshow" of some importance to the new administration. The United States invested heavily in the idea that the two bands of Communists, the Cambodians and the Vietnamese, were united. In March 1969 Nixon ordered American B-52s to begin bombing Cambodia.[8] Code-named "Operation Breakfast" for the setting in which National Security Adviser Henry Kissinger and U.S. military advisers drafted their bombing plans, the mission was kept top secret for fear of domestic protest. When the bombers failed to locate the Communists' bases, Nixon expand-

ed the mission. He authorized secret attacks on other sanctuaries and followed up Operation Breakfast with further unappetizing missions, named
Operations Lunch, Snack, Dinner, Dessert, and Supper. In the first phase of
the bombing campaign, which lasted fourteen months and was known as
Menu, U.S. bombers flew 3,875 sorties.[9]

President Nixon did not stop there. In April 1970, frustrated by the elu-
siveness of the North Vietnamese, he ordered U.S. ground troops to "clean
out" North Vietnamese strongholds in Cambodia. Nixon warned, "If,
when the chips are down, the world's most powerful nation—the United
States of America—acts like a pitiful, helpless giant, the forces of totalitarianism and anarchy will threaten free nations and free institutions throughout the world." Some 31,000 American and 43,000 South Vietnamese
forces surged into Cambodia, ostensibly to prevent the Communists there
from staging "massive attacks" on U.S. troops in Vietnam.[10] The invasion,
which Nixon insisted was only an "incursion," had nothing to do with the
Cambodians and everything to do with the U.S. war with Vietnam.
Defense Secretary James Schlesinger later testified to Congress, "The value
of Cambodia's survival derives from its importance to the survival of South
Vietnam."[11]

The month before the U.S. ground attack on Cambodia, the United
States had welcomed a coup by the pro-American prime minister, Lon
Nol, against Cambodia's longtime ruler, Prince Norodom Sihanouk.
Sihanouk, the father of independent Cambodia, had acquired the aura of
an ancient Angkor *deva-raj,* or god-king, since he had assumed the throne
in 1941. A bon vivant, Sihanouk was a movie director, a gourmet, and a
womanizer, as well as a popular head of state. But he had alienated the
United States by striking up a friendship with China, America's foe at the
time. He had also irritated President Nixon by trying to keep Cambodia
neutral in the U.S. war with Vietnam. U.S. officials believed Lon Nol would
be far more malleable to American designs.

But the United States had backed a loser. Lon Nol was pro-American,
but like many U.S.-sponsored dictators of the period, he was also corrupt,
repressive, and incompetent. He secluded himself in his villa in the
Cambodian capital of Phnom Penh and remained woefully out of touch
with the affairs of his state. He depended on the mystical advice of a
visionary monk named Mam Prum Moni, or "Great Intellectual of Pure
Glory." The only assertive moves Lon Nol made were those designed to
increase his own power. He stripped citizens of basic freedoms, suspended

parliament, and announced in October 1971 that it was time to end "the sterile game of outmoded liberal democracy." In 1972 he declared himself president, prime minister, defense minister, and marshal of the armed forces. The United States cared only that Lon Nol was a staunch anti-Communist. The United States spent some $1.85 billion between 1970 and 1975 propping up his regime—evidence, in President Nixon's words, of "the Nixon Doctrine in its purest form."[12]

The U.S. ground invasion of April 1970 occurred at the beginning of Cambodia's five-year civil war, a merciless war that the genocidal Khmer Rouge would win. On one side were Lon Nol and the United States. On the other side stood the Vietnamese Communists and the small, mysterious group of radical Cambodian Communist revolutionaries. The leaders of the Khmer Rouge, or Red Khmer, had been educated in Paris, studied Maoist thought, and received extensive political and military support from China. They were youths who had been driven to Communist resistance out of frustration with Prince Sihanouk's earlier, authoritarian rule. Under the leadership of Saloth Sar, who later assumed the pseudonym Pol Pot, they had left Cambodia's cities in the 1960s to plot revolution from the Cambodian and Vietnamese countryside.[13] It had been Sihanouk's tyranny that drove them to arms, but when Lon Nol seized power in the 1970 coup, the KR began fighting Lon Nol's government forces instead and made their former nemesis Prince Sihanouk the figurehead leader of an unlikely coalition. This earned them support from the millions of Cambodians who trusted Sihanouk, the likable man who had brought them independence. Although doubts emerged in 1973 and 1974 about whether the more moderate Sihanouk spoke for the KR, Cambodians trusted his judgment. "I do not like the Khmer Rouge and they probably do not like me," the prince said in 1973. " But they are pure patriots. . . . Though I am a Buddhist, I prefer a red Cambodia which is honest and patriotic than a Buddhist Cambodia under Lon Nol, which is corrupt and a puppet of the Americans."[14]

Even backed by the United States, the Lon Nol regime did not stand much of a chance in battle. Its forces were equipped for parades, not war-fare.[15] In 1972 Lon Nol famously had airplanes sprinkle blessed sand around Phnom Penh's perimeters to ward off his ungodly Communist enemies. Lon Nol's officers exaggerated Cambodian army troop strength, listing phantom troops and using U.S. aid to pad their pockets, stuff foreign bank accounts, and build themselves glamorous homes. Regular army soldiers, by contrast, frequently went unpaid and deserted. And though the Cambodian army enjoyed a huge numerical edge over the rebels, many were unenthusiastic about fighting on behalf of Lon Nol. Those who did fight were dependent on U.S. bombing and, later, U.S. military aid.

U.S. interest in Cambodia during the civil war was completely derivative of U.S. designs on Vietnam. So when U.S. troops withdrew from Vietnam in January 1973, the bombing of Cambodia became harder to justify. In August 1973 Congress finally stepped in to ban the air campaign. President Nixon was furious. He blamed Congress for weakening regional security and "raising doubts in the mind of both friends and adversaries" about U.S. "resolve." All told, between March 1969 and August 1973, U.S. planes dropped 540,000 tons of bombs onto the Cambodian countryside.[16] The United States continued to supply military and financial assistance to Lon Nol, warning that a "bloodbath" would ensue if the KR were allowed to triumph.

The U.S. B-52 raids killed tens of thousands of civilians.[17] Villagers who happened to be away from home returned to find nothing but dust and mud mixed with seared and bloody body parts. Lon Nol's ground forces used massive heavy artillery barrages to pacify areas or villages where some enemy activity was suspected. By 1973, inflation in Cambodia topped 275 percent, and 40 percent of roads and one-third of all bridges had been rendered unusable.[18] With the local economy dysfunctional, U.S. aid came to count for 95 percent of all of Lon Nol's income.

The U.S. bombing did little to weaken the Vietnamese or the Cambodian Communists. Instead, it probably had the opposite effect. Cambodians who resented America's demolition derby were captive both to the promise of peace and the anti-Americanism of the Khmer Rouge. British journalist William Shawcross and others have argued that the Khmer Rouge ranks swelled primarily because of the U.S. intervention. Chhit Do, a Khmer Rouge leader from northern Cambodia who later defected, described the effect of U.S. bombing:

> Every time after there had been bombing, they would take the people to see the craters, to see how big and deep the craters were, to see how the earth had been gouged out and scorched. . . . The ordinary people . . . sometimes literally shit in their pants when the big bombs and shells came. . . . Their minds just froze up and they would wander around mute for three or four days. Terrified and half-crazy, the peo-

ple were ready to believe what they were told. . . . That was what made it so easy for the Khmer Rouge to win the people over. . . . It was because of their dissatisfaction with the bombing that they kept on cooperating with the Khmer Rouge, joining up with the Khmer Rouge, sending their children off to go with them.[19]

Prince Sirik Matak, once a Lon Nol ally, warned U.S. officials not to back the unpopular Lon Nol regime. "If the United States continues to support such a regime," he warned, "you help the Communists."[20] American intervention in Cambodia did tremendous damage in its own right, but it also indirectly helped give rise to a monstrous regime.

The Unknowable Unknown

Before it begins, genocide is not easy to wrap one's mind around. A genocidal regime's intent to destroy a group is so hideous and the scale of its atrocities so enormous that outsiders who know enough to forecast brutality can rarely bring themselves to imagine genocide. This was true of many of the diplomats, journalists, and European Jews who observed Hitler throughout the 1930s, and it was certainly true of diplomats, journalists, and Cambodians who speculated about the Khmer Rouge before they seized power. The omens of imminent, mass violence were omnipresent but largely dismissed.

Before the fall of Phnom Penh in April 1975, Cambodia's Communists were well enough known to cause some Americans alarm. In June 1973 Kenneth Quinn, a thirty-two-year-old U.S. foreign service officer, was introduced to the Khmer Rouge quite by accident. For six years, he had worked in Vietnam as an American provincial adviser, and he had spent his last two years posted in Chou Doc, the Vietnamese province bordering Cambodia on the Mekong River. One day, Quinn hiked up a mountain outside Chou Doc that allowed him to survey the terrain for 10 miles around. In scanning the Cambodian horizon, he encountered a scene that both stunned and chilled him. "The villages in Cambodia are clustered in circles," Quinn recalls. "When I looked out, I saw that every one of these clusters was in flames and there was black smoke rising from each one. I didn't know what was going on. All I knew was that as far as the eye could see, every single village in Cambodia was on fire."

Confused, Quinn hand-wrote a description of the scene, stuffed it into an envelope, and put it on the plane that flew to the nearest U.S. consular headquarters, where it was typed up and sent back to the United States as a spot report. He also set out to learn more about Cambodia's internal divisions. In the subsequent weeks he interviewed dozens of Cambodian refugees who had fled to Vietnam, including a former KR official. The refugees described such brutality and the visual image of the burning horizon was so memorable that Quinn had what he calls a "eureka moment." He concluded that although the Khmer Rouge may have been well-behaved "boy scout revolutionaries" when they began their military campaign in 1970, in June 1973 they had launched a far more radical program designed to communalize the entire Cambodian society overnight. The KR were deporting people from their ancestral homes to new communes and were burning the old villages to enforce the policy.

In February 1974 he sent to Washington a forty-five-page classified report, "The Khmer Krahom [Rouge] Program to Create a Communist Society in Southern Cambodia." Quinn wrote: "The Khmer Krahom's programs have much in common with those of totalitarian regimes in Nazi Germany and the Soviet Union, particularly regarding efforts to psychologically reconstruct individual members of society." He described KR attacks on religion and on parental and monastic authority as well as the widespread use of terror. "Usually people are arrested and simply never show up again, or are given six months in jail and then die there," he reported. The "crimes" that "merited" this treatment were fleeing KR territory and questioning KR policies.[21] Today Quinn's voice still betrays shock at the bloodiness of the KR approach to social transformation: "They were forcing everybody to leave their homes and build new collectivized living communities. They were setting fires to everything the people owned so they would have nothing to go back to. They were separating children from parents, defrocking monks, killing those who disobeyed and creating an irrevocable living arrangement."

Quinn's reporting stood out from that of his State Department colleagues because at that time U.S. government officials rarely interviewed refugees. Instead they relied almost exclusively on official, government-to-government sources. But Quinn also urged his superiors to begin distinguishing between Communists in Cambodia and those in Vietnam. Vietnam had certainly supplied the KR with weapons, military advisers, and direct combat and logistical help in the past, but the two groups had begun to feud. Quinn sent detailed accounts of the KR's purge of Vietnamese civilians from Cambodia and their disruption of Vietnamese supply lines. Quinn's analysis was at complete odds with the prevailing view in Washington, which held that the Khmer Rouge were simply an extension of the North Vietnamese and the Vietcong. Quinn's reports were never heeded. Quinn recalls his rude awakening:

> It was of course disappointing to me. I was young and didn't know how government worked. I thought I would write this huge report and everybody would read it, but it was just another piece of paper. When I got back to Washington, people were still analyzing Cambodia in the old way, as if it were run by Hanoi. People would hear me out, and then just say, "Yeah, but . . . ."

Although the American press, too, occasionally mentioned "infighting" among the different Communist "factions," the myth of monolithic communism died hard. U.S. involvement in Cambodia was justifiable because the various Communist forces were joined in revolution. The KR rebels had shrouded their leadership in a thick cloak of mystery, and Quinn's hilltop survey was not going to sway Americans who assumed all Communists were in cahoots.

But others were beginning to stop lumping the two neighbors together. Elizabeth Becker became a "stringer" for the *Washington Post* in 1972. She was twenty-five when she arrived, and with her short blond hair, petite frame, and unending inquisitiveness, she might have been mistaken for a teenager. Most of the eager young correspondents had flocked to neighboring Vietnam to make their professional fortunes, but Becker had chosen to cover Cambodia, the sideshow. Permanently based in Phnom Penh, she did not depart for mini-sabbaticals or alternate assignments. Unlike her more senior, established colleagues, she lived among the Cambodian people and was thus better positioned to pick up stray gossip.

By the time Becker arrived in Cambodia, only 25,000 U.S. troops were left in Vietnam, and U.S. correspondents from the major news outlets were heading home. Initially, Becker joined her other American colleagues in defining the rebels according to the regime they opposed (as "anti–Lon Nol insurgents") or by the generic ideology they pursued ("Cambodian Communists" or "indigenous Communist rebels," to distinguish them from the North Vietnamese rebels who were presumed to direct them). The reporters used shorthand references that gave no hint of the aims or the character of the revolutionary force.

In early 1974, around the time Quinn was circulating his detailed report, Becker had begun to notice that Cambodians in Phnom Penh were becoming increasingly alarmed by what they learned about the mysterious rebels storming across Cambodia. The KR already occupied 85 percent of the country, and they seemed certain to take the rest. Becker saw that pedi-cab drivers, riverboat captains, and politicians alike were devouring the contents of a small book distinguishable by its cover, which depicted Cambodia shaped like a heart torn in two by the Mekong River. The book, *Regrets of the Khmer Soul,* was the published diary of Ith Sarin, a former Phnom Penh schoolteacher who had traveled through KR territory for nine months in 1972 and 1973, interviewing KR soldiers and peasants. Becker and Ishiyama Koki, a Japanese friend and colleague, paid to have Sarin's diary translated. Becker thought it time to ask a question that no American reporter to date had posed. She wrote a story for the *Post* entitled "Who Are the Khmer Rouge?" and answered the question in a way that few afterward would believe.

Becker's long feature, to which the *Post* gave a full-page spread in March 1974, drew heavily on Cambodian government and Western diplomatic sources, as well as Ith Sarin's diary. In her exposé, Becker quoted Sarin's description of the KR's appealing discipline and daunting severity. "I paid attention to the great help the Khmer Rouge gave to the people; building dikes, harvesting crops, building houses and digging bunkers," Sarin noted. "I also saw them force all people to wear black clothes, forbid idle chatter and severely punish any violations of their orders."[22]

Becker also quoted Cambodians who had defected from KR zones to the dwindling patch of territory controlled by the government. Becker's article was the first to mention Pol Pot, who was then still known by his given name of Saloth Sar. It was the first to note that relations between the KR and the Vietnamese Communists were strained. And it was the first to describe the cruelty of KR rule.

But if Becker depicted life under the KR as spartan, she did not depict it as savage. And if she described their rule as clinically disciplined, they did not come across as criminally disposed. In places Becker herself seemed taken with the egalitarian premises of the organization, which attracted Cambodians and foreigners alike. When the disreputable Lon Nol government captured KR women soldiers, Becker wrote, the government generals were appalled by the women's self-possession. Becker quoted one diplomat as say-ing, "They complained of the audacity of these virgins who had the nerve to look a man straight in the eye and who didn't shuffle their feet demurely like good women." Becker did not suggest that life under KR rule would be fun. But she also did not imply that life would not be permitted.[23]

Becker's description proved too bold for most American Cambodia observers. Sydney Schanberg of the *New York Times* faulted her for running a story without ever having toured KR territory. Since it was the KR that denied access, she said she could not ignore the horror stories simply because she could not see for herself. She told Schanberg, "We have to publish what we can find out." Back in the United States, she was severely criticized by both the right and left. U.S. government officials said she had been duped into believing the KR were not Vietnamese puppets, whereas leftist intellectuals chided her for falling for Central Intelligence Agency (CIA) warnings of an imminent KR-induced bloodbath. Much more serious than any of these crit-icisms was another consequence of the research: Her close friend and col-league Ishiyama Koki followed up his story on Sarin's diary by attempting to become the first journalist to visit the KR side. "It was strange," Becker recalls. "The sum result of my learning more about the Khmer Rouge was that I knew I never wanted to see these guys up close. The sum result for Koki was that he wanted to meet them and learn more." Koki vanished behind KR lines, as did another of Becker's Japanese colleagues shortly thereafter.

For the remainder of 1974 and into 1975, journalists attempted to shed light upon the KR leadership, but Pol Pot and his leading associates, Khieu Samphan and Ieng Sary, operated behind the scenes in complete isolation. With the KR resolutely unknowable, their mystery received almost as much attention as the misery they inflicted upon Cambodians. Even Lon Nol's government had no idea with whom it was dealing. In April 1974, when the Khmer Rouge's Khieu Samphan visited New York, Becker's reports focused not on what Samphan had to say at the United Nations but on whether he was in fact Samphan, who was rumored to have been exe-cuted by Prince Sihanouk. Becker wrote: "Some Cambodians say he is too fat in the photos, his voice is too high, and that he gave only one speech in French in Pyongyang, which they find suspicious since he holds a doctor-ate in economics from Paris."[24] The sternly secretive Khmer Rouge bewil-dered even the most informed Cambodia observers.

The presence of the soothing Sihanouk at the head of the KR front also continued to throw people off. As one Western diplomat put it, "They know it is Sihanouk's army out there and they think once that army gets inside everything will be all milk and honey—or rice and dried fish if you will—again."[25] In 1974 Sihanouk sent several Democrats in the U.S. Congress a letter in which he described rumors of an imminent Khmer Rouge massacre of Lon Nol and his supporters as "absurd." Sihanouk assured the legislators that the KR front would not establish a socialist republic upon taking power, "but a Swedish type of kingdom."[26] His was the public face of the coalition, but it was difficult to judge whether the public face had influence over the private soul of the movement.

However worrying the rumors that swirled before the KR victory, few Cambodia watchers grasped what lay ahead before it was too late.

Wishful Thinking

As foreigners collected their impressions of the Khmer Rouge, they deferred, as foreigners do, to the instincts of their local friends and colleagues. If anybody had the grounds to anticipate systematic brutality, it seems logical that it would be those most immediately endangered. Yet those with the most at stake are in fact often the least prone to recognize their peril. The Cambodian people were frightened by the reports of atrocities in the KR-occupied countryside, but they retained resilient hope.

François Ponchaud was a French Jesuit priest who spoke Khmer and lived among the Cambodians. He heard the chilling local gossip that preceded the KR's capture of Phnom Penh. "They kill any soldiers they capture, and their families too," Cambodians said. "They take people away to the forest," they warned. But in the mental duel that was fought in each and every Cambodian's mind, it was the concrete features of a horrifying, immediate war that won out over the more abstract fear of the unknown. The toll of the civil war on Cambodia's civilians had been immense. Some 1 million Cambodians had been killed.[27] Both sides got into the habit of taking no prisoners in combat, unless they planned to torture them to extract military intelligence. Cannibalism was widespread, as soldiers were told that eating the livers of captured enemies would confer the power of the vanquished upon the victor. The country's rice crop had been obliterated. More than 3 million Cambodians had been displaced, causing the population of the capital to swell from 600,000 to over 2 million by 1975. The daily privations were such that Cambodians naturally preferred the idea of the KR to the reality of Lon Nol. Moreover, most assumed that the KR excesses were the product of the heat of battle, and not the result of ideology or innate callousness. The most ominous warnings about the KR were dismissed as Lon Nol propaganda. As Ponchaud later noted, "Khmers were Khmers, we thought; [the KR] would never go to such extremes with their own countrymen. Victory was within their grasp: what psychological advantage could they gain by taking wanton reprisals?"[28]

The kinds of conversations that went on in Phnom Penh in the months preceding its fall resembled those that Lemkin had struck up as he toured eastern Poland, Latvia, and Lithuania as a refugee during World War II. Why would Hitler round up defenseless people? Why would he divert precious resources from the eastern front during World War II so that he could finish them off? Because the extermination of the Jews constituted its own victory, and it was the triumph for which he was sure he would be remembered. Similarly, Pol Pot would treat as discrete policy objectives the eradication of those associated with the old regime, as well as the educated, the Vietnamese, the Muslim Cham, the Buddhist monks, and other "bourgeois elements." Violence was not an unfortunate byproduct of the revolution; it was an indispensable feature of it. But like so many targeted peoples before them, Cambodians were consoled by the presumption of reasonableness.

As the KR rebels closed in on the capital, ordinary people dared to visualize the end of deprivation, bombs, and bullets. Once the civil war between Lon Nol and the KR ended and they were rid of foreign interference, they told themselves, they could return to their Buddhist, peaceable heritage. Since high politics was the province of the elite, most Cambodians assumed that the politicians would settle scores with the "traitorous clique" of seven senior officials in the Lon Nol government and everybody else would be left alone, free at last to resume normal life. "I have no ideas about politics," My Vo, a twenty-nine-year-old Cambodian, was quoted as saying two weeks before Phnom Penh fell to the KR. "I am just a man in the middle. . . . If this side wins, I'll be an office assistant. If the other wins, I'll be an office assistant. I don't care which side wins."[29] What mattered to Cambodians was that the fighting stop.

Having known only conflict for five years, the Cambodians considered the KR promise of peace an appealing alternative. The Communists talked about justice to a people who had known nothing but injustice. They spoke of order to a people who knew only corruption. And they pledged a brighter future free of imperialists, whereas the Lon Nol government promised only more of the dim present. Having watched their leaders cozy up to the United States and the United States repay them by bombing and invading their country, Cambodians longed for freedom from outside interference.

Major U.S. newspapers reflected the optimistic mood. Once the KR won the war, Schanberg wrote, "there would be no need for random acts of terror."[30] He, too, made rational calculations about what was "necessary." He recalls:

> We knew the KR had done some very brutal things. Many reporters went missing and didn't come back. But we all came to the conclusion—it wasn't a conclusion, it was more like wishful thinking—that when the Khmer Rouge marched into Phnom Penh, they'd have no need to be so brutal. There'd be some executions—of those on the Khmer Rouge's "Seven Traitors List"—but that was it. We were talking to people—talking to our Cambodian friends who want to believe the best. Nobody believes they will get slaughtered. It is unthinkable and you don't wrap your mind around it.

Schanberg, *Times* photographer Al Rockoff, and British reporter Jon Swain were so incapable of "wrapping their minds around" what lay ahead that they chose to remain in Cambodia after the U.S. embassy had evacuated its citizens. They stayed to report on the "transition" to postwar peace.[31] Hope and curiosity outweighed fear.

A Bloodbath?

Alarming reports of atrocities are typically met with skepticism. Usually, though, it is the refugees, journalists, and relief workers who report the abuses and U.S. government decision-makers who resist belief. Some cannot imagine. Others do not want to act or hope to defer acting and thus either downplay the reports or place them in a broader "context" that helps to subsume their horror. In Cambodia atrocity warnings were again minimized, but it was not officials in the U.S. government who dismissed them as fanciful.

In early 1975 senior U.S. policymakers in the administration of Gerald Ford reiterated earlier warnings that a bloodbath would follow a KR triumph. In March 1975 President Ford himself predicted a "massacre" if Phnom Penh fell to the Khmer Rouge.[32] A National Security Council fact sheet, which was distributed to Congress and the media the same month, even invoked the Holocaust. The briefing memo warned, "The Communists are waging a total war against Cambodia's civilian population with a degree of systematic terror perhaps unparalleled since the Nazi period—a clear precursor of the blood bath and Stalinist dictatorship they intend to impose on the Cambodian people."[33] The U.S. ambassador in Phnom Penh, Dean, said he feared an "uncontrolled and uncontrollable solution" in which the KR would kill "the army, navy, air force, government and Buddhist monks."[34]

But few trusted the warnings. The Nixon and Ford administrations had cried wolf one time too many in Southeast Asia. In addition, because the KR were so secretive, America's warnings were by definition speculative, based mainly on rumors and secondhand accounts. To the extent that the apocalyptic warnings of U.S. government officials were sincere, many Americans believed they stemmed from the Ford administration's anti-Communist paranoia or its desire to get congressional backing for an $82 million aid package for the Lon Nol regime. They did not believe that the administration had any tangible evidence that the Communists were murdering their own people. In the aftermath of Watergate and Vietnam, Americans doubted whether any truth existed in politics.

On April 13, 1975, on the eve of the fall of Phnom Penh, Schanberg published a dispatch titled "Indochina Without Americans: For Most, a Better Life." "It is difficult to imagine," he wrote, how the lives of ordinary Cambodians could be "anything but better with the Americans gone."[35]

Many members of Congress agreed. U.S. legislators felt lied to and burned by their previous credulity. To warn of a new bloodbath was no excuse to continue the bloody civil war. As Bella Abzug (D.–N.Y.), who had just returned from Cambodia, told a House hearing:

> It is argued that we must give military aid because if we do not there will be a bloodbath. One thing we did discover, there is no greater bloodbath than that which is taking place presently and can only take place with our military assistance. . . . Suppose we were asked to address either 75,000 or 100,000 of those Cambodians who may very well lose their lives or be maimed by our military assistance for the next 3-month period . . . and they said to you, "Why do I have to die?" . . . or "Why should my body be mangled?"—What would you tell them? That we are doing it in order to avoid a bloodbath?[36]

Abzug suggested that if the United States would only change its policy, it could likely work with the Khmer Rouge and "arrange for an orderly transfer of power."[37] Senator George McGovern (D.–S. Dak.), a leader of the antiwar movement, trusted nothing the U.S. government said about the Cambodian Communists. He expected the KR to form a government "run by some of the best-educated, most able intellectuals in Cambodia."[38] The editorial pages of the major newspapers and the congressional opposition were united in the view, in the words of a *Washington Post* editorial, that "the threatened 'bloodbath' is less ominous than a continuation of the current bloodletting."[39] Western journalists in Phnom Penh sang a song to the tune of "She Was Poor but She Was Honest":

> *Oh will there be a dreadful bloodbath*
> *When the Khmer Rouge come to town?*
> *Aye, there'll be a dreadful bloodbath*
> *When the Khmer Rouge come to town.*

Becker, the young *Post* reporter who had offered one of the earliest depictions of the Khmer Rouge, was pessimistic. She departed Cambodia ahead of the KR capture of Phnom Penh, as she did not want to be around for what she knew would come next. Besides fearing the worst for Cambodians and her colleagues who had disappeared, Becker also sensed the impossibility of generating outside interest in the story. This was a region whose problems the world was anxious to put behind it. She predicted that she would be unable to cover the ensuing horrors, and the outside world would do nothing to stop them. She was right on both counts.

Recognition

From Behind a Blindfold

Although most foreigners hoped for the best in advance of the fall of Phnom Penh, most of those with passports from non-Communist countries did not remain to test the new regime. Nearly all American and European journalists had left Phnom Penh by early April 1975. Twenty-six reporters had already gone missing.[40] Most of the others had come to agree with Becker that something extremely ugly lay ahead. The U.S. embassy kept its evacuation plans secret until the morning that U.S. Marines secured a helicopter landing area in the outskirts of the capital. On April 12, in Operation Eagle Pull, diplomatic staff and most U.S. correspondents left aboard the U.S. helicopters. President Ford said that he had ordered the American departure with a "heavy heart."

Not all the signs from Phnom Penh were grim. Prince Sihanouk, the titular leader of the KR coalition, had sent mixed signals all along. On the one hand, he had spoken confidently of the KR's intention to establish a democratic state. On the other hand, he had cautioned that the KR would have little use for him: "They'll spit me out like a cherry pit," he once said.[41] But in the immediate aftermath of the KR triumph, Sihanouk was less interested in prophesying than in gloating. "We did what they said we could never do," he boasted. "We defeated the Americans."[42] The day after the harrowing evacuation of Phnom Penh began, bewildered Western reporters led their stories by again posing the question that the *Post*'s Becker had posed a full year before, "Who are the Khmer Rouge?"

A few hundred brave, foolish, or unlucky foreigners stayed in Phnom Penh. On April 17 they heard the same unforgiving commands that jolted their Cambodian friends into flight. They did not believe KR claims that American B-52s were going to bomb the town, but they attempted to offer rational explanations for the exodus. The KR would be unable to feed the swollen population in the capital, and dispersal to the countryside would move the people closer to food sources. The dislocation would make it easier for the KR to distinguish allies of the old regime from ordinary Cambodians. Or maybe the KR leaders simply wanted their pick of housing in the capital. All assumed the evacuation would be temporary. Cambodians would surely return to their homes once the new Communist government felt secure.

Forbidden to move around the city, the remaining foreigners huddled at the French embassy, awaiting KR clearance to leave.[43] The best early intelligence on the nature of the new KR regime consisted of mental snapshots that these reporters, aid workers, and diplomats had gathered before they were confined at the embassy. Most had seen the fearsome KR cadres driving trembling Cambodians out of town, but they had not witnessed killings. "There were no massacres committed in front of us," recalls Schanberg, who was very nearly executed, along with his colleagues Rockoff and Swain, while snooping around a hospital on the day of the

KR victory. "We did see these people from another planet. You had the feeling that if you did something they didn't like they would shoot you. But we had no awareness of what was to come."

On May 6 a final caravan of trucks carrying Schanberg and the last Western witnesses to KR rule left Cambodia. The evacuees peered out from behind their blindfolds on the stifling hot journey. The KR had been in charge less than three weeks, but the signs of what we would later understand to be the beginning of genocide were already apparent. All of Cambodia's major towns had already been emptied of their inhabitants. The rice paddies, too, were deserted. The charred remains of cars lay gathered in heaps. Saffron-robed monks had been put to work in the fields. Decomposed bodies lay by the side of the road, shot or beaten to death. KR soldiers could be spotted with their heads bowed for their morning "thought sessions."[44] The overriding impression of those who drove through a country that had bustled with life just weeks before was that the Cambodian people had disappeared.

Once the final convoy of foreigners had been safely evacuated, the departed journalists published stark front-page accounts. They acknowledged that the situation unfolding was far more dire than they had expected. In a cover story for the *New York Times,* Schanberg wrote: "Everyone—Cambodians and foreigners alike—looked ahead with hopeful relief to the collapse of the city. . . . *All of us were wrong.* . . . That view of the future of Cambodia—as a possibly flexible place even under Communism, where changes would not be extreme and ordinary folk would be left alone—turned out to be a myth."[45] Schanberg even quoted one unnamed Western official who had observed the merciless exodus and exclaimed, "They are crazy! This is pure and simple genocide. They will kill more people this way than if there had been hand-to-hand fighting in the city."[46] That same day the *Washington Post* carried an evacuation story that cited fears of "genocide by natural selection" in which "only the strong will survive the march."[47]

Although Schanberg and others were clearly spooked by their chilling final experiences in Cambodia, they still did not believe that American intelligence would prove right about much. In the same article in which Schanberg admitted he had underestimated the KR's repressiveness, he noted that official U.S. predictions had been misleading. The U.S. government had said the Communists were poorly trained, Schanberg noted, but the journalists had encountered a well-disciplined, healthy, organized force. The intelligence community had forecast the killing of "as many as 20,000 high officials and intellectuals." But Schanberg's limited exposure to the KR left him convinced that violence on that scale would not transpire. He wrote:

> There have been unconfirmed reports of executions of senior military and civilian officials, and no one who witnessed the take-over doubts that top people of the old regime will be or have been punished and perhaps killed or that a large number of people will die of the hardships on the march into the countryside. But none of this will apparently bear any resemblance to the mass executions that had been predicted by Westerners.[48]

Once the reporters had departed, the last independent sources of information dried up. Nine friendly Communist countries retained embassies in Phnom Penh, but even these personnel were restricted in movement to a street around 200 yards long and accompanied at all times by official KR "minders."[49] For the next three and a half years, the American public would piece together a picture of life behind the Khmer curtain from KR public statements, which were few; from Cambodian radio, which was propaganda; from refugee accounts, which were doubted; and from Western intelligence sources, which were scarce and suspect.

Official U.S. Intelligence, Unofficial Skepticism

When the KR first took power, U.S. officials eagerly disclosed much of what they knew. The Ford administration condemned violent abuses, reminding audiences that its earlier forecasts of a Khmer Rouge bloodbath were being borne out by fact. The day after the fall of Phnom Penh, Kissinger testified on Capitol Hill that the KR would "try to eliminate all potential opponents."[50] In early May 1975, President Ford said he had "hard intelligence," including Cambodian radio transmissions, that eighty to ninety Cambodian officials and their spouses had been executed.[51] He told *Time* magazine, "They killed the wives, too. They said the wives were just the same as their husbands. This is a horrible thing to report to you, but we are certain that our sources are accurate." *Newsweek* quoted a U.S. official saying "thousands have already been executed" and suggested the

A Khmer Rouge guerrilla orders store owners to abandon their shops in Phnom Penh on April 17, 1975, the day the city fell into rebel hands.

figure could rise to "tens of thousands of Cambodians loyal to the Lon Nol regime." With intercepts of KR communications in hand, U.S. officials were adamant about the veracity of their intelligence. "I am not dealing in third-hand reports," one intelligence analyst told *Newsweek*. "I am telling you what is being said by the Cambodians themselves in their own communications."[52] Syndicated columnists Jack Anderson and Les Whitten, who would regularly relay reports of atrocities over the next several years, published leaked translations of these secret KR radio transmissions in the *Washington Post*. "Eliminate all high-ranking military officials, government officials," one order read. "Do this secretly. Also get provincial officers who owe the Communist Party a blood debt." Another KR unit, relaying orders from the Communist high command, called for the "execution of all military officers from lieutenant to colonel, with their wives and their children."[53] In a press conference on May 13, Kissinger accused the KR of "atrocity of major proportions."[54] President Ford again cited "very factual evidence of the bloodbath that is in the process of taking place."[55]

But the administration had little credibility. Kissinger had bloodied Cambodia and blackened his own reputation with past U.S. policy. Just as critics heard the Ford administration's earlier predictions of bloodshed as thinly veiled pretexts for supplying the corrupt Lon Nol regime with more U.S. aid, many now assumed that American horror stories were designed to justify the U.S. invasion of Cambodia and Vietnam. Events elsewhere in Southeast Asia were only confirming the unreliability of U.S. government sources. The United States had similarly warned that the fall of Saigon would result in a slaughter, but when the city fell on April 30, 1975, the handover was far milder than expected. The American public had learned to dismiss what it deemed official rumor-mongering and anti-Communist propaganda. It would be two years before most would acknowledge that this time the bloodbath reports were true.

The U.S. government also lost reliable sources inside Cambodia. One of the side effects of the closing of U.S. embassies in times of crisis is that it ravages U.S. intelligence-gathering capabilities. Cambodia was especially cut off because journalists, too, were barred from visiting. Because the perpetrators of genocide are careful to deny observers access to their crime scenes, journalists must rely on the eyewitness or secondhand accounts of refugees who manage to escape. Reporters trained to authenticate their stories by visiting or confirming with multiple sources thus tend initially to shy away from publishing refugee accounts. When they do print them, they routinely add caveats and disclaimers: With almost every condemnation or citation of intelligence that appeared in the press about Cambodia in 1975 and 1976, reporters included reminders that they had only "unconfirmed reports," "inconclusive accounts," or "very fragmentary information." This caution is warranted, but as it had done during the Armenian genocide and the Holocaust, it blurred clarity and tempered conviction. It gave those inclined to look away further excuse for doing so. "We simply don't know the full story," readers said. "Until we do, we cannot sensibly draw conclusions." By waiting for the full story to emerge, however, politicians, journalists, and citizens were guaranteeing they would not get emotionally or politically involved until it was too late.

If this inaccessibility is a feature of most genocide, Cambodia was perhaps the most extreme case. The Khmer Rouge may well have run the most secretive regime of the twentieth century. They sealed the country completely. "Only through secrecy," a senior KR official said, could the KR "win victory over the enemy who cannot find out who is who."[56] When Pol Pot emerged formally as KR leader in September 1977, journalists hypothesized out loud about his identity. "Some say he is a former laborer on a French rubber plantation, of Vietnamese origin," AFP reported. "Others say he is actually Nuong Suon, a onetime journalist on a Communist newspaper who was arrested by Prince Norodom Sihanouk in the 1950s."[57] When Pol Pot's photo was released by a Chinese photo news agency, analysts noted that he bore a "marked resemblance" to Saloth Sar, the former Communist Party secretary-general. The resemblance was of course not coincidental.[58]

The KR did have a voice. They spurred on their cadres over the radio, proclaiming, "The enemy must be utterly crushed"; "What is infected must be cut out"; "What is too long must be shortened and made the right length."[59] The broadcasts were translated daily by the U.S. Foreign Broadcast Information Service, but they were euphemisms followed by the KR's glowing claims about the "joyous" planting of the rainy season rice crop, the end of corruption, and the countrywide campaign to repair U.S. bomb damage.

In the United States, the typical editorial neglect of a country of no pressing national concern was compounded exponentially by the "Southeast Asia fatigue" that pervaded newsrooms in the aftermath of Vietnam. The horde of American journalists who had descended on the region while U.S. troops were deployed in Vietnam dwindled. Only the three major U.S. newspapers—the *New York Times, Washington Post,* and *Los Angeles Times*—retained staff correspondents in Bangkok, Thailand, and they were tasked with covering Vietnam, Laos, and Cambodia (known as VLCs, or "very lost causes") as well. As soon as U.S. troops returned home, the American public's appetite for news from the region shrank. Journalists who did publish stories tended to focus on the Vietnamese boat people and the fate of American POWs and stay-behinds. Responsible for such broad patches of territory, they were slow to travel to the Thai-Cambodian border to hear secondhand tales of terror.[60] Those who did make the trip found that many of the Cambodian refugees had experienced terrible suffering, hunger, and repression, but few had witnessed massacres with their own eyes. Soon after seizing the capital, the KR had hastily erected a barbed-wire barrier to prevent crossing into Aranyaprathet, Thailand, and had laid mines all along the border. The Cambodians with the gravest stories to tell were, by definition, dead or still trapped inside the country. U.S. officials estimated that only one in five who attempted to reach Thailand survived.

The dropoff in U.S. press coverage of Cambodia was dramatic. During Cambodia's civil war between 1970 and 1975, while the United States was still actively engaged in Southeast Asia, the *Washington Post* and *New York Times* had published more than 700 stories on Cambodia each year. In the single month of April 1975, when the KR approached Phnom Penh, the two papers ran a combined 272 stories on Cambodia. But in December 1975, after foreigners had left, that figure plummeted to eight stories altogether.[61] In the entire year of 1976, while the Khmer Rouge went about destroying its populace, the two papers published a combined 126 stories; in 1977 they ran 118.[62] And these figures actually exaggerate the extent of American attention to the plight of Cambodians. Most of the stories in this period were short, appeared in the back of the international news section, and focused on the geopolitical ramification of Cambodia's Communist rule rather than on the suffering of Cambodians. Only two or three stories a *year* focused on the human rights situation under the Khmer Rouge.[63] In July 1975 the *Times* ran a powerful editorial asking "what, if anything" the outside world could do "to alter the genocidal policies" and "barbarous cruelty" of the KR. The editorial argued that U.S. officials who had rightly criticized Lon Nol now had a "special obligation to speak up," as "silence certainly will not move" Pol Pot.[64] But the same editorial board that called on the United States to break the silence did not itself speak again on the subject for another three years.

Cambodia received even less play on television. Between April and June 1975, when one might have expected curiosity to be high, the three major networks combined gave Cambodia just under two and a half minutes of airtime. During the entire three and a half years of KR rule, the networks devoted less than sixty minutes to Cambodia, which averaged less than thirty seconds per month per network. ABC carried one human rights story about Cambodia in 1976 and did not return to the subject for two years.[65]

American editors and producers were simply not interested, and in the absence of photographs, video images, personal narratives that could grab readers' or viewers' attention, or public protests in the United States about the outrages, they were unlikely to become interested. Of course, the public was unlikely to become outraged if the horrors were not reported.

Plausible Deniability: "Propaganda, the Fear of Propaganda, and the Excuse of Propaganda"

Some of the guilt that Americans might have had over ignoring the terror behind KR lines was eased by a vocal group of atrocity skeptics who questioned the authenticity of refugee claims. They were skeptical for many of the usual reasons. They clung to the few public statements of senior KR officials, who consistently refuted bloodbath claims and confirmed observers' hopes that only the elite from the last regime had reason to fear. "You should not believe the refugees who came to Thailand," said Ieng Sary, deputy premier in charge of foreign affairs, in November 1975, while visiting Bangkok, "because these people have committed crimes." He urged the refugees in Thailand to return to Cambodia, where they would be welcomed.[66] In September 1977 Pol Pot said in Phnom Penh that "only the smallest possible number" out of the "1 or 2 percent" of Cambodians who opposed the revolution had been "eradicated." Conceding some killings gave the KR a greater credibility than if they had denied atrocities outright, and many observers were taken in by these concessions.[67]

Another factor that blunted understanding of the evil of the regime was that many Cambodians died of starvation and malnutrition, which outsiders associated with "natural" economic and climatic forces. This probably helped obscure the human causes of the disaster. In addition, refugees who told horror stories were presumed to be affiliated with the old regime. International relief workers in Thailand were said to be politically motivated as well because many were funded by the U.S. Agency for International Development or were thought to be anti-Communist.[68]

Leading voices on the American left, a constituency that in other circumstances might have been the most prone to shame the U.S. government into at least denouncing the KR, ridiculed the early atrocity claims as conservative "mythmaking." They pursued the speculative bloodbath debate that had preceded the KR victory with even greater ferocity. The directors of the antiwar Indochina Resource Center, George Hildebrand and Gareth Porter, released a study in September 1975 that challenged claims that the evacuation of Phnom Penh had been an "atrocity" causing famine. Instead they said it was a response to Cambodians' "urgent and fundamental needs" and "it was carried out only after careful planning for provision of food, water, rest and medical care."[69] The following year they published the widely read *Cambodia: Starvation and Revolution.* Without ever having visited the country, they rejected atrocity reports. The city evacuations, they argued, would improve the welfare of Cambodians, whose livelihoods had been devastated by the Nixon years. They were convinced that American and European media, governments, and anti-Communists were colluding to exaggerate KR sins for Cold War propaganda purposes. This account was read widely at the State Department and received backing from Noam Chomsky and Edward Herman, who, in an article in the *Nation,* "Distortions at Fourth Hand," praised Hildebrand and Porter. As the title of their article indicates, Chomsky and Herman faulted reporters for their third- and fourth-hand sourcing.[70]

The motives of the skeptics varied. A few leftists were so eager to see an egalitarian band of Communist revolutionaries taking control of yet another Southeast Asian state that they paid little attention to reports of terror. But many who in fact cared about the welfare of Cambodians were relieved that the corrupt, abusive Lon Nol had been deposed. Most had learned to doubt any claim that emerged from a U.S. government source. But above all, politics and recent history aside, they possessed a natural, human incapacity to take their imaginations where the refugees demanded they go.

Within a decade and a half, human rights organizations would gather refugee testimony and shame governments that committed abuses, as well as the outside powers that ignored them. At the time of the Cambodian genocide, however, Amnesty International, the largest human rights organization in the world, was not yet oriented to respond forcefully. Founded in 1961 with a budget of $19,000, it had increased its annual expenditures to about $660,000. As a letter-writing organization best suited to getting political prisoners freed from jail, the organization's reporting from the 1970s tended to focus on a small number of specific victims whose names were known; it had never before responded to systematic, large-scale slaughter like that alleged in Cambodia. The organization did not dispatch monitors to the Thai-Cambodian border but instead relied mainly upon tentative press reports. A September 1975 Amnesty report stated that "allegations of mass executions were impossible to substantiate." Amnesty's research department noted that a number of allegations were based on "flimsy evidence and second-hand accounts."[71] The following year the organization's annual report devoted a little over one page to Cambodia. It noted "allegations of large scale executions" but added that "few refugees seem to have actually witnessed executions."[72]

An internal policy document sent in March 1977 from Amnesty's London headquarters to national chapters explained the organization's reticence. Amnesty was mistrustful of "conservative opinions" and refugee testimony alike. "Allegations made by refugees must be examined with care in view of their possible partiality and the fact that they often give only fragmentary information and have a tendency to generalize," the document said.[73] Of course, the dead had not lived to tell their tales, and the living, the refugees, could describe only the abuses they had suffered, which were often "lesser" crimes, or those that they had witnessed but could not substantiate.

Even when they had reliable evidence in hand, Amnesty officials operated very much like the committees the United Nations had established to monitor human rights: They avoided public shaming when possible and approached governments directly. Amnesty's 1977 policy report described its tactics: "In view of the existing international attention and of the polemical aspects of the public debate on Cambodia," it would be better to establish private contact with the KR than to embarrass them publicly.[74] Each year the organization sent letters to the regime requesting further information on specific reports of torture and disappearances. When the Pol Pot regime failed to respond, Amnesty ritually included a complaint about its unresponsiveness in the following year's annual report. Only in 1978, three years after the killing and starvation campaign had begun, did the organization finally accept refugee claims and seek avenues for more public shaming.

Other atrocity skeptics concentrated on the impossibility of resolving debates over the number of Cambodians killed. They insisted, accurately, that the estimates of dead and wounded were arbitrary. Ben Kiernan, a young Australian historian who later became a prominent critic of the Khmer Rouge, objected to the lack of "evidence to support anything like the figures quoted," saying that "huge figures have been plucked out of the air for numbers of victims."[75] Journalists joined the numbers debate by noting shifts in estimates, sometimes in a self-satisfied tone. In the *Washington Post* Lewis Simons observed in July 1977 that the estimates of deaths had dropped dramatically. Once, he wrote, "it was popular to say that anywhere between 800,000 and 1.4 million Cambodians had been executed by vengeful Communist rulers," but suddenly Western observers had begun "talking in terms of several hundred thousand deaths from all causes."[76] Observers of the Khmer Rouge from 1975 to 1979 did pass figures and anecdotes from one account to the next. And often these figures were unconfirmed, but circumstances also rendered them unconfirmable. Because Cambodia was completely inaccessible, analysts could give only their best guess of the scale of the violence, and those guesses tended to vary wildly.

With so much confusion about the precise nature of the KR reign, apathy became justified by what journalist William Shawcross later called "propaganda, the fear of propaganda and the excuse of propaganda."[77]

Those who believed refugees argued that the sameness of their accounts revealed a pattern of abuses across Cambodia. Yet for those who wanted to turn away or who were unsure of the utility of turning toward Cambodia, this very sameness offered proof of scripting.

"This Is Not 1942"

Many came around once they had personal contact with the traumatized refugees. Charles Twining was a thirty-three-year-old foreign service officer who had served in Vietnam and—to the bemusement of his State Department colleagues—had spent 1974 diligently learning the Khmer language. In June 1975 he was posted to the U.S. embassy in Bangkok, and within a week of his arrival his new-found language skill proved all too useful. He was dispatched to the Thai-Cambodian border to interview refugees who were arriving exhausted, emaciated, and petrified. Twining initially could not bring himself to trust the stories he heard. "The refugees were telling tales that you could only describe as unbelievable," he remembers. "I kept saying to myself, 'This can't be possible in this day and age. This is not 1942. This is 1975.' I really thought that those days, those acts, were behind us."[78] After his first trip Twining did not even file a report because he found the refugees' recollections literally "inconceivable" and felt he would be laughed at back in Washington. But every time he took the four-hour car journey to the border, he found it harder to deny the reality of the atrocities. The Cambodians had heard the howls of their starving infants. They had watched KR cadres use plastic bags to suffocate Buddhist monks. They had seen their loved ones murdered by teenage warriors who mechanically delivered the blow of a hoe to the back of the neck.

Twining pointed to a small milk can and asked the refugees to indicate the amount of rice the Khmer Rouge fed them each day. They said that they had been given rice that would have filled about half of this palm-sized implement. When Twining argued that they would not have been able to live on such portions, they agreed but told him that anybody who complained was dragged away to what the KR called *Angkar Loeu. Angkar* was the nameless and faceless "organization on high," which prided itself on never erring and on having "as many eyes as a pineapple."[79] At first most Cambodians believed that those who disappeared were being taken to

Angkar for reeducation or extra training and study. Despite the agony of daily life and the rumors of daily death, they had again hoped for the best. Often the truth became clear only when they stumbled upon a huge pile of bones in the forest. After encountering these concrete artifacts of evil, most accepted that a summons by *Angkar* meant certain death, a realization that was enough to cause only some to risk flight.

One refugee, Seath K. Teng, was only four years old when she was separated from her family. She later remembered fierce hunger pain as the KR forced four children to share one rice porridge bowl. "Whoever could eat the fastest got more to eat," she recalled:

> We worked seven days a week without a break. The only time we got
> off work was to see someone get killed, which served as an example
> for us. . . . In the center of the meeting place was one woman who
> had both of her hands tied behind her. She was pregnant and her
> stomach bulged out. Before her stood a little boy who was about six
> years old and holding an ax. In his shrill voice he yelled for us to look
> at what he was going to do. He said that if we didn't look, we would
> be the next to be killed. I guess we all looked, because the woman was
> the only one killed that day. The little boy was like a demon from
> hell. His eyes were red and he didn't look human at all. He used the
> back of his ax and slammed it hard on the poor woman's body until
> she dropped to the ground. He kept beating her until he was too tired
> to continue.[80]

By August 1975 Twining had heard enough of these stories to become a convert:

> I remember there was one moment. I was in a place in Thailand called
> Chantha Buri, a province that borders the Cambodian town of Pailin.
> I was sitting in this little dark house on the border, and suddenly
> twenty or thirty Cambodians appeared like ghosts out of the forest.
> They told me stories of such hardship and horror that it just hit me.
> Somebody afterwards said to me, "you know they rehearsed their sto-
> ries." But these Cambodians had just arrived from weeks on the road.
> They were lean, tanned. They had been wearing the same clothes for
> days. They were smelly, if I dare say it. And the one thing I knew was
> that they were genuine. Genuine. From that point on, I believed. . . .

After he was jolted into belief by the smell of the distraught survivors, Twining filtered future testimony through the prism of the Holocaust. "My mind wanted, needed, some way of framing the thing," he recalls, "and the Holocaust was the closest thing I had. This sounded to me like extermination—you wipe out a whole class of people, anyone with glasses, anyone with a high school education, anyone who is Buddhist. I mean, the link was natural." Although there were similarities between the Nazis and the KR, he and others at the border gradually assembled an understanding of the specifics of KR brutality. They learned that in the new Cambodia freedom had become undesirable, dissent intolerable, and joy invisible. All facets of life had been mandated by *Angkar*, which made the rules. By the end of 1975, those who had once known enough to fear but had hoped enough to deny had come to accept the contours of the hell that had befallen Cambodia.

Refugees told them:

- Citizens could not move. Travel passes were required even to cross town. Cities were evacuated at gunpoint.
- They could not feed themselves. In most areas the state supplied a tin or less of rice each day.
- They could not learn what they chose. Only KR tracts were permitted. Libraries were ravaged. And speaking foreign languages signaled "contamination" and earned many who dared to do so a death sentence.
- They could not reminisce. Memories of the past life were banned. Families were separated. Children were "reeducated" and induced to inform on parents who might be attempting to mask their "bourgeois" pasts. "Cambodia," a colonial term, was replaced by "Democratic Kampuchea."
- They could not flirt. Only *Angkar* could authorize sexual relationships. The pairings for weddings were announced en masse at the commune assemblies.
- They could not pray. Chapels and temples were pillaged. Devout Muslims were often forced to eat pork. Buddhist monks were defrocked, their pagodas converted into grain silos.
- They could not own private property. All money and property were abolished. The national bank was blown up. Radios, tele-

phones, televisions, cars, and books gathered in the central
squares were burned.

- And they could not make contact with the outside world.
  Foreign embassies were closed; telephone, telegraph, and mail
  service suspended.

Work was prized to a deadly extent. Cambodians were sent to the countryside, where an average day involved planting from 4 a.m. to 10 a.m., 1
p.m. to 5 p.m., and then again from 7 p.m. to 10 p.m. Communist cadres
transported annual harvests to central storage sites but refused to distribute
the fruits of the harvests to those who had done the reaping. Health was
superfluous to the national project, and starvation and disease quickly
engulfed the country. Upon taking power, the Khmer Rouge terminated
almost all foreign trade and rejected offers of humanitarian aid.

"Enemies" were eliminated. Pol Pot saw two sets of enemies—the
external and the internal. External enemies opposed KR-style socialism;
they included "imperialists" and "fascists" like the United States as well as
"revisionists" and "hegemonists" like the Soviet Union and Vietnam.
Internal enemies were those deemed disloyal.[81] Early on the Khmer Rouge
had instructed all military and civilian officials from the Lon Nol regime to
gather at central meeting posts and had murdered them without exception.
Another child, Savuth Penn, who was eleven years old when the evacuation was ordered, recalled:

> They shipped my father and the rest of the military officers to a
> remote area northwest of the city . . . then they mass executed them,
> without any blindfolds, with machine guns, rifles, and grenades. . . .
> My father was buried underneath all the dead bodies. Fortunately, only
> one bullet went through his arm and two bullets stuck in his skull. The
> bullets that stuck in his skull lost momentum after passing through the
> other bodies. My father stayed motionless underneath the dead bodies
> until dark, then he tried to walk to his hometown during the
> night. . . . The Khmer Rouge threatened that if anyone was hiding the
> enemy, the whole family would be executed. My father's relatives were
> very nervous. They tried to find a solution for my family. They dis-
> cussed either poisoning my father, hiding him underground, or giving
> us an ox cart to try to get to Thailand. . . . The final solution was

reached by my father's brother-in-law. He informed the Khmer Rouge soldiers where my father was. . . . A couple of soldiers climbed up with their flashlights and found him hiding in the corner of our cabin. . . . The soldiers then placed my father in the middle of the rice field, pointed flashlights, and shot him.[82]

This was the kind of killing that journalists and U.S. embassy officials in Phnom Penh had expected—political revenge against those the Khmer Rouge called the traitors. What was unexpected was the single-mindedness with which the regime turned upon ethnic Vietnamese, ethnic Chinese, Muslim Chams, and Buddhist monks, grouping them all traitors. Xenophobia was not new in Cambodia; the Vietnamese, Chinese, and (non-Khmer) Cham had long been discriminated against. But it was Pol Pot who set out to destroy these groups entirely. Buddhist monks were an unexpected target, as Buddhism had been the official state religion and the "soul" of Cambodia. Yet the KR branded it "reactionary." The revolutionaries prohibited all religious practice, burned monks' libraries, and destroyed temples, turning some into prisons and killing sites. Monks who refused to disrobe were executed.

More stunning still in its breadth, as Twining had gathered at the border, the Khmer Rouge were wiping out "class enemies," which meant all "intellectuals," or those who had completed seventh grade. Paranoid about the trustworthiness of even the devout radicals, the KR also began targeting their own supporters, killing anybody suspected of even momentary disloyalty. Given the misery in which Cambodians were living at the time, this covered almost everyone. As a witness against Pol Pot later testified, Brother Number One (as Pol Pot was known) saw "enemies surrounding, enemies in front, enemies behind, enemies to the north, enemies to the south, enemies to the west, enemies to the east, enemies in all eight directions, enemies coming from all nine directions, closing in, leaving no space for breath."[83] Citizens lived in daily fear of *chap teuv,* or what people in Latin America call being "disappeared." Bullets were too precious and had to be spared; the handles of farming implements were preferred.

The key ideological premise that lay behind the KR revolution was that "to keep you is no gain; to kill you is no loss."[84] Liberal societies preach a commitment to individual liberty embodied in the mantra, "Better ten guilty men go free than one innocent man be convicted." Khmer Rouge revolutionary society was predicated on the irrelevance of the individual.

The KR even propagated the adage, "It is better to arrest ten people by mistake than to let one guilty person go free."[85] It was far more forgivable to kill ten innocent men than to leave one guilty man alive, even if he was "guilty" simply of being less than overjoyed by the terms of service to *Angkar*.

Soon after the fall of Phnom Penh, Henry Kamm of the *New York Times* visited three refugee camps at the Thai border, none of which was in contact with the others. He wrote a long piece in July 1975, which the paper accompanied with an editorial that compared the Khmer Rouge practices to the "Soviet extermination of kulaks or . . . the Gulag Archipelago."[86] In February 1976 the *Post*'s David Greenway filed a front-page story describing the harsh conditions. "For Westerners to interpret what is going on is like the proverb of the blind men trying to describe an elephant," Greenway wrote. "Skepticism about atrocity stories is necessary especially when talking to refugees who tend to paint as black a picture as they can, but too many told the same stories in too much detail to doubt that, at least in some areas, reprisals occurred."[87] Collectively, although all were slow to believe and none gave the terror the attention it deserved, diplomats, non-governmental workers, and journalists did gather ghastly accounts of death marches, starvation, and disease in 1975 and 1976. The media did not lead with these reports, and the politicians did not respond to them, but the stories did appear.

The most detailed and eventually the most influential examination of KR brutality was prepared by the French priest François Ponchaud. Ponchaud, a Khmer speaker, had lived in Cambodia for ten years before he was evacuated from the French embassy in early May 1975. He debriefed refugees at the Thai border and then later in Paris, and he translated Cambodian radio reports. In February 1976, less than a year after the Khmer Rouge seized power, *Le Monde* published his findings, which said some 800,000 had been killed since April 1975.[88] For Elizabeth Becker, then a metro reporter in Washington, this was enough. "As soon as his stories came out, I believed," she recalls. "You have to know your shepherds. In Cambodia the French clerics had lived the Khmer life, not the foreigners' life. It took Ponchaud to wake the world up." Soon thereafter, a former KR official came forward in Paris claiming to have helped execute some 5,000 people by pickax. He estimated that 600,000 had already been killed.[89] In April 1976, a year into the Khmer Rouge reign, *Time* ran a story, soon followed by other accounts, that included graphic drawings of the executions and described Cambodia as the "Indochinese Gulag Archipelago." "A year after the takeover, Cambodia is still cocooned in silence—a silence, it is becoming increasingly clear, of the grave," *Time* wrote. "There is now little doubt that the Cambodian government is one of the most brutal, backward, and xenophobic regimes in the world."[90]

Even when the diplomats, journalists, and relief workers no longer assumed the Cambodians were exaggerating, it was another step entirely for them to move along the continuum toward understanding. One need only recall the exchange during World War II between Polish witness Jan Karski and U.S. Supreme Court justice Felix Frankfurter in which Frankfurter told the eyewitness, "I do not mean that you are lying. I simply said I cannot believe you." Holocaust survivor Elie Wiesel has spoken of the difference between "information" and "knowledge." In Cambodia observers had initially resisted certifying the refugee accounts even as "information." The words were available, describing death marches, road-side executions, and the murder of the rich, the intellectuals, and even office assistants. But the first photos were not smuggled out of Cambodia until April 1977, and they depicted harsh, forced labor conditions but not the systematic elimination of whole ethnic groups and classes.[91] With the country sealed tight, statesmen and citizens could take shelter in the fog of plausible deniability. But even once they accepted the information, the moral implications of that information did not really sink in. For those back in Washington, 10,000 miles from the refugee camps at the Thai border, it would take years to promote the raw, unconfirmed data to the status of knowledge.

Response

Options Ignored; Futility, Perversity, Jeopardy

Those who argued that the number of Cambodians killed was in the hundreds of thousands or those who tried to generate press coverage of the horrors did so assuming that establishing the facts would empower the United States and other Western governments to act. Normally, in a time of genocide, op-ed writers, policymakers, and reporters root for a distinct outcome or urge a specific U.S. military, economic, legal, humanitarian, or diplomatic response. Implicit indeed in many cables and news articles, and explicit in most editorials, is an underlying message, a sort of "if I were czar, I would do X or Y." But in the first three years of KR rule, even the Americans most concerned about Cambodia—Twining, Quinn, and Becker among them—internalized the constraints of the day and the system. They knew that drawing attention to the slaughter in Cambodia would have reminded America of its past sins, reopened wounds that had not yet healed at home, and invited questions about what the United States planned to do to curb the terror. They were neither surprised nor agitated by U.S. apathy. They accepted U.S. noninvolvement as an established background condition. Once U.S. troops had withdrawn from Vietnam in 1973, Americans deemed all of Southeast Asia unspeakable, unwatchable, and from a policy perspective, unfixable. "There could have been *two* genocides in Cambodia and nobody would have cared," remembers Morton Abramowitz, who at the time was an Asia specialist at the Pentagon and in 1978 became U.S. ambassador to Thailand. During the Khmer Rouge period, he remembers, "people just wanted to forget about the place. They wanted it off the radar."

From the mountains of Vietnam, foreign service officer Ken Quinn had spotted early indicators of the Khmer Rouge's brutality back in 1974 and had since been rotated back to the United States, where he served as the Indochina analyst at the National Security Council. Quinn remembers the impossibility of generating constructive ideas after the U.S. withdrawal from Vietnam:

> The country was in a state of shock. There was a great sense that we were powerless. We were out. We were done. We had left. It was painful, but it was over. . . . Vietnam had been such an emotional, wrenching, painful experience that there was just a huge national relief and a sense the country needed to be put back together. *Our* country.

Those who retained curiosity about the region continued to do so with the aim, in military parlance, of "fighting the last war." Most observers remained unable or unwilling to look at events as they transpired or to see Cambodia as anything other than a stepchild of Vietnam. They interpreted events on the ground accordingly. As Becker later wrote:

Too many people in and out of government had staked their reputations, their careers, and their own self-esteem on the positions they took during the [Vietnam] war. Each side wanted the postwar era to shore up those old positions and prove them correct. News was [seen] . . . as potential ammunition against old American opponents, as proof of America's guilt or honor.[92]

Certainly, it is impossible to overstate the importance of the historical context in dictating America's response to atrocities in Cambodia. Neither President Ford nor President Carter, who took office in January 1977, was going to consider sending U.S. troops back to Southeast Asia. But it is still striking that so many Americans concluded that *nothing at all* could be done. Even the "soft" response options that were available to the United States were passed up.

The United States barely denounced the massacres. The Ford administration had initially done so, but official U.S. reprimands proved short-lived, as Washington tuned out. Twining, the designated Cambodia watcher at the U.S. embassy in Bangkok, continued collecting and passing along hefty and chilling refugee accounts.[93] But these reports led only to a low-key U.S. government request to Amnesty International to begin investigations. A confidential June 8, 1976, policy paper on human rights from the State Department to embassy posts contained the following press guidance:

We share the concern about reported conditions in Cambodia. . . . We are prepared to support any effective action that might be taken to inquire further into the question of violations of human rights in Cambodia. . . . Reports of conditions in Cambodia are . . . difficult to verify. Information available to the [U.S. government] is not significantly different from that obtained by journalists and comes primarily from refugees. Nevertheless, these reports are too numerous to ignore and sufficient information certainly exists for further inquiry by appropriate international or private humanitarian organizations.

. . . We have already urged Amnesty International to investigate the situation in Cambodia but have avoided any public actions which would give the appearance of leading a campaign against Cambodia or would lend credence to Cambodian allegations that we are behind reports of their transgressions.[94]

Apart from casual appeals for "further inquiry," the United States did not itself launch its own determined inquiry or act upon the facts already acquired.

U.S. officials could have publicly branded Pol Pot's killings as genocide. But they did not do so. Indeed, I have not found a U.S. official who remembers even reading the genocide convention to see if events in Cambodia met its requirements. Because the treaty excluded political groups and so many of the KR murders were committed against perceived political enemies, it was actually a harder fit than one would expect. But even though many killings met the law's terms, no faction emerged inside the Carter administration arguing for any change in U.S. policy toward Cambodia. Thus, it is not surprising that nobody thought to ask the State Department legal adviser's office to issue a legal finding of genocide. Such a finding would have been moot in the face of the "reality" of U.S. nonengagement. And since the United States was not a party to the convention, a genocide proclamation would have created no legal obligation to act.

The United States could have urged its allies to file genocide charges at the International Court of Justice. The court could not weigh in on individual criminal guilt and had no enforcement powers to ensure its rulings were heeded. But if it had determined that genocide was under way, the ICJ could have issued a declaratory judgment on Cambodia's responsibility and demanded that provisional measures be taken. This would have signaled to Cambodians that at least one institution was prepared to judge the KR slaughter.

Proxmire hoped that the United States might turn to the ICJ for a genocide finding, but he knew U.S. ratification of the genocide convention had to come first. By the beginning of 1977, it had been a decade since he had started delivering his daily speech urging ratification. In ten years he had stood up 1,761 times, drawing frequently upon the "textbook case of genocide" being committed by the Khmer Rouge.[95] In 1977 and 1978 Proxmire ratcheted up his attention to the KR. "The destruction of 2 million Cambodians is the numerical equivalent of murdering every man, woman, and child in the entire state of Colorado," he declared. "Every human being in Boston, Massachusetts. Every person in Washington, DC—and that includes you and me." The numbers of victims was still disputed, but he knew he would be better off estimating than waiting. "As we leave the Senate tonight, the Khmer Rouge will be awakening for another bloody day's business," he said. "The noose of genocide will tighten with a jerk around the necks of another 1,577 Cambodian peasants."[96] Even those countries that had ratified the convention deferred to diplomatic niceties among states; other countries resisted and refused to challenge a fellow member of the club of nations in court. Cambodia, which itself had ratified the genocide treaty in 1951, never had to answer to genocide charges.

Apart from bilaterally denouncing the KR for its terror or attempting to get an ally to file a genocide case in the World Court, the United States might have condemned the crime in the UN General Assembly, the Security Council, or one of the multiple committees at the UN that had sprung up since Lemkin's day. Neither the United States nor its European allies did this. Israel became the first country to raise the issue of Cambodia at the United Nations. Representative Chaim Herzog, knowing that much of the violence was Khmer on Khmer, warned of "auto-genocide."[97] And finally, in March 1978, Britain's UN representative responded to popular pressure from the main churches of England by raising the subject before the UN Commission on Human Rights (UNCHR). He called for the appointment of a special human rights rapporteur to investigate.[98] The Khmer Rouge dismissed the Human Rights Commission as an imperialist, partisan body of which it would make "mincemeat."[99] And true to form, the Soviet Union, Yugoslavia, and Syria teamed up to block even this rhetorical route, delaying consideration of Cambodia's human rights record for another full year. By three years into the genocide, no official UN body had condemned the slaughter.

Economist Albert Hirschman observed that those who do not want to act cite the futility, perversity, and jeopardy of proposed measures. The United States and its allies defended their reticence on the grounds that speaking out or applying soft sanctions to such a reclusive regime would be futile. Normal diplomatic demarches, symbolic acts, and criticisms were unlikely to affect radical revolutionaries who were committing atrocity on this scale. In testimony on Capitol Hill, foreign service officer Twining noted, "I am not sure that the Cambodian leadership would care a hoot about what we . . . say."[100] Because the United States gave the KR regime no support, it could not suspend trade or military aid.

Bilateral denunciations by the United States may well have had little effect on the Khmer Rouge's internal practices. Unfortunately, because so few U.S. officials spoke out publicly against the genocide, we cannot know. But contrary to American claims, the Khmer Rouge were not completely oblivious to outside commentary. Isolated though they were, KR leaders still piped up to refute allegations made by foreign powers. When the British raised the issue of Cambodian human rights violations at the UN Commission in Geneva, the KR responded by claiming that British citizens enjoyed only the right to be slaves, thieves, prostitutes, or unemployed. In April 1978 the KR's Ieng Sary submitted a letter to the UN, denouncing the "propaganda machine of the imperialists, the expansionists, annexationists" who charged them with mass killing. He made a logical argument about why the KR could never kill on the scale suggested: "There is no reason for the [KR] to reduce the population or to maintain it at its current level," he wrote, "since today's population of 8 million is well below the potential of the country, which needs more than 20 million."[101]

U.S. policymakers also cited the possibly perverse results of taking a more outspoken approach. Public rebukes would likely anger the Khmer Rouge, causing them to intensify their violence against innocents or withdraw even further into darkness. Diplomats fell into the trap of believing (because they hoped) that the KR were on the verge of emerging from their isolation.[102] It is of course possible that outside expressions of interest in the KR's treatment of its citizens would have made the regime more barbarous and xenophobic, but it is hard to imagine how much worse the regime could have become. Often choosing a policy of isolation can deprive a concerned state of its only means of influencing a violent regime. But in this case the United States had nothing to risk losing by speaking the truth. A far steadier stream of condemnations could conceivably have convinced those educated KR officials who maintained covert radio links to the outside world to press for a more humane policy or even to revolt against Pol Pot and his clan.

The United States might also have pressured China, the KR's main backer, to use its considerable leverage to deter the KR from its murderousness. But the Carter administration was determined not to jeopardize its burgeoning relationships with either of the KR's regional allies: Thailand and China. Thailand was anti-Communist, but it maintained civil relations with the Khmer Rouge because its top priority was containing Vietnam. And China, which viewed the Khmer Rouge as a natural and ideological ally, had occupied center-stage in U.S. foreign policy circles since Nixon's 1972 trip to Beijing. The Chinese had long been supplying the KR with military advisers, light arms, and ammunition. In early 1978 Chinese military aid to the Khmer Rouge reportedly increased to include

100 light tanks, 200 antitank missiles, a number of long-range 122- and 130-millimeter guns, and more than a dozen fighter aircraft. Despite the gruesome reports of KR terror, the United States did not protest the transaction.[103] In May 1977 President Carter called the U.S.-Chinese relationship "a central element of our global policy" and China a "key for global peace."[104] Although China was the state most likely able to affect KR behavior, the Carter administration was not about to risk normalization by carping about the KR's human rights abuses.

Analogy and Advocacy

U.S. policy toward Cambodia was not contested within the executive branch. Nothing could be done, State Department and White House officials assumed, and virtually nothing was done. It took a handful of members of Congress to begin demanding that the United States take a more expansive view of the land of the possible. Stephen Solarz was a Democratic House member from New York who had won election in 1974 on an antiwar platform and had earlier helped block further U.S. funding to the Lon Nol regime. Unlike most of his colleagues, Solarz had not lost interest in the region with the cutoff of U.S. funds. In August 1975 he had traveled with a House delegation to Thailand, where he had taken a helicopter ride with the embassy's Twining to Aranyaprathet. There, the man who would become known as the "Marco Polo" of Congress for all his foreign travel, heard tales that reminded him of the forced deportation of Jews in World War II. As a Jew and as a politician—his district contained more Holocaust survivors than any other in the country—he became incensed. "They were killing anyone who wore glasses," Solarz remembers, "because if they wore glasses, it suggested they knew how to read, and if they knew how to read, it suggested they had been infected with the bourgeois virus. It was a Great Leap Forward that made the Great Leap Forward under Mao look like a tentative half-step."

In 1976, despite reports of nearly a million dead, no congressional hearings had been held specifically on human rights abuses in Cambodia. Solarz and a few other avid legislators had settled for including the grim press articles in the *Congressional Record* and occasionally condemning the KR in floor debates. Senator Claiborne Pell, who partnered with Proxmire in pushing the genocide convention and who would later do more than any other senator to try to punish Saddam Hussein for gassing Iraqi Kurds, took a parallel interest in Cambodia. On the floor of the Senate in 1976, he declared:

> [If estimates of 1 million killed are] true, approximately one-fifth of the Cambodian population has been annihilated—a record of barbarous butchery which is surpassed in recent history only by the Nazi atrocities against the Jews during World War II. . . . I am amazed that so little has been done to investigate and condemn what is happening in Cambodia. The UN Human Rights Commission has so far ignored the situation in that country.[105]

By 1977, Solarz, Pell, and others had finally generated enough interest to stage hearings on Capitol Hill devoted exclusively to Cambodian atrocities. In one of those hearings, much of Solarz's frustration over the U.S. policy of silence and the ongoing squabbles over numbers of dead burst forth. Indochina specialist Gareth Porter testified, again denouncing the "wild exaggeration and wholesale falsehood" of allegations of KR terror. Porter insisted that it was a "myth" that "one-to-two million Cambodians [had] been the victims of a regime led by genocidal maniacs." Solarz exploded. "It is beyond belief to me that anyone could seriously argue that this hasn't been going on," he exclaimed.[106] For the next year and a half, Solarz attempted to get the House to pass a resolution calling on President Carter to turn his attention to curbing the killings.

Solarz was one of several Americans who, in drawing attention to the KR horrors, linked his advocacy to the Holocaust. Seated more than two decades later in a study lined with shelves filled with 123 books on the Holocaust and another fifty-two on Hitler and Nazi Germany, Solarz reflects, "The Holocaust is the key to the whole thing. It is the Rosetta stone. For me, the Holocaust was the central fact of the twentieth century and has had more of an influence on my view of the world and America's role in it than anything else."

By the mid- and late-1970s, Hitler's destruction of the Jews was at last becoming the subject of scholarly and public focus. The term "Holocaust" had not entered into popular usage until the late 1960s, but in 1970 two books analyzed the U.S. indifference to the Holocaust for the first time: Arthur Morse's *While Six Million Died: A Chronicle of American Apathy* and Henry Feingold's *Politics of Rescue: The Roosevelt Administration, 1939–1945*. One of the most pivotal instruments for "popularizing" the Final

Solution was the four-part, nine-and-a-half-hour television dramatization *Holocaust,* starring James Woods and Meryl Streep, which some 120 million viewers watched in 1978. The same year President Carter appointed a special commission on Holocaust remembrance and education and decided to build a monument to the horror on the National Mall in Washington, D.C.

By 1977, because it had become widely accepted that a bloodbath was indeed taking place in Cambodia, advocates of U.S. engagement tried to jar decisionmakers and ordinary citizens by likening Pol Pot's atrocities to those of Hitler. Syndicated columnists Jack Anderson and Les Whitten published a total of fifteen opinion pieces on Cambodia, most of which invoked the Holocaust.[107] On July 21, 1977, they wrote, "The uproar over human rights has ignored the world's most brutal dictatorship. Adolf Hitler at his worst was not as oppressive as the Communist rulers of tiny Cambodia."[108] Several months later, Anderson and Whitten called the KR terror "the greatest atrocity since the Nazis herded Jews into the gas chambers."[109] When the *Holocaust* docudrama aired in 1978, Anderson noted that "another Holocaust story, every bit as stark as the recent TV saga" was ongoing. The Nazis had disguised their crimes with euphemisms such as "resettlement," "removal," and "special action," Anderson wrote. So, too, the Khmer Rouge had introduced a sanitized language. "The Khmer word for 'kill, assassinate, execute' was never spoken when the annihilation policy was discussed," he noted. "The Khmer term used was 'baoh, caol,' literally 'sweep, throw out' or 'sweep, discard.'"[110] The next day Anderson penned another column, entitled "Cambodia: A Modern-Day Holocaust," in which he condemned President Carter for averting his gaze from the extermination of Cambodians.[111]

Others chimed in, also adopting the analogy. The *Economist* described "brutality that would make Hitler cringe."[112] In an April 1978 *New York Times* editorial, "Silence is Guilt," William Safire also referred to the *Holocaust* miniseries and asked why the world was doing nothing. "In terms of numbers of people killed," Safire wrote, "this generation's rival to Adolf Hitler is the leader of Communist Cambodia, Pol Pot."[113] Leo Cherne of the International Rescue Committee and Freedom House wrote in the *Wall Street Journal* on May 10, 1978, that "the ruthlessness in each country has come about in service to an ideal—of racial purity in Nazi Germany, of political purity in Democratic Kampuchea." A May 1978 front-page *New York Times* story said that refugees in Thailand "recall concentration camp survivors in Europe of 1945."

As the months passed, Capitol Hill became more engaged. Senator Bob Dole (R.–Kans.) was moved by the story of a Cambodian refugee who had visited him. He compared the Cambodian crisis to "the death camps in Nazi Germany, and the excesses of Stalinist Russia."[114] Pleading as always for the ratification of the genocide convention and denouncing the KR, Proxmire noted the parallels with the destruction of the Jews: "This is no ordinary genocide. There are no concentration camps and gas chambers disguised as showers. This is genocide without technology."[115]

Donald Fraser (D.–Minn.), the Hill's most vocal human rights advocate, chaired a House International Relations Subcommittee hearing in July 1977. Ken Quinn, who in 1977 was tapped as special assistant to the new assistant secretary for East Asian and Pacific affairs, Richard Holbrooke, told his boss, "This is a chance to go public with all we know." Holbrooke and Twining appeared on Capitol Hill and ended the State Department's two-year policy of silence. Holbrooke noted that "journalists and scholars guess that between half a million and 1.2 million have died since 1975." U.S. intelligence indicated that "for every person executed several have died of disease, malnutrition, or other factors, which would have been avoidable if the Government itself had not followed . . . a policy which seeks to completely transform the society by the most Draconian measures possible."[116] Holbrooke concluded that "we should speak out," even though, as he admitted, he was unsure "what the impact of our words" would be.[117] This was the first time Twining had been publicly summoned to relay his graphic findings. The U.S. government had detailed knowledge of Pol Pot's atrocities. A February 13, 1978, State Department cable reported plainly, "A renewed emphasis was placed on completely eliminating all vestiges of the former government and completing the executions of all people who were not from the poor farmer-working class."[118] Still, Twining recalls his attitude at the time of the hearing. "It was easy to come before Congress because I was so sure about what was going on," he says. "When it came to 'what to do,' though, I just had this overwhelming feeling of helplessness."

With American editorial writers weighing in on the subject with some frequency in 1978, and with congressional pressure mounting, the daily press coverage of human rights abuses finally expanded. In the summer of 1978, the *Washington Post* and *New York Times* began running two to three news stories a month on human rights in Cambodia, still a small number but far more than the two or three per year they had run in 1975, 1976, and 1977. By late 1978 death estimates that had earlier been referred to as "reports of mass death" became "hundreds of thousands, possibly 2½ million" and "one to three million killed."[119]

Not until 1978 did nongovernmental actors urge that trying and failing to influence the KR would be preferable to making no effort at all. "One may not be able to triumph over evil, but one need not remain silent in its presence," syndicated columnist Smith Hempstone wrote in the *Washington Post* in May 1978. "President Carter might speak up more than once on the subject. He might instruct Andrew Young to walk out of the United Nations General Assembly whenever the representative of 'Democratic Kampuchea' rises to speak. At every time and in every available forum, those who speak for the United States could call on the conscience of the world to condemn those who commit such atrocities."[120] None of these steps were taken.

President Carter's first firm public denunciation came in April 1978 when he sent a message to an independent commission examining the atrocity reports in Oslo:

> America cannot avoid the responsibility to speak out in condemnation of the Cambodian government, the worst violator of human rights in the world today. Thousands of refugees have accused their government of inflicting death on hundreds of thousands of Cambodian people through the genocidal policies it has implemented over the past three years. . . . It is an obligation of every member of the international community to protest the policies of this or any nation which cruelly and systematically violates the right of its people to enjoy life and basic human dignities.[121]

Sixteen months had passed since his inauguration and three years since the fall of Phnom Penh.

In early June 1978, a group calling itself United People for Human Rights in Cambodia fasted and protested in front of the White House, and Freedom House convened a colloquium in Washington, "Cambodia: What Can America Do?" Amnesty International appealed more adamantly for scrutiny of Cambodia's record. Its 1977–1978 report removed many of its earlier disclaimers. The report cited Ponchaud's claim that 100,000 was the absolute minimum number of Cambodians executed and said it was possible that "two or three times as many" had been murdered.[122] Rather than simply writing privately to the KR, Amnesty called upon the regime to allow independent investigators to deploy to Cambodia and made its own submission to the UN Human Rights Commission.[123] Citing refugee and press accounts, the submission stated that although many allegations remained "uncorroborated," their number and consistency "give cause for great concern."[124] Public and political groups were finally taking notice of a people in dire need.

Although elite opinion had concluded "something had to be done," the "something" remained narrowly defined. Behind the scenes, U.S. ambassador Andrew Young urged United Nations Secretary-General Kurt Waldheim to visit Cambodia, and Secretary of State Cyrus Vance instructed U.S. embassies to discuss with host countries the possibility of raising the issue of Cambodia in the UN General Assembly. Warren Christopher, Carter's deputy secretary of state, criticized the KR for its massive human rights abuses but pledged only to support "international efforts to call attention to this egregious situation."[125] The U.S. foreign policy establishment remained persistently passive, issuing only a handful of public statements and never investing its political capital in a serious attempt to alter KR behavior.

Military What? George Who?

As press coverage steadily picked up and as the U.S. legislature responded with hearings, one lonely American official argued that an outside military force should intervene in Cambodia to dislodge the Khmer Rouge. That person was a Democratic senator from South Dakota named George McGovern—the same George McGovern who had captured the Democratic Party's nomination in the 1972 presidential election and run on a platform of opposition to the Vietnam War. McGovern had spearheaded congressional efforts to proscribe funding for U.S. military operations in Indochina, and he had initiated the passage of the War Powers Act. He said he carried Vietnam "in my stomach and heart and mind for ten years above any other concern in public life."[126] His antiwar credentials were unimpeachable.

But McGovern had come to the conclusion that events in Cambodia amounted to genocide, and for him this carried steep and unavoidable consequences. McGovern felt such a diagnosis meant first that the United States had to condemn the KR, which it had done hardly at all since the terror began. But it also meant that the United States had to contribute its military might to stopping the horrors. In August 1978 Senator McGovern publicly urged the Carter administration to consider deploying an international military force to launch a humanitarian intervention. It was time for the United States and its allies to ask, "Do we sit on the sidelines and watch an entire people be slaughtered, or do we marshal military forces and move in quietly to put an end to it?"[127] The press corps darted for the telephones. "They thought this was big news," he recalls. "They wondered, 'How could this dove have become a raving hawk?'" A *Wall Street Journal* editorial lambasted McGovern for his "truly mind-boggling" stance. For the next several weeks, he deployed three staff aides to answer the phones, which rang off the hook. Some Americans called to denounce him for his opposition to the war in Vietnam and to blame Cambodia's misery on the U.S. withdrawal from the region. But most telephoned either to applaud him for his proposal or, in the case of old friends, to ask, somewhat shyly, for clarification.

McGovern saw the duty to oust the Khmer Rouge as an outgrowth of, not a challenge to, the United States' duty to get and stay out of Vietnam. The American role in the war in Vietnam only heightened U.S. responsibility, as he believed the rise of the Khmer Rouge was one of the greatest single costs of U.S. involvement in Indochina. McGovern understood the apparent irony of his position. But at the hearings, he, too, alluded to the parallel to the Holocaust:

> I am the last person to be enthusiastic about military intervention except under the most extreme circumstances, but it does seem to me that these are the most extreme I have heard of. If anything close to 2.5 million people have been killed in a few years' time out of a population of seven million, percentage-wise that makes Hitler's oppressions look rather tame.[128]

McGovern argued that the United States should take the lead politically and militarily. To him Vietnam and Cambodia had little, apart from geography, in common. In Vietnam U.S. forces had squared off against an indigenous independence movement headed by a popularly backed leader, Ho Chi Minh. In Cambodia, by contrast, Pol Pot and a "handful of fanatics" were imposing their vision on millions of Cambodians. In light of Pol Pot's "bloodthirsty" rule, his victimized populace could not possibly support him; indeed, McGovern believed the Cambodians would welcome rescue from the "murderous, slaughtering regime."[129]

McGovern was not the first American to make such a proposal. The previous year conservative essayist William F. Buckley Jr., perhaps the least likely of all of McGovern's possible bedfellows, made a similar recommendation in the *Los Angeles Times*. "I am quite serious," Buckley wrote. "Why doesn't Congress authorize the necessary money to finance an international military force to overrun Cambodia?" The force, he argued, should be composed of Asian units from Malaysia, Thailand, Japan, the Philippines, and even Vietnam. The troops did not have to establish a democratic state. They simply had to "go there and take power away from one, two, three, perhaps as many as a half-dozen sadistic madmen who have brought on their country the worst suffering, the worst conditions brought on any country in this bloody century."[130]

The McGovern-Buckley premise—that a barbarous, beatable small clan of murderers could be quickly vanquished—was challenged by the State Department. Douglas Pike, a foreign service officer and Indochina expert who testified at the 1978 Senate hearings, agreed that the Pol Pot regime was savage. But he said Cambodian troops loyal to the Khmer Rouge were fighting extremely effectively against their one-time allies, the Vietnamese. "If the regime is as bad as it is portrayed," Pike asked, "why do the people fight?" He insisted that international forces would face tough resistance: "I think we should not entertain the idea that a quick indochop in Phnom Penh could put things right," Pike testified. "To control Cambodia and the government, you would have to control the villages, all of them. You would have to put forces into the villages. The idea of just trying to take off the head in Phnom Penh sounds good . . . but it isn't."[131]

Robert Oakley, deputy assistant secretary for East Asian and Pacific Affairs, was present when McGovern made his appeal for intervention. He was dumbstruck. So far as the Carter administration was concerned, Oakley testified, multilateral military intervention was not a "live option." The United States would not consider generating or participating in an invasion. In reading Oakley's testimony today, one can hear the loss of confidence in the U.S. capacity to shape the world or even accurately to diagnose its developments. "We don't have the sort of intelligence on that that we sometimes in the past told ourselves that we had," Oakley said, reminding the committee members, "We have learned a lot about the degree of appropriate U.S. involvement in the internal affairs of other countries, as well as an ability to influence them."[132]

McGovern was puzzled. He had heard a great deal about why the situation was more complicated than it seemed, about how difficult it would be to dislodge Khmer Rouge cadres at the village level. And he could find nobody at all prepared to use outside force to end the slaughter. McGovern did not mention the genocide convention. For him, it was not the law but the atrocities that necessitated acts aimed at suppressing the crime:

> It just strikes me that we ought not to dismiss out of hand the responsibility of the international community to stop this kind of indiscriminate slaughter. I realize it is a long way from home. These are people with different colored skins and so on. But nevertheless, one would think that the international community would at least be considering the possibility of intervening in what seems to be a clear case of genocide.[133]

Two political dissidents facing trial in the Soviet Union were then being celebrated, their imprisonment denounced. Yet, he observed, Americans were ignoring the killing of at least a million Cambodians. Instead of fighting the "last war," McGovern believed, the United States should pay attention to the current genocide. "I hate needless and ill-conceived military ventures," he said. "That is why I opposed our military intervention . . . in Vietnam. But to hate a needless and foolish intervention that served no good purpose does not give us the excuse to do nothing to stop mass murder in another time and place under vastly different circumstances."[134] Later he remembered the glee with which some of his former adversaries greeted his alleged "reversal" and the grief he got at the time:

> Dean Rusk was by then out of office, but I remember he gave a public statement after he heard I had called for military intervention in which he said, "Now *there* is irony." The implication of Rusk's statement was that I had finally come around. Of course I've never been a pacifist. I always thought there was a time when military intervention was necessary. I never regretted for one minute my time as a bomber pilot in World War II. Fighting genocide is one cause worth fighting for.[135]

McGovern's proposal went nowhere. The State Department issued a statement that the Carter administration was focusing attention on the "monstrous" situation in Cambodia but that it had no intention of resolving "the terrible situation in Kampuchea by military force." It added, "Nor are we aware of any international support for [such] a plan."[136] In truth McGovern had not expected that states would rush to respond to his summons, but he had hoped the "old shock technique" would at least spark a discussion of the horrors that the Carter administration, the general public, and the international community had resisted to date.[137] The appeal did cause a ripple effect in certain quarters, as even the KR, who so many had argued did not care about the opinion of outsiders, felt compelled to respond. On August 26, 1978, McGovern received a letter from the radical regime, slamming him for his "wanton and shameless attacks" and rebutting the genocide charge with the claim that it was the United States that had committed genocide in Cambodia.

In October 1978 McGovern did succeed in getting most of his fellow senators to sign on to a letter to Secretary of State Vance.[138] Eighty senators called for international action to halt the Cambodian genocide, urged the secretary to introduce the issue immediately at the UN Security Council, and criticized the Carter administration's lethargy. In August 1978 the United States had finally submitted to the UN Human Rights Commission a 667-page report on the atrocities based on refugee testimony, but the senators noted that this belated, written submission "seems to be a rather low-key approach in light of the enormity of the crimes being committed in Cambodia."[139]

The First Visit

By 1978 the Khmer Rouge were feeling more vulnerable to the outside world. They had moved from scapegoating their own citizens to scapegoating their neighbors. The KR had begun trying to infiltrate and occupy southern Vietnam in 1977, and border skirmishes had intensified. In early December 1977, Vietnam, fed-up with Pol Pot's attacks and backed by the Soviet Union, had sent some 60,000 troops just inside the Cambodian border.[140] A propaganda war between the two sides had ensued, publicly confirming Ken Quinn's 1974 conclusion that no Communist monolith existed in Indochina. On December 31, 1977, the Cambodian Foreign Ministry, which had kept past clashes with Vietnam silent, denounced Vietnam's "ferocious and barbarous" aggression, comparing it to Hitler's annexation of Czechoslovakia. Pol Pot severed relations with Vietnam. Throughout 1978 the Khmer Rouge took measures aimed at improving their public image, inviting diplomatic visitors and friendship delegations, pledging reforms, and quietly relaxing their xenophobic stance toward the outside world. In March 1978 Pol Pot announced that Cambodia was "open to our friends. . . . We invite them to visit our country."[141]

Elizabeth Becker, the *Washington Post* metro reporter, had been clamoring to get back into Cambodia since she left in 1974. She had written more than a dozen letters paying what she remembers as "disgusting" homage to the KR's "glorious revolution" in the hopes of winning a visa. Whenever Ieng Sary visited the United Nations for the annual General Assembly session, Becker trekked up to New York to appeal to him in person. In November 1978 she received a telegram from the KR (postmarked from Beijing) inviting her to Cambodia. She was one of three Western guests chosen.

Becker did not hesitate for a second. All of the fears that had driven her from the country in 1974 had been overtaken by a desperate desire to peer behind the Khmer curtain. She felt as if she had been "put in a coffin" since the KR sealed the country. She remembers:

> I hadn't guessed they would isolate themselves like they did. I mean, the idea that you could go to an airport and it would never say "Phnom Penh" on the departures board—that broke my heart. I had to go back to see what was happening. Since the KR were busy killing their own people, I didn't think they would make time for us. Nobody said, "Don't go."

Becker and Richard Dudman of the *St. Louis Post-Dispatch* became the first American journalists to enter the country since the Khmer Rouge had seized Phnom Penh in April 1975. Joined by Scottish academic Malcolm Caldwell, a leftist sympathizer with the KR regime, they arrived on a biweekly flight from China, the only country that retained landing rights in Cambodia. For the next ten days, Becker, Dudman, and Caldwell were given an "incubated tour of the revolution" that included immaculate parks, harangues about Vietnamese aggression, and screenings of propaganda films.[142] Throughout their stay, the three foreigners were forbidden from independently exploring. They spoke only with those who had been handpicked by *Angkar* to represent the KR, and even these meetings were

Elizabeth Becker

From left: Elizabeth Becker, Richard Dudman, and Malcolm Caldwell at
the Angkor Wat temples in December 1978.

steered by a guide who was present at all times. Nothing Becker's group
saw resembled either what she remembered or what the refugees at the
Thai border had described. Fishermen, rubber plantation workers, weavers,
all were wheeled out to speak of the joys of the revolution and the bounty
of their productivity.

Only when Becker sneaked out of her compound did she get a sense of
what lay behind the Potemkin village. If Phnom Penh's main Monivong
Boulevard was clean-shaven for the consumption of visitors, the surrounding streets were littered with stubble. Shops and homes had been weeded
over. Furniture and appliances were stacked haphazardly. Just as many religious shrines in Bosnia would later be reduced to rubble overnight, so, too,
the French cathedral and the picturesque pagodas had vanished without a
trace. Even when she participated in the KR's regimented activities, Becker
observed a country that was missing everything that signaled life. She later
recalled, "There were no food-stalls, no families, no young people playing
sports, even sidewalk games, no one out on a walk, not even dogs or cats
playing in alleyways."[143] When she spotted people out in the countryside,

they were working joylessly, furiously, without contemplating rest. The country's stunning Buddhist temples had been converted into granaries.

It is difficult to imagine how confused Becker and the others must have been at that time. They had heard refugee reports of massacres and starvation. They suspected the number killed was in the hundreds of thousands. But they knew virtually nothing specific about the bloody Pol Pot regime. Becker was unable to muster the practical or moral imagination needed to envision the depths of what was happening behind the pristine and cheery front presented. She recalled:

> We were the original three blind men trying to figure out the elephant. At that time no one understood the inner workings of the regime—how the zones operated; how the party controlled the country; how the secret police worked; that torture and extermination centers . . . even existed; the depth of the misery and death. . . . We had the tail, the ears, the feet of the monster but no idea of its overall shape. . . .[144]

By the time the two-week trip began winding down, the luster of being the first to visit had long since worn off. On December 22, 1978, the group's last full day in the country, Becker became the first American journalist ever to interview the famed Pol Pot. Although she had heard of Brother Number One's charisma, his smile was far more endearing and his manner more polished than she had predicted. But it was not long before he turned off his charm, treating Becker and colleague Dudman as if he had granted them an audience, not an interview. Pol Pot delivered a one-hour stinging and paranoid indictment of Vietnam, forecasting a war between NATO and the Warsaw Pact over Cambodia. He warned: "A Kampuchea that is a satellite of Vietnam is a threat and a danger for Southeast Asia and the world . . . for Vietnam is already a satellite of the Soviet Union and is carrying out Soviet strategy in Southeast Asia."[145] Ironically, as American decisionmakers formed their policy in the coming months, they operated on assumptions that mirrored Pol Pot's.

Caldwell, the Scottish Marxist, was granted a separate interview with the supreme revolutionary leader. When he later traded notes with Becker, he delighted in describing Pol Pot's mastery of revolutionary economic theory. Before retiring for the evening, Becker sparred with her zealous colleague one last time about the veracity of refugee accounts, which he still refused to believe, and the worthiness of the revolution, in which he refused to abandon belief. She was awakened in the middle of the night by the sound of tumult and gunfire outside her room. A half dozen or more shots were fired, and an hour and a half of the longest, most terrifying silence of Becker's life passed. When she finally heard the voice of her KR guide, she emerged trembling into the hall. Dudman was fine, she was told. Caldwell, the true believer, had been murdered.

Becker did not know why Caldwell had been killed, but she suspected that one faction wanted either to embarrass another or to plug the crack of an opening to the outside world before it widened. A murder would deter meddlesome foreigners from visiting again. On December 23, 1978, Becker and Dudman arrived in Beijing with the wooden casket containing Caldwell's body. Two days later Vietnam launched a full-scale invasion of Cambodia.

Aftermath

"Humanitarian" Rescue

Kassie Neou, one of Cambodia's leading human rights advocates today, survived Pol Pot's madness and the outside world's indifference. An English teacher before the genocide, he posed as a taxi driver, shedding his eyeglasses and working around the clock to develop a "taxi-driver manner." He had to make the KR believe that he had not been educated. Captured nonetheless, Neou was tortured five times and spent six months in a KR prison with thirty-six other inmates. Of the thirty-seven who were bound together with iron clasps, only Neou's hope of survival was rewarded. The young guards executed the others but spared him because they had grown fond of the Aesop's fables he told them as bedtime stories. When Neou discusses the terror today, he lifts up his trouser leg and displays the whitened, rough skin around his ankle where a manacle held him in place. The revolutionaries' crimes were so incomprehensible that some part of him seems relieved to be left with tangible proof of his experience.

During his imprisonment, though he had been highly critical of the earlier U.S. involvement in Cambodia, Neou was one of many

Cambodians who could not help but dream that the United States would rescue his people. "When you are suffering like we suffered, you simply cannot imagine that nobody will come along to stop the pain," he remembers. "Everyday, you would wake up and tell yourself, 'somebody will come, something is going to happen.' If you stop hoping for rescue, you stop hoping. And hope is all that can keep you alive." Survivors of terror usually recall maintaining similar, necessary illusions. Without them, they say, the temptation to choose death over despair would overwhelm.

Neou had fantasized that the United States would spare him certain death, but it was Vietnam, the enemy of the United States, that in January 1979 finally dislodged the bloody Communist radicals. In response, the United States, which in 1978 had at last begun to condemn the KR, reversed itself, siding with the Cambodian perpetrators of genocide against the Vietnamese aggressors.

Vietnam's invasion had a humanitarian consequence but was not motivated by humanitarian concerns. Indeed, for a long time Vietnam and its Soviet backer had blocked investigation into the atrocities committed by their former partner in revolution. In 1978, however, as KR incursions into Vietnam escalated, Vietnam had begun detailing KR massacres. Vietnamese officials used excerpts from Ponchaud's book, *Year Zero,* as radio propoganda. They called on Cambodians to "rise up for the struggle to overthrow the Pol Pot and Ieng Sary clique" who were "more barbarous . . . than the Hitlerite fascists." Vietnam also began reindoctrinating and training Khmer Rouge defectors and Cambodian prisoners seized in territory taken from Cambodia. It crept ever closer to the Soviet Union, joining the Council for Mutual Economic Assistance (COMECON), signing a twenty-five-year treaty of friendship and cooperation with the Soviets, and receiving ever larger military shipments from them. The Soviet Union joined Vietnam's anti-KR campaign, condemning the KR "policy of genocide."

For the previous year, the United States had been flirting with restoring relations with Vietnam but was not keen on seeing it overrun its neighbor.[146] From the U.S. embassy in Bangkok, Ambassador Morton Abramowitz wrote in a secret August 1978 cable to the State Department: "Neither the Khmers nor the world would miss Pol Pot. Nonetheless, the independence of Kampuchea, particularly its freedom from a significant Hanoi presence or complete Hanoi domination, is a matter of importance to us."[147] Far from encouraging the overthrow of the KR, as Neou and others would have hoped, U.S. officials urged the Vietnamese to think twice.

In November 1978 Secretary of State Vance sent a message to the Vietnamese: "Don't you see what lies ahead if you invade Cambodia? This is not the way to bring peace to the area. Can't we try some UN instrument, use the UN in some way?"[148]

The United States had its own reasons for frowning upon a Vietnamese triumph. It planned to restore diplomatic relations with China on January 1, 1979. China's hostility toward Vietnam and its Soviet military and political sponsor greatly influenced the U.S. reaction to the invasion. For neither the first nor the last time, geopolitics trumped genocide. Interests trumped indignation.

Aware of the Khmer Rouge's isolation and unpopularity in the West, Hanoi thought it would earn praise if it overthrew Pol Pot. It also concluded that regardless of the outside world's opinion, it could not afford to allow continued KR encroachments into the Mekong Delta. By December 22, 1978, Vietnamese planes had begun flying forty to fifty sorties per day over Cambodia. And on December 25, 1978, twelve Vietnamese divisions, or some 100,000 Vietnamese troops, retaliated against KR attacks by land. Teaming up with an estimated 20,000 Cambodian insurgents, they rolled swiftly through the Cambodian countryside. Despite U.S. intelligence predictions that the KR would constitute a potent military foe, McGovern's earlier forecast of rapid collapse turned out to be prescient. Lacking popular support, the Khmer Rouge and its leaders fled almost immediately to the northern jungle of Cambodia and across the Thai border.

The Vietnamese completed their lightning-speed victory with the seizure of Phnom Penh on January 7, 1979.

Skulls, Bones, and Photos

Upon seizing the country, the Vietnamese found evidence of mass murder everywhere. They were sure this proof would strengthen the legitimacy of their intervention and their puppet rule. In the months and years immediately after the overthrow, journalists who trickled into Cambodia were bombarded by tales of horror. Every neighborhood seemed to unfurl a mass grave of its own. Bones could still be seen protruding from the earth. Anguished citizens personalized the blame. "Pol Pot killed my husband," or "Pol Pot destroyed the temple," they said. Rough numerical estimates of deaths emerged quickly. All told, in the three-and-a-half-year rule of the

Khmer Rouge, some 2 million Cambodians out of a populace of 7 million were either executed or starved to death.[149] National minorities were special targets of the regime. The Vietnamese minority was completely wiped out. Of the 500,000 Muslim Cham who lived in Cambodia before Pol Pot's victory, some 200,000 survived. Of 60,000 Buddhist monks, all but a thousand perished.

The Tuol Sleng Examination Center in Phnom Penh, which was code-named Office S-21, quickly became the most notorious emblem of the terror.[150] A pair of Vietnamese journalists discovered the center nestled in a part of the capital known as Tuol Svay Prey, or "hillock of the wild mango." While roaming the neighborhood with Vietnamese troops the day after they had seized the capital, they smelled what they thought was rotting flesh and poked their heads into the lush compound that had once served as a girls' high school. They quickly discovered that of the 16,000 Cambodians who had arrived there, only five had departed alive.[151]

The Tuol Sleng complex consists of four triple-story, whitewashed concrete buildings, lined on the top floor by a Motel 6–like balcony-corridor and overlooking identical grassy courtyards, once playgrounds for the young schoolgirls. A single-floor wooden building divides the compound in two. Some time in late 1975, Kang Keck Ieu (known as "Duch"), a former schoolteacher, took over the management of the facility and helped turn a seat of innocence into a seat of inhumanity. Most of the instruments found in Tuol Sleng were primitive, "dual-use" garden implements. Building A, which contained individual prison cells, was divided into small rooms, each containing a metal bed frame, an ammunition box to collect the prisoners' feces, and garden shears, lead pipes, and hoes. When the Vietnamese journalists first entered these rooms in 1979, they found these tools beside bloodied victims whose cadavers lay shackled to the bed posts. The prisoners' throats had been slit, and their blood still dripped slowly from the beds onto the mustard-and-white-tiled floors.

When the Vietnamese wandered around the ravaged compound, they found other adornments, including bulkier torture implements and busts of Pol Pot. They also rummaged through surrounding houses and came across thousands of documents, notebooks, and photos. Years later this paper trail would be used to spur prosecution of the aging former KR leaders for genocide and crimes against humanity.

Like the Nazis, those who ran the extermination center were bureaucratically precise. A prisoner's time at Tuol Sleng consisted of four basic

Stephen Solarz

Rep. Stephen Solarz (D.–N.Y.) with Joel Pritchard (R.–Wash.) at the Tuol Sleng Museum in Phnom Penh in 1981.

activities. The prisoners were photographed, either upon arrival or upon death. They were tortured, often electrocuted as they hung by their feet, their heads submerged in jars of water. They were forced to sign confessions affirming their status as CIA or Vietnamese agents and to prepare lists of their "networks of traitors." Then they were murdered. Low-ranking prisoners were usually disposed of quickly, whereas more senior inmates were typically kept alive for protracted torture sessions. The highest daily tally was May 27, 1978, when 582 people were executed. A day's targets were often clustered according to their affiliation. For example, on July 22, 1977, the KR "smashed" those from the Ministry of Public Works.[152] The photos and confessions of four Americans were also found. The men had disappeared in 1978 while sailing yachts off the coast of Cambodia. Hoping to convince their brutal torturers to relent, the men wrote detailed, bizarre accounts of their elaborate CIA plots to destabilize Cambodia.

If ever there was a document that captured the regimental tenor and terror of the KR regime, it was the set of instructions for inmates that had been posted at the Tuol Sleng interrogation center. It read in part:

1) You must answer in conformity with the questions I asked you. Don't try to turn away my questions.

2) Don't try to escape by making pretexts according to your hypocritical ideas.

3) Don't be a fool for you are a chap who dares to thwart the revolution.

4) You must immediately answer my questions without wasting time to reflect. . . .

6) During the bastinado or the electrification you must not cry loudly.

7) Do sit down quietly. Wait for the orders. If there are no orders, do nothing. If I ask you to do something, you must immediately do so without protesting. . . .

9) If you disobey [any] point of my regulations you will get either ten strokes of the whip or five shocks of electric discharge.[153]

An "interrogator's manual" was another of the many damning documents left behind. A forty-two-page guide for Tuol Sleng torturers, it reminded them they should use both political pressure and torture on prisoners. "Prisoners," the guide said, "cannot escape from torture. The only difference is whether there will be a lot of it or a little. . . . We must hurt them so that they respond quickly. Don't be so bloodthirsty that you cause their death quickly. You won't get the needed information."[154]

The Vietnamese-installed regime was savvy enough to create a Tuol Sleng Museum almost as soon as it had solidified control of the capital city. The new leaders turned the snapshots of murdered prisoners into perhaps the most vivid visual indictment of evil in the second half of the twentieth century. The photos had been taken of boys and girls and men and women of all shapes, shades, and sizes. Some have been beaten; others seem clean-shaven and calm. Some look crazed, others resigned. As in the German concentration camps, all wear numbers. And all display a last gasp of individuality in their eyes. It is with these eyes that they interrogate the interrogator. That they plead. That they grovel. That they accuse. That they accost. That they mock. And for those who visit, that they remind. It is in their eyes, much more than in the stacks of skulls gathered in villages throughout Cambodia, that visitors are prodded to confront the extremity of the victims' last days. With their eyes, most of the Cambodians signal that they remained very much alive and that they hoped to stay that way.

U.S. Policy: Choosing the Lesser Evil

The existence of the torture center testified to the depravity of the KR regime.[155] Cambodia was not widely visited immediately following the KR overthrow, but enough evidence of KR brutality emerged for many Americans to know that they should celebrate their defeat. Senator McGovern, the new humanitarian hawk, learned of the Vietnamese victory and thought it offered the real irony. "After all those years of predictions of dominos falling and Communist conspiracies," he remembers, "it was *Vietnam* that went in and stopped Pol Pot's slaughter. Whatever their motivation, the Vietnamese were the ones who supplied the military force to stop the genocide. They should have gotten the Nobel Peace Prize." Foreign service officer Charles Twining, who by then had been transferred to the Australia–New Zealand desk at the State Department, was overjoyed at reports of the Vietnamese victory. He recalls, "I didn't see how else change would have happened. Those of us who knew about the Khmer Rouge cheered, but we quickly realized that everyone else just heard it as 'Vietnam, our enemy, has taken over Cambodia.'" Some prominent U.S. officials confessed publicly to being torn. The U.S. ambassador to the United Nations, Andrew Young, told reporters in New York: "I almost always think it's always wrong for a country to transgress the borders of another country, but in the case of Cambodia I'm not terribly upset. . . . It is a country that has killed so many of its own people, I don't know if any American can have a clear opinion of it. . . . It's such a terribly ambiguous moral situation."[156]

But rational, interest-based calculations led the United States to different official conclusions, which quickly overtook these isolated bursts of relief among Cambodia watchers. The Vietnamese victory presented President Carter with a difficult moral and political choice. Which was the lesser evil, a regime that had slaughtered some 2 million Cambodians or a Communist regime backed by the Soviet Union that had flagrantly violated an international border and that now occupied a neighboring state? After weighing the politics of the choice, Carter sided with the dislodged Khmer Rouge regime. The United States had obvious reasons for opposing the expansion of Vietnamese (and, by proxy, Soviet) influence in the region. It also said it had an interest in deterring cross-border aggression anywhere in the world. But this principle was applied selectively. In 1975, when its ally, the oil-producing, anti-Communist Indonesia, invaded East

Timor, killing between 100,000 and 200,000 civilians, the United States looked away.[157] In the Cambodia case perhaps the most important factor behind Carter's choice was U.S. fondness for China, which remained the prime military and economic backer of Pol Pot's ousted government. National Security Adviser Zbigniew Brzezinski saw the problem through the Sino-Soviet prism. Since U.S. interests lay with China, they lay, indirectly, with the Khmer Rouge. Slamming the KR might jeopardize the United States' new bond with China. Slamming the Vietnamese would cost the United States nothing.

With the policy decided and the tilt toward China firm, Secretary of State Vance called immediately for the Vietnamese to "remove their forces from Cambodia." Far from applauding the KR ouster, the United States began loudly condemning Vietnam. In choosing between a genocidal state and a country hostile to the United States, the Carter administration chose what it thought to be the lesser evil, though there could hardly have been a greater one.

The new government in Phnom Penh was led by Heng Samrin and Hun Sen, two former Khmer Rouge officials who had defected to Vietnam in 1977. Meanwhile, the KR regrouped at the border, thanks to military and medical aid from Thailand, China, Singapore, Britain, and the United States.[158] With the Soviet Union arming Vietnam and the Heng Samrin government, China opened up the Deng Xiaoping Trail for Chinese arms deliveries to the KR guerrillas through Thailand.[159] Brzezinski told Becker: "I encouraged the Chinese to support Pol Pot. I encouraged the Thai to help the [Khmer Rouge]. . . . Pol Pot was an abomination. We could never support him but China could."[160] The military and political conflict took on the flavor of a Sino-Soviet proxy war. Vietnam and the states that made up the Soviet bloc argued that the will of the Cambodian people had been gratified and it was absurd to support a genocidal regime. On the other side were China, most members of ASEAN, and the jilted Khmer Rouge officials themselves, who argued that whatever the abuses of the past regime, nothing could excuse a foreign invasion.

The Khmer Rouge did their part, launching an image campaign of sorts. Khieu Samphan replaced Pol Pot as prime minister in December 1979 and invited journalists to hear his version of events. Rejecting charges of genocide, he said, "To talk about systematic murder is odious. If we had really killed at that rate, we would have no one to fight the Vietnamese."[161] Yet now that the evidence of the horrors had surfaced, Samphan could not deny abuse outright. He shrewdly acknowledged some 10,000 executions under Pol Pot, and admitted "mistakes" and "shortcomings." Samphan swore that if the KR returned to power, they would not again evacuate the cities, restrict movement and religion, or eliminate currency. In pursuit of U.S. help, he also brushed aside mention of America's prior sins. "These things are in the past," he said, referring to Nixon's invasion of Cambodia, "and should not be brought up."[162] Well aware that it was American hostility toward Vietnam rather than any love of the KR that earned the KR U.S. support, he warned that without U.S. help and with the backing of Moscow, "The Vietnamese will go further—toward the rest of Southeast Asia, the Malacca Strait, toward control of the South Pacific and Indian oceans."[163] He spoke the fashionable language of falling dominoes.

The Carter administration's policy choice was made easier because at home no voices cried out to support Vietnam. America's most ardent anti-Communists were still angry at Vietnam for the U.S. defeat. American leftists were mostly disengaged. Die-hard Communists were befuddled by the seemingly sudden division of Southeast Asia into two rival and bitterly contested Communist camps. The mass protests in the United States in the 1960s were a reaction against American imperialism and the loss of American lives. With neither at stake in the 1979 Vietnam-Cambodia conflict, the activists who had once made it to the mainstream did not resurface. The administration was able to reduce its policy calculus to pure geopolitics without rousing dissent.

The issue was not simple. Cambodians themselves were elated to be rid of the KR but opposed to the Vietnamese occupation. The Vietnamese had brought about a liberation from hell, but they did not usher in the freedom for which Cambodians longed. Vietnam's claims to have invaded simply to stop atrocity and to defend its borders from Cambodian attacks were proven more hollow with the passage of time. Some 200,000 Vietnamese troops patrolled the Cambodian countryside, and Vietnamese advisers clogged the Cambodian governmental ministries. The Vietnamese-backed regime earned further criticism because of its mishandling of a potential famine. It initially dismissed as Western propaganda reports that Cambodians faced imminent starvation because of disruption of planting and poor cultivation. Then, when outside aid was clearly needed, the regime was more intent on using food as a political weapon than ensuring Cambodians were fed. Kassie Neou, the former English teacher who had long fantasized about rescue, remembers his reaction to the Vietnamese invasion: "My first response was raw. It was a simple, 'Phew, we survived.' My second thought, upon understanding that our land was occupied, was, 'Uh-oh.' Basically, the Vietnamese saved us from sure death, and they deserved our thanks for that. But years later, we felt like saying, 'We already said thank you. So why are you still here?'"

Prince Sihanouk, once the nominal leader of the KR front, had been placed under house arrest soon after the KR seized Phnom Penh. In the course of Pol Pot's rule, he had lost three daughters, two sons, and fifteen grandchildren. Sensing yet another political opening, he emerged from the shadows after the KR's ouster to criticize both the KR and the Vietnamese. "It is a nightmare," he said. "The Vietnamese, they are like a man who has a very delicious piece of cake in his mouth—Cambodia—and all that man can do is swallow the cake."[164] For many Cambodians, the occupation by the Vietnamese quickly came to feel like a "liberation" similar to that of Poland by the Soviets after Nazi rule.

A Regime Less "Stinky"?

The UN Credentials Committee, an obscure nine-member body based at UN headquarters in New York, became the unlikely forum for the international debate on what to do about Cambodia. The Credentials Committee routinely met twice a year to determine whether states had the "credentials" to occupy their UN seats. In September 1979, when the committee convened, both the vanquished KR regime and the victorious Vietnamese-backed regime submitted applications. UN delegates from the Communist and non-Communist worlds sparred over which regime should be recognized and which violation of international law was more egregious.

Three layers of geopolitics made it unlikely that the U.S. representative was going to favor stripping the Khmer Rouge of their UN seat. First, of course, the United States was determined not to condone the Vietnamese invasion. Second, it wanted to please China. And third, as a matter of standing policy, the United States wanted the Credentials Committee to remain a pro forma paperwork clearinghouse rather than a political body that would weigh in on the relative "goodness" or "badness" of a regime. If the committee moved away from ritual rubber-stamping and began judging the merits and demerits of member states, the United States feared, the committee might next strip UN credentials from Israel.

Robert Rosenstock was the lawyer who represented the United States on the Credentials Committee. The Secretariat tried to select people who would treat the granting of credentials as a technical issue, not a substantive one. They wanted people, he says, who would not "start carrying on if a government was obnoxious." Rosenstock did not find the Cambodia vote especially difficult:

> We at the Credentials Committee . . . don't make waves. . . . For us to go against our long-standing mode of operating, somebody in Washington would have had to call us up, and say, "Listen these Khmer Rouge guys really stink and the new guys, the Vietnamese, stink a little less so let's take away the credentials of the stinkier regime." That didn't happen. Washington looked at it as, "They all stink, so let's support the status quo."

Rosenstock duly argued that what was at issue was not the conduct of a government toward its own nationals. Since the KR credentials had been accepted at the 1978 session of the General Assembly, they should be accepted again. The committee had a "technical" task to perform and not a political one.

On September 19, 1979, after some heated debate and despite the submission by Congo of a compromise proposal that would have left Cambodia's UN seat open, the committee voted 6–3 to award UN credentials to the KR regime. The committee did not even review the credentials of the Vietnamese-backed Heng Samrin government.[165]

"I was told to engineer the result on the Credentials Committee," says Rosenstock, "so I engineered the result." The happiest and most surprised man in New York on the day of the vote was the KR's Ieng Sary.[166] He came bounding up to Rosenstock after the tally and extended his hand. "Thank you so much for everything you have done for us," Ieng said. Rosenstock instinctively shook the extended hand and then muttered to a colleague, "I think I now know how Pontius Pilate must have felt."

The battle was not yet won, as the debate over the two regimes' competing moral and legal claims simply shifted from the Credentials Committee to the General Assembly two days later. Here multiple critics spoke out against the Credentials Committee's recommendation that the KR regime be recognized. UN delegates, mainly from the Soviet bloc, argued that the KR's brutality was of such magnitude that they had forfeited their claim to sovereignty. These UN representatives contended that the new regime controlled Cambodia's territory, represented the people's will, and therefore earned the rank of legitimate sovereign. Some pointed to the Holocaust. The Grenada representative compared the Vietnamese liberators to the Allied liberators who administered Germany after defeating it. The Soviet and Byelorussian delegates cited the terms of the genocide convention, which they said required withholding recognition from the genocidal regime. Far from deserving to occupy the UN seat, they said, Pol Pot and Ieng Sary, who had fled to the Thai border, should be extradited back to Cambodia to be tried for genocide under the convention.

The debate was highly charged, as blistering condemnations of the old and new regimes were traded across the floor. Although the majority of the speakers supported the U.S. and Chinese view that Vietnam's invasion should not be recognized, none contested the atrocities committed by Pol Pot. Indeed, all were quick to preface their support for maintaining recognition of the KR with disclaimers that they "held no brief" for the Pol Pot regime, "did not condone their human rights record," and "did not excuse their abominable crimes." Their votes to seat the KR government, they stressed, "did not mean agreement with the past policies of its leaders."[167]

The United States carried Rosenstock's arguments from the Credentials Committee to the General Assembly. "For three years," U.S. representative Richard Petree said, "we have been in the forefront of international efforts to effect fundamental changes in these practices and policies by peaceful means." In the absence of a "superior claim," however, the regime seated by the previous General Assembly should be seated again.[168] Moral values were at stake—a commitment to peace, stability, order, and the rule of law, as well as the insistence that states carry out their obligations under the UN charter. The UN charter had made noninterference in sovereign states a sacred principle. No doctrine of humanitarian intervention had yet emerged to challenge it.

Most of the arguments made by those who voted for seating the KR were internally contradictory. They first insisted that recognizing the Vietnamese-installed regime would mean condoning external intervention and licensing foreign invasions by big powers into small states, thus making the world a "more dangerous place." Yet they next claimed that maintaining recognition of the Pol Pot government would not mean condoning genocide or licensing dictators elsewhere to believe they could treat their citizens as abusively as they chose.

Nonetheless, the U.S. position prevailed. The first debate of many, on September 21, 1979, lasted six and a half hours, and the assembly voted 71–35 (34 abstentions, 12 absences) to endorse the Credentials Committee resolution. The KR's Khieu Samphan was quoted later on the front page of the *Washington Post,* saying, "This is a just and clear-sighted stand, and we thank the U.S. warmly."[169]

Although it would take years for Pol Pot to enter the ranks of the maniacs of our century, where he is ritually placed now, even by 1979 many grasped the depth of his terror. Those who visited were able to tour Tuol Sleng, witness the skeletal remains that lay stubbornly scattered throughout the country, tabulate death counts, and speak with their Cambodian friends, who would often simply burst into tears without a moment's notice. Rosenstock remembers, "I realized enough at the time to feel that there was something disgusting about shaking Ieng Sary's hand. I wasn't in the habit of comparing myself to Pontius Pilate. I mean, I felt like throwing up when the guy shoved his hand in my face. Oooh, it was awful." Yet not so awful as to cause him or his more senior colleagues to challenge U.S. policy, which was driven by U.S. distaste for Vietnam and its interest in pleasing China.

Even with the 1979 vote behind the United States, the presence of KR officials at the UN continued to upset many Americans. In advance of the Credentials Committee vote in 1980, ten U.S. senators signed a letter calling for the United States to abstain on the vote in order to "stand apart from both" brutal regimes. A *Washington Post* editorial urged the United States to hold the seat open, as nothing about the U.S. policy of recognizing the KR was working. "Geopolitically, it has brought the United States no evident gains," the editorial said. "Politically, it has been used by Hanoi to justify both its support of Heng Samrin and its suspicion of U.N. relief efforts. Morally, it is beyond characterization."[170] A subsequent editorial, entitled "Hold-Your-Nose Diplomacy," noted, "There are many close calls in foreign policy, but this is not one of them."[171] Yet no American lobby really pressed the empty-seat solution and, on the other side of the issue, the five ambassadors from the ASEAN countries (Indonesia, Malaysia,

Singapore, Thailand, and the Philippines) urged the White House to stand its ground. In an effort to win support for the Khmer Rouge claim to the UN seat, they also held a secret meeting with members of the House Asian and Pacific Affairs Subcommittee.[172] After a brief period of suspense, Secretary of State Edmund Muskie announced that since Vietnam continued to refuse to withdraw from Cambodia, the United States would again support the seating of Pol Pot's government. He stressed that the U.S. decision "in no way implies any support or recognition" of the Khmer Rouge regime. "We abhor and condemn the regime's human rights record," Muskie said.[173] The General Assembly voted 74–35, with 32 abstentions. By the following year, the debate over whether to recognize the KR had become pro forma.[174]

In 1982, under ASEAN pressure, the Khmer Rouge joined in a formal coalition that included the non-Communist forces, the so-called National Army of Sihanouk, and the Khmer People's National Liberation Front under Son Sann. This coalition shared the UN seat. At the request of the United States, China supplied Sihanouk and Son Sann with arms, and in 1982 the United States began to provide nonlethal covert assistance. Estimated initially at $5 million a year, this funding grew to $12 million by 1985, when Congress authorized up to $5 million in overt aid.

The Khmer Rouge coalition continued to occupy the UN seat as its guerrillas battled the Heng Samrin regime from the countryside. KR tactics changed little. KR soldiers captured and executed foreign tourists and inflicted terror upon those Cambodians who had the misfortune to live under KR control.[175] The consequences of international recognition were significant. The legitimate KR coalition received international financial and humanitarian support, whereas the illegitimate Vietnam-installed regime in Phnom Penh was treated like a pariah. The Cambodian people who had so recently been isolated by the paranoid KR were now isolated by the United States and its allies.[176]

Ignoring all the evidence available in Cambodia and their commitments to punish genocide, UN member states continued to refuse to invoke the genocide convention to file genocide charges at the International Court of Justice against the Cambodian government. Indeed, official UN bodies still refrained even from condemning the genocide. Only in 1985 were bureaucratic inertia and political divides briefly overcome so that a UN investigation could finally be conducted. By then, because it had emerged that the

Khmer Rouge had killed huge percentages of Muslim Chams, Buddhist monks, and Vietnamese *as such,* it proved relatively easy to show that the regime was guilty of genocide against distinct ethnic, national, and religious groups. Once the UN chair of the Subcommission on Prevention of Discrimination and Protection of Minorities had thoroughly documented the crimes, the 1985 final report described the atrocities as "the most serious that had occurred anywhere in the world since Nazism." The subcommission noted that the horrors were carried out against political enemies as well as ethnic and religious minorities but found that this did not disqualify the use of the term "genocide." Indeed, in the words of Ben Whitaker, the UN special rapporteur on genocide, the KR had carried out genocide "even under the most restricted definition."[177]

Yet nothing changed as a result of the declaration. The Khmer Rouge flag continued to fly outside the United Nations, and KR foreign minister Ieng Sary continued to represent Cambodia at the UN as if the KR terror had never happened. Only with the thawing of the Cold War and the visit of Soviet premier Mikhail Gorbachev to former arch-enemy China in May 1989 did Cambodia cease to be a pawn on the superpowers' chessboard. With the Chinese and the Soviets no longer interested in fighting a proxy war through the KR and the Vietnamese, the United States had no reason to maintain support for the KR. Not until July 1990 did Secretary of State James Baker write a letter to Senate majority leader George Mitchell laying out a new U.S. policy toward the KR at the UN. Henceforth, the United States would vote against the KR coalition at the United Nations and at last support the flow of humanitarian aid into Vietnam and Cambodia.[178] Still, during negotiations in Paris aimed at brokering a peace deal among the rival factions, the United States sided with China and the KR in opposing the word "genocide" in the Paris peace accords. This led to an embarrassing moment in the midst of an all-night negotiation in which, according to U.S. officials present, Prince Sihanouk stood up and said, "I am for genocide, I am for genocide, I am for genocide." Because the U.S. position again prevailed, the accords referred not to genocide, but to "the universally condemned policies and practices of the past."[179]

Chapter 7

Speaking Loudly and Looking for a Stick

"We, as a nation, should have been first to ratify the Genocide Convention. . . . Instead, we may well be near the last."
—U.S. Supreme Court Chief Justice Earl Warren[1]

"One Hand Tied"

Senator Proxmire had enjoyed little success using his speech-a-day genocide convention ritual to draw attention to the Cambodia genocide. But he had even less luck generating support for the convention itself. A small group of extremists were unrelenting in their opposition to U.S. ratification. The Liberty Lobby, which the Anti-Defamation League called the "strongest voice of anti-Semitism in America," published a weekly tabloid, the *Spotlight,* that claimed 330,000 paid subscribers and boasted a radio network of 425 stations in forty-six states. The lobby slammed U.S. efforts to denaturalize and deport Nazi collaborators and war criminals living in the United States. It claimed that ratification of the genocide convention would allow missionaries to be tried before an international tribunal for genocide "on grounds that to convert cannibals in Africa to Christianity is to destroy a culture." Other ultra-rightist groups chimed in. The John Birch Society called the convention a "vicious communist perversion."[2] Convention critics resurrected the old argument that the treaty's passage would mean that "you or I may be seized and tried in Jerusalem or

Moscow or somewhere in Punjab . . . if we hurt the feelings of a Jew or other minority."[3]

What was surprising, at least at first glance, was the vast and disproportionate influence these groups were exerting on the legislative process. Proxmire said the groups criticizing the treaty were a "politician's dream of what each of us dearly wish we could identify with our opponent."[4] In a fashion not unusual for Capitol Hill, the lobbies were making themselves more vocal and thus more effective in their opposition than mainstream American groups that supported the law in a passive way. "Let's not kid ourselves," Proxmire declared in 1986, the so-called discredited organizations can be "astonishingly effective."

He identified the challenge:

> Responsible, respected, prestigious supporters of the treaty rarely discuss it. When they do discuss it, they talk about it in factual, low key, unemotional, reasonable terms. This doesn't excite anyone. The overwhelming majority of Americans agree with the treaty's supporters but they aren't excited about it. They are not moved emotionally. They rarely listen. So what's the result? We go home to our States. The only time we hear the Genocide Treaty brought up, it's brought up by intense, bitter people who know the treaty only through what they read in Liberty Lobby's *Spotlight* or some publication of the John Birch Society.[5]

Human rights advocates had placed great hope in the presidency of Jimmy Carter. They expected him to galvanize a broader and more spirited base of support for the convention. Carter did attempt to resuscitate the law in a March 1977 speech before the United Nations. He was aided in 1978 when Proxmire and others used the airing of the *Holocaust* television series to spark a Senate debate. But the issue again dropped quickly out of public discourse. Carter opted to use his legislative leverage instead to secure U.S. ratification of the Panama Canal Treaty in 1977 and Start II in 1979. "Carter's problem was that he had so many other problems," says William Korey, the former director of International Policy Research for B'nai B'rith, who was then actively involved in the Ad Hoc Committee for the Ratification of the Human Rights and Genocide Treaties, which had been formed in the 1960s to raise support for the unratified UN treaties.

In the early 1980s, despite their exhaustion and exasperation, Proxmire, Korey, and other treaty supporters began to sense a newfound American receptivity to the convention. The American Bar Association, the most important longtime opponent of ratification, had dropped its opposition in 1976. Korey helped draw a short burst of attention to Lemkin's life. In 1964, after writing a *Saturday Review* article (entitled "An Embarrassed American") about the U.S. failure to ratify, Korey had received a call from Robert Lemkin, a cousin of Raphael Lemkin, who lived and worked as a dentist and amateur sculptor in Hempstead, Long Island. Robert Lemkin turned over a treasure trove of his cousin's belongings—his correspondence, notebooks, drafts of his genocide book, and a bust of the surly Polish American that Robert had sculpted. Korey asked Vartan Gregorian, head of the New York Public Library, whether he might host an exhibit on Lemkin's unheralded life. Gregorian, who happens to be of Armenian descent, agreed. In December 1983 Kathleen Teltsch, Lemkin's old friend from their days together at the early United Nations, wrote a short *New York Times* story on the New York exhibition.[6] After the three-month exhibit, Korey published several op-ed pieces on the need for ratification in America's major dailies.[7]

With the Holocaust now a topic for public discussion and debate, convention advocates began doing what Cambodia advocates had done: They linked their efforts to the Holocaust. Proxmire did so frequently. He trumpeted the tales of ordinary Poles who had refused to "stand idly by" during the Holocaust. "Mr. President, can we do any less than the Chrosteks and the Walter Ukalos? They did what they could to stop the monstrous actions of the Nazis. Will we do what we can to prevent a future Holocaust? Are we willing, at long last, to join the other 96 nations which have ratified the Genocide Convention?"[8] He invoked the death of Anne Frank. On her birthday he declared,

> Mr. President, no treaty signed by this country could ever make up for the loss of Anne Frank and 6 million others who perished in the Holocaust. But we have an obligation to join with the other nations that have already ratified the Genocide Treaty to make clear to them that we share their sorrow at the tragedy that claimed Anne Frank's life. We need to make clear, Mr. President, our intention to prevent

such a tragedy from ever happening again. We need to make clear that
we will bring those who would commit genocide to justice.[9]

Around the fortieth anniversary of the Allied liberation of the Nazi concentration camps, Proxmire specifically highlighted America's wartime
indifference. During Hitler's Third Reich, he noted, seventy-eight speeches
had been made in the U.S. House of Representatives about the persecution
of the Jews in Europe. "Yet despite the speeches and the resolutions," he
said, "the killings went on, the cries of the dying went unheeded, and our
immigration policies remained unchanged. Is it any wonder that Hitler dismissed foreign outrage with the quip, 'Who remembers the Armenians?'"[10]
When Holocaust survivor and author Elie Wiesel made his first trip to
Germany, Proxmire linked it, too, to ratification. "How can we sympathize
with Mr. Wiesel's cause without taking action? The Genocide Convention
establishes the mechanisms for action. . . ."[11]

Although Proxmire cultivated the image of himself as apolitical, he
made an acutely political case for passage. Neither he nor the other supporters of the convention relied primarily upon moral argumentation,
which was slowly drifting out of fashion. Like Lemkin, they went out of
their way to demonstrate that nonratification was damaging America's
interests. If Lemkin had instinctively wooed government representatives
by describing the cultural losses *they* would endure, Proxmire and other
advocates argued that American nonratification was undermining U.S.
Cold War diplomacy. "It's clear that our failure to ratify . . . has been one
of the most useful propaganda clubs the Soviet Union has ever had,"
Proxmire said in a 1986 speech, "and we've handed it to them on a silver
platter." UN ambassador Jeane Kirkpatrick had testified before the Senate
Foreign Relations Committee the previous fall. "It is contrary to our
national interest," Kirkpatrick said, to fuel anti-American propaganda by
refusing "to reaffirm clearly and unequivocally U.S. support for the
objectives of the Convention." Proxmire quoted Kirkpatrick and asked,
"Is Ambassador Kirkpatrick some type of one-worlder internationalist? Is
she easily duped by Soviet or Communist trickery?"[12] The Soviet Union
had ratified the genocide convention in 1954, an act the *New York Times*
described as analogous to Al Capone's joining the "anti-saloon league."[13]
Proxmire agreed that the Soviets were hypocrites who had no intention
of heeding international law simply because they had agreed to it. Still,

he believed the United States should not remain aloof from the international framework. It was the only major power that had not ratified the convention.

The Soviet representative at the UN Human Rights Commission and at the review conferences for the Helsinki accords frequently undercut U.S. criticisms by saying a country that had not even contracted to the genocide convention had no right to lecture the Soviet Union on human rights. "Why permit Communist nations, which all too often only give lip service to these obligations, to take the moral high ground in these debates?" Proxmire asked. The United States could use the convention in its diplomatic arsenal. "It is unlikely that genocide will be committed in any Western democratic nation. It is more likely that genocide will occur in non-democratic, totalitarian or Communist states," he said. "We cannot do moral battle against genocide with one hand tied behind our backs."[14]

Proxmire's staff collected a running tally of embarrassing clashes between U.S. and Soviet representatives in international settings, which they showered upon senators. At one meeting of the UN Subcommission on the Prevention of Discrimination, Proxmire recalled that Morris Abrams, the U.S. member of the commission, had urged the need for "forceful measures of implementation" to confront racial discrimination. The Soviet delegate promptly turned to Abrams to inquire whether the United States had ratified the genocide convention, the most basic of all human rights treaties. Chastened, Abrams quietly stated his "regret, of course, that my country has not ratified the convention on genocide."[15]

Rita Hauser, President Nixon's delegate to the UN Human Rights Commission, had testified before the 1970 Senate Committee:

> We have frequently invoked the terms of this Convention . . . in our continued aggressive attack against the Soviet Union for its practices, particularly as to its Jewish communities, but also as to the Ukrainians, Tartars, Baptists and others. It is this anomaly . . . [that] often leads to the retort in debates plainly put, "Who are you to invoke a treaty that you are not a party to?"[16]

Although Proxmire had relayed many of these tales on the Senate floor and the Soviet tactic had long been publicized, he believed President Reagan, the renowned Cold Warrior, would be more annoyed by the Soviet debater's move than his predecessors had been. Reagan would not wish to allow the "Evil Empire" to claim any patch of moral high ground.

Proxmire was backed by the grassroots ad hoc committee, which tried to generate bottom-up pressure. With the November 1984 presidential election approaching, Korey worked behind the scenes to lobby the foreign policy advisers of the incumbent Reagan and challenger Walter Mondale. He struck out with the Mondale campaign, but in early September one of Reagan's foreign policy advisers casually called to say that the president was prepared to change his position on the genocide convention and support ratification. Korey was floored.

In each presidential election cycle, it had become a tradition that the candidates would use the B'nai B'rith annual convention as an opportunity to address the Jewish community. On the eve of the 1984 convention, State Department spokesman John Hughes publicly announced that President Reagan would endorse the genocide convention. "The commitment of our country to prevent and punish acts of genocide is indisputable," Hughes said. "Yet our failure to ratify this treaty . . . has opened the United States to unnecessary criticism in various international fora."[17] In his first term Reagan had not supported the convention. In fact, when Republican Senator Charles Percy, chairman of the Senate Foreign Relations Committee, held hearings on the treaty in 1981, not a single representative of the Reagan administration had turned up to testify. But in his B'nai B'rith speech, thanks partly to the lobbying of nongovernmental advocates and the proven unwillingness of Proxmire to let the issue drop on Capitol Hill, the president (and candidate) changed course. The Soviet rebuttals irritated him. Reagan's advisers also believed that the president could gain at least a few Jewish votes by supporting the measure. But perhaps most crucial, with only three weeks remaining in the Senate session, the Reagan team knew that the treaty would not come up for passage until after his reelection. "This was a shrewd move by the Administration," a Senate aide said at the time. "There is no time for floor debate in which the President would have to take on the conservatives, but there is time for political benefits for the President."[18]

Reagan's belated shift was a small victory for convention advocates. But it actually only brought him into line with all previous American presidents except Eisenhower. The administration gave no signs that President Reagan was prepared to invest the political capital needed to bring about full Senate ratification. But that was before Reagan blundered at Bitburg.

Bitburg

In April 1985 the White House announced that President Reagan planned to lay a wreath at West Germany's Bitburg Cemetery the following month. Reagan's trip was meant to commemorate the fortieth anniversary of the end of World War II. But when the press reported that forty-nine Nazi Waffen SS officials were buried at the site and that Reagan had declined requests to visit Holocaust memorials, the president was lambasted for his insensitivity. The *Washington Post* and *New York Times* demanded he drop the visit, calling it "one of the most embarrassing and politically damaging episodes of his Administration."[19] The American Legion, which represented 2.5 million U.S. war veterans, said it was "terribly disappointed."[20] Some eighty senators in the Republican-controlled Senate called on Reagan to "reassess his itinerary."[21] Senate Republican leader Bob Dole issued his own public appeals for cancellation. More than 250 House representatives wrote German chancellor Helmut Kohl directly, asking him to spare the U.S. president humiliation by changing the venue. And Jewish organizations protested fiercely. The main pro-Israel lobbying group, the American Israel Public Affairs Committee (AIPAC), the U.S. Holocaust Memorial Council, Jewish survivor organizations, and most prominent Jewish American leaders expressed anger and alarm. Holocaust survivor Wiesel said he had "rarely seen such outrage" among Jewish groups and condemned what he termed the "beginning . . . of the rehabilitation of the SS."[22] At a White House ceremony coincidentally honoring Wiesel, Reagan tried to appease him by citing the "political and strategic reasons" for visiting Bitburg. But in his public remarks Wiesel rejected Reagan's defense. "The issue here is not politics, but good and evil. And we must never confuse them. For I have seen the SS at work. And I have seen their victims. They were my friends. They were my parents," Wiesel said.[23]

Reagan defended the planned trip on a variety of grounds. He hoped to "cement" the German-U.S. friendship. He had to stand by his commitment to Chancellor Kohl. It was important to move beyond German guilt. In one interview Reagan claimed that the German soldiers were "victims" of the Nazis "just as surely as the victims in the concentration camps."[24] In response to the outrage, Reagan tacked on a visit to the Bergen-Belsen concentration camp, but he refused to do the one thing that might have

AP/Wide World Photos

At an April 16, 1985, news conference in New York, Elie Wiesel expresses his "deep anguish" over President Reagan's plan to visit the Bitburg cemetery. He is accompanied by leaders of Jewish and veterans' groups.

curbed the criticisms: cancel the visit. He preferred plunging poll ratings to the appearance of bowing to public pressure. "All it would do is leave me looking as if I caved in the face of some unfavorable attention,"[25] Reagan said, blaming the reporters for stirring the controversy. "They've gotten hold of something, and like a dog . . . they're going to keep on chewing on it." The president plowed ahead, ignoring the predictions by his Republican strategists that the Bitburg visit would cost him Jewish support. On the day of Reagan's Bitburg stopover, May 5, 1985, protests were held in Boston, Miami, Atlanta, Milwaukee, Philadelphia, Newark, West Hartford, and New Haven.

Harold Koh was a twenty-nine-year-old lawyer at the U.S. Department of Justice. In 1984 he had supplied the Reagan administration with a fifty-page legal analysis on why the United States could ratify the genocide convention with few risks to U.S. citizens. He had never heard back from the

White House. "There was zero interest in getting the Convention passed," Koh recalls. "Proxmire was the only man in town talking about it." When the Bitburg storm clouds burst, however, Koh received a panicked phone call from a National Security Council (NSC) staffer who said the president planned to push for immediate ratification of the genocide law. "Bitburg wasn't *a* reason for the shift," Koh says; "it was the only reason." Koh stayed up all night to prepare the press guidance and drove it personally to the White House, where the NSC official, a uniformed military officer, came out to receive it. That man, Koh later learned, was Lieutenant Colonel Oliver North. President Reagan had become determined to appease his critics by bullying the treaty through Congress. This gave the convention its best chance of passage since 1948.

Through the years, many American presidents had supported the measure. But when Ronald Reagan did so sincerely, it undermined the long-standing Republican opposition on the Senate Foreign Relations Committee. "We couldn't have done it without Reagan," Proxmire says. "He cut the ground right out from under the right wing."

Reservations

Despite Reagan's support, the Republican critics of the convention did not disappear. They simply channeled their hostility in a different direction, stalling a full Senate vote and insisting upon a slew of conditions to U.S. ratification that they knew would weaken the treaty's force. Recognizing that President Reagan's support for the law made passage inevitable, Senators Jesse Helms (R.–N.C.), Orrin Hatch (R.–Utah), and Richard Lugar (R.–Ind.) introduced a stringent Senate "sovereignty package" that included "RUDs," or reservations, understandings, and declarations. These interpretations of and disclaimers about the genocide convention had the effect of immunizing the United States from being charged with genocide but in so doing they also rendered the U.S. ratification a symbolic act.

One reason advocates lobbied for U.S. ratification was to give the United States the legal standing to do what it had been unable to do during the Cambodia genocide: file genocide charges at the International Court of Justice. The convention's reference to the ICJ was typical of the dispute resolution procedures stipulated in more than eighty bilateral and multilateral treaties and international agreements. But in April 1984 Nicaragua had sued the United States at the ICJ for mining its harbors. When the court sided with Nicaragua and accepted jurisdiction, the United States walked out of the case. Neither the Republicans on the Senate Foreign Relations Committee nor the president was prepared to see the United States judged by an international court, so they now conditioned their acceptance of the genocide convention on a potent reservation, an à la carte "opt-out" clause. The reservation held that before the United States could be called as a party to any case before the ICJ, the president would have to consent to the court's jurisdiction. Only the United States would decide whether it would appear before the World Court. It was the equivalent of requiring an accused murderer to give his consent before he could be tried. If the convention stood any chance of resembling, in John Austin's phrase, "law, properly so-called," states had to give the ICJ advance consent so that judges would be empowered to interpret and apply the genocide convention independently, without requesting a state's permission each time.

The legal consequence of the U.S. reservation was that if the United States henceforth suspected that another state was committing genocide and attempted to bring the matter before the ICJ, the accused country could assert the American reservation against the United States under something called the doctrine of reciprocity. The United States was effectively blocked from ever filing genocide charges at the court against perpetrator states.[26] Proxmire battled against the reservations in the same way he had fought on behalf of the convention. He took to the familiar floor, spelling out the consequences of the American position:

> Under this reservation, the Pol Pots [and] the Idi Amins . . . could escape any efforts we would make to bring them before the Court to account for their actions. Why? Because under international law, they could invoke our reservation against us. If we get to decide which cases go before the Court, so do they. It is that simple.
>
> If this treaty had been drafted and signed before World War II, would Senator Helms and Lugar argue that Hitler should choose which cases go before the World Court? Does anyone in this Chamber really believe that? I doubt it.[27]

Proxmire got strong support from Senator Pell, who, along with seven other senators, prepared a detailed critique of the reservations. "The [sovereignty] package as a whole taints the political and moral prestige that the United States would otherwise gain by ratification of this landmark in international law," Pell's report noted. The United States was "defensively embracing a shield that to date has largely been adopted only by countries that may well have reason to fear charges of genocide."[28]

The Senate Foreign Relations Committee split largely along party lines. Nine Republicans and one Democrat voted for the treaty with the reservations; the eight remaining Democrats protested by voting only "present." One of the few avenues the genocide convention created for enforcement would remain completely off-limits to the United States.

On February 11, 1986, Senator Dole brought up the U.S. version of the genocide treaty for a full Senate vote, declaring, "We have waited long enough . . . as a nation which enshrines human dignity and freedom. . . . We must correct our anomalous position on this basic rights issue."[29] A week later, thirty-eight years since the unanimous UN General Assembly passage of the law and thirty-seven years after President Truman had requested the Senate's "advice and consent," the Senate finally and overwhelmingly adopted a ratification resolution—eighty-three in favor, eleven against, and six not voting. Ninety-seven nations had ratified the convention ahead of the United States.

Senate supporters gave credit where they believed it was due. Patrick Moynihan (D.–N.Y.) likened Proxmire's struggle to that of Lemkin and thanked him for an effort that was "without parallel" in the history of the U.S. Senate:

> For 15 years [sic], William Proxmire has asked this body to do what in conscience it ought to have done nearly 40 years ago. . . . When it was not adopted immediately, the man who coined the word "genocide," Mr. Raphael Lemkin . . . made it his business. . . . He succeeded in bringing about the adoption by the general assembly of the convention, and then he saw the Senate of his own country, his newly adopted country, refuse to agree to ratification. It broke his heart. He died alone and in poverty, and uncomprehending that we could not ratify the treaty. Indeed, we never would have done so were it not for the advent of William Proxmire in this body, who is a kind of person

who says if something is worth doing, it does not matter to him that it takes 15 years to do it.

I would like to salute the Senator, and say to him that he has enlarged the quality of this body, and certainly has made this Senator prouder still to be a Member of it.[30]

Proxmire had in fact been speaking daily for nineteen years, or 3,211 times. When we break down this figure into a year-by-year tally, the numbers are daunting. The following table illustrates the number of speeches the senator gave each year.

Year	No. of Speeches	Year	No. of Speeches
1967	199	1977	178
1968	158	1978	159
1969	176	1979	168
1970	208	1980	166
1971	186	1981	165
1972	162	1982	147
1973	184	1983	150
1974	168	1984	131
1975	178	1985	170
1976	142	1986	16

Senators who had opposed the convention throughout its tortured floor history applauded the reservations that had so eviscerated U.S. ratification of the treaty. Senator Helms, who would later warn that the 1998 treaty to create an International Criminal Court to prosecute perpetrators of genocide, war crimes, and crimes against humanity would be "dead on arrival" at the U.S. Senate, voted with eleven others against even the watered-down ratification package. Yet he applauded its toothlessness. Thanks to the reservations, he claimed, "the sovereignty of our Nation and the freedom of our people have been protected against assault by the World Court." He said, "We might as well be voting on a simple resolution to condemn genocide—which every civilized person does."[31]

Some on Proxmire's staff were relieved. Howard Schumann, the senator's chief of staff, who worked for the senator for twenty-seven years, recalls his sense of gratification in 1988. "We worked so long—it felt like we were watching paint dry all those years," Schumann says. "When ratification finally came, it was a great event, like the birth of a first child." But for the staffer most intimate with the law, the victory was as bitter as it was sweet. Larry Patton had devoted a decade and a half of his life to meeting the legal objections, and he found the triumph tainted because the version that actually survived the committee was not the one he had fought for. "We lost the reservations fight," Patton remembers. "I thought that they took away one of the few mechanisms in place to make the Convention effective." Still, the Proxmire team decided to accept and support the flawed ratification resolution. "At least as a state that had finally ratified the law," Patton says, "we could henceforth use our diplomacy to denounce genocide and maybe even stop it."

Remarkably, though it seemed the long struggle was over, Senate critics continued to stall. Full ratification required the passage of "implementing legislation" that would make genocide a crime under U.S. federal law. The months passed, and Proxmire grew angry as the treaty lay fallow. "Why do I rise today to speak on this subject?" Proxmire asked in February 1988. "I rise because it is now two years since the Senate of the United States by an overwhelming 82 to 11 vote ratified the Genocide Convention. In that two-year period the Congress has failed to finish the job. This is incredible. In fact, it is a disgrace to this U.S. Senate." Proxmire noted that the implementing legislation had been drafted and the respective chairmen of the House and Senate Judiciary Committees had introduced the measure, but no hearings had followed. Indeed, Proxmire said he had heard "not a whisper indicating any concern or any action." The irony was bitter. The genocide convention had finally earned Reagan's sincere support in 1985. It had won the overwhelming backing of the Senate in 1986. And here it was 1988, and, in Proxmire's words, the Congress had gone "sound to sleep": "We should take a special international prize for gross hypocrisy. The Senate resoundingly passes the ratification of the Genocide Treaty. We thereby tell the world that we recognize this terrible crime. Then, what do we do about it? We do nothing about it. We speak loudly but carry no stick at all."[32]

It was not until October 1988 that the Senate got around to passing the Genocide Convention Implementation Act, which named the "Proxmire Act." The U.S. law made genocide punishable in the United

States by life imprisonment and fines of up to $1 million. It passed only after Strom Thurmond (R.–S. Car.), a longtime opponent of the convention, gave up on his insistence that the death penalty be required. Thurmond dropped his objection only in exchange for the confirmation of Republican judges whose appointments had been stalled in the Senate Judiciary Committee.

President Reagan signed the implementing legislation in Chicago, credited Lemkin for his role, and declared, "We finally close the circle today. I am delighted to fulfill the promise made by Harry Truman to all the people of the world—and especially to the Jewish people."[33] Proxmire says he was not invited to the signing.

The sovereignty package revealed a go–it–alone approach to treaty ratification and a hostility to international law that was not new, but that rubbed U.S. allies the wrong way. By December 1989, nine European countries (Denmark, Finland, Ireland, Italy, the Netherlands, Norway, Spain, Sweden, and the United Kingdom) had filed formal objections to several of the conditions the United States included in its ratification resolution.

Although Proxmire believed that ratification of the genocide ban would spur Senate ratification of other human rights treaties such as the International Covenant on Economic, Social, and Cultural Rights; the Convention on the Elimination of All Forms of Discrimination Against Women; the Convention on the Rights of the Child; and later the international treaty to ban land mines, none has passed.

On October 19, 1988, Proxmire stood up in a deserted Senate chamber to speak about the genocide convention one last time. He noted that the belated Senate passage had prompted *New York Times* columnist A. M. Rosenthal, the man whom Lemkin had hounded in the late 1940s and early 1950s at the United Nations, to write a column entitled, "A Man Called Lemkin." Proxmire, then seventy-two, rose a little more slowly than he had twenty-one years before, when he had pledged to carry forward Lemkin's crusade. Proxmire requested that Rosenthal's article be published in the *Congressional Record*. "It is a tribute to a remarkable man named Raphael Lemkin," Proxmire said, "one individual who made the great difference against virtually impossible odds. . . . Lemkin died 29 years ago. . . . He was a great man."[34]

With the Reagan administration's support, the U.S. Senate had finally ratified the genocide convention. But when the president and the Senate got their first chance to enforce the law, strategic and domestic political concerns caused them to side *with* the genocidal regime of Saddam Hussein. Far from making the United States more likely to do more to stop genocide, ratification seemed only to make U.S. officials more cautious about using the term.

A Kurdish widow holding up photographs of family members "disappeared" by Iraqi forces.

Chapter 8

Iraq: "Human Rights and Chemical Weapons Use Aside"

In March 1987, a year after the U.S. Senate ratified the genocide convention, Iraqi president Saddam Hussein appointed his cousin Ali Hassan al-Majid as secretary-general of the Northern Bureau, one of five administrative zones in Iraq. The Iraqi dictator vested in al-Majid supreme authority. "Comrade al-Majid's decisions shall be mandatory for all state agencies, be they military, civilian [or] security," Hussein declared. The new Northern Bureau chief set out to use these absolute powers, in his words, to "solve the Kurdish problem and slaughter the saboteurs."[1]

Ever since Iraq had gone to war with Iran in 1980, Hussein had been especially concerned about his "Kurdish problem." Kurds made up more than 4 million of Iraq's population of 18 million. Although Hussein's security forces could control those in the towns, Baghdad found it difficult to keep a close watch on rural areas inhabited by Kurds. Armed Kurds used the shelter of the mountains to stage rebellions against Iraqi forces. Some even aligned themselves with Iran. Hussein decided that the best way to stamp out rebellion was to stamp out Kurdish life.

Al-Majid ordered Kurds to move out of the homes they had inhabited for centuries and into collective centers, where the state would be able to monitor them. Any Kurd who remained in the so-called "prohibited zones" and refused to resettle in the new government housing complexes would henceforth be considered a traitor and marked for extinction. Iraqi special police and regulars carried out al-Majid's master plan, cleansing, gassing, and killing with bureaucratic precision. The Iraqi offensive began in 1987 and peaked between February and September 1988 in what was known as the Anfal campaign. Translated as "the spoils," the Arabic term *anfal* comes from the eighth sura of the Koran, which describes Muhammad's revelation in 624 c.e. after routing a band of nonbelievers. The revelation announced: "He that defies God and His apostle shall be sternly punished by God. We said to them: 'Taste this. The scourge of the Fire awaits the unbelievers.'" Hussein had decreed that the Kurds of Iraq would be met by the scourge of Iraqi forces. Kurdish villages and everything inside became the "spoils," the booty from the Iraqi military operation. Acting on Hussein's wishes, and upon al-Majid's explicit commands, Iraqi soldiers plundered or destroyed everything in sight. In eight consecutive, carefully coordinated waves of the Anfal, they wiped out (or "Saddamized") Kurdish life in rural Iraq.

Although the offensive was billed as a counter-insurgency mission, armed Kurdish rebels were by no means the only targets. Saddam Hussein aimed his offensive at every man, woman, and child who resided in the new no-go areas. And the Kurdish men who were rounded up were killed not in the heat of battle or while they posed a military threat to the regime. Instead, they were bussed in groups to remote areas, where they were machine-gunned in planned mass executions.

Hussein did not set out to exterminate every last Kurd in Iraq, as Hitler had tried against the Jews. Nor did he order all the educated to be murdered, as Pol Pot had done. In fact, Kurds in Iraq's cities were terrorized no more than the the rest of Iraq's petrified citizenry. Genocide was probably not even Hussein's primary objective. His main aim was to eliminate the Kurdish insurgency. But it was clear at the time and has become even clearer since that the destruction of Iraq's rural Kurdish population was the means he chose to end that rebellion. Kurdish civilians were rounded up and executed or gassed not because of anything they as individuals did but simply because they were Kurds.

In 1987–1988 Saddam Hussein's forces destroyed several thousand Iraqi Kurdish villages and hamlets and killed close to 100,000 Iraqi Kurds, nearly all of whom were unarmed and many of whom were women and children. Although intelligence and press reports of Iraqi brutality against the Kurds surfaced almost immediately, U.S. policymakers and Western journalists treated Iraqi violence as if it were an understandable attempt to suppress rebellion or a grisly collateral consequence of the Iran-Iraq war. Since the United

States had chosen to back Iraq in that war, it refrained from protest, denied it had conclusive proof of Iraqi chemical weapons use, and insisted that Saddam Hussein would eventually come around. It was not until September 1988 that the flight of tens of thousands of Kurds into Turkey forced the United States to condemn the regime for using poisonous gas against its own people. Still, although it finally deplored chemical weapons attacks, the Washington establishment deemed Hussein's broader campaign of destruction, like Pol Pot's a decade before and Turkey's back in 1915, an "internal affair."

Between 1983 and 1988, the United States had supplied Iraq with more than $500 million per year in credits so it could purchase American farm products under a program called the Commodity Credit Corporation (CCC). After the September 1988 attack, Senator Claiborne Pell introduced a sanctions package on Capitol Hill that would have cut off agricultural and manufacturing credits to Saddam Hussein as punishment for his killing of unarmed civilians. Influenced by his foreign policy aide Peter Galbraith, Pell argued that not even a U.S. ally could get away with gassing his own people. But the Bush administration, instead of suspending the CCC program or any of the other perks extended to the Iraqi regime, in 1989, a year *after* Hussein's savage gassing attacks and deportations had been documented, doubled its commitment to Iraq, hiking annual CCC credits above $1 billion. Pell's Prevention of Genocide Act, which would have penalized Hussein, was torpedoed.

Despite its recent ratification of the genocide convention, when the opportunity arose for the United States to send a strong message that genocide would not be tolerated—that the destruction of Iraq's rural Kurdish populace would have to stop—special interests, economic profit, and a geopolitical tilt toward Iraq thwarted humanitarian concerns. The Reagan administration punted on genocide, and the Kurds (and later the United States) paid the price.

Warning

Background: No Friends but the Mountains

The Kurds are a stateless people scattered over Turkey, Iran, Syria, and Iraq. Some 25 million Kurds cover an estimated 200,000 square miles. The Kurds are divided by two forms of Islam, five borders, and three Kurdish languages and alphabets. The major powers promised them a state of their own in 1922, but when Turkey refused to ratify the Treaty of Sèvres (the same moribund pact that would have required prosecution of Turks for their atrocities against the Armenians), the idea was dropped. Iraqi Kurds staged frequent rebellions throughout the century in the hopes of winning the right to govern themselves. With a restless Shiite community comprising more than half of Iraq's population, Saddam Hussein was particularly determined to neutralize the Kurds' demands for autonomy.

The Kurdish fighters adopted the name *peshmerga,* or "those who face death." They have tended to face death alone. Western nations that have allied with them have betrayed them whenever a more strategically profitable prospect has emerged. The Kurds thus like to say that they "have no friends but the mountains."

U.S. policymakers have long found the Iraqi Kurds an infuriating bunch. The Kurds have been innocent of desiring any harm to the Iraqi people, but like Albanians in Kosovo throughout the 1990s, they were guilty of demanding autonomy for themselves. Haywood Rankin, a Middle East specialist at the U.S. embassy in Baghdad, made a point of visiting Kurdish territory several times each year. "You have to understand," Rankin says. "The Kurds are a terribly irksome, difficult people. They can't get along with one another, never mind with anybody else. They are truly impossible, an absolute nightmare to deal with."

Through decades of suffering and war, Iraqi Kurds have not just had to worry about repressive rule and wayward allies; they have had to keep one eye on each other. They have squabbled and indeed even warred with one another as often as they have attempted to wriggle free of their Baghdad masters. *Washington Post* correspondent Jonathan Randal dubbed the rivalry between Kurdish Democratic Party (KDP) leader Massoud Barzani and Patriotic Union of Kurdistan (PUK) leader Jalal Talabani as the Middle Eastern version of the Hatfields and the McCoys. As Randal wrote and as many U.S. foreign policymakers would agree, "Kurdistan exists as much despite as because of the Kurds."[2]

Iraq's most violent campaign against the rural Kurds, which began in 1987 and accelerated with the Anfal in 1988, was new in scale and precision, but it was the most forceful manifestation of a long-standing effort by Iraq to repress the Kurds. In 1970 Iraq offered the Kurds significant self-rule in a Kurdistan Autonomous Region that covered only half of the territory Kurds considered theirs and that excluded Kurdish-populated oil-rich provinces. After the Kurds rejected the offer, Saddam Hussein imposed the plan unilaterally in 1974. The Kurds trusted they would receive support from Iran, Israel, and the United States (which was uneasy about Iraq's recent friendship treaty with the Soviet Union), and they revolted under their legendary leader Mullah Mustafa Barzani (the grandfather of Massoud). In 1975, however, with U.S. backing, Iran and Iraq concluded the Algiers agreement, temporarily settling a historic border dispute: Iraq agreed to recognize the Iranian position on the border, and the shah of Iran and the United States withdrew their support for the Kurds. Betrayed, Barzani's revolt promptly collapsed. Henry Kissinger, U.S. secretary of state at the time, said of the American reversal of policy and the Kurds' reversal of fortune, "Covert action should not be confused with missionary work."[3] For his part, Saddam Hussein publicly warned, "Those who have sold themselves to the foreigner will not escape punishment."[4] He exacted swift revenge.

Hussein promptly ordered the 4,000 square miles of Kurdish territory in northern Iraq Arabized. He diluted mixed-race districts by importing large Arab communities and required that Kurds leave any areas he deemed strategically valuable. Beginning in 1975 and continuing intermittently through the late 1970s, the Iraqis established a 6–12-mile-wide "prohibited zone" along their border with Iran. Iraqi forces destroyed every village that fell inside the zone and relocated Kurdish inhabitants to the *mujamma'at,* large army-controlled collective settlements along the main highways in the interior. Tens of thousands of Kurds were deported to southern Iraq. In light of how much more severe Hussein would later treat the Kurds, this phase of repression seems relatively mild: The Iraqi government offered compensation, and local Kurdish political and religious leaders usually smoothed the relocation, arriving ahead of the Iraqi army and its bulldozers and guns. In addition, many of the Kurdish men who were deported to the Iraqi deserts actually returned alive several years later. Still, the evacuations took their toll. According to the Ba'ath Party newspaper *Al-Thawra* ("The Revolution"), 28,000 families (as many as 200,000 people) were deported from the border area in just two months in the summer of 1978. Kurdish sources say nearly half a million Kurds were resettled in the late 1970s.[5]

When Iraq went to war with Iran in 1980, the Kurds' prospects further plummeted. The war began after Iraq turned its back on the 1975 Algiers agreement that had briefly settled its border dispute with Iran. In reviving its claim to the entire Shatt al-Arab waterway, Iraq wanted to demonstrate to the new regime of the Ayatollah Khomeini that it was the regional strongman. It also wished to signal its displeasure with Iran for continuing to support Kurdish rebels in Iraq. Iran's Khomeini in turn began urging Iraqi Shiites to rise up against Hussein. Iraq countered by pledging to support Iranian rebel movements. Border skirmishes commenced. In April 1979 Iraq executed the leading Shiite clergyman, Ayatollah Muhammad Bakr al-Sadr. And on September 4, 1980, Iran began shelling Iraqi border towns. To this day, when Iraqis celebrate the war, they mark its beginning as September 4. But it was not until September 22 that Iraq launched a strike into the oil-rich Iranian province of Khuzistan. Hussein expected that the Iranian defenses would crumble instantly. For neither the first nor the last time, the Iraqi dictator miscalculated. Caught off-guard by the invasion and still reeling from the revolution, Iran did founder at the start, in part because the ayatollah had destroyed the shah's professional military. But Iran bounced back and counterattacked in what would become one of the most bloody, futile wars of the twentieth century—a war that gave Saddam pretext, motivation, and cover to target Iraq's Kurdish minority.

U.S. Prism: The Enemy of My Enemy

The U.S. refusal to bar the genocidal Khmer Rouge from the United Nations during the 1980s was an explicit outgrowth of U.S. hostility toward Vietnam. So, too, in the Middle East, the U.S. response to Iraq's atrocities against the Kurds stemmed from its aversion toward revolutionary Iran. The United States was aghast at the prospect of Iraqi oil reserves falling into the Ayatollah Khomeini's hands; it feared that radical Islam would destabilize the pro-American governments in Saudi Arabia and the Gulf emirates. Thus, with each Iranian battlefield victory, the United States inched closer to Iraq—a warming that had tremendous bearing on the American response to Saddam Hussein's subsequent atrocities against the Kurds.

During the Armenian genocide, the Holocaust, and the Khmer Rouge terror, the United States had been neutral or, eventually, in World War II, at war with the genocidal regime. Here, the United States ended up aligned with one. Unwilling to see an Iranian victory, the Reagan administration began in December 1982 to intervene to offset Iranian gains. In what Secretary of State George Shultz called "a limited form of balance-of-power policy," the United States provided Iraq with an initial $210 million in agricultural credits to buy U.S. grain, wheat, and rice under the CCC. This figure soon climbed to $500 million per year. The credits were essential because Iraq's poor credit rating and high rate of default made banks reluctant to loan it money.[6] The United States also gave Iraq access to export-import credits for the purchase of goods manufactured in the United States.[7] And after Baghdad expelled the Abu Nidal Black June terrorist group, the United States removed Iraq from its list of countries sponsoring terrorism. In November 1984 the United States and Iraq restored diplomatic relations, which had been severed during the 1967 Arab-Israeli war. U.S. officials had detailed knowledge of Hussein's reliance on torture and executions, but the United States could not allow Iran to defeat him.[8]

Because both Iran and Iraq were stockpiling weapons and ideological resentments that could hurt the United States, U.S. leaders did not protest much as the two sides destroyed one another. A clear victory by Iraq would not be terribly good for U.S. interests either. Iran might collapse, allowing the brutal Hussein to dominate the Gulf. Americans lapsed into thinking about the conflict (to the extent that they thought of it at all) as one between Saddam Hussein and the Ayatollah Khomeini. They thought little of the poorly trained teenagers being hurled into battle.

As Iraq gathered favor with the United States, the Kurds continued to lose favor with Iraq. In 1982 Baghdad began clearing more Kurdish territories, forcing many of those who had been relocated into housing complexes to move again. The prohibited zones were expanded inward from the border and the resettlement policies intensified. Because Iraq wanted to move all Kurds it did not control, any Kurds who did not live along the main roads or in the major towns were targets. This time, when Hussein's regime deported the Kurds, it paid no compensation to those who left, and it cut off all services and banned trade for those who stayed. Because Iraq was concentrating its military resources on Iran, however, its enforcement of the zones remained somewhat erratic.

The Kurds had always been opportunists, and as the Iraq-Iran conflict wore on, both major Kurdish political parties opted to team with Iran. In 1983 one of the two main Kurdish factions (loyal to Barzani) helped the Iranian fighters capture an Iraqi border town, Haj Omran. Iraqi forces swiftly responded, rounding up some 8,000 Kurdish men from the Barzani clan. Among them were 315 children, aged between eight and seventeen. "I tried to hold on to my youngest son, who was small and very sick," remembered one mother. "I pleaded with them, 'You took the other three, please let me have this one.' They just told me, 'If you say anything else, we'll shoot you,' and then hit me in the chest with a rifle butt. They took the boy. He was in the fifth grade." The men (and boys) were loaded onto buses, driven south, and never seen again. The women, who became known as the "Barzani widows," still carry framed photographs of their missing husbands, sons, and brothers and remain, like their spiritual sisters in Buenos Aires and Bosnia, desperate to learn the fates of their men. Saddam Hussein was not shy about admitting what his forces had done. In a speech reminiscent of Turkish interior minister Talaat's public boastings in 1915, Hussein proclaimed, "They betrayed the country and they betrayed the covenant, and we meted out a stern punishment to them and they went to hell."[9] Although the Kurds attempted to press their case in Western circles, neither the United States nor its allies protested the killings.

The American tendency to write off the region was so pronounced that the United States did not even complain when Hussein acquired between 2,000 and 4,000 tons of deadly chemical agents and began experimenting with the gasses against the Iranians.[10] Policymakers responded as if the ayatollah had removed the Iranian people (and especially Iranian soldiers) from the universe of moral and legal obligation. Iraq used chemical weapons approximately 195 times between 1983 and 1988, killing or wounding, according to Iran, some 50,000 people, many of them civilians.[11] One Iraqi commander was quoted widely saying, "for every insect there is an insecticide."[12] These weapons instilled such psychological terror that even well-equipped troops tended to break and run after small losses.[13]

The United States had much to lose from the use and proliferation of chemical weapons. But still the State Department and even the Congress largely let the Iraqi attacks slide. Reports of Iraq's chemical use against Iran first reached Secretary of State Shultz in late 1983. It was not until March 5, 1984, that the State Department spokesman finally issued a condemnation. And even then he tempered the sting of the démarche by rendering it two-sided. "While condemning Iraq's resort to chemical weapons," the spokesman said, "the United States also calls on the government of Iran to accept the good offices offered by a number of countries and international organizations to put an end to the bloodshed."[14] And even this even-handed statement went too far for many in the U.S. intelligence community. On March 7, 1984, an intelligence analyst complained: "We have demolished a budding relationship [with Iraq] by taking a tough position in opposition to chemical weapons."[15] Internal efforts to promote a new international treaty banning chemical weapons production, use, and transfer met with stiff resistance from the Washington national security community and from allies like West Germany, which were profiting handsomely from the sale of chemical agents. The most that the international community mustered was a 1987 UN Security Council Resolution that generally "deplored" chemical weapons use.[16]

U.S. officials justified their soft response to Iraqi chemical weapons use on several grounds. They portrayed it as a weapon of last resort deployed only after more traditional Iraqi defenses were flattened. Although Iraq carried out first-use attacks, the operations were frequently presented as defensive attacks designed mainly to deflect or disrupt Iranian offensives, not to gain ground.[17] This, of course, was a fine line to walk, as proponents of the preemptive, defensive rationale might have applied the same logic to rationalize nuclear first use.

A typical U.S. response to reports of chemical attacks was to demand further investigation. On several occasions the UN dispatched fact-finding teams, which verified that the Iraqis had used mustard and tabun gas. But policymakers greeted their reports with an insistence that both sides were guilty.[18] Once Hussein saw he would not be sanctioned for using these weapons against Iran, the Iraqi dictator knew he was on to something.

A Friend Beyond the Mountains

Peter Galbraith monitored developments in the Gulf from Capitol Hill, where he was a staff member on the Senate Foreign Relations Committee. Galbraith, the son of Harvard economist John Kenneth Galbraith, was an unusual Washington operator. On the one hand, he earned widespread respect for his conviction and his willingness to explore foreign hot spots in person. On the other hand, he was notorious for arriving late to meetings, for dressing sloppily, and for acquiring tunnel vision on behalf of his causes. I met him for the first time in 1993, five years after the Anfal campaign, at a plush Washington breakfast in honor of Turkish president Turgut Ozal. The guest list was refined, including Pamela Harriman, Jeane Kirkpatrick, and chairman of the Joint Chiefs of Staff Colin Powell. When Powell arrived at the breakfast, the waters seemed to part before him. He had height, width, grooming, and striking confidence, a marked contrast to the frazzled thirty-something man who rushed into the room after the guests had moved from their breakfast fruit plates to their second cups of coffee. When Galbraith noted that the only empty seat was at the head table, he maneuvered clumsily toward the front of the banquet hall. It was early morning, but his tie was already as loose as one that has freed itself at the end of a draining day. One side of his shirt was untucked in the front. His straight, thinning brown hair stood on end. General Powell eyed Galbraith skeptically as the young Senate staffer plopped down beside him.

In the question-answer session that followed Ozal's presentation, most of the distinguished guests inquired politely about the future of U.S.-Turkish ties or heaped profuse praise upon the Turkish leader for his country's cooperation during the 1991 Gulf War. Galbraith quickly assumed the role of spoiler, posing the only taxing question of the morning. "The first goal of Kurds in northern Iraq is independence," Galbraith said. "Their second preference is some kind of affiliation with Turkey. The last thing they want is to remain part of Iraq. What is your view?"

The audience gasped at what they feared was a characteristically undiplomatic question. In fact, Galbraith knew Ozal to have had a Kurdish grandmother and to be relatively sympathetic. The Turkish president gave an animated, lengthy response.

The Kurdish cause was not the first that had made Galbraith alienate official Washington. His first significant contribution to American law and humanitarian relief had been the McGovern amendment, which he drafted in the summer of 1979 to allow U.S. humanitarian assistance to Cambodia after the country had fallen to the Vietnamese. The law had passed, but Galbraith complained so bitterly about the committee's changes that he was one of the first to be laid off when cutbacks were needed in December 1979. "I was my usual self back then, neither impressing people nor making friends," he remembers. "They had the rap on me right away—I was concerned with a flaky issue, and I was not really a foreign policy professional. I cared too much about the humanitarian aspect, I didn't dress particularly well, and I didn't comb my hair properly." McGovern intervened personally to have Galbraith rehired, this time to work directly for Senator Pell, who was thought to be similarly concerned with flaky issues. It was not long before Galbraith discovered the Kurds.

Galbraith traveled to Iraq for the Senate Foreign Relations Committee for the first time in 1984. Although he would later become the Kurds' leading advocate in Washington, initially he, like everyone else, allowed his diagnosis of Hussein's behavior to be affected by what he knew to be the overall U.S. objectives in the region. Galbraith agreed with the Reagan administration's assessment that America's highest priority should be making sure that Iran did not win the war, which it seemed on the verge of doing. The young Senate staffer arrived in Iraq knowing nothing about the Kurds and little about the Middle East. He spotted tanned men with baggy pants in the hills, but they barely left an impression. Geopolitics and the interests of the United States dominated his perspective almost entirely.

In 1987 Galbraith made a second committee trip to Iraq. This time he saw scenes that made him more prone to believe subsequent allegations of Iraqi genocide against Kurds. What is surprising, in retrospect, is that Iraq, which had stepped up its brutal counter-insurgency campaign in March 1987, permitted access to American visitors at all. Because Iraq had never been sanctioned for prior atrocities against the Kurds, the regime must have been confident it would pay no price for exposure. In addition, Hussein had become alarmed by recent press reports about American backroom arms deals with Iran.[19] The Iraqi ambassador in Washington, Nizar Hamdoon, hoped that by rolling out the red carpet to Galbraith, he would tip the balance back toward Iraq.

Galbraith took up Hamdoon's offer to visit Iraq in early September 1987, joining the U.S. embassy's Haywood Rankin on an eight-day fact-finding trip. Travel for diplomats and journalists anywhere in Iraq was severely circumscribed. Those diplomats who wished to leave Baghdad had to apply forty-eight hours in advance to the Iraqi Foreign Ministry. They were sure to be followed. Western journalists were granted visas to the country only rarely, and if they wrote critically, they knew they would be barred from return. But the biggest obstacle to intelligence gathering was fear—fear for one's own life and fear of endangering Iraqis. Rankin traveled beyond Baghdad more than any other Western diplomat, but he never lost sight of the risks. "Getting killed in an ambush or running over a land mine weren't high on anybody's list of things to do," Rankin recalls. "I guess it took people either as curious or as dumb as Peter and me to go wandering into the north." Even once they were out of Baghdad, Rankin notes, "we had to be careful not to let our desire for information interfere with the desire of ordinary people to stay alive." A 1984 amendment to the Iraqi penal code prescribed the death penalty for anyone who even "communicated" with a foreign state if it resulted in "damage to the military, political or economic position of Iraq."[20] Like their counterparts in the

Khmer Rouge's Cambodia, Iraqis deemed critical of the regime would rarely escape with their lives. Indeed, the paranoia of the regime was such that a British civil engineer was arrested, beaten, and tortured for accidentally causing a picture of Saddam Hussein to fall to the ground when he leaned against a wall at a construction site.[21] The Kurds were so frightened by Iraqi officialdom that there was only so much a pair of American sleuths were going to learn as they roamed the countryside. But they could gather stark visual impressions.

Since Galbraith's previous trip, more deadly signs of the war with Iran had cropped up—children disfigured by shell fire and coffins draped in the Iraqi colors strapped to the tops of the country's trademark orange-and-white taxis. Black flags also flapped in the wind, bearing the names of dead soldiers and the dates and locations of their passing. As if to compensate, even more monuments to Saddam had sprouted—Saddam as general, as businessman, as Bedouin Arab in headdress, as comforter of children, as man in prayer, as cigar-smoking politician, and even decked out in traditional pantaloons, as Kurd.[22]

On September 6, 1987, several days into their trip, Galbraith and Rankin left Baghdad and headed north in a Chevy S10 Blazer. Because he had visited three years before, Galbraith could conduct an informal, before-and-after comparison. In 1984 he had been able to drive undiverted up to a town called Shaqlawa. But the very same checkpoints and military fortifications along the road that had then been largely deserted were now bustling with forbidding military guards. It seemed the prohibited zones were suddenly being strictly enforced.

Driving through a dust storm, the Americans reached a checkpoint outside Jalawla, the last sizable Arab town on the road north. Jalawla lies fifteen miles from the Iranian border. They were told to turn back. When they presented their travel permit signed by the Iraqi deputy prime minister, the soldier at the checkpoint was flabbergasted. Finally, after two hours making dozens of confused, frantic phone calls and against his better judgment, the Iraqi guard allowed the pair to proceed under heavily armed escort. An army truck led the way with one soldier holding a rocket-propelled grenade, six other helmeted men in the back, two more in the front. Behind them a handful of soldiers and an antiaircraft gun completed the caravan.

While Rankin drove, Galbraith tracked their route on the map. Once they proceeded a few miles up the road, he began to fear that they had taken a wrong turn. Nothing on the map appeared before them. He scanned the horizon for the next village but spotted no sign of life. This became the rule. Kurdish village upon Kurdish village that appeared as specks on the map and that had once stood on the road from Baghdad to Jalawla to Darbandikhan to Sulaymaniyah to Kirkuk had vanished. "On the right-hand side," Galbraith recalls, "you'd see nothing but rubble. On the left side you'd see empty buildings waiting for destruction. It was chilling." No more than a handful of villages were left standing along the main road, and these straggler villages looked doomed, as bulldozers hovered nearby, expectantly. Occasionally a few stray electric poles offered a hint of past life. In the 1990s these lifeless, rubbled scenes would become familiar to journalists, diplomats, and aid workers in Bosnia, but in 1987 neither Galbraith nor Rankin had heard of "ethnic cleansing" or seen anything comparable. In certain areas the Iraqis were knocking down the villages and all traces that the villages—many of which had been inhabited since the beginning of civilization—had ever existed. Even cemeteries and orchards were mowed to bits.

The only places along the road that remained intact were the Iraqi Arab villages, which stood untouched, and the newly erected "victory cities," or ghettos, where the Iraqi soldiers continued to "concentrate" the forcibly displaced Kurds. In a journal he prepared after the trip, Rankin described Kalar, one such city, "as a spectacle of new construction—an ugly beehive, all in cement laid out on a grid pattern, grotesque and squalid."[23] Driving along the road that day, the two Americans saw twenty-three destroyed towns and villages in all. Some were just rubble heaps, with no walls left standing. As they drove further north, the natural bounty that greeted them was considerable: oleander, olive, and pomegranate trees. But the human presence was negligible—they came across not a single herdsman.

The brutality of the Iran-Iraq war and the sight of the Kurdish villages (or absence thereof) made a deep impression on Galbraith. But the different brands of violence and despair—among Iraqis, Kurds, and Iranians—blended together in his mind. As memorable to him as the demolished Kurdish villages was what he had seen in the southern port of Basra, once Iraq's most glorious city. In the town's dilapidated Republican Hospital, where some of the sheets were bloodstained and where cats and flies wandered in and out of the wards, corpses were casually wheeled in and out of the compound. Rankin's journal recorded their encounters. "Most patients seemed passive and fatalistic," the American wrote. "Some spoke matter-of-

Peter Galbraith

Peter Galbraith of the Senate Foreign Relations Committee standing with
Kurds in front of a destroyed village in northern Iraq.

factly about the simultaneous death of a wife or child or grandparent, as if
it was a daily and expected occurrence."[24] The Iranian attack on Basra had
begun in January 1987. By the time the battle for the town had ground to
an unceremonious halt that June, analysts estimate that 40,000 Iranians and
25,000 Iraqis had been killed, making it the bloodiest battle in the bloodiest war since World War II.

In its senselessness and savagery, the conflict between Iran and Iraq bore
striking parallels with World War I. The Iraqis employed chemical weapons
against the Iranians; the fronts remained static for years; and in vicious
trench warfare, wave after wave of Iranian soldier went over the top, obliterating a generation of young men and boys. The ayatollah encouraged
martyrdom, which gave him spiritual cover to mask the ridiculous losses
and the hollow cause.[25] He famously deployed Iranian children as mines-
weepers, tying them together to walk across fields and across no-man's-
land. He instructed them to wear around their necks plastic keys that
would enable them to unlock the gates of paradise. Often the children
were sent with no training in full frontal charge across open terrain against

enemy machine-gun posts. In this context, the "mere" demolition of Kurdish villages, the displacement of Kurdish civilians, and the implications of prohibiting life in rural Kurdistan did not really stand out.

Although Galbraith had absorbed the human costs of the bloody Iran-Iraq war and the onslaught against Kurdish villages, he devoted his portion of a 1987 report on the conflict—sixteen pages out of forty-nine—mainly to U.S. interests in Iraq. "War in the Persian Gulf: The U.S. Takes Sides" argued that despite Baghdad's brutality, the United States still could not afford for Iraq to lose the war.

Galbraith recommended that the United States pursue economic sanctions against Iran and work through the United Nations to bring the war to a close. He did not urge that Saddam Hussein be punished for his harsh repression of the Kurds. Indeed, he hardly mentioned the Kurds. When he did, they came across not as a people that mattered in their own right but as a group whose rebellion underscored Iraqi vulnerability to Iran. The Kurdish problem might "prove the Achilles heel of Iraq's defense," Galbraith worried. "The Kurdish insurgency has gained enormous strength, and now poses a major military threat to Iraqi control of the Kurdish region."[26] The report hinted at the nature of what Rankin and Galbraith had seen, describing the destroyed villages, but it blared none of the alarms that might have alerted readers to the severity of the repression and the potential for further brutality. Galbraith considered the Kurds "rebels," "insurgents," and "Iranian allies." That far more Kurds were unarmed than armed did not alter his perception. And the report made note of the oft-repeated fact that Iraq had, until recently, treated its Kurdish minority better than any of its neighbors. The pressing concern was that Iraq's Kurdish nuisance was then drawing some 150,000 Iraqi troops away from the Iranian front. Iraq was facing a war of attrition from both south (Iran) and north (Iran plus Iranian-backed Kurds). *This* was deemed bad for the United States.

Official Knowledge, Official Silence

Although Galbraith's insight into the destruction of the Kurds was derived anecdotally from his two trips to the country, U.S. officials at the State Department were also systematically monitoring Iraqi troop movements and had a far deeper understanding of Saddam Hussein's brutal resettlement campaign. "Our reporting from Iraq was very good," remembers

Larry Pope, then State Department office director for Iran and Iraq. "There
was a lag of a couple weeks at most. We knew that something dreadful was
going on. We knew al-Majid was running the show. We had the satellite
overhead that showed the villages razed." The State Department's 1987
unclassified human rights report described "widespread destruction and
bulldozing of Kurdish villages, mass forced movement of Kurds, and exile of
Kurdish families into non-Kurdish parts of Iraq."[27] Yet whatever the broad
knowledge of the facts, the U.S. embassy in Baghdad gave the impression
that the demolition and population transfers were both justified and likely
soon to subside. The embassy argued that al-Majid would soon cease the
offensive against the Kurds. Instead of wasting "at least a battalion of soldiers" per village, one April 1987 embassy cable noted, he "will resettle and
raze some of them and then slow down or stop such activity in the summer,
as part of a 'carrot and stick' approach."[28] The U.S. embassy presumed, as
usual, that Iraq was run by rational actors who would be so intent on winning war that they would not expend precious resources on inflicting seemingly gratuitous suffering on civilians. Already U.S. officials reporting on the
attacks had acquired a matter-of-fact tone, describing the harsh treatment of
Kurds as routine. Al-Majid was coordinating "ruthless repression, which also
includes the use of chemical agents," the embassy noted casually.[29]

The U.S. media did not press the matter. The few correspondents who
cared about the region had great difficulty getting inside Iraq. The
Washington Post's Randal had visited in 1985, but he could not persuade his
editors that another trip would be worth the expense, the risk, and the has-
sle. Once, when he tried to get the *Post* to publish a picture of a gassed
Kurd, his editor asked, "Who will care?" Randal maintained contacts with
émigré Kurds in London and Paris and urged them to buy themselves a
few secondhand camcorders so they could record evidence of the atrocities
for the networks. "I told them that even a monkey could take footage of
some seriously dead people," Randal recalls, "but they were proud that they
had a telex connection to Cyprus. They were way behind the curve tech-
nologically. The people calling the shots had been in the mountains so
long that they did not know how the world worked."

Hussein, by contrast, did know how the world worked. Having seen
how effective chemical weapons could be against his external foe, Hussein
turned them next against his chief internal enemy. In May 1987 Iraq
became the first country ever to attack its own citizens with chemical
weapons. Iraqi Kurds who fled to Iran claimed that Hussein's planes had

dropped mustard gas on some two dozen Kurdish villages along the Iranian-Iraqi border.[30] The headquarters of the two main Kurdish political parties had also been bombed with poison gas. Similar reports trickled out of the region for the rest of 1987 and into 1988.

Iraq's destruction of villages by more conventional means was also reported in the media. In September 1987 the *New York Times* noted that Iraq had dynamited some 500 villages in the previous six months. Still, back in the United States the accounts continued to be processed as if they were an ordinary feature of war. *Times* reporter Alan Cowell described the onslaught not as an offensive that killed innocent people but as a "ruthless drive to deny sanctuary to Kurdish guerrillas."[31] The absence of protest again seemed to embolden the Iraqis. Al-Majid, whom Kurds later dubbed "Anfal Ali" and who continued to oversee the purge of the rural Kurds, quickly gathered that the United States prized its relationship with Iraq and did not intend to use its leverage to curb his campaign. Transcripts later retrieved of al-Majid's conversations reveal that he operated with scant fear of consequence. In a May 26, 1988, meeting, al-Majid described a planned gas attack against the Kurds. "I will kill them all with chemical weapons!" he exclaimed. "Who is going to say anything? The international community? Fuck them!"[32] Al-Majid carried on with impunity, ravaging Iraq's Kurds.

States are constantly signaling one another. One can often discern moments before genocide in which outside powers, by reacting timidly or invitingly to initial abuses, reveal a lack of concern about the repressive tactics of a friend or foe. The American responses to Iraqi chemical weapons' use against Iran, early reports of use against the Kurds, and ongoing Iraqi bulldozing of Kurdish villages was extremely tame.[33] Nothing in U.S. behavior signaled Hussein that he should think twice about now attempting to wipe out rural Kurds using whatever means he chose.

Recognition

Kurdish Hiroshima

Galbraith did not recommend that the United States change its policy after he toured the wasteland of northern Iraq in 1987, but the images of destruction stayed with him. He had a nagging suspicion that Saddam

Hussein's bulldozing campaign was more sinister and widespread than he initially thought. If Hussein only wanted to keep irksome armed Kurds at bay, Galbraith wondered, why was he targeting places inhabited mainly by civilians? Galbraith's fears deepened in March 1988 when Iraqi forces gassed the Kurdish town of Halabja.

The Iraqi demolition of villages around Halabja in 1987 had caused the town's population to swell from 40,000 to nearly 80,000. Halabja constituted a special source of irritation and rage for Northern Bureau chief al-Majid. Kurdish rebel *peshmerga* had made it a stronghold of sorts, frequently teaming up with Iranian Revolutionary Guards who seeped across the nearby border. Halabja also lay just seven miles east of a strategically vital source of water for Baghdad.

In mid-March 1988, a joint Kurdish-Iranian operation routed Iraqi soldiers in Halabja. Overnight Iranian soldiers replaced the Iraqis in the border town. Kurdish civilians, the pawns in the struggle between the neighborhood's two big powers, were gripped by a wave of chilling apprehension. On March 16, Iraq counterattacked with deadly gases. "It was different from the other bombs," one witness remembered. "There was a huge sound, a huge flame and it had very destructive ability. If you touched one part of your body that had been burned, your hand burned also. It caused things to catch fire."[34] The planes flew low enough for the petrified Kurds to take note of the markings, which were those of the Iraqi air force. Many families tumbled into primitive air-raid shelters they had built outside their homes. When the gasses seeped through the cracks, they poured out into the streets in a panic. There they found friends and family members frozen in time like a modern version of Pompeii: slumped a few yards behind a baby carriage, caught permanently holding the hand of a loved one or shielding a child from the poisoned air, or calmly collapsed behind a car steering wheel. Not everybody who was exposed died instantly. Some of those who had inhaled the chemicals continued to stumble around town, blinded by the gas, giggling uncontrollably, or, because their nerves were malfunctioning, buckling at the knees. "People were running through the streets, coughing desperately," one survivor recalled. "I too kept my eyes and mouth covered with a wet cloth and ran. . . . A little further on we saw an old woman who already lay dead, past help. There was no sign of blood or any injury on her. Her face was waxen and white foam bubbled from the side of her mouth."[35] Those who escaped serious exposure fled toward the Iranian border. When reports of the attack reached the outside world, the Iraqi government attributed the assault to Iran.

Halabja quickly became known as the Kurdish Hiroshima. In three days of attacks, victims were exposed to mustard gas, which burns, mutates DNA, and causes malformations and cancer; and the nerve gases sarin and tabun, which can kill, paralyze, or cause immediate and lasting neuropsychiatric damage. Doctors suspect that the dreaded VX gas and the biological agent aflatoxin were also employed. Some 5,000 Kurds were killed immediately. Thousands more were injured. Iraq usually justified its attacks against the Kurds on the grounds that it aimed to destroy the saboteurs aligned with the Iranians. But in Halabja most of the Kurdish *peshmerga* who had worked with Iran had obtained gas masks. It was unarmed Kurdish civilians who were left helpless.

Halabja was the most notorious and the deadliest single gas attack against the Kurds, but it was one of at least forty chemical assaults ordered by al-Majid. A similar one followed that spring in the village of Guptapa. There, on May 3, 1988, Abdel-Qadir al-'Askari, a chemist, heard a rumor that a chemical attack was imminent. He left the village, which was situated on low ground, and scrambled up a distant hilltop so he might warn his neighbors of imminent danger. When he saw Iraqi planes bombing, he sprinted back down to the village in order to help. But when he reached his home, where he had prepared a makeshift chemical attack shelter, nobody was inside. He remembered:

> I became really afraid—convinced that nobody survived. I climbed up from the shelter to a cave nearby, thinking they might have taken refuge there. There was nobody there, either. But when I went to the small stream near our house, I found my mother. She had fallen by the river; her mouth was biting into the mud bank. . . . I turned my mother over; she was dead. I wanted to kiss her but I knew that if I did, the chemicals would be passed on. Even now I deeply regret not kissing my beloved mother.[36]

He searched desperately for his wife and children:

> I continued along the river. I found the body of my nine-year-old daughter hugging her cousin, who had also choked to death in the

water. . . . Then I went around our house. In the space of 200–300 square meters I saw the bodies of dozens of people from my family. Among them were my children, my brothers, my father, and my nieces and nephews. Some of them were still alive, but I couldn't tell one from the other. I was trying to see if the children were dead. At that point I lost my feelings. I didn't know who to cry for anymore and I didn't know who to go to first. I was all alone at night.[37]

Al-Askari's family contained forty people before the attack and fifteen after. He lost five children—two boys, one sixteen, the other six; and three girls, aged nine, four, and six months. In Guptapa some 150 Kurds were killed in all. Survivors had witnessed the deaths of their friends, their spouses, and their children.

When word of the gas attacks began spreading to other villages, terrified Kurds began fleeing even ahead of the arrival of Iraqi air force bombers. Al-Majid's forces were fairly predictable. Jets began by dropping cluster bombs or chemical cocktails on the targeted villages. Surviving inhabitants fled. When they reached the main roads, Iraqi soldiers and security police rounded them up. They then often looted and firebombed the villages so they could never be reoccupied. Some women and children were sent to their deaths; others were moved to holding pens where many died of starvation and disease. Many of the men simply disappeared, never to be heard from again. In the zones that Saddam Hussein had outlawed, Kurdish life was simply extinct.

Official Skepticism

In Washington skepticism greeted gassing reports. Americans were so hostile toward Iran that they mistrusted Iranian sources. When Iraq had commenced its chemical attacks against the Kurds in early 1987, the two major U.S. papers had carried scattered accounts but had been quick to add that that they were relaying Iranian "allegations" of gassing. Baghdad was said to have "struck back" or "retaliated" against Kurdish rebels.[38] The coverage of Halabja in 1988 was initially similar. The first reports of the attack came from the Islamic Republic News Agency in Teheran, and U.S. news stories again relayed "Iranian accounts" of Iraqi misdeeds. They gave Iraqi officials ample space for denial. Two days after the first attack, a short *Washington*

Post news brief read: "Baghdad has denied reports of fighting. It said it withdrew from Halabja and another town, Khormal, some time ago."[39]

The Kurds, like many recent victims of genocide, fall into a class of what genocide scholar Helen Fein calls "implicated victims." Although most of the victims of genocide are apolitical civilians, the political or military leaders of a national, ethnic, or religious group often make decisions (to claim basic rights, to stage protests, to launch military revolt, or even to plot terrorist attacks) that give perpetrators an excuse for crackdown and bystanders an excuse to look away. Unlike the Jews of 1930s Europe, who posed no military or even political threat to the territorial integrity of Poland or Germany (given their isolation or assimilation in much of Europe), the Kurds wanted out—out of Hussein's smothering grasp and, in their private confessions, out of his country entirely. Kurds were in fact doubly implicated. Not only did some take up arms and rebel against the Iraqi regime, which was supported by the United States, but some also teamed up with Iran, a U.S. foe. As "guerrillas," the Kurds thus appeared to be inviting repression. And as temporary allies of Iran, they were easily lumped with the very forces responsible for hostage-taking and "Great Satan" berating.

The March 1988 Halabja onslaught did more than any prior attack to draw attention to the civilian toll of Hussein's butchery. In part this was because the loss of some 5,000 civilians made it the deadliest of all the Iraqi chemical assaults. But it was also the accessibility of the scene of the crime that caused outsiders to begin to take notice. Halabja was located just fifteen miles inside Iraq, and Western reporters were able to reach the village wasteland from Iran. They could witness with their own eyes the barbarous residue of what otherwise might have been unimaginable. Reporters had the chance to provide rare, firsthand coverage of a fresh, postgenocidal scene.

Iran, which was still struggling to win its war with Iraq, was eager to present evidence of the war crimes of its nemesis. European and American correspondents visited Iranian hospitals, where they themselves interviewed victims with blotched, peeling skin and labored breathing. The Iranians also offered tours of Halabja, where journalists saw corpses that Iranian soldiers and Kurdish survivors had deliberately delayed burying. The *Washington Post* and *Los Angeles Times* ran stories on their front pages on March 24, 1988, and U.S. television networks joined in by prominently covering the story over the next few days. The journalists were aghast, and

Western journalists filming a Kurdish man and his infant son killed in
the March 1988 Iraqi chemical attack on Halabja.

the dispatches reflected it. Patrick Tyler's *Washington Post* story described
"the faces of the noncombatant dead: four small girls in traditional dress
lying like discarded dolls by a trickling stream below the small hamlet of
Anap; two women cuddling in death by a flower garden; an old man in a
turban clutching a baby on a door-step."[40] For the first time, Kurdish faces
were on display. They were no longer abstract casualty figures or mere
"rebels."

U.S. officials insisted that they could not be sure the Iraqis were responsible for the poisonous gas attacks. Western journalists, who had little experience with Iraq and none with the Kurds, hedged. The disclaimers
resurfaced. "More than 100 bodies of women, children and elderly men
still lay in the streets, alleys and courtyards of this now-empty city," Tyler
wrote, "victims of *what Iran claims* is the worst chemical warfare attack on
civilians in its 7½-year-old war with Iraq."[41] The *New York Times* March 24
story buried on page A11 was titled, "Iran Charges Iraq with Gas Attack."
Newsweek wrote: "Last week the Iranians had a grisly opportunity *to make
their case* when they allowed a few Western reporters to tour Halabja, a city
in eastern Iraq recently occupied by Iranian forces after a brief but bloody

siege. *According to Iran,* the Iraqis bombarded the city with chemical weapons after their defeat. *The Iranians said* the attack killed more than 4,000 civilians."[42] This was not fact; this was argument, and Iranian argument at that. The victims themselves could tell no tales. The journalists were privy to the aftermath of a monstrous crime, but they had not witnessed that crime and refrained from pointing fingers. Thus, the requisite caveats again blunted the power of the revelations.

The Iraqis further muddied the waters by leading their own tours of the region. The regime denied the atrocities and reminded outsiders that bad things happen during war. Around the time of Halabja, Iraq's ambassador to France told a news conference: "In a war, no one is there to tell you not to hit below the belt. War is dirty."[43] Yet "war" also implies two or more sets of combatants, and Hussein's chemical weapons attacks were carried out mainly against Kurdish civilians. But Iraq had its cover: Kurdish rebels had fought alongside Iranians, Iraq was at war with Iran, and the war, everyone knew, was brutal. The fog of war again obscured an act of genocide.

The U.S. official position reflected that of its allies in Europe. But whereas they were almost completely mute about Halabja, the State Department issued a statement that confined its critique to the weapons used. "Everyone in the administration saw the same reports you saw last night," White House spokesman Marlin Fitzwater told reporters. "They were horrible, outrageous, disgusting and should serve as a reminder to all countries of why chemical warfare should be banned."[44]

The United States issued no threats or demands. American outrage was rooted in Hussein's use of deadly chemicals and brazen flouting of the 1925 Geneva Protocol Against Chemical Warfare. The *New York Times* editorial page condemned the Iraqi gas attack and called upon Washington to suspend support to Baghdad if chemical attacks did not stop. On Capitol Hill Senator George Mitchell (D.–Maine) introduced a forceful Senate resolution decrying Iraqi chemical weapons use. Jim Hoagland of the *Washington Post* condemned Iraq for calling out the "Orkin Squadron" against civilians. Hoagland, who happened to have been with Mullah Mustafa Barzani in the mountains of Kurdistan in March 1975 when the United States abandoned him, now urged America to use all the influence it had been storing up with Hussein to deter further attacks.[45]

Human rights groups were more numerous, more respected, and better financed than they had been during Cambodia's horrors. Helsinki Watch had been established in 1978, and it added Americas Watch in 1981 and

Asia Watch in 1985. But it did not have the resources to set up Middle East Watch until 1990. As a result, the organization refrained from public comment on the gassing of Kurds. "We didn't have the expertise," explains Ken Roth, who today directs an organization of more than 200 with an annual budget of nearly $20 million but who was then deputy director of a team of no more than two dozen people. "None of us had been to the region, and we felt we could not get in the business of saying things that we could not follow through on. We would only have raised expectations that there was no way we could meet." Amnesty International had re-searchers in London who had established contacts with Iraqi Kurds who confirmed the horror of the press reports, but Amnesty staff were unable to enter Iraq. Shorsh Resool, a thirty-year-old Kurdish engineer and Anfal survivor, had never been abroad but wondered why news of the slaughter was never reported on the BBC's Arabic service. He was told that people in the West did not believe the Kurdish claims that 100,000 people had disappeared. The figure sounded abstract and random. Resool resolved to make it concrete. Between October 1988 and October 1999, he walked through northern Iraq, dodging Iraqi troop patrols and systematically interviewing tens of thousands of Anfal survivors. He assembled a list of names of 16,482 Kurds who had gone missing. When he extrapolated his statistical survey, he concluded that between 70,000 and 100,000 Kurds had in fact been murdered. But when he presented this evidence to the Amnesty researcher in London, she asked, "Do you really expect people to believe that that many Kurds could disappear in a year without anybody knowing about it?"

Amnesty did circulate photographs of the victims as well as the names of those it could confirm had disappeared. But as Curt Goering, Amnesty-USA deputy director, says, "The problem then, as now, was getting our grassroots base to have any actual influence in Washington."

U.S. officials claimed that the proof of Iraqi responsibility was inconclu-sive and blamed "both sides."[46] U.S. officials cited "indications" that Iran had also used chemical artillery shells against Iraq, although they had to concede that the evidence was unconvincing. State Department spokesman Charles Redman issued a forward-looking, even-handed proclamation. He said, "We call upon Iran and Iraq to desist immediately from any further use of chemical weapons, which are an offense to civilization and humanity."[47] Nearly three weeks after the Halabja attack, the *Washington Post* ran a front-page story citing Defense Department claims that "it wasn't a one-way show."[48] At the UN Security Council, the United States blocked an Iranian attempt to raise the question of responsibility for the Halabja attack.[49]

Whatever the surface confusion, Kurdish refugees were adamant about what they witnessed and experienced. David Korn, a State Department Middle East specialist who later interviewed dozens of Kurdish survivors, recalls, "The facts were available, but you don't get the full facts unless you want the full facts." The facts of the larger campaign of destruction were undeniable. A Defense Intelligence Agency cable, dated April 19, 1988, reported that "an estimated 1.5 million Kurdish nationals have been reset-tled in camps"; that "approximately 700–1000 villages and small residential areas were targeted for resettlement"; that "an unknown but reportedly large number of Kurds have been placed in 'concentration' camps located near the Jordanian and Saudi Arabian borders."[50] But these horrors cap-tured no headlines. Thus, U.S. officials never hurried to gather details on the conditions in the camps or the welfare of the men they knew had been taken away. The story of Halabja died down as quickly as it had popped up, and the State Department maintained full support for Iraq.

Mass Executions

Iraqi gas attacks received the public attention, but most Kurds who died in the Anfal were killed in mass executions. U.S. officials knew throughout the 1987–1988 offensive that Iraqi men who were captured were led away and imprisoned. It is unclear when these officials learned of the ritualized mass killing. Senior Reagan administration officials had made it plain that the fate of the Kurds was not their concern, so it would not be surprising if U.S. intelligence officers did not attempt to track the prisoners' condition at the time the massacres were happening. Several Kurds who survived Iraqi firing squads later came forward to describe the horror that befell those who ended up in al-Majid's custody.

Some Kurds who were rounded up in the prohibited zones during the Anfal campaign were dumped at the sprawling Topzawa detention center near the oil-rich town of Kirkuk. Survivors said that some 5,000 Kurds occupied Topzawa at one time, but the turnover was rapid, as busloads of men were removed and arrived daily. Through the barred windows, women and children watched the men in the courtyard outside being handcuffed and beaten savagely. Usually after no more than a day or two, the guards read off a list of names, and the men were packed, stripped to their shorts, bound together, and forced into windowless green-and-white vehicles, which reminded many of ambulances. The elderly (those between fifty and ninety) were driven twelve to fifteen hours to the Pit of Salman, or Nugra Salman, an abandoned, lice-infested fortified prison, where an average of four or five men died each day from starvation, disease, and physical abuse.[51] The men of fighting age met fates even more sinister.

In April 1988 Ozer, an unmarried, twenty-five-year-old construction worker, had ended up in Topzawa after Iraqi shelling and bulldozers forced him from his home for a second time. At about 8:00 one morning, he and several hundred others were dragged onto sealed vehicles that were thick with old urine and human feces and steamy hot. After a full day on the road, Ozer's nine-vehicle convoy made its way onto a dirt path, ahead of which he spotted only desert and darkness. Ozer and the other men knew the end was near and began to pray, to weep, and in keeping with the Islamic tradition, to ask one another for forgiveness.[52] The prisoners could hear the steady melody of nearby gunfire, the sounds of screams, followed by the groan of bulldozer engines. The driver of Ozer's bus turned on his highbeams so the Iraqi police would have an easier time killing the men in the bus ahead. Ozer and his fellow prisoners watched as Kurdish men were dragged in front of the light, shot by a uniformed firing squad, and thrown into a freshly dug pit.

Confronted with the visual reality of their destiny and unable to take solace in wishful thinking, Ozer's busload did something quite unusual: They attempted forcibly to resist their execution, injuring one of the guards in a scuffle. But the prisoners were outnumbered, and the guards outside simply emptied their guns, again and again, into the bus. Ozer was grazed by a flying piece of shrapnel but lay coiled on the bus floor as dead bodies piled up around him and as he listened to the steady patter of blood dripping from the porous vehicle. Ozer eventually stole away into the safety of the dark desert night. Unable to see clearly, he stumbled into a trench with some 400 bleeding bodies. But he crawled out and found his way to the Kurdish quarter of Kirkuk.

The Iraqis tended to vary their methods. As Middle East Watch later found:

> Some groups of prisoners were lined up, shot from the front and
> dragged into pre-dug mass graves; others were shoved roughly into

trenches and machine-gunned where they stood; others were made to lie down in pairs, sardine-style, next to mounds of fresh corpses, before being killed; others were tied together, made to stand on the lip of the pit, and shot in the back so that they would fall forward into it—a method that was presumably more efficient from the point of view of the killers. Bulldozers then pushed earth or sand loosely over the heaps of corpses.[53]

In some areas women and children who had been removed from their homes also became targets. Taimour Abdullah Ahmad, a twelve-year-old, became the Kurds' most famous survivor. In April 1988 he lived with his parents; eleven-year-old sister, Gaylas; ten-year-old sister, Leyla; and nine-year-old sister, Serwa. Iraqi troops swept through their town and rounded up his family and brought them to Topzawa, where Taimour thought himself fortunate not to be housed with the men. By peering through a small hole in the compound wall, he saw his father being stripped down to his underclothes, manacled to his nearest neighbor, and dragged out of the compound with the other men. Other women and families were competing for access to the same hole, and Taimour remembered wives, mothers, and daughters screaming, shouting, beating themselves, and pulling at their hair in agony.[54]

Taimour remained in the compound with his mother and sisters for a month, living off a piece of bread per day, until one morning in late May the guards summoned them, checking their names off a list and hustling them onto the green-and-white buses. Taimour drove with some fifty or sixty women and children who were seated the length of the bus. They drove in sweltering silence—three children died of dehydration on the way—until nightfall. When the guards threw open the rear doors, Taimour, who had removed his blindfold saw that each of the thirty or so vehicles in his convoy had been positioned next to its own desert burial pit, each of which was about fifteen feet square and a yard deep. A mound of mud was stacked precipitously on the far side of each pit. Before Taimour had time to process the grim scene, the guards pushed him and the others into the pits, separating him from his mother and sisters.[55]

When Taimour was hit by a bullet in the left shoulder, he began to stagger toward the man who shot him, reaching out with his hands. He remembered the look in the soldier's eyes. "He was about to cry," Taimour said three years later, mechanically reciting a narrative he had learned to tell and retell, "but the other one shouted at him and told him to throw me back in the pit. He was obliged to throw me back."[56] The officer ordered the soldier to fire again, which he did, hitting Taimour for a second time, this time on the right side of his back, just above the waist. The boy lay still. When the guards had walked away, he felt a young girl move next to him. "Let's run," he whispered, but she declined, too frightened of the soldiers.

Taimour emerged from the pit and stole one last look behind him, spotting his mother, three sisters, and three aunts piled like cordwood. He inched his way away from the grave, avoiding the sweeping headlights of the guards' land-cruisers. With blood pouring from his wounds, he passed out behind one of the dirt mounds. When he regained consciousness, the pits had been filled and smoothed flat. He escaped and was sheltered by an Arab family for two years. Only with the Kurdish uprising in 1991 was he repatriated to the north. There he learned he had lost twenty-eight relatives in the Anfal.[57]

A Pair of Iraqi Victories

U.S. and European policymakers had long refused to meet officially with Iraqi Kurdish leaders for fear of irritating Saddam Hussein. But the high-profile gassing of Halabja and the disappearance and suspected massacres of tens of thousands of unarmed Kurds caused Jalal Talabani, the leader of one of the Iraqi Kurds' two main political parties, to believe he might at last gain an audience with Western officialdom. In June 1988 Talabani, a fifty-four-year-old former journalist and lawyer, decided to test his luck and left the Middle East for the first time in eight years. He traveled to London where, along with Latif Rashid, his party's representative there, he pored over a copy of the genocide convention. "We knew 'genocide' was a very sensitive term, and we wanted to be very careful that we were using it correctly," Rashid remembers. After reviewing the text, debating its terms, and comparing it to the facts of the Anfal, Talabani announced publicly that Iraq was "waging a genocide campaign against our people through the daily use of poison gas."[58]

A few weeks later, Talabani visited Washington. He claimed that Iraq had destroyed more than 1,000 villages in the previous year alone and offered gruesome accounts of gassing. Wearing a pinstriped suit and a paisley tie,

Talabani did not conform to the image of the pantalooned, bullet-laden Kurdish rebel. More politically savvy than expected, Talabani deftly made the case that Hussein's genocide was downright historic. "It's the first time in history a government has used chemical weapons against its own citizens who are not at the battlefront," he told Elaine Sciolino of the *New York Times*. He also defended the alliance that his forces had made with Iran on the grounds that "when you are facing a war of genocide, it is your duty to fight back in any way you can."[59]

Larry Pope, the State Department's Iran-Iraq office director, favored the Reagan administration's chosen policy of engagement with Iraq. But he was sufficiently revolted by the images out of Halabja that he felt the United States should register its disapproval by agreeing to meet Talabani at the State Department. This meant ignoring the long-standing "self-denying ordinance" that required all contact with the Kurds to occur off U.S. government property. Talabani was delighted. He and Pope met for an hour in the State Department's fortress at Foggy Bottom. The first burst of outrage came not from the Iraqis but from Turkish president Kenan Evren, who happened to be in Washington to meet with Secretary of State Shultz. Evren, who feared that any encouragement given Iraqi Kurds would embolden Turkey's 10 million Kurds, went ballistic. Shultz knew nothing of the Talabani-Pope meeting and demanded to know, "Who the hell had this bright idea?" The Iraqis, predictably, were also irate. Iraqi foreign minister Tariq Aziz canceled his long-planned meeting with Shultz, accusing the U.S. government of interfering in Iraqi internal affairs. Iraq was most sensitive to U.S. statements and maneuvers. The State Department scrambled to appease Iraq by declaring publicly: "The United States does not interfere in the internal affairs" of those countries with a Kurdish minority.[60] Pope was reprimanded, and the department reiterated its policy of meeting with the Kurdish leadership only off-site. "At first, we were so popular. Everyone was so gracious and interested," remembers Rashid, the Talabani aide. "Then suddenly, overnight, the doors closed and we were shut out." In the end Pope believes his gesture—tame as it was—backfired. "Rather than send a message of disapproval to Iraq, we sent the message that our relations with Iraq and Turkey were more important than anything Hussein did internally," he recalls.

Talabani had quickly learned the value the United States placed on its relationship with Iraq. Still, the trip paid some dividends. He got to know several members of Congress and became acquainted for the first time with Galbraith. He also helped nudge along Senator Mitchell's resolution condemning Iraqi chemical weapons use, which passed unanimously (91–0) on June 24, 1988.[61] But because no sticks were attached to the resolution and because Hussein could be confident the White House was still on his side, he was not deterred. In late June and July the Iraqis staged chemical weapons attacks throughout Kurdish territory.

The United States had concentrated its diplomatic efforts in 1987–1988 on isolating and securing an arms embargo against Iran. It had also supplied concrete assistance to Iraq. Although it did not sell Baghdad weapons, the United States provided intelligence gathered from AWACS early-warning aircraft, which included damage estimates on Iraqi strikes and reports of Iranian troop movements.[62] Partly as a result of U.S. support, Iraq turned the tide in its war with Iran. Iran may have blundered by highlighting the gruesome effects of Iraqi chemical weapons. Instead of mobilizing public opinion, the testimony of survivors convinced potential volunteers to steer clear of the recruiting offices. Khomeini agreed to a cease-fire in July 1988. Teheran radio broadcast a statement in his name that hinted at the role of the poisonous chemicals. "Taking this decision was more deadly than taking poison," the ayatollah said. "I have sold my honor. I have swallowed the poison of defeat."[63] More than 1 million soldiers and civilians on both sides had died in the war.[64] Not an inch of land had changed hands.

On August 20, 1988, Iran and Iraq signed an armistice ending their bloody struggle. Despite the vivid images from Halabja and the brief flurry of Western interest in the Kurds, their suffering had faded from public view. Al-Majid continued his ruthless drive to empty rural Kurdistan throughout the summer, dragging away any Kurd who dared remain in the prohibited areas. On August 25 Iraq launched a new attack on Kurdish villages, using aircraft, fixed-wing helicopters, tanks, and tens of thousands of Iraqi troops. It was the "final" offensive in al-Majid's six-month Anfal campaign.

After ignoring Iraqi attacks for so long, senior U.S. officials had to take notice of this one. Perched at the U.S. embassy in Baghdad, Rankin remembers his reaction to the news:

> We at the embassy thought that once the Iran-Iraq war ended, Hussein would bring his country and his people, who had so much potential and who had suffered for so long, out of oblivion. We told ourselves that if he no longer had to fight Iran, he could become the man we wished he could be. But when he signed the cease-fire with

Iran and *then* gassed the Kurds, he lost his cover. It was clear he could never be that man. He was a monster. These attacks had nothing to do with his Iranian security threat. They had to do with killing Kurds.

The final offensive against the Kurds was widely known. Two days after it began, the *New York Times* reported that in late July Iraq had dispatched at least 20,000 elite forces to the north and quoted one regional expert as saying, "We get the impression that the Iraqis wanted to finish the whole business." A long front-page story on September 1, 1988, described the deployment of more than 60,000 troops and led with the sentence, "Iraq has begun a major offensive [meant to] crush the 40-year-long insurgency once and for all."[65] The media gave this offensive more intensive coverage than previous Iraqi assaults because it quickly sent 65,000 Kurdish victims and survivors flooding into Turkey. The Turkish government was none-too-pleased by the destabilizing Kurdish influx, but it set up encampments along its border and refused to grant Iraq the reciprocal right of "hot pursuit" that Turkish forces had invoked so often to track down armed Turkish Kurds in northern Iraq. The Kurdish refugees did what Cambodians had done: They poured out their stories to journalists, who had full and free access to southern Turkey. These stories got Galbraith's attention immediately and that of the U.S. secretary of state eventually.

"Genocide"

Galbraith had kept his eye out for bad news from northern Iraq since March, when he had learned of the Halabja attack. There was no question that Hussein's recent deeds suggested a ruthlessness that boded extremely ill for the Kurdish people: the elimination of the Kurdish villages, the widespread disappearances (and probable execution) of Kurdish men, and Hussein's repeated, brazen use of chemical weapons. Galbraith had begun to wonder whether Hussein was committing genocide.

Galbraith saw a certain internal logic in Hussein's piecemeal campaign. He believed the Iraqi dictator might be husbanding the full might of his armed forces, knowing that a more gradual campaign against the Kurds would enable him to keep his soldiers committed, forestall a more spirited international reaction, and enable the local economy (fueled largely by Kurds) to remain afloat.

On Galbraith's trip to Iraq in 1987, he had seen dozens of villages and small cities demolished far from the sensitive border with Iran. He also knew that al-Majid's dragnet was sweeping up women and children as well. All Kurds in rural Kurdistan were vulnerable, regardless of their political sympathies. Loyalty to the Baghdad regime was no protection, as the Kurdish *jash,* those who worked for the Iraqi government, discovered. At a meeting in 1987, al-Majid told one *jash,* "I cannot let your village stay. . . . I will attack it with chemical weapons. Then you and your family will die."[66]

But it was with Hussein's August offensive, launched *after* the end of his war with Iran, that Galbraith's worst suspicions were confirmed. On August 28, 1988, tucked away in Vermont for a relaxing Labor Day weekend, Galbraith came across a short *New York Times* report buried back on page A15. The piece, "More Chemical Attacks Reported," described Iraqi Kurds crossing into Turkey and reporting gas attacks.[67] He froze, as images of the rubbled remains of Kurdish life flashed into his mind. He read the same sixty-three words over and over again, draining the news item for any details that might be lurking between the lines.

Galbraith was sure that the reports of chemical attacks were true. Although he could not gauge precisely the breadth of the brutal campaign of gassing, execution, and depopulation under way, Galbraith believed Hussein's regime had set out to destroy Iraqi Kurds. It was genocide.

> It was just one of those moments of recognition. I just knew it was true. . . . I knew then that we could never be fully certain that Hussein wanted to destroy the Kurds, but we would also never be more certain.

Unlike the Cambodia watchers of the late 1970s or most of Washington's Iraq watchers at the time, Galbraith knew that the genocide convention did not require an intent to exterminate every last Iraqi Kurd. Working for Senator Pell, one of Proxmire's co-conspirators in pushing for U.S. ratification of the convention, Galbraith had come to appreciate some of the nuances inherent in the law's notion of "destruction." He had surveyed Lemkin's writings and the drafting history of the genocide convention, and he knew that a perpetrator did not have to be executing attacks as holistic in scope as the Holocaust to qualify as genocide. The category of genocide was valuable because it described an ongoing or outstanding intent, whereas the "Holocaust" described a singulary monstrous event that had already happened. "These things accelerate," Galbraith says. "Hitler, when he took power in 1933, did not have a plan to exterminate all the Jews in Europe. Evil begets evil." Hussein and Hitler were both fascist ideologues intent on destroying groups they found distasteful or, for their own reasons, threatening. Hussein's aims were clearly more limited than Hitler's. It was only Kurds in the "prohibited areas" who had thus far been marked for destruction. But Galbraith believed the million or more Kurds living in Baghdad would eventually be targeted as well: "While at that time the extermination campaign was focused on Kurds in rural areas and small towns, I thought that the logic of his program could culminate in the elimination of the entire Kurdish population of Iraq."

Galbraith raced back to Washington to begin making his case on Capitol Hill. He knew a great deal about Lemkin's law, but he knew almost nothing about his lobbying. Yet within days Galbraith had drafted a new law and begun pursuing its passage with all the blunt zeal of his Polish predecessor.

Response

Sanctioning Saddam

When word of the August offensive broke, the Reagan administration had a number of options available. It could have condemned the new wave of gas attacks. It could have demanded that its ally stop destroying rural Kurdish life. It could have urged that the men and women taken away in the previous offensives be released. And it could have threatened to suspend some of the economic perks it had been extending to Baghdad for the past five years.

Because Congress controlled the purse strings, Galbraith understood that legislators could have considerable influence on how the United States used its economic leverage abroad. Senate staffers were not permitted to speak on the record to the press. Nor could they publish articles under their own names. Yet with the backing of a powerful senator, they could do something far more influential: They could draft U.S. law. Most U.S. laws are proposed by the executive branch. Some are drafted by lobbyists and adopted by the Senate. And many more are drafted by House and Senate staff, especially the committee staff. Having worked for Pell on the Senate Foreign Relations Committee for more than a decade, Galbraith knew that the senator, the son of the Roosevelt administration's representative to the Allied War Crimes Commission, would want to use U.S. law to take a stand. He was right.

After its month-long August recess, the Senate returned for its last weeks of business of the year on September 7, 1988. At the urging of his boss, Galbraith dashed off the draft law in an hour, writing in English that all could understand (a gift he attributed to avoiding law school). "This was not a deeply reflective process," Galbraith remembers. "I included every sanction that I could think of"; indeed, his bill contained harsher sanctions than those imposed against apartheid South Africa. The sanctions package barred Iraqi oil imports, worth $500 million per year; instructed U.S. officials to vote against Iraqi loans at the IMF and World Bank; eliminated $500 million in annual CCC credit guarantees to Iraq for the purchase of U.S. agricultural foodstuffs; terminated $200 million in annual export-import credits for manufactured goods; and prohibited exports to Iraq of any item that required an export license (e.g., sensitive technology or any item with possible military use).

One of the boldest features of the bill was also one of its most novel. Instead of requiring the president to prove that genocide was being committed, which is always hard to do while atrocities are still under way and which an administration aligned with Saddam Hussein had no incentive to demonstrate, Pell's legislation reversed the burden: President Reagan was required to certify that Iraq was *not* using chemical weapons against the Kurds and that it was *not* committing genocide.[68] If Reagan wished to avoid sanctions, he would have to defend Iraqi conduct affirmatively.

Senator Pell asked the ranking member of the Senate Foreign Relations Committee, Jesse Helms, to cosponsor the bill, which he did. Helms had battled Pell and Proxmire over the genocide convention, but he often took a strong stand against flagrantly abusive regimes. In this instance he and his wife had been moved by an encounter with three Kurds who were on hunger strikes to protest the Iraqi atrocities, whom they met through their church, the First Baptist in Alexandria, Virginia.[69] Four other senators—Proxmire, Al Gore (D.–Tenn.), Wendell Ford (D.–Ky.), and Senate majority leader Robert Byrd (D.–W.Va.)—heard of the draft law and joined in introducing it. Pell and Helms were able to "hotline" the measure, bypassing the Foreign Relations Committee, which had already held its last business meeting of the year. This gave staff members and senators virtually no time to review the bill. Galbraith had named the law the "Prevention of Genocide Act," a title that he thought would resonate. "I wanted a title that would call attention to the crimes taking place and rally support for the legislation," Galbraith recalls. He also wanted to make it less likely that senators would in fact read the bill. If he had called the measure the "Iraqi Sanctions Act," he knew U.S. business lobbies would read and scuttle it. Additionally, because of the "moral high-tone" of the label, senators might assume that this bill, like others in such a tenor, was merely hortatory.

Galbraith had something unseemly working in his favor. Since April 1987 Hussein had been purging and killing Kurds with a variety of weapons. But this most recent offensive involved chemical weapons, which killed in a more grisly way than machine guns and captured the imagination of U.S. lawmakers. Ensconced in a country attacked only once in the twentieth century, most Americans did not feel vulnerable when foreign slaughter was discussed. Before September 11, 2001, most Americans believed that the large-scale murder of civilians could only occur miles from home. But chemical weapons were different. They had crept into American consciousness because they did not respect national rankings and were unimpressed by geographic isolation. No matter how thick U.S. defenses, the gasses could penetrate. The horrors of gassing entered the Western imagination back in April 1915, when British soldiers were subjected to what Churchill called the "hellish poison" of German mustard gas. At the Battle of Ypres in Belgium, these gases wounded 10,000, killed some 5,000, and ushered in a tit-for-tat series of chemical attacks that left more than 100,000 dead. The gasses blistered the skin and singed the lungs. The deaths were slow; the last days of life ghastly. British poet Wilfred Owen, who was himself exposed to the chemicals, lived the horror of the trenches and brought it vividly home to postwar Britain with his wrenching "Dulce et Decorum Est." The poem describes the "helpless sight" of stricken soldiers, "guttering, choking, drowning," and "gargling from froth-corrupted lungs." Decades later, Owen's words remained artifacts of a substance to be abhorred and a weapon to be avoided. Gassing could happen to us because it *had* happened and because victims of gassing attacks, scientists, and artists have detailed the vomiting, blistering, choking, singeing, and peeling associated with chemical weapons.

U.S. senators knew that chemical weapons had become all too easy to acquire in the 1980s. Nuclear weapons required either plutonium or highly enriched uranium, which had few suppliers, and sophisticated chemical and engineering processes and equipment were needed to convert the fissionable material. Chemical weapons, by contrast, were cheap and said to take a garage and a little high school chemistry to make. They were the poor man's nuke. The news media were filled with accounts of rogue states and terrorist groups that had stockpiled deadly chemicals.

Galbraith recognized that generic fears about chemical weapons use and proliferation could be a kind of Trojan horse by which he could muster congressional support for punishing Iraq for its broader campaign of destruction aimed at the Kurds. Like Lemkin and Proxmire, he made a prudential, interest-based case for the Pell-Helms bill, emphasizing the gassing more than Hussein's other means of killing. "Right now the Kurds are paying the price for past global indifference to Iraqi chemical weapons use," he wrote. "The failure to act now could ultimately leave every nation in peril."[70] In private Galbraith worried that if a pro-sanctions Senate coalition were held together only because of Hussein's use of poisons, the Iraqi dictator might simply revise his tactics and massacre civilians in other ways. "Most of those senators were concerned not with the Kurds but with the instrument of death, the chemical weapons," Galbraith remembers. "I wasn't concerned with the use of chemical weapons as such but with their use as a way of destroying the Kurdish people. These weapons were not any more evil than guns." Nevertheless, he needed all the help he could get on the sanctions legislation, and he took it.

One week after the Kurdish refugees had begun pouring into Turkey, the sanctions bill, which kept the name "Prevention of Genocide Act," was introduced on the Senate floor. It passed the Senate the next day on a unanimous voice vote. Because senators did not hold a roll-call vote, they were not on the written record as having supported the bill, which would subsequently enable them to squirm more easily out of their commitments. On September 9, 1988, though, Galbraith noticed only the remarkable tally. It looked to him and most observers as if, to paraphrase Holocaust survivor Primo Levi, it was the good fortune of Iraqi Kurds to be attacked with chemical weapons. The bill needed only to clear the House before it became law.

A "Reorganization of the Urban Situation"

If Galbraith was relieved by the vote, the Reagan administration was alarmed. U.S. officials knew of Saddam Hussein's general designs. The State Department's cable traffic from the first week of September continued to report on Iraq's campaign of destruction against the Kurds. On September 2, 1988, a full week ahead of the passage of the Prevention of Genocide Act in the Senate, Morton Abramowitz, the former U.S. ambassador to Thailand who was then assistant secretary of state for intelligence and research, sent a top-secret memo to the secretary of state entitled, "Swan Song for Iraq's Kurds?" Abramowitz cited evidence that Iraq had used chemical weapons against the Kurds on August 25, writing, "Now, with cease-fire [with Iran], government forces appear ready to settle Kurdish dissidents once and for all. . . . Baghdad is likely to feel little restraint in using chemical weapons against the rebels and against villages that continue to support them." Abramowitz acknowledged that "the bulk" of Kurdish villages were vulnerable to attack.[71] Hussein's forces would consider Kurdish civilians and soldiers alike fair game.

But this made little difference in a State Department and White House determined to avoid criticizing Iraq. A September 3 cable from the State Department to the U.S. embassy in Baghdad urged U.S. officials to stress to Hussein's regime that the United States understood the Kurds had aligned with Iran and that the problem was a "historical one." U.S. diplomats were told to explain that they had "reserve[d] comment" until they had been able to take Baghdad's view "fully into account."[72] Still, the conduct of Iraq's campaign was causing international outcry that was becoming embarrassing for the United States. In consultation with Iraqi foreign ministry undersecretary Nizar Hamdoon the following day, Ambassador April Glaspie warned that Iraq had "a major public relation problem." She noted that the lead story on the BBC that morning had been the gas attacks and said, "If chemical warfare is not being used and if Kurds are not herded into WWII concentration camps," then Iraq should permit independent observers access to Kurdish territory. Hamdoon denied chemical weapons use but said the access she requested was "impossible" just then. Besides, the fighting would be over "in a few days." The embassy "comment" on the meeting was that "it has been clear for many days that Saddam has taken the decision to do whatever the army believes necessary to fully pacify the north."[73]

In public, State Department officials betrayed little of this behind-the-scenes grasp of Iraq's agenda. Picking up on wire reports of gas attacks that started running August 10, journalists had begun pressing State Department spokespersons for comment on the attacks on August 25. Day after day spokesperson Phyllis Oakley said she had "nothing" to substantiate the reports. Her colleague Charles Redman said on September 6 that he could not confirm the news stories. Sensing the reporters' exasperation, Redman did add a hypothetical condemnation. "If they were true, of course *we would strongly condemn* the use of chemical weapons, as we have in the past," he said. "The use of chemical weapons is deplorable. It's barbaric."[74]

U.S. officials reluctant to criticize Iraq again took refuge in the absence of perfect information. They noted that the reports from the Turkish border were not unanimous. Bernard Benedetti, a doctor with Médecins du Monde, had found no chemical weapons cases. "That's a false problem," he told the *Washington Post,* referring to chemical weapons. "The refugees here are suffering from diarrhea and skin rash which are spreading because of overcrowding and unsanitary conditions."[75] Turkey likewise insisted that forty doctors and 205 other health personnel had found no proof of the atrocities. One Turkish doctor told the *New York Times* that the blisters on the face of a three-year-old Kurdish boy came from "malnutrition" and "poor cleanliness."[76] But neither source was reliable. Physicians with the international aid agencies had no expertise on diagnosing the side effects of exposure to chemical weapons, and Turkey got most of its oil from Iraq and conducted $2.4 billion in annual trade with its neighbor.[77] It also frequently partnered with Iraq to suppress Kurdish rebels.

Shaken refugees in Turkey found their claims rudely challenged. Clyde Haberman of the *New York Times* described a "reluctant subject," thirteen-year-old Bashir Semsettin, who after suffering a gas attack and landing in Turkey found "his thin body pulled and prodded like an exhibit . . . for the benefit of curious visitors." Bashir's chest and upper back were scarred in a "marbled pattern" of burns, with streaks of dark brown juxtaposed beside large patches of pink. While he was pent up in a Turkish medical tent, a Turkish MP arrived with an entourage of assistants and began poking at Bashir's wounds.

"What are these?" the lawmaker asked.
"Burns," replied the Turkish government physician.

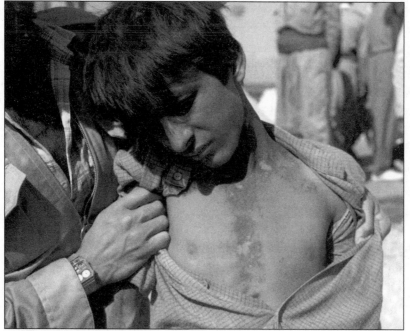

Peter Galbraith

Bashir Semsettin, Kurdish survivor of an Iraqi chemical attack.

"What sort of burns?" the MP pressed.

"Who can say?" the physician answered. "I know these are first-degree burns from a heat source other than flames," he said. "If they were flames, his hair and eyebrows would also be burned. But I can't say if they're from chemicals. They can be from anything."[78]

The Reagan administration had been conciliatory toward Iraq for years, always preferring double condemnations of Iraq and Iran and requests for additional fact finding. Yet at the time of the massive Kurdish flight in September, the State Department consensus at last began to crack. The State Department's Bureau for Near Eastern Affairs (NEA), run by Richard Murphy, and the Bureau for Intelligence and Research (INR), run by Abramowitz, took different positions. Within several days of the launching of the final Anfal, INR intercepted Iraqi military communications in which the Iraqis themselves confirmed that they were using chemical weapons against the Kurds. A pair of U.S. embassy officials also spent two days conducting interviews with refugees from twenty-eight villages at the Turkish border. The refugees and the intercepts together left little doubt. But Murphy's bureau, which managed the U.S. political relationship with

Iraq, remained unconvinced. Murphy may have mistakenly trusted Iraqi denials of responsibility and thus discounted the overwhelming evidence of Iraqi poison attacks. Or he may have willfully cast doubt on the information because he believed the U.S.-Iraq relationship would be harmed if the United States condemned the gassing. "I certainly don't recall deliberate slanting," Murphy says today. "I think that we did what we are supposed to do with intelligence: We challenged it. We said, 'Where did you get it?'; 'Who were your sources?'; 'How do you know you can trust those sources?'" Whatever the bureau's motives, NEA officials contested INR's findings long after the intelligence officers found the evidence of Iraqi responsibility overwhelming.

After nearly two weeks of heated internal debate, the INR view finally prevailed. It had been nearly eighteen months since al-Majid had begun his vicious counter-insurgency campaign. The United States had long known about the destruction of Kurdish villages and disappearances of Kurdish men. But only after the high-profile refugee flight and the deluge of press inquiries did Secretary of State Shultz decide to speak out. "As a result of our evaluation of the situation," spokesman Redman declared authoritatively on September 8, 1988, "the United States government is convinced that Iraq has used chemical weapons in its military campaign against Kurdish guerrillas."[79] When he was challenged to account for why the United States had been so reticent about responding to chemical weapons attacks in the past, Redman noted, "All of these things have a way of evolving. And it's simply a matter of the course of events."[80]

On the same day Secretary Shultz confirmed Iraqi chemical use, he raised the matter with Saddoun Hammadi, Iraqi minister of state for foreign affairs, delivering what Murphy and others present described as a fifty-minute harangue. Hammadi denied the U.S. charge three times during the meeting, calling the allegations "absolutely baseless."[81] But he said Iraq had a responsibility to "preserve itself, not be cut to pieces." The Iraqi perspective, like that of most perpetrators, was grounded in a belief that the collective could be punished for individual acts of rebellion. Baghdad had to "deal with traitors." Shultz suggested they be arrested and tried, not gassed.[82] Britain, which up to this point had been mute, quickly followed the U.S. lead with a similar statement.

Iraqi Foreign Minister Tariq Aziz, too, vehemently denied allegations of wrongdoing. Aziz did not dispute that the Iraqi government was relocating a number of Kurds who lived near the Iranian border. But sounding an awful lot like Talaat Pasha, the Ottoman minister of the interior in 1915, he stressed, "This is not a deportation of people, this is a reorganization of the urban situation."[83]

Iraq's defense minister, General Adnan Khairallah, was more revealing in his statements. Iraq was entitled to defend itself with "whatever means is available." When confronting "one who wants to kill you at the heart of your land," he asked, "will you throw roses on him and flowers?" Combatants and civilians looked alike: "They all wear the Kurdish costume, and so you can't distinguish between one who carries a weapon and one who does not."[84]

The Iraqi regime was watching Washington carefully. Indeed, the September 9 Senate passage of the sanctions bill and the Shultz condemnation gave rise to the largest anti-American demonstration in Baghdad in twenty years. Some 18,000 Iraqis turned out in a rigged "popular" protest. The Iraqi media inflated the figure to 250,000, and said a "large group" of Kurds also attended. Each evening Iraq's state-run television broadcast clips of Vietnamese civilians who had been burned by U.S. napalm bombs, as well as images of Japanese victims of Hiroshima and Nagasaki.[85] Baghdad media derided the sanctions as the handiwork of "Zionists" and other "potentates of imperialism and racism."[86] The Reagan administration saw Iraq's propaganda as a testament to the peril to U.S.-Iraqi relations; Galbraith considered it proof of the potential for American influence.[87]

Iraq had recently spent vast energy and resources fending off criticisms in Geneva, New York, and Washington. In 1985 the Iraqi embassy in Washington had hired a public relations firm, Edward J. Van Kloberg and Associates, to help it renovate its reputation. Ambassador Nizar Hamdoon agreed to pay the firm $1,000 for "every interview with [a] distinguished American newspaper" that could be arranged. The company had organized television interviews and succeeded in placing articles favorable to Iraq in the *Washington Post, New York Times, Washington Times*, and *Wall Street Journal*.[88] Desperate for foreign investment and reconstructive aid, Iraq was promoting the image of a "new Iraq." It cared about the outside world's opinion.

Iraq's ambassador to the United States, Abdul-Amir Ali al-Anbari invited any journalist to northern Iraq "to see for himself the truth." This was a typical delay tactic: Visitors are promised access but then denied it once the act of granting permission has deflated outrage. In some instances, after endless delays, independent observers are allowed to visit the prohibited territory, but then, like Becker in Cambodia, they are trailed at all times by a "security escort" handpicked by the regime. Iraqi officials who offered access to an impartial international inquiry quickly added that such a mission would have to be delayed until "active military operations" in northern Iraq had been concluded.[89] In late September twenty-four Western journalists were let in, but only on a carefully supervised government helicopter tour. The trip proved embarrassing for Baghdad: Iraq airlifted journalists to an outpost on the Iraq-Turkey border to witness the return of 1,000 refugees. But the Kurds failed to show, and the journalists spotted an Iraqi truck whose driver and passengers were hidden behind gas masks.[90]

Unhappy with Shultz's September 8 condemnation, U.S. Middle East specialists tried to "walk the Secretary back" to a more conciliatory position.[91] When Ambassador Glaspie met again September 10 with Hamdoon, she acknowledged that in 1977 in Cairo she herself had seen people with burns and nausea from mere tear gas. In a secret cable back to Washington, the embassy credited Iraq for the "remarkably moderate and mollifying mode of its presentation" and an "atypical willingness to gulp down their pride and give us assurances even after we publicly announced our certainty of their culpability."[92]

In Search of "Proof"

Although Pell's Prevention of Genocide Act had sailed through the Senate, Pell came under immediate pressure to retreat. Those who criticized the bill initially said they were simply uncertain that Iraq was responsible. Galbraith was determined to put this excuse to rest and to expose the real reasons for U.S. opposition. On September 10, 1988, the day after the Senate unanimously cleared the stiff sanctions bill, he boarded a plane for Turkey and traveled to the crowded border with Iraq, where thousands of tents housing refugees had sprouted. He was accompanied by Chris Van Hollen, a younger colleague on the Senate Foreign Relations Committee. The two staffers scurried from camp to camp, interviewing witnesses.

The Americans began tentatively, almost shyly. At each site a flood of arrivals quickly descended upon them, desperate to tell their stories. It is never clear just what refugees expect from their encounters with Western intruders. Some probably believe the foreigners will bring some form of salvation—that they will deliver the chilling accounts to the higher-ups and that justice will thus be dispensed, property retrieved, or, in this case, gassings forcibly suspended. Many traumatized civilians simply want to be heard. The Cambodian refugees who crossed into Thailand and spoke to Charles Twining, the Muslims who would survive the Serb concentration camps of 1992 or the Srebrenica massacre of 1995, all revealed that same intense desire to let people know what had happened to them. Only later, when the great white hopes returned again and again empty-handed, did the patience of these eager refugees wear thin.

Dazed Kurdish men and women clustered around Galbraith and Van Hollen. The refugees pointed with animation to the detailed U.S. government maps of the region and groped for the familiar to tell of their experiences. They compared their sensations to the everyday sights, sounds, and smells that they knew and that they knew the Americans would know. The mustard, cyanide, and nerve gases carried odors so distinct that survivors were desperate to describe them. Abdulressiak Salih described for Galbraith a smell "like garlic and cologne." Kahar Mikhail Mahmood remembered a whiff of "rotten apples." And most earnest but least helpful, Asiye Babir recalled "an unpleasant smell, like burnt nylon. Like burnt ants."[93]

Survivors of Iraqi attacks had hidden in caves or plunged into nearby streams to avoid contamination. Although the frenzy of flight made it impossible for them to compare notes, their responses did not vary much by locale. Each remembered a haunting chain of events: Planes and helicopters overhead. Flares released to gauge wind direction. Bombs dropped from the sky. A popping sound. Yellow or brown fumes and mist. Birds falling and tumbling to the earth. Screams. Burning. Vomiting. Bleeding. Slow death of loved ones expedited only occasionally by a hail of follow-up machine-gun fire. Galbraith and Van Hollen documented chemical weapons attacks on forty-nine Kurdish villages, and they spoke only with Kurds who were lucky enough to have made it to Turkey.

Galbraith knew how skeptically "mere" testimony was received back in Washington. In March he had seen the way public outrage about Halabja had been muted when U.S. officials raised doubts about Iraq's responsibility. In this instance, although Secretary Shultz had recently condemned Iraq, the administration remained loath to punish its ally. Thus they would likely seize upon the inevitable uncertainty surrounding survivor stories.

Galbraith hoped he could bring home physical evidence that would elevate the tales to fact. But it was difficult to find refugees who bore physical symptoms of the gassing. Most Kurds who were able to cross into Turkey bore few traces of the gasses. Some had fled not gassing but rumors of imminent gassing; in the five months since Halabja, the Kurdish Hiroshima had become notorious. Others had managed to avoid the deadly fumes but witnessed the result upon emerging from shelters or returning to their villages. "Most of the Kurds who were exposed to nerve gas died on the spot," Galbraith says, "and many of those who streamed into Turkey wanted to avoid that fate."

Around the same time Galbraith was puzzling over the dearth of physical evidence at the border, Assistant Secretary Abramowitz was explaining the evidentiary paradox to the secretary of state. In a September 17 memo, Abramowitz wrote:

> It is prudent to point out that victims of immediate lethal doses of chemical weapons agents obviously would not have escaped Iraq. . . . There is a good chance that on-site inspection in northern Iraq could provide evidence of mustard agent attacks, but there is little chance of finding physical or medical evidence of attacks with non-persistent nerve agent or non-lethal agents. These agents dissipate rapidly, making it difficult to find residual traces in the soil, on a victim's body, or even on expended munitions. The U.S. Government is convinced that Iraq used chemical agents in the late August offensive against the Kurds, it recognizes it will be difficult in this case to provide physical and medical evidence that will be acceptable in the public arena.[94]

Whereas Abramowitz had Iraqi military intercepts to draw upon, the two Senate staffers knew they would have to confirm and reconfirm accounts from as many disparate voices as possible. After they talked to the men, they attempted to speak alone as well with the women and children, who would have been less likely to have been organized in advance by camp leaders. The faces of the Kurdish refugees only rarely bore signs of emotion. "This was just days after the event. People were numb as they told the stories," Galbraith recalls. "They did not sob or break down." Virtually all had lost loved ones and had no prospect of returning home.

By coincidence, after joining the Senate Foreign Relations Committee, Galbraith had taken his first official trip abroad in March 1980 to the Thai-Cambodian border. There, he had heard refugees describe atrocities carried out by the Khmer Rouge. He had also heard skeptics claim that the refugees were exaggerating. Some foreigners probably brought an innate snobbery about the capacity of uneducated Kurds to truth-tell. "We tell ourselves these are people who are not thoughtful," says Galbraith. "There is a certain racism and classism here that tells us that we should not take seriously the words of peasants or that we should look down on them." But he had seen the doubters proven wrong once outsiders visited Cambodia in the early 1980s. "The real lesson of my experiences in these camps over the years is that refugees don't lie," Galbraith reflects. "This is not to say that we should accept one account from one refugee, but in the case of the Cambodians, the Kurds, and later the Bosnians, there were thousands and thousands of witnesses to the crimes. We must learn to believe them."

Amnesty International had learned its lesson in Cambodia as well. Whatever its internal skepticism about Kurdish claims, instead of publicly casting doubt on refugee reports, the organization did something no non-governmental group had ever done: It appealed directly to the UN Security Council to act immediately to stop the slaughter of Kurdish civilians. It made what was then a radical, new argument: When a state committed mas-sacres inside its borders, the killings constituted "a threat to international peace and security" and thus, according to the UN charter, became the responsibility of the Security Council. The organization did not invoke the genocide convention. It argued only what it could prove definitively. Researchers did not want a debate over the aptness of the genocide label to distract policymakers from crimes that were undeniable.

With the sanctions bill pending back in Washington, Galbraith went scavenging for proof besides the refugees' consistent oral accounts. One day, driving along the Turkish border, he and Van Hollen met some Turkish beekeepers who invited them to a dinner of homemade bread and home-grown honey. The beekeepers' Spartan settlement boasted a single electric wire that led directly to a 27-inch television set, where the Americans were treated to an episode of *All in the Family* in Turkish. The beekeepers also supplied them with something that they were sure would prove Iraqi chemical weapons use once and for all—dead bees that they said had died as a result of Saddam Hussein's gas attacks nearby. Galbraith brought the bees back home for analysis. Realizing that clearing customs with Ziploc bags of bee corpses might be tricky, he secured special clearance from the secretary of agriculture himself. Galbraith found himself checking the "yes" box by "animal products" on the U.S. customs declaration for the first and last time. On the plane back to the United States, with plastic baggies of dead bees tucked into his briefcase, he happened upon a short blurb in the *International Herald Tribune* that reported the emergence of a mite that was killing southeastern European bees. Undaunted, Galbraith handed over several of the bags to the CIA. Not trusting the intelligence services, he kept one sample for himself, which he stored in the same refrigerator at the Senate Foreign Relations Committee where his colleagues stored their lunches. Only a year later, long after the CIA results had come back negative, did somebody throw out Galbraith's moldy bee corpses.

Assistant Secretary Murphy and others at the State Department who were highly critical of Galbraith's sanctions effort to begin with greeted the news of his bee corpses as proof that he had gone mad. "I never saw the bees myself," remembers Murphy, "but when we heard he had come back with these baggies, we all just groaned and thought, 'There's Peter, at it again.'"

On the plane back to the United States, Galbraith drafted a report on his trip, including testimony from some thirty-five refugees. He was haunted by his memory of the old men who stoically described the deaths of their children and grandchildren and the families seated by tiny bundles that now constituted the sum of their lives' possessions. Surely Congress would punish Hussein, even if it meant resisting the pressure of the State Department and White House.

Analogy and Advocacy

Galbraith was not without his supporters. As in Cambodia, the most out-spoken U.S. officials were those on Capitol Hill not required to adopt the administration line. They, too, invoked Holocaust imagery. When Senator Pell, the Senate Foreign Relations Committee chairman, introduced the law imposing sanctions, he declared:

> For the second time in this century a brutal dictatorship is using
> deadly gas to exterminate a distinct ethnic minority. . . . There can be
> no doubt but that the Iraqi regime of Saddam Hussein intends this
> campaign to be a final solution to the Kurdish problem. While a peo-
> ple are gassed, the world is largely silent. . . . Silence, however, is com-
> plicity. A half century ago, the world was also silent as Hitler began a
> campaign that culminated in the near extermination of Europe's Jews.
> We cannot be silent to genocide again.[95]

The analogy was made all the more resonant by Hussein's choice of lethal weapon. The next day Pell noted that although the sanctions bill would hurt some American businesses, Americans should be prepared to make sacrifices for a "moral issue of the greatest magnitude":

> To do the right thing the American people have in the past been willing to pay the price. After the holocaust that consumed Europe's Jewish population, the world said "never again." Sadly, it is happening again in Iraqi Kurdistan. We must do whatever we can to let the Iraqi dictatorship know that the United States will not stand idly by while they massacre the Kurds. This bill sends that message.[96]

Having read Galbraith and Van Hollen's account of their interviews with refugees, Pell grew impatient with those still demanding physical evidence of the gassing. The senator mentioned the dead bees, but when reporters kept pressing, Pell snapped, "They did not bring back a corpse, if that's your question."[97]

In the House, Representative James Bilbray (D.–Nev.) rejected the argument that because U.S. allies would not sanction Hussein, the United States should not do so either. He wondered aloud if his colleagues would have allowed Hitler to proceed just because others chose not to confront him. "Are we going to show our children and our grandchildren we sat by while an entire race was exterminated?"[98]

Naturally, the bill also got some help from Senator Proxmire, who called upon colleagues to act on behalf of this "forgotten people" that had "little or no constituency in the West." Proxmire noted the double standard of U.S. policy and the importance of responding to genocide wherever it occurs:

> Mr. President, if Nicaragua were using chemical agents against its own population or a neighboring state, the outcry by the public, politicians, and our own Government would drown all other news. The president would be speaking out about such barbarity as would the Secretary of State and certainly the Defense Department would not remain silent. We would be pounding the doors of the United Nations and the world community. We should expect no less when genocide is being conducted against a people far away, of faint famil-

iarity, who do not touch our daily lives, but who are no less victim to the inhumanity of chemical warfare.[99]

Editorial writers teamed up with these outraged senators and representatives. The Kurdish people had acquired a few prominent friends in the media over the years. William Safire of the *New York Times* and Jim Hoagland of the *Washington Post* performed the role that syndicated columnists Jack Anderson and Les Whitten had played describing Khmer Rouge terror. Safire lambasted the United States government for its passivity. In a September 5, 1988, op-ed, Safire wrote angrily, "A classic example of genocide is under way, and the world does not give a damn." Singled out for special opprobrium were television journalists, who he knew would be indispensable to sparking and sustaining public support for American reprisals. Although some 60,000 Kurds had gathered in tent cities on the Turkish border and though Saddam Hussein "may yet pass Pol Pot in megamurders," Safire wrote, the media was absent. Film crews were ignoring a "genocidal campaign against a well-defined ethnic group that has been friendless through modern history and does not yet understand the publicity business." He argued that "inaccessibility" was "no excuse for ignoring the news." Indeed, he wrote, "the ability of color cameras to bring home the horror of large-scale atrocities imposes a special responsibility on that medium to stake out murder scenes or get firsthand accounts from refugees."[100] Safire was concrete. The United States should gather additional testimony from the refugees, launch a Security Council investigation, threaten to pull out American ships from the Persian Gulf, and if all else failed, "slip Stinger missiles to [Kurdish rebel leader] Massoud Barzani in the hills to bring down the gassing gunships."[101] The *New York Times* editorial board agreed: "Not just a whiff but the stench of genocide" drifts from Kurdish territory, it said, "sovereignty cannot legitimize genocide. . . . Enough silence."[102]

Hoagland's September 8 editorial in the *Washington Post* was entitled "Make No Mistake—This Is Genocide." Hoagland noted that the "Iraqi version of genocide . . . does not have the maniacal pace or organization of Hitler's Germany or Pol Pot's Cambodia," but urged that the United States stop shrinking "from branding Iraq's actions with the horrible word." The State Department's low-key "expressions of concern" to the Baghdad government would do little to comfort the Kurds, who he wrote were being dynamited, bulldozed, and gassed to oblivion.[103] In a later editorial,

Hoagland stuck with the Holocaust theme. Hussein's attack on the Kurds was "the most ghastly case of the use of poison gas since the Nazi death camps." The Reagan administration's endless search for "evidence" provided a familiar fig leaf for inaction. "Reports of massive gassing of Jews by the Nazis were regularly dismissed because they lacked 'evidence,'" he wrote. "Those who did not want to know, or act, in World War II were always *able to find the lack of proof at the right moment*."[104] The *Washington Post* editorial board followed Hoagland's lead. "In a world in which many things are muted, this one is clear," the *Post* said. "If gas is not to be considered beyond the limits, then there are no limits."[105]

Galbraith maintained periodic contact with Safire and Hoagland during this period because he knew that a single editorial would be more valuable in the legislative fight than an entire committee report.

Galbraith also invoked the Holocaust when possible. He named the report from his trip "Iraq's Final Solution." But Gerald Christianson, staff director of the Senate Foreign Relations Committee, wanted to shy away from the controversy that Galbraith seemed to court and insisted that the committee report title be changed to "Iraq's Final Offensive." Christianson thought that the Holocaust analogy would alienate some members of Congress and that those it moved would not need such blatant cues. He argued that the combination of gas, haggard refugees, and destruction would be enough to stir the association.

Special Interests, National Interest

Galbraith found bedlam on Capitol Hill on the day of his return from Turkey. Some eighty yellow message slips lay scattered on his desk. The sanctions bill faced steep opposition from the White House and State Department, which he had expected, but also from the House. Most disappointing, many of the senators who had supported the measure a week before had since been clued into its contents and consequences. They were now reconsidering.

Some of the opposition on the Hill was structural. The House Foreign Affairs Committee leadership tended to be more deferential than the Senate Foreign Relations Committee to the foreign policy prerogatives of the executive branch, which opposed sanctions in this case. Representative

Bill Frenzel (R.–Minn.) testified to this concern, asking, "How can our government provide effective leadership, moral and otherwise, if the administration must always be second-guessed by a Congress which wants to make its own foreign policy with splashy headlines?"[106] The White House blanched every time Congress went about making foreign policy. Similarly, the House Ways and Means Committee, which has jurisdiction over trade, frowned upon using trade as a political tool and thus generally objected to sanctions bills.

But the real opposition derived from an excessive faith in diplomacy and, more fundamentally, from a desire to advance U.S. economic interests. First, the Reagan White House could not accept that years of investment in Iraq would not create a kinder, gentler dictator. "They were sure they were going to convert Saddam Hussein and make him 'my fair lady,'" says David Korn, the former State Department Middle East specialist. Some genuinely believed carrots would achieve more than sticks. They spoke of Iraq's assurances as if they were reliable. Iraq was coming around. "If [our objective] is to prevent the further use of chemical weapons in Kurdistan in the immediate future, this may no longer be an issue," one analyst wrote on September 9, 1988. "We have been told in Baghdad that the campaign against the Kurds is coming to an end, and as a practical matter, there will be little or no need for continued Iraqi use of chemical weapons once the Kurdish insurgence has been suppressed."[107] Private overtures were paying dividends. Iraqi foreign minister Tariq Aziz said on September 17 that Iraq "respects" its obligations under international law. In the weeks ahead, the administration repeatedly referred back to Aziz's single, incomplete statement as evidence that Washington's gentle persuasion was working. Aziz's credibility had apparently not suffered for having repeatedly denied that Iraq had used poison gas in the first place.[108] U.S. officials even filled in the blanks left open in Iraq's renunciation. "We take this statement to mean that Iraq forswears the use of chemical weapons in internal as well as international conflicts," State Department spokesman Charles Redman said.[109] The United States would neither punish past use of chemical weapons nor threaten punishment for future use. The farthest it went was to warn that additional attacks would cause the department to "reconsider" its opposition to sanctions.[110] Representative Tom Lantos (D.-Calif.), a Holocaust survivor, declared:"I am intrigued by the logic which views a criminal act, sweeps it aside and focuses on the intent of the criminal to engage in further criminal acts."[111]

But the Reagan administration continued to act as though economic incentives and warm ties would influence Saddam Hussein's regime. James Baker, then secretary of the treasury, wrote later:

> Diplomacy—as well as the American psyche—is fundamentally biased toward "improving relations." Shifting a policy away from cooperation toward confrontation is always a more difficult proposition—particularly when support for the existing policy is as firmly embedded among various constituencies and bureaucratic interests as was the policy toward Iraq.[112]

The Defense Intelligence Agency was issuing predictions that Hussein would likely try to "defeat decisively" or crush "once and for all" the Kurds, but U.S. diplomats downplayed the campaign against the Kurdish minority and hoped for the best.[113]

U.S. patience would have worn thin far sooner if not for American farming, manufacturing, and geopolitical interests in Iraq. The policy of engagement was virtually uncontested at the State Department and White House. Internal memoranda thus tended to lament Iraqi repression only parenthetically:"Human rights and chemical weapons use aside, in many respects our political and economic interests run parallel with those of Iraq."[114]

One-quarter of the rice grown in Arkansas, Galbraith swiftly gathered, was exported to Iraq. Approximately 23 percent of overall U.S. rice output went there. One staffer representing Senator John Breaux of Louisiana actually appeared before Galbraith in tears and accused him of committing genocide against Louisiana rice growers. U.S. farmers also annually exported about 1 million tons of wheat to Iraq. As economist John Kenneth Galbraith, the father of the author of the sanctions package, mused to me years later, "The one thing you don't want to do is take on the American farmer. There aren't many left, but you've got to take care of them." The administration got immediate assistance from U.S. farm and industry lobbyists who had read the *Congressional Record* and were horrified that the sanctions bill had slipped quietly by their Senate friends. With a hideous lack of irony, several chemical companies also called to inquire how their products might be affected if sanctions were imposed to punish chemical weapons use.

What is both remarkable and typical about the shift in Senate sentiment toward the bill is that the senators who had voted for the sanctions bill on

September 9, 1988, changed their votes without even taking the time to substantiate that a vote for the Prevention of Genocide Act would necessarily cost them the support of the special interests. Committee Staff Director Christianson recalls that this happened often on Capitol Hill:

> In many cases the Senators and their staffs overreact in terms of what they feel needs to be done to placate the special interests. They go one better. Or they anticipate a problem even before somebody has complained. They are so sensitive. They don't say to themselves, "We vote with this lobby nine out of ten times, so we can afford to go our own way this time." It is not a rational calculation. They feel that *nothing* is worth the risk of losing the support.

Although these sources of opposition were obvious at the time, none of the bill's critics dared argue that it was wrong to stop Hussein's gassing of the Kurds; they "simply" argued that, "unfortunately," the *means* that Senators Pell and Helms had selected—economic sanctions—and the place that foreign policy was being made—Capitol Hill—were inappropriate.

The stories the U.S. officials told themselves are by now familiar and can be grouped into Hirschman's futility, perversity, and jeopardy categories of justification. From the futility perspective, the Iraqi regime had already retreated into isolation and would not respond to outside pressure. What's more, farmers and manufacturers from other countries would quickly fill the vacuum, so Hussein would end up with all the farm goods, credits, and trade he needed. From the perversity standpoint, slapping sanctions on Iraq would only anger the Iraqi dictator and make him more likely to punish the Kurds of northern Iraq. Economic sanctions would be "useless or counterproductive," the Near Eastern Affairs Bureau argued. They would reduce U.S. influence over Iraq and allow European and Japanese businesses to help Iraq rebuild its economy.[115] "If it wasn't us," the State Department's Larry Pope insists today, "it would have been someone else." France had a thriving arms business with Iraq. Germany nonchalantly sold insecticide and other chemicals to Baghdad. Britain's commercial interests also took priority. One secret State Department briefing memo listed a set of sanctions, ranging from economic to diplomatic—for example, placing Iraq back on the terrorism list, withdrawing the U.S. ambassador from Baghdad, or suspending the military intelligence liaison relationship. The U.S. analyst concluded: "The disadvantages of all of these actions are obvious. In differing degrees, they would have a sharp negative impact on our ability to influence the Iraqi regime, and set in motion a downward spiral of action and reaction which would be unpredictable and uncontrollable."[116] U.S. diplomats in Baghdad warned, "If [Hussein] perceives a choice between correct relations with the USA and public humiliation, he will not hesitate to let the relationship fall completely by the wayside."[117]

Nowhere in the internal debates about the sanctions package can one find U.S. officials arguing that Hussein was more vulnerable to economic levers than ever before. After the war with Iran, Iraq was looking to roll over some $70 billion in debt, one of the highest per capita debts in the world. The Prevention of Genocide Act, which would have required Washington to vote against loans to Iraq at international financial institutions, could have ravaged Iraq's credit rating and provoked a massive financial crisis that Hussein surely hoped to avoid.

The United States had tremendous leverage with Iraq. Apart from supplying hefty agricultural and manufacturing credits, the United States was Iraq's primary oil importer. But the Reagan administration viewed U.S. influence as something to be stored, not squandered.

The administration and the special interests got help making their case for futility, perversity, and jeopardy from Middle East analysts. One scholar, Milton Viorst, wrote an op-ed piece in the *Washington Post* entitled "Poison Gas and 'Genocide': The Shaky Case Against Iraq." Nearly a full month after Shultz had confirmed Iraqi chemical attacks, Viorst urged Congress not to impose sanctions against Iraq because the punishment would be exacted for a crime "which, according to some authorities, may never have taken place." He suggested that Iraqi radio intercepts were likely "subject to conflicting interpretations" and hinted that the United States might be adopting its new stand simply to placate Iran or to secure the release of U.S. hostages. Having spent a whole week in Iraq "looking into the question," Viorst described the findings he had gathered from an Iraqi helicopter. He explained away the ruins of hundreds of Kurdish villages he had seen by arguing that the Iraqi army was simply denying sanctuary to Kurdish rebels. He could not say for sure that lethal gas had not been used, but even though he had been serviced and escorted by the Iraqi authorities, he felt confident enough to "conclude that if lethal gas was used, it was not used genocidally." Without mentioning that any Kurd in Iraq who spoke to the press risked execution, Viorst noted, "If there had been large-scale killing, it is likely they would know and tell the world about it. But neither I nor any westerner I encountered heard such allegations." He wrote, "In Baghdad, I attended a gala Kurdish wedding, where the eating, drinking and dancing belied any suggestion that the community was in danger."[118]

Opposing "Inaccurate Terms"

The State Department's Bureau of Near Eastern Affairs had lost the fight with INR over Iraq's culpability. But it succeeded in convincing Shultz to offend Iraq no further. "Our condemnation of Iraq's use of chemical weapons against the Kurdish insurgency has shaken the fragile U.S.-Iraqi relationship and been heavily criticized in the Arab world," NEA head Murphy wrote. "We need to move quickly to ensure that our action is seen as anti–[chemical weapons], not anti-Iraq or pro-Iran." "Specifically," Murphy urged, "we should oppose legislation which uses inaccurate terms like genocide."[119] He offered no suggestions as to how the United States might influence Iraq so that it would refrain from attacking the rural Kurdish populace. The bureau's focus was on preservation of the U.S.-Iraq relationship.

Shultz's State Department heeded Murphy's advice and framed virtually all criticism of Iraq in terms that focused on the particular weapons employed rather than the attacks themselves. Both publicly and in private meetings with senior Iraqis, Shultz described steep stakes to allowing chemical weapons use and proliferation. "For a long while this genie had been kept in the bottle," Shultz said, explaining the diplomatic assault. Now, he added, "it's out."[120] President Reagan used his final speech before the United Nations to propose the staging of an international conference that would nourish and reinforce the commitment of signatories to the 1925 Geneva protocol ban on chemical weapons use. His spokesman, Marlin Fitzwater, stressed that U.S. relations with Iraq had warmed considerably in recent years. "We want to see those relations continue to develop," he said. "Our position that we've taken on chemical warfare, chemical weapons, is in no way intended to diminish our interest in those bilateral relations."[121]

The Bureau of Near Eastern Affairs had conducted its own internal review of the genocide question and concluded that Iraq was putting down a rebellion and not committing genocide. "The Iraqi military campaign, brutal as it was, sought to reclaim territories occupied for years by rebels closely allied with, and financed, armed and reinforced by, Iran as a second front," Assistant Secretary Murphy wrote. He insisted that since there was no evidence that Hussein intended to exterminate the Kurds, the genocide claim was far-fetched. "We see no evidence of an attempt to wipe out the Kurds as a whole," Murphy proceeded. He has not changed his mind. "Genocide is something different," he argues. "We knew he was doing brutal things to the Kurds, but you have to use the term 'genocide' very carefully, and it was clear to me that Hussein had no intention of exterminating all Kurds." Murphy had never read the genocide convention and thus equated genocide with Hitler's holistic campaign to wipe out every last Jew in Europe.

Murphy's NEA Bureau received support for this interpretation from Patrick E. Tyler in the *Washington Post*. On September 25, 1988, Tyler wrote a piece entitled simply, "The Kurds: It's Not Genocide." Although Iraq's "massive and forced relocation" of Kurds was "horrible and historic," Tyler wrote, "genocide, the extermination of a race of people and their culture. . . is not an accurate term for what is happening in this part of Iraq."[122] Tyler, too, ignored the legal definition of "genocide." He also extrapolated on the basis of a superficial, strictly supervised tour of several major Kurdish towns. The article was datelined Batufa, one of many Kurdish cities untouched by the Anfal campaign. Only the rural Kurdish population had been targeted for extinction, and Tyler did not visit rural territory. The *Washington Post*'s Jonathan Randal testily describes the tendency of journalists inexperienced in the region to generalize wildly and irresponsibly. "All journalists seem to believe that life begins when they arrive. They get off the plane and expect to be instant experts," he says. "The parties on the ground know when our deadlines are and play us like violins." Western reporters saw bustling city life, but rural Kurds depended on their mountain life, which was off-limits. As one Kurdish spokesman said:

> The Kurds have a saying: "Level the mountains, and in a day the Kurds would be no more." To a Kurd the mountain is no less than the embodiment of the deity: mountain is his mother, his refuge, his protector, his home, his farm, his market, his mate—and his only friend. . . . Kurds who settle in the cities outside the mountains—even those within Kurdistan proper—soon lose their true Kurdish identities.[123]

At no point during the eighteen-month Iraqi campaign of destruction did Reagan administration officials condemn it, and they did all they could to kill the Senate sanctions package. Still, the Near Eastern Affairs Bureau continued to claim it had the same ends as the human rights advocates. "We should balance all our interests in this increasingly important country in order to achieve *what we all seek* in terms of [chemical weapon] restraints and human rights performance," Murphy wrote.[124] At a House hearing, he said, "Our opposition, I can assure you, is every bit as strong and outraged as your own. . . . We share the same goal, which is to end the use of chemical weaponry by Iraq [and] by any other state which has the capabilities. There is no daylight between us in what we are trying to accomplish."[125] The difference, as always, was one of "means."

Defeat

When the Khmer Rouge starved and bludgeoned nearly 2 million people to death in Cambodia, journalists like Becker and Schanberg cared passionately about the place and the people, and U.S. diplomats like Twining and Quinn were revolted by the brutality of the new regime. But these journalists and diplomats had no hope that they could overcome the country's Southeast Asia fatigue and generate an American response to KR terror. They felt their wisdom would land like a snowflake on the Potomac. Thus, although they diligently documented the horrors, they did not really lobby for U.S. engagement. Deep down, they seemed to doubt that the United States could ameliorate conditions on the ground. After Vietnam and Watergate, Americans retained little faith in the system.

Galbraith began his crusade to have Saddam Hussein punished for genocide against the Kurds in 1988, nearly a decade after the KR ouster. In a short time much had changed on the international stage. The Cold War was thawing, and President Reagan had none of President Carter's shyness about throwing U.S. weight around the world. But the United States was no more likely to try to curb a strategic partner's human rights abuses, especially if doing so could harm U.S. economic interests.

U.S. politicians were notoriously captive to special interests.[126] Walter Lippmann once wrote of U.S. legislators, "They advance politically only as they placate, appease, bribe, seduce, bamboozle, or otherwise manage to manipulate the demanding threatening elements in their constituencies.

The decisive consideration is not whether the proposition is good but whether . . . the active-talking constituents like it immediately."[127]

But Galbraith believed that the Senate was an institution that, for all of its horse-trading, could act on principle. It need not become a "mere collection of local potato plots and cabbage grounds."[128] The Senate's early vote for the Prevention of Genocide Act seemed to confirm that the body could do the right thing for the right reasons. But as the fallout from the bill's initial Senate passage intensified, Galbraith began to fear the wrong result for the wrong reasons.

The person most responsible for sabotaging the sanctions effort once it moved from the Senate to the House was Dan Rostenkowski (D.–Ill.), the chairman of the House Ways and Means Committee who would later be brought down in a corruption scandal. Influenced by the storm of protests on Capitol Hill, Rostenkowski moved to have Galbraith's Prevention of Genocide Act "blue-slipped," or returned to the Senate as a money bill unconstitutionally originating in the Senate.[129] Rostenkowski's argument was a weak one, but, as Lemkin had once said, "If somebody doesn't like mustard, they will find a reason for opposing it." Rostenkowski did not like this brand of mustard, and he killed the Pell-Helms Prevention of Genocide Act. Galbraith was stunned. "I thought the House would take this bill, mark it up, and make it law," he remembers. "I didn't think that business interests would kick in when such an abhorrent thing was taking place." The Senate bill, many Congressmen said, had "gone a little too far." For Galbraith, such euphemisms were code for criminal capitulation.

All was not lost. The House developed its own version of the law, which supporters called "a measured response" to chemical weapons use. The House sanctions bill shifted the burden of proof away from the White House and omitted any reference to genocide. After successive rounds of ravaging in committee, the only sanctions the law retained were the ban on export-import credits used to purchase U.S. manufactured goods and the sale of chemicals that could be used in the production of chemical weapons. And lawmakers continued to object to these because they said U.S. manufacturers would be harmed.

Galbraith scratched the backs of those he thought could be swayed. But his aggressiveness and his single-mindedness did not charm all those who encountered him. "There was a lot of backlash against anything Peter did," Christianson, his boss at the Senate Foreign Relations Committee, remembers. "He rubbed a lot of people the wrong way. They would pooh-pooh

him as 'emotional.' Whether it was out of jealousy or because they were disdainful of his aggressiveness, he was not their favorite person." Galbraith's
message was also not one lawmakers or State Department officials wanted
to hear, as he was proposing something that promised no conceivable material gain and several prospective tangible losses. "Peter was, . . . well, Peter
was Peter," remembers Larry Pope of the State Department. "He was a pain
in the neck and a real thorn in the side of our policy of engagement."

Whatever the Reagan administration's objections, the half-measure
soared through the House on September 27, 1988, with a huge bipartisan
majority, 388–16. On October 11 the Senate approved, by a vote of 87–0, a
revised bill almost identical to the one passed by the House. Although the
bill was not very punishing, Galbraith thought it would signal at least some
degree of disapproval of Hussein's brutality and force President Reagan
into the awkward position of deciding whether he opposed punishing
Hussein enough to veto the congressional measure. On October 21, 1988,
however, Galbraith learned that in a last-minute round of parliamentary
maneuvering before the autumn adjournment, Representative Dante
Fascell (D.–Fla.) had removed the sanctions bill from a tax bill that was certain to become law. Instead, in an effort to preserve his committee's jurisdiction, Fascell put it into a freestanding bill that, because of its other
provisions, had no chance of passage. The economic sanctions package
never made it off Capitol Hill.

In keeping with the natural workings of the U.S. political process, the
question of whether to denounce, punish, or attempt to deter chemical
weapons attacks against a largely defenseless minority was never explained
to the American people. It was settled, as it usually is, behind closed doors,
where special interests ruled the day and where narrow versions of national interest helped rationalize inhumanity.

The trouble was not just that special interests spoke loudly against
action; it was that, apart from these lobbies that were especially interested,
there were no competing voices making phone calls on behalf of the Kurds.
When the genocide convention had come up for ratification, a small group
of vocal, isolationist, southern senators had managed to block its passage.
During the Khmer Rouge's bloody rule in Cambodia, likewise, the loudest
voices were those that cast doubt on the refugee claims. With Iraq, too, the
major human rights organizations, Amnesty International and Human
Rights Watch, were still operating out of dingy offices on small budgets and
focusing principally on jailed political dissidents, in the case of Amnesty, and

abuses committed in Latin America and Asia, in the case of Human Rights Watch. One Boston-based group, Physicians for Human Rights (PHR), had sent a medical team to the Turkish border October 7–16. After systematically debriefing refugees, PHR doctors had issued the first independent report documenting widespread chemical weapons use and describing the Iraqi offensive as a "genocidal assault." The report, which attracted a large but short burst of media attention, had not been picked up by influential actors in Washington.[130]

The loudest political support Galbraith received was from a group of steelworkers from Baytown, Texas, whose plant was scheduled to be shut down and shipped to Iraq, costing them hundreds of jobs. When they learned that the sanctions bill would block the factory move, they were ecstatic. They phoned up the frazzled Galbraith and offered him enthusiastic moral support, which counted for little when measured against the potent U.S.-Iraqi Business Council. Representative Howard Berman (D.–Calif.) had been pushing legislation to limit trade with Iraq since the mid-1980s, but the deck was stacked in the wrong direction. "There was no grassroots campaign," he said. "The American people weren't aware of, or that interested in, our policy toward Iraq at that time." When the bill came up for passage, and hearing nothing from their constituents, most thought in terms of economic and strategic interests alone.

Some of the most potent lobbies in U.S. political life today are of course those that speak for various ethnic interests. The Armenian American community has lobbied for decades to secure a day of remembrance to commemorate the Armenian genocide and in November 2000, over Turkish objections, very nearly gained official U.S. recognition of the genocide. Jewish American groups have been extremely influential, helping secure the allocation of billions of dollars worth of aid to Israel and the establishment of the Holocaust Museum on the Mall in Washington, D.C. While the atrocities were actually being perpetrated in Turkey and Nazi-occupied Europe, however, these lobbies did not exist. During the Cambodian genocide, similarly, few Cambodian expatriates or descendants lived in the United States. Those who did were not organized politically to attract much attention to the cause of their compatriots. In the case of the Kurds, when Galbraith's sanctions measure stood poised for passage in the Congress, neither Kurds nor Kurdish Americans had joined forces to set up a Washington lobby. When Talabani visited Washington in June 1988 for the first time, his party did not reinforce the trip by establishing a D.C.

office or liaison. Latif Rashid, who ran the party's London office, remembers, "Because we had no representatives based in Washington, it was easy for American leaders to pretend the Kurds didn't exist."

The U.S. media can sometimes play a role in helping draw public attention to an injustice abroad or to the stakes of a legislative sequence. When it came to Iraq's repression of the Kurds, however, the March 1988 Halabja attack and the September 1988 exodus received some attention, but neither the larger Iraqi campaign to destroy Kurds in rural Iraq nor the legislative toing and froing around the Prevention of Genocide Act on Capitol Hill generated much press interest. This spotty reporting helped ensure that lawmakers and administration officials could oppose the sanctions bill without attracting negative publicity.

Senator Pell delivered a postmortem on the Prevention of Genocide Act:

> Occasionally our legislative process works in a way the American people can understand and appreciate. September 9, 1988, was such an occasion. On that day the Senate unanimously passed sweeping sanctions against Iraq in response to its poison gas attacks on its Kurdish minority. . . . Now we are in a situation where a . . . couple of senior members in the House of Representatives were able to thwart the overwhelming majorities in both the House and Senate that favored taking a stand against Iraq's use of poison gas. This is . . . the sort of thing that makes so many Americans skeptical about our legislative process.[131]

The United States did not summon a special meeting of the UN Security Council, as advocates urged, but instead joined nine other nations in calling on the UN to send a team of experts to Iraq to investigate, urging that the fact-finding mission be modeled on past UN chemical weapons inquiries (which had confirmed Iraqi use against Iran). U.S. officials made this recommendation without noting that these prior investigations offered staunch testimony to the ineffectiveness of a policy of inquiry alone. Such UN teams had "concluded" in 1986, 1987, and 1988 that Iraq had used chemical weapons against Iran.[132]

In November 1988 Iraq expelled Haywood Rankin, the same U.S. foreign service officer who had accompanied Galbraith into Kurdish territory in 1987, because he had taken another trip to northern Iraq to inquire about Iraq's poison gas use. Baghdad said it was expelling him for "talking to Kurds."[133] The State Department responded by expelling an Iraqi diplomat from the Iraqi embassy in Washington, but it did not publicly announce the expulsion or link it to chemical weapons use or the destruction of rural Kurds.[134]

Saddam Hussein had been destroying rural Kurdish areas for more than eighteen months. The deadly Anfal campaign had lasted more than six months. In that period, although the State Department received a steady stream of intelligence on the destruction of the Kurdish villages and the gas attacks against Kurdish civilians, officials in the Reagan administration spoke out only when forced to do so by the media and the feisty sanctions effort on Capital Hill. Even then, they worded their criticism so narrowly that they made it clear Hussein was free to attack the Kurds with means besides chemical weapons. Senator Pell initiated the sanctions effort because he considered stopping genocide more important than the geopolitical, agricultural, manufacturing, or oil interests at stake. Yet the opponents of sanctions did not pose the question as one of principle versus interest. "People don't like to admit they are weighing a hard principle against a hard constituent interest," Christianson observes. "They are much happier weighing a soft principle against a hard constituent interest. So it is better to keep the principle hazy, or on the horizon, and not let it crystallize."

Thus, those who did not want to punish Hussein told themselves that the crime was not necessarily genocide, that the Kurds had invited repression upon themselves, and that the evidence of gassing was not foolproof. The United States had intelligence that distinguished Iraqi military engagement with armed Kurds from Iraqi destruction of whole communities. And although senior policymakers were right that the information flow was imperfect, U.S. policy is rarely predicated on foolproof evidence. U.S. officials certainly knew enough to know that Saddam Hussein was prepared to use any means available to him to solve his "Kurdish problem."

Aftermath

Life (and Death) After Anfal

Saddam Hussein wound down his Anfal campaign just after Galbraith's abortive sanctions effort in the fall of 1988. Those Kurds from prohibited areas who had been relocated but not executed were forced to sign or place a thumbprint on a statement that read: "I, the undersigned, _____, testify that I live in the governorate of_____, in the section of _____, residence number_____, and I recognize that I will face the death penalty should the information indicated be false, or should I alter my address without notifying appropriate administration and authorities."[135] The Kurds from the forbidden areas were crammed into more than a dozen complexes, each containing some 50,000 people, each composed mainly of Anfal survivors, or *Anfalakan*.[136] Kurds still in Iraqi jails were said to have amnesty, but some were executed anyway. Others were freed under the condition that they "shall not be treated on an equal footing with other Iraqis in terms of rights and duties, unless they can effectively match good intentions with proper conduct and demonstrate that they have ended all collaboration with the saboteurs. . . ." They would be monitored, the authorities said, "through the placement of thorough and diligent inform- ers in their midst."[137]

Having performed his brutal mission with alacrity, al-Majid was deter- mined that the gains not be lost. "There shall be a prompt and decisive response to any incidents that may occur," he said, "with the scale of the response being out of proportion to the scale of the incident, no matter how trivial the latter may be."[138]

By 1989 only a few hundred villages remained standing in Hussein's "Kurdish autonomous region." Some 4,049 villages had been destroyed since Iraq demarcated the prohibited zones.[139] In April 1989 al-Majid handed over the Northern Bureau to his successor. At a kind of pass-the- torch (so to speak) ceremony, he reflected on his handiwork while profess- ing to have retained his humanity:

> I would like to admit that I am not and will not be the right person
> for the current stable situation in the North. . . . I cry when I see a
> tragic show or movie. One day I cried when I saw a woman who was
> lost and without a family in a movie. But I would like to tell you that
> I did what I did and what I was supposed to do. I don't think you
> could do more than what I could do.[140]

When George Bush Sr. took over the White House in January 1989, his foreign policy team undertook a preliminary strategic review of U.S. poli- cy toward Iraq. The study, completed at the same time al-Majid departed northern Iraq, deemed Iraq a potentially helpful ally in containing Iran and nudging the Middle East peace process ahead. The "Guidelines for U.S.-Iraq Policy" swiped at proponents of sanctions on Capitol Hill and a few human rights advocates who had begun lobbying within the State Department. The guidelines noted that despite support from the Agriculture, Commerce, Defense, and State Departments for a profitable, stable U.S.-Iraq relationship, "parts of Congress and the Department would scuttle even the most benign and beneficial areas of the relationship, such as agricultural exports."[141] The Bush administration would not shift to a policy of dual containment of both Iraq and Iran. Vocal American businesses were adamant that Iraq was a source of opportunity, not enmity. The White House did all it could to create an opening for these companies. "Had we attempted to isolate Iraq," Secretary of State James Baker wrote later, "we would have also isolated American businesses, particularly agricultural interests, from significant commercial opportunities."[142] Hussein locked up another $1 billion in agricultural credits. Iraq became the ninth largest purchaser of U.S. farm products; he was a favorite with midwestern farm-state politicians. As Baker put it gently in his memoirs, "Our administration's review of the previous Iraq policy was not immune from domestic economic considerations."[143]

The Bush administration's guidelines revealed a worry that Iraqi transgressions would be harder to justify publicly now that its war with Iran had ended. "Clouding the issue, the immediate threat of Iranian expansion has faded, and with it the shield that protected Iraq from western criticism," the guidelines noted. "This has allowed human rights to become the battleground for those wanting to justify severing or greatly limiting relations with Iraq." The State Department maintained the view that the Kurds had earned repression with their rebellions. As the author of the guidelines advised, "In no way should we associate ourselves with the 60-year-old Kurdish rebellion in Iraq or oppose Iraq's legitimate attempts to suppress it."[144] The U.S. official did not explain how legitimate suppression could be distinguished from illegitimate suppression, but the United States was under no illusion about the nature of the regime. "Saddam Hussein will continue to eliminate those he regards as a threat," the guidelines stated, "torture those he believes have secrets to reveal, and rule without any real concessions to democracy. . . . Few expect a humane regime [will] come to Iraq any time soon." But when twelve Western states joined together in 1989 at the UN Human Rights Commission and sponsored a strongly worded resolution that called for the appointment of a special rapporteur to "make a thorough study of the human rights situation in Iraq," the United States refused to join.[145]

On October 2, 1989, a year after some 60,000 Kurds had tumbled into Turkey fleeing gas attacks, President Bush signed National Security Directive 26 (NSD-26), which concluded that "normal relations between the United States and Iraq would serve our longer-term interests and promote stability in both the Gulf and the Middle East." Thus, the administration would "pursue, and seek to facilitate, opportunities for U.S. firms to participate in the reconstruction of the Iraqi economy." The devastation caused by the Iran-Iraq war would create vast opportunities. In other settings, such as South Africa and later China, the United States justified its support for economic engagement on the grounds that greater prosperity and Western contacts would eventually improve respect for the human rights of the South Africans and Chinese. But with Iraq the case for foreign investment was made with almost no reference to the "long-term human rights benefits" to Iraqi Arabs and Kurds. With Saddam Hussein in office, it was clear, there would be none.

In a brochure welcoming visitors to the U.S. pavilion at the 1989 Baghdad international trade fair, U.S. Ambassador Glaspie wrote that the embassy "places the highest priority on promoting commerce and friendship between our two nations." A number of major U.S. companies, including AT&T International, General Motors, Xerox, Westinghouse, and Wang Laboratories, participated in the fair and others worked to form the U.S.-Iraq Business Forum, which lobbied in Washington to promote trade ties.[146]

Certain members of Congress refused to let the issue of Hussein's brutality against his people rest. In 1989, thanks to the pestering of Representative Berman, Senator Pell's ally on the House side, Congress finally agreed to ban Export-Import Bank financing for exports to Iraq. It attached a waiver, however, allowing the Bush administration to ignore the ban if national security requirements dictated. The president took advantage of this loophole two months later. On January 17, 1990, Bush overrode congressional opposition and signed a directive authorizing an Export-Import Bank line of credit worth nearly $200 million. If the Congress and the Bush White House were driven by special interests, the administration justified its stand on the grounds of advancing the U.S. national interest. Neither the Bush nor the Reagan administration ever spoke out against the forced relocation of the Kurds.

Burn Israel, Burn Bridges

Saddam Hussein's behavior grew so bold in early 1990 that President Bush had to work to justify warm ties. In March Iraq executed a British journalist it claimed spied for Israel. Reports began pouring in that Iraq was strengthening its nuclear and chemical weapons capability. On April 2, 1990, Hussein crossed the Rubicon in a speech to the general command of his armed forces. He confirmed that Iraq possessed chemical weapons and warned that if Israel attacked Iraq, "By God, we will make fire eat up half of Israel."[147] This became known as the "Burn Israel" speech, and it earned him the special ire of American supporters of Israel, specifically, New York Republican senator Alphonse D'Amato. D'Amato hurriedly enlisted Galbraith to draft another sanctions package, this one known as the Iraq International Law Compliance Act of 1990.

The Bush administration continued to hope that Hussein would come around. He got backing from some powerful senators. A congressional delegation that included Bob Dole and Alan Simpson (R.–Wyo.) returned from Iraq in mid-April 1990 having met with Hussein for two and a half hours. They cheerily proclaimed him a leader with whom the United States could work.[148] In the meeting Hussein complained that "a large-scale campaign is being launched against us from the United States and Europe." Senator Dole assured him, "Not from President Bush," insisting that Bush would veto sanctions legislation if it ever passed both houses of Congress. Still, the challenges from Capitol Hill grew louder. At a House hearing Representative Lantos challenged Murphy's successor as assistant secretary of state for Near Eastern affairs, John Kelly. "At what point will the administration recognize that this is not a nice guy?" Lantos boomed. Kelly clung to the U.S. position: "We believe there is still a potentiality for positive alterations in Iraqi behavior."[149]

The Senate opposition continued to cite futility, perversity, and jeopardy as grounds for remaining silent. But others had awoken to the humanitarian and national security implications of allowing Hussein to dictate the terms of the relationship. In 1990 they said what they had not said in 1988. Senator William Cohen (R.–Maine) decried U.S. timidity. "It is the smell of oil and the color of money that corrodes our principles," Cohen remarked.[150] To those senators who argued that unilateral sanctions would do no good, Cohen said that if the United States avoided penalizing Hussein because it feared its allies would not follow, "we are left with the argument that we must follow the herd, follow it right down the path of feeding Saddam Hussein while he continues to terrorize, attack, or simply threaten to do so." Cohen invoked Hitler: "At one point in our history we heard the tap, tap, tap of Neville Chamberlain's umbrella on the cobblestones of Munich," Cohen said, just before a July 27 Senate vote on the new sanctions bill. "Now we are about to hear the rumble of the farm tractor on the bricks of Baghdad."[151]

Senator Nancy Kassebaum hailed from Kansas, which exported 1 million tons of wheat annually to Iraq. But moved by Amnesty International's report about human rights abuses against children in Iraq and remorseful at the Senate's tardiness in confronting Hussein, she memorably declared that, farm state or not, Kansas should support the sanctions bill. "I cannot believe that any farmer in this nation would want to send his products . . . to a country that has used chemical weapons and to a country that has tortured and injured their children," she said.[152] The Senate passed the D'Amato amendment 88–12 on July 27, 1990. It prohibited the United States from extending any sort of financial credit or assistance, including CCC guarantees, and from selling arms to Iraq, unless the president were to certify that Iraq was in "substantial compliance" with the provisions of a number of international human rights conventions, including the genocide convention. The Senate tabled an amendment put forth by Texas Republican Phil Gramm that would have allowed the Bush administration to waive its terms if it found that the sanctions hurt U.S. businesses and farmers more than they hurt Iraq.

A week after the sanctions bill finally cleared the Senate, Iraq invaded Kuwait, and Saddam Hussein named Ali al-Majid (aka "Chemical Ali") military governor of the occupied province.

Within hours of Iraq's invasion, Representative Berman's long-stalled proposal to deny export-import credits to Iraq passed the House, 416–0. At this point virtually nobody contested the measure. The cross-border invasion trampled the sovereignty of a U.S. ally and threatened U.S. oil supplies. House Foreign Affairs Committee Chairman Fascell scrambled to attach an executive order just penned by President Bush, which called for a total embargo on Iraq and a freeze on its assets in the United States.

U.S. government-guaranteed loans had totaled $5 billion since 1983. The credits had freed up currency for Hussein to fortify and modernize his more cherished military assets, including his stockpile of deadly chemicals. American grain would keep the Iraqi army fed during its occupation of Kuwait.

The Kurdish Uprising

The U.S. bombing of Baghdad began on January 17, 1991. U.S. ground troops routed Iraqi Republican Guards soon thereafter. Galbraith received a phone call from Kurdish leader Jalal Talabani, pledging to relay intelligence on Iraqi troop movements. Galbraith arranged for these reports to be radioed out of northern Iraq to Damascus and then faxed in Kurdish to a dentist in Detroit, who translated them and faxed them to Washington. But Galbraith quickly learned there were no takers in the Bush administration. The United States may have been at war with Iraq, but the war had not made the Bush administration any more inclined to deal with the Kurds. State Department officials informed Galbraith that the intelligence the Kurds were gathering would be of little use. When Talabani visited Washington in person, the low-level State Department officials who agreed to see him insisted on meeting him not in the building but at a nearby coffee shop.

On February 15, 1991, however, President Bush did speak for the first time of changing the Iraqi regime. He gave a speech that Kurds to this day can quote verbatim. "There's another way for the bloodshed to stop," Bush said, "and that is for the Iraqi military and the Iraqi people to take matters into their own hands and force Saddam Hussein, the dictator, to step aside."[153] The Kurds had wanted out of Iraq for so long that they heard the Bush speech as encouragement to launch a full-fledged revolt. On February 27, 1991, Bush declared a cease-fire only 100 hours after the ground war began. Alarmed at the prospect of "another Vietnam," Bush had deferred to the wisdom of General Colin Powell, chairman of the Joint Chiefs of Staff, in calling off the war before sealing Hussein's doom. Iraq was left with some 300,000 combat-ready troops and 2,000 tanks. Trusting in allied support and underestimating Baghdad's resources, however, Iraqi Shiites began a rebellion in southern Iraq on March 2, and the Kurds rose up in the north on March 6.

Informed by Talabani of Kurdish plans for a revolt, Galbraith got the Senate Foreign Relation Committee's permission to tour the Middle East on a fact-finding mission. His main aim was to enter Kurdish territory to assess what Washington should be doing to aid the Kurds. But he kept that part of his itinerary to himself, knowing his supervisors would never approve such a dangerous scheme. More intimate than most Americans with the Iraqi dictator's brutality, Galbraith knew that the current was unpredictable and that Hussein's fury could be pronounced. The day before he left Damascus, Syria, he scribbled a note to his thirteen-year-old son, Andrew:

> Dear Andrew,
>
> I hope you never receive this note, but if you do there are some things I want you to know.
>
> First, I traveled to Kurdistan because I believe in helping the victimized. The Kurds are in rebellion against an evil regime and their people need help, including above all food and medicine. By going there I thought I could help convince the Congress to provide the help.
>
> Second, I am most sorry I won't see you grow up. Your Mom and I divorced when you were a baby and so you and I never really were a family. But I love you very much and know you will be a fine, loving man. Live a good, kind, caring life.
>
> Love,
>
> Dad

Galbraith traveled the first part of the journey with a *Newsweek* journalist. The pair came under sporadic mortar fire as they crossed the Tigris River in a small boat. Galbraith filmed his ungraceful entrance and the vast destruction of Kurdish lands on a Hi-8 video camera. He found a celebration among Kurds. It was March 30, 1991, and the Kurds had been in rebellion for nearly three weeks. They had taken control of nearly all of Iraqi Kurdistan. In Zakho the streets were crowded and loudspeakers proclaimed, "We liberated Kurdistan!" Kurds used earth-moving equipment to drag abandoned Iraqi trucks into repair sheds. They brandished documents and videotapes they had captured from the Iraqi secret police archives. At an evening celebration with Talabani, Galbraith offered a toast, declaring, "President Woodrow Wilson promised the peoples of the world self-determination, and the Treaty of Sèvres gave that right to the Kurds. I am pleased to be the first American government official to stand on territory governed by the Kurds themselves." Yet at 6:15 a.m., Galbraith was awoken and told simply, "It's time to go." Hussein was crushing the rebellion.

The Kurds had banked on U.S. military support and overestimated the damage already inflicted on the Iraqi army by the allied attack. A brutal Iraqi counteroffensive involving tanks, armored vehicles, heavy artillery, and aircraft was under way, and virtually the entire Kurdish populace had taken flight.[154]

When the United States had negotiated its cease-fire with Iraq earlier in the month, it had not insisted upon banning Iraqi military helicopter flights. U.S. commander Norman Schwarzkopf later said he had been "suckered" into permitting their limited use for liaison purposes only. It was these helicopters that now became Iraq's ultimate terror weapon against the Kurds. Because the helicopters had delivered poison gas against the Kurds in 1987 and 1988, many Kurds fled ahead of Iraqi counter-attacks.

Although theirs was an oil-rich region, after eight months of economic sanctions and two months of war, the Kurds had little gasoline to fuel their flight. Most refugees walked in long, winding columns. Some 1.3 million Kurds streamed into the Iraqi mountains bordering Iran and Turkey. The Iraqis had systematically dynamited and bulldozed Kurdish villages along the way, so refugees could find no shelter en route. Galbraith met one man on the road who was carrying a bag of grain that had earlier been coated with rat poison. This was all his village had to eat, and he was attempting to wash the poison off the grain.

After a stay of only thirty-six hours in "liberated" Kurdistan, Galbraith made his way back to the Syrian border, which was under heavy artillery fire. As shells landed all around him, he dashed across the mudflats to a sandbagged position at the edge of the river. From there a small boat took him to Syria. The Iraqis seized the border crossing the next day.

Although Galbraith was teased for the unsteadiness of his camera work, his Hi-8 images, the first of the collapse of the Kurdish uprising, led U.S. news programs on April 1, 1991. It took Kurdish refugees several more days to reach the Turkish border, but Galbraith telephoned Morton Abramowitz, the former INR assistant secretary who had since become U.S. ambassador in Turkey, to warn him that close to a million people would soon be at his doorstep. On April 2 Galbraith prepared a detailed memo for Senators George Mitchell and Daniel Patrick Moynihan, reporting that the Kurds were in danger of being massacred. Perhaps the most significant outcome of Galbraith's unsuccessful 1988 effort to get sanctions imposed against Iraq was that by 1991, when the Kurds again faced slaughter, people in Washington had at least heard of the unlucky minority. Having raised the genocide issue in 1988, Senator Pell also had greater authority warning that if the allies did not act, the Kurds could be wiped out.

In entering Iraq without Senate approval, Galbraith had broken one of the Senate Foreign Relations Committee's cardinal rules. After seeing what he saw in Kurdistan, he began breaking others. Staff members were not allowed to make media appearances, but Galbraith appeared on *Nightline* on April 1, April 4, and again on April 18. He also wrote a cover story for the *New Republic* on the failed uprising. Senator Moynihan spoke on Galbraith's behalf on the Senate floor on April 17. He urged that Congress should reward "service above and beyond the call of duty." Noting that members of the Senate staff usually went unrecognized, he said, "This is no dereliction on our part. It is simply that in two and more centuries we have not seen the likes of young Galbraith: The indifference to his own welfare and safety; the all-consuming concern for the welfare and safety of an oppressed people caught up in a ghastly travail."[155]

Some 400,000 Kurdish refugees had reached Turkey by mid-April, and it was feared an additional half a million were en route.[156] Galbraith's new-found cachet made him less rather than more tactful. He found Washington speaking as if humanitarian aid agencies would solve the problem. Responding to questions about the security of Kurds in Turkey, Secretary of State Baker said, "It is hoped that the presence of humanitarian relief workers will act as a deterrent to future harassment and persecution of these people."[157] At one relief meeting attended by forty to fifty crisis experts, Galbraith exploded. "Are you telling me that a bunch of unarmed Swedes at feeding stations are going to give the Kurds enough confidence to come down from the mountains to face a man our president has likened to Hitler? I suppose your solution to Auschwitz would have been to ensure that some Swedish girls in shorts would have been made available to give the Jews food!" His outburst was met with silence. This was not how business was done. Galbraith was told he had become too emotionally attached to the issue.

But Galbraith's proposed alternative—allied military intervention—was gaining support. Prime Minister John Major of Britain began urging the Bush administration to act. William Safire attacked the president for his "loss of nerve."[158] He wrote, "People like the too trusting Kurds now know they can get killed by relying on Mr. Bush."[159] Still, Bush held firm, responding by authorizing $10 million for relief. One top White House aide said, "A hundred Safire columns will not change the public's mind. There is no political downside to our policy."[160]

But Turkey, a U.S. ally, vociferously disagreed. It needed U.S. help to get rid of the sprawling Kurdish presence in southern Turkey. Secretary of State Baker took a helicopter ride to the Turkish border on April 7 and in a seventeen-minute stopover saw some 50,000 Kurds hugging the surrounding mountains. It was a public relations disaster that he feared would negate all the gains the Gulf War had brought the Bush White House. It was also a humanitarian catastrophe that moved him. Some 1,000 Kurds were estimated to be dying per day. "We can't let this go on," Baker said. "We've got to do something—and we've got to do it now."[161]

On April 16, 1991, the United States joined with its allies and launched Operation Provide Comfort, carving out a "safe haven" for Kurds north of the thirty-sixth parallel in northern Iraq. Allied ground forces would set up relief camps in Iraq, and U.S., British, and French aircraft would patrol from the skies.[162]

Provide Comfort was perhaps the most promising indicator of what the post–Cold War world might bring in the way of genocide prevention. Under the command of Lieutenant General John M. Shalikashvili, some 12,000 U.S. soldiers helped patrol the region as part of a 21,000-troop allied ground effort. This marked an unprecedented intervention in the internal affairs of a state for humanitarian reasons. Thanks to the allied effort, the Iraqi Kurds were able to return home and, with the protection of NATO jets overhead, govern themselves.

Justice?

Today women Kurdish survivors crunched into resettlement complexes cling to rumors that their male *Anfalakan* remain alive in secret jails in the desert. Some inquiries have been met with cold precision, others with evasion. On September 25, 1990, the following directive was issued by Iraqi authorities in Erbil: "The phrase 'We do not have any information about their fate' will replace the phrase 'They were arrested during the victorious Anfal operation and remain in detention.'"[163]

The entrance to the ravaged town of Halabja is marked by a statue of a father dying as he tries to shield his two sons from the gas attack. More than 70,000 Kurds have returned to the town where VX, sarin, and mustard gas were combined in deadly cocktails. Survivors remain blinded from corneal scarring from mustard gas burns.[164] Miscarriages and birth defects such as cleft palates and harelips recur in the maternity ward of the Martyrs Hospital. Christine Gosden, a British geneticist, has attempted to investigate and raise money to treat the ailments. "Not only do those who survived have to cope with memories of their relatives suddenly dying in their arms," Gosden noted, "they have to try to come to terms with their own painful diseases and those of their surviving friends and relatives."[165] Gosden says infant deaths are more than four times greater than in neighboring Sulaymaniyah. Leukemia and lymphomas are ravaging the community at rates Kurdish doctors claim are four times higher than in unexposed areas. No chemotherapy or radiotherapy is available. More profound, Gosden believes, the congenital malformations in children born after the Halabja attacks suggest that the chemical agents have produced permanent genetic mutations in those exposed. Preliminary medical findings indicate that the occurrence of these mutations is comparable with those who were about one to two miles from the epicenter of the Hiroshima and Nagasaki atomic bombs. The Anfal technically ended in 1988, but Gosden calls it "the persistent genocide." Succeeding generations will pay a price.

In their failed revolt against Baghdad in 1991, the Kurds stormed secret police buildings and recovered huge piles of government records. The files had been stuffed randomly into plastic flour sacks, tea boxes, and binders. Others were tied loosely with staples, strings, laces, or pins. Handwritten ledgers were covered with flowered wallpaper, and some of the Arab titles had been penned in psychedelic, calligraphic script filled in with colored felt-tip pens by bored Iraqi bureaucrats.[166] The Kurds who gathered the evidence were not thinking about prosecuting Iraqi officials or even documenting a genocide for posterity. Rather, they hoped to learn the identity of informers. Although many of the documents were destroyed or lost in the rebellion, Iraqis were so meticulous about their bureaucratized killing and cleansing machine that an abundance of evidence was recovered.

In May 1992 Galbraith helped negotiate the transfer of fourteen tons of captured documents to the National Archives in Washington for safekeeping. Human Rights Watch (HRW), the parent organization to all the regional "watch" groups, which itself secured the shipment of an additional four tons from the Kurdish Democratic Party, was granted exclusive access to the documents and launched an unprecedented investigation. The more than 4 million pages covered not only the Anfal but Iraqi repression from the 1960s forward. There were explicit shoot-to-kill orders, such as the June 14, 1987, order from the Ba'ath Party People's Command in Zakho. "Dear Comrades," reads the order, "The entry of any kind of human cargo, nutritional supplies, or mechanical instruments into the security-prohibited villages under the second stage [of the operation] is strictly prohibited. . . . It is

Dr. Clyde Snow, forensic anthropologist, exhumes the blindfolded skull of a Kurdish teenager from a mass grave in Erbil, northern Iraq, December 1991.

the duty of the members of the military forces to kill any human being or animal found in these areas."[167] There were proud tallies of individuals and villages eliminated, minutes of meetings, arrest warrants, notes on phone surveillance, and decrees ordering mass execution.

Human Rights Watch dispatched its researchers to Iraqi Kurdistan in 1992 and 1993, where they interviewed some 350 survivors and witnesses to the slaughter. These investigators teamed up with scientists from Physicians for Human Rights who exhumed mass graves and gathered forensic material, such as traces of chemical weapons found in soil samples and bomb shrapnel, as well as the skeletons of the victims themselves. Excavators found rope still tying the hands of the decomposed men, women, and children. One foray yielded a fully preserved woman's braid.[168]

The eighteen-month investigation by Human Rights Watch (aided by Physicians for Human Rights) was the most ambitious ever carried out by a nongovernmental organization. It was the kind of study that a U.S. government determined to stop atrocities might well have attempted while the crimes were under way. The human rights group legitimated the earli-

er estimate of Shorsh Resool, the amateur investigator into the operation.
The group found that between 50,000 and 100,000 Kurds (many of whom
were women and children and nearly all of whom were noncombatants)
were executed or disappeared between February and September 1988
alone. Hundreds of thousands of Kurds were forcibly displaced. The numbers of those eliminated or "lost" cannot be confirmed because most of the
men who were taken away were executed by firing squad and buried in
unexhumed, shallow mass graves in southwest Iraq, near the border with
Saudi Arabia. The Kurdish leadership claims 182,000 were eliminated in
the Anfal campaign. Mahmoud 'Uthman, the leader of the Socialist Party
of Kurdistan, tells of a 1991 meeting at which the Anfal's commander, al-
Majid, grew enraged over this number. "What is this exaggerated figure of
182,000?" he snapped. "It couldn't have been more than 100,000."[169]

For the first time in its history, Human Rights Watch found that a country had committed genocide. Often a large number of victims is required
to help show an intent to destroy a group. But in the Iraqi case the confis-
cated government records explicitly recorded Iraqi aims to wipe out rural
Kurdish life.

Having documented the genocide, Human Rights Watch assigned
lawyer Richard Dicker to draw up a legal case in the spring of 1994. He
hoped to get Canada, the Netherlands, or a Scandinavian state to enforce
the genocide convention by at least filing genocide charges before the
International Court of Justice. "My role was to make it happen by preparing a tight case and persuading a state to take it on," Dicker remembers.
"Of course I failed spectacularly." Diplomats initially argued that Iraq had
not committed genocide. "They would say, 'Gee, this doesn't look like the
Holocaust to me!'" Dicker recalls. But once they became familiar with the
law, most officials dropped that objection and worried out loud about the
consequences of scrutinizing a fellow state in an international court.

If a genocide case were filed at the ICJ, the court could recommend that
Iraqi assets be seized or that Iraqi perpetrators be punished at home,
abroad, or in some international court. International criminal punishment
had not been levied since Nuremberg, but human rights lawyers hoped
that the Iraq case would renew interest in prosecution. After several years
of badgering by Dicker and colleague Joost Hiltermann, two governments
confidentially accepted the challenge, but they refused to file the case
unless a European state would join them. To this day no European power
has agreed.

The U.S. Senate had ratified the genocide convention, but Dicker and others believed that the United States should keep a "low profile" on any ICJ genocide case against Iraq because of its nettlesome reservations to the treaty. Advocates feared that Hussein might use the American reservations to deny the ICJ jurisdiction.[170] Although Human Rights Watch did not request American participation in the case, it did hope the United States would support the effort. After initially opposing the campaign, the State Department legal adviser received innumerable legal briefs and evidentiary memos from Dicker and Hiltermann, and changed his mind. In July 1995 Secretary of State Warren Christopher signed a communiqué that found Iraq had committed genocide against Iraq's rural Kurds and that endorsed Human Rights Watch's efforts to file a case against Iraq.

To this day, however, no Iraqi soldier or political leader has been punished for atrocities committed against the Kurds.

Muslim and Croat prisoners in the Serb concentration camp of Trnopolje.

Ron Haviv-VII

Chapter 9

Bosnia: "No More than Witnesses at a Funeral"

"Ethnic Cleansing"

If the Gulf War posed the first test for U.S. foreign policy in the post–Cold War world, the wars in the Balkans offered a second. Before 1991 Yugoslavia was composed of six republics. But in June of that year, when Serbian president Slobodan Milosevic began to stoke nationalist flames and increase Serb dominance, the republic of Slovenia seceded, sparking a relatively painless ten-day war. Croatia, which declared independence at the same time, faced a tougher exit. Because Croatia had a sizable Serb minority and a picturesque and lucrative coastline, the Yugoslav National Army (JNA) refused to let it go. A seven-month war left some 10,000 dead and 700,000 displaced from their homes. It also introduced the world to images of Serb artillery pounding civilians in towns like Dubrovnik and Vukovar. By late 1991 it was clear that Bosnia (43 percent Muslim, 35 percent Orthodox Serb, and 18 percent Roman Catholic Croat), the most ethnically heterogeneous of Yugoslavia's republics, was in a bind. If Bosnia remained a republic within rump Yugoslavia, its Serbs would receive the plum jobs and educational opportunities, whereas Muslims and Croats would be marginalized and likely physically abused under Milosevic's

Map of Yugoslavia, depicting Serb gains, 1991–1995.

oppressive rule. But if it broke away, its Muslim citizens would be especially vulnerable because they did not have a parent protector in the neighborhood: Serbs and Croats in Bosnia counted on Serbia and Croatia for armed
succor, but the country's Muslims could rely only upon the international
community.

The seven members of the Bosnian presidency (two Muslims, two
Serbs, two Croats, and one Yugoslav) turned to Europe and the United
States for guidance on how to avoid bloodshed. Western diplomats
instructed Bosnia's leadership to offer human rights protections to minorities and to stage a "free and fair" independence referendum. The Bosnians
by and large did as they were told. In March 1992 they held a referendum
on independence in which 99.4 percent of voters chose to secede from
Yugoslavia. But two Serb members of the presidency, who were hard-
liners, had convinced most of Bosnia's Serbs to boycott the vote.[1] Backed
by Milosevic in Belgrade, both Serb nationalists in the presidency resigned
and declared their own separate Bosnian Serb state within the borders of

the old Bosnia. The Serb-dominated Yugoslav National Army teamed up with local Bosnian Serb forces, contributing an estimated 80,000 uniformed, armed Serb troops and handing almost all of their Bosnia-based arsenal to the newly created Bosnian Serb Army. Although the troops changed their badges, the army vehicles that remained behind still bore the traces of the letters "JNA." Compounding matters for the Muslims and for those Serbs and Croats who remained loyal to the idea of a multiethnic Bosnia, the United Nations had imposed an arms embargo in 1991 banning arms deliveries to the region. This froze in place a gross imbalance in Muslim and Serb military capacity. When the Serbs began a vicious offensive aimed at creating an ethnically homogenous state, the Muslims were largely defenseless.

In 1991 Germany had been the country to press for recognizing Croatia's independence. But in April 1992 the EC and the United States took the lead in granting diplomatic recognition to the newly independent state of Bosnia. U.S. policymakers hoped that the mere act of legitimating Bosnia would help stabilize it. This diplomatic act would "show" President Milosevic that the world stood behind Bosnian independence. But Milosevic was better briefed. He knew that the international commitment to Bosnia's statehood was more rhetorical than real.

Bosnian Serb soldiers and militiamen had compiled lists of leading Muslim and Croat intellectuals, musicians, and professionals. And within days of Bosnia's secession from Yugoslavia, they began rounding up non-Serbs, savagely beating them, and often executing them. Bosnian Serb units destroyed most cultural and religious sites in order to erase any memory of a Muslim or Croat presence in what they would call "Republika Srpska."[2] In the hills around the former Olympic city of Sarajevo, Serb forces positioned heavy antiaircraft guns, rocket launchers, and tanks and began pummeling the city below with artillery and mortar fire.

The Serbs' practice of targeting civilians and ridding their territory of non-Serbs was euphemistically dubbed *etničko čišcenje,* or "ethnic cleansing," a phrase reminiscent of the Nazis' *Säuberung,* or "cleansing," of Jews. Holocaust historian Raul Hilberg said of the Nazi euphemism: "The key to the entire operation from the psychological standpoint was never to utter the words that would be appropriate to the action. Say nothing; do these things; do not describe them."[3] The Khmer Rouge and Iraqi Northern Bureau chief al-Majid had followed a similar rule of thumb, and Serb nationalists did the same.

As the war in Bosnia progressed, outsiders and insiders relied on the phrase "ethnic cleansing" to describe the means and ends employed by Serb and later other nationalistic forces in Bosnia. It was defined as the elimination of an ethnic group from territory controlled by another ethnic group. Although the phrase initially chilled those who heard it, it quickly became numbing shorthand for deeds that were far more evocative when described in detail.

The phrase "ethnic cleansing" meant different things on different days in different places. Sometimes a Serb radio broadcast would inform the citizenry that a local factory had introduced a quota to limit the number of Muslim or Croat employees to 1 percent of the overall workforce. Elsewhere edicts would begin appearing pasted around town, as they had in 1915 in the Ottoman Empire. These decrees informed non-Serb inhabitants of the new rules. In the town of Celinac, near the northern Bosnia town of Banja Luka, for instance, the Serb "war presidency" issued a directive giving all non-Serbs "special status." Because of "military actions," a curfew was imposed from 4 p.m. to 6 a.m. Non-Serbs were forbidden to:

- meet in cafes, restaurants, or other public places
- bathe or swim in the Vrbanija or Josavka Rivers
- hunt or fish
- move to another town without authorization
- carry a weapon
- drive or travel by car
- gather in groups of more than three men
- contact relatives from outside Celinac (all household visits must be reported)
- use means of communication other than the post office phone
- wear uniforms: military, police, or forest guard
- sell real estate or exchange homes without approval.[4]

Sometimes Muslims and Croats were told they had forty-eight hours to pack their bags. But usually they were given no warning at all. Machine-gun fire or the smell of hastily sprayed kerosene were the first hints of an imminent change of domicile. In virtually no case where departure took place was the exit voluntary. As refugees poured into neighboring states, it was tempting to see them as the byproducts of war, but the purging of non-Serbs was not only an explicit war aim of Serb nationalists; it was their primary aim.

Serb gunmen knew that their violent deportation and killing campaign would not be enough to ensure the lasting achievement of ethnic purity. The armed marauders sought to sever permanently the bond between citizens and land. Thus, they forced fathers to castrate their sons or molest their daughters; they humiliated and raped (often impregnating) young women. Theirs was a deliberate policy of destruction and degradation: destruction so this avowed enemy race would have no homes to which to return; degradation so the former inhabitants would not stand tall—and thus would not dare again stand—in Serb-held territory.

Senior officials within the Bush and later the Clinton administrations understood the dire human consequences of Serb aggression. This was Europe and not a crisis that could be shoved on to the desks of midlevel officials. More than ever before, Lemkinian voices for action were heard within the State Department, on Capitol Hill, and on America's editorial pages. A swarm of Western journalists in Bosnia supplied regular, graphic coverage. Yet despite unprecedented public outcry about foreign brutality, for the next three and a half years the United States, Europe, and the United Nations stood by while some 200,000 Bosnians were killed, more than 2 million were displaced, and the territory of a multiethnic European republic was sliced into three ethnically pure statelets.

The international community did not do nothing during the vicious war. With the Cold War behind it, the United Nations became the forum for much collective activity. The UN Security Council pointed fingers at the main aggressors, imposed economic sanctions, deployed peacekeepers, and helped deliver humanitarian aid. Eventually it even set up a war crimes tribunal to punish the plotters and perpetrators of mass murder. What the United States and its allies did not do until it was too late, however, was intervene with armed force to stop genocide. So although the European location of the crime scene generated widespread press coverage, a far more vocal elite lobby for intervention, and the most bitter cleft within the U.S. government since the Vietnam War, these factors did not combine to make either President Bush or President Clinton intervene in time to save the country of Bosnia or its citizens from destruction.

Warning

"Bloody as Hell"

Serb brutality in Bosnia came with plenty of warning. Intelligence officials are severely scolded and embarrassed if they fail to anticipate a crisis, but they face less opprobrium if they offer a "false positive" by predicting a crisis that does not unfold. The intelligence community is thus more prone to raise too many flags than too few. U.S. intelligence had already failed to forecast Saddam Hussein's 1990 invasion of Kuwait and the 1991 breakup of the Soviet Union. When it came to the Balkan wars, U.S. analysts were therefore especially careful to position themselves well out in front of the carnage. The brief war in Slovenia and the longer and more bloody one in Croatia in 1991 led officials in the U.S. government to predict that Bosnia's ethnic diversity and the Muslim plurality's defenselessness would make the next war the deadliest of all. Although reporters spoke later of the Bosnian conflict's "erupting," it would be more apt to say the Bosnian conflict arrived. Indeed, many felt it was a war that arrived virtually on schedule. The war's viciousness had been forecast so regularly and so vividly as to desensitize U.S. officials. By the time the bloodshed began, U.S. officials were almost *too* prepared: They had been reading warning cables for so long that nothing could surprise them.

Jim Hooper, a fastidious U.S. foreign service veteran, worked as the deputy director of the Office of East Europe and Yugoslav Affairs in the State Department's European Bureau from 1989 to 1991. He had joined the U.S. government in 1971 and spent the late 1980s consumed with the right kind of turbulence and upheaval—the historic roundtable negotiations that helped bring about the end of communism in Poland, the fall of the Berlin Wall, the velvet passage to democracy in Czechoslovakia. But ever since he read an article in the *Economist* in early 1989 that predicted the violent breakup of Yugoslavia, Hooper had been worried. In 1991, with Balkan leaders sounding ever more belligerent and nationalist militias sprouting, Hooper urged Deputy Secretary of State Lawrence Eagleburger to travel to the region. Eagleburger had served as U.S. ambassador to Yugoslavia from 1977 to 1981 and consulted on business there throughout the 1980s in partnership with Henry Kissinger. He spoke Serbo-Croatian and was enamored of the verdant landscape. In February 1991 Eagleburger

paid a visit to the region and warned Milosevic against violence. When he
returned, he said to Hooper, "I thought you were exaggerating, that you
were giving me the usual bureaucratic hype. But now that I've been there,
I think you were much too optimistic. It is going to be bloody as hell."
Eagleburger thought there was nothing the United States could do, that it
was Europe's problem, and that any attempt to get involved would fail *and*
harm the United States in the process.

Some of the loudest early-warning sirens and moral sermons came from
Capitol Hill. Some, like Republican senator Bob Dole, brought a prior
interest in the region. During World War II, the young Kansan had led an
attack on a German machine-gun nest in Po Valley, Italy. When Dole saw
his radioman go down, he crawled out of his foxhole to retrieve him. As he
did, a shell exploded nearby, shattering his shoulder and his vertebrae.
Shipped from Italy to Russell, Kansas, in a full-body cast, the young war
hero earned press coverage that caught the eye of Dr. Hampar Kelikian, a
Chicago reconstructive surgeon. Kelikian wrote to Dole and told him that
if the young veteran could find the train fare, he would perform the necessary surgery at no cost. Dole's neighbors chipped in, filling an empty cigar
box propped up in the window of the local drug store where Dole had
served as a soda jerk. Kelikian not only operated on Dole in Chicago but
also kept him company in the long recovery period by regaling him with
stories about the Turkish slaughter of the Armenians. Kelikian had escaped
to America as a boy after three of his sisters were massacred in the genocide.[5] Dole, who had never before heard of these crimes, was shocked.
When he joined the Senate, he kept an eye trained on the Balkans.

Dole began denouncing Yugoslavia's human rights record in 1986. He
introduced Senate resolutions expressing special concern about the state's
systematic persecution of Albanians, who made up 90 percent of the population in Kosovo, Serbia. Each year Serb forces stepped up their violence
against the Albanians, and Dole in turn amplified his denunciations. By
1990, with the rest of Eastern Europe liberalizing, Dole was describing the
Yugoslav government as a "symbol of tyranny and repression" that was
"murdering, maiming and imprisoning" its citizens.[6]

But none of the Kansas senator's rhetorical litanies had prepared him for
the official visit he paid to Kosovo in August 1990. At first the Serb authorities tried to keep Dole and six Senate colleagues from entering Serbia's
southern province, prompting Dole to storm out of a Belgrade meeting.
They next tried to supply the group with a Serbian watchdog who would

prevent them from speaking freely to Albanians. In the end the Belgrade regime supplied a Serb driver who roared into Kosovo's capital at break-neck speed in order to block the American lawmakers from viewing the grim police state. As the bus entered Pristina, thousands of ethnic Albanians lined the streets and began chanting, "USA, USA." Dole later recalled "appalling and unforgettable" scenes of hundreds of people running across the fields to wave to the speeding bus, while police with guns and clubs mauled them.[7] After returning, Dole told the *Washington Post* of "tanks and troops everywhere, hundreds of demonstrators fleeing in all directions, try-ing to avoid the club-wielding security forces, and tear gas rising over the confusion and carnage." Scores were injured and hundreds arrested.[8] On the Senate floor Dole declared, "The United States cannot sit this out on the sidelines, we have a moral obligation to take a strong stand in defense of the individual rights of Albanians and all of the people of Yugoslavia."[9] Dole's act of "witnessing" conditioned his response to future reports of atrocity. As his chief foreign policy adviser, Mira Baratta, notes, "It is one thing to have a natural inclination to care about human rights, but it is another thing entirely when you see people who only want to wave at Americans getting pummeled before your own eyes. Once you have seen that, you just can't look away."

Congressman Frank McCloskey, a Democrat from Indiana, also dates his awakening to a weeklong trip he took to the Balkans during the war in Croatia in December 1991. The congressman had four experiences on the trip that, in hindsight, ably illustrate the nature of the entire Yugoslav mess and prepared him for Milosevic's double-dealings in Bosnia. They also altered the course of his political career and life. First, he was shelled by Serb forces while visiting the Croatian city of Osijek, a university town that reminded him of his own Bloomington. Second, he came upon the remains of a massacre that had been committed around the Croatian town of Vocin, some seventy miles southeast of the capital of Zagreb. Forty Croatian vic-tims, most over the age of sixty, had been dismembered with chain saws, and McCloskey, who was one of the first to arrive on the scene, was revolted by the piles of mutilated body parts. Third, when he personally traveled to Belgrade to confront the Serbian authorities, President Milosevic told McCloskey solemnly that no matter what he had seen or thought he had seen, Osijek had not been shelled and no massacre had been committed in Vocin. "He was very smooth and polished, and described himself as a peace-loving man," McCloskey remembers. Milosevic told him that the corpses were "part of a show" put on by the Croatian government. And fourth, a U.S. embassy official in Belgrade had warned him that although the ongoing war in Croatia was bad, the conflict in Bosnia would produce a "real slaughter." The war would rarely deviate from this text: shelling, massacre, straight-faced lies, and plenty of early warning of worse to come.

Wishful Thinking

American policymakers have often fallen prey to wishful thinking in the face of what they later recognized to be genocide. But history has shown that this phenomenon is more human than American. Before the war began in Bosnia, many of its citizens, too, dismissed omnipresent omens. They were convinced that bloodshed could not happen there, that it could not happen then, or that it could not happen to them. In order to maintain this faith amid mounting evidence of horror, Bosnians found ways to link the widespread tales of terror to circumstances that did not apply to them. When Serb forces began targeting Croatian civilians in 1991, many Muslims in Bosnia told themselves that it was Croatian president Franjo Tudjman who was the nationalist and the obstructionist making it impossible to resolve the conflict peacefully. *Bosnia's* leaders would be more sensible and moderate. Besides, even if the Serb response to Croatia's declaration of independence was unduly violent, their beloved Yugoslavia would never turn on Bosnia, an ethnically jumbled microcosm of Yugoslav leader Marshal Tito's larger dream. Even once it was clear that war was consuming Bosnia and the radio brimmed with gruesome reports of summary executions and rapes, Muslims continued to console themselves that the war could never infect their neighborhoods. "That's a long way off," they would say. "*We* have been living together for years."

In retrospect, when Serb radio began broadcasting reports that Bosnian towns had been attacked by "Muslim extremists," non-Serbs might have checked their history books. The extremists tended to be those who made such announcements, justifying preemptive assaults. But Bosnians were not prepared for either the crackle of evening gunfire or the suddenly stern, familiar radio voice telling them, "Citizens are requested to remain in their homes and apartments for the sake of their own security."

Most Bosnians did as they were told. Under Tito's forty-five-year Communist rule, they had grown accustomed to listening to strongmen. In many the muscle that twitches in defiance, or at least in apprehension, of state authority had atrophied for lack of use. Some might have questioned the source, but few dared to challenge it. The instructions made sense: danger outside; safety inside. Unfortunately, they made sense to those who issued them as well. Because the Muslims stayed indoors, they could be found playing cards, folding linen, or simply sleeping when the Serb police or militia arrived.

Bosnians were not especially naive or gullible. They erected what Primo Levi likened to a cordon sanitaire to shield them from murderous events they felt powerless to stop or avoid. They were confronted with a choice that for most was too awful to contemplate: fight or flight. Bosnia's Muslims were militarily unprepared to make war, but, like the Kurds who remained in Saddam Hussein's prohibited zones, they stared out at the fields they had tilled or the hills they had roamed for generations and could not bring themselves to take leave. In the primarily rural country, many clung to the cold walls that they or their ancestors had assembled brick by brick. They claimed even the patch of sky overhead. Every Bosnian seemed to have a river of his or her own—the Sava, the Una, the Sana, the Miljacka, the Drina—in which they had bathed as children, by which they had nestled romantically for the first time as teenagers. There was, they said, "a special bond between heart and grass."

Because the national story in Tito's era was one of "brotherhood and unity" in which ethnic identity was discounted and even disparaged, and because the communities had lived intermingled or in neighboring villages for so many years, many found it even harder to take seriously the threat from their neighbors. They maintained a faith in the power of familiarity, charm, and reason. They believed that individual destiny and personality would count for something.

As remarkable as the existence of this faith is its durability. In Cambodia even those subjected daily to the rigors and horrors of Khmer Rouge rule persisted in hoping that those who were hauled away were only being reeducated. In Bosnia, even two years into the war, when more than 100,000 of their neighbors had been killed and the bloodiest of displacements had taken place, thousands of Muslims and Croats refused to leave Serb-held territory. Some had no money, and by then the Serbs had begun charging an "exit tax" of nearly $1,000. But most who remained found the fear of death preferable to the reality of abandoning their homes. Foreign visitors would plead with them, remind them of the lunacy (patently obvious to our transient, cosmopolitan eyes) of their perseverance. Those who tested the neighborhood thugs inevitably lost their homes and many, eventually, their lives. One month foreign visitors would meet an elderly family that would dip into its emergency stock of bread, cheese, and Turkish coffee and produce photos of missing family members. Several months later the visitors could return to find the quaint cul-de-sac reduced to blackened rubble. Or they might discover the Muslims' bungalow intact but occupied by Serbs who hung a Serb flag from the window, as protective lamb's blood had once been splashed above doorways. The Muslim occupants had vanished.

Human rights groups were quicker than they had ever been to document atrocities. Helsinki Watch, the European arm of what would become known as Human Rights Watch, had begun dispatching field missions to the Balkans in 1991. When the war in Bosnia broke out in 1992, the organization was thus able to call quickly on a team of experienced lawyers. In the early months of the war, Helsinki Watch sent two teams to the Balkans, the first from March 19 to April 28, 1992, the second from May 29 to June 19. Investigators interviewed refugees, government officials, combatants, Western diplomats, relief officials, and journalists. Aryeh Neier, executive director of Helsinki Watch, edited the impressive 359-page report, which contained gruesome details of a systematic slaughter. Neier found himself presiding over an organization-wide debate over whether the Serb atrocities amounted to genocide.

Neier had moved to the United States from Germany at age eleven as a refugee after World War II. As president of the history club at Stuyvesant High School in New York City, he had heard about the exploits of a fellow refugee, Raphael Lemkin, who had coined a new word. In 1952, forty years before the Bosnian war, Neier, a presumptuous sixteen-year-old, rode the subway to the new UN headquarters and tracked down Lemkin in one of its unused offices. Neier asked the crusader if he would come to speak to the Stuyvesant history club some afternoon. Never one to turn down a speaking engagement, Lemkin agreed, giving the future founder of Helsinki Watch his first introduction to the concept of genocide.

In the Helsinki Watch report, published just four months into the war in August 1992, the organization found that the systematic executions, expulsions, and indiscriminate shelling attacks at the very least offered "*prima facie* evidence that genocide is taking place." Neier had learned Lemkin's lessons well. The report said: "Genocide is the most unspeakable crime in the lexi-

con. . . . The authorization that the Convention provides to the United
Nations to prevent and suppress this crime carries with it an obligation to
act. The only guidance the Convention provides as to the manner of action
is that it should be 'appropriate.' We interpret this as meaning it should be
effective."[10]

Helsinki Watch had a mandate different from that of Amnesty
International. It criticized both the perpetrator state *and* the Western powers that were doing so little to curb the killing. But for all of their outrage,
many individuals within the organization were uncomfortable appealing to
the United States to use armed force. "We were in a real bind," Neier
remembers. "The organization had never called for military intervention,
and we couldn't bring ourselves to do so. Yet we could also see that the
atrocities would not be stopped by any other means. What we ended up
with was a kind of tortured compromise." In the report Helsinki Watch
described U.S. policy as "inert, inconsistent and misguided."[11] It became
the first organization to call upon the United Nations to set up an international war crimes tribunal to prosecute those responsible for these crimes.
But when it came to the question of military intervention, it punted:

> It is beyond the competence of Helsinki Watch to determine all the
> steps that may be required to prevent and suppress the crime of geno-
> cide. It may be necessary for the United Nations to employ military
> force to that end. It is not the province of Helsinki Watch to deter-
> mine whether such force is required. Helsinki Watch believes that it is
> the responsibility of the Security Council to address this question.[12]

The Security Council was made up of countries, including the United
States, steadfastly opposed to using armed force.

A U.S. Policy of Disapproval

When Yugoslavia had disintegrated in June 1991, European leaders claimed
they had the authority, the strength, and the will to manage the country's
collapse. Europeans had high hopes for the era of the Maastricht Treaty and
the creation of a borderless continent that might eventually challenge U.S.
economic and diplomatic supremacy. Jacques Poos, Luxembourg's foreign
minister, proclaimed "If anyone can do anthing here, it is the EC. It is not

Ron Haviv-VII

Serb Paramilitaries in Bijeljina, Bosnia, Spring 1992.

the U.S. or the USSR or anyone else."[13] The United States happily stepped aside. "It was time to make the Europeans step up to the plate and show that they could act as a unified power," Secretary of State James Baker wrote later. "Yugoslavia was as good a first test as any."[14] Whatever the long-term promise of the European Union (EU), it was not long into the Balkan wars before European weaknesses were exposed. By the time of the Bosnian conflict in April 1992, most American decisionmakers had come to recognize that there was no "European" diplomacy to speak of. They were left asking, as Henry Kissinger had done, "What's Europe's phone number?" Yet anxious to avoid involvement themselves, they persisted in deferring to European leadership that was nonexistent.

U.S. and European officials adopted a diplomatic approach that yielded few dividends. Cyrus Vance, secretary of state under President Carter, and David Owen, a former British Labour Party leader, were appointed chairmen of a UN-EU negotiation process aimed at convincing the "warring parties" to settle their differences. But nationalist Serbs in Bosnia and Serbia were intent on resolving difference by eliminating it. The "peace process" became a handy stalling device. Condemnations were issued. U.S. diplomats warned Milosevic that the United States regarded his military support for rebel Bosnian Serbs with the "utmost gravity." But because warnings were not backed by meaningful threats, Milosevic either ignored them or dissembled. "For Milosevic the truth has a relative and instrumental rather than absolute value," the U.S. ambassador to Yugoslavia, Warren Zimmermann, observed. "If it serves his objectives, it is put to use; if not, it can be discarded."[15] Although Milosevic struck some as a habitual liar, most U.S. and European diplomats continued to meet his undiplomatic behavior with diplomatic house calls. Milosevic did not close off the diplomatic option as the Khmer Rouge had done. Instead, he shrewdly maintained contact with Western foreign servants, cultivating the impression from the very start of the conflict that peace was "right around the corner."

Most diplomats brought a gentlemen's bias to their diplomacy, trusting Milosevic's assurances. This was not new. Most notorious, Adolf Hitler persuaded Neville Chamberlain that he would not go to war if Britain and France would allow Germany to absorb the Sudetenland. Just after the September 1938 meeting, where the infamous Munich agreement was signed, Chamberlain wrote to his sister: "In spite of the hardness and ruthlessness, I thought I saw in his face, I got the impression that here was a man who could be relied upon when he gave his word."[16] When it came to Milosevic, Ambassador Zimmerman noted, "Many is the U.S. senator or congressman who has reeled out of his office exclaiming, 'Why, he is not nearly as bad as I expected!'"[17] Milosevic usually met U.S. protests with incredulous queries as to why the behavior of Bosnian Serbs in Bosnia had anything to do with the president of Serbia, a neighboring state. He saw that the Bush administration was prepared to isolate the Serbs and brand them pariahs but not intervene militarily. This the Serbian leader deemed an acceptable risk.

Washington's foreign policy specialists were divided about the U.S. role in the post–Cold War world. One camp believed in the idealistic promise of a new era. They felt that the Gulf War eventually fought against Saddam Hussein in 1991 and the subsequent creation of the safe haven for the Kurds of northern Iraq signaled a U.S. commitment to combating aggression. Where vital American interests *or* cherished values were imperiled and where the risks were reasonable, the United States should act. They were heartened by Bush's claim that the Gulf War had "buried once and for all" America's Vietnam syndrome. The United States had a new credibility. "Because of what's happened," President Bush had said soon after the U.S. triumph, "I think when we say something that is objectively correct—like 'don't take over a neighbor or you're going to bear some responsibility'— people are going to listen."[18] Still, for all the talk of a "new world order," Bush was in fact ambivalent. To be sure, the United States had made war against Iraq, a state that "took over a neighbor." But the United States had always frowned upon and occasionally even reversed aggression that affected U.S. strategic interests. Although Serbia's aggression against the internationally recognized state of Bosnia clearly made the Bosnian war an international conflict, top U.S. officials viewed it as a civil war. And it was still not clear whether the rights of individuals *within* states would have any higher claim to U.S. protection or promotion than they had for much of the century.

The other camp vying to place its stamp on the new world order was firm in the belief that abuses committed inside a country were not America's business. Most of the senior officials in the Bush administration, including Secretary of State Baker, Secretary of Defense Richard Cheney, National Security Adviser Brent Scowcroft, and Chairman of the Joint Chiefs of Staff Colin Powell, were traditional foreign policy "realists." The United States did not have the most powerful military in the history of the world in order to undertake squishy, humanitarian "social work." Rather, the foreign policy team should focus on promoting a narrowly defined set of U.S. economic and security interests, expanding American markets, curbing nuclear proliferation, and maintaining military readiness. Although these were the same men who had waged the Gulf War, that war was fought in order to check Hussein's regional dominance and to maintain U.S. access to cheap oil. Similarly, when they established the safe haven for Kurds in Operation Provide Comfort, the Bush administration had been providing comfort to Turkey, a vital U.S. ally anxious to get rid of Iraqi Kurdish refugees.

With ethnic and civil conflict erupting left and right and sovereignty no longer the bar on U.S. intervention it had been in Morgenthau's day, Bush's foreign policy team saw that the United States would need to develop its own criteria for the use of military force. In 1984 President Reagan's defense secretary, Caspar Weinberger, had demanded that armed intervention (1) be used only to protect the vital interests of the United States or its allies; (2) be carried out wholeheartedly, with the clear intention of winning; (3) be in pursuit of clearly defined political and military objectives; (4) be accompanied by widespread public and congressional support; and (5) be waged only as a last resort.[19] Powell, chairman of the Joint Chiefs, now resurrected this cautious military doctrine and amended it to require a "decisive" force and a clear "exit strategy."[20] Iraq had eventually threatened U.S. oil supplies, whereas Yugoslavia's turmoil threatened no obvious U.S. national interests. The war was "tragic," but the stakes seemed wholly humanitarian. It met very few of the administration's criteria for intervention.

Several senior U.S. officials may have also been influenced by personal idiosyncrasies in their handling of the Bosnian war. Secretary Baker relied heavily on his deputy, Eagleburger, whose diagnosis may have stemmed, in the words of Zimmerman, from "understanding too much." Knowing that Croatian president Tudjman was a fanatical nationalist and frustrated that the lovely Yugoslavia was being torn apart, Eagleburger seemed to adopt a kind of "pox on all their houses" attitude, which, according to several of his State Department colleagues, he fed Baker. This was not uncommon. Journalists and diplomats who had served time in Belgrade tended to bring a Yugo-nostalgia for "brotherhood and unity" to their analysis, which made them more sympathetic to the alleged effort of Yugoslav forces to preserve the federation than toward the nationalistic, breakaway republics that seemed uncompromising. They were right that the leaders of Croatia, Slovenia, and Bosnia were inflexible, and Tudjman was in fact a fanatic. But however blighted, the leaders of the secessionist states clued into Milosevic's ruthlessness faster than anyone in the West. The repressive policies of the Serbian president left no place in Yugoslavia for non-Serbs.

An "action memorandum" sent to Deputy Secretary of State Eagleburger two weeks into the Bosnian war in April 1992 proposed a variety of detailed economic and diplomatic measures designed to isolate the Belgrade regime. Eagleburger's signature appears at the bottom of the document—beside the word "disapprove."[21] Critics of the Bush administration's response branded it a "policy of appeasement," but it might better be dubbed a "policy of disapproval," a phrase that testifies more accurately to the abundance of "soft" and "hard" intervention proposals that were raised and rejected.

U.S. policymakers had a number of options. Most made their way onto the editorial pages of the nation's major dailies. The United States might have demanded that the arms embargo be lifted against the Bosnian Muslims, making a persuasive case at the UN Security Council. "I completely agree with Mr. Bush's statement that American boys should not die for Bosnia," Bosnia's Muslim president Alija Izetbegovic said in early August 1992. "We have hundreds and thousands of able and willing men ready to fight, but unfortunately they have the disadvantage of being unarmed. We need weapons." The United States might have helped arm and train the Muslims, using its leverage to try to ensure the arms were used in conventional conflict and not against Serb or, later, Croat civilians. But President Bush was opposed to lifting the UN embargo. "There are enough arms there already," he said. "We've got to stop the killing some way, and I don't think it's enhanced by more and more [weapons]."[22]

If the Bush administration had been serious about stopping the killing of unarmed Bosnians, U.S. troops alone or in coalition (à la the Gulf War or Operation Provide Comfort) might have seized Sarajevo and enough surrounding territory to protect the airport against artillery attack. They might have fanned out from the capital to create a ground corridor to the port city of Split, Croatia, where aid could be delivered. U.S. fighter planes acting alone or with their NATO allies could have bombed the hills around Sarajevo to stop Serb mortar and artillery fire on the capital or to protect humanitarian relief flights. They might have bombed Serb military and industrial targets in Bosnian Serb territory or even in Serbia proper with the aim of deterring Serb aggression. Or most radical, they might have waged all-out war, reversing Serb land gains and allowing Bosnia's 2 million displaced persons to return home.

Instead, the Bush administration took a number of tamer steps aimed mainly at signaling its displeasure. In addition to withdrawing Ambassador Zimmerman from Belgrade, the United States closed its two consulates in Serbia, expelled the Yugoslav ambassador from the United States, and moved military forces to the Adriatic to begin enforcing the arms embargo and UN economic sanctions. But the Bush White House did nothing that caused the Serbs to flinch. Diplomatic and economic jabs were worth enduring if the reward for that endurance was an independent, ethnically pure Serb "statelet" in Bosnia.

Recognition

What Did the United States Know?

No other atrocity campaign in the twentieth century was better monitored and understood by the U.S. government. U.S. analysts fed their higher-ups detailed and devastating reports on Serbian war aims and tactics. One classified April 14 information memorandum, for instance, described the Serbs'

> clear pattern of use of force, intimidation, and provocation to violence aimed at forcibly partitioning [Bosnia] and effecting large forced transfers of population. . . . The clear intent of Serbian use of force is to displace non-Serbs from mixed areas (including areas where Serbs are a minority) to consolidate Bosnian Serb claims to some 60% of Bosnian territory . . . in a manner which would create a "Serbian Bosnia."[23]

Balkan watchers also knew Milosevic well enough to alert their superiors to his favorite stalling tactics. In the same memo the analyst wrote, "Belgrade practiced the strategy of the hyena in Croatia, curbing its most aggressive actions during peak moments of international scrutiny and condemnation but resuming them as soon as possible."[24] This was written just a week into the war.

Jon Western, an analyst in the State Department's Bureau of Intelligence and Research, was one of many U.S. officials charged with processing Serb brutality on a daily basis. Western was on the fast track in the department. Fair-haired, blue-eyed, and nothing if not earnest, Western had joined the government in 1988. His first day's journal entry from INR, dated July 15, 1990, read: "This is the job I've always dreamed of." Western had grown up in North Dakota and never in his life seen a dead body. Yet suddenly in 1992 he found himself confronted by reports and photos that depicted human beings who "looked like they had been through meat grinders." From the beginning of the war, he was tasked with sifting through some 1,000 documents on Bosnia a day—open source reports from foreign and American journalists and international human rights groups, local press translations, classified cables from the field, satellite intelligence, refugee testimony, and telephone and radio intercepts. He used the data to prepare Secretary of State Baker's morning intelligence summary.

In his training for the post of intelligence analyst, Western had been taught to greet reports with skepticism. And the stories emerging from Bosnia certainly seemed to warrant disbelief. One cable described a nine-year-old Muslim girl who had been raped by Serb militiamen and left lying in a pool of blood for two days while her parents watched, from behind a fence, as she died. He did not believe it. "You're taught to be objective," he remembered. "You're trained not to believe everything you hear."[25] Following in the footsteps of Morgenthau in Constantinople and Twining on the Cambodia-Thai border, Western confronted images he could not process. But the refugees kept talking, making themselves heard. The very same report about the Muslim girl crossed his desk a second time when a separate group of witnesses confirmed it independently to U.S. investigators.[26]

Some of the images were superficially mild. For instance, Western saw satellite photos that looked like they depicted the night sky—hundreds of luminous little stars dotted a black canvas. But the young analyst knew that the stars were not stars at all but the glowing embers of small fires that proud Europeans expelled from their homes built in their makeshift encampments in the woods. In June 1992 he found himself assigned to conduct a frame-by-frame analysis of television footage of the Sarajevo "breadline massacre," in which a Serb shell blew twenty-two shoppers apart. His was a taxing visual odyssey. Marshall Harris, Western's colleague in the State Department, remembers, "Jon had it the worst. He had to read everything that came in, no matter how horrific. The rest of us got a summarized version of the brutality, but he had to process every minute detail."

However gruesome his tasks, Western had a job to do. Beginning in late May, he set out to see if there might be a pattern in the refugee accounts and in the Serb military advance. He was leery of leaping to conclusions because the Bosnian Muslims had already gained a reputation for manipulating international sympathy. Western demanded corroboration. Could the refugees provide more descriptive detail about the weather on a particular day? Did they recall the color of the buildings in the so-called concentration camps? Could they describe the clothes of their supposed assailants?

Over the July 4 weekend in 1992, Western and a CIA colleague worked around the clock for three days, poring over mounds of classified and unclassified material. Gathering military intelligence and refugee reports from all across Bosnia, they acquired the most clear-cut evidence yet of a vast network of concentration camps. The Serb tactics in Brcko in northern Bosnia resembled those in Zvornik in eastern Bosnia and Prijedor in western Bosnia. This suggested that the ethnic cleansing and the military attacks had been planned and coordinated. Bosnian Serb artillery would begin by unleashing a barrage on a given village; Serb paramilitaries would launch infantry assaults, killing armed men, rounding up unarmed men, and sending trembling women and children into flight. When most Serb forces moved to the next village, a cadre of paramilitaries and regulars stayed behind to "mop up." Within hours, they had looted valuables, shot livestock, and blown roofs off houses. Non-Serb life in Serb territory was banned. Some 10,000 Bosnians were fleeing their homes each day.[27]

The Serbs' next moves were spookily easy to predict. As Western remembers:

> We could see the attacks coming by watching our computer terminal screens, by scanning the satellite imagery, or often just by watching television. We knew exactly what the Bosnian Serbs were going to do next, and there was nothing we could do. Imagine you could say, "In two days this village is going to die," and there was nothing you could do about it. You just sat there, waited for it to happen and dutifully reported it up the chain.

But the chain was missing some links. The question about what could be done, which was burning inside junior and midlevel officials, had already been answered by senior officials within the administration. Powell, Baker, Scowcroft, Cheney, Eagleburger, and Bush had decided the United States would not intervene militarily. That case was closed. John Fox of the State Department's Policy Planning Office recalls a climate that eschewed mention of the possibility of U.S. intervention. "For most of 1992, we couldn't send memos that called for the use of American force," Fox remembers. "The best we could do was to write arresting things that led inexorably to the conclusion that force would have to be used."

An ever-expanding posse of like-minded State Department officials piped cable upon cable up the State Department food chain in the hopes that one senior official would bite. There were no takers. The young hawks recognized that they had several forces working against them. First, their

higher-ups had narrowly circumscribed what everybody within the building understood to be "possible." There would be no U.S. military intervention in Bosnia. This was a fact, not a forecast. This shaped the thinking of
those who sat before their computers or bumped into one another in the
department's drab cafeteria and decided whether and how to appeal.
Second, they were dealing with bureaucrats like themselves who were protective of turf and career and not at all in the habit of rocking the boat.
Third, they knew that their strongest argument for intervention was a
moral argument, which was *necessarily* suspect in a department steeped in
the realist tradition. Fox remembers diversifying his written appeals, offering "something for everyone":

> I used history, arguing that we had allowed fascism to triumph before
> in this building, and that it had proven not to be such a good idea. I
> argued that we should intervene because it was "the right thing to
> do." This is an argument you almost never make in government if you
> know what you are doing. It virtually guarantees that you don't get
> invited to the next meeting and that you gain a reputation for moral-
> ism. I warned them that if we let these killings happen this time
> around, they would be the ones stuck holding the smoking gun. Of
> the three types of argument—the historical, the moral, and the "cover
> your ass" kind—the latter was of course the most compelling.

U.S. foreign service officers knew that Secretary of State Baker believed
that the United States did not "have a dog in this fight." But undaunted by
their superiors' indifference, they kept the analysis coming. One of the
most memorable overviews of the situation came from the pen of
Ambassador Zimmerman, who, one month into the war, submitted a confidential cable to the secretary of state entitled "Who Killed Yugoslavia?"
The cable was divided into five sections, each headed by a verse from
"Who Killed Cock Robin?" Zimmerman had been recalled to Washington
on May 16, 1992, and writing it was his last official act as ambassador. He
argued that nationalism had "put an arrow in the heart of Yugoslavia" and
placed the blame squarely on Balkan leaders like Croatia's "narrow-mind-
ed, crypto-racist regime" and the Milosevic dictatorship in Belgrade:

> Innocent bystanders . . . never had a chance against Milosevic's com-
> bination of aggressiveness and intransigence. Historians can argue

about the role of the individual in history. I have no doubt that if
Milosevic's parents had committed suicide before his birth rather than
after, I would not be writing a cable about the death of Yugoslavia.
Milosevic, more than anyone else, is its gravedigger.

Western leaders, he observed, were "no more than witnesses at Yugoslavia's
funeral."[28]

Zimmerman asked Jim Hooper, recently promoted to become the State
Department's director of the Office of Canadian Affairs, to join him in
developing a menu of concrete policy options for Bosnia. Hooper was
skeptical that Deputy Secretary Eagleburger would take his initiatives seriously. He thought Zimmerman was the one who needed to argue for air
strikes, but Zimmerman insisted he would lose his access. "This was the
classic bureaucratic trap," says Hooper. "If you go to the boss with bad
news, the boss won't want to see you anymore." Hooper's wife urged him
to accept anyway. "If you don't take this," she said, "you'll wonder for the
rest of your life whether you could have made a difference." Hooper
accepted the offer and spent the second half of 1992 running the Office of
Canadian Affairs and, on a pro bono basis, trying to rally department support for intervention.

U.S. diplomats who worked day to day on Bosnia became eager to see a
Western military intervention. They had not become so engaged with
Cambodia or Iraq in part because they had been blocked from entering
either country and directly witnessing the carnage. Newspaper coverage
had been sparse, as journalists, too, were denied access. Americans were also
probably less prone to identify with Kurds and Cambodians than they were
with Europeans. But the most significant difference was that the Cold War
had ended, and there was no geopolitical rationalization for *supporting* Serb
perpetrators. Thus, for the first time in the twentieth century, U.S. military
intervention to stop genocide was within reach.

But internal appeals alone were unlikely to make a dent in the consciousness of senior policy-makers so firmly opposed to intervening. The
State Department dissenters needed help from American reporters, editorial boards, and advocacy groups. Initially, they did not really get it. Between
April and early August many of the journalists who swooped into Bosnia
had never visited the country before and compensated for their ignorance
with an effort to be "even-handed" and "neutral." Many recall scavenging
to dig up stories about atrocities committed by "all sides." Many did not

portray the war as a top-down attempt by Milosevic to create an ethnically pure Greater Serbia.

In early August 1992, however, the proponents of intervention within the U.S. government gained a weapon in their struggle: The Western media finally won access to Serb concentration camps. Journalists not only began challenging U.S. policy, but they supplied photographic images and refugee sagas that galvanized heretofore silent elite opinion. Crucially, the advocates of humanitarian intervention began to win the support of both liberals committed to advancing human rights as well as staunch Republican Cold Warriors, who believed the U.S. had the responsibility and the power to stop Serb aggression in Europe. The Bush administration's chosen policy of nonintervention suddenly came to feel politically untenable.

Response (Bush)

"Concentration Camps in Europe"

In the notorious Serb-run camps in northern Bosnia, Muslim and Croat detainees were inhumanly concentrated. Onetime farmers, factory workers, and philosophers were pressed tightly into barracks. One prisoner's nose nestled into the armpit or the sweaty feet of the eighty-five-year-old inmate beside him. The urine bucket filled, spilled, and remained in place. Parched inmates gathered their excretion in cupped hands to wet their lips.

The camps of Bosnia were not extermination camps, though killing was a favorite tool of many of the commanders in charge. Nor could they really be called death camps, though some 10,000 prisoners perished in them. Not every Bosnian Muslim was marked for death as every Jew had been in the Holocaust. Although injury and humiliation were inevitable, death was only possible. *Concentration* camps is what they were. Forever linked with gas chambers, concentration camps were not a Nazi invention. The Spaniards had used them in Cuba during a local rebellion in 1896, the British in South Africa during the Boer War at the beginning of the twentieth century.[29]

Thanks to its spy satellites, radio and phone communications, and agents on the ground, the United States had known of the Serb camps since May 1992. But midlevel and junior U.S. officials remember the offices above them were a "black hole." "We would send things up and nothing would

A woman is evacuated from Sarajevo in 1993 on a special convoy arranged for Bosnia's Jewish community.

come back," said Western. "The only time we would get a response was when the press covered a particular event."[30] U.S. analysts knew that Muslim and Croat men were being incarcerated and abused, but Bush administration officials never publicly condemned the camps or demanded their closure. It would take public outrage to force their hand.

When Western journalists first heard reports of the camps' atrocities, they did not know whether the accounts were reliable. The first convoy of Muslim and Croat refugees from northern Bosnia crossed into Croatia in June. Laura Pitter, a freelance journalist, remembers her reaction to the horrors described by the first wave of refugees:

> They were talking about women being put in rape camps. They were talk-
> ing about all these killings—some said they'd personally seen things, but
> when we probed deeper it was clear they had actually only heard about
> them. They talked about people being thrown off cliffs, men being held
> and tortured and starved in camps. We stayed up talking to them until 2
> a.m. So many different people from different places were describing these
> incredibly similar things. They seemed credible, but I still wondered if they
> were all just repeating the same rumors. No matter how much I heard, I
> just found it hard to believe. I couldn't believe. In fact, I didn't believe.

Pitter sat around her colleague's apartment that night debating the veracity of the reports. She filed stories over the course of the next week about the refugee crisis but talked only generally of the refugees' "allegations" of atrocities. A few weeks later she finally found an eyewitness—a man who had escaped from a Serb-run camp with the help of a Serbian Orthodox priest. The camp, in the northwestern Bosnian town of Brcko, was situated in a slaughterhouse. The same machines formerly used to kill cattle were being used to kill his fellow prisoners, the witness said. But when Pitter filed her story with United Press International, the news agency refused to run it, citing legal concerns and saying that they needed more than one witness before they felt comfortable putting the story into print.

One Muslim, Selma Hecimovic, took care of Muslim and Croat women in Bosnia who had been raped at camps the Serbs established specifically for that purpose. She recalled the ways journalists and human rights workers pressed the victims and witnesses of torture:

> At the end, I get a bit tired of constantly having to *prove*. We had to prove genocide, we had to prove that our women are being raped, that our children have been killed. Every time I take a statement from these women, and you journalists want to interview them, I imagine those people, disinterested, sitting in a nice house with a hamburger and beer, switching channels on TV. I really don't know what else has to happen here, what further suffering the Muslims have to undergo . . . to make the so-called world react.[31]

The first high-profile press reports of Serb detention camps appeared in July, and American and European journalists flooded to Bosnia. *Newsday's* Roy Gutman, a British film crew from the Independent Television News (ITN), and the *Guardian's* Ed Vuillamy led the way. On July 19, 1992, Gutman published an article from the Manjaca camp, where he accompanied representatives of the International Committee for the Red Cross (ICRC), then performing its first inspection. Supervised at all times by Serb escorts, Gutman was allowed to speak only with eight handpicked prisoners. Still, he managed to piece together—mainly from those inmates who had been recently released—tales of beatings, torture, and mass executions. One seventeen-year-old survivor described being hauled to the camp in a covered truck along with his father, grandfather, brother, and 150 others. He said eighteen people in the six-truck convoy died from asphyxiation.[32] In a story entitled "There Is No Food, There Is No Air," Gutman relayed a Muslim relief worker's account that six to ten people were dying daily in the Omarska camp near the Serb-held town of Prijedor. On July 21 Gutman's *Newsday* story, "Like Auschwitz," described the deportation of thousands of Muslim civilians in sweltering, locked freight cars.[33] Gutman, who later won the Pulitzer Prize for his dispatches on the camps, used terms such as "sealed boxcars" and "deportations," which could only remind readers of events of fifty years before. He quoted a Muslim student who said, "We all felt like Jews in the Third Reich."[34]

Gutman relied on refugee testimony to give readers a glimpse of Omarska, the worst of the Serbs' camps, where several thousand Muslim and Croat civilians, including the entire leadership of the town of Prijedor, were held in metal cages and killed in groups of ten to fifteen every few days. A former inmate, Alija Lujinovic, a fifty-three-year-old electrical engineer, had been held in a northeastern Bosnian facility where he said some 1,350 people were slaughtered between mid-May and mid-June. Not surprisingly, just like the Khmer Rouge and the Iraqi government, the Serbs denied access to relief officials and journalists who wanted to investigate. On August 2, 1992, Gutman filed a story in which Lujinovic, the survivor, offered grim details of Serbs slitting the throats of Muslim prisoners, stripping them, and throwing them into the Sava River or grinding them into animal feed.

The following day U.S. State Department spokesman Richard Boucher finally confirmed that the United States possessed evidence of the camps. He admitted that the administration knew "that the Serbian forces are maintaining what they call detention centers" and that "abuses and torture and killings are taking place." But he insisted that the Serbs were not alone, adding, "I should also note that we have reports that Bosnians and Croatians also maintain detention centers." The United States did not have evidence that similar atrocities had occurred in the other camps, but Boucher still broadened the appeal for access. "*All parties* must allow international authorities immediate and unhindered access to all the detention centers," he said. "We've made clear right from the beginning of this that there were various parties involved in the fighting; that there were people *on all sides* . . . that were doing bad things."[35]

Even Boucher's diluted condemnation proved too much for his bosses. The following day, on instructions from Eagleburger, Assistant Secretary of State for Europe Tom Niles backtracked, testifying on Capitol Hill that the administration in fact did not have "thus far substantiated information that would confirm the existence of these camps."[36] Boucher's admissions had caused a spike in elite pressure for intervention. A senior State Department official said at the time, "Our intention was to move the ball forward one step, and the [news] reports moved it forward two steps."[37] With Niles's retreat, the Washington-based journalists became furious. The *Washington Post*'s veteran correspondent Don Oberdorfer wrote in his journal, "I had rarely seen the State Department press corps—or what was left of it in August—so agitated."[38] From then on, the reporters assumed the administration was obfuscating or lying outright. Congressman Tom Lantos, the Holocaust survivor who had found the Bush administration's response to Iraqi atrocities "nauseating," was again enraged. He confronted Niles by grabbing the morning's *New York Times,* which led with the headline about the camps. "You remember the old excuse that while the gas chambers were in full blast killing innocent people, we could say, not very honestly, 'we don't know,'" Lantos challenged Niles. "Now, either Mr. Boucher is lying or you are lying, but you are both working for [Secretary of State] Jim Baker, and we are not going to read Boucher's statement in the *New York Times* and listen to you testify to the exact opposite."[39] Since no reporter had yet visited the Omarska death camp, the Bush administration could still claim that the refugee claims were unconfirmed.

On August 5 Boucher said Red Cross officials had visited nine camps and reported "very difficult conditions of detention." But he said, "they have not found any evidence of death camps." The Holocaust standard, he implied, had not been met. Boucher went on to note that the Red Cross had not yet been allowed to visit the most notorious camps. Asked what the United States would do when evidence had been gathered against those responsible, Boucher said he did not know of any plans for a war crimes tribunal. And no, he stressed, the administration was not considering using force.[40]

President Bush remained immobile on the question of U.S. intervention. In an interview published the same day, he was quoted as saying that military force "is an option that I haven't thought of yet." He met the objections of critics by falling back on the Powell-Weinberger doctrine. "Now we have some people coming at me saying, 'Commit American forces,'" Bush said. "Before I'd commit forces to a battle, I want to know what's the beginning, what's the objective, how's the objective going to be achieved and what's the end."[41] These were of course reasonable questions, but there was no indication that anyone at the upper levels of the U.S. government was trying to supply answers.

Analogy and Advocacy

Bill Clinton, the Democratic challenger in the upcoming presidential election, was clocking miles and racking up promises as he toured the country. On August 5, 1992, the day after Niles stammered his way through his House hearings, Clinton told an audience of black teenagers at a school in East St. Louis, Illinois, with regard to Serb concentration camps, "We may have to use military force. I would begin with air power against the Serbs to try to restore the basic conditions of humanity."[42] Clinton was a committed multilateralist. He said the UN demands that Serb camps be closed and aggression halted "should be backed by collective action, including the use of force, if necessary." The United States, he said, should "be prepared to lend appropriate support, including military, to such an operation."[43]

Clinton was more of a hawk than Bush on Bosnia, but one could see signs that the former antiwar protester was deeply uncomfortable with the idea of *American* military action. Even as Clinton delivered his sternest warnings to Serb forces, he also sounded nervous that Yugoslavia might steal center stage from the domestic agenda that was far dearer to him. Both his faith in the United Nations and his privileging of the home front were evident in his remarks to the Illinois children:

> I want us to be focused on the problems of people at home. I'm worried about kids being killed on the streets here at home. I think we'll have more people killed in America today than there are killed in Yugoslavia, or what used to be Yugoslavia, probably.
>
> But I think that we cannot afford to ignore what appears to be a deliberate, systematic extermination of human beings based on their ethnic origin. The United Nations was set up to stop things like that, and we ought to stop it.[44]

Like many liberal internationalists, Clinton referred to the United Nations as if it might someday become an institution with a mind, a body, and a bank account of its own. But the UN was dependent on the United

States for one-quarter of its budget, on the Security Council for authorization and financing of its missions, and on member states for peacekeepers.

Still, Clinton, the challenger, slashed at what he saw was a Bush Achilles'
heel. Whatever his squeamishness about force, with all of the media attention suddenly focused on Serb atrocities, Clinton was not going to pass up
a chance to criticize the incumbent for his idleness. Clinton campaigned
on an interventionist plank, criticizing Bush in a written statement for his
inaction on the grounds that "if the horrors of the Holocaust taught us
anything, it is the high cost of remaining silent and paralyzed in the face of
genocide."[45] Clinton advocated tightening economic sanctions, using force
to facilitate the delivery of humanitarian aid and to open Serb camps to
inspections, and bombing the Serb units that were pummeling Sarajevo.

Clinton's pressure was reinforced by shocking revelations from Bosnia,
where Penny Marshall and Ian Williams of British Independent Television
News and Ed Vulliamy of the *Guardian* finally managed to reach Omarska.
Bosnian Serb leader Radovan Karadzic had visited London in late July. At
a press conference he had denied the atrocity allegations and challenged
journalists "to come and see for themselves." He was sure he could empty
the worst of the camps before the television crews arrived, but he miscalculated, and the British journalists beat him to northern Bosnia.

Initially, local Serb officials blocked the ITN and *Guardian* reporters'
visit by denying permission. Then the Bosnian Serbs stationed soldiers in
the woods near the camps who began firing at the journalists' car. The
Serbs claimed that "Muslim mujahideen" were doing the firing, making
the visit too dangerous. But finally, on August 5, Marshall, Williams, and
Vulliamy were granted limited access to what was rumored to be a death
camp. Allowed into the canteen, the journalists saw wafer-thin men with
shaven heads eating watery bean stew. From across a courtyard, they spotted rows of men being drilled by harsh Serb taskmasters. But they were not
allowed to visit the prisoners' sleeping quarters or the notorious "White
House," which they had heard was a veritable human abattoir.
Disappointed to have been so limited in their access, the journalists were
bundled into the car and out of the camp. As they departed, however, they
drove past another camp, Trnopolje, where they happened to spot a group
of prisoners who had just arrived from the camp of Keraterm, which had a
reputation similar to Omarska's. The new arrivals were in terrible shape,
and ITN's Williams and Marshall leaped out of the car and began filming
the ghastly scene. The ITN news producer who met his camera team in

Hungary deliberately chose the footage most reminiscent of the Holocaust. "After viewing their ten tapes, I advised that the image that would shake the world was of skeletal men behind barbed wire," he said. "They sparked thoughts of Auschwitz and Belsen."[46]

ITN broadcast the first television pictures from Trnopolje on August 6, 1992. The images of wilting Muslims behind barbed wire concentrated grassroots and elite attention and inflamed public outrage about the war like no postwar genocide. In July 45 percent of Americans had disapproved of U.S. air strikes and 35 percent approved. Now, without any guidance from their leaders, 53 percent of Americans approved, whereas 33 percent disapproved. Roughly the same percentage supported contributing U.S. forces to a humanitarian or peacekeeping mission.[47] While the Bush administration had portrayed the "Bosnia mess" as insoluble, editorialists now met the administration head-on. "It is not merely an 'ethnic conflict,'" the New Republic editors wrote. "It is a campaign in which a discrete faction of Serbian nationalists has manipulated ethnic sentiment in order to seize power and territory. . . . There have been too many platitudes about the responsibility of 'all factions' for the war. This lazy language is an escape hatch through which outside powers flee their responsibilities."[48]

Even Jon Western, the intelligence officer who had been dutifully documenting the horrors, was stunned when he first came face to (televised) face with the Muslim prisoners he had long been monitoring from afar. "There is an enormous difference between reading about atrocities and seeing those images," Western says. "We had all the documentation we needed before. We knew all we needed to know. But the one thing we didn't have was videotape. We had never *seen* the men emaciated behind barbed wire. That was entirely new." As had occurred when television reporters gained access to the frozen, bluish remains of Kurdish victims in Halabja, popular interest and sympathy were aroused by pictures far more than they had been by words. Between August 2 and August 14, the three major networks broadcast forty-eight news stories on atrocities in Bosnia, compared to just ten in the previous twelve days.[49]

Even with the camps exposed, the tales of the refugees were still difficult to confirm, and the stories, as always, sounded far-fetched. Newsweek's Joel Brand visited the Manjaca camp and interviewed a gaunt prisoner in the presence of the camp commandant. Brand asked the man how he had lost so much weight. The prisoner's voice shook as he eyed the forbidding Serb commander. He blamed his condition on hospital confinement and not starvation. Only when the prisoner turned his head did Brand see that his left ear had been seared off. The interview was abruptly terminated.[50]

Reporters and television producers followed ITN's lead, relaying images that evoked heightened Holocaust sensitivity among viewers. Television producers often accompanied their daily Bosnia coverage with scenes from Holocaust newsreels. Vulliamy, who gave some fifty-four radio interviews the day he broke the camp story in the *Guardian,* was himself frustrated by the tendency to make linkages to the Holocaust. When one radio station led into his interview by playing Hitler thundering at the Nuremberg rallies, Vulliamy hung up the phone. "I had to spend as much time saying, 'This is not Auschwitz,' as I did saying, 'This is unacceptably awful,'" Vulliamy recalls. Two years later, when he met Holocaust Museum Director Walter Reich, Vulliamy asked Reich if he thought the phrase "echoes of the Holocaust" was appropriate. "Yes," Reich said, "very loud echoes."

In newspapers around the country, the analogy recurred. The *Cincinnati Enquirer's* Jim Borgman depicted Croat and Muslims skeletons walking from the "Serbian concentration camp" through a door labeled "SHOWERS" and into a room with one showerhead.[51] *U.S. News and World Report* described "locked trains . . . once again carrying human cargoes across Europe," noting that "the West's response to this new holocaust has been as timid as its reactions to the beginnings of Hitler's genocide."[52] An August *Washington Post* editorial declared: "Images like these have not come out of Europe since a war whose depredations and atrocities—it has been agreed again and again—would never be allowed to recur."[53] The *New York Times* editorial the next day read: "The chilling reports from Bosnia evoke this century's greatest nightmare, Hitler's genocide against Jews, Gypsies and Slavs." The *Chicago Tribune* editorial asked: "Are Nazi-era death camps being reprised in the Balkans? Unthinkable, you say?" and answered, "Think again. . . . The ghost of World War II genocide is abroad in Bosnia."[54] However disturbing viewers and readers found images from prior genocides, there was nothing quite like their discomfort that such horrors could occur again *in Europe.*

Journalists generally reported stories that they hoped would move Western policymakers, but pundits and advocates openly clamored for force. Jewish survivors and organizations put aside Israel's feud with Muslims in the Middle East and were particularly forceful in their criticism of U.S. idleness. In a private meeting with National Security Adviser Brent

Scowcroft, American Jewish leaders pressed for military action. The American Jewish Committee, the American Jewish Congress, and the Anti-Defamation League published a joint advertisement in the *New York Times* headlined, "Stop the Death Camps." The ad declared:

> To the blood-chilling names of Auschwitz, Treblinka, and other Nazi death camps there seem now to have been added the names of Omarska and Brcko. . . . Is it possible that fifty years after the Holocaust, the nations of the world, including our own, will stand by and do nothing, pretending we are helpless? . . . We must make it clear that we will take every necessary step, including the use of force, to put a stop to this madness and bloodshed.[55]

On August 10, 1992, President Bush met with Israeli prime minister Yitzhak Rabin, who also likened the camps to those of the Nazis. The same day thousands of Jewish American protesters marched on the White House.

The Holocaust analogy was also invoked with regard to the allies' handling of the crisis. The interminable and seemingly fruitless Vance-Owen peace process caused many to draw comparisons between the Western "appeasers" of 1992 and those who had kowtowed to Hitler in Munich in 1938. For example, *Time* magazine wrote, "The ghastly images in newspapers and on television screens conjured up another discomfiting memory, the world sitting by, eager for peace at any price, as Adolf Hitler marched into Austria, carved up Czechoslovakia."[56] Anthony Lewis of the *New York Times* called President Bush a "veritable Neville Chamberlain."[57]

This public commentary aided dissenters within the bureaucracy. They began filtering much of what they read and saw through the prism of the Holocaust. Fox recalls:

> It was the shock of recognition of those images. It was the visual memory that most of us had through documentaries. It was the likeness of the thing. It didn't add anything to our knowledge to know about the camps in August. There was much more death after they were revealed than before. . . . But we had all sat through 500 documentaries on the Holocaust. I had been to Auschwitz. We had all experienced the college curriculum. The Holocaust was part of the equipment that one brought to the job.

Jim Hooper had delved into the history of the State Department's weak response to the Holocaust. He pressed his government colleagues to read British historian Martin Gilbert's *Auschwitz and the Allies* and supplied them with a stream of facts about parallels with the Holocaust that they could use internally. Twining, Solarz, Galbraith, and other advocates of an interventionist, humanitarian policy had invoked the Holocaust before, but neither Cambodia nor Iraq had resonated like Bosnia. The Bosnian war brought both a coincidence of European geography and imagery.

"We Will Not Rest Until. . . "

The association of the television imagery with the Holocaust and the outrage of elite opinion-makers forced President Bush to speak out. Three months before an election, with Clinton snapping at his heels, he had to confront the possibility of intervening. Bush held a press conference on Friday, August 7. Fox vividly recalls the moment when Bush made his remarks: "I remember hearing Bush say, 'We will not rest.' And I thought to myself, 'How on earth is he going to finish this sentence?' Will he say, 'We will not rest until we liberate the camps'? 'We will not rest until we close the camps'? 'We will not rest until we rest'? I knew he didn't want to do anything, so I wondered what on earth he could say." In fact, Bush himself made the Holocaust link:

> The pictures of the prisoners rounded up by the Serbian forces and being held in these detention camps are stark evidence of the need to deal with this problem effectively. And the world cannot shed its horror at the prospect of concentration camps. The shocking brutality of genocide in World War II, in those concentration camps, are burning memories for all of us, and that can't happen again. And we will not rest until the international community has gained access to any and all detention camps.[58]

Bush's pledge not to rest until the international community gained access to the camps left the administration ample room for maneuver. Would the access demand be satisfied by a single international visit? Would it entail stationing foreign observers in or near the enclosed premises? Even if helped in the short term, would prisoners be punished more in the long term?

The camp story had sent shock waves through Foggy Bottom. But many of the midlevel officials within the State Department who lobbied for intervention were concerned that all the attention paid to the camps risked drowning out the larger truth: The Serbs were killing or expelling non-Serbs from any territory they controlled or conquered. Still, in a parallel to Peter Galbraith's decision to tap American outrage over chemical weapons' use in Iraq, the Bosnia hawks within the department opted to take what they could get. They reasoned that attention to the concentration camps and the Holocaust parallels might succeed in drawing attention to the wider campaign of genocide.

Richard Holbrooke, who had served as assistant secretary of state for East Asian and Pacific affairs under President Carter, was a board member of the International Rescue Committee, America's largest nongovernmental relief organization. He decided to visit Bosnia just after the camp story broke. There he encountered an angry British aid worker, Tony Land, who expressed his amazement at the sudden attention to the camps. "For six months, we have seen Sarajevo systematically being destroyed without the world getting very upset," Land told Holbrooke. "Now a few pictures of people being held behind barbed wire, and the world goes crazy."[59] Holbrooke videotaped the results of Serb ethnic cleansing, filming house upon house that had been blown up by Serb soldiers and militia. He saw petrified Muslims handing over their property deeds to the local Serb authorities in exchange for bus passage out of the country. And he interviewed refugees who recounted the abduction and disappearance of Muslim men. When he returned to the United States, Holbrooke wrote an article in *Newsweek* that urged lifting the arms embargo against the Muslims and bombing Serb bridges and military facilities. He also asked rhetorically, "What would the West be doing now if the religious convictions of the combatants were reversed, and a Muslim force was now trying to destroy two million beleaguered Christians and/or Jews?"[60] Knowing that Clinton had spoken out on Bosnia and sensing an opening, Holbrooke wrote a memo to Clinton and vice presidential candidate Al Gore in which he stressed: "This is not a choice between Vietnam and doing nothing, as the Bush Administration has portrayed it. . . . Doing nothing now risks a far greater and more costly involvement later."[61]

Although President Bush's statement resolved little on the ground in Bosnia, it did require U.S. bureaucrats to begin a high-level intelligence scramble to gather all available data on the camps.[62] Within six weeks of

Bush's pledge, the intelligence community had compiled a list of more than 200 camps that included the names of commanders. Because of America's top-flight technical intelligence-gathering capabilities, this information had been available to any interested party all along. But before the August public "shaming," senior Bush administration officials had placed no premium on knowing. There was no point in receiving details about crimes that they did not intend to confront. When Jon Western had conducted his investigation, he had done so juggling a portfolio that included Poland, Croatia, and Bosnia. Nobody above him had ordered—or much welcomed—his July 4 weekend intelligence scramble. But now the president had commissioned a well-staffed search. The sequencing was quite typical. As Fox notes: "The intelligence community is responsive to what the bosses want to know. You could say 'I'm deeply interested in a green-eyed abominable snowman,' and you'd get all the briefings you could ever want. But when the higher-ups are blaming the killings on the victims, you aren't going to get much intelligence."

U.S. Policy: Diplomacy, Charity, Futility, Perversity, Jeopardy

The United States did not couple its new public commitment to document Serb aggression with a plan to stop it. As a way of defusing the pressure stirred up by the camp images, U.S. and European officials pointed optimistically to a UN-EU peace conference scheduled for late August in London. There "the parties" would be convinced to stop fighting. Eagleburger pledged $40 million of U.S. humanitarian aid and said he expected the London agreements to produce "a substantial diminution" in the shelling of Sarajevo.

Under public fire the Bush administration made another move that seemed more consequential. On August 13, 1992, the United States and its allies passed a Security Council resolution authorizing "all necessary measures" to facilitate the delivery of humanitarian aid. Many believed that this was a precursor to military intervention against the Serbs. But in fact it only paved the way for reinforcing a small UN contingent that had been positioned in Bosnia since the beginning of the war in April 1992. On top of 100 UN monitors already on the ground, an additional 6,000 peacekeepers, including some 1,800 British troops, deployed. U.S. public support

for contributing its share of peacekeepers was high (80 percent), and the
U.S. Senate even approved money for U.S. participation in a UN military
force. But the Bush team refused requests for troops, choosing instead to
finance relief and transport missions carried out by others.[63] The Security
Council resolution, which implied a willingness to use force, was intended
to frighten the Serbs into ceasing the slaughter. But even the deterrent
value of the threat was undermined when assistant secretary Niles admitted, "The hope is that the adoption of the resolution would obviate the
need for force."[64] When asked about the concentration camps, President
Bush said the United States would use relief to address "these tremendous
humanitarian problems."[65] Events, Americans were told, constituted civil
war or a humanitarian "nightmare," but not a genocide.

As pressure picked up, the Bush administration also developed a spin on
events in the Balkans that helped temper public enthusiasm for involvement. Three portrayals emerged in the daily press guidance and in the
statements of administration officials. The language muddied the facts and
quenched some of the moral outrage sparked by the camp photos. Because
the American public and the Washington elite began with no prior understanding of the region and because the conflict was indeed complicated,
the administration was able to inscribe its version of events onto a virtually
blank slate.

First, senior officials viewed and spun the violence as an insoluble
"tragedy" rather than a mitigatable, deliberate atrocity carried out by an
identifiable set of perpetrators. The war, they said, was fueled by bottom-
up, ancient, ethnic or tribal hatreds (not by the top-down political machinations of a nationalistic or opportunistic elite), hatreds that had raged for
centuries (and, by implication, would rage for centuries more). This of
course invited a version of Hirschman's futility justification for inaction.[66]
Defense Secretary Cheney told CNN, "It's tragic, but the Balkans have
been a hotbed of conflict . . . for centuries."[67] Bush said the war was "a
complex, convoluted conflict that grows out of age-old animosities [and]
century-old feuds."[68] Eagleburger noted, "It is difficult to explain, but this
war is not rational. There is no rationality at all about ethnic conflict. It is
gut, it is hatred; it's not for any common set of values or purposes; it just
goes on. And that kind of warfare is most difficult to bring to a halt."[69]

Bosnia was racked by a "civil war" (not a war of aggression) in which
"all sides" committed atrocities against the others. "I have said this 38,000
times," said Eagleburger, "and I have to say this to the people of this coun-

try as well. . . . The tragedy is not something that can be settled from outside and it's about damn well time that everybody understood that. Until
the Bosnians, Serbs, and Croats decide to stop killing each other, there is
nothing the outside world can do about it."[70]

Second, administration officials argued there would be perverse consequences to confronting the Serbs. Military engagement or the lifting of the
arms embargo could endanger the delivery of humanitarian aid. It could
cause the Serbs to retaliate against Muslim civilians or European peacekeepers. And thus such well-meaning steps would in fact do more harm
than good.

Third, owing to the ancient hatreds and to the particular topography of
the region, military intervention would bring about a Vietnam-like quagmire, putting U.S. soldiers in jeopardy. Reporters pressed Bush on
whether the United States would use force, and the president downplayed
the possibility:

> Everyone has been reluctant, for very understandable reasons, to use
> force. There is a lot of voices out there in the United States today that
> say "use force," but they don't have the responsibility for sending
> somebody else's son or somebody else's daughter into harm's way.
> And I do. I do not want to see the United States bogged down in any
> way into some guerrilla warfare—we lived through that.[71]

One deterrent to U.S. involvement was the estimated steep cost of intervening. The U.S. military's authoritative monopoly on estimating likely
casualties lowered the prospects for intervention. Since Vietnam, U.S. generals had opposed U.S. military involvement in virtually all wars and had
never favored intervention on mere humanitarian grounds. In the summer
of 1992, the Bush administration debated whether or not to contribute
U.S. military aircraft to a humanitarian airlift for Sarajevo. Military planners
said that some 50,000 U.S. ground troops would be needed to secure a
thirty-mile perimeter around the airport.[72] In fact, the airlift eventually was
managed with a light UN force of some 1,000 Canadian and French forces
at Sarajevo airport. At an August 11 Senate hearing, Lieutenant General
Barry McCaffrey, assistant to the chairman of the Joint Chiefs of Staff,
Colin Powell, told Congress 400,000 troops would be needed to enforce a
cease-fire.[73] Scowcroft concedes that the military's analysis was "probably"
inflated but says that "armchair strategists" could not very well challenge

the Joint Chiefs.[74] Ambassador Zimmerman remembers his frustration at the military trump card that the Joint Chiefs played time and again. "They never said, 'No, we won't,' or 'No, we can't,'" he recalls. "They just tossed around figures on what it would take that were both unacceptable and, because of who was supplying them, uncontestable."

When humanitarian land corridors were proposed, according to Scowcroft, the "troops-to-task" estimate came back at 300,000. This was a daunting figure that many independent observers deemed utterly disproportionate to the quality and commitment of the Serb troops attacking unarmed civilians in Bosnia. But military experts proliferated and pontificated, repeatedly citing the impenetrability of the mountainous landscape and the heroic fortitude of Tito's Partisans in World War II, who tied down the Nazis in pitched battle for months. Powell and Defense Secretary Cheney convinced the President that the risks of military engagement were far too high—even to use U.S. airpower to facilitate the delivery of humanitarian aid to Bosnia's hungry civilians.

The one-word bogey "Vietnam" became the ubiquitous shorthand for all that could go wrong in the Balkans if the United States became militarily engaged.[75] For some, the war in Vietnam offered a cause for genuine concern, as they feared any operation that lacked strong public support, implicated no "vital interests," and occurred on mountainous terrain. But many opponents of intervention proffered the Vietnam analogy less because they saw a likeness between the two scenarios than because they knew of no argument more likely to chill public enthusiasm for intervention.

The Bosnian Serbs took their cue, taunting the Americans whenever the prospect of intervention was raised. They warned of casualties and "mission creep." Bosnian Serb leader Radovan Karadzic exploited allied anxiety, threatening to retaliate against UN peacekeepers in Bosnia if NATO bombed from the air: "We'll determine the time and the targets, doing our best to make it very painful," Karadzic warned, daring the United States to act.[76] "The United States sends 2,000 marines, then they have to send 10,000 more to save the 2,000," he said. "That is the best way to have another Vietnam."[77] The same message was delivered by nationalists in Serbia itself. After ringing the bells of the Serb Orthodox churches and raising black flags emblazoned with skulls, Serb Radical Party leader Vojislav Seselj jeered at the Americans, saying, "We would have tens of thousands of volunteers, and we would score a glorious victory. The Americans would have to send thousands of body bags. It would be a new Vietnam."[78]

The fact that one of the handful of senior officials that opposed intervention was General Colin Powell was especially important. Powell, who
had won a Bronze Star and Purple Heart in Vietnam, was fresh off his Gulf
War blitz. It is usually forgotten, but when the Bush administration had
debated going to war with Iraq, Powell had lobbied against it. Because he
could not pinpoint an exit strategy for U.S. forces ahead of time, he argued,
it was better to stay home. After the United States won the Gulf War, however, Powell's dominance was undisputed. Those who argued that Bosnia
would not deteriorate into Vietnam could not compete with the highly
respected veteran. Many of the "Balkan hawks" had not served in Vietnam.
Their recent experience in the Balkans counted for little. Zimmerman
remembers: "I hadn't served in Vietnam, but I knew the Serbs. And they
bore no resemblance to the Vietnamese Communists. They didn't have the
commitment to the cause of Bosnia. Theirs wasn't a holy crusade. Theirs
was a land-grab. They weren't the same quality of soldiers. They were
weekend warriors, and many of them were drunk a lot of the time. It was
just very, very different."

General Powell, who opposed any U.S. role in delivering humanitarian
aid or enforcing a no-fly zone over Bosnia, made an unusually public pitch
to keep U.S. troops and airplanes grounded. He first called Michael
Gordon of the *New York Times* into his office to deliver a lecture on why an
intervention in Bosnia would not work. "As soon as they tell me it is limited," Powell told Gordon, "it means they do not care whether you achieve a
result or not. As soon as they tell me 'surgical,' I head for the bunker."[79]
Then, when a *New York Times* editorial criticized the U.S. military's "no-
can-do" attitude, Powell fired back, himself publishing an op-ed in the
paper that argued against deploying U.S. troops in harm's way "for unclear
purposes" in a conflict "with deep ethnic and religious roots that go back a
thousand years."[80]

With the November 1992 election approaching, Powell did not have to
win many converts within the administration. Bush was unwilling to risk
American lives in Bosnia in any capacity. Senior U.S. officials in the
Administration said they viewed Bosnia as a "tar baby" on which nobody
wanted their fingerprints.[81]

One way the administration deflected attention away from Bosnia was
to focus on another humanitarian crisis, in Somalia. President Bush learned
of the famine not from international media coverage, which was initially
belated and thin, but from the personal appeals of U.S. ambassador Smith

Hempstone in Kenya and those of Senators Paul Simon (D.–Ill.) and Nancy Kassebaum (R.–Kans.).[82] The Joint Chiefs instinctively opposed sending U.S. troops to Somalia. But on August 14, 1992, Bush abruptly altered course, ordering a very limited intervention. U.S. C-130 cargo planes, not ground troops, were deployed to aid in the relief effort. Bush also pledged to help transport 500 Pakistani peacekeepers to the embattled country. According to senior officials involved in the planning, the White House saw an opportunity to demonstrate it had a heart, to respond to domestic criticisms on the eve of the Republican Party's national convention, and to do it relatively cheaply. The nightly news coverage of Bosnia from the middle to the end of August dropped to one-third of what it had been earlier in the month.[83] Even though U.S. troops would not deploy to Africa for several months, the Somalia famine had already begun drawing attention away from the Balkans.

Within the bureaucracy the State Department's cold exterior continued to be hotly contested. On August 25, 1992, George Kenney, the acting Yugoslav desk officer, stunned the Beltway by resigning from the State Department. News of Kenney's departure made the front page of the *Washington Post*. "I can no longer in clear conscience support the Administration's ineffective, indeed counterproductive, handling of the Yugoslav crisis," the foreign service officer wrote in his letter of resignation, which the newspaper quoted. "I am therefore resigning in order to help develop a stronger public consensus that the U.S. must act immediately to stop the genocide."[84] Kenney, like so many, favored lifting the arms embargo and bombing the Bosnian Serbs. In London for the UN-EU peace conference, Eagleburger asked, "Who knows Kenney?" He then publicly dismissed the act of the junior official, saying, "To my mind that young man has never set foot in the former Yugoslavia."[85] But Kenney's exit gave the public its first taste of the battle raging inside the department. And U.S. officials who remained disgruntled by the U.S. policy were introduced to a new option. "When you're in the foreign service," Kenney's counterpart on Bosnia, Marshall Harris, notes, "every part of the institution and the culture frowns on leaving. It just isn't seen as an option. The fact that George had done it awakened us to thinking of resignation as a real possibility."

With the November 1992 election nearing, foreign policy had been demoted. James Baker and a few of his top foreign policy advisers had been transferred to the White House, where they managed the president's reelection campaign. Eagleburger had been promoted to acting secretary of state. Many U.S. officials thought Eagleburger had long been making the Bosnia policy; now his title reflected his influence.

Hooper requested a meeting with the new secretary and surprised his colleagues by being granted one. At a half-hour session in mid-September, Eagleburger appeared willing to listen. At the end of the meeting, he asked Hooper to prepare a memo that explicitly spelled out his recommendations for a new policy. Hooper and his colleague Richard Johnson, another career foreign service officer, prepared a twenty-seven-page memo and employed the dissent channel to be sure it reached Eagleburger's desk. The State Department had introduced the channel at the end of the Vietnam War so that those who disagreed with policy could make their views known to senior officials without having to clear them with their immediate bosses. "This was the one thing we could do that didn't have to be cleared," recalls Hooper. "Nobody could stop you from sending it—not your boss, not the secretary of state, not anybody." Eagleburger did not respond until after the election, but on Veteran's Day, November 11, 1992, he summoned Hooper and Johnson to his office. After a two-and-a-half-hour session in which Eagleburger peppered the men with questions, he escorted them out of his office and commended them for their critique. "Thanks for telling me my policy is full of horseshit," a grinning Eagleburger said. The normally lugubrious Hooper was speechless. Johnson said wearily, "I see you were listening."

Both dissenters were surprised that their message had not been delivered by other sources. Bill Montgomery, Eagleburger's office director, told Hooper, "You're the only ones. Nobody else in the bureaucracy is telling him this." The department's officials who cared about America's Bosnia policy could be divided into three groups—the dissenters who favored U.S. intervention (mainly in the form of air strikes), the senior policymakers who actively opposed it, and most numerous, the officials who supported bombing but assumed it would not happen so did nothing.

President Bush himself never paid much attention to the conflict in Bosnia. National Security Adviser Scowcroft remembers that about once a week Bush would turn to him and say, "Now tell me again what this is all about?" This was at a time when some 70,000 Bosnians had been killed in seven months.

Scowcroft speaks very candidly about the formulation of the Bush administration's response, expressing no regret. If he had to formulate policy all over again, the calculus would yield the same outcome. The atrocities were awful, but they occurred in a country whose welfare was simply not in the U.S. national interest:

> We could never satisfy ourselves that the amount of involvement we thought it would take was justified in terms of the U.S. interests involved. . . . We were heavily national interest oriented, and Bosnia was of national interest concern only if the war broke out into Kosovo, risking the involvement of our allies in a wider war. If it stayed contained in Bosnia, it might have been horrible, but it did not affect us.

War that spread was deemed threatening to the United States. Regardless of how many civilians died, one that remained internal was not.

Genocide?

Although the Holocaust analogy was employed frequently in this period, the question of whether events constituted genocide or not was controversial as always. The killings, the rapes, the torture, the camps, the cleansing together convinced lawyers at Helsinki Watch to use the term. The Serbs had set out to destroy the Bosnian Muslim population, and even if they were not exterminating every person, they were ravaging the Muslim community and doing all they could to ensure it would never recover.

The Bush administration assiduously avoided using the word. "Genocide" was shunned because a genocide finding would create a moral imperative. The day after the ITN footage of Keraterm aired, Bush told a news conference: "We know there is horror in these detention camps. But in all honesty, I can't confirm to you some of the claims that there is indeed a genocidal process going on there."[86] Policymakers preferred the phrase "ethnic cleansing."

Scowcroft believes genocide would have demanded a U.S. response, but ethnic cleansing, which is the label he uses for what occurred in Bosnia, did not:

> In Bosnia, I think, we all got ethnic cleansing mixed up with genocide. To me they are different terms. The horror of them is similar, but

the purpose is not. Ethnic cleansing is not 'I want to destroy an ethnic group, wipe it out.' It's 'They're not going to live with us. They can live where they like, but not with us.' . . . There is a proscription on genocide, but there is not a proscription on killing people. . . . Therefore there is something of a national interest in preventing genocide because the United States needs to appear to be upholding international law.

During the reign of the Khmer Rouge, a small-scale debate over applying the word genocide had been played out mainly on America's editorial pages. It did not occur in the U.S. government, where such a finding was considered moot in the face of a determined U.S. policy of nonengagement. When Iraq targeted the rural Kurds, Galbraith's claim of genocide was rejected by the Reagan administration on the grounds Hussein was not exterminating all Kurds but was suppressing rebellion. The Bosnia debate over "genocide" was notable because it was the most wide-ranging, most vocal, and most divisive debate ever held on whether Lemkin's term should apply.

Some U.S. officials who debated the "is it" or "isn't it" saw it simply as a question of truth. The Serbs were systematically killing and expelling Muslim and Croat civilians from territory they controlled. The talk of "ancient hatreds" implied a degree of inevitability and spontaneity belied by the carefully coordinated, top-down nature of the killing, which was better signaled by the term "genocide." These officials wanted to gather and publish evidence of atrocities in order to set the record straight and show that a group of individuals had *decided* to target non-Serbs for destruction. Others hoped to see Serb attacks labeled "genocide" so as to trigger the genocide convention, which the United States had ratified and which they read to legally oblige a U.S. military response. They knew as well from polls and instinct that the term "genocide" moved Americans. A later poll showed that while 54 percent of Americans favored military intervention in Bosnia, that figure rose to 80 percent when those surveyed were told that an independent commission had found genocide under way.[87] This was a key point: Whatever America's legal obligations, U.S. officials hoped a finding of genocide might at least frighten politicians into thinking they would pay some political price for inaction. Both reasons for pursuing application of the word "genocide"—to clarify the nature of the violence and to generate or tap public outrage—were motivated by a desire to make the higher-ups act. They believed that a dominant majority in the United States would support intervention to stop a murderous minority in the Balkans if they only knew what it was they were stopping.

Richard Johnson, the foreign service officer who had accompanied Hooper to meet with Eagleburger, set out to investigate why the "g-word" controversy persisted when the separating of the men from the women and children; the beatings, rapes, and murders; and the specific targeting of the educated and political elites satisfied the convention's requirements. He cornered sixteen State Department and NSC officials for formal interviews. He found that any confusion over the Serbs' genocidal intent stemmed from the State Department's reluctance to stir moral outrage and its failure to devote the human or material resources needed to collect evidence of a systematic attempt to destroy a substantial part of the Bosnian Muslim group. The White House never issued a directive calling for research and analysis to determine whether a genocide case could be made against Serbian president Milosevic or against rump Yugoslavia (composed of Serbia and Montenegro).

In the waning days of the Bush administration, the focus of State Department dissenters shifted from rescue to punishment. Jon Western, for one, intensified his effort to collect proof of atrocities. He hoped to turn the heaps of evidence that had been gathered since April into "courtroom-ready" intelligence. Although no international criminal court existed, the frustration with international impotence, the relentlessness of some spirited advocates of prosecution (such as Neier at Helsinki Watch), and probably also the resonance of the crimes in Bosnia with those of World War II caused European and U.S. policymakers to begin considering setting up a tribunal. By December 1992 Western and others had set out to answer two questions: Was there sufficient evidence of war crimes to think about prosecuting perpetrators, and did these crimes constitute a legal genocide? Western took a plodding approach to tackling the issue, which was unpopular with some of his colleagues. "I felt we weren't going to get a smoking gun," recalls Western. "Milosevic was never going to call up his henchmen and say, 'Go commit genocide.' We had to develop the case by showing the systematic nature of the campaign. Only by working backwards could we show intent."

Western had company. In October 1992, upon the recommendation of Tadeusz Mazowiecki, the UN Human Rights Commission's special rapporteur for ex-Yugoslavia, the allies had created an impartial commission of experts to assess the atrocity reports.[88] The five-member War Crimes Commission convened for the first time in December 1992 in Geneva. Coincidentally, this inaugural session was held in the same building as one of the many cease-fire negotiations sponsored by the Vance-Owen, UN-EU "International Conference for the Former Yugoslavia." By this time the defeated Bush administration was concerning itself with its legacy, which, when it came to Yugoslavia, needed quick repair. At that meeting Eagleburger urged several new steps, including enforcement of a no-fly zone, possibly lifting the arms embargo against the Muslim-led Bosnian government, and accountability for suspected war criminals. Eagleburger declared:

> We have, on the one hand, a moral and historical obligation not to stand back a second time in this century while a people faces obliter-ation. But we have also, I believe, a political obligation to the people of Serbia to signal clearly the risk they currently run of sharing the inevitable fate of those who practice ethnic cleansing in their names. . . . They need, especially, to understand that a second Nuremberg awaits the practitioners of ethnic cleansing, and that the judgment and opprobrium of history awaits the people in whose name their crimes were committed.[89]

What made Eagleburger's December 1992 remarks significant was that the top U.S. diplomat "named names." An unlikely midwife to the justice movement, Eagleburger said that the United States had identified ten war crimes suspects that should be brought to trial. His list included the promi-nent Serb warlords Zelko "Arkan" Raznjatovic and Vojislav Seselj, as well as the Serb political and military leaders Milosevic, Karadzic, and Ratko Mladic.[90] Eagleburger also described specific crimes—such as the Serb siege of Sarajevo, the Yugoslav army's destruction of the Croatian city of Vukovar in 1991, and the Serb murder of 2,000–3,000 Muslims near Brcko.

According to Eagleburger, though he had supported the idea of a court for several months, it had been Holocaust survivor Elie Wiesel who con-vinced him to speak out. Wiesel had visited the region in November, mak-ing stops in Belgrade, Sarajevo, and Banja Luka, including the Manjaca concentration camp. When Wiesel returned home, he had what he called a "long talk" with Eagleburger in which he convinced him that speaking out was a moral obligation. But Eagleburger made it clear he was not calling for the forcible seizure of the men he named. Karadzic, one of those just branded, freely wandered the halls outside the main conference hall in Geneva.[91] He would remain a valued negotiating partner for two and a half more years. In addition, the United States did not follow up on Eagleburger's statement by assigning officials within the State Department or U.S. intelligence community to build legal cases against these leaders. According to Johnson, when the State Department finally began submitting evidence to the UN War Crimes Commission, it assigned the task to a foreign service officer in the Human Rights Bureau with no knowledge of Balkan affairs and to a short-term State Department intern just out of college.[92]

The closest the Bush administration came to acknowledging genocide was on December 18, 1992, when the United States joined a long UN General Assembly resolution that held Serbian and Montenegrin forces responsible for aggression and for "the abhorrent policy of 'ethnic cleansing,' which is a form of genocide."[93] The American voice was one of many. It was probably not heard and certainly not heeded.

Around the same time, Hooper and Johnson entered a second memo into the State Department dissent channel arguing for a legal finding of genocide. The memo was circulated on December 20, 1992. It quickly garnered signatures from the assistant secretaries of state for INR, legal affairs, European affairs, and International Organizations. With those signatures in place, however, the department practically shut down for the holidays until January 3, 1993. A memo that found that the Serbs were committing genocide sat unexamined for two weeks while State Department officials celebrated Christmas and the New Year. When Secretary Eagleburger returned, he said at last that he agreed. But he also said that it would be unfair for the Bush administration to issue a finding of genocide just as the next administration was taking over. As Western put it: "The last act of the Bush administration was not going to be, 'Oh, by the way, this is genocide. We haven't been doing anything about it. Oops. It's all yours!'" On January 19, 1993, the last day of the Bush administration, Patricia Diaz Dennis, the assistant secretary of state for human rights and humanitarian affairs equivocated unintelligibly:

> In Bosnia, our report describes widespread systematic atrocities, including the rapes and killings of civilian victims to the extent that it probably borders on genocide. We haven't yet decided whether or not

it's a legal matter. The conduct in Bosnia is genocide, but clearly the abuses that have occurred there over the last year are such that they, as I said, border on that particular legal term.[94]

Before leaving office, President Bush did something that woud have grave bearing on the Clinton administration's foreign policy: he sent 28,000 U.S. troops to feed starving civilians in Somalia. Although President Bush viewed the Somalia mission as purely humanitarian, National Security Advisor Scowcroft saw two national interests present that were "intimately connected with our decision not to intervene in Yugoslavia." He argued at the time, first, that the United States had to demonstrate that "it was not that we were afraid to intervene abroad; it was just that the circumstances weren't right in Bosnia." Second, Scowcroft believed that the United States had to show Muslim nations that the U.S. decision to stay out of Bosnia was not rooted in the victims' Muslim faith. "For me, Somalia gave us the ability to show they were wrong," he says. "It was a Southern Hemisphere state; it was black; it was non-Christian; it was everything that epitomized the Third World." When asked why the Third World mattered at all to U.S. vital interests, Scowcroft says, "The opinions of leaders in the Third World matter because to be a 'world leader,' you have to convince people it is in their interest to follow. If everyone hates you, it is hard to be a world leader."

The Somalia intervention made it far less likely that the United States would do something to curb the killing in Bosnia. Bush had ordered a humanitarian intervention; U.S. troops were otherwise engaged.

Meanwhile, the war raged on in Bosnia. The only good news Bosnians received as they endured their first winter of war was that their interventionist ally Bill Clinton had won the U.S. presidential election. Help, they felt sure, was on the way.

Response (Clinton)

"An Early and Crucial Test"

If Americans have learned to shrug off campaign pledges, the potential beneficiaries of those promises overseas are often less jaded. Clinton the presidential candidate had argued that the United States did have a dog in

the Bosnian fight. And even though President Bush had used the bully pul-
pit to argue against action, by the time of Clinton's inauguration in January
1993, some 58 percent of Americans believed military force should be used
to protect aid deliveries and prevent atrocities.[95] Clinton chose as his top
foreign policy adviser Anthony Lake. Lake had earned a reputation as a
man of conscience for resigning from the National Security Council to
protest President Nixon's 1970 decision to send U.S. troops into
Cambodia. In *Foreign Policy* magazine in 1971, Lake and a colleague had
reflected on the process by which Americans of noble character could have
allowed themselves to wage the Vietnam War, which had such immoral
consequences: "The answer to that question begins with a basic intellectual approach which views foreign policy as a lifeless, bloodless set of abstractions," they wrote:

> A liberalism attempting to deal with intensely *human* problems at
> home abruptly but naturally shifts to abstract concepts when making
> decisions about events beyond the water's edge. "Nations," "interests,"
> "influence," "prestige"—all are disembodied and dehumanized terms
> which encourage easy inattention to the real people whose lives our
> decisions affect or even end.[96]

When Lake and his Democratic colleagues were put to the test, however, although they were far more attentive to the human suffering in Bosnia,
they did not intervene to ameliorate it.

Soon after being tapped to become national security adviser, Lake
received a lengthy memo from Richard Holbrooke, who had just returned
from Bosnia. On this trip, his second, taken just after Christmas 1992,
Holbrooke visited Sarajevo, where he saw the town's Muslims burning
books in an effort to warm their frigid homes. He stayed in the Holiday
Inn, whose rooms were still stained with blood left over from the early
killings. He also interviewed survivors of Serb camps in northern Bosnia.
One man who described the horror of life in the Manjaca camp fished out
two wooden figures from beneath his mattress. The figures, which he had
carved with a piece of broken glass, depicted prisoners as they had been
forced to stand: with their heads down and hands tied behind their backs.
When Holbrooke had made a motion to hand them back, the former prisoner stopped him. "No," he said. "Please take them back to your country
and show them to your people. Show the Americans how we have been

treated. Tell America what is happening to us." On January 1, 1993, while Holbrooke waited at Sarajevo airport for Serb clearance to depart, he wrote in his journal: "If I don't make my views known to the new [Clinton] team, I will not have done enough to help the desperate people we have just seen; but if I push my views, I will appear too aggressive. I feel trapped."[97] He returned to the United States and carried the carved figures around with him, appearing with them on the Charlie Rose show and getting them photographed and printed in a full-page, color spread in the *New York Times Magazine*. In his memo to Lake and Clinton's new secretary of state, Warren Christopher, Holbrooke offered to serve as a U.S. mediator in the Balkans. He never received a response to his offer.

The Clinton foreign policy team did undertake a thorough Bosnia policy review. The foreign service veterans who had served in the Bush administration needed time to adjust to the new sense of possibility. "Career officers, who had been conditioned to temerity through two years of Bush administration inaction, inattention, and pre-election jitters, did not seem to realize that they could now speak openly and even favorably of military solutions," Bosnia desk officer Harris later observed.[98]

The Clinton team at least seemed prepared to offer a candid diagnosis of the conflict. On February 10, 1993, ten months after the start of the war and with some 100,000 estimated dead, Secretary Christopher, another veteran of the Carter administration, issued a statement far sterner than any of those of senior Bush administration officials:

> This conflict may be far from our shores, but it is certainly not distant from our concerns. We cannot afford to ignore it. . . . Bold tyrants and fearful minorities are watching to see whether ethnic cleansing is a policy the world will tolerate. If we hope to promote the spread of freedom, if we hope to encourage the emergence of peaceful ethnic democracies, our answer must be a resounding no.[99]

The secretary then vividly described Serb ethnic cleansing "pursued through mass murders, systematic beatings, and the rape of Muslims and others, prolonged shellings of innocents in Sarajevo and elsewhere, forced displacements of entire villages, [and] inhuman treatment of prisoners in detention camps." He said he recognized that the world's response would constitute "an early and crucial test of how it will address the critical concerns of ethnic and religious minorities in the post–Cold War world."

But Christopher's prescriptions were weak. He vowed to bring "the full weight of American diplomacy to bear on finding a peaceful solution."[100] He did not deliver an ultimatum to the Serbs. He did not mention military force. The Serbs faced only the familiar obligation to turn up for peace talks. Deprived at home of running water, gas, electricity, and basic goods, most Balkan officials welcomed the opportunity to take diplomatic (and shopping) trips to plush hotels in New York, London, and Geneva.

Although interventionists within the State Department were distraught at the vagueness of the newly unveiled policy, they attempted to put a positive spin on the announcement. "We saw we had started with this horrible Christopher statement," Harris recalls. "But we knew things were bad and weren't going to get better, particularly after Milosevic himself saw this statement. At least this administration understood what was going on over there. We figured events would quickly force Christopher to revise our policy."

Open Dissent

On the eve of Christopher's much-anticipated policy announcement, career foreign service officers Hooper and Johnson had stepped up to the microphone at the State Department's "open forum," a program that enables department employees and guests of employees to speak in small or large settings about pressing policy dilemmas. Kurdish leader Jalal Talabani had used the same forum to urge the United States to respond to Saddam Hussein's Anfal offensive against the Kurds. Whereas just two dozen people had turned up to hear Talabani in 1988, however, more than 200 gathered to hear Hooper and Johnson in 1993. In Hooper's ten-minute speech, which he had agonized over for weeks, he relayed the message he had received earlier from Eagleburger's office director: Overwhelming support for intervention among the department's rank and file was not being communicated up the chain. Just because his colleagues were hearing people by their watercoolers speaking about Bosnia did not mean that the message was reaching the seventh floor, where power (in the form of the secretary and his or her most senior advisers) is concentrated.

Hooper denounced the Western powers' reliance on mere negotiations, declaring:

If the conflict reflected legal and constitutional differences over the breakup of Yugoslavia, creative diplomacy and split-the-difference negotiations would offer promise. We could rely on the tools of our profession—memos, cables, communiqués, meetings, visits, and talking points—to facilitate a genuine peace process. But the conflict is driven by a Serb bid for racial and national supremacy. As such, it can be halted, reversed, and defeated *only* by military force.

This was the first time in a twenty-year bureaucratic career that Hooper had allowed his frustration to erupt in public. He likened America's "self-deluding" faith in the peace process to that of the Allies before World War II, reminding listeners, "The problem with Munich wasn't its clauses or the map." Hooper referenced the history books he had been reading, playing up the department's quietude during Hitler's genocide. "Not every institution gets a second chance," Hooper said, pausing for effect. "This is our second chance." The department should declare "unequivocally, officially, and publicly" that Serbia was practicing genocide. Hooper's remarks were unclassified and disseminated via cable to all diplomatic posts. "You would not believe the number of people in the department who came up to me after that speech to thank me," he recalls.

Still, Hooper knew that few of his concerned colleagues would dare to challenge their superiors. He decided to enlist a voice of moral authority from outside the building: Elie Wiesel. Wiesel had already played a key role convincing Eagleburger to name names in December 1992. And on April 22, 1993, at the opening ceremony for the Holocaust Museum in Washington, Wiesel spoke extemporaneously to President Clinton, who was seated behind him. "Mr. President, I cannot *not* tell you something," Wiesel memorably declared, turning away from the podium to face the president. "I have been in the former Yugoslavia last fall. I cannot sleep since what I have seen. As a Jew I am saying that. We must do something to stop the bloodshed in that country."[101]

President Clinton was quick to distinguish the two crimes. "I think the Holocaust is on a whole different level," he told reporters later in the day. "I think it is without precedent or peer in human history." U.S. inaction over Bosnia could not be compared with the U.S. failure to bomb the railroads to the Nazi camps. Still, he acknowledged that "ethnic cleansing is the kind of inhumanity that the Holocaust took to the nth degree," and said, "I think you have to stand up against it. I think it's wrong." But then he again revealed his ambivalence, cautioning, "That does not mean that the United States or the United Nations can enter a war."[102]

On April 28, 1993, at Hooper's request, Wiesel spoke out again—this time to a packed Dean Acheson Auditorium at the State Department. More than 300 people assembled to hear Wiesel critique U.S. idleness. The most dramatic moment occurred not in the auditorium but at a small lunch gathering after the event. Wiesel remembers turning to Peter Tarnoff, the undersecretary for political affairs and exclaiming, "These are camps, for heaven's sake! Can't you just liberate one of them?" Tarnoff did not respond, but Ralph Johnson, the principal deputy assistant secretary for European affairs, attempted to defend the administration. "We're afraid that if we did try to liberate them, there would be retaliation and the prisoners inside would be killed," Johnson said. After a long, awkward silence, Wiesel looked up, eyes flashing, and he said quietly, "Do you realize that that is precisely what the State Department said during World War II?"

As Hooper, Wiesel, and others continued to try to provoke a more aggressive policy by pointing to the Holocaust, Clinton's team entered an ungainly wiggle campaign to avoid calling events genocide.

On March 30, 1993, at a Senate Foreign Operations Subcommittee hearing, Senator Dennis DeConcini (D.–Ariz.) challenged Christopher: "Is there any doubt in your mind that indeed genocide has occurred in Bosnia-Herzegovina?" he asked. The secretary of state responded: "There's no doubt in my mind that rape and ethnic cleansing and other almost indescribable acts have taken place and it certainly rises to the level that is tantamount to genocide. The technical definition is not perhaps what's important here, but what is important is that it is atrocious conduct, it is atrocity after atrocity and must be stopped."[103] Both Clinton and Christopher tended to speak about the conflict as if they were still on the campaign trail and not the individuals best positioned to bring about the stoppage.

Congressman McCloskey, the Democrat from Indiana, became the Hill's most forceful crusader to see the term applied. In November 1992 McCloskey had traveled for a second time to the region, this time to Bosnia, where he saw that the dire predictions issued to him in Belgrade the previous year had been borne out. He heard tales of rapes, beatings, and castrations with gardening shears that invigorated his efforts on the House Armed Services Committee. "The stories of the people were unbelievable," McCloskey recalls. "It was almost a Pol Pot–like scenario in terms of what the Serbs were doing to the intellectuals, the teachers, the engineers." McCloskey was particularly moved by an eighty-one-year-old Muslim woman who took McCloskey aside and described watching the Serbs kill her entire family. Before the Serbs entered her home, she had begged her son to shoot her to spare her what she knew she would witness. But he refused, and she had to watch Serb militiamen butchering him. When she met McCloskey, she was so devastated by her memories that she faulted her son for lacking the courage to kill her.

When McCloskey returned to the United States, he told this woman's story again and again to relay not only the savagery of the Bosnian war but the tragedy of its legacy. Atrocity survivors were often bracketed as the "lucky ones," but many were left with parting images of their loved ones so horrific that they envied the dead. The memories were doubly devastating. A friend or relative being bludgeoned, stabbed, or shot. And the sight of the person reduced in their final moments to primal behavior. In Bosnia, where gardens were so often turned into killing fields and homes became infernos, families who were minding their own business inside were rarely prepared for the late-night knock on the door. And for those executed in the middle of the night, it was this very lack of preparedness—the fact that they were enacting their humanity until the very end—that ensured they had tasted life too recently to surrender it. They had not yet given up either on the possibility of persuasion or the killer's capacity for mercy. Although they felt shame in doing so, they went to unseemly lengths to hang on. While the victims' hopes were rewarded with a bullet down the throat or a knife in the groin, the survivors' memories of those last moments drowned out all others.[104] Instead of remembering friends and loved ones for the ways they lived, survivors remembered them for the ghastly ways they died.

McCloskey replayed his unexpected and unwanted bloody Balkan anec-dotes often enough to irritate his colleagues on the Hill. All told he made nearly a dozen trips to the region during the three-and-a-half-year war. On his return McCloskey chased potential allies around the halls. "Staking out these issues, people looked at you like you were living on the moon," he recalls. "They would say to me, 'But that has nothing to do with Decatur, Illinois,' or 'My constituency isn't interested in that.'" Most of McCloskey's colleagues found ways to avoid him. McCloskey was especial-ly disappointed when his colleagues attacked him personally for his stand. Ron Dellums (D.–Calif.), the chairman of the Armed Services

Committee, castigated McCloskey as a warmonger. McCloskey recalls: "I almost walked out of the meeting and resigned right then and there from the committee. There was no justice to allowing people to be killed and mutilated. To me it was a very obvious issue. I guess I could understand somebody not agreeing with me, but to call me a 'warmonger,' that was just too much."

McCloskey had secured a copy of the genocide convention and frequently returned to its text. "There are degrees of genocide and different genocidal leaders have different capabilities for destruction," McCloskey recalls. Like Lemkin and Galbraith, McCloskey was adamant that the Holocaust not be treated as the threshold for action. "I had to show people there was nothing in the genocide convention that says a crime has to hit Nazi proportions to count as genocide."

On April 1, 1993, at a House International Operations Subcommittee hearing, McCloskey began the first of a memorable series of exchanges with Secretary Christopher on the use of what became known as the "g-word":

> **Rep. McCloskey:** Previously to the Congress in response to a question as to whether or not genocide has taken place in Bosnia, the reply from State was that acts tantamount to genocide have taken place. I think that's not a clear answer to a very important and policy-driving question. Would you order a clear, explicit determination, yes or no, if the outrageous Serb systematic barbarism amounts to genocide?
>
> **Sec. Christopher:** With respect to the definition of the circumstances in Bosnia, we certainly will reply to that. That is a legal question that you've posed. I've said several times that the conduct there is an atrocity. The killing, the raping, the ethnic cleansing is definitely an atrocious set of acts. Whether it meets the technical legal definition of genocide is a matter that we'll look into and get back to you.[105]

Later that month outgoing department spokesman Richard Boucher asked Bosnia desk officer Harris to draft a statement that said that "the United States Government believes that the practice of 'ethnic cleansing' in Bosnia includes actions that meet the international definition of genocide." But the statement was killed—according to Harris—by incoming spokesman Thomas Donilon after he consulted with Secretary Christopher.

A Healthy Exchange

As the policy horizon became clear, those who worked the issue day to day grew more, not less, uneasy. Harris, an eight-year veteran of the State Department, decided he had little to lose by openly challenging the administration's timidity. Soon after Christopher's appearance on Capitol Hill, just as the Serbs looked destined to overrun the Muslim-held town of Srebrenica, Harris drafted a letter to Christopher that noted that the United States was trying to stop a Serb "genocide" with political and economic pressures alone. "In effect," the letter said, "the result of this course has been Western capitulation to Serbian aggression."[106] The policy had to change. Every State Department country officer that Harris approached agreed to sign the letter—desk officers for Serbia and Montenegro, Albania, Romania, Bulgaria, Macedonia, Croatia, Slovenia, as well as several officials involved in East European affairs and U.S. policy at the United Nations—forming a group that became known as the "dirty dozen." Harris believes he could have got many more signatures if he had had the time to do so. "When you are in a bureaucracy, you can either put your head down and become cynical, tired and inured," Harris observes. "Or you can stick your head up and try to do something."

The junior and midlevel officials were aided by their influential allies outside the State Department. The "dirty dozen" dissent letter was leaked, and the message of the dissenters was reinforced by a chorus of appreciative cries from elite opinion-makers. The war was dragging on, and many prominent Americans were distressed by Clinton's passivity. Well-known hawks from across the Atlantic weighed in. In a television interview former British prime minister Margaret Thatcher, who had admonished President Bush not to "go all wobbly" after Saddam's invasion of Kuwait, said of Bosnia: "I never thought I'd see another holocaust in my life again." She later wondered whether she should get into the "rent-a-spine business."[107]

Senator Joseph Biden (D.–Del.) had partnered with Dole in a bipartisan Senate campaign to aid the besieged Muslims. Under President Bush, the pair had introduced legislation that would have authorized the provision of up to $50 million in Defense Department stocks of military weapons and equipment to the Bosnian Muslims as soon as the embargo was lifted. Biden visited Sarajevo in April and, on his return, his rage intensified. Sounding a lot like Theodore Roosevelt three-quarters of a century earlier,

Biden accused the Clinton administration of placing relief workers and peacekeepers in circumstances in which they did not belong and then using their presence as an excuse for inaction. The new world order was in shambles, he declared, because the United States and its allies were giving a new meaning to collective security. "As defined by this generation of leaders," Biden said, "collective security means arranging to blame one another for inaction, so that everyone has an excuse. It does not mean standing together; it means hiding together."[108]

In May 1993, as a result of pressure from inside and outside, Clinton finally agreed to a new U.S. policy, known as "lift and strike." The president dispatched Secretary Christopher on a high-profile trip to Europe to "sell" America's allies on lifting the arms embargo against the Bosnian Muslims and bombing the Serbs, the two measures recommended by Hooper and Johnson in their twenty-seven-page dissent the previous year and by Holbrooke and countless others in the media. The Bosnian Muslim leadership continued to stress that it did not want U.S. troops, only an end to U.S. support for a UN sanction that tied their hands and left the Serbs with an overwhelming military advantage.

But Clinton's support for the plan proved shallow and Christopher's salesmanship nonexistent. According to journalist Elizabeth Drew, Hillary Clinton gave her husband a copy of Robert Kaplan's *Balkan Ghosts,* a deftly written travel book that portrays people in the Balkans as if they were destined to hate and kill.[109] Fearful of a quagmire in an unmendable region, Clinton reportedly "went south" on lift and strike. One NATO official who was present at the meeting between Secretary Christopher and NATO secretary-general Manfred Woerner remembers Christopher's singular lack of enthusiasm for the policy. He never lifted his nose from his notes. "Christopher started talking about the proposed U.S. policy of lift and strike, but doing it in a way that emphasized the disadvantages rather than the advantages," the official recalls. "There was a moment when Woerner realized what was going on: He was being invited to think the policy was a bad idea. The problem was he didn't think it was a bad idea at all." Christopher returned to the United States saying he had enjoyed a healthy "exchange of ideas," with his European counterparts. There had indeed been a healthy exchange. As Richard Perle, a former Bush administration Defense Department official put it, "Christopher went over to Europe with an American policy and he came back with a European one." The lift and strike policy was abandoned.

In the wake of Christopher's visit, the United States and the other powers on the UN Security Council settled upon a compromise policy. Instead of lifting the embargo and bombing the Serbs, they agreed to create "safe areas" in the Muslim-held eastern enclave of Srebrenica, in the capital city of Sarajevo, and in four other heavily populated civilian centers that were under Serb siege. UN Secretary General Boutros Boutros-Ghali told the Security Council that 30,000 troops would be needed to protect them. Thanks largely to the American refusal to contribute soldiers and fatigue among European states with troops already in Bosnia, only a tiny fraction of the forces needed to man, monitor, and defend these pockets arrived. President Clinton himself called the safe areas "shooting galleries." The problem remained unsolved, the Serbs remained virtually unimpeded, and the outrage that had briefly focused Clinton's attention on the tragedy gradually subsided. The world's gaze shifted. And the safe areas were left lightly tended and extremely vulnerable.

When the lift and strike plan surfaced, the young foreign service officers had believed that the system might reward them for their dissent. They were devastated by the safe-area compromise. They had seen the Christopher trip as the last, best hope to change the policy and save the shrinking country of Bosnia. Senator Dole, the Senate minority leader, took to the editorial pages, criticizing Clinton for finally coming up with a "realistic" Bosnia policy and then dropping it "when consensus did not magically appear on his doorstep." Dole warned that even if it seemed that only humanitarian interests were at stake in Bosnia, in fact *American* interests were under siege as well. If Clinton stood by in the face of Serb atrocities in Bosnia, Milosevic would soon turn on Albanians in Kosovo, provoking a regional war. Islamic fundamentalists were using Western indifference to Muslim suffering as a recruiting device. And global instability was on the rise because the United States and its allies had signaled that borders could be changed by force with no international consequence. "The United States, instead of leading, has publicly hesitated and waffled," Dole wrote. "This shirking and shrinking American presence on the global stage is exactly the type of invitation dictators and aggressors dream of." He urged Clinton to summon his NATO allies and issue an ultimatum: The Serbs must adhere to the latest cease-fire accord, permit the free passage of all humanitarian convoys, place its fearsome heavy weapons under UN control, and disband its paramilitary forces. If they failed to meet the U.S. demands, air strikes should begin and the arms embargo against the

Bosnian Muslims should be lifted so that the Muslims themselves could protect the vulnerable safe areas.[110]

Dole was ignored right along with the State Department's in-house hawks.

"A Long Way from Home"

The Clinton White House deplored the suffering of Bosnians far more than had the Bush White House, but a number of factors caused Clinton to back off from using force. First, the U.S. military advised against intervention. Clinton and his senior political advisers had little personal experience with military matters. The Democrats had not occupied the White House since 1980. General Colin Powell, who remained chairman of the Joint Chiefs until the end of September 1993, was still guided by a deep hostility to humanitarian missions that implicated no vital U.S. interests. Clinton was particularly deferential to Powell because the president had been publicly derided as a "draft dodger" in the campaign and because he had bungled an early effort to allow gay soldiers to serve in the U.S. armed forces.

Second, Clinton's foreign policy architects were committed multilateralists. They would act only with the consent and active participation of their European partners. France and Britain had deployed a combined 5,000 peacekeepers to Bosnia to aid the UN delivery of humanitarian aid, and they feared Serb retaliation against the troops. They also trusted that the Vance-Owen negotiation process would eventually pay dividends. With the Serbs controlling some 70 percent of the country by 1993, many European leaders privately urged ethnic partition. Clinton was also worried about offending the Russians, who sympathized with their fellow Orthodox Christian Serbs.

Third, Clinton was worried about American public opinion. As the Bush team had done, the Clinton administration kept one eye on the ground in Bosnia and one eye fixed on the polls. Although a plurality in the American public supported U.S. intervention, the percentages tended to vary with slight shifts in the questions asked. And U.S. officials did not trust that public support would withstand U.S. casualties. The more poll-conscious officials were criticized for adopting a "Snow White approach" to foreign policy. In effect, they asked, "Mirror, mirror on the wall, how can we get the highest poll numbers of them all?" And they worked to dampen moral outrage, steering senior officials to adopt the imagery and wording of "tragedy" over that of "terror." "Many people, while sympathizing with the Bosnian Muslims, find the situation too confusing, too complicated and too frustrating," said Defense Secretary William Perry. "They say that Bosnia is a tragedy, but not our tragedy. They say that we should wash our hands of the whole situation." According to Perry, there was "no support, either in the public or in the Congress, for taking sides in this war as a combatant, so we will not."[111]

Americans have historically opposed military campaigns abroad except in cases where the United States or its citizens have been attacked or in instances where the United States has intervened and then appealed to the public afterward, when it has benefited from the "rally-around-the-flag" effect. In the absence of American leadership, the public is usually ambivalent at best. Six months before Pearl Harbor, 76 percent of Americans polled favored supplying aid to Britain, but 79 percent opposed actually entering World War II.[112] Once the United States was involved, of course, support soared. Two months before the invasion of Panama in 1989, just 26 percent of Americans supported committing troops to overthrow military strongman Manuel Noriega, but once it came, 80 percent backed the decision to invade.[113] A week after Saddam Hussein invaded Kuwait in August 1990, before President Bush had mobilized support for U.S. combat, a majority of Americans opposed invading Iraq or even staging air strikes against Iraqi military bases. Four out of ten went so far as to say that the United States "should not get involved in a land war in the Middle East even if Iraq's invasion means that Iraq permanently controls Kuwait."[114] Even after the president had deployed troops to the Gulf and demonized Hussein as "Hitler," Americans preferred to stick with economic and diplomatic sanctions. Asked directly in November 1990 if the United States should go to war, 58 percent said no. Some 62 percent considered it likely that the crisis could "bog down and become another Vietnam situation."[115] When the prospect of U.S. casualties was raised, support dropped further.[116] Yet when U.S. troops battled the Iraqi Republican Guard, more than 80 percent backed Bush's decision to fight.[117]

Instead of leading the American people to support humanitarian intervention, Clinton adopted a policy of nonconfrontation. The administration would not confront the Serbs, and just as fundamentally, they would not confront opponents of intervention within the U.S. military or the Western alliance. Clinton's foreign policy team awaited consensus and drifted into the habits of its predecessor. Clinton himself testified to what would be his deep ambivalence about a U.S. role in the Balkans: "The U.S. should always seek an opportunity to stand up against—at least *speak out against*—inhumanity," he said.[118]

Thus, the administration's language shifted from that of moral imperative to that of an amoral mess. The "futility" imagery of tribal hatreds returned. Secretary of State Christopher said, "The hatred between all three groups . . . is almost unbelievable. It's almost terrifying, and it's centuries old. That really is a problem from hell. And I think that the United States is doing all we can to try to deal with that problem."[119] British foreign secretary Neville Chamberlain once called the strife over Czechoslovakia "a quarrel in a foreign country between people of whom we know nothing." In May 1993 Secretary Christopher described the war in Bosnia as "a humanitarian crisis a long way from home, in the middle of another continent."[120]

Many senior officials found it difficult to argue with their junior officers about the magnitude of the moral stakes at play in Bosnia. But as had happened with regard to the Holocaust, Cambodia, and northern Iraq, they resolved their internal conflicts by telling themselves that other interests and indeed other values trumped those involved in the Balkans. Intervention in Bosnia might have perverse consequences for the very people the United States sought to help. The more peacekeepers who were present in Bosnia helping deliver relief or deterring attacks against safe areas, the more Western policy became hostage to concerns about the peacekeepers' welfare. If the arms embargo were lifted or the Serbs bombed, humanitarian aid would be suspended, UN peacekeepers withdrawn, negotiations canceled, and the intended beneficiaries, Bosnia's Muslims, made far worse off.

Some very cherished goods at home would also be jeopardized. After more than a decade of Republican rule in the White House, leading Democrats spoke about the importance of carrying out domestic reforms. Jimmy Carter had squandered his opportunity by getting mired in a hostage crisis in Iran, people said; Clinton could not forfeit this historic moment. Dick Morris, Clinton's erstwhile pollster who liked to dabble in foreign policy decisionmaking, made noninvolvement in Bosnia a "central element" of his advice. "You don't want to be Lyndon Johnson," he said to Clinton early on, "sacrificing your potential for doing good on the domestic front by a destructive, never-ending foreign involvement. It's the

Democrats' disease to take the same compassion that motivates their domestic policies and let it lure them into heroic but ill-considered foreign wars."[121] Sure, the moral stakes were high, but the moral stakes at home were even higher.[122]

Atrocities "on All Sides"

To quell the unease that lurked in the halls of Foggy Bottom, senior officials drifted into the familiar "blame-the-victim" approach invoked whenever one's morals collide with one's actions. No genocide since the Holocaust has been completely black and white, and policymakers have been able to accentuate the grayness and moral ambiguity of each crisis. The Armenians and Kurds were not loyal to the state. In Bosnia the Muslim army carried out abuses, too. "All sides" were again said to be guilty. President Clinton said, "Until these folks get tired of killing each other, bad things will continue to happen." In the *New Republic* Anna Husarska noted the illogic of Clinton's position. "I guess if President Clinton had been around during the 1943 uprising in the Warsaw ghetto, he would also have called it 'those folks out there killing each other,'" she wrote. "How would he describe the brief armed rebellion in the Treblinka concentration camp?"[123]

Bosnia desk officer Harris remembers his supervisor Mike Habib's questioning reports on Serb shelling:

> He didn't want us to be seen pointing the finger when we weren't going to do anything. So he'd say, "How do you know it's the Serbs?" I would say that the Serbs were positioned outside the town with heavy weapons and the town was being shelled, so the Serbs were shelling the town. That wasn't good enough. I had to write, "There was shelling" or "There were reports of shelling." It was as if there was spontaneous combustion across Bosnia.

It is probably no coincidence that the less-experienced U.S. officials were likelier to let their human response to the carnage bubble over. These low-ranking officials did not allow their understanding of the slim odds of American intervention to cloud or alter their assessments of the problem. But their internal analysis and ongoing appeals met silence. They sent reports daily from intelligence officers, embassy staff, and journalists in the field up the chain of command and watched them become more sanitized at each rung of the ladder. By the time the analysis reached the secretary of state—when it did—the reports would have been unrecognizable to their original drafters. "The Clinton policy was unrealistic, but nobody wanted to change it," says Harris. "So those who defended it consciously and unconsciously contorted the reality on the ground in Bosnia to make the chosen policy seem sensible." Unwilling to alter the policy, officials in the Clinton administration had to reinterpret the facts.

On May 18, 1993, Christopher delivered unfathomable remarks to the House Foreign Affairs Committee in which he stunned listeners by insinuating that the Bosnian Muslims themselves had committed genocide:

> First, with respect to the moral case that you make, one of the just absolutely bewildering parts of this problem is that the moral case is devastating and clear that there are atrocities, but there are atrocities on all sides. As I said in my statement, the most—perhaps the most serious recent fighting has been between the Croats and the Muslims . . . you'll find indication of atrocities by all three of the major parties against each other. The level of hatred is just incredible. So, you know, it's somewhat different than the holocaust. It's been easy to analogize this to the holocaust, but I never heard of any genocide by the Jews against the German people.[124]

Before this testimony, according to one State Department official, Christopher had sent an urgent appeal to the department's Human Rights Bureau, requesting evidence of Bosnian Muslim atrocities.[125]

In Bosnia, as time passed, the conflict did take on more and more of the appearances of a civil war. During the Bush era, Serb paramilitaries, police, and regular armies had rounded up unarmed civilians and hauled them into camps; they had shelled city centers, looted homes, raped women, and expelled nearly 2 million Muslims and Croats from their homes. By the time Clinton took office, the Serbs had completed much of their ethnic cleansing and occupied almost three-quarters of the country. The Muslims had gradually assembled a ragtag army. They had also developed a smuggling network that enabled them to endure the Serbs' frequent suspensions of humanitarian aid and to begin equipping their defenders with light arms. A Serbo-Croatian expression says, "It takes two spoons to make noise." Although the Muslims had begun to make noise by meeting Serb attacks, they mustered only a teaspoon against a shovel, and only in certain areas of the country. By the time Clinton's cabinet began rummaging to prove parity, the Muslims had lost additional favor by going to war with Croats in central Bosnia (largely on the Croats' instigation). This complicated the picture by creating multiple aggressors. When the Muslims had no arms, no army, and no chance against the high-powered Serbs in 1992, the Bush administration had been careful to stress there were "no good guys." By mid-1993, when those same Muslims had acquired arms, an army, and a second front, it is not surprising that the language of "factions" and "warring parties" predominated.

The reality of the Bosnian "resistance" was far more pathetic. The heavily armed Serb forces donned crisp uniforms donated by the Yugoslav National Army from which they descended, whereas the Bosnian Muslim forces looked as though they had pieced together their uniforms by touring a host of garage sales, plucking garments of all shapes, sizes, and colors from a variety of different neighborhoods. Nothing fit or matched. Their efforts seemed so amateur that they evoked George Orwell's descriptions of the antifascists' attempt to defend the town of Barcelona against an attack by Franco's forces. The motley group in Spain had sought to shore up their positions by stacking sandbags outside their defenses and uprooting heavy cobblestones from the central plaza. Yet lacking the required mercenary instinct, they had patiently stopped to number each cobblestone with chalk so that they could return the stones to their rightful slots after the fighting had subsided.

One reason Western negotiators and U.S. policymakers succumbed to the temptation to equate all sides might be that they were equally frustrated by all sides. Diplomats quickly discerned that none of the Balkan leaders—Muslim, Serb, or Croat—were particularly concerned about the fate of their own people. With few exceptions, the political leaders did not seem moved by the ways their intransigence in negotiations doomed those on the battlefield or in the streets. This divide between warmakers and war casualties was not new. In 1917 when Siegfried Sassoon refused to return to the French front, he prepared a "A Soldier's Declaration," arguing that politicians who did not themselves suffer the conflict would deliberately prolong it. In the letter, printed in the *Times*, Sassoon said he hoped he might "help to destroy the callous complaisance with which the majority of those at home regard the continuance of the agonies which they do not share and have not sufficient imagination to realize."[126] The callousness and lack of imagination that characterized Bosnia's wartime Serb, Croat, and Muslim leaders gave Western diplomats legitimate grounds for despair.

But American and European frustration stemmed mainly from the foreigners' impatience with the Muslim refusal to quit. The cherished but churlish "peace process" hinged upon the Muslims' agreeing to surrender much of the territory from which they had been brutally expelled. Many diplomats felt that the Muslims should sign away the country in the interest of peace. Because the Serbs took so much territory so quickly, they were able to portray themselves as positively pacifist, whereas the Muslims wanted to take back their homes.

A subsequent CIA study found that Serbs were "responsible for the vast majority of ethnic cleansing in Bosnia." Croats and Muslims had committed "discrete" atrocities, the CIA found, but theirs lacked "the sustained intensity, orchestration, and scale of the Bosnian Serbs' efforts."[127] Hardly a partisan of U.S. intervention, the CIA concluded that "90 percent" of the atrocities committed during the three-and-a-half-year war were the handiwork of Serb paramilitary and military forces.

"No National Interest"

In July 1993 the Olympic city of Sarajevo came under fierce artillery fire and looked poised to fall. The U.S. press abounded with stories on the human toll of the carnage. As the world looked to the United States for leadership and solutions, Secretary Christopher came clean with the thinking that had come to inform and justify Clinton policy. When a reporter asked what the United States would do to stop what seemed to be the imminent fall of Sarajevo, Christopher responded: "That's a tragic, tragic situation in Bosnia, make no mistake about that. It's the world's most difficult diplomatic problem I believe. It defies any simple solution. The United States is doing all that it can consistent with our national interest."[128] Christopher was a veteran of the Carter foreign policy team that had helped introduce the rhetoric of human rights into foreign policy. But here only national interests, narrowly defined, would count, and Bosnia was not one. The United States would do what it could to help provide humanitarian relief, to maintain economic sanctions against Serbia, and to support diplomatic efforts. When the journalist continued to press him,

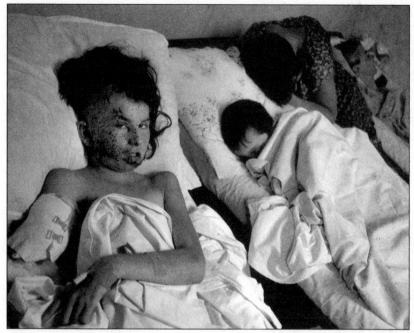

©Gilles Peress/Magnum

Muslim children injured in a 1994 shelling attack lying in the hospital
in East Mostar, Bosnia.

Christopher bristled: "I would ask you to go back and either look at what I
said or I'll say it again. What I said was the United States is doing all that it
can consistent with its national interest, and I've discussed before at some
length what our national interest is in this situation."

A few of the State Department junior officials who worked daily on the
former Yugoslavia were watching Christopher on television in their offices.
While their boss foundered under the reporters' continued grilling, they
joked that the secretary seemed to be "scouring the room for a black or
Asian face" so that he could call on somebody who might steer the discussion away from the "problem from hell." The following day, the Bosnian
Serbs fired 3,777 shells into Sarajevo in a sixteen-hour period, one of the
highest counts ever recorded.[129]

Between the outbreak of war in April 1992 and July 1993, America's
new breed of "conscientious objectors" had continued to believe in the
possibility of changing policy from inside the U.S. government. The interventionists within the ranks were not told to their faces that their ideas
were off the wall. Bureaucratic ritual had become better at incorporating
dissent, and they were shrewdly "domesticated" or assigned the role of
"official dissenters." They argued positions that were predictable and thus

easier to dismiss. Former National Security Council official James C. Thomson Jr., who resigned the NSC over Vietnam, described the ways the Johnson administration had once "warmly institutionalized" Undersecretary of State George Ball as the "inhouse devil's advocate" on Vietnam. Ball had been urged to speak his piece. Thomson remembered,

> Ball felt good, I assume (he had fought for righteousness); the others felt good (they had given a full hearing to the dovish option); and there was minimal unpleasantness. The club remained intact; and it is of course possible that matters would have gotten worse faster if Mr. Ball had kept silent, or left before his final departure in the fall of 1966.

According to Thomson, the president greeted the arrival at meetings of Bill Moyers, his dissenting press secretary, with an affectionate, "Well, here comes Mr. Stop-the-Bombing."[130]

By the summer of 1993 the Bosnia dissenters in the State Department and on Capitol Hill, too, had been "heard" and discounted. In this case Clinton and his senior officials might well have greeted a hawk like McCloskey and Dole on Capitol Hill or Harris, Hooper, and Western in the State Department as "Mr. *Start*-the-Bombing."

Exit

The State Department is difficult to leave. As with most hierarchical institutions, rituals entrench the solidarity of "members." Stiff "initiation costs" include fiercely competitive foreign service exams, tedious years of stamping visas in consular offices around the world, and dull desk jobs in the home office. Because of the association of service with "honor" and "country," exit is often seen as betrayal. Those few who depart on principle are excommunicated or labeled whistle-blowers. U.S. foreign policy lore is not laden with tales of the heroic resignee.

A further deterrent to exit is that the very people who care enough about a policy to contemplate resigning in protest often believe their departure will make it less likely that the policy will improve. Bureaucrats can easily fall into the "efficacy trap," overestimating the chances they will succeed in making change.[131] Dropping out can feel like copping out. The perverse result is that officials may exhibit a greater tendency to stay in an institution the worse they deem its actions.

By August 1993, despite all of these factors weighing against exit, existence within the State Department had become so insufferable for a small group of young officers that they took their leave. They found the U.S. policy so timid, so passive, and so doomed to fail that they chose to disassociate themselves from the administration and to go public with their discontent.

For Marshall Harris, the Bosnia desk officer and the lead author of the April 1993 dissent letter, there was nothing conscientious about objecting to a policy that would never change. In July Harris had drafted an "action memorandum" that outlined options for easing the siege of Sarajevo. By the time it had arrived on the seventh floor, however, the memo had been demoted to a "discussion paper." Christopher's "no national interests" pronouncement on July 21 was the last straw. On August 4, 1993, one year after the skeletal figures in the concentration camps had appeared on television and foreign service officer George Kenney had resigned, Harris followed suit. He quit only after he had lined up a job with Congressman McCloskey, who had turned criticizing the administration's Bosnia policy into a nearly full-time pursuit. "I was lucky," Harris recalls. "I could at least go straight to a job where I felt like I still had an official voice and might still influence policy." In a letter addressed to Secretary Christopher, Harris wrote, "I can no longer serve in a Department of State that accepts the forceful dismemberment of a European state and that will not act against genocide and the Serbian officials who perpetrate it."[132]

Harris was tired of the hypocrisy of Clinton's rhetoric. The administration refused to lead either the American people or its European allies and then complained that its policy was constrained by a lack of support from both. Speaking at a press conference the day after his resignation, Harris, thirty-two, delivered his first public verdict on the administration:

> If [President Clinton] were to lead, that would bring the American public along, that would bring along the congressmen who are reluctant to do anything, and it could inspire our European allies to do more. . . . I think the administration would be surprised what it could accomplish if it confronts this issue head on. When it adopts a defeatist mode . . . it's going to get defeatist results.[133]

Like Kenney, Harris was quickly disparaged by his higher-ups. Some said he quit because he had been shut out of the policy loop. State Department spokesman Mike McCurry shrugged off the impact of the resignation, pointing out that Harris was easily replaceable and saying, "We will fill the position with someone who is interested in working on the Administration's more aggressive policy to save Sarajevo and Bosnia from demise."[134] But Harris's colleagues within the department congratulated him for his courage and thanked him for giving voice to their frustration.

Jon Western, the State Department intelligence analyst, was driving with his wife into work from their home in Alexandria, Virginia, when he learned the news. Glancing at the *New York Times,* he saw a front-page story on Harris's departure. Western was stunned. Beneath the morning paper, he happened to be carrying his own detailed letter of resignation. Christopher's declaration that carnage in Bosnia was not a national interest had pushed him over the edge as well. The thirty-year-old could no longer sleep at night, reading about fathers and sons orally castrating one another or preteen girls raped in front of their parents. This was not a civil war, as Christopher kept saying; it was genocide. Western had been mulling resignation for several months, as he knew the daily death beat was getting the best of him. A few weeks before the Christopher press conference, he had visited the Holocaust Museum and heard the narrator, television journalist Jim Lehrer, recite the words of the Department spokesmen from 1943 and 1944 saying they had information on concentration camps in Europe but had "no ability to confirm the reports." Immediately he found himself transported to August 1992, when Assistant Secretary Tom Niles had said the administration did not have "substantiated information that would confirm the existence of these camps." Western himself had supplied Niles with all the evidence he needed.

On August 6, 1993, after reading the story about Harris's departure, Western went ahead and submitted his resignation letter. "I am personally and professionally heartsick by the unwillingness of the United States to make resolution of the conflict in the former Yugoslavia a top foreign policy priority," Western wrote. He took the elevator from his office on the fourth floor up to the seventh floor and handed the letter to the secretary of state's secretary. Word traveled so fast that by the time he had returned to his office minutes later, his phone had begun ringing off the hook. Harris was in Geneva when he heard about his colleague's exit and was surprised and pleased. Western was simply exhausted. In his journal entry that day, he described himself as "thoroughly demoralized and depressed."

Two weeks later Steven Walker, the Croatia desk officer, became the third diplomat to depart the State Department that month. On August 23, 1993,

Walker wrote, "I can no longer countenance U.S. support for a diplomatic process that legitimizes aggression and genocide."[135] Criticized for his testy response to the earlier exits, Christopher had convened a meeting with Balkan officials on August 13 to clear the air. Now with yet another exit, the secretary had begun to wonder whether the cascade of resignations would ever subside. This time he was far more conciliatory. His spokesman McCurry described Walker's exit as "an honorable form of protest" and said the Bosnian war was "just as frustrating for the secretary as it is for people at the country-desk-officer level who work on the problem."[136]

Nothing like this had happened before. It was the largest wave of resignations in State Department history. The departure of so many promising young officers reflected a degree of despair but also a capacity for disappointment among officials not evident in the previous genocides. In the past, U.S. officials had internalized the policy constraints and the top-level indifference. There were few feuds. But Bosnia caused an enormous policy rift that played itself out in the morning papers, which in turn bolstered the confidence and legitimated the outrage of officials who opposed U.S. policy from within.

After the three resignations, the State Department tried to improve morale by redecorating the offices, putting in new furniture and carpet, and shortening the tours of duty. As Harris remembers, "I guess they thought if they gave us soothing blue walls, people wouldn't be prone to fly off the handle and leave." But it was the policy, not the interior design, that was the problem.

National Security Adviser Lake, who had himself once resigned in protest, was now architect of a policy that was causing others to flee. In his *Foreign Policy* article "The Human Reality of Realpolitik," written in 1971, two decades before he became national security adviser, Lake had complained that the human dimensions of a policy were rarely discussed. "It simply is not *done*," Lake wrote. "Policy—good, steady policy—is made by the 'tough-minded.' . . . To talk of suffering is to lose 'effectiveness,' almost to lose one's grip. It is seen as a sign that one's rational arguments are weak." He had urged that policymakers elevate human costs and benefits to the category of "one of the principal and unashamedly legitimate considerations in *any* decision." In the 1990s, nearly a half century after the Holocaust and two decades since Vietnam, many believed that under Lake's leadership the U.S. foreign policy establishment would be more sensitive to human consequences. Yet at the State Department, officials say, to talk of human suffering remained something that was "not done." Those who complained about the human consequences of American decisions (or here, nondecisions) were still branded emotional, soft, and irrational. The language of national interest was Washington's lingua franca, and so it would remain.

Lake says he was torn when he heard of the departures:

> On the one hand, I agreed with them. They realized that the United States needed to do more, and they were willing to put their careers on the line on behalf of principle. If I had completely disagreed with them, then I could have just dismissed them as grandstanders. But I didn't have that option. On the other hand, I thought they were making it sound easier than it was to change course. There was no unanimity within the government on the issue, never mind with our European allies.

Lake devoted much of his time at the White House to managing the U.S. response to the crisis in the Balkans. Although he chaired a lot of meetings and generated a dense paper trail, he coordinated more than he led. "If you want to take ownership of an issue," one senior U.S. official says, "you have to do more than hold meetings and express your moral convictions. You have to make risky decisions and prove you have the courage of your convictions." Lake personally favored intervention, but did not recommend it to the president because he could not get consensus within the cabinet. With Secretaries Christopher and Perry as well as the chairman of the Joint Chiefs opposed to NATO air strikes, Lake opted for diplomacy and humanitarian relief, all the while attempting to reconcile these tame measures with the president's public promises never to tolerate ethnic cleansing. The endless, seemingly fruitless meetings led another high-level U.S. official to reflect, "It wasn't policy-making. It was group therapy—an existential debate over what is the role of America."[137] Lake did not go toe-to-toe against Pentagon officers and civilians who argued that air-power alone could not halt Serb terror. "When our senior military guys were saying, 'This mission can't be done,'" Lake explains, "it's hard to say, 'Listen, you professionals, here's an amateur's view of how and why it can be done.'"

Clinton's always awkward relations with the military were deteriorating further because the U.S. intervention in Somalia staged by Bush before he left the White House had begun spiraling out of control. In March 1993 the time had seemed ripe for U.S. troops deployed in December 1992 to slip away. UN peacekeeping forces would remain to preserve the peace and continue the relief operation. But just as the bulk of U.S. forces were withdrawing, the Security Council, at the urging of the United States, expanded the peacekeepers' mandate to include disarming the militias and restoring law and order. On June 5 the faction headed by Mohammed Farah Aideed ambushed lightly armed Pakistani peacekeepers, killing two dozen of them. The Americans lobbied for and U.S. special forces carried out a manhunt aimed at tracking down and punishing the Pakistanis' assailants. On October 3, 1993, U.S. Army rangers and Delta special forces attempted to seize several of Aideed's top advisers. Somali militia retaliated, killing eighteen U.S. Soldiers, wounding seventy-three, and kidnapping one Black Hawk helicopter pilot.[138] The American networks broadcast a video interview with the trembling, disoriented pilot and a gory procession in which the naked corpse of a U.S. ranger was dragged through a Mogadishu street.

On receiving word of these events, President Clinton cut short a trip to California and convened an urgent crisis-management meeting at the White House. When an aide began recapping the situation, an angry president interrupted him. "Cut the bullshit," Clinton snapped. "Let's work this out." "Work it out" meant walk out. Republican congressional pressure was intense. Clinton appeared on television the next day, called off the manhunt for Aideed, and announced that all U.S. forces would be home within six months. Bosnian Serb television gleefully replayed the footage of the U.S. humiliation, knowing that it made U.S. intervention in Bosnia even less likely. A week after the Mogadishu firefight, U.S. forces suffered further humiliation in Haiti, as angry anti-American demonstrators deterred the USS *Harlan County* from landing troops to join a UN mission there. The Pentagon concluded that the president would not stand by them when U.S. forces got into trouble. Multilateral humanitarian missions seemed to bring all risk and no gain.

Although a U.S. ground invasion of the Balkans was never proposed even by the most hawkish Bosnia defenders, the Pentagon feared that what began as a limited U.S. involvement in Bosnia would end up as a large, messy one. The "active measures" proposed to punish ethnic cleansing would send the United States "headlong down a slippery slope," Defense Secretary Perry said. "At the bottom of that slope will be American troops in ground combat."[139]

The combination of the departures of three internal (if junior) advocates and the persistence of the ineffectual U.S. policy left the department far more hopeless and cynical than it had been before. The junior officers who replaced the resignees worked around the clock as their predecessors had done, but in the words of one, they were not "emotionally involved, only morally involved." It is hard to know what this distinction means exactly, except that it hints at the way the three resignees were branded after they took their leave. They were publicly hailed as honorable men, but a whisper campaign blasphemed them for their unprofessional stands.

The State Department quieted down. The longer Clinton served in office, the greater the distance that grew between him and his campaign promises and the less sensible it seemed to continue to contest what appeared to be an entrenched policy of noninvolvement. The use of the Holocaust analogy diminished. "The State Department wanted professionals who would not think what Warren Christopher was doing was the equivalent of not bombing the railroads to Auschwitz," says one Balkan desk officer. The State Department Balkan team was there to do "damage control" for the administration. They were not there to kick up a fuss.

Defeat on All Fronts

Not everyone quieted down. Like a broken record, Congressman McCloskey continued to seize every opportunity to badger administration officials. When Christopher blamed all sides as a way of explaining the weak U.S. policy, McCloskey pounced, slamming Christopher's attempt to posit "moral equivalency." In what was becoming a ritual between the two men, the Indiana congressman asked again for the State Department's position on the term "genocide." "I know—you know that my request is still pending right now," McCloskey said. A skilled lawyer, Christopher agreed that the Serbs were aggressors, which was irrefutable, but again seized the opportunity to obfuscate. Christopher responded:

> Mr. McCloskey, thank you for the question and for giving me an opportunity to say that I share your feeling that the principal fault lies with the Bosnian Serbs, and I've said that several times before. They are the most at fault of the three parties. But there is considerable fault

on all three sides, and . . . atrocities abound in this area as we have seen in the last several days and weeks. But I agree that the aggression coming from Serbia is the . . . principal perpetrator of the problem in the area.

With respect to genocide, the definition of genocide is a fairly technical definition. Let me just get it for you here. I think I can get it in just a moment.

Christopher paused, read from the convention, and then said:

I would say that some of the acts that have been committed by various parties in Bosnia, principally by the Serbians, could constitute genocide under the 1948 convention, if their purpose was to destroy the religious or ethnic group in whole or in part. And that seems to me to be a standard that may well have been reached in some of the aspects of Bosnia. Certainly some of the conduct there is tantamount to genocide.[140]

As he had done in March, Christopher called the atrocities "tantamount to genocide" but refused to deliver a formal finding to that effect. Other U.S. officials were thus left to squirm for themselves.

During a September 15, 1993, hearing of the House Europe and Middle East Subcommittee, McCloskey pressed Assistant Secretary of State for European and Canadian Affairs Stephen Oxman, who stuck to the qualifier of "tantamount":

Rep. McCloskey: As you know, since April, I've been trying to get an answer from State as to whether these activities by the Bosnian Serbs and Serbs constitute genocide. Will I get a reply on that today?
Mr. Oxman: I learned, just today, that you hadn't had your response. And the first thing I'm going to do when I get back to the Department is find out where that is. We'll get you that response as soon as we possibly can. But to give you my personal view, I think that acts tantamount to genocide have been committed. Whether the technical definition of genocide—I think this is what the letter that you're asking for needs to address.
Rep. McCloskey: Right.
Mr. Oxman: And I think you're entitled to an answer.

Rep. McCloskey: This word tantamount floats about. I haven't looked it up in a dictionary, though. I'm derelict on that. I don't know how—I guess I have a subjective view as to how to define it, but it's an intriguing word. But I'll look forward to your reply.[141]

Behind the scenes soon thereafter, Assistant Secretary of State for Intelligence and Research (INR) Toby Gati sent Secretary Christopher classified guidance on the genocide question. Although Gati's memo left Christopher some wiggle room, its overall message was clear: Undoubtedly, the analysis stated, the Serbs had carried out many of the acts listed in the convention—killing, causing serious bodily or mental harm, inflicting conditions of life calculated to bring about physical destruction, imposing measures to prevent births—against Bosnia's Muslims because they were Muslims. What proved challenging, as always, was determining whether the Serbs possessed the requisite intent to "destroy, in whole or in part," the Muslim group. The memo noted that proving such intent without intercepting written policies or orders was difficult, but it suggested that intention could be "inferred from the circumstances." It noted several of the circumstances present in Bosnia:

- the expressed intent of individual Serb perpetrators to eradicate the Muslims
- the publicly stated Serb political objective of creating an ethnically homogeneous state
- the wholesale purging of Muslims from Serb-held territory, with the aim of ensuring ethnic homogeneity
- the systematic fashion in which Muslims, Muslim men, or Muslim leaders are singled out for killing

The "overall factual situation," the memo said, provided "a strong basis to conclude that killings and other listed acts have been undertaken with the intent of destroying the Muslim group as such." The secretary was informed that one of the understandings the U.S. Senate attached to its ratification of the genocide convention required an intent to destroy a "substantial" part of a group. The Senate had defined "substantial" to mean a sufficient number to "cause the destruction of the group as a viable entity." In Bosnia, the memo concluded, the "numbers of Muslims subjected to killings and other listed acts . . . can readily be considered substantial."[142]

Responding to the widespread perception that a finding of genocide would carry severe consequences for U.S. policymakers, the INR analysis observed that the convention's enforcement requirements were in fact weak. It relayed the legal adviser's judgment that a genocide finding would carry no "particular legal benefits (or, for that matter, legally adverse consequences)":

> Some have argued that . . . the United States is obligated to take further measures in order to "prevent" genocide in Bosnia, once and if it is determined to be genocide. In our view, however, this general undertaking . . . *cannot* be read as imposing an obligation on outside states to take all measures whatsoever as may prove necessary— including the use of armed force—in order to "prevent" genocide.[143]

The United States was already meeting its obligations under the convention: "The United States and other parties are attempting to 'prevent and punish' such actions," the memo said, adding sheepishly, "even though such measures may not be immediately wholly effective."[144]

On October 13, 1993, a year and a half after the conflict began, Christopher finally approved the drafting of a letter by the assistant secretary for congressional relations acknowledging "acts of genocide." But Christopher pulled his approval several days later when Congressman McCloskey published an editorial in the *New York Times* calling for his resignation.[145] Upon reading the editorial, Christopher reportedly picked up the memo authorizing a finding of genocide and wrote in large letters "O.B.E.," for "overtaken by events." In the culmination of a series of exchanges, the pair traded bitter words in a House Foreign Affairs Committee hearing the following month.[146] With the behind-the-scenes help of his new staffer, Marshall Harris, who had been uncorked to vent his frustration, McCloskey prepared a statement summing up the collapse of the administration's Balkan policy:

> On February 10th, three weeks after President Clinton took office, Secretary Christopher stated that this administration had to address the circumstances as it found them in Bosnia. He further stated that the administration was resolved to do so. Just last month, however, he stated that the administration "inherited" the problem. Also on February 10th, Secretary Christopher stated that the United States [had] "direct strategic concerns in Bosnia." . . . When I heard those

remarks, I was proud of my president, proud of this administration, proud and grateful to Mr. Christopher and proud of my country. Unfortunately, the administration began an about-face soon after that was . . . abysmally shameful.

. . . It acquiesced to European objections to allowing the Bosnians to defend themselves, it signed on to . . . a meaningless plan which called for safe areas that we all know—we all know—and two weeks ago I was in Sarajevo—we all know that Sarajevo and the other so-called safe enclaves to this day are still not safe. In fact, 50 years after Buchenwald and Auschwitz, there are giant concentration camps in the heart of Europe.

. . . On July 21st, Secretary Christopher said this administration was doing all it could in Bosnia consistent with our national interests. The very next day, consistent with that statement, the Serbs launched one of their largest attacks ever in the 17-month-old siege of Sarajevo. Last month, the Serbs resumed their shelling of Sarajevo and killed dozens more innocent civilians. Bosnian Serb terrorist leaders . . . were quoted in the *New York Times* as saying that they renewed their bloody attacks because they knew after American fiascoes in Haiti and Somalia the Clinton administration would not respond. They were right. Our only response was another warning to Milosevic.

We've been warning these people, Mr. Secretary, for nearly two years, and I guess I appreciate your warnings, but I'd like to see some effect at some point. Unlike the shells raining down on innocent men, women and children in the Bosnian capital, these warnings ring absolutely hollow. Even now, we won't lift the sieges [of the safe areas], and I think this is very important.

. . . All these things happened or are happening on the Secretary's watch. The situation in Bosnia stopped being an inherited problem in January '93. Since then, several hundred thousand Bosnians have been driven out of the country or into internal exile, thousands of inno-cent civilians have been murdered, tens of thousands of ill-equipped Bosnian soldiers have been killed because we won't arm them, thou-sands more women have been raped as a systematic campaign by the Bosnian Serbs.

The administration continues to profess . . . that it wants a negoti-ated solution to this war of aggression even if it means dismembering the sovereign U.N.-member state of Bosnia. It also says this is a tragic, complex situation with no easy answers. We all want a negotiated solution. We all know perfectly well that it's tragic and that nothing will come easily in addressing the crisis, but these are empty posturings in the administration's grievously inadequate foreign policy. Hundreds of thousands of lives hang in the balance as we say we support the enlargement of democracies and do little more.

Genocide is taking place in Bosnia, and I think it's very important—Mr. Christopher knows this, but Secretary Christopher won't say so. On at least two occasions of which I am aware, State Department lawyers and representatives of other relevant bureaus have recommended that he state this publicly, but we still do not have an answer. That request was first made publicly and in writing about 200 days ago.

Mr. Chairman, I won't go on. I appreciate the time. But when the history books are written, we cannot say that we allowed genocide because health care was a priority. We cannot say that we allowed genocide because the American people were more concerned with domestic issues. History will record, Mr. Secretary, that this happened on our watch, on your watch, that you and the administration could and should have done more. I plead to you, there are hundreds of thousands of people that still can die. . . . I plead for you and the administration to make a more aggressive—to take a more aggressive interest in this.

Secretary Christopher responded to McCloskey's assault with a rare burst of anger. He faulted McCloskey for proposing a massive U.S. ground invasion, which in fact the congressman had never recommended. Christopher said:

At rock bottom, you would be willing to put hundreds of thousands of American troops into Bosnia to compel a settlement satisfactory to the Bosnian government. I would not do so. I don't think our vital interests are sufficiently involved to do so. I don't see any point in our debating this subject further. You and I have discussed it several times in this forum. We have got fundamental differences of opinion. I do not believe that we should put hundreds of thousands of troops into Bosnia in order to compel a settlement. I'd go on to say, Mr.

McCloskey, that it seems to me that your very strong feelings on this
subject have affected adversely your judgment.[147]

McCloskey's concerns about the wars in the Balkans, sparked in 1991,
had only deepened with time. Indeed, the congressman was so haunted by
the carnage that in at least fifteen hearings he raised questions about U.S.
policy in Bosnia.[148] To some, McCloskey's hawkish Bosnia fervor seemed at
odds with his leftist politics, his outspoken opposition to the war in
Vietnam in the early 1970s, and his vote in Congress against the 1991
Persian Gulf War. Others were surprised to see him take on fellow
Democrats. Indeed, he voted for Clinton's programs 86 percent of the
time, the highest rating within the Indiana congressional delegation. But
during the Bosnian war, the man the *Almanac of American Politics* described
as "a man of earnest, plodding demeanor" metamorphosed into the unlikely conscience of the U.S. House of Representatives.[149]

The Clinton team had been much more forceful than the Bush team
about condemning the Serbs as aggressors. When sixty-eight Muslim shoppers and vendors were killed in a Sarajevo marketplace massacre in
February 1994, for instance, Clinton denounced the "murder of innocents." In a transient interlude, Clinton even took the lead in issuing a
NATO ultimatum that banned Serb heavy weapons from around the capital. "The United States," he said, "will not stand idly by in the face of a conflict that affects our interests, offends our consciences, and disrupts the
peace." The risks entailed in NATO bombing, he assured the American
people, were "minimal." "If we can stop the slaughter of civilians," Clinton
said, "we ought to try it."[150]

Because Clinton warned, "No one should doubt NATO's resolve," initially nobody did. For several months, Sarajevans lived free of artillery and
sniper fire. But when the Serbs resumed shelling the safe areas, the president's attention had drifted elsewhere and NATO did not bomb.

Beginning in April 1994, the allies did occasionally launch what became
known as "pinprick" air strikes—usually a single strike against aged Serb
military hardware delivered with plenty of advanced warning. But whenever the Serbs answered by intensifying attacks on Muslim civilians or rounding up UN peacekeepers as hostages (as they did in November 1994 and
May and June 1995), the United States, along with its allies, caved. U.S. policymakers spent endless hours working to devise a solution for Bosnia, but
they never took charge of the diplomatic process. They could not admit

either to the Muslims or to themselves the limits of what they were willing to risk on behalf of their moral commitments. And they were not prepared to barrel ahead with a strategy or to invest the political capital that would have been needed to get international support for military action. Instead, they wrung their hands. "The Europeans were waiting for American leadership," says Holbrooke, "but they didn't get it for three years."

Those who did own the issue paid a price. Any relationship Frank McCloskey maintained with the Clinton administration was severed after his highly public demand for Christopher's resignation. Although McCloskey occupied a seat in the most hotly contested district in the entire country, he seemed oblivious to the polls and the likely repercussions of his crusade. He ignored the appeals of his staff members to stop making so many visible trips to the Balkans. Ahead of the November 1994 election, he told a reporter that he didn't care if his Bosnia efforts cost him his seat in office: "This thing is beyond politics for me and beyond election or reelection." To another journalist, he said, "I would rather actively try to stop the slaughter than run and continue to win, knowing that I didn't face this."[151]

Back in Indiana, though, McCloskey's Republican challenger made him pay, deriding him for being "more concerned about Bosnia than Evansville." Republican National Committee chairman Haley Barbour visited Evansville, the largest city in McCloskey's district, and happily noted, "People are coming out of the woodwork to run."[152] McCloskey's constituents by and large opposed military intervention. Recalling constituent letters that poured into the office, Marshall Harris remembers, "They would say, 'Bosnia is far from our concern.' They always sounded a lot like Warren Christopher." In the end, after electing him to six terms in office, sour voters sent McCloskey packing in the November 1994 Republican sweep. The race was tight, 51–49, and although McCloskey, then fifty-five, says he does not regret a moment he spent lobbying for intervention in Bosnia, he does wonder if a few more trips back to his district on weekends instead of those across the Atlantic to Bosnia might have made the difference. The *Indianapolis Star* attributed his defeat to his Balkan fixation. In McCloskey's southern Indiana district, the *Star* noted, "Hoosiers were much more interested in local events than the problems of a region half a world away."

Before he was voted out of office, McCloskey had a bizarre encounter with President Clinton that taught him all he needed to know about the president's now notorious tendency to compartmentalize. At a black-tie Democratic fund-raising dinner in Washington, McCloskey stood in a rope line to greet the president, whom he had been criticizing fiercely. Like Lemkin, McCloskey was never one to waste an opportunity. The congressman took Clinton's hand and said, "Bill, bomb the Serbs. You'll be surprised how good it'll make you feel." Unflustered, Clinton nodded thoughtfully for a few seconds and then blamed the Europeans for their hesitancy. "Frank, I understand what you're saying," the president said. "But you just don't understand what bastards those Brits are." Clinton slid along the rope line, shaking more hands and making more small talk, and McCloskey thought the exchange was over. But a few minutes later the president spun around and walked back to where McCloskey was standing. "By the way, Frank," Clinton proclaimed cheerily, "I really like what you're doing. Keep it up!" "The problem with Bill Clinton," McCloskey observes, "was that he didn't realize he was president of the United States."

During the Bosnian war, during both a Republican and a Democratic administration, the UN Security Council passed resolutions deploring the conduct of the perpetrators. It created the UN-EU International Conference on the Former Yugoslavia as a formal negotiation channel. It called upon states and international human rights organizations to document human rights violations. It deployed UN peacekeepers (though no Americans). And it funded the longest-running humanitarian airlift since the Berlin airlift.

In addition, in its most radical affront to state sovereignty, the Security Council invoked the genocide convention and created the first international criminal tribunal since Nuremberg.[153] The court would sit in The Hague and try grave breaches of the Geneva conventions, violations of the law or customs of war, crimes against humanity, and, at long last, genocide. One of the most tireless supporters of the court was Madeleine Albright, the U.S. ambassador at the UN. If her colleagues looked to Vietnam for policy guidance, Albright liked to say, "My mindset is Munich." She was the rare official in the Clinton team who lobbied relentlessly for NATO bombing and who laced her public condemnations of Serb "extermination" and expulsion with Holocaust references. When the Security Council voted to establish an international tribunal, Albright declared, "There is an echo in this Chamber today. The Nuremberg Principles have been reaffirmed. . . . This will be no victors' tribunal. The only victor that will prevail in this endeavor is the truth."[154]

But in the Bosnian war, the truth had never been in short supply. What was missing was U.S. willingness to risk its own soldiers on the ground or to convince the Europeans to support NATO bombing from the air. As a result, the ethnic cleansing and genocide against the country's Muslims proceeded apace, and more than 200,000 Bosnians were killed.

In June 1995 President Clinton and Vice President Gore appeared on *Larry King Live* and defended their policy. "This is a tragedy that has been unfolding for a long time, some would say for 500 years," Gore said. Clinton did him one better: "Their enmities go back 500 years, some would say almost a thousand years." He also claimed that 130,000 people were killed in 1992, whereas fewer than 3,000 were murdered in 1994. "That's still tragic," the president noted, "but I hardly think that constitutes a colossal failure."[155]

Jim Hooper, who had worked within both administrations and had chosen not to resign, juxtaposes the struggles:

> The Bush administration did not have to be persuaded it was OK to intervene. They had done so in the Gulf. They just had to be persuaded that this was the right place to do it. With the Clinton administration we had to convince them that it was OK to intervene *and* that this was the right place to do so. Their starting point was that military intervention was never OK. This made it doubly difficult.

In the immediate aftermath of Clinton's election victory, the former British foreign secretary and European negotiator Lord David Owen had warned the Bosnians not to rely on U.S. promises. In December 1992, standing on the tarmac at Sarajevo airport, his cheeks flush with the winter cold, Owen had declared: "Don't, don't, don't live under this dream that the West is going to come in and sort this problem out. Don't dream dreams."[156] However cold the sentiment, Owen honestly and accurately urged Bosnians to assume they were on their own. Clinton administration officials often spoke sternly about Serb brutality and criticized European and UN peace plans that would have divided Bosnia and "rewarded aggression." But if Clinton managed to keep the dream of rescue alive, for the first two and a half years of his presidency he left the Bosnians to their own meager devices. It was not until July 1995 that Clinton would act. By then, another genocide would have killed 800,000 people in Rwanda.

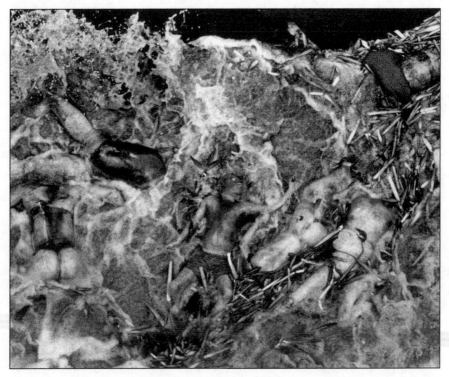

Rwandan bodies floating down the Kagera River.

Chapter 10

Rwanda: "Mostly in a Listening Mode"

"I'll Never Be Tutsi Again"

On the evening of April 6, 1994, two years to the day after the beginning of the Bosnian war, Major General Romeo Dallaire was sitting on the couch in his bungalow residence in Kigali, Rwanda, watching CNN with his assistant, Brent Beardsley. Beardsley was preparing plans for a national sports day that would match Tutsi rebel soldiers against Hutu government soldiers in a soccer game. Dallaire, the commander of the UN mission, said, "You know, Brent, if the shit ever hit the fan here, none of this stuff would really matter, would it?" The next instant the phone rang. Rwandan president Juvénal Habyarimana's Mystère Falcon jet, a gift from French president François Mitterrand, had just been shot down, with Habyarimana and Burundian president Cyprien Ntaryamira aboard. When Dallaire replaced the receiver, the phone rang again instantly. Indeed, the UN phones rang continually that night and the following day, averaging 100 phone calls per hour. Countless politicians, UN local staff, and ordinary Rwandans were calling out for help. The Canadian pair hopped in their UN jeep and dashed to Rwandan army headquarters, where a crisis meeting was under way. They never returned to their residence.

When Dallaire arrived at the Rwandan army barracks, he found Colonel Théoneste Bagosora, the army staff director, a hard-line Hutu, seated at the head of a U-shaped table. Appearing firmly in command, Bagosora announced that the president's death meant the government had collapsed and the army needed to take charge. Dallaire interjected, arguing that in effect the king had died, but the government lived on. He reminded the officers assembled that Prime Minister Agathe Uwilingiyimana, a leading moderate, had become the lawful head of state. Many of the stone-faced officers gathered around the table began to snicker at the prospect.

Back in Washington, Kevin Aiston, the Rwanda desk officer at the State Department, knocked on the door of Deputy Assistant Secretary of State Prudence Bushnell and told her that the presidents of Rwanda and Burundi had been killed in a plane crash. "Oh, shit," she said. "Are you sure?" In fact nobody was sure at first, but Dallaire's forces supplied confirmation within the hour. The Rwandan authorities quickly announced a curfew, and Hutu militias and government soldiers erected roadblocks around the capital. Radio Mille Collines, the Hutu extremist radio station, named ethnic Tutsi, those they called *Inyenzi,* or "cockroaches," the targets.

Bushnell drafted an urgent memo to Secretary of State Warren Christopher. She was concerned about a probable outbreak of killing in both Rwanda and its neighbor Burundi. The memo read: "If, as it appears, both Presidents have been killed, there is a strong likelihood that widespread violence could break out in either or both countries, particularly if it is confirmed that the plane was shot down. Our strategy is to appeal for calm in both countries, both through public statements and in other ways."[1] A few public statements proved to be virtually the only strategy that Washington would muster in the weeks ahead.

Lieutenant General Wesley Clark, who later commanded the NATO air war in Kosovo, was the director of strategic plans and policy for the Joint Chiefs of Staff at the Pentagon. On learning of the crash, Clark remembers, staff officers asked, "Is it Hutu and Tutsi or Tutu and Hutsi?" He frantically telephoned around the Pentagon for insight into the ethnic dimension of events in Rwanda. Unfortunately, Rwanda had never been of more than marginal concern to Washington's most influential planners.

America's best-informed Rwanda observer was not a government official but a private citizen, Alison Des Forges, a historian and a board member of Human Rights Watch, who lived in Buffalo, New York. Des Forges had been visiting Rwanda since 1963. She had received a Ph.D. from Yale in African history, specializing in Rwanda, and she could speak the Rwandan language, Kinyarwanda. Half an hour after the plane crash Des Forges got a phone call from a close friend in Kigali, the human-rights activist Monique Mujawamariya. Des Forges had been worried about Mujawamariya for weeks because the hate-propagating Radio Mille Collines had branded her "a bad patriot who deserves to die." Mujawamariya had sent Human Rights Watch a chilling warning a week earlier: "For the last two weeks, all of Kigali has lived under the threat of an instantaneous, carefully prepared operation to eliminate all those who give trouble to President Habyarimana."[2]

Now Habyarimana was dead, and Mujawamariya knew instantly that the hard-line Hutu would use the incident as a pretext to begin mass killing. "This is it," she told Des Forges on the phone. For the next twenty-four hours, Des Forges called her friend's home every half hour. With each conversation Des Forges could hear the gunfire grow louder as the Hutu militia drew closer. Finally the gunmen entered Mujawamariya's home. "I don't want you to hear this," Mujawamariya said softly. "Take care of my children." She hung up the phone.

Mujawamariya's instincts were correct. Within hours of Habyarimana's death, armed Hutu took command of the streets of Kigali. Dallaire quickly grasped that supporters of a Hutu-Tutsi peace process were being targeted. Rwandans around the capital begged peacekeepers at the headquarters of the UN Assistance Mission for Rwanda (UNAMIR) to come and get them. Dallaire was especially concerned about Prime Minister Uwilingiyimana, the reformer who had become the titular head of state. Just after dawn on April 7, five Ghanaian and ten Belgian peacekeepers arrived at the prime minister's home in order to deliver her to Radio Rwanda, so that she could broadcast an emergency appeal for calm.

Joyce Leader, the second-in-command at the U.S. embassy, lived next door to Uwilingiyimana. She spent the early hours of the morning behind the steel-barred gates of her embassy-owned house as Hutu killers hunted and dispatched their first victims. Leader's phone rang. Uwilingiyimana was on the other end. "Please hide me," she begged. Leader had not known Uwilingiyimana well. "She was a prime minister," the American recalls, "I was just a lowly diplomat." But they had become acquainted through diplomatic functions, and once, when the electricity supply had cut out, Uwilingiyimana had come over to Leader's home to do her hair. It was considered an emergency.

Minutes after the phone call a UN peacekeeper attempted to hike the prime minister over the wall separating their compounds. When Leader heard shots fired, she urged the peacekeeper to abandon the effort. "They can see you!" she shouted. Uwilingiyimana managed to slip with her husband and children into another compound, which was occupied by the UN Development Program. But the militiamen hunted them down in the yard, where the couple surrendered. There were more shots. Leader recalls, "We heard her screaming and then, suddenly, after the gunfire, the screaming stopped, and we heard people cheering." Hutu gunmen in the presidential guard that day systematically tracked down and eliminated virtually all of Rwanda's moderate politicians.

The raid on Uwilingiyimana's compound not only cost Rwanda a prominent supporter of peace and power-sharing, but it also triggered the collapse of Dallaire's UN mission. In keeping with a prior plan, Hutu soldiers rounded up the peacekeepers at Uwilingiyimana's home, took them to a military camp, led the Ghanaians to safety, and then killed and savagely mutilated the ten Belgians. Because the United States had retreated from Somalia after the deaths of eighteen U.S. soldiers, the Hutu assailants believed this massacre would prompt a Belgian withdrawal. And indeed, in Belgium the cry for either expanding UNAMIR's mandate or immediately pulling out was prompt and loud.

Only at 9 p.m. on April 7 did Dallaire learn that the Belgians had been killed. He traveled to Kigali Hospital, where more than 1,000 dead Rwandan bodies had already been gathered. Dallaire entered the darkened morgue and shone his flashlight on the corpses of his men, who were heaped in a pile. At first he wondered why there were eleven bodies when he had been told that ten were killed. Then he realized that their bodies had been so badly cut up that they had become impossible to count. Dallaire negotiated with the Rwandan authorities to lay their corpses out with more dignity and to preserve what was left of their uniforms.

Most in the Pentagon greeted the news of the Belgians' death as proof that the UN mission in Rwanda had gone from being a "Somalia waiting to happen" to a Somalia that was happening. For many, the incident fed on and fueled ingrained biases about UN peacekeeping because the Belgians had allowed themselves to be disarmed. James Woods, deputy assistant secretary of defense for Africa since 1986, recalled:

Well, there was horror and consternation at the deaths and, particularly, that they died badly. But there was also consternation that they
did not defend themselves. They did not draw their pistols. I think it
tended to confirm in the minds of those people who were following
UN peace operations that there was a lot of romantic nonsense built
into some of the ground rules and this was another reason to steer
clear of UN peacekeeping operations. . . . I heard one person say,
"Well, at least, you know, our rangers died fighting in Somalia. These
guys, with their blue berets, were slaughtered without getting a shot
off."[3]

A fever descended upon Rwanda. Lists of victims had been prepared
ahead of time. That much was clear from the Radio Mille Collines broadcasts, which read the names, addresses, and license plate numbers of Tutsi
and moderate Hutu. "I listened to [it]," one survivor recalled, "because if
you were mentioned over the airways, you were sure to be carted off a
short time later by the Interahamwe. You knew you had to change your
address at once."[4]

In response to the initial killings by the Hutu government, Tutsi rebels of
the Rwandan Patriotic Front, stationed in Kigali under the terms of a
recent peace accord, surged out of their barracks and resumed their civil
war against the Hutu regime. But under the cover of that war were early
and strong indications that systematic genocide was taking place. From
April 7 onward, the Hutu-controlled army, the gendarmerie, and the militias worked together to wipe out Rwanda's Tutsi. Many of the early Tutsi
victims found themselves specifically, not spontaneously, pursued. A survivor of a massacre at a hospital in Kibuye reported that he heard a list read
over a loudspeaker before the attack began. Another survivor said that once
the killing was finished:

They sent people in among the bodies to verify who was dead. They
said, "Here is the treasurer and his wife and daughter, but where is the
younger child?" Or, "Here is Josue's father, his wife and mother, but
where is he?" And then, in the days after, they tried to hunt you down
if they thought you were still alive. They would shout out, "Hey Josue,
we see you now" to make you jump and try to run so that they could
see you move and get you more easily.[5]

In Kigali in the early days, the killers were well-equipped government soldiers and militiamen who relied mainly on automatic weapons and grenades. In the countryside, where the slaughter gradually spread, the killing was done at first with firearms, but as more Hutu joined in the weapons became increasingly unsophisticated—knives, machetes, spears, and the traditional *masu,* bulky clubs with nails protruding from them. Later screwdrivers, hammers, and bicycle handlebars were added to the arsenal. Killers often carried a weapon in one hand and a transistor radio piping murder commands in the other.

Tens of thousands of Tutsi fled their homes in panic and were snared and butchered at checkpoints. Little care was given to their disposal. Some were shoveled into landfills. Human flesh rotted in the sunshine. In churches bodies mingled with scattered hosts. If the killers had taken the time to tend to sanitation, it would have slowed their efforts to "sanitize" their country.

Because the Hutu and Tutsi had lived intermingled and, in many instances, intermarried, the outbreak of killing forced Hutu and Tutsi friends and relatives into life-altering decisions about whether or not to desert their loved ones in order to save their own lives. At Mugonero Church in the town of Kibuye, two Hutu sisters, each married to a Tutsi husband, faced such a choice. One of the women decided to die with her husband. The other, who hoped to save the lives of her eleven children, chose to leave. Because her husband was Tutsi, her children had been categorized as Tutsi and thus were technically forbidden to live. But the machete-wielding Hutu attackers had assured the woman that the children would be permitted to depart safely if she agreed to accompany them. When the woman stepped out of the church, however, she saw the assailants butcher eight of the eleven children. The youngest, a child of three years old, pleaded for his life after seeing his brothers and sisters slain. "Please don't kill me," he said. "I'll never be Tutsi again." But the killers, unblinking, struck him down.[6]

The Rwandan genocide would prove to be the fastest, most efficient killing spree of the twentieth century. In 100 days, some 800,000 Tutsi and politically moderate Hutu were murdered. The United States did almost nothing to try to stop it. Ahead of the April 6 plane crash, the United States ignored extensive early warnings about imminent mass violence. It denied Belgian requests to reinforce the peacekeeping mission. When the massacres started, not only did the Clinton administration not send troops to

Rwanda to contest the slaughter, but it refused countless other options. President Clinton did not convene a single meeting of his senior foreign policy advisers to discuss U.S. options for Rwanda. His top aides rarely condemned the slaughter. The United States did not deploy its technical assets to jam Rwandan hate radio, and it did not lobby to have the genocidal Rwandan government's ambassador expelled from the United Nations. Those steps that the United States did take had deadly repercussions. Washington demanded the withdrawal of UN peacekeepers from Rwanda and then refused to authorize the deployment of UN reinforcements. Remembering Somalia and hearing no American demands for intervention, President Clinton and his advisers knew that the military and political risks of involving the United States in a bloody conflict in central Africa were great, yet there were no costs to avoiding Rwanda altogether. Thus, the United States again stood on the sidelines.

Warning

Background: The UN Deployment

If ever there was a peacekeeper who believed wholeheartedly in the promise of humanitarian action, it was the forty-seven-year-old major general who commanded UN peacekeepers in Rwanda. A broad-shouldered French Canadian with deep-set, sky blue eyes, Dallaire has the thick, callused hands of one brought up in a culture that prizes soldiering, service, and sacrifice. He saw the United Nations as the embodiment of all three.[7]

Before his posting to Rwanda, Dallaire had served as the commandant of an army brigade that sent peacekeeping battalions to Cambodia and Bosnia, but he had never seen actual combat himself. "I was like a fireman who has never been to a fire, but has dreamed for years about how he would fare when the fire came," Dallaire recalls. When, in the summer of 1993, he received the phone call from UN headquarters offering him the Rwanda posting, he was ecstatic. "It's very difficult for somebody not in the service to understand what it means to get a command. He'd sell his mother to do it. I mean, when I got that call, it was answering the aim of my life," he says. "It's what you've been waiting for. It's *all* you've been waiting for."

Canadian Major General
Romeo Dallaire, commander of
UN peacekeeping forces in
Rwanda.

Romeo Dallaire

Dallaire was sent to command a UN force that would help to keep the peace in Rwanda, a nation the size of Vermont, with a population of 8 million, which was known as "the land of a thousand hills." Before Rwanda achieved independence from Belgium in 1962, the Tutsi, who made up 15 percent of the populace, had enjoyed a privileged status. But independence ushered in three decades of Hutu rule, under which Tutsi were systematically discriminated against and periodically subjected to waves of killing and ethnic cleansing. In 1990 a group of armed exiles, mainly Tutsi, who had been clustered on the Ugandan border, invaded Rwanda. Over the next several years the rebels, known as the Rwandan Patriotic Front (RPF), gained ground against Hutu government forces. In 1993, with the support of the major Western powers, Tanzania brokered peace talks, which resulted in a power-sharing agreement known as the Arusha accords. Under its terms the Rwandan government agreed to govern with Hutu opposition parties and the Tutsi minority. UN peacekeepers would be deployed to patrol a cease-fire and assist in demilitarization and demobilization as well as to help provide a secure environment, so that exiled Tutsi could return. The hope among moderate Rwandans and foreign diplomats was that Hutu and Tutsi would at last be able to coexist in harmony.

Hard-line elements within the Rwandan government and Hutu extremists outside it found the Arusha agreement singularly unattractive. They saw themselves as having everything to lose, everything to fear, and nothing obvious to gain by complying with the terms of the peace deal. The Hutu had dominated the Rwandan political and economic scene for three decades, and they were afraid that the Tutsi, who had long been persecuted, would respond in kind if given the chance again to govern. The accord did not grant past killers amnesty for their misdeeds, so those Hutu leaders who had blood on their hands were concerned that integrating Tutsi political and military officials into the government would cost them their freedom or their lives. The Hutu memories of preindependence Rwanda had been passed down through the generations, and Hutu children could recite at length the sins the Tutsi had committed against their forefathers.

Hutu extremists opposed to Arusha set out to terrorize the Tutsi and those who supported power-sharing. Guns, grenades, and machetes began arriving by the planeload.[8] By 1992, Hutu militia had purchased, stockpiled, and begun distributing an estimated eighty-five tons of munitions, as well as 581,000 machetes—one machete for every third adult Hutu male.[9] The situation deteriorated dramatically enough in 1993 for a number of international and UN bodies to take interest. In early 1993 Mujawamariya, executive director of the Rwanda Association for the Defense of Human Rights, urged international human rights groups to visit her country in the hopes of deterring further violence. Des Forges of Human Rights Watch was one of twelve people from eight countries who composed the International Commission of Investigation. The commission spent three weeks in Rwanda, interviewing hundreds of Rwandans. The crimes that were being described even then were so savage as to defy belief. In one instance the investigators met a woman who said that her sons had been murdered by Hutu extremists and buried in the mayor's back garden. When the authorities denied the woman's claims, the team knew they had to obtain concrete proof. They descended upon the mayor's doorstep, demanding they be allowed to dig up his garden; the mayor nonchalantly agreed on the condition that they reimburse him for the price of the beans that would be uprooted. The investigators, most of whom were lawyers and none of whom had ever dug up a grave (or even done much gardening), began digging. "We dug and dug and dug," remembers Des Forges, "while the mayor sat there and watched us amateurs with a big smirk on his face."

With the sides of the pit on the verge of collapsing inward, the team had found nothing and was prepared to give up. Only the sight of the woman waiting nearby kept them going. "This woman is a mother," Des Forges told her colleagues. "She may get a lot of things wrong, but the one thing she won't get wrong is where her sons are buried." Minutes later the investigators unearthed a foot. More body parts followed.

The commission's March 1993 report found that more than 10,000 Tutsi had been detained and 2,000 murdered since the RPF's 1990 invasion.[10] Government-supported killers had carried out at least three major massacres of Tutsi. Extremist, racist rhetoric and militias were proliferating. The international commission and a UN rapporteur who soon followed warned explicitly of a possible genocide.[11]

Low-ranking U.S. intelligence analysts were keenly aware of Rwanda's history and the possibility that atrocity would occur. A January 1993 CIA report warned of the likelihood of large-scale ethnic violence. A December 1993 CIA study found that some 4 million tons of small arms had been transferred from Poland to Rwanda, via Belgium, an extraordinary quantity for a government allegedly committed to a peace process. And in January 1994 a U.S. government intelligence analyst predicted that if conflict restarted in Rwanda, "the worst case scenario would involve one-half million people dying."[12]

The public rhetoric of the hard-liners kept pace with the proliferation of machetes, militias, and death squads. In December 1990 the Hutu paper *Kangura* ("Wake up!") had published its "Ten Commandments of the Hutu." Like Hitler's Nuremberg laws and the Bosnian Serbs' 1992 edicts, these ten commandments articulated the rules of the game the radicals hoped to see imposed on the minority:

1. Every Hutu should know that a Tutsi woman, wherever she is, works for the interests of her Tutsi ethnic group. As a result, we shall consider a traitor any Hutu who:
   - marries a Tutsi woman;
   - befriends a Tutsi woman;
   - employs a Tutsi woman as a secretary or concubine.
2. Every Hutu should know that our Hutu daughters are more suitable and conscientious in their role as woman, wife and mother of the family. Are they not beautiful, good secretaries and more honest?

3. Hutu women, be vigilant and try to bring your husbands, brothers and sons back to reason.
4. Every Hutu should know that every Tutsi is dishonest in business. His only aim is the supremacy of his ethnic group. As a result any Hutu who does the following is a traitor:
   - makes a partnership with a Tutsi in business;
   - invests his money or the government's money in a Tutsi enterprise;
   - lends or borrows money from a Tutsi;
   - gives favors to a Tutsi in business (obtaining import licenses, bank loans, construction sites, public markets . . .)
5. All strategic positions, political, administrative, economic, military and security should be entrusted to Hutu.
6. The education sector (school pupils, students, teachers) must be majority Hutu.
7. The Rwandese Armed Forces should be exclusively Hutu. The experience of the October [1990] war has taught us a lesson. No member of the military shall marry a Tutsi.
8. The Hutu should stop having mercy on the Tutsi.
9. The Hutu, wherever they are, must have unity and solidarity, and be concerned with the fate of their Hutu brothers.
   - The Hutu inside and outside Rwanda must constantly look for friends and allies for the Hutu cause, starting with their Bantu brothers;
   - They must constantly counteract the Tutsi propaganda;
   - The Hutu must be firm and vigilant against their common Tutsi enemy.
10. The Social Revolution of 1959, the Referendum of 1961, and the Hutu Ideology, must be taught to every Hutu at every level. Every Hutu must spread this ideology widely. Any Hutu who persecutes his brother Hutu for having read, spread and taught this ideology, is a traitor.[13]

Staunch Hutu politicians made plain their intentions. In November 1992 Leon Mugesera, a senior member of Habyarimana's party, addressed a gathering of the National Revolutionary Movement for Development Party (MRND), saying: "The fatal mistake we made in 1959 was to let [the Tutsi] get out. . . . They belong in Ethiopia and we are going to find them

a shortcut to get there by throwing them into the Nyabarongo River. I
must insist on this point. We have to act. Wipe them all out!"[14] When the
Tutsi-dominated RPF invaded Rwanda in February 1993 for a second
time, the extremist Hutu media portrayed the Tutsi as devils and, alluding
to Pol Pot's rule in Cambodia, identified them as "Black Khmer." As genocidal perpetrators so often do as a prelude to summoning the masses, they
began claiming the Tutsi were out to exterminate Hutu and appealing for
preemptive self-defense.[15] Although the threats against the Tutsi and the
reports of violence did not generate mainstream Western press coverage,
they were reported regularly in the Foreign Broadcast Information Service
and in diplomatic cables back to Washington.

But Dallaire knew little of the precariousness of the Arusha accords.
When he made a preliminary reconnaissance trip to Rwanda, in August
1993, he was told that the country was committed to peace and that a UN
presence was essential. It is hardly surprising that nobody steered Dallaire
to meet with those who preferred the eradication of Tutsi to the ceding of
power. But it was remarkable that no UN officials in New York thought to
give Dallaire copies of the alarming reports prepared by the International
Commission of Investigation or even by a rapporteur from the United
Nations itself.

The sum total of Dallaire's intelligence data before that first trip to
Rwanda consisted of one encyclopedia's summary of Rwandan history,
which Major Beardsley, Dallaire's executive assistant, had snatched at the
last minute from his local public library. Beardsley says, "We flew to
Rwanda with a Michelin road map, a copy of the Arusha agreement, and
that was it. We were under the impression that the situation was quite
straightforward: There was one cohesive government side and one cohesive
rebel side, and they had come together to sign the peace agreement and
had then requested that we come in to help them implement it."

Although Dallaire gravely underestimated the tensions brewing in
Rwanda, he still believed that he would need a force of 5,000 to help the
parties implement the terms of the Arusha accords. But the United States
was unenthused about sending any UN mission to Rwanda. "Anytime you
mentioned peacekeeping in Africa," one U.S. official remembers, "the cru-
cifixes and garlic would come up on every door." Washington was nervous
that the Rwanda mission would sour like those in Bosnia, Somalia, and
Haiti were then doing. Multilateral initiatives for humanitarian purposes
seemed like quagmires in the making. But President Habyarimana had

traveled to Washington in 1993 to offer assurances that his government was committed to carrying out the terms of the Arusha accords. In the end, after strenuous lobbying by France (Rwanda's chief diplomatic and military patron), U.S. officials accepted the proposition that UNAMIR could be the rare "UN winner." Even so, U.S. officials made it clear that Washington would give no consideration to sending U.S. troops to Rwanda and would not pay for 5,000 troops. Dallaire reluctantly trimmed his written request to 2,500. He remembers, "I was told, 'Don't ask for a brigade, because it ain't there.'" On October 5, 1993, two days after the Somalia firefight, the United States reluctantly voted in the Security Council to authorize Dallaire's mission.[16]

Once he was actually posted to Rwanda in October 1993, Dallaire lacked not merely intelligence data and manpower but also institutional support. The small Department of Peacekeeping Operations in New York, run by the Ghanaian diplomat Kofi Annan (who later became UN secretary-general), was overwhelmed. Madeleine Albright, the U.S. ambassador to the UN and a leading advocate of military intervention in Bosnia, recalls, "The global 9-1-1 was always either busy or nobody was there." At the time of the Rwanda deployment, with a staff of a few hundred, the UN was posting 70,000 peacekeepers on seventeen missions around the world.[17] Amid these widespread crises and logistical headaches, the Rwanda mission had low status.

Life was not made easier for Dallaire or the UN peacekeeping office by the United States' thinning patience for peacekeeping. The Clinton administration had taken office better disposed toward peacekeeping than any other administration in U.S. history. But Congress owed half a billion dollars in UN dues and peacekeeping costs. It had tired of its obligation to foot one-third of the bill for what had come to feel like an insatiable global appetite for mischief and an equally insatiable UN appetite for missions. The Clinton White House agreed that the Department of Peacekeeping Operations needed fixing and insisted that the UN "learn to say no" to chancy or costly missions.

In the aftermath of the Somalia firefight, Senate Republicans demanded that the Clinton administration become even less trusting of the United Nations. In January 1994 Senator Bob Dole, a leading defender of the Bosnian Muslims at the time, introduced legislation to limit U.S. participation in UN peacekeeping missions.[18] Against the backdrop of the Somalia meltdown and the congressional showdown, the Clinton administration accelerated the development of a formal U.S. peacekeeping doc-trine. The job was given to Richard Clarke of the National Security Council, a special assistant to the president who was known as one of the most effective bureaucrats in Washington. In an interagency process that lasted more than a year, Clarke managed the production of a presidential decision directive, PDD-25, which listed sixteen factors that policymak-ers needed to consider when deciding whether to support peacekeeping activities: seven factors if the United States was to vote in the UN Security Council on peace operations carried out by non-American sol-diers, six additional and more stringent factors if U.S. forces were to par-ticipate in UN peacekeeping missions, and three final factors if U.S. troops were likely to engage in actual combat. U.S. participation had to advance U.S. interests, be necessary for the operation's success, and garner domestic and congressional support. The risk of casualties had to be "acceptable." An exit strategy had to be shown.[19] In the words of Representative David Obey of Wisconsin, the restrictive checklist tried to satisfy the American desire for "zero degree of involvement, and zero degree of risk, and zero degree of pain and confusion."[20] The architects of the doctrine remain its strongest defenders. "Many say PDD-25 was some evil thing designed to kill peacekeeping, when in fact it was there to save peacekeeping," Clarke says. "Peacekeeping was almost dead. There was no support for it in the U.S. government, and the peacekeepers were not effective in the field." Although the directive was not publicly released until May 3, 1994, a month into the genocide in Rwanda, the considerations encapsulated in the doctrine and the administration's frus-tration with peacekeeping greatly influenced the thinking of U.S. officials involved in shaping Rwanda policy.

Back in the United States, Rwanda was extremely low on the list of American priorities. When Woods of the Defense Department's African affairs bureau suggested that the Pentagon add Rwanda-Burundi to its list of potential trouble spots, his bosses told him, in his words, "Look, if some-thing happens in Rwanda-Burundi, we don't care. Take it off the list. U.S. national interest is not involved and we can't put all these silly humanitari-an issues on lists. . . . Just make it go away."[21]

Every aspect of Dallaire's UNAMIR was run on a shoestring. It was equipped with hand-me-down vehicles from the UN's Cambodia mission, and only eighty of the 300 that turned up were usable. When the medical supplies ran out, in March 1994, New York said there was no cash for resupply. Very few goods could be procured locally, given that Rwanda was one of Africa's poorest nations. Spare parts, batteries, and even ammunition could rarely be found. Dallaire spent some 70 percent of his time battling UN logistics.[22]

Dallaire had major problems with his personnel as well. He commanded troops, military observers, and civilian personnel from twenty-six countries. Although multinationality is meant to be a virtue of UN missions, the diversity yielded grave discrepancies in resources. Whereas Belgian troops turned up in Rwanda well armed and ready to perform the tasks assigned to them, the poorer contingents showed up "bare-assed," in Dallaire's words, and demanded that the United Nations suit them up. "Since nobody else was offering to send troops, we had to take what we could get," he says. When Dallaire expressed concern, a senior UN official instructed him to lower his expectations. He recalls, "I was told, 'Listen, General, you are NATO-trained. This is not NATO.'" Although some 2,500 UNAMIR personnel had arrived by early April 1994, few of the soldiers had the kit they needed to perform even basic tasks.

The signs of militarization in Rwanda were so widespread that, even though Dallaire lacked much of an intelligence-gathering capacity, he was able to learn of the extremists' sinister intentions. In December high-ranking military officers from within the Hutu government sent Dallaire a letter warning that Hutu militias were planning massacres. Death lists had become so widely known that individuals had begun paying local militias to have their names removed. In addition to broadcasting incitements against Tutsi, Radio Mille Collines had begun denouncing UN peacekeepers as Tutsi accomplices.

In January 1994 an anonymous Hutu informant, said to be high up in the inner circles of the Rwandan government, came forward to describe the rapid arming and training of local militias. In what is now referred to as the "Dallaire fax," Dallaire relayed to New York the informant's claim that Hutu extremists "had been ordered to register all the Tutsi in Kigali." "He suspects it is for their extermination," Dallaire wrote. "Example he gave was that in 20 minutes his personnel could kill up to 1,000 Tutsis."

"Jean-Pierre," as the informant became known, said that the militia planned first to provoke and murder a number of Belgian peacekeepers, in order to "guarantee Belgian withdrawal from Rwanda." The informant was prepared to identify major arms caches littered throughout Rwanda, including one containing at least 135 weapons, but he wanted passports

©Gilles Peress/Magnum

The Hutu killers who fled Rwanda after the genocide were required by Zairean border guards to leave their weapons behind. These machetes were piled up outside a customs house on the Rwandan side of the border.

and protection for his wife and four children. Dallaire admitted the possibility of a trap but said he believed the informant was reliable. He and his UN forces were prepared to act within thirty-six hours. "Where there's a will, there's a way," Dallaire signed the cable. "Let's go."[23] He was not asking for permission; he was simply informing headquarters of the arms raids that he had planned.

Annan's deputy, Iqbal Riza, cabled back to Dallaire on behalf of his boss, rejecting the proposed arms raids. "We said, 'Not Somalia again,'" Riza remembered later. "Now in Somalia, those troops—U.S., Pakistani—they were acting within their mandate when they were killed. Here, Dallaire was asking to take such risks going outside his mandate. And we said no."[24] The Annan cable suggested that Dallaire focus instead on protecting his forces and avoiding escalation. The Canadian was to notify Rwandan President Habyarimana and the Western ambassadors in Kigali of the informant's claims. Dallaire contested the decision, battling by telephone with New York and sending five faxes on the subject. Even after Dallaire had confirmed the reliability of the informant, his political masters told him plainly and consistently that the United States in particular would not support such an aggressive interpretation of his mandate. "You've got to let me do this," Dallaire pleaded. "If we don't stop these weapons, some day those

weapons will be used against us." In Washington Dallaire's alarm was discounted. Lieutenant Colonel Tony Marley, the U.S. military liaison to the
Arusha process, respected Dallaire but knew he was operating in Africa for
the first time. "I thought that the neophyte meant well, but I questioned
whether he knew what he was talking about," Marley recalls.

Even a rise in political assassinations in the spring of 1994 could not
attract mainstream attention to Rwanda. On February 21, 1994, right-
wing extremists assassinated Felicien Gatabazi, the minister of public
works. Martin Bucyana, president of the hard-line Hutu Coalition pour la
Défense de la République (Coalition for the Defense of the Republic, or
CDR), was killed in the southern Rwandan town of Butare the next day,
giving outsiders the impression of tit-for-tat skirmishes rather than a trial
balloon for something more ambitious.[25] Dallaire wanted to investigate
these murders, but he could do little but watch as the feared *Interahamwe*
units became more conspicuous around town, singing, blowing whistles,
wearing colorful uniforms, and toting weapons. Machetes hung from belts
around their waists, as guns once hung in cowboys' holsters. Grenades were
available at the market for next to nothing. On February 23 Dallaire
reported that he was drowning in information about death squad target
lists. "Time does seem to be running out for political discussions," he
wrote, noting that "any spark on the security side could have catastrophic
consequences."[26]

The Peace Processors

The United States was alarmed enough about the deterioration for the
State Department's Bureau for African Affairs to send Deputy Assistant
Secretary Bushnell and Central Africa Office Director Arlene Render to
Rwanda in late March. The daughter of a diplomat, Bushnell had joined
the foreign service in 1981, at the age of thirty-five. With her agile mind
and sharp tongue, she had earned the attention of George Moose when she
served under him at the U.S. embassy in Senegal. When Moose was named
the assistant secretary of state for African affairs in 1993, he made Bushnell
his deputy. In meetings with President Habyarimana, the able Bushnell
warned him that failure to implement Arusha might cause the United
States to demand the withdrawal of UN peacekeepers, whose mandate was
up for review on April 4. Bushnell ran through all of PDD-25's "factors for

involvement." She described the congressional mood in the United States. Before leaving, Bushnell said, "President Habyarimana, your name will head this chapter of Rwandan history. It is up to you to decide whether it will be a chapter of glory or a chapter of tragedy."[27] Before she departed Rwanda, Bushnell received a handwritten note from the mercurial president in which he promised to comply with the Arusha agreement and set up the transitional government the following week.

For all the concern of the U.S. officials familiar with Rwanda, their diplomacy suffered from several weaknesses. First, it continued to reveal its natural bias toward states and negotiations. Because most diplomatic contact occurs between representatives of states, U.S. officials are predisposed to trust the assurances of government officials. In the case of Rwanda, several of these officials were plotting genocide behind the scenes. Those in the U.S. government who knew Rwanda best viewed the escalating violence with a diplomatic prejudice that left them both institutionally oriented toward the Rwandan government and reluctant to do anything to disrupt the peace process. This meant avoiding confrontation. An examination of the cable traffic from the U.S. embassy in Kigali to Washington, between the signing of the Arusha agreement and the downing of the presidential plane, reveals that setbacks were perceived as "dangers to the peace process" more than as "dangers to Rwandans." As was true in the Iran-Iraq war and the Bosnian war, American criticisms were steadfastly leveled at "both sides," although here Hutu government and militia forces were usually responsible.

The U.S. ambassador in Kigali, David Rawson, proved especially vulnerable to such bias. Rawson had grown up in Burundi, where his father, an American missionary, had set up a Quaker hospital. He entered the foreign service in 1971. When in 1993, at age fifty-two, he was given the embassy in Rwanda, his first, he could not have been more intimate with the region, the culture, or the peril. He spoke the local language—almost unprecedented for an ambassador in central Africa. But Rawson found it difficult to imagine the Rwandans who surrounded the president as conspirators in genocide. He issued pro forma démarches about Habyarimana's obstruction of power-sharing, but the cable traffic shows that he accepted the president's assurances that he was doing all he could. The U.S. investment in the peace process gave rise to a wishful tendency to see peace "around the corner." Rawson remembers,

We were naive policy optimists, I suppose. The fact that negotiations can't work is almost not one of the options open to people who care about peace. We were looking for the hopeful signs, not the dark signs. In fact, we were looking away from the dark signs. . . . One of the things I learned and should have already known is that once you launch a process, it takes on its own momentum. I had said, "Let's try this, and then if it doesn't work, we can back away." But bureaucracies don't allow that. Once the Washington side buys into a process, it gets pursued, almost blindly.

Even after the Hutu government began exterminating the country's Tutsi in April 1994, U.S. diplomats focused most of their efforts on "re-establishing a cease-fire" and "getting Arusha back on track."

In order to do so, U.S. and UN officials often threatened to pull out UN peacekeepers as punishment for bad behavior or failure to implement Arusha's terms.[28] The trouble with this approach, which Western officials adopted in Bosnia as well, was that extremists who believed in ethnic purity wanted to see nothing more than a UN withdrawal. As one senior U.S. official remembers, "The first response to trouble is, 'Let's yank the peacekeepers.' But that is like believing that when children are misbehaving the proper response is, 'Let's send the babysitter home,' so the house gets burned down."

The second problematic feature of U.S. diplomacy before and during the genocide was a tendency toward blindness bred by familiarity: The few people in Washington who were paying attention to Rwanda before Habyarimana's plane was shot down were those who had been tracking Rwanda for some time and had thus come to expect a certain level of ethnic violence from the region. And because the U.S. government had tolerated the deaths of some 50,000 civilians in Burundi in October 1993, these officials also knew that Washington would not get exercised over substantial bloodshed. When the massacres began in April, some U.S. regional specialists initially suspected that Rwanda was undergoing "another flare-up" that would involve another "acceptable" (if tragic) round of ethnic murder.

Rawson had read up on genocide before his posting to Rwanda, surveying what had become a relatively extensive scholarly literature on its causes. But although he expected internecine killing, he did not anticipate the scale at which it occurred. "Nothing in Rwandan culture or history could have led a person to that forecast," he says. "Most of us thought that if a war broke out, it would be quick, that these poor people didn't have the resources, the means, to fight a sophisticated war. I couldn't have known that they would do each other in with the most economic means." Assistant Secretary Moose agrees: "We were psychologically and imaginatively too limited."

Dallaire, for one, quickly saw that withdrawal threats only encouraged the militants. They knew that if they pushed harder, disrupted longer, they could get rid of the UN peacekeepers who were implementing the agreement they hoped to sabotage. UN withdrawal was a carrot, not a stick. But as the Canadian officer resisted the political approach of his colleagues, he was scolded and scoffed. "The general attitude," remembers Beardsley, "was, 'Shut up. You're a soldier. Let the experts handle this.'"

But within weeks the "experts" had vanished, and Dallaire was on his own.

Recognition

Crimes Against Humanity

In the first days after the checkpoints were hoisted and the massacres began on April 6, 1994, Dallaire maintained his contacts with Colonel Bagosora and other Rwandan army officials. But these men, the ringleaders of the slaughter, assured Dallaire and foreign diplomats that they were committed to stopping the killing and continuing the peace process. They even appealed to Dallaire for help in brokering a cease-fire. They claimed, as had Talaat and Milosevic, that they needed time to rein in the "uncontrolled elements."

Initially, although Dallaire was aghast at the killings, he believed that the Hutu gunmen and militia were only pursuing their "political enemies." In the first few days, moderate Hutu and leading Tutsi politicians had been the main targets of attack. As in Cambodia, this gave rise to the notion that the killings were narrowly tailored reprisals rather than harbingers of a broadly ambitious genocide. Ordinary people, Dallaire and others hoped, would be left alone.

Dallaire and other foreign observers passed through two phases of recognition. The first involved coming to grips with the occurrence not only of a conventional war but of massive crimes against humanity. All Tutsi were targets. The second involved understanding that what was taking place was genocide.

The first wave of recognition swept through UN headquarters—and was relayed back to Western capitals—very quickly. Two days after the plane crash, on April 8, Dallaire sent a cable to New York indicating that ethnicity was one of the dimensions behind the killing. The telegram detailed the political killings, which then included not only ten Belgian peacekeepers and Prime Minister Uwilingiyimana, but also the chairman of the Liberal Party, the minister of labor, the minister of agriculture, and dozens of others. It refuted the impression (and the claim by the Hutu authorities) that the violence was uncontrolled. Dallaire described instead a "very well-planned, organized, deliberate and conducted campaign of terror initiated principally by the Presidential Guard"; he urged that UN forces make protecting government leaders their "major task."[29] Dallaire still considered the killings mainly as political adjuncts to a civil war and his own role as broker of a cease-fire.

The following day, though, Dallaire's thinking shifted. Beardsley, Dallaire's executive assistant, got a frantic call by radio from a pair of Polish UN military observers who were at a church run by Polish missionaries across town. "Come get us," the UN officials said. "They are massacring people here." Beardsley got permission from Dallaire to take a Bangladeshi armored personnel carrier through the front lines. He passed about twenty roadblocks and reached the church.

> When we arrived, I looked at the school across the street, and there were children, I don't know how many, forty, sixty, eighty children stacked up outside who had all been chopped up with machetes. Some of their mothers had heard them screaming and had come running, and the militia had killed them, too. We got out of the vehicle and entered the church. There we found 150 people, dead mostly, though some were still groaning, who had been attacked the night before. The Polish priests told us it had been incredibly well organized. The Rwandan army had cleared out the area, the gendarmerie had rounded up all the Tutsi, and the militia had hacked them to death.

Beardsley left a first-aid kit and his ration of water for the wounded. He promised to come back later in the evening with help. But by the time he managed to clear dozens of additional roadblocks, the militia had finished off the survivors. The Polish priests, who had been pinned up to the wall with a barrel of the gun, were broken-hearted. Beardsley remembers, "They kept repeating, over and over, 'These were our parishioners.'" All Beardsley could do was make sure the details of the massacre were communicated back to headquarters in New York.

By the fourth day, April 10, 1994, Dallaire had concluded that Bagosora and the Hutu militants were ordering a massive campaign of crimes against humanity, against anybody carrying a Tutsi identity card. "Only when I saw with my own eyes the militias at the roadblocks pulling people out of their vehicles did it really become clear," he says. "At that point you couldn't argue anymore that it was just politically motivated slaughter." Hutu officers kept insisting that the violence was a product of war, but Dallaire had come to see that the civil war between the RPF rebels and the government forces was a separate problem. "I saw that one side was eliminating civilians behind the lines," Dallaire explains. "And what was going on at the front had nothing much to do with the killings of civilians going on in the back."

Dallaire did not then imagine a full-scale, countrywide genocide. Indeed, although he quickly grasped the savage nature of the violence, his imagination was hemmed in by his knowledge of the region's "last war," which had occurred between Tutsi and Hutu in neighboring Burundi. "Burundi had just blown up, and 50,000 had been killed in just a few days," Dallaire explains. "So when the plane went down, we actually expected around 50,000 plus dead. Can you imagine having that expectation in Europe? Racism slips in so it changes our expectations." Still, with the smell of decomposing flesh already intolerable, Dallaire knew that regardless of the numbers likely to be killed, he would need outside help.

On April 10 Dallaire made the most important request of his life. He telephoned New York and asked for reinforcements so as to double his troop strength to 5,000. Just as crucial, he appealed for a more forceful mandate so he could send his peacekeepers to intervene to stop the killings. If he did not get a positive response, he knew he had neither the soldiers, the ammunition, the fuel, the vehicles, the communication equipment, nor even the water or food—what few survival rations he had were rotten and inedible—to mount any sustained opposition to the militiamen. He could do nothing but await his instructions. The United States, more than any other country, would dictate the UN reply.

The Intervention That Wasn't

David Rawson was sitting with his wife in their residence watching a taped broadcast of the *MacNeil/Lehrer News Hour* when he heard the back-to-back explosions that signaled the downing of President Habyarimana's plane. As the U.S. ambassador, Rawson was concerned primarily for American citizens, whom, he feared, would be killed or injured in any outbreak of fighting. The United States made the decision to withdraw its personnel and nationals on April 7. Penned within his house, Rawson did not think his presence was of any use. Looking back, he says, "Did we have a moral responsibility to stay there? Would it have made a difference? I don't know, but the killings were taking place in broad daylight while we were there. I didn't feel that we were achieving much."

Still, about 300 Rwandans from the neighborhood had gathered at Rawson's residence seeking refuge, and when the Americans cleared out, the local people were left to their fates. Rawson recalls, "I told the people who were there that we were leaving and the flag was coming down, and they would have to make their own choice about what to do. . . . Nobody really asked us to take them with us." Rawson says he could not help even those who worked closest to him. His chief steward, who served dinner and washed dishes, called the ambassador from his home and pleaded, "We're in terrible danger. Please come and get us." Rawson says, "I had to tell him, 'We can't move. We can't come.'" The steward and his wife were killed.

Assistant Secretary of State for African Affairs Moose was away from Washington, so Bushnell, the acting assistant secretary, was made the director of the task force that managed the Rwanda evacuation. Her focus, like Rawson's, was on the fate of U.S. citizens. "I felt very strongly that my first obligation was to the Americans," she recalls. "I was sorry about the Rwandans, of course, but my job was to get our folks out. . . . Then again, people didn't know that it was a genocide. What I was told was, 'Look, Pru, these people do this from time to time.' We thought we'd be right back."

At a State Department press conference on April 8, Bushnell made an appearance and spoke gravely about the mounting violence in Rwanda and the status of Americans there. After she left the podium, Michael McCurry, the department spokesman, took her place and criticized foreign governments for preventing the screening of the Steven Spielberg film *Schindler's List*. "This film movingly portrays. . . the twentieth century's most horrible catastrophe," McCurry said. "And it shows that even in the midst of genocide, one individual can make a difference." McCurry urged that the film be shown worldwide. "The most effective way to avoid the recurrence of genocidal tragedy," he declared, "is to ensure that past acts of genocide are never forgotten."[30] No one made any connection between Bushnell's remarks and McCurry's. Neither journalists nor officials in the United States were focused on the Tutsi.

On April 9 and 10, in five different convoys, Ambassador Rawson and 250 Americans were evacuated from Kigali and other points. "When we left, the cars were stopped and searched," Rawson says. "It would have been impossible to get Tutsi through." All told, thirty-five local employees of the U.S. embassy were killed in the genocide.

Secretary of State Warren Christopher knew little about Africa. At one meeting with his top advisers, several weeks after the plane crash, he pulled an atlas off his shelf to help him locate the country. Belgian foreign minister Willie Claes recalls trying to discuss Rwanda with his American counterpart and being told, "I have other responsibilities." Christopher appeared on the NBC news program *Meet the Press* the morning the U.S. evacuation was completed. "In the great tradition, the ambassador was in the last car," Christopher said proudly. "So that evacuation has gone very well." Christopher stressed that although U.S. marines had been dispatched to Burundi, there were no plans to send them into Rwanda to restore order: They were in the region as a safety net, in case they were needed to assist in the evacuation. "It's always a sad moment when the Americans have to leave," he said, "but it was the prudent thing to do."[31] The Republican Senate minority leader, Bob Dole, agreed. "I don't think we have any national interest there," Dole said on April 10. "The Americans are out, and as far as I'm concerned, in Rwanda, that ought to be the end of it."[32]

Dallaire, too, had been ordered to make the evacuation of foreigners his priority. At the UN, Kofi Annan's Department of Peacekeeping Operations, which had rejected the field commander's proposed raid on arms caches in January, sent an explicit cable: "You should make every effort not to compromise your impartiality or to act beyond your mandate, but [you] may exercise your discretion to do [so] should this be essential for the evacuation of foreign nationals. This should not, repeat not, extend to participating in possible combat except in self-defense."[33] Neutrality was essential. Avoiding combat was paramount, but Dallaire could make an exception for non-Rwandans.

While the United States evacuated overland without an American military escort, the Europeans sent troops to Rwanda so that their personnel could exit by air. On April 9 Dallaire watched covetously as just over 1,000 French, Belgian, and Italian soldiers descended on the Kigali airport to begin evacuating their expatriates. These commandos were clean-shaven, well fed, and heavily armed, in marked contrast to Dallaire's exhausted, hungry, ragtag peacekeeping force.

If the soldiers ferried in for the evacuation had teamed up with UNAMIR, Dallaire would have had a sizable deterrent force. He commanded 440 Belgians, 942 Bangladeshis, 843 Ghanaians, 60 Tunisians, and 255 others from twenty countries. He could also call on a reserve of 800 Belgians in Nairobi. If the major powers had reconfigured the 1,000-man European evacuation force and the 300 U.S. Marines on standby in Burundi and contributed them to Dallaire's mission, he would finally have had the numbers to stage rescue operations and to confront the killers. "Mass slaughter was happening, and suddenly there in Kigali we had the forces we needed to contain it, and maybe even to stop it," he recalls. "Yet they picked up their people and turned and walked away."

The consequences of the exclusive attention to foreigners were felt immediately. In the days after the plane crash, some 2,000 Rwandans, including 400 children, had grouped at the *Ecole Technique Officielle* under the protection of about ninety Belgian soldiers. Many of the Rwandans were already suffering from machete wounds. They gathered in the classrooms and on the playing field outside the school. Rwandan government and militia forces lay in wait nearby, drinking beer and chanting, "Pawa, pawa," for "Hutu power." On April 11 the Belgian peacekeepers were ordered to regroup at the airport to aid the evacuation of European civilians. Knowing they were trapped, several Rwandans pursued the jeeps, shouting, "Do not abandon us!" The UN soldiers shooed them away from their vehicles and fired warning shots over their heads. When the peacekeepers had departed out through one gate, Hutu militiamen entered through another, firing machine guns and throwing grenades. Most of the 2,000 gathered there were killed.[34]

In the three days during which some 4,000 foreigners were evacuated, about 20,000 Rwandans were killed. After the American evacuees were safely out and the U.S. embassy had been closed, Bill and Hillary Clinton visited the U.S. officials who had manned the emergency-operations room at the State Department and offered congratulations on a "job well done."

What Did the United States Know?

Just when did Washington learn of the sinister Hutu designs on Rwanda's Tutsi? As always, the precise nature and extent of the slaughter was obscured by the civil war, the withdrawal of U.S. diplomatic sources, some confused press reporting, and the lies of the perpetrator government. Nonetheless, both the testimony of U.S. officials who worked the issue day to day and the declassified documents unearthed by the National Security Archive indicate that plenty was known about the killers' intentions. Those officials who were quickest to diagnose genocide looked not at the numbers killed, which were, as always, difficult to ascertain. They looked instead at the perpetrators' intent: Were Hutu forces attempting to destroy Rwanda's Tutsi? The answer to this question was available quickly: "By 8 a.m. the morning after the plane crash, we knew what was happening, that there was systematic killing of Tutsi," Joyce Leader, the deputy chief of mission, recalls. "People were calling me and telling me who was getting killed. I knew they were going door-to-door." Back at the State Department, she explained to her colleagues that three kinds of killing were going on: casualties in war, politically motivated murder, and genocide. Dallaire's early cables to New York likewise described the armed conflict that had resumed between rebels and government forces and also stated plainly that savage "ethnic cleansing" of Tutsi was occurring. U.S. analysts warned that mass killings would increase. In an April 11 memo prepared for Frank Wisner, the undersecretary of defense for policy, in advance of a dinner with Henry Kissinger, a key talking point was that "unless both sides can be convinced to return to the peace process, a massive (hundreds of thousands of deaths) bloodbath will ensue."[35]

Whatever the inevitable imperfections of U.S. intelligence early on, the reports from Rwanda were severe enough to distinguish Hutu killers from ordinary combatants in civil war. And they certainly warranted a heightened intelligence gathering operation to snap satellite photos of large gatherings of Rwandan civilians or of mass graves, to intercept military communications, and to infiltrate the country in person. In fact, in a shocking new revelation, some two dozen U.S. special forces were sent on a one-day reconnaissance mission to Kigali within a few days of the beginning of the murder campaign. According to one U.S. officer, the Marines returned from Kigali "white as ghosts," describing "so many bodies on the streets that you could walk from one body to the other without touching the ground." They reported that the metal leaf-springs of cars were being sharpened into knives, and that the scale of the slaughter was mammoth. The men were debriefed immediately, and the report was sent to European Command Headquarters in Stuttgart, Germany. On April 26, 1994, an unattributed intelligence memo titled "Responsibility for Massacres in Rwanda" reported that the ringleaders of the genocide, Colonel Bagosora and his crisis committee, were determined to liquidate their opposition and exterminate the Tutsi populace. A May 9 Defense Intelligence Agency report stated plainly that the Rwandan violence was not spontaneous but was directed by the government, with lists of victims prepared well in advance. The agency observed that an "organized parallel effort of genocide [was] being implemented by the army to destroy the leadership of the Tutsi community."

Dallaire was acutely conscious of the importance of the media. Although he had had no previous occasion in his military career to court press attention, he says he immediately saw that a "reporter with a line to the West was worth a battalion on the ground." Between juggling the safety of his own peacekeepers and the protection of Rwandans, Dallaire shuttled reporters around Kigali whenever possible. "At that point," he recalls, "the journalists were really all I had." He permitted Mark Doyle of the BBC to live with the peacekeepers and file two stories a day from Dallaire's satellite phone.

Not all the reporting helped clarify the nature of the violence for the outside world. If all the reports portrayed the killing as extensive, many also treated the violence as typical. During the conflict in Bosnia, U.S. officials had tried to convince journalists that the conflict was the product of "ancient tribal hatreds"; in Rwanda reporters in the field adopted this frame on their own. Asked what caused such violence, CNN's Gary Streiker reported by telephone from Nairobi that "what's behind this story is probably the worst tribal hostility in all of Africa, hostility that goes back centuries long before European colonization."[36] Also reporting from Nairobi, Michael Skoler of NPR told of Tutsi killing Hutu as well as Hutu killing Tutsi.[37] When NPR's Daniel Zwerdling interviewed Georges Nzongola-Ntalaja, an associate professor of African studies at Howard University, Zwerdling simply could not accept Ntalaja's nuanced explanation of the violence:

Zwerdling: Why are things in Africa so bad? Why is tribal violence so deep?

Ntalaja: Most of it has been exacerbated by politicians hungry for more power.

Zwerdling:... Well, of course, politicians can exacerbate what tensions already exist. I mean, you're not arguing, are you, that these tribal hatreds were not already there before modern politicians came along?

Ntalaja: I'm saying that the ethnic groups do have prejudices and people do tend to feel they may be different from other groups. But it's not enough to make a person pick up a knife or a gun and kill somebody else. It is when politicians come and excite passion and try to threaten people—make people believe that they are being threatened by other groups that are going to be extinguished.

Zwerdling: Of course, in most of these battlegrounds, though, there is ancient ethnic hatred and something that surprises me actually is that you're blaming modern, contemporary African politicians for this divide and conquer, playing one tribe against another.[38]

Still, for all the flaws in the coverage (especially by those stationed *outside* Rwanda), the major media gave anybody reading or watching cause for grave alarm. From April 8, 1994, onward, reporters described the widespread targeting of Tutsi and the corpses piling up on Kigali's streets. American journalists relayed stories of missionaries and embassy officials who had been unable to save their Rwandan friends and neighbors from death. An April 9 front-page *Washington Post* story quoted reports that the Rwandan employees of the major international relief agencies had been executed "in front of horrified expatriate staffers."[39] On April 10 a *New York Times* front-page article quoted the Red Cross claim that "tens of thousands" were dead, 8,000 in Kigali alone, and that corpses were "in the houses, in the streets, everywhere."[40] The *Post* the same day led its front-page story with a description of "a pile of corpses six feet high" outside the main hospital.[41] On April 12 the American evacuees, many of whom were Christian missionaries, described what they had seen. Phil Van Lanen, a relief worker with the Seventh-Day Adventist Church mission in Rwanda, wept openly when he told William Schmidt of the *Times* of the murder of the eight Tutsi girls who used to work in his dental clinic.[42] Chris Grundmann, an American evacuee who worked for the Center for Disease Control, was quoted as saying, "It was the most basic terror." He told how he and his family hunkered down in their house with mattresses against the windows and listened to the ordeals of Rwandan victims over a two-way radio. "The UN radio was filled with national staff screaming for help," he said. "They were begging: 'Come save me! My house is being blown up,' or 'They're killing me.' There was nothing we could do. At one point we just had to turn it off."[43]

On April 16 the *New York Times* reported the shooting and hacking to death of nearly 1,200 men, women, and children in the church where they had sought refuge.[44] On April 19 Human Rights Watch, which, through Des Forges, had excellent sources on the ground in Rwanda, estimated the number of dead at 100,000 and called on the Security Council to use the term "genocide."[45] The 100,000 figure (which proved to be a gross under-estimation) was picked up immediately by the Western media, endorsed by the Red Cross, and featured on the front page of the *Washington Post*.[46] On April 24 the *Post* reported how "the heads and limbs of victims were sorted and piled neatly, a bone-chilling order in the midst of chaos that harkened back to the Holocaust."[47] The Red Cross issued the most authoritative statement on the killings on April 26, declaring that "at least 100,000, but perhaps as many as 300,000" Rwandans had already been killed. On April 28 the British aid agency Oxfam warned that these estimates were too low and that 500,000 people had been reported missing.[48]

The Tutsi rebels in the Rwandan Patriotic Front publicly appealed for a Western response. On April 13 they accused the Rwandan government of carrying out genocide. They invoked the Holocaust. In an April 23 letter to the head of the Security Council, the RPF representative, Claude Dusaidi, reminded Security Council members and the secretary-general, "When the institution of the UN was created after the Second World War, one of its fundamental objectives was to see to it that what happened to the Jews in Nazi Germany would never happen again."[49] But as Kurdish leader Jalal Talabani had found in Iraq and as the Bosnian government was learning around the same time, those who are suffering genocide are deemed to be biased and unreliable. Besides, the analogy that most gripped American minds at the time was not the Holocaust but Somalia. Dusaidi met with Albright, the U.S. ambassador, four times during the genocide. He did not know it, but Albright was aware of her constraints going into the meetings. Before one of them, she received a briefing memo that reminded her, "You should be mostly in a listening mode during this meeting. You can voice general sympathy for the horrific situation in Rwanda, but should not commit the USG to anything."[50]

The "G-Word"

The putrid smell in Kigali told Dallaire all he needed to know about the scale of the murders. Once he had made the mental leap from viewing the violence as war to viewing it as crimes against humanity, he had begun to employ the phrase "ethnic cleansing" to describe the ethnically motivated killing, a phrase he was familiar with from having presided over the dispatch of Canadian troops to the former Yugoslavia.[51] He recalls his thought process:

> I was self-conscious about saying the killings were "genocidal" because, to us in the West, "genocide" was the equivalent of the Holocaust or the killing fields of Cambodia. I mean millions of people. "Ethnic cleansing" seemed to involve hundreds of thousands of people. "Genocide" was the highest scale of crimes against humanity imaginable. It was so far up there, so far off the charts, that it was not easy to recognize that *we* could be in such a situation. I also knew that if I used the term too early, I'd have been accused of crying wolf and I'd have lost my credibility.

Two weeks into the killing, Dallaire telephoned Philippe Gaillard, who ran the International Committee for the Red Cross mission in Rwanda, and asked him for a book on international law. Dallaire leafed through the Geneva conventions and the genocide convention and looked up the relevant definitions. "I realized that genocide was when an attempt was made to eliminate a specific group," Dallaire says, "and this is precisely what we saw in the field. . . . I just needed a slap in the face to say, 'Holy shit! This is genocide, not just ethnic cleansing.'"

Dallaire included the term for the first time in his situation report during the last week in April. Reuters quoted him on April 30 warning, "Unless the international community acts, it may find it is unable to defend itself against accusations of doing nothing to stop genocide."[52] And he began using the term confidently in May. Even after he had adopted the label however, he left the semantic battles to others. "I didn't get bogged down in the debate over the genocide terminology," he remembers. "We had enough proof that it was genocide, and for those who didn't agree, we had crimes against humanity on a massive scale. What more did we need to know what we had to do?"

Even after the reality of genocide in Rwanda had become irrefutable, when bodies were shown choking the Kagera River on America's nightly news, the brute fact of the slaughter failed to influence U.S. policy except in a negative way. As they had done in Bosnia, American officials again shunned the g-word. They were afraid that using it would have obliged the United States to act under the terms of the 1948 genocide convention. They also believed, rightly, that it would harm U.S. credibility to name the crime and then do nothing to stop it. A discussion paper on Rwanda, prepared by an official in the Office of the Secretary of Defense and dated May 1, testifies to the nature of official thinking. Regarding issues that might be brought up at the next interagency working group, it stated, "1. Genocide Investigation: Language that calls for an international investigation of human rights abuses and possible violations of the genocide convention. *Be Careful. Legal at State was worried about this yesterday—Genocide finding could commit [the U.S. government] to actually 'do something.'"*[53]

At an interagency teleconference in late April, Susan Rice, a rising star on the NSC who worked under Richard Clarke, stunned a few of the officials present when she asked, "If we use the word 'genocide' and are seen as doing nothing, what will be the effect on the November [congressional] election?" Lieutenant Colonel Marley remembers the incredulity of his colleagues at the State Department. "We could believe that people would wonder that," he says, "but not that they would actually voice it." Rice does not recall the incident but concedes, "If I said it, it was completely inappropriate, as well as irrelevant."

The Clinton administration opposed use of the term. On April 28 Christine Shelly, the State Department spokesperson, began what would be a two-month dance to avoid the g-word, a dance that brought to mind Secretary Christopher's concurrent semantic evasion over Bosnia. U.S. officials were afraid that the use of the stinging term would cause demands for intervention that the administration did not intend to meet. When a reporter asked her for comment on whether Rwanda was genocide, she sounded an awful lot like her boss:

> Well, as I think you know, the use of the term "genocide" has a very precise legal meaning. . . . Before we begin to use [the] term, we have to know as much as possible about the facts of the situation, particularly about the intentions of those who are committing the crimes. . . . I'm not an expert on this area, but generally speaking there—my understanding is that there are three types of elements that we look at in order to make that kind of a determination.

Shelly suggested that the United States had to examine "the types of actions" and the "kind of brutality" under way. It had to look at who was committing the acts and against whom (i.e., "whether these are particular groups, social groups, ethnic groups, religious groups"). And it needed to assess "extremely carefully" the intent of the perpetrators and whether they were trying to eliminate a group in whole or in part. "This one," Shelly said, "is one which we have to undertake a very careful study before we can make a final kind of determination."

It was clear that copies of the genocide convention had been circulating within the department, as Shelly possessed an impressive familiarity with its contents. In applying the convention's terms, Shelly said, "Now, certainly, in those elements there are actions which have occurred which would fit." She agreed that killings were being directed toward particular ethnic groups. The problem lay in gauging intent. Here she gave a largely indecipherable account and refused to commit herself or the U.S. government:

> The intentions, the precise intentions, and whether or not these are just directed episodically or with the intention of actually eliminating groups in whole or in part, this is a more complicated issue to address. . . . I'm not able to look at all of those criteria at this moment and say yes, no. It's something that requires very careful study before we can make a final determination.

When asked whether a finding of genocide would oblige the United States to stop it, Shelly again referred back to the terms of the genocide convention, saying that the law did not contain an "absolute requirement . . . to intervene directly." Pressed again to reveal whether the United States viewed events as genocide, Shelly stalled:

> Well, I think it's—again, I was trying to get the point across that this is—in order to actually attach the genocide label to actions which are going on, that this is a process that involves looking at several categories of actions. And as I've said, certain of the actions very clearly fall into some of the categories that I've mentioned. But whether you can wrap this all up in a way that then brings you to that conclusion, I'm simply not in a position to make that judgment now.[54]

The UN Security Council was becoming bitterly divided over whether to use the word. Czech Ambassador Karel Kovanda had begun complaining that 80 percent of the council's time was focused on whether and how to withdraw Dallaire's peacekeepers, the other 20 percent on getting a cease-fire to end the civil war, which he compared to "wanting Hitler to reach a cease-fire with the Jews."[55] None of their energy was concentrated on the genocide. When the president of the Security Council drew up a statement that named the crime "genocide," the United States objected. The original draft read: "The Security Council reaffirms that the systematic killing of any ethnic group, with intent to destroy it in whole or in part constitutes an act of genocide. . . . The council further points out that an important body of international law exists that deals with perpetrators of genocide."[56]

But the United States was having none of it. In a cable sent from New York to the State Department, a political adviser wrote:

> The events in Rwanda clearly seem to meet the definition of geno-
> cide in Article II of the 1948 Convention on the Prevention and
> Punishment of the Crime of Genocide. However, if the council
> acknowledges that, it may be forced to "take such action under the
> charter as they consider appropriate for the prevention and suppres-
> sion of acts of genocide" as provided for in Article VIII.[57]

On American (and British) insistence, the word "genocide" was exclud-ed from the Security Council statement. In a gesture that testified to both Lemkin's success in imbuing the term with moral judgment and his failure to change the policymakers' political calculus, the final statement read:

> The Security Council condemns all these breaches of international
> humanitarian law in Rwanda, particularly those perpetrated against
> the civilian population, and recalls that persons who instigate or par-
> ticipate in such acts are individually responsible. In this context, the
> Security Council recalls that the killing of members of an ethnic
> group with the intention of destroying such a group in whole or in
> part constitutes a crime punishable under international law.[58]

The testy genocide debate started up in U.S. government circles the last week of April, but it was not until May 21, six weeks after the killing in Rwanda began, that Secretary Christopher gave his diplomats permission to use the term "genocide"—sort of. The UN Human Rights Commission was about to meet in special session, and the U.S. representative, Geraldine Ferraro, needed guidance on whether to join a resolution stating that genocide had occurred. The stubborn U.S. stand had become untenable internationally.

The case for a label of genocide was the most straightforward since the Holocaust. The State Department's assistant secretary for intelligence and research, Toby Gati, who had analyzed whether Bosnian Serb atrocities were genocide, again undertook the analysis, which she summarized in a May 18 confidential memo: Lists of Tutsi victims' names and addresses had reportedly been prepared; Rwandan government troops and Hutu militia and youth squads were the main perpetrators; massacres were reported all over the country; humanitarian agencies were now "claiming from 200,000 to 500,000 lives" lost. Gati offered the Intelligence Bureau's view: "We believe 500,000 may be an exaggerated estimate, but no accurate figures are available. Systematic killings began within hours of Habyarimana's death. Most of those killed have been Tutsi civilians, including women and children."[59] The terms of the genocide convention had been met. "We can never know precise figures," Gati says, "but our analysts had been reporting huge numbers of deaths for weeks. We were basically saying, 'A rose by any other name. . . .'" The word-processing file containing the intelligence memo was titled "NONAMERWANDAKILLLGS."[60]

Despite this matter-of-fact assessment, Christopher remained reluctant to speak the obvious truth. When he issued his guidance, on May 24, fully a month after Human Rights Watch had identified the killings as "genocide," Christopher's instructions were hopelessly muddied:

> The delegation is authorized to agree to a resolution that states that "acts of genocide" have occurred in Rwanda or that "genocide has occurred in Rwanda." Other formulations that suggest that some, but not all of the killings in Rwanda are genocide . . . e.g. "genocide is taking place in Rwanda"—are authorized. Delegation is not authorized to agree to the characterization of any specific incident as genocide or to agree to any formulation that indicates that all killings in Rwanda are genocide.[61]

Notably, Christopher confined permission to acknowledge full-fledged genocide to the upcoming session of the Human Rights Commission.

In July 1994, after Hutu refugees were struck by a fatal wave of cholera in Goma, Zaire, a French Army bulldozer gathered the deceased for a mass burial.

Outside that venue State Department officials were authorized to state publicly only that "acts of genocide" had occurred.

State Department spokesperson Shelly returned to the podium on June 10, 1994. Challenged by Reuters correspondent Alan Elsner, she attempted to follow the secretary's guidance:

> **Elsner:** How would you describe the events taking place in Rwanda?
>
> **Shelly:** Based on the evidence we have seen from observations on the ground, we have every reason to believe that acts of genocide have occurred in Rwanda.
>
> **Elsner:** What's the difference between "acts of genocide" and "genocide"?
>
> **Shelly:** Well, I think the—as you know, there's a legal definition of this. . . . Clearly not all of the killings that have taken place in Rwanda are killings to which you might apply that label. . . . But as to the distinctions between the words, we're trying to call what we have seen so far as best as we can; and based, again, on the evidence, we have every reason to believe that acts of genocide have occurred.

Elsner: How many acts of genocide does it take to make genocide?

Shelly: Alan, that's just not a question that I'm in a position to answer.[62]

The same day, in Istanbul, Warren Christopher, by then under severe internal and external pressure to come clean, relented: "If there is any particular magic in calling it genocide, I have no hesitancy in saying that."[63]

Response

"Not Even a Sideshow"

Once the Americans had been evacuated from Rwanda, the massacres there largely dropped off the radar of most senior Clinton administration officials. In the situation room on the seventh floor of the State Department, a map of Rwanda had been hurriedly pinned to the wall when Habyarimana's plane was shot down, and eight banks of phones had rung off the hook. Now, with U.S. citizens safely home, the State Department chaired a daily interagency meeting, often by teleconference, designed to coordinate midlevel diplomatic and humanitarian responses. Cabinet-level officials focused on crises elsewhere. National Security Adviser Anthony Lake, who happened to know Africa, recalls, "I was obsessed with Haiti and Bosnia during that period, so Rwanda was, in journalist William Shawcross's words, a 'sideshow,' but not even a sideshow—a no-show." At the NSC the person who managed Rwanda policy was not Lake but Richard Clarke, who oversaw peacekeeping policy and for whom the news from Rwanda only confirmed a deep skepticism about the viability of UN deployments. Clarke believed that another UN failure could doom relations between Congress and the United Nations. He also sought to shield the president from congressional and public criticism. Donald Steinberg managed the Africa portfolio at the NSC and tried to look out for the dying Rwandans, but he was not an experienced infighter, and, colleagues say, he "never won a single argument" with Clarke.

The Americans who wanted the United States to do the most were those who knew Rwanda best. Joyce Leader, Rawson's deputy in Rwanda, had been the one to lock the doors to the U.S. embassy for the final time.

When she returned to Washington, she was given a small room in a back office and told to prepare the State Department's daily Rwanda summaries, drawing on press and U.S. intelligence reports. Incredibly, despite her expertise and her contacts in Rwanda, she was rarely consulted and was instructed not to deal directly with her sources in Kigali. Once an NSC staffer did call to ask, "Short of sending in the troops, what is to be done?" Leader's response, unwelcome, was "Send in the troops."

Throughout the U.S. government, Africa specialists had the least clout of all regional specialists and the smallest chance of affecting policy outcomes. In contrast, those with the most pull in the bureaucracy had never visited Rwanda or met any Rwandans.

The dearth of country or regional expertise in the senior circles of government not only reduces the capacity of officers to assess the "news" but also increases the likelihood—a dynamic identified by Lake in his 1971 *Foreign Policy* article—that killings will become abstractions. "Ethnic bloodshed" in Africa was thought to be regrettable but not particularly unusual. U.S. officials spoke analytically of "national interests" or even "humanitarian consequences" without appearing gripped by the human stakes.

As it happened, when the crisis began President Clinton himself had a coincidental and personal connection with the country. At a coffee at the White House in December 1993 Clinton had met Monique Mujawamariya, the Rwandan human rights activist. He had been struck by the courage of a woman who still bore facial scars from an automobile accident that had been arranged to curb her dissent. Clinton had singled her out, saying, "Your courage is an inspiration to all of us."[64] On April 8, two days after the onset of the killing, the *Washington Post* published a letter that Alison Des Forges had sent to Human Rights Watch after Mujawamariya had hung up the phone to face her fate. "I believe Monique was killed at 6:30 this morning," Des Forges had written. "I have virtually no hope that she is still alive, but will continue to try for more information. In the meantime. . . please inform everyone who will care."[65] Word of Mujawamariya's disappearance got the president's attention, and he inquired about her whereabouts repeatedly. "I can't tell you how much time we spent trying to find Monique," one U.S. official remembers. "Sometimes it felt as though she was the only Rwandan in danger." Miraculously, Mujawamariya had not been killed; she had hidden in the rafters of her home after hanging up with Des Forges and eventually managed to talk and bribe her way to safety. She was evacuated to Belgium, and on April 18 she joined Des Forges in the United States, where the pair began lobbying the Clinton administration on behalf of those left behind. With Mujawamariya's rescue, reported in detail in the *Post* and the *New York Times,* the president apparently lost his personal interest in events in Rwanda.

It is shocking to note that during the entire three months of the genocide, Clinton never assembled his top policy advisers to discuss the killings. Anthony Lake likewise never gathered the "principals"—the cabinet-level members of the foreign policy team. Rwanda was never thought to warrant its own top-level meeting. When the subject came up, it did so along with, and subordinate to, discussions of Somalia, Haiti, and Bosnia. Whereas these crises involved U.S. personnel and stirred some public interest, Rwanda generated no sense of urgency and could safely be avoided by Clinton at no political cost.

The UN Withdrawal

When the killing had begun, Romeo Dallaire expected and appealed for reinforcements. Within hours, he had cabled UN headquarters in New York: "Give me the means and I can do more." He was sending peacekeepers on rescue missions around the city, and he felt it was essential to increase the size and improve the quality of the UN's presence. But the United States opposed the idea of sending reinforcements, no matter where they were from. The fear, articulated mainly at the Pentagon, was that what would start as a small engagement by foreign troops would end as a large and costly one by Americans. This was the lesson of Somalia, where U.S. troops had gotten into trouble after returning to bail out the beleaguered Pakistanis. The logical outgrowth of this fear was an effort to steer clear of Rwanda entirely and be sure others did the same. Only by yanking Dallaire's entire peacekeeping force could the United States protect itself from involvement down the road. One senior U.S. official remembers,

> When the reports of the deaths of the ten Belgians came in, it was clear that it was Somalia redux, and the sense was that there would be an expectation everywhere that the U.S. would get involved. We thought leaving the peacekeepers in Rwanda and having them confront the violence would take us where we'd been before. It was a

foregone conclusion that the United States wouldn't intervene and that the concept of UN peacekeeping could not be sacrificed again.

"A foregone conclusion." What is most remarkable about the American response to the Rwandan genocide is not so much the absence of U.S. military action as that during the entire genocide the possibility of U.S. military intervention was never even debated. Indeed, the United States resisted even diplomatic intervention.

The bodies of the slain Belgian soldiers were returned to Brussels on April 14. One of the pivotal conversations in the course of the genocide took place around that time, when Willie Claes, the Belgian foreign minister, called the State Department to request "cover." "We are pulling out, but we don't want to be seen to be doing it alone," Claes said, asking the Americans to support a full UN withdrawal. Dallaire had not anticipated that Belgium would extract its soldiers, removing the backbone of his mission and stranding Rwandans in their hour of greatest need. "I expected the ex-colonial white countries would stick it out even if they took casualties," he remembers. "I thought their pride would have led them to stay to try to sort the place out. The Belgian decision caught me totally off guard. I was truly stunned."

Belgium did not want to leave ignominiously, by itself. Warren Christopher agreed to back Belgian requests for a full UN exit. Policy over the next month or so can be described simply: no U.S. military intervention, robust demands for a withdrawal of all of Dallaire's forces, and no support for a new UN mission that would challenge the killers. Belgium had the cover it needed.

On April 15 Secretary Christopher sent Ambassador Albright at the UN one of the most forceful documents produced in the entire three months of the genocide. Christopher's cable instructed Albright to demand a full UN withdrawal. The directions, which were heavily influenced by Richard Clarke at the NSC and which bypassed Steinberg, were unequivocal about the next steps. Saying that the United States had "fully" taken into account the "humanitarian reasons put forth for retention of UNAMIR elements in Rwanda," Christopher wrote that there was "insufficient justification" to retain a UN presence:

The international community must give highest priority to full, orderly withdrawal of all UNAMIR personnel as soon as possible. . . .

We will oppose any effort at this time to preserve a UNAMIR presence in Rwanda. . . . Our opposition to retaining a UNAMIR presence in Rwanda is firm. It is based on our conviction that the
Security Council has an obligation to ensure that peacekeeping operations are viable, that they are capable of fulfilling their mandates, and
that UN peacekeeping personnel are not placed or retained, knowingly, in an untenable situation.[66]

"Once we knew the Belgians were leaving, we were left with a rump mission incapable of doing anything to help people," Clarke remembers.
"They were doing nothing to stop the killings."

But Clarke underestimated the deterrent effect that Dallaire's very few
peacekeepers were having. Although many soldiers hunkered down, terrified, others scoured Kigali, rescuing Tutsi, and later established defensive
positions in the city, opening their doors to the fortunate Tutsi who made it
through roadblocks to reach them. One Senegalese captain, Mbaye
Daigne, saved 100 or so lives single-handedly. Some 25,000 Rwandans
eventually assembled at positions manned by UNAMIR personnel. The
Hutu were generally reluctant to massacre large groups of Tutsi if foreigners (armed or unarmed) were present. It did not take many UN soldiers to
dissuade the Hutu from attacking. At the Hotel des Mille Collines, ten
peacekeepers and four UN military observers helped to protect the several
hundred civilians sheltered there for the duration of the crisis. About
10,000 Rwandans gathered at the Amohoro Stadium under light UN
cover. Beardsley, Dallaire's executive assistant, remembers, "If there was any
determined resistance at close quarters, the government guys tended to
back off." Kevin Aiston, the Rwanda desk officer at the State Department,
was keeping track of Rwandan civilians under UN protection. When
Deputy Assistant Secretary Bushnell told him of the U.S. decision to
demand a UNAMIR withdrawal, he turned pale. "We can't," he said.
Bushnell replied, "The train has already left the station."

On April 19 the Belgian colonel Luc Marchal delivered his final salute
to Dallaire and departed with the last of his soldiers. The Belgian withdrawal reduced UNAMIR's troop strength to 2,100. What was more crucial, Dallaire lost his best troops. Command and control among Dallaire's
remaining forces became tenuous. Dallaire soon lost every line of communication to the countryside. He had only a single satellite phone link to the
outside world.

The UN Security Council now made a decision that sealed the Tutsi's fate and signaled to the Hutu militia that they would have free rein. The U.S. demand for a full UN withdrawal had been opposed by some African nations as well as Albright, so the United States lobbied instead for a dramatic drawdown in troop strength. On April 21, amid press reports of some 100,000 dead in Rwanda, the Security Council voted to slash UNAMIR's force size to 270.[67] Albright went along, publicly declaring that a "small, skeletal" operation would be left in Kigali to "show the will of the international community."[68]

After the UN vote, Clarke sent a memorandum to Lake reporting that language about "the safety and security of Rwandans under UN protection had been inserted by US/UN at the end of the day to prevent an otherwise unanimous UNSC from walking away from the at-risk Rwandans under UN protection as the peacekeepers drew down to 270." In other words, the memorandum suggested that the United States was leading efforts to ensure that the Rwandans under UN protection were not abandoned. The opposite was true.

Most of Dallaire's troops were evacuated by April 25. Although he was supposed to keep only 270 peacekeepers, 503 remained. By this time Dallaire was trying to deal with a bloody frenzy. "My force was standing knee-deep in mutilated bodies, surrounded by the guttural moans of dying people, looking into the eyes of children bleeding to death with their wounds burning in the sun and being invaded by maggots and flies," he later wrote. "I found myself walking through villages where the only sign of life was a goat, or a chicken, or a songbird, as all the people were dead, their bodies being eaten by voracious packs of wild dogs."[69]

Dallaire had to work within narrow limits. He attempted simply to keep the positions he held and to protect the 25,000 Rwandans under UN supervision while hoping that the member states on the Security Council would change their minds and send him some help while it still mattered.

By coincidence Rwanda held one of the rotating seats on the Security Council at the time of the genocide. Neither the United States nor any other UN member state ever suggested that the representative of the genocidal government be expelled from the council. Nor did any Security Council country offer to provide safe haven to Rwandan refugees who escaped the carnage. In one instance Dallaire's forces succeeded in evacuating a group of Rwandans by plane to Kenya. The Nairobi authorities allowed the plane to land, sequestered it in a hangar, and echoing the

American decision to turn back the USS *St. Louis* during the Holocaust, then forced the plane to return to Rwanda. The fate of the passengers is unknown.

Throughout this period the Clinton administration was largely silent. The closest it came to a public denunciation of the Rwandan government occurred after personal lobbying by Human Rights Watch, when Anthony Lake issued a statement calling on Rwandan military leaders by name to "do everything in their power to end the violence immediately." When he is informed six years after the genocide that human rights groups and U.S. officials point to this statement as the sum total of official public attempts to shame the Rwandan government, he seems stunned. "You're kidding," he says. "That's truly pathetic."

At the State Department the diplomacy was conducted privately, by telephone. Prudence Bushnell regularly set her alarm for 2:00 a.m. and phoned Rwandan government officials. She spoke several times with Augustin Bizimungu, the Rwandan military chief of staff. "These were the most bizarre phone calls," she says. "He spoke in perfectly charming French. 'Oh, it's so nice to hear from you,' he said. I told him, 'I am calling to tell you President Clinton is going to hold you accountable for the killings.' He said, 'Oh, how nice it is that your president is thinking of me.'" When she called Tutsi rebel commander Paul Kagame, he would say, "Madame, they're killing my people."

The Pentagon "Chop"

The daily meeting of the Rwanda interagency working group was attended, either in person or by teleconference, by representatives from the various State Department bureaus, the Pentagon, the National Security Council, and the intelligence community. Any proposal that originated in the working group had to survive the Pentagon "chop." "Hard intervention," meaning U.S. military action, was obviously out of the question. But Pentagon officials routinely stymied initiatives for "soft intervention" as well.

The Pentagon May 1 discussion paper on Rwanda, referred to earlier, ran down a list of the working group's six short-term policy objectives and carped at most of them. The fear of a slippery slope was pervasive. Next to the seemingly innocuous suggestion that the United States "support the UN and others in attempts to achieve a cease-fire" the Pentagon official

responded, "Need to change 'attempts' to 'political efforts'—without 'political' there is a danger of signing up to troop contributions."[70]

The one policy move the Defense Department supported was a U.S.
effort to achieve an arms embargo. But the same discussion paper acknowledged the ineffectiveness of this step: "We do not envision it will have a
significant impact on the killings because machetes, knives and other hand
implements have been the most common weapons."[71]

Dallaire never spoke to Bushnell or to Tony Marley, the U.S. military
liaison to the Arusha process, during the genocide, but they separately
reached the same conclusions. Seeing that no troops were forthcoming,
they turned their attention to measures short of full-scale deployment that
might alleviate the suffering. Dallaire pleaded with New York, and Bushnell
and her team recommended in Washington, that something be done to
"neutralize" Radio Mille Collines.

The country best equipped to prevent the genocide planners from
broadcasting murderous instructions directly to the population was the
United States. Marley offered three possibilities. The United States could
destroy the antenna. It could transmit "counterbroadcasts" urging perpetrators to stop the genocide. Or it could jam the hate radio station's broadcasts. This could have been done from an airborne platform such as the Air
National Guard's Commando Solo airplane. Anthony Lake raised the matter with Secretary of Defense William Perry at the end of April. Pentagon
officials considered all the proposals nonstarters. On May 5 Frank Wisner,
the undersecretary of defense for policy, prepared a memo for Sandy
Berger, the deputy national security adviser. Wisner's memo testifies to the
unwillingness of the U.S. government to make even financial sacrifices to
diminish the killing:

> We have looked at options to stop the broadcasts within the
> Pentagon, discussed them interagency and concluded jamming is an
> ineffective and expensive mechanism that will not accomplish the
> objective the NSC Advisor seeks.
>
> International legal conventions complicate airborne or ground
> based jamming and the mountainous terrain reduces the effectiveness
> of either option. Commando Solo, an Air National Guard asset, is the
> only suitable DOD jamming platform. It costs approximately $8500
> per flight hour and requires a semi-secure area of operations due to its
> vulnerability and limited self-protection.

I believe it would be wiser to use air to assist in Rwanda in the
[food] relief effort.[72]

The U.S. plane would have needed to remain in Rwandan airspace
while it waited for radio transmissions to begin. "First we would have had
to figure out whether it made sense to use Commando Solo," Wisner
recalls. "Then we had to get it from where it was already and be sure it
could be moved. Then we would have needed flight clearance from all the
countries nearby. And then we would need the political go-ahead. By the
time we got all this, weeks would have passed. And it was not going to
solve the fundamental problem, which was one that needed to be addressed
militarily." Pentagon planners understood that stopping the genocide
required a military solution. Neither they nor the White House wanted
any part in a military solution. Yet instead of undertaking other forms of
intervention that might at least have saved some lives, they justified inaction by arguing that a military solution was required.

It was clear that radio jamming would have been no panacea, but most
of the delays Wisner cites could have been avoided if senior administration
officials had followed through. Instead, justifications for standing by
abounded. In early May the State Department Legal Adviser's Office issued
a finding against radio jamming, citing international broadcasting agreements and the American commitment to free speech. When Bushnell
raised radio jamming yet again at a meeting, one Pentagon official chided
her for naiveté: "Pru, radios don't kill people. *People* kill people!"

The Defense Department was disdainful both of the policy ideas being
circulated at the working-group meetings, and, memos indicate, of the
people circulating them. A memo by one Defense Department aide
observed that the State Department's Africa bureau had received a phone
call from a Kigali hotel owner who said that his hotel and the civilians
inside were about to be attacked. The memo snidely reported that the
Africa bureau's proposed "solution" was "Pru Bushnell will call the
[Rwandan] military and tell them we will hold them personally responsible
if anything happens (!)."[73] (In fact the hotel owner, who survived the genocide, later acknowledged that phone calls from Washington played a key
role in dissuading the killers from massacring the inhabitants of the hotel.)

However significant and obstructionist the role of the Pentagon in April
and May, Defense Department officials were stepping into a vacuum. As
one U.S. official put it, "Look, nobody senior was paying any attention to

this mess. And in the absence of any political leadership from the top, when you have one group that feels pretty strongly about what shouldn't be done, it is extremely likely they are going to end up shaping U.S. policy." Lieutenant General Wesley Clark looked to the White House for leadership. "The Pentagon is always going to be the last to want to intervene," he says. "It is up to the civilians to tell us they want to do something and we'll figure out how to do it."

But with no powerful personalities or high-ranking officials arguing forcefully for meaningful action, midlevel Pentagon officials held sway, vetoing or stalling on hesitant proposals put forward by midlevel State Department and NSC officials. If Pentagon objections were to be overcome, the president, Secretary Christopher, Secretary Perry, or Lake would have had to step forward to "own" the problem, which did not happen.

The deck was stacked against Rwandans, who were hiding wherever they could and praying for rescue. The American public expressed no interest in Rwanda, and the crisis was treated as a civil war requiring a cease-fire or as a "peacekeeping problem" requiring a UN withdrawal. It was not treated as a genocide demanding instant action. The top policymakers trusted that their subordinates were doing all they could do, while the subordinates worked with an extremely narrow understanding of what the United States would do.

Society-Wide Silence

The Clinton administration did not actively consider U.S. military intervention, it blocked the deployment of UN peacekeepers, and it refrained from undertaking softer forms of intervention. The inaction can be attributed to decisions and nondecisions made at the National Security Council, at the State Department, in the Pentagon, and even at the U.S. mission to the UN. But as was true with previous genocides, these U.S. officials were making potent political calculations about what the U.S. public would abide. Officials simultaneously believed the American people would oppose U.S. military intervention in central Africa and feared that the public might support intervention if they realized a genocide was under way. As always, they looked to op-ed pages of elite journals, popular protest, and congressional noise to gauge public interest. No group or groups in the United States made Clinton administration decisionmakers feel or fear that they would pay a political price for doing nothing to save Rwandans. Indeed, all the signals told them to steer clear. Only *after* the genocide would it become possible to identify an American "constituency" for action.

At the height of the war in Bosnia, the op-ed pages of America's newspapers had roared with indignation; during the three-month genocide in Rwanda, they were silent, ignorant, and prone fatalistically to accept the futility of outside intervention. An April 17 *Washington Post* editorial asked "what if anything might be done" about the killings. "Unfortunately, the immediate answer to the last question," the editors wrote, "appears to be: not much":

> The United States has no recognizable national interest in taking a role, certainly not a leading role. In theory, international fire-engine service is available to all houses in the global village. Imagine a fire department that would respond only to the lesser blazes. But in a world of limited political and economic resources, not all of the many fires will be equally tended. Rwanda is in an unpreferred class.[74]

An April 23 *New York Times* editorial acknowledged that genocide was under way but said that the Security Council had "thrown in the bloodied towel":

> What looks very much like genocide has been taking place in Rwanda. People are pulled from cars and buses, ordered to show their identity papers and then killed on the spot if they belong to the wrong ethnic group. . . . It is legally if not morally easy to justify pulling out since the unevenly trained U.N. force was meant to police a peace, not take sides in a civil war. Somalia provides ample warning against plunging open-endedly into a "humanitarian" mission. . . . The horrors of Kigali show the need for considering whether a mobile, quick-response UN force under UN aegis is needed to deal with such calamities. Absent such a force, the world has little choice but to stand aside and hope for the best.[75]

A May 4 *Nightline* program began with anchorman Ted Koppel's asking: "Rwanda: Is the world just too tired to help?" The segment included a comment from President Clinton, who had been asked about Rwanda that day. Clinton invoked Somalia: "Lesson number one is, don't go into one of these things and say, as the U.S. said when we started in Somalia, 'Maybe we'll be done in a month because it's a humanitarian crisis.' . . . Because there are almost always political problems and sometimes military conflicts, which bring about these crises."[76]

American newspapers included graphic descriptions of the atrocities, but although the coverage was steady, it was not heavy. In South Africa in early May 1994, some 2,500 reporters congregated for the historic elections that officially dismantled apartheid and brought Nelson Mandela to power. In Rwanda at the height of coverage of the killings, between April and June, the number of reporters present never exceeded fifteen.[77] Editors make judgments about where, when, and why to deploy their "troops" in much the same way commanders-in-chief make theirs. And since U.S. or European military intervention in Rwanda was seen as highly unlikely, none of the major Western media outlets made coverage of the crisis a priority. Of course, as in Cambodia, because press coverage was light, public and elite pressure for military intervention remained faint.

Capitol Hill was likewise quiet. Some in Congress were glad to be free of the expense of another flawed UN mission. Senator Dole had introduced the Peace Powers Act in Congress in January and made his opposition to U.S. involvement widely known. Other members of Congress were not hearing from their constituents. On April 30 Representative Patricia Schroeder (D.–Colo.) described the relative silence in her district. "There are some groups terribly concerned about the gorillas," she said, noting that Colorado was home to a research organization that studied Rwanda's imperiled gorilla population. "But—it sounds terrible—people just don't know what can be done about the people."[78]

Around the time of President Habyarimana's plane crash in Rwanda, Randall Robinson of TransAfrica started a hunger strike to protest the Clinton administration's automatic repatriation of Haitians fleeing the coup that had ousted Jean-Bertrand Aristide. Robinson was quoted in the *Washington Post* on April 12, 1994, a week after the Rwandan massacres had begun, talking about America's Haitian refugee policy: "I can't remember ever being more disturbed by any public policy than I am by this one. I can't remember any American foreign policy as hurtful, as discriminatory, as racist as this one. It is so mean, it simply can't be tolerated."[79] Some 10,000 Rwandans had been killed that week in Kigali alone. On April 21 six members of the U.S. Congress were arrested in front of the White House for protesting the administration's decision to turn back the Haitian refugees.[80] Robinson was briefly hospitalized for dehydration on May 4; Clinton officially changed his policy on repatriation on May 9.

A few members of the Africa subcommittees and the Congressional Black Caucus (CBC) did eventually appeal tamely for the United States to play a role in ending the violence. But again, they did not dare urge U.S. involvement on the ground, and they did not kick up a public fuss. The CBC staged no hunger strikes and no marches; no members were arrested in front of the White House; and in the end, after a few isolated television appearances, three letters, and a handful of private contacts, the caucus had no effect on U.S. policy. Holly Burkhalter of Human Rights Watch acknowledges the CBC's lethargy but notes, "We can't forget that the White Caucus, which is a lot bigger, wasn't very effective either."

The phones in congressional offices were not ringing. Representative Alcee Hastings (D.–Fla.) later recalled, "In my constituency, I'm first to admit that the primary focus is on Haiti. You have to remember that I come from south Florida, and . . . we have suffered the megashocks of refugee influx. Africa seems so far away, and there is no vital interest that my constituency sees." Representative Maxine Waters, the California Democrat, later said she had trouble following what was going on. "I don't know whether the Hutus or the Tutsis were correct. I couldn't tell anybody what I thought they should do," she recalled. "A lot of people were like me; they didn't know from crap."[81] No significant Rwandan diaspora lived in the United States; few African Americans identify specific ancestral homelands and lobby on their behalf in the way Armenians, Jews, or Albanians might. On May 13 Senator Paul Simon (D.–Ill.), chairman of the Senate Foreign Relations Subcommittee on Africa, and Senator James Jeffords of Vermont, the ranking Republican on the subcommittee, telephoned General Dallaire in Kigali and asked what he needed. A desperate Dallaire told them if he had 5,000 troops he could end the massacres. The senators immediately drafted and hand-delivered a note to the White House requesting that the U.S. get the Security Council to authorize the deployment of troops. "Obviously there are risks involved," the letter read, "but we cannot continue to sit idly by while this tragedy continues to unfold." The senators got no reply. When they called to follow up ten days later, they were unable to reach National Security Adviser Lake but were told by another official, "We don't feel there is a base of public support for taking any action in Africa." "This might have been accurate," Simon noted later, "but if there is no base for public support, the president can get on television and explain our reasons for responding and build a base. Even then, if public support still is not strong, leadership demands action in this type of situation."[82] Simon believes public pressure might have altered the U.S. response. "If every member of the House and Senate had received 100 letters from people back home saying we have to do something about Rwanda, when the crisis was first developing, then I think the response would have been different," Simon said.[83] He wishes he had telephoned Clinton personally or at least staged a press conference: "I remember I considered calling in the press, but I just assumed nobody would show up." Clinton did not write back to the senators until June 9, and in his letter he defended U.S. policy, listing all of the important steps the United States had taken, ranging from paying for medical supplies to pressing for a cease-fire. "I have spoken out against the killings," the president wrote. "We have called for a full investigation of these atrocities."[84]

Although Human Rights Watch supplied exemplary intelligence to the U.S. government and lobbied in one-on-one meetings, it lacked the grassroots base from which it might have mobilized the crucial domestic pressure everyone agreed was missing. When Des Forges, Mujawamariya, and Burkhalter of Human Rights Watch visited the White House on April 21 and asked Lake how they might alter U.S. policy, he shrugged his shoulders. "If you want to make this move, you will have to change public opinion," Lake said. "You must make more noise."[85] But the only noise that could be heard was the sound of machetes slicing their way through Rwanda's Tutsi population.

PDD-25 in Action

No sooner had most of Dallaire's forces been withdrawn, in late April 1994, than a handful of nonpermanent members of the Security Council, aghast at the scale of the slaughter, pressed the major powers to send a new, beefed-up force (UNAMIR II) to Rwanda.

When Dallaire's troops had first arrived, in the fall of 1993, they had done so under a fairly traditional peacekeeping mandate known as a Chapter VI deployment—a mission that assumes a cease-fire and a desire on both sides to comply with a peace accord. The Security Council now had to decide whether it was prepared to move from peacekeeping to peace enforcement—that is, to a Chapter VII mission in a hostile environment. This would demand more peacekeepers with greater resources, more aggressive rules of engagement, and an explicit recognition that the UN soldiers were there to protect civilians.

Two proposals emerged. Dallaire submitted a plan that called for joining his remaining peacekeepers with about 5,000 well-armed soldiers he hoped could be gathered quickly by the Security Council. He wanted to secure Kigali and then fan outward to create safe havens for Rwandans around the country who had gathered in large numbers at churches and schools and on hillsides. The United States was one of the few countries that could supply the rapid airlift and logistic support needed to move reinforcements to the region. In a meeting with UN Secretary-General Boutros Boutros-Ghali on May 10, Vice President Al Gore pledged U.S. help with transport.

But Richard Clarke and Tony Lake at the NSC and representatives of the Joint Chiefs challenged Dallaire's idea. "How do you plan to take control of the airport in Kigali so that the reinforcements will be able to land?" Clarke asked. He argued instead for an "outside-in" strategy, as opposed to Dallaire's "inside-out" approach. The U.S. proposal would have created protected zones for refugees at Rwanda's borders. It would have kept any U.S. pilots involved in airlifting the peacekeepers safely out of Rwanda. "Our proposal was the most feasible, doable thing that could have been done in the short term," Clarke insists. Dallaire's proposal, in contrast, "could not be done in the short term and could not attract peacekeepers." The U.S. plan—which was modeled on the allies' 1991 Operation Provide Comfort for the Kurds of northern Iraq—seemed to assume that the people in need were refugees fleeing to the border, but most endangered Tutsi could not make it to the border. The most vulnerable Rwandans were those clustered together, awaiting salvation, deep inside Rwanda. Dallaire's plan would have had UN soldiers make their way to the Tutsi in hiding. The U.S. plan would have required civilians to move to the safe zones, negotiating murderous roadblocks on the way. "The two plans had very different objectives," Dallaire says. "My mission was to save Rwandans. Their mission was to put on a show at no risk."

America's new peacekeeping doctrine, which Clarke had helped shape, was unveiled on May 3, and U.S. officials applied its criteria zealously. PDD-25 did not merely circumscribe U.S. participation in UN missions; it also limited U.S. support for other states that hoped to carry out UN missions. Before such operations could garner U.S. approval, policymakers had to meet the PDD's requirements, showing U.S. interests at stake, a clear mission goal, acceptable costs, Congressional, public, and allied support, a clear command-and-control arrangement, and an exit strategy.

The United States haggled at the Security Council and with the UN Department of Peacekeeping Operations for the first two weeks of May. U.S. officials pointed to the flaws in Dallaire's proposal without offering the resources that would have helped him to overcome them. On May 13 Deputy Secretary of State Strobe Talbott sent Madeleine Albright instructions on how the United States should respond to Dallaire's plan. Noting the logistic hazards of airlifting troops into the capital, Talbott wrote, "The U.S. is not prepared at this point to lift heavy equipment and troops into Kigali." The "more manageable" operation would be to create the protected zones at the border, secure humanitarian aid deliveries, and "promot[e] restoration of a ceasefire and return to the Arusha Peace Process." Talbott acknowledged that even the minimalist American proposal contained "many unanswered questions":

> Where will the needed forces come from; how will they be transported; . . . where precisely should these safe zones be created; . . . would UN forces be authorized to move out of the zones to assist affected populations not in the zones; . . . will the fighting parties in Rwanda agree to this arrangement; . . . what conditions would need to obtain for the operation to end successfully?

Nonetheless, Talbott concluded, "We would urge the UN to explore and refine this alternative and present the Council with a menu of at least two options in a formal report from the [secretary-general] along with cost estimates before the Security Council votes on changing UNAMIR's mandate."[86] U.S. policymakers were asking valid questions. Dallaire's plan certainly would have required the intervening troops to take risks in an effort to reach the targeted Rwandans or to confront the Hutu militia and government forces. But the business-as-usual tone of the American inquiry did not seem appropriate to the unprecedented and utterly unconventional crisis that was under way.

On May 17, by which time most of the Tutsi victims of the genocide were already dead, the United States finally acceded to a version of Dallaire's plan. But few African countries stepped forward to offer troops. Even if troops had been immediately available, the lethargy of the major powers would have hindered their use. Although Vice President Gore had committed the United States to provide armored support if the African nations provided soldiers, Pentagon stalling resumed. On May 19 the UN formally requested fifty armored personnel carriers from the United States. On May 31 U.S. officials agreed to send the APCs from Germany to Entebbe, Uganda.[87] But squabbles between the Pentagon and UN planners arose. Who would pay for the vehicles? Should the vehicles be tracked or wheeled? Would the UN buy them or simply lease them? And who would pay the shipping costs? Compounding the disputes was the Department of Defense regulation that prevented the U.S. Army from preparing the vehicles for transport until contracts had been signed. The Defense Department demanded that it be reimbursed $15 million for shipping spare parts and equipment to and from Rwanda. In mid-June the White House finally intervened. On June 19, a month after the UN request, the United States began transporting the APCs, but they were missing the radios and heavy machine guns that would be needed if UN troops came under fire. The APCs did not arrive in Rwanda until July.

"Interventions"

In June, France, perhaps the least appropriate country to intervene because of its warm relationship with the genocidal Hutu regime, announced its plan to send 2,500 soldiers to set up a "safe zone" in the southwest of the country.[88] Operation Turquoise was intended to serve as a "bridge action" until UNAMIR II arrived.[89] French troops were deployed extremely quickly, entering Rwanda on June 23 and illustrating the pace at which a determined state could move. Although they undoubtedly saved lives, mop-up killings proceeded in the French protected zone. When the Hutu moved their Radio Mille Collines transmitter into the area, French forces seized neither the hate-propagating equipment nor the individuals responsible for orchestrating the genocide. Yet President Mitterrand was quick to claim credit, alleging the operation had saved "tens of thousands of lives." France bore no responsibility for events, he said, because the massacres happened after France left Rwanda and because France could not intervene during the genocide, as this was the job of the United Nations.[90]

It was Tutsi (RPF) rebels under the command of Paul Kagame who eventually brought the genocide to a halt. In so doing, they sent Hutu perpetrators, among an estimated 1.7 million Hutu refugees, fleeing into neighboring Zaire and Tanzania. On July 19, the day the RPF government of national unity was sworn in and nearly two months after the Security Council's reinforcements resolution, Dallaire commanded the same 503 soldiers as he had since late April. Not a single additional UN soldier had been deployed.

Only after the RPF had seized virtually all of Rwanda (except the French zone) did President Clinton finally order the Rwandan embassy in Washington closed and its assets frozen. Clinton said the United States could not "allow representatives of a regime that supports genocidal massacres to remain on our soil."[91] On August 25, 1994, the Security Council ruled that Rwanda would not take its turn as president of the council.[92]

Clinton did in fact send U.S. forces to the Great Lakes region. Rwandan refugees, mainly Hutu fleeing the RPF advance, were ravaged by hunger, thirst, and cholera in neighboring Zaire. They had begun dying at a rate of 2,000 per day. President Clinton requested $320 million in emergency relief funds from Congress and announced the deployment of 4,000 U.S. troops to aid refugees in the camps in Zaire. The *New York Times* editorial on July 23, 1994, was titled: "At Last, Rwanda's Pain Registers."[93] On July 29 President Clinton ordered 200 U.S. troops to occupy the Kigali airport so that relief could be flown directly into Rwanda. Ahead of their arrival, Dallaire says he got a phone call. A U.S. officer was wondering precisely how many Rwandans had died. Dallaire was puzzled and asked why he wanted to know. "We are doing our calculations back here," the U.S. officer said, "and one American casualty is worth about 85,000 Rwandan dead."[94]

These troops, Clinton administration officials insisted, would aid in the provision of humanitarian relief; they would not keep peace. Somalia was *not* the model. Indeed, peacekeeping had become a four-letter word. "Let me be clear about this," the president said on July 29, 1994. "Any deployment of United States troops inside Rwanda would be for the immediate and sole purpose of humanitarian relief, not for peacekeeping." He assured Americans, "Mission creep is not a problem here."[95]

The U.S. Senate authorized only $170 million of the $320 million Clinton requested and wrote into the legislation that all forces be withdrawn by October 1 unless Congress specifically approved a longer stay. Although cost had been one of several factors behind U.S. opposition to sending UN reinforcements to Rwanda ahead of and during the genocide, its peacekeeping contribution would probably have hovered around $30 million; it ended up spending $237 million on humanitarian relief alone.[96]

In late August U.S. ambassador David Rawson held a press conference back in Kigali. Even after the deaths of 800,000 people, he remained committed to the Arusha peace process:

Since they all speak the same language, have basically the same culture and the same history, the reality of it is if they all want to live in Rwanda, then they have to at some point sit around a table and figure out the formulas that will make this happen. We believe that the Arusha formulas, negotiated over a very intense year of negotiations in Arusha, provide that kind of power-sharing formula that would make that happen. And the closer that, even with all the horror that has happened, the current arrangements can hew to the Arusha formulas, we believe, the more chance there is for success.[97]

In one of his parting cables, Dallaire summed up his experience in UNAMIR:

What we have been living here is a disgrace. The international community and the UN member states have on the one hand been appalled at what has happened in Rwanda while, on the other hand, these same authorities, apart from a few exceptions, have done nothing substantive to help the situation. . . . The [UN] force has been prevented from having a modicum of self-respect and effectiveness on the ground. . . . I acknowledge that this mission is a logistical nightmare for your [headquarters], but that is *nothing* compared to the living hell that has surrounded us, coupled with the obligation of standing in front of both parties and being the bearer of so little help and credibility. . . . Although Rwanda and UNAMIR have been at the centre of a terrible human tragedy, that is not to say Holocaust, and although many fine words had been pronounced by all, including members of the Security Council, the tangible effort . . . has been totally, completely ineffective.[98]

The Stories We Tell

It is not hard to conceive of how the United States might have done things differently. Ahead of the April killing, as violence escalated, it could have agreed to Belgian pleas for UN reinforcements. Once the killing of thousands of Rwandans a day had begun, the president could have deployed U.S. troops to Rwanda. The United States could have joined Dallaire's beleaguered UNAMIR forces, or, if it feared associating with shoddy UN peacekeeping, it could have intervened unilaterally with the

Security Council's backing, as France did in June. The United States could also have acted without the UN's blessing, as it would do five years later in Kosovo. Securing congressional support for U.S. intervention would have been extremely difficult, but by the second week of the killing, Clinton, one of the most eloquent presidents of the twentieth century, could have made the case that something approximating genocide was under way, that an inviolable American value was imperiled by its occurrence, and that U.S. contingents at relatively low risk could stop the extermination of a people.

Even if the White House could not have overcome congressional opposition to sending U.S. troops to Africa, the United States still had a variety of options. Instead of leaving it to midlevel officials to communicate with the Rwandan leadership behind the scenes, senior officials in the administration could have taken control of the process. They could have publicly and frequently denounced the slaughter. They could have branded the crimes "genocide" at a far earlier stage. They could have called for the expulsion of the Rwandan delegation from the Security Council. On the telephone, at the UN, and over the Voice of America, they could have threatened to prosecute those complicit in the genocide, naming names when possible. They could have deployed Pentagon assets to jam—even temporarily—the crucial, deadly radio broadcasts.

Instead of demanding a UN withdrawal, quibbling over costs, and coming forward (belatedly) with a plan better suited to caring for refugees than to stopping massacres, U.S. officials could have worked to make UNAMIR a force to contend with. They could have urged their Belgian allies to stay and protect Rwandan civilians. If the Belgians insisted on withdrawing, the United States could have done everything within its power to make sure that Dallaire was immediately reinforced. Senior officials could have spent U.S. political capital rallying troops from other nations and could have supplied strategic airlift and logistic support to a coalition that it had helped to create. In short, the United States could have led the world.

It is striking that most officials involved in shaping U.S. policy were able to define the decision not to stop genocide as ethical and moral. The administration employed several devices to dampen enthusiasm for action and to preserve the public's sense—and more important, its own—that U.S. policy choices were not merely politically astute but also morally acceptable. First, administration officials exaggerated the extremity of the possible responses. Time and again U.S. leaders posed the choice as between staying out of Rwanda and "getting involved everywhere." In addition, they often presented the choice as one between doing nothing and sending in hundreds of thousands of marines.

Second, administration policymakers appealed to notions of the greater good. They did not simply frame U.S. policy as one contrived in order to advance the national interest or avoid U.S. casualties. Rather, they often argued against intervention from the standpoint of people committed to protecting human life. Owing to recent failures in UN peacekeeping, many humanitarian interventionists in the U.S. government were concerned about the future of America's relationship with the United Nations generally and peacekeeping specifically. They believed that the UN and humanitarianism could not afford another Somalia. Many internalized the belief that the UN had more to lose by sending reinforcements and failing than by allowing the killings to proceed. Their chief priority, after the evacuation of the Americans, was looking after UN peacekeepers, and they justified the withdrawal of the peacekeepers on the grounds that it would ensure a future for humanitarian intervention. In other words, Dallaire's peacekeeping mission in Rwanda had to be destroyed so that peacekeeping might be saved for use elsewhere.

A third feature of the response that helped to console U.S. officials at the time was the sheer flurry of Rwanda-related activity. U.S. officials with a special concern for Rwanda took their solace from minivictories, working on behalf of specific individuals such as Monique Mujawamariya or groups like the Rwandans gathered at the hotel and the stadium. "We were like the child in the ghetto who focuses all of her energy on protecting her doll," says one senior official. "As the world collapses around her, she can't bear it, but she takes solace in the doll, the only thing she can control." Government officials involved in policy met constantly and remained, in bureaucratic lingo, "seized of the matter"; they neither appeared nor felt indifferent. Although little in the way of effective intervention emerged from midlevel meetings in Washington or New York, an abundance of memoranda and other documents did.

Finally, the almost willful delusion that what was happening in Rwanda did not amount to genocide created a nurturing ethical framework for inaction. "War" was "tragic" but created no moral imperative.

One U.S. official kept a journal during the crisis. In late May, exasperated by the obstructionism pervading the bureaucracy, the official dashed off this lament:

A military that wants to go nowhere to do anything—or let go of their toys so someone else can do it. A White House cowed by the brass (and we are to give lessons on how the armed forces take orders from civilians?). An NSC that does peacekeeping by the book—the accounting book, that is. And an assistance program that prefers whites (Europe) to blacks. When it comes to human rights we have no problem drawing the line in the sand of the dark continent (just don't ask us to do anything—agonizing is our specialty), but not China or any place else business looks good.

We have a foreign policy based on our amoral economic interests run by amateurs who want to stand for something—hence the agony—but ultimately don't want to exercise any leadership that has a cost.

They say there may be as many as a million massacred in Rwanda. The militias continue to slay the innocent and the educated. . . . Has it really cost the United States nothing?

Aftermath

Guilt

The genocide in Rwanda cost Romeo Dallaire a great deal. It is both paradoxical and natural that the man who probably did the most to save Rwandans feels the worst. By August 1994 Dallaire had a death wish. "At the end of my command, I drove around in my vehicle with no escort practically looking for ambushes," Dallaire recalls. "I was trying to get myself destroyed and looking to get released from the guilt."

Upon his return to Canada, he behaved initially as if he had just completed a routine mission. As the days passed, though, he began to show signs of distress. In late 1994 the UN Security Council established a war crimes tribunal for Rwanda modeled after one just set up to punish crimes committed in the former Yugoslavia. When the UN tribunal called Dallaire to take the stand in February 1998, four years after the genocide, he plunged back into his memories.[99] Pierre Prosper, the UN prosecutor, remembers the scene: "He carried himself so proudly and so commanding. Just like a soldier. He saluted the president of the tribunal. All of his answers were 'Yes, sir,' 'No, sir.' He was very stoic. And then, as the questioning progressed, you could just see it unraveling. It was as though he was just reliving it right there in front of us." As Dallaire spoke, it became clear how omnipresent the genocide was in his life. On one occasion, as he described his operational capacity, he said, "I had a number of bodies on the ground"—but then paused and corrected himself: "Forgive me—a number of troops on the ground." His voice cracked as he struggled to find words to match his shock and disappointment: "It seems . . . inconceivable that one can watch . . . thousands of people being . . . massacred . . . every day in the media . . . and remain passive."[100]

Dallaire seemed to be searching the courtroom for answers. He still could not understand how the major powers could have sent troops to the region with a genocide under way, extracted their civilian personnel and soldiers, and stranded the people of Rwanda and the UN peacekeepers. Dallaire stared straight ahead and said stiffly that the departure of those military units "with full knowledge of the danger confronting the emasculated UN force, is inexcusable by any human criteria."[101]

The defense attorney at the tribunal interjected at this point: "It seems as though you regret that, Major General." Dallaire glanced up as if the trance had been broken, fixed his gaze on the interrogator, and responded, "You cannot even imagine."

At a news conference after his testimony, Dallaire said, "I found it very difficult to return to the details. . . . In fact, at one point yesterday, I had the sense of the smell of the slaughter in my nose and I don't know how it appeared, but there was all of a sudden this enormous rush to my brain and to my senses. . . . Maybe with time, it will hurt less."[102] He hoped to visit Rwanda after testifying. "Until I can see many of those places, until I can see some of the graves, until I can see those hills and those mountains and those villages," he said. "I don't think I'll ever have closure."[103] He hoped to bring his wife.

President Clinton visited Rwanda a month after Dallaire testified. With the grace of one grown practiced at public remorse, he issued something of an apology. "We in the United States and the world community did not do as much as we could have and should have done to try to limit what occurred," Clinton said. "It may seem strange to you here," he continued, "but all over the world there were people like me sitting in offices, day after day after day, who did not fully appreciate the depth and the speed with which you were being engulfed by this unimaginable terror."[104] But Clinton's remorse came too late for the 800,000 Rwandans who died, and for Dallaire, who often feels sorry he lived.

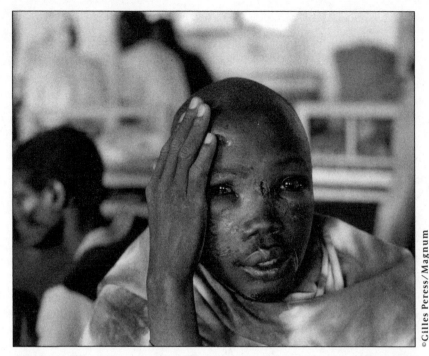

©Gilles Peress/Magnum

A Tutsi survivor of a machete attack nurses his wounds at a hospital in Kabgai, Rwanda.

Some of Dallaire's colleagues speculated that he was reacting emotionally to his experience in Rwanda because the Belgian press and the families of the deceased Belgian soldiers had vilified him. He claims to be reconciled to his decisions. "I've been criticized by the Belgians for sending their troops to a 'certain death' by directing them to protect Prime Minister Agathe," he notes. "I'll take that heat, but I could not take the heat of having hunkered down and not having tried to give Agathe the chance to call to the nation to avert violence. You couldn't let this thing go by and watch it happen."

His bigger problem is his guilt over the Rwandans. They entrusted their fate to the UN and were murdered: "I failed my mission," he says. "I simply cannot say these deaths are not mine when they happened on my mission. I cannot erase the thousands and thousands of eyes that I see, looking at me, bewildered. I argued, but I didn't convince, so I failed."

In an effort to help Canadians deal with the stress of their military experiences, Dallaire agreed to produce a thirty-minute video, "Witness the Evil." In the video he says it took two years for the experiences to hit him but that eventually he reached a point where he couldn't "keep it in the drawer" any longer:

I became suicidal because . . . there was no other solution. I couldn't live with the pain and the sounds and the smell. Sometimes, I wish I'd lost a leg instead of having all those grey cells screwed up. You lose a leg, it's obvious and you've got therapy and all kinds of stuff. You lose your marbles, very, very difficult to explain, very difficult to gain that support that you need.[105]

As the passage of time distanced Dallaire from Rwanda, the nights brought him closer to his inner agony. He carried a machete around and lectured cadets on post-traumatic stress disorder, he slept sparingly, and he found himself nearly retching in the supermarket, transported back to Rwandan markets and the bodies strewn within them. In October 1998 Canada's chief of defense staff, General Maurice Baril, asked Dallaire to take a month of stress-related leave. Dallaire was shattered. After hanging up the phone, he says, "I cried for days and days." He tried to keep up a brave public front, sending a parting e-mail to his subordinates that read: "It has been assessed essential that I recharge my batteries due to a number of factors, not the least being the impact of my operational experience on my health. . . . Don't withdraw, don't surrender, don't give up."[106]

Dallaire returned from leave, but in December 1999 Baril called again. He had spoken with Dallaire's doctors and decided to force a change with an ultimatum: Either Dallaire had to abandon the "Rwanda business" and stop testifying at the tribunal and publicly faulting the international community for not doing more, or he would have to leave his beloved armed forces. For Dallaire, only one answer was possible: "I told them I would never give up Rwanda," he says. "I was the force commander and I would complete my duty, testifying and doing whatever it takes to bring these guys to justice." In April 2000 Dallaire was forced out of the Canadian armed services and given a medical discharge.

Dallaire had always said, "The day I take my uniform off will be the day that I will also respond to my soul." But since becoming a civilian he has realized that his soul is not readily retrievable. "My soul is in Rwanda," he says. "It has never, ever come back, and I'm not sure it ever will." He feels that the eyes and the spirits of those killed continue to watch him.

In June 2000 a brief Canadian news wire story reported that Dallaire had been found unconscious on a park bench in Hull, Quebec, drunk and alone. He had consumed a bottle of scotch on top of his daily dose of pills for post-traumatic stress disorder. He was on another suicide mission. After recovering,

Dallaire sent a letter to the Canadian Broadcast Corporation thanking them for their sensitive coverage of this episode. His letter was read on the air:

> Thank you for the very kind thoughts and wishes.
>
> There are times when the best medication and therapist simply can't help a soldier suffering from this new generation of peacekeeping injury. The anger, the rage, the hurt, and the cold loneliness that separates you from your family, friends, and society's normal daily routine are so powerful that the option of destroying yourself is both real and attractive. That is what happened last Monday night. It appears, it grows, it invades, and it overpowers you.
>
> In my current state of therapy, which continues to show very positive results, control mechanisms have not yet matured to always be on top of this battle. My doctors and I are still [working to] establish the level of serenity and productivity that I yearn so much for. The therapists agree that the battle I waged that night was a solid example of the human trying to come out from behind the military leader's ethos of "My mission first, my personnel, then myself." Obviously the venue I used last Monday night left a lot to be desired and will be the subject of a lot of work over the next while.

Dallaire remained a true believer in Canada, in peacekeeping, in human rights. The letter went on:

> This nation, without any hesitation nor doubt, is capable and even expected by the less fortunate of this globe to lead the developed countries beyond self-interest, strategic advantages, and isolationism, and raise their sights to the realm of the pre-eminence of humanism and freedom . . . . Where humanitarianism is being destroyed and the innocent are being literally trampled into the ground . . . the soldiers, sailors, and airpersons . . . supported by fellow countrymen who recognize the cost in human sacrifice and in resources will forge in concert with our politicians . . . a most unique and exemplary place for Canada in the league of nations, united under the United Nations Charter.
>
> I hope this is okay.
>
> Thanks for the opportunity.
>
> Warmest regards,
>
> Dallaire

Ron Haviv-VII

A defaced photograph of a Muslim family found when they returned to their home after the Dayton agreement. The Serbs had
looted the family's furniture, appliances, cabinets, sinks, and window panes. The photo was virtually all that remained.

Chapter 11

Srebrenica: "Getting Creamed"

On July 11, 1995, a year after Tutsi rebels finally halted the Rwandan genocide and a full three years into the Bosnian war, Bosnian Serb forces did
what few thought they would dare to do. They overran weak UN defenses
and seized the safe area of Srebrenica, which was home to 40,000 Muslim
men, women, and children.

The Srebrenica enclave had been declared "safe" back in the spring of
1993, just after the Clinton administration abandoned its proposal to lift
the arms embargo against the Muslims and bomb the Serbs. Srebrenica was
one of six heavily populated patches of Muslim territory that the UN
Security Council had sent lightly armed peacekeepers to protect.

The UN had hoped that enough peacekeepers would be deployed to
deter Serb attacks, but President Clinton had made it clear that the United
States would not send troops, and the European countries that had already
deployed soldiers to Bosnia were reluctant to contribute many more
peacekeepers to a failing UN effort. Those blue helmets that did deploy
had a tough time. Sensing a Western squeamishness about casualties after
Somalia and Rwanda, outlying Serb forces frequently aimed their sniper
rifles at the UN soldiers. They also repeatedly choked off UN fuel and
food. By the time of the July attack on Srebrenica, the 600 Dutch peacekeepers were performing most of their tasks on mules and were living off
emergency rations. So few in number, they knew that if the Bosnian Serbs

ever seriously attacked, they would need help from NATO planes in the sky. In 1994 the Western powers had established a process by which UN peacekeepers in Bosnia could appeal for "close air support" if they themselves came under fire, and they could request air strikes against preselected targets if the Muslim-populated safe areas came under serious attack. In a cumbersome command-and-control arrangement meant to limit the risk to peacekeepers, the NATO foreign ministers agreed that "dual keys" had to be turned before NATO jets would be sent to assist UN troops in Bosnia. The civilian head of the UN mission, Yasushi Akashi, had to turn the first key. If this happened, then NATO commanders would need to turn the second. Most requests were stalled at the initial stage, as UN civilians were openly skeptical of NATO bombing. They believed it would destabilize the peace process and cause the Serbs to round up UN hostages, as they had done in November 1994 and May 1995.

When the Serbs called the international community's bluff in July 1995, their assault went virtually uncontested by the United Nations on the ground and by NATO jets in the sky. At 4:30 p.m. on July 11, the ruddy-faced, stout commander of the Bosnian Serb army, Ratko Mladic, strolled into Srebrenica. General Radislav Krstic, the chief of staff of the Drina corps, which had executed the attack, accompanied him. Krstic had lost his leg the year before when he ran over a mine planted by Muslim forces. So the victory was particularly sweet. With Krstic standing nearby, Mladic announced on Bosnian Serb television, "Finally, after the rebellion of the Dahijas, the time has come to take revenge on the [Muslims] in this region."[1]

Over the course of the following week, Mladic separated the Muslim men and boys of Srebrenica from the women. He sent his forces in pursuit of those Muslims who attempted to flee into the hills. And all told, he slaughtered some 7,000 Muslims, the largest massacre in Europe in fifty years. The U.S. response, though condensed in time, followed the familiar pattern. Ahead of and during the Serb assault, American policymakers (like Bosnian civilians) again revealed their propensity for wishful thinking. Once the safe area had fallen, U.S. officials narrowly defined the land of the possible. They placed an undue faith in diplomacy and reason and adopted measures better suited to the "last war." But a major difference between Srebrenica and previous genocides in the twentieth century was that the massacres strengthened the lobby for intervention and the understanding, already ripening within the Clinton administration, that the U.S. policy of nonconfrontation had become *politically* untenable. Thus, in the aftermath of the gravest single act of genocide in the Bosnian war, thanks to America's belated leadership, NATO jets engaged in a three-week bombing campaign against the Bosnian Serbs that contributed mightily to ending the war.

Warning

"The Sitting-Duck Position"

Diplomats, journalists, peacekeepers, and Bosnian Muslims had lived for a long time with the possibility that the Serbs would seize the vulnerable safe areas of eastern Bosnia. The enclaves were so unviable that U.S. intelligence analysts placed bets on how long they would survive. Richard Holbrooke had finally become involved in shaping America's Bosnia policy in September 1994 when he was appointed assistant secretary of state for European and Canadian affairs. He says he told the queen of the Netherlands that Dutch troops in Srebrenica were in the "Dien Bien Phu of Europe" facing a "catastrophe waiting to happen."

In June 1995 the UN force commander Bernard Janvier had unveiled a proposal at the Security Council to withdraw the blue helmets from the three eastern enclaves. He argued that peacekeepers were too lightly armed and few in number to protect Muslim civilians. U.S. ambassador Albright, a strong defender of what was left of Bosnia, exploded. She said Janvier's plan to "dump the safe areas" was "flatly and completely wrong." Albright had lost countless battles at the National Security Council to convince the president to order the bombing of the Serbs. Now, though she was rejecting Janvier's proposal as inhumane, she knew she could offer no suggestions as to how either the Muslim civilians or the lightly armed peacekeepers would survive in the face of Serb attack. The reality, obvious to all, was that the safe areas would be safe only as long as the Serbs chose to leave them so.

Many western policymakers secretly wished Srebrenica and the two other Muslim safe areas in eastern Bosnia would disappear. By the summer of 1995, both the Bosnian Serbs and the Muslim-led government were exhausted, and western negotiators thought they were closer than ever to reaching a settlement. But because the three eastern enclaves did not abut other Muslim-held territory, they were a recurrent sticking point in negotiations. The international community could not very well ask the Muslims, the war's main victims, to leave the enclaves voluntarily, especially since most of the Muslims inhabiting them had already been expelled from their homes in neighboring villages. The Muslim government would be lambasted by its own citizens if it handed over to the Serbs any of the few towns still in Muslim hands. And the Serb nationalists were not about to agree to a peace deal that preserved Muslim enclaves, which tied down Serb troops and kept nettlesome Muslims in their midst. The whole idea behind Republika Srpska had been the creation of an ethnically pure Serb state.

Whatever the West's secret hopes or stated fears that the enclaves would crumble, when the Serbs began their attack on Srebrenica on July 6, 1995, nobody besides the besieged Dutch peacekeepers and the Muslims within Srebrenica took it especially seriously. Mladic's forces began the attack by firing tank rounds at the white UN lookout cabins and sending the Dutch scrambling from their observation posts. The Serbs took Dutch hostages and stole their weapons, body armor, vehicles, and blue helmets and berets.

UN peacekeepers in Srebrenica were probably the least well informed of all the interested parties. Like Dallaire's hamstrung forces in Rwanda, the UN troops in Bosnia lacked an intelligence-gathering capacity of their own. The UN military observers (UNMOs) who provided the mission with its visual intelligence rarely spoke Serbo-Croatian and paraded around the countryside in luminous white four-wheel drives. Anybody interested in hiding anything could do so at the sight of the lumbering vehicles approaching. Thus, UN commanders depended upon intelligence input from the more powerful UN member states, who rarely delivered. If U.S. spy satellites or NATO planes picked up visual evidence or word of Serb troop advances toward Srebrenica, they did not share it with UN peacekeepers. Just as Dallaire's troops had to encounter militias in person if they hoped to document their activities, so, too, here, Dutch peacekeepers interested in learning the location of Serb troops had to patrol until they met up with Serb gunfire.[2] It was a twisted, Balkan game of blindman's bluff.

At the morning press conference in Sarajevo on July 8, the garrulous UN spokesman Gary Coward mechanically rattled off the names of the Dutch UN observation posts around Srebrenica that the Serbs had seized. When I approached him after the press conference and asked for his best estimate of the Serb objectives, he shrugged, grabbed a sheet of scrap paper from a nearby table, and drew a large, oblong circle meant to represent the safe area. "We think the Serbs want to do this," he said, blotting out the bottom third of the circle with scribbles. By taking control of the southern portion of the pocket, Coward and other UN analysts were predicting, the Bosnian Serbs could secure the hills that overlooked a crucial supply road. Coward then drew a second circle. "But we are afraid the Serbs want to do this," he said, scribbling out the entire circle so that nothing remained. "We simply don't know." The following day, when I asked Bosnian prime minister Haris Silajdzic to gauge Serb intentions, the prime minister pointed to the large map on the wall behind him. "You see those green dots?" he said, indicating the three specks representing the UN-declared safe areas in eastern Bosnia that were stranded apart from the rest of Muslim holdings. I nodded. "The Serbs want those to disappear," he said.

The Muslim-led government had cried wolf in the past often enough that it was difficult to know when to rely on its warnings. Silajdzic seemed to have received general alarms about Srebrenica's peril, but he did not know precisely what lay in store for the enclave's inhabitants. Certainly it seemed obvious that as winter approached the Serbs would seek to establish even more favorable "facts on the ground." Although the Serbs still controlled 70 percent of the country, the Muslim army had begun nibbling away at Serb gains. Deserted by Western nations, the Sarajevo government had begun receiving arms and advice from Islamic groups and governments around the world, and looked to get stronger with time. The Serbs needed to free up the 1,000 or so troops that ringed Srebrenica. Even without any intelligence, one only had to look at the map to know the Bosnian Serbs' strategic objectives.

Still, the Serbs' day-to-day plans were another matter. However untenable the isolated islands of thinly guarded territory, the map had also come to seem oddly destined to endure. Some combination of Serb caution, UN deterrence, NATO airpower, Muslim resistance, and historic inertia would leave the safe areas intact. No major Bosnian town had changed hands in the past two years, and most Balkan watchers had difficulty imagining outright conquest. Srebrenica in particular was a place that had captured headlines in 1993 when it was declared one of the six safe areas. But it had since faded from public concern.

Prime Minister Silajdzic's warning sounded more like a sigh than a siren. Bosnia's Muslims had suffered for so long and so prominently that after years of protestations—"How could you let this happen to us?"—most now seemed resigned to the outside world's indifference. The UN arms embargo remained in place. NATO planes flew overhead but had only undertaken a handful of pinprick bombings against Serb forces shelling the safe areas. Whenever the Serbs had rounded up and humiliated UN peacekeepers, the NATO powers had simply backed down. Western policymakers clung to their neutrality in the conflict and refused to line up behind the Muslims. Silajdzic's caustic fatalism reflected the mood in the capital, where people no longer dashed behind barricades at the hint of flying metal or moved circuitously around town to avoid deadly junctions. Most now chose the quickest route to their destinations. "If you run, you hit the bullet," the Sarajevo saying went. "If you walk, the bullet hits you." Foreigners who remained in the city had once been welcomed as messengers, but now they were reminders of an outside world that had watched Bosnia perish. Doors were slammed in the faces of reporters; the UN Protection Force (UNPROFOR) was mocked as the UN *Self*-Protection Force. With so many broken promises and broken lives, nothing could surprise the Bosnians. The prime minister sounded like a man who had run out of options:

> To whom am I supposed to talk at this stage? We know the American people have a sympathy for the underdog. They know what is happening to us, and it bothers them. But the American government talks only about its interest—which is to do as little as possible. Bosnia is not a vital U.S. interest, so why would America risk its name, credibility, and prestige here?

Yet there was defiance in Silajdzic's tone as well. "In the first year of the war, we were in great danger of disappearing from the earth, but Bosnia has escaped execution," he said. "We are now like men walking the streets saying hello to people who had seen us hanging from the gallows the day before." In fact, although many in the country had escaped death, the men of Srebrenica would not.

U.S. intelligence analysts had predicted Srebrenica could not survive, but when the attack began, they underestimated Serb intentions. At the CIA the *National Intelligence Daily* on July 9, 1995, stated that the Serb offensive against Srebrenica was "most likely to punish the Bosnian government for offensives in Sarajevo." It was also "a means to press a cease-fire." On July 10 the CIA assessment remained the same—the Serbs would not try to take the town because they would not want to deal with its inhabitants.[3]

They would "neutralize" the safe area rather than overrun it altogether. And on July 11 the chargé at the U.S. embassy in Sarajevo sent a cable at 6:11 p.m., nearly two hours after the enclave had already fallen, relaying the views of a "drained and downcast" Prime Minister Silajdzic:

> No consensus has formed among government and diplomatic contacts here as to the ultimate Serb military strategy, but most think it is interactive—that is, the [Bosnian Serb army] probes resistance and pushes until it locates an opportunity. [Muslim] officials now fear the Serb aim in Srebrenica is to "expel and occupy," the former being pursued with brutality. . . . Another contact summed up the Serbs' objective, "They want it all."[4]

Evidence gathered later indicates that the Serbs did in fact begin their offensive intending only to seize the southern section. But when they realized, to their amazement, that the Western powers would not resist, they opted to plow ahead and gobble the whole pocket.

The normally ambulatory and zealous press corps paid little attention to Srebrenica in advance of its fall. The American and European journalists based in Bosnia in the summer of 1995 had not visited the town, which the Serbs had sealed off since the spring of 1994. In addition, trapped in Sarajevo, journalists were stuck relying inordinately on the United Nations. And senior UN officials, long impressed with what they said was General Mladic's military acumen, had been conned by Serb assurances. The Dutch in Srebrenica first appealed to UN force commander Janvier to summon NATO air support on July 6. But he turned down that request and four others that followed, including a pivotal request the night before the Serbs' final push. Janvier did not believe the Serbs would go all the way. Indeed, even when the Serbs fired on Dutch forces on the ground, clearly warranting the use of force in self-defense, the French general remained frozen by his mistrust of NATO airpower and his trust of Serb promises. "I spoke to [Bosnian Serb general Zdravko] Tolimir and he says they do not intend to take the enclave," Janvier told a UN crisis team on July 10. "I believe him. If they do take the enclave, I'll draw my conclusions." Janvier also believed the Serbs when they claimed that Dutch peacekeepers had not been taken hostage. Tolimir had told him that any Dutch in Serb custody had "asked to be taken in . . . for their own safety."[5] In fact more than thirty Dutch peacekeepers had been forcibly disarmed and incarcerated.

By this stage in the war, Janvier and other UN officers processed intelligence through a lens of a preexisting prejudice that held that the Bosnian Muslims were the ones destabilizing the peace and provoking the Serbs. At this same July 10 meeting, Janvier stressed that it was the Bosnian Muslims who were attacking the Serbs and the Dutch in an effort to "push us into a path that we don't want." His civilian counterpart, Yasushi Akashi, shared this perspective, which helped justify UN refusals to summon NATO airpower. "The [Muslim army] initiates actions and then calls on the UN and international community to respond and take care of their faulty judgement," Akashi said. By 1995 senior UN officials spoke as if almost everything the Serbs did was merely "retaliatory," while everything the Muslims did was "a provocation."

There was a grain of truth to much of the UN rhetoric. The Bosnian Muslims did stage attacks from safe areas, which were supposed to be demilitarized. Indeed, for Bosnians and foreigners alike, there was no worse feeling than hearing a hefty Bosnian artillery piece being wheeled just outside their window and then fired into the Sarajevo night; the incoming barrage was always disproportionately punishing. But most of the raids were forays to retrieve food and supplies from neighboring Serb villages, revenge attacks for the sieges to which the Serbs were subjecting them, or efforts to recapture lands from which they had been purged. Sergio Vieira de Mello, who spent 1993 living under siege in Sarajevo as the head of UN civil affairs, recalls approaching the Bosnian Serbs about a particularly heavy week of shelling. Vieira de Mello first contacted Bosnian Serb political leader Radovan Karadzic to complain that for every sixty outgoing Bosnian rounds, the city of Sarajevo was earning 600 incoming. Karadzic claimed not to know what Vieira de Mello was talking about and referred him to Bosnian Serb military commander Mladic. When Vieira de Mello registered the same complaint with Mladic, the Serb general looked up and snorted, "*That* is the appropriate ratio."

If the first bout of wishful thinking occurred in not predicting that the Serbs would attack Srebrenica when they did, the second lay in not anticipating the speed with which the Serbs would seize the safe area. Seeing no response from Washington or New York, the Serbs, like the Rwandan Hutu government and militia before them, kept pressing. Many Muslims in Srebrenica expected the Serb assault would be temporary and the international community would intervene. One fifty-five-year-old Muslim later recalled:

> By July 11, UNPROFOR soldiers were in a constant retreat. . . . I
> locked the door of my house and joined the retreating civilians and
> soldiers. . . . So many people like myself thought that what was hap-
> pening would only be a temporary thing. . . . "It was a U.N. 'safe
> haven,' there is no way it will be allowed to fall," I thought. That's why
> I didn't take anything with me when I left my house. I just locked my
> door and figured I'd be back in a few hours or a few days at the
> longest. Now all I have with me—of all the things I owned—are the
> keys to the front of my house.[6]

While Muslim civilians coddled their house keys and mistakenly
looked to the UN for protection, the peacekeepers expected the town's
largely unarmed Muslim defenders to offer the first line of defense and
NATO airpower to supply the second. But crammed into what amounted
to an ethnic ghetto for more than two years and disgusted by the corruption of their local leaders, the morale of Srebrenica's Muslims had plummeted. Reluctant to fight, they were told for a long time they would not
have to. Up until hours before the Serbs entered Srebrenica, Colonel Tom
Karremans, the Dutch commander of UN troops in Srebrenica, promised
NATO air strikes. On July 10 Karremans met with Muslim military leaders and assured them that forty to sixty NATO planes would soon arrive
to stage a "massive air strike." "This area will be a zone of death in the
morning," Karremans told the desperate Muslim leaders, pointing to a
broad swath of territory that the Serbs had just occupied south of
Srebrenica. "NATO planes will destroy everything that moves," he said.[7]
That night Dutch peacekeepers and Bosnian soldiers and civilians kept
one eye on the sky, longing to see NATO bombers, and the other eye on
Serb trucks, armored personnel carriers, tanks, and infantrymen closing in
on the town. Because the United Nations had promised bombing, the
Muslims had not reclaimed the tanks and antiaircraft guns they turned
over to the UN in 1993 as part of a demilitarization agreement. They
knew that on their own they would eventually be overrun by Serb forces.
They needed the UN and NATO, and they feared that if they took back
their weapons, the blue helmets would use this as an excuse to shirk their
duty to defend the pocket.[8]

Finally, around midday on July 11, four hours after the Dutch commander in Srebrenica had submitted that day's futile request for NATO
assistance and five days after he had made his first appeal, a NATO posse of

eighteen jets set off from their base in Italy. Muslim civilians had already begun fleeing the town. When the NATO planes arrived overhead, one pair of U.S. F-16s could not find the Serb targets and another NATO pair bombed near a Serb tank with little effect. The Serbs threatened to kill Dutch hostages if air attacks continued, and the Dutch government and the United Nations commanders opted to negotiate a surrender.

While the bombers were roaring across the Balkans toward Srebrenica, at 2:30 p.m. Bosnian time, 8:30 a.m. back in the United States, President Clinton was deflecting a question from a reporter about the Serb attack.

"Sir," the reporter asked, "the Bosnian Serbs are moving into Srebrenica fast, according to reports. Is it time for NATO air strikes?"

"We may have something to say on that later today," the President said. "But let me say I'm concerned about the people who are there, and I'm also concerned about the UNPROFOR troops—the Dutch—who are there."[9]

Meanwhile, some 15,000 Muslims—most of whom were men, fewer than one-third of whom were armed, and none of whom believed that the UN would protect them—had taken to the hills in anticipation of Mladic's arrival. They had little chance of surviving a thirty-mile night-time journey through dense forests, scattered minefields, and Serb shell and machine-gun fire. Still, they preferred their dim odds to entrusting their fates to the Serb general who had commanded the brutal Serb war effort since 1992. Some 25,000 others, including the town leaders, remained in the enclave, certain that the international community would preside over their evacuation. They spent the evening of the 11th pressed up against a UN base in the small village of Potocari, four miles north of Srebrenica center, clambering to be allowed behind the protective UN sheath. Dutch commander Karremans reported to his UN superiors that the Muslims who had gathered outside UN gates were "in an extremely vulnerable position: the sitting duck position."[10]

Bosnian Serb general Mladic held the fate of Srebrenica's Muslims in his hands. Soon after seizing the town on July 11, he summoned Colonel Karremans for a pair of meetings at the local Hotel Fontana. Mladic delivered a blistering harangue and then insisted Karremans drink with him "to a long life," an image of amiability that was broadcast around the world. Off-camera, Mladic warned that if NATO planes reappeared, the Serbs would shell the UN compound in Potocari, where the refugees had gathered. Later, with Karremans looking on, Mladic asked the Muslim representative of the Bosnian government who had been called to negotiate whether the Muslims wanted to survive or "disappear."

AP/Wide World Photos

Bosnian Serb army General Ratko Mladic, left, drinks with Dutch Col. Tom Karremans, the commander of UN peacekeepers in Srebrenica, on July 12, 1995, the day after Serb forces seized the UN-declared "safe area."

Recognition

"They're All Going Down"

General Mladic arrived back in Srebrenica the next day, television cameras in tow. Looking well rested and tanned from the summer offensive, he urged the Muslims of Srebrenica gathered before him to be patient. He and his men were filmed passing out chocolates to young Muslim children. "Those who want to leave can leave," Mladic said. "There is no need to be frightened." Patting the head of a terrified young boy, Mladic offered soothing words that did not come easily to a man brusque by nature who was surrounded by thousands of people he had come to despise. "You'll be taken to a safe place," he said, assuring the anxious throngs that women and children would go first. Under general Krstic's logistic leadership, some fifty to sixty buses and trucks arrived in the next twenty-four hours to carry out the deportation.

The Serbs initially allowed Dutch peacekeepers to ride on the buses, but they quickly changed their minds. When a peacekeeper tried to prevent a

bus from being loaded without UN supervision, General Mladic grinned
and said, "I am in charge here. I'll decide what happens. I have my plans and
I'm going to carry them out. It will be best for you if you cooperate."[11]

In the next several hours at Potocari, the Serb general ordered men separated from women and children. While the UN soldiers looked on, armed
Serbs ripped fathers, brothers, and sons from the hysterical grip of the
women. Mladic claimed he was simply screening Muslim men for "war
crimes" or detaining them for a prisoner exchange. Eventually, they would
all be reunited in safety. Those who contested Mladic's order were brutally
punished. One Muslim woman described her horrific experience at the
UN base:

> At 4:00 [on July 12], they took my husband away. And then my son
> Esmir. . . . It is just so hard to talk about this, I can't, it just breaks my
> heart. . . . I was holding him in my arms. . . . We were hugging, but
> they . . . grabbed him and just slit his throat. They killed him. I just
> can't say anymore, I just can't, you have to understand that it is break-
> ing my heart. I'm still hoping the authorities or anyone can still get
> my other son or my husband free.[12]

Many westerners quickly overlooked Mladic's brazen deceits of recent
days and trusted Serb promises to adhere to the Geneva conventions. But
others saw the writing on the wall. Christina Schmidt, a German-born
nurse with Doctors Without Borders, sent her July 12 journal entry to the
organization's Belgrade office, which publicly transmitted it. "Everybody
should feel the violence in the faces of the [Bosnian Serb] soldiers directing
the people like animals to the buses," Schmidt wrote. "A father with his
one-year-old baby is coming to me, crying, accompanied by [Serb soldiers].
He doesn't have anybody to take care of the baby and [the Serbs] selected
him for . . . ? It's a horrible scene—I have to take the baby from his arm—
writing down his name and feeling that he will never see his child again."[13]

The Dutch around Potocari began finding bodies on July 12. One fourteen-year-old girl was found hanging from a rafter. The night before she
had been taken away by Serb soldiers for an hour and had returned with
blood running down her legs. A young Muslim boy led two Dutch soldiers to nine Muslims who had been executed. The boy waited quietly
while the peacekeepers snapped photos of the bodies. In the vicinity of the

town of Nova Kasaba, the Dutch drove by a soccer field and spotted thousands of Muslim men on their knees with their hands on their heads. A table had been set up to register them, and their small knapsacks and bags lay in the grass. When these same Dutch later heard single gunshots from the field, some began to suspect, in the words of one sergeant, "They're all going down."[14] Others allowed themselves to believe the tales told them by the Serbs: The gunshots were a "celebration" of enlistment of a new recruit. Or the areas the Dutch might like to inspect were "too dangerous," as "Muslim attacks" were ongoing.

UN officials at headquarters focused on the damage the fall of the safe area would do to the UN's reputation. At a July 12 meeting, Akashi, the top UN civilian, blamed the Muslims for their "provocation" and said, "It would help if we had some TV pictures showing the Dutch feeding refugees."[15] When asked at a press conference that day whether the fall of Srebrenica represented the UN's biggest failure in Bosnia, Secretary-General Boutros-Ghali answered: "No, I don't believe that this represents a failure. You have to see if the glass is half full or half empty. We are still offering assistance to the refugees . . . and we have been able to maintain the dispute within the borders of the former Yugoslavia."[16]

Unlike Dallaire, who rapidly relayed grisly reports from Rwanda and who seized any microphone placed in his vicinity, UN officials in the former Yugoslavia resisted publicizing atrocity reports. Officials at UN headquarters in New York ended up learning more from journalists than they did from their own delegates in the field. A piqued July 18 cable from headquarters to Akashi inquired: "What about the reports of mass murder coming from refugees? They are widespread and consistent and have been given credence by a variety of international observers. We have, however, received nothing on the subject from UNPROFOR."[17]

The women, children, and elderly the Serbs forced onto buses endured a ghastly journey from Potocari to just outside Tuzla, another of the Muslim-held towns that had been declared "safe" in 1993. On the two-and-a-half-hour drive, many pressed their faces up to the glass of the bus windows in the hopes of spotting their men. Bodies were strewn along the roadside, some mutilated, many with their throats slit. Trembling young Muslim men were coerced into giving the three-finger Serb salute. Large clusters of men, hands tied behind their backs, heads between their knees, sat awaiting instructions. The buses were frequently stopped along the way so that Serb gunmen could select the young, attractive women for a roadside rape. By 8 p.m. on July 13, the UN base near Srebrenica had been virtually emptied.

Citizens and policymakers in the United States and Europe followed this entire sequence. The western media reported the fall of the enclave, the alleged "screening" of the Muslim men for war crimes, and the terror of the bus journey.[18] The first suggestions of summary executions appeared on July 14. Although reporters were typically reluctant to extrapolate on the basis of individual reports of murders, Bosnian Muslim officials and refugees offered a devastating picture.

Reporters at the State Department asked spokesman Nicholas Burns whether he could verify that the Serbs were separating the men from the women, the children, and the elderly. Burns replied:

> I don't have specific information about elderly people, women, and children being separated from males. I do have information that a great number of people are being herded into a football stadium. Considering what happened three or four years ago in the same area at the hands of the same people, the Bosnian Serb military, we are obviously concerned, greatly concerned, gravely concerned about this situation. And we are sending a public message today to the Bosnian Serbs that they have a humanitarian responsibility to treat these people well.

Yet the only threat he issued on behalf of the United States was that Serb gunmen would eventually be held accountable at the UN war crimes tribunal.[19] President Clinton made no threats.

The Bosnian ambassador to the UN, Mohammed Sacirbey, received reports of massacres that were more disturbing than any he had heard before. He had been told that the men General Mladic brought to the stadium had been killed en masse. Sacirbey telephoned Ambassador Albright with the report. A cable from the U.S. embassy in London to the State Department on July 13 related Sacirbey's "alarming news" that the Bosnian Serbs were committing "all sorts" of atrocities. It was public knowledge that women between fifteen and thirty-five were being singled out and removed from buses, while boys and men were being taken away to unknown destinations.

For all the outrage among world leaders over what the Serbs had done, policymakers did not readily make the leap from the dismay over the Serbs' seizure of UN-protected territory to alarm about the fate of the people who had lived within it. Ambassador Sacirbey attempted to keep the focus at the UN on the safe area's living contents. "The most important thing to keep in mind," Sacirbey kept telling people, was that "the safe area is gone, but the safe area was not the land; it was the people, and they can still be saved." But as they had done during the genocide in Rwanda, senior U.S. and UN officials behaved as if they were conducting business as usual. UN special representative Akashi sent a bland cable to New York on July 14 that described the food stocks and the shelter needs of the women and children arriving in Tuzla and the status of Dutch hostages. Only in the eighth paragraph of the second page did Akashi casually reference the missing Muslim men, stating, "We are beginning to detect a short-fall in [the] number of persons expected to arrive in Tuzla. There is no further information on the status of the approximately 4,000 draft age males."[20] In the U.S. government, none of the atrocities that had occurred in Bosnia or Rwanda in the previous three years had made the threat to distant foreigners any less abstract. "People are very far from these issues," Holbrooke says. "Very few people in Washington have ever visited a refugee camp. They feel really detached from the stakes." The capacity and willingness of Western policymakers to imagine what was occurring out of range of the cameras was limited. But this could not be forgiven by the limits of experience alone. "Going to a refugee camp might help," National Security Adviser Anthony Lake notes. "But not having gone to a refugee camp is not an excuse for not having an imagination."

John Menzies, a foreign service officer who had long favored bombing the Serbs and had signed the "dirty dozen" letter prepared by Bosnia desk officer Harris back in April 1993, had recently been nominated to become U.S. ambassador to Bosnia. On July 13, 1995, he met with Hasan Muratovic, the Bosnian president's chief confidant. Menzies remembers Muratovic, a typically unflappable operator, "utterly flapped." Muratovic made wild appeals for NATO planes to drop radios into the Srebrenica enclave so the disoriented men who were trying to escape might use them to find a safe exit out of the woods. "He was at a loss for constructive ideas," Menzies recalls. "I had never seen this level of helplessness." Over the next several days, Menzies could do nothing more than relay Muslim distress signals to Washington. He heard little encouragement from his political masters.

Response

The Constraint: The Rules of the Road

When the safe area fell, U.S. policymakers considered themselves constrained by two fundamental facts. First, as a policy matter, the United States would not deploy its troops on the ground in the Balkans to wage war; that remained nonnegotiable. Second, though many in the Clinton cabinet backed the idea of NATO air strikes from the skies, they believed the United States was at the mercy of the "dual-key" arrangement that had placed one key in the hands of UN officials (backed by European governments) determined to stay neutral in the conflict. U.S. officials "did not like" the mechanism, they said, but the "rules of the road" had been established and the United States had to live with them. Reporters were told to steer their inquiries toward the Europeans who had peacekeepers in Bosnia. Clinton's campaign promises long forgotten, Spokesman Burns said the United States was "not a decisive actor" in the debate:

> We've chosen not to put troops on the ground because we don't believe it is in the vital interests of the United States to do so, which should always be the standard when a decision is made to put American troops into battle, combat situations. We took that decision, the last administration took that decision, this administration has reconfirmed, reaffirmed that decision, and that is United States policy. So therefore, the United States has influence on the margins.[21]

There was much the United States might have done. It might have used the Serb seizure of Srebrenica and the ghastly television images to convince its European allies to rewrite the rules of the road in urgent fashion. It might have threatened to bomb the Serbs around Srebrenica and elsewhere in Bosnia if their troops did not depart the enclave, turn over the male prisoners unharmed, or at the very least stop shelling the Muslims who were in the woods trying to escape. It might have acted preemptively, warning the victorious Serbs that they would be met with stiff retaliation if they turned their sights on Zepa, the safe area just south of Srebrenica, which was home to 16,000 vulnerable Muslims. If the United States failed to win support for such an aggressive response, and if the allies refused to support bombing, senior U.S. officials might, at the very least, have made the fate of the Muslim men their chief diplomatic priority. They might have warned Serbian president Slobodan Milosevic that economic sanctions would be stiffened and prolonged if the men in Mladic's custody were ill treated. They might have carefully tracked the whereabouts of the prisoners so as to send a signal to Mladic, Krstic, and the other Serb officers that they were being watched. Instead, the United States did none of the above.

With the preexisting constraints on policy internalized, U.S. officials did not take a very active role in tending to the crisis. As Sandy Vershbow, the director for European Affairs on the National Security Council at the time, recalls, "We assumed the worst. We weren't on a war footing around the clock. We just sort of watched helplessly from the sidelines."

The day after Srebrenica's fall, French president Jacques Chirac, known as "Le Bulldozer," called for the reestablishment of the safe area by force. Bosnian Serb political leader Karadzic scoffed, saying, "There will be no withdrawal. Srebrenica belongs to us."[22] UN and U.S. officials also dismissed the French idea as "unfeasible." Chirac kept at it, calling President Clinton on July 13 to say the separation of the sexes reminded him of World War II. "We must do something," Chirac said. "Yes," Clinton agreed. "We must act."

But "action" was a relative term. To Chirac it meant using U.S. helicopters to ferry French troops into the enclave to recapture Srebrenica. To Clinton this scheme was harebrained, and no other actions leapt to mind. After hanging up the telephone, Clinton muttered that only NATO bombing seemed to produce results. He turned to the young naval aide who had arranged the phone meeting with Chirac. "What do you think we should do on Bosnia?" the president asked. "I don't know, Mr. President," the aide stammered.[23]

While the Clinton administration watched helplessly, the Muslim men hoped helplessly. By the evening of July 13, in the words of a subsequent UN investigation, the Muslim men of Srebrenica belonged to one of four categories: those alive and trying to escape through the woods; those killed on that journey; those who had surrendered to the Serbs and had already been killed; those who had surrendered and who would soon be killed.[24]

The United States, which had some five spy satellites operating in space at all times, snapping some 5,000 images per day, did not even concentrate on tracking the fate of the men. Each time a satellite camera clicked, it captured a 100-square-mile chunk of territory. When analysts knew precisely what they were looking for and, better yet, where they were looking, photo images could be invaluable. They could depict foreign troop locations, additional buildings at suspect nuclear weapons sites, and even mass graves. But competition to secure images was fierce, as the satellites were accounted for every minute of every day. The satellites over Bosnia took pictures from an SMO, or support-to-military-operations, perspective. They tried to detect Serb troop movements or locate Serb air defense systems that could take aim at NATO overflights. Unless explicitly instructed to do so, intelligence analysts did not spend their days counting specks that looked like men in stadiums or speculating about faint shadows that might hint at recently overturned earth around burial pits. Somebody senior in the U.S. policy community would have had to request a shift in the flight pattern and a reorientation of the analysts. This did not happen. "We weren't analyzing these pictures in real time for atrocity," Assistant Secretary of State for Intelligence and Research Toby Gati recalls. "We were analyzing whether NATO pilots were vulnerable." The analysts of intelligence data are trained to tell policy planners what they want to know, not necessarily what they should know. They are warned not to volunteer information or to make policy recommendations. Indeed, the CIA even boasts an ombudsman to guard against politicization and deter analysts from overreaching or drifting into advocacy of any kind. As one CIA official said, however, "It is tough to draw the line between what is politicized analysis and what is an agent simply saying, 'You're stupid and wrong.'"

Even if intelligence officials had been told to find evidence of atrocities, they might not have been able to detail the killings immediately. Sifting through the available data, analysts say, can be the equivalent of trying to drink water from a fire hose.[25] Gati claims that even a concerted campaign to track the fate of the men could have left them stumped: "Say we had taken these photographs and noticed the men disappear from the fields. No people can mean they've been taken somewhere. No people can mean the Serbs are beating the crap out of them. But no people doesn't necessarily mean the Muslims are dead." Still, an administration that announced it was monitoring the Bosnian Serbs and their captives might at least have made some Serbs think twice before they obeyed Mladic's murderous orders.

Srebrenica's missing men and boys were not entirely forgotten. After one of her conversations with Ambassador Sacirbey in New York, Ambassador Albright did make inquiries. On July 14, 1995, she phoned Deputy National Security Adviser Sandy Berger and, on his suggestion, asked the intelligence community to try to find evidence corroborating Sacirbey's tip. It is not entirely clear what happened next. Perhaps the National Photographic Interpretation Center's special team that analyzes satellite and U-2 spy-plane imagery did not get around to it until later, as some have reported.²⁶ Or perhaps the photo analysts reviewed their images quickly and reported back that they could not corroborate the reports. Either way, no senior administration official remained on top of the issue, demanding daily updates on the location (and welfare) of the men in Mladic's custody. If the photo analysts looked, they looked without urgency. As one former senior U.S. intelligence official put it, "It's one thing to say, 'Hey, take a look, if you don't mind.' It's another thing entirely to say, 'God damn it, these men are in danger and may even be dead. Let's find out immediately! I mean *now!*'"

Fighting the Last War

The United States has a tendency to "fight the last war" in response to genocide. U.S. officials processed Cambodia through the prism of Vietnam, the Kurdish slaughter through the Iran-Iraq war, and Rwanda through Somalia. With Srebrenica, the precedent that informed international humanitarian and U.S. policy judgments was not an actual war. It was the August 1992 battle for access to Serb concentration camps. Then, when *Newsday*, ITN, and the *Guardian* produced photos of emaciated prisoners and refugee accounts of torture, starvation, and executions, the Bush administration had tailored its threats to secure inspection visits. "We will not rest . . . until we get access to the camps," President Bush had said. And in fact, though the vast majority of Bosnian citizens continued to live under terrifying siege, American and European demands for access did enable the Red Cross to begin inspections. The harshest of the camps were closed down, and the treatment of prisoners in some of the others was said to have improved.

By 1995 Western policymakers were experienced in dealing with Serb brutality and atrocity, and they expected to see patterns repeated. At the July 12, 1995, State Department press briefing, Nicholas Burns responded to a reporter's grilling by saying that "given past practice," the United States did "have a number of concerns about the capacity and the inclination of the Bosnian Serb forces to treat well and justly captives." In 1992, he said, the Serbs "displayed for all the world to see brutal tendencies" toward Muslim prisoners. "They should not repeat those very grave and serious mistakes now," he warned. "They should treat these people well."[27] Burns never imagined that captivity would not be an option open to Srebrenica's Muslim men and boys.

Western officials focused their diplomatic efforts on demanding access for the International Committee for the Red Cross. They expected slowly but eventually to ameliorate camp conditions. "We had the Omarska model in our mind," remembers John Shattuck, U.S. assistant secretary of state for human rights. "We assumed we would eventually get access to these guys and that they'd be badly roughed up." Many would be beaten in slow torture, they would be starved, they would be humiliated, and some would even be killed. But most would be kept alive to dig trenches or to serve as booty in a prisoner exchange. The Serbs were presumed rational actors, who followed predictable patterns. "There was nothing in the history of that war, brutal as it was," Gati recalls, "that would indicate Mladic would kill every last one of them."

Senior officials in the United States who were now focusing on Bosnia around the clock did not really consider the possibility of extermination. National Security Adviser Lake remembers: "I had been paying attention long enough to imagine the Serbs would do something truly awful, but I wasn't imagining 'a Srebrenica' because it hadn't happened before. There was still room for shock. It was like Vietnam: You knew how terrible it was, you came to expect the worst, but you could still be shocked by My Lai."

Assistant Secretary Holbrooke rejects the claim that what followed in Srebrenica could have surprised senior Clinton administration officials. "We didn't need specific intelligence to know that something terrible was going on," Holbrooke says. "In fact, the search for intelligence is often a deliberate excuse to avoid or at least to delay action. We knew what needed to be done. If we'd bombed these fuckers as I had recommended in November and in May, Srebrenica wouldn't have happened."

The United States and its European allies responded generously to the 20,000 Muslim refugees who were arriving harried but alive in Muslim territory. They erected a sprawling tent city on the Tuzla air base, where Muslim women and children were fed, sheltered, and given medical care. Muslim men were conspicuously absent.

The State Department ranks had been emptied of some of the young officers who might have risen in the open forum to clamor for rescue. And the policy divisions within Clinton's cabinet were predictable. Even the most activist of Clinton's senior advisers had accepted that although they would like to change U.S. policy, they could not do so in time to affect the fates of the Muslims purged from Srebrenica. "Once the men were in Mladic's custody," one State Department official explains, "we forgot about them because we knew we could no longer address their futures."

In the week after the fall of Srebrenica, the traditional division of labor unfolded. Relief organizations, human rights groups, and UN agencies attempted to process the sea of Muslim displaced persons in Tuzla. Diplomats and politicians weighed the geopolitical implications of the fall of the safe area and debated how to respond to the Serb assault on Zepa and likely future attacks on other Muslim territory. UN officials thought first and foremost about the fate of Dutch peacekeepers who remained in Mladic's custody. And it was left to the Swiss-based ICRC to tend to the fates of the Muslim prisoners from Srebrenica. The ICRC was a small nongovernmental organization with no muscle behind it and a library of conventions that had gone unheeded in the past. It was tapped to perform the function it had always performed—negotiating access with the Serbs, compiling lists of missing, and inspecting prisoner conditions. When its requests for access were ignored, the organization did not blare an alarm. Red Cross officials, who operate on the basis of the consent of all parties and who try to keep a low profile, hoped that the next day would bring better luck.

Just as the Iraqi government had done while it was gassing the Kurds, the Serbs stalled brilliantly during this period, employing tactics that they had mastered in the war. They never *refused* access to international observers; they granted it so as not to arouse suspicions but then blocked or "postponed" it on the grounds that they could not guarantee the safety of visitors. Despite the repetitiveness of the sequence, diplomats and ICRC officials joined the pantomime, failing to grasp that they had a very short time to influence Serb behavior.

Murder

The vivid and consistent testimony about murder continued to pour in from Muslim refugees, and the suspicions of a handful of U.S. government officials were stirred. On July 16 the *Washington Post* began reporting gruesome refugee accounts of mass executions. A teenager, Senada Cvrk, recalled watching some twenty young Muslim men be taken away on the evening of July 12. The following morning, before her bus left, she went to fetch water in a field outside an old car battery factory where the refugees had sought shelter. There she found her friends stacked in a pile, dead, their hands tied behind their backs.[28] Other Muslims described to the American media rapes and throat-slittings carried out before their eyes. The major newspapers and television outlets brimmed with graphic depictions of Serb butchery. On July 17 the CIA's Bosnia Task Force wrote in its classified daily report that although it lacked "authoritative, detailed information," refugee accounts of atrocities "provide details that appear credible."[29]

In 1993 President Clinton had appointed Peter Galbraith as U.S. ambassador to Croatia. Galbraith's heroics in northern Iraq in 1991 had earned him plaudits from the influential senators Al Gore and Daniel Patrick Moynihan. At the time of the seizure of Srebrenica, Galbraith happened again to be back in Vermont, where he had read the *New York Times* story about the gassing of the Kurds seven years before. Like Holbrooke, Galbraith had visited Bosnia, including the Manjaca concentration camp, in 1992. He had interviewed Muslim refugees and survivors for the Senate Foreign Relations Committee and had recommended using NATO airpower to stop Serb aggression. Galbraith was now incredulous that the United States could be allowing the fall of the safe area, the deportation of more than 20,000 Muslim women and children, and the detention and possible execution of the Muslim men. On the basis of his experience with Cambodians and Kurds, he quickly surmised that the men in Mladic's custody had already been murdered. "People don't just disappear," he recalls. "Once we didn't hear from them and once we couldn't get access to the area, we knew. How could we not know?" He says he spent much of that week on the phone with Assistant Secretary Holbrooke. Both men spoke of resigning out of despair over the U.S. response to the safe area's fall. Holbrooke arranged a meeting for Galbraith with Secretary of State Christopher on July 17, the first one-on-one meeting Galbraith had ever been granted with the secretary, who made his dislike for the outspoken ambassador known. Galbraith feared that neither Srebrenica's land nor Srebrenica's Muslim men could be saved. He did not believe that he had a prayer of convincing Christopher to roll back Serb gains. But he spoke out against the massacres because he did believe that credible U.S. threats of bombing were still needed to save Muslims in the nearby safe area of Zepa, which Mladic had begun attacking on July 14 and which was guarded by just seventy-nine peacekeepers. Galbraith met with a stone wall. Christopher and virtually all other U.S. officials were already convinced that Zepa could not be saved. It was, they said, "indefensible." Action would be futile.

The following day Vice President Al Gore, another of the administration's longtime proponents of bombing, joined the high-level conversation. He said he believed events in Bosnia constituted genocide. "The worst solution would be to acquiesce to genocide and allow the rape of another city and more refugees," Gore said in a Clinton cabinet meeting. "We can't be driven by images, because there's plenty of other places that aren't being photographed where terrible things are going on," Gore acknowledged. Nonetheless, he added, "We can't ignore the images either." The cause of consistency could not be allowed to defeat that of humanity.

The *Washington Post*'s John Pomfret had just filed an arresting report on the atrocities from Tuzla. The piece began:

> The young woman died with no shoes on. Sometime Thursday night she climbed a high tree near the muddy ditch where she had camped for 36 hours. Knotting a shabby floral shawl together with her belt, she secured it to a branch, ran her head of black hair through the makeshift noose and jumped. . . . She had no relatives with her and sobbed by herself until the moment she scaled the tree.[30]

Gore told the Clinton cabinet that in the photo that accompanied Pomfret's story, the woman looked around the same age as his daughter. "My twenty-one-year-old daughter asked about that picture," Gore said. "What am I supposed to tell her? Why is this happening and we're not doing anything?" Srebrenica provided Gore, Albright, and Holbrooke with an opening to restart the conversation about NATO bombing. Although Gore gave every appearance of challenging the president, witnesses say his remarks were in fact less geared to convert Clinton than they were aimed at senior officials in the Pentagon, who remained unconvinced of the utility of using airpower. "My daughter is surprised the world is allowing this to happen," Gore said, pausing for effect. "I am too." Clinton said the United States would take action and agreed, in Gore's words, that "acquiescence is not an option."[31]

A Muslim refugee from Srebrenica who hanged herself
in despair. The woman, who
was in her early twenties,
was found hanging by a torn
blanket at the Tuzla air base
on July 14, 1995.

AP/Wide World Photos/Darko Bandic

On July 19, in a confidential memorandum Assistant Secretary for
Human Rights Shattuck delivered a preliminary account of the Serb abuses and argued that the other safe areas should be protected:

> The human rights abuses we are seeing hearken back to the very
> worst, early days of "ethnic cleansing." In Bratunac [a town near
> Srebrenica], 4,000–5,200 men and boys are incarcerated and the
> Bosnian Serbs continue to deny access to them. Another 3,000 sol-
> diers died as they fled Srebrenica, some taking their own lives rather
> than risking falling into Serb hands. There are credible reports of sum-
> mary executions and the kidnapping and rape of Bosnian women.[32]

Shattuck urged the protection of the remaining safe areas, arguing that the
Muslims in Bosnia's safe areas had relied on the "international community's
promise," which was "clear, proper and well-considered." He argued that a
failure to act would mean not only the fall of the safe areas but a UN withdrawal. If the Europeans pulled out their peacekeepers, the United States
would have to follow through on prior pledges to assist in their evacuation.

This would be messy and humiliating. Shattuck warned, "U.S. troops will be on the ground helping the UN force pull out while Bosnian Serbs . . . fire upon them, and fearful Muslim civilians try to block their exit." This was the image that most haunted U.S. policymakers, and Shattuck hoped the threat of bloody U.S. involvement down the road would tip the balance in favor of immediate intervention.

The most detailed early evidence of the Bosnian Serbs' crimes came on July 20, 1995, when three Muslim male survivors staggered out of the woods with the bullet wounds to prove what to that point had simply been feared: Mladic was systematically executing the men in his custody.

A lack of food, water, and sleep and a surfeit of terror had left the men delirious. But they told their stories first to Bosnian Muslim police and then to Western journalists. Each account defied belief. Each survivor had prayed and assumed that his experience had not been shared by others. There were uncanny parallels in the killing tactics described at three different sites. Some massacres took place two by two; others twenty by twenty. The men were ordered to sit on buses or in warehouses as they waited their turn. One man remembered the night of July 13, which he spent on a bus outside a school in Bratunac. The Serbs pulled people off the buses for summary execution. "All night long we heard gunshots and moaning coming from the direction of the school," the man said. "That was probably the worst experience, just sitting in the bus all night hearing the gunfire and the human cries and not knowing what will happen to you." He was relieved the following morning when a white UN vehicle pulled up. But when the four men dressed as UN soldiers delivered the Serb salute and spoke fluent Serbian, he realized his hoped-for rescuers were in fact Serb reinforcements who had stolen Dutch uniforms and armored personnel carriers.[33]

At the Grbavici school gym, several thousand men were gathered and ordered to strip down to their underwear. They were loaded in groups of twenty-five onto trucks, which delivered them to execution sites. Some of the men pulled off their blindfolds and saw that the meadow they approached was strewn with dead Muslim men. One eyewitness, who survived by hiding under dead bodies, described his ordeal:

> They took us off a truck in twos and led us out into some kind of meadow. People started taking off blindfolds and yelling in fear because the meadow was littered with corpses. I was put in the front row, but I fell over to the left before the first shots were fired so that

bodies fell on top of me. They were shooting at us . . . from all different directions. About an hour later I looked up and saw dead bodies
everywhere. They were bringing in more trucks with more people to
be executed. After a bulldozer driver walked away, I crawled over the
dead bodies and into the forest.[34]

The Serbs marched hundreds of Muslim prisoners toward the town of
Kravica and herded them into a large warehouse. Serb soldiers positioned
themselves at the warehouse's windows and doorways and fired their
rifles and rocket-propelled grenades and threw hand grenades into the
building, where the men were trapped. Shrapnel and bullets ripped into
the flesh of those inside, leaving emblazoned upon the walls a montage of
crimson and gray that no amount of scrubbing could remove. The soldiers finished off those still twitching and left a warehouse full of corpses
to be bulldozed.[35]

Remarkably, Muslim survivors of the massacre continued to hope. Only
hours after Serb soldiers had shot up the warehouse and its human contents,
one Serb returned and shouted, "Is anyone alive in there? Come out. You're
going to be loaded onto a truck and become part of our army." Several men
got up, believing. The Serbs returned again a while later, this time promising
an ambulance for the wounded. Again, survivors rose and left the warehouse. One Kravica survivor who laid low and eventually escaped remembers his shock at the credulity of his peers. He also remembers his own
disappointment on hearing successive rounds of gunshots outside.[36]

Graves

On July 21, 1995, the allied leaders gathered in London for an emergency
conference meant to iron out a new Bosnia policy. The Zepa enclave still
hung in the balance, and the evil in Srebrenica had been broadly publicized. But the allies stunned Bosnia's Muslims by issuing what became
known as the London declaration. The declaration threatened "substantial
and decisive air-power," but only in response to Serb attacks on the safe
area of Gorazde, one of the few Bosnian safe areas *not* then under fire. The
declaration did not mention Sarajevo, which continued to withstand fierce
artillery siege; Zepa, which had not yet fallen; or the men of Srebrenica,
some of whom were still alive.

A convoy of Dutch peacekeepers departed Srebrenica the same day. They arrived to a heroes' welcome at UN headquarters in Zagreb. At a press conference the Dutch defense minister announced that the Dutch had seen Muslims led away and heard shooting. He also said they had heard that some 1,600 Muslims were killed in a local schoolyard. The rumors, he said, were too numerous and "too authentic" to be false. Yet this was the first the Dutch had spoken publicly about their suspicions. Moreover, apart from the defense minister's grim reference, he presented a relatively mild general picture. He complained that the Serbs were still denying the Red Cross access to some 6,000 Muslim prisoners. When the dazed Dutch commander Karremans spoke, he praised Mladic for his "excellently planned military operation" and reflected that "the parties in Bosnia cannot be divided into 'the good guys' and 'the bad guys.'"[37] That night at a festive UN headquarters in Zagreb, the Dutch drank and danced well into the early morning.

On July 24 the UN special rapporteur for human rights for the former Yugoslavia, onetime Polish prime minister Tadeusz Mazowiecki, described the findings of his week-long investigation. He said 7,000 of Srebrenica's 40,000 residents seemed to have "disappeared." He appealed to the Western powers to ensure that Zepa's 16,000 residents not meet the same fate. Zepa's Muslim defenders continued to hang on, even though the UN had already announced that it would not summon air strikes to aid their defense.[38]

On July 27, 1995, Mazowiecki announced his resignation. He was sickened by the UN refusal to stand up to the Serbs in Srebrenica and Zepa. In his resignation letter, he wrote:

> One cannot speak about the protection of human rights with credibility when one is confronted with the lack of consistency and courage displayed by the international community and its leaders. . . . Crimes have been committed with swiftness and brutality and by contrast the response of the international community has been slow and ineffectual. . . . The very stability of international order and the principle of civilization is at stake over the question of Bosnia. I am not convinced that the turning point hoped for will happen and cannot continue to participate in the pretense of the protection of human rights.[39]

When Galbraith returned to his post in Croatia, he received even more damning news about the Srebrenica men. His fiancée, a UN political officer, happened to be in Tuzla, where she overheard a UN interview with one

of the male survivors of a mass execution. On July 25, 1995, Galbraith sent
Secretary Christopher a highly classified, "No Distribution" cable headed,
"Possible Mass Execution of Srebrenica Males Is Reason to Save Zepa":

> 1. A UN official has recounted to me an interview she conducted of a
> Srebrenica refugee in Tuzla. The account, which she felt was highly
> credible, provides disturbing evidence that the Bosnian Serbs have
> massacred many, if not most, of the 5,000 plus military age men in
> their custody following the fall of Srebrenica.
> 2. If the Bosnian Serb army massacred the defenders of Srebrenica, we
> can be sure a similar fate awaits many of the 16,000 people in Zepa. The
> London Declaration implicitly writes off Zepa. In view of the numer-
> ous accounts of atrocities in Srebrenica and the possibility of a major
> massacre there, I urge reconsideration of air strikes to help Zepa. . . .
> 3. If this account is accurate, there may be no survivors of the men
> rounded up in Srebrenica. We should redouble efforts to see these
> men. If the Serbs refuse access, the implications are obvious.
> 4. Again, it is not too late to prevent a similar tragedy at Zepa. Zepa's
> defenders valiantly continue to hold on. Undoubtedly they realize the
> fate that awaits them. They should not be abandoned.

The cable had no effect on UN or NATO policy toward Zepa, which surrendered two days later. Most of the men there who entrusted their fates to
the Serb authorities were murdered.

Immediately after receiving Galbraith's cable, Secretary Christopher dispatched Assistant Secretary for Human Rights Shattuck and Assistant
Secretary of State for Refugees Phyllis Oakley to Tuzla to verify the survivors' claims. The United States was far quicker to debrief survivors and
witnesses than it had been in Charles Twining's days at the Cambodian
border. Shattuck prepared a detailed report on the basis of two days of
interviews with a dozen Muslim refugees, including two survivors of mass
executions—a teenage boy, and a fifty-five-year-old crippled man.
Shattuck reported back to Washington: "It is impossible at this point to
estimate accurately how many have been killed, but clearly that number is
very substantial. The accounts that I have heard . . . indicate that there is
substantial new evidence of genocide." Yet knowing that the United States
did not intend to deploy ground troops, bomb unilaterally, or immediately
rally its European allies into multilateral action, the only recommendation

Shattuck mustered was that further war crimes indictments be issued at the UN criminal tribunal that had been set up at The Hague.[40]

Shattuck's findings finally prompted a serious review of U.S. intelligence data for evidence of mass executions. Since the Muslim survivors had supplied Shattuck with the precise names and locations of alleged killing sites, the CIA could scan the aerial photos that its satellites had snapped over the past few weeks with geographic coordinates in mind. On August 2, 1995, a CIA imagery analyst stayed up all night examining the hundreds of aerial photos around the small village of Nova Kasaba near Srebrenica. He noticed severe discrepancies. In one spy photo several hundred prisoners were gathered at the neighborhood soccer field where the Dutch had spotted them. Several days later the prisoners had vanished and four mounds of earth, testaments to fresh digging, appeared nearby. The *National Intelligence Daily* reported this evidence on August 4, and Albright pressed for its public release. At a closed session of the UN Security Council on August 10, Albright presented enlargements of the photographs that showed the movement of earth. The evidence indicated these were mass graves:

- newly disturbed earth where refugees were known to have been;
- heavy vehicle tracks where there were none shortly before;
- no apparent military, industrial, or agricultural reason for such tracks or disturbed earth;
- multiple, confirming reports from refugees; and
- no vegetation on the site.

Albright concluded, "The Bosnian Serbs have executed, beaten, and raped people who were defenseless. They have carried out a calculated plan of atrocities far from a battlefield and with the direct involvement of high-level Bosnian Serb Army officials. There can be no excuse."[41] Albright declared:

Innocent lives remain at stake. Some 10,000 civilians from Srebrenica and around 3,000 from Zepa are missing and unaccounted for. Some may be in hiding. Some may be in detention. Some are most certainly dead. We have a responsibility to investigate, to find out what we can, to see that those in hiding are granted safe passage; that those in detention are well-treated or released; that the names of those who died or who have been killed are made known to their families; and

that those responsible for illegal and outrageous activities are brought
to justice.

Something evil had transpired, but even those most prepared to believe the
worst could not have believed *how* evil.[42]

No amount of wishful thinking or reenergized U.S. diplomacy could
change a most grisly fact: In the month since Srebrenica had fallen, and
mainly in the ten days after the Muslim surrender, Ratko Mladic and his
associate Radislav Krstic had overseen the systematic slaughter by ambush
or execution of more than 7,000 Muslim men and boys.

It would not have mattered if the United States had predicted precisely
when the Serbs would attack Srebrenica. Zepa fell more than a fortnight
after Srebrenica in plain view of the international community, revealing
that the will to confront the Serbs was absent in the face of full knowledge.
"The failure was not an intelligence failure," says Assistant Secretary Gati.
"Ethnic cleansing was not a priority in our policy. . . . When you make the
original decision that you aren't going to respond when these kinds of
things happen, then, I'm sorry, but these things are going to happen."

The United States tried to defend its intelligence and its policy failure.
This was difficult. Clinton officials were reluctant to admit they knew the
Serbs were going to do what they did and yet had done nothing about it.
But to admit that they had not predicted the Serb onslaught revealed other
weaknesses. Several weeks after the Serb victory, the State Department circulated a "bottom lines" memo, which supplied officials with press guidance. When challenged, U.S. officials were to say the United States knew
no more in advance than the United Nations about any Serb plan to take
the enclave, and it did not have evidence of Bosnian Serb troop movements. One U.S. official scribbled a reminder to himself in the corner of
the memo that Srebrenica had been besieged for nearly three years and the
Bosnian Serbs could have launched a military attack at any time. "We did
assess that all of the eastern enclaves were indefensible unless reinforced by
ground units and supported by close air support," the note said. On the
question of the likelihood of atrocities, U.S. officials were urged to fudge
their response by saying, "We did not have any information on any
[Bosnian Serb] intent to commit atrocities against the Muslim defenders or
population of Srebrenica. We did know of the possibility of such activity
given the history of genocide and ethnic cleansing in the Balkans."[43] State
Department and White House officials and others deplored the "failure,"

the "tragedy," and the "imperfect reality." But they were careful not to accept responsibility for the demise of the enclave, as they did not want to own the problem, which showed no signs of subsiding.

A few days after Srebenica's fall, White House spokesman McCurry entered into an exchange with a reporter over whether the United States was ashamed:

> McCurry: I think everybody in this government has consistently said that it's a devastating situation and nobody is satisfied with the performance of those who have been entrusted with the will of the international community to keep the peace.
> Reporter: But do we feel—do we accept the fact that we bear some responsibility for what happened?
> McCurry: There's no way to assess responsibility for all the tragedy that is Bosnia. You have to look back over the work of this administration, the previous administration; frankly, you've got to look back into decisions taken by many governments in many different places.[44]

Meanwhile, State Department spokesman Burns claimed that the administration was working behind the scenes with its European allies to develop a military strategy. Moreover, he said, much as had U.S. spokespersons during the Rwanda genocide, that the United States was providing an additional $5 million to deliver food, shelter, and water to "meet immediate needs in Srebrenica."[45] Burns stressed that the United States was on the ball. "We will meet any request that they give to us," he continued, "because we do feel a sense of urgency."[46]

But feeling a sense of urgency and acting urgently were two different matters. In order for the Clinton administration to *act* on its feeling, the war in Bosnia would have to become caught up in American domestic politics. It was Bob Dole, the seventy-two-year-old, wisecracking Republican senator from Kansas, who brought Bosnia home.

Aftermath

Bob Dole, the Senate majority leader, had been committed to a more activist U.S. foreign policy in the Balkans since 1990, when he had watched

Serb police maul the throngs of Kosovo Albanians who had come out to greet his American delegation. Dole's own witnessing had sparked a sustained engagement with the region. His chief foreign policy adviser, Mira Baratta, a Croatian American attuned to Serb aggression, spurred him on further. Dole had been consistently critical of U.S. policy under Bush and Clinton. By the summer of 1995, he was regarded as the chief Republican challenger to Bill Clinton in the 1996 presidential election. Thus, he was well positioned to make the fall of Srebrenica a subject for American politics. This was the first time in the twentieth century that allowing genocide came to feel politically costly for an American president.

All along, the central criticism of U.S. policy made by human rights advocates, engaged members of Congress, and dissenters within the State Department had been that it was timid. The central criticism of the same policy made by UN officials and America's European allies was that it was rhetorically tough, practically weak or indifferent, and thus doing more harm to the Bosnian Muslims than if the United States had stayed uninvolved entirely.

A shift in U.S. policy had been in the works even before Srebrenica's demise. Indeed, by the spring of 1995, it was already clear that the UN peacekeeping mission in Bosnia could not survive. In mid-June, at a Bosnia briefing meeting with his senior advisers, President Clinton had been testy about the way the United States had floated along without a policy. It had allowed nationalists in the Balkans to dictate the course of change. "We need to get the policy straight," he had snapped, "or we're just going to be kicking the can down the road again. Right now we've got a situation, we've got no clear mission, no one's in control of events."[47] Most outside observers thought the president was in control.

After Mladic conquered Srebrenica on July 11, the pressure on Clinton to do more came from a number of sources, both domestic and foreign. First, congressional criticism, which had always been harsh but never overwhelming, rose to a fever pitch. With Dole's leadership, it culminated in a decisive congressional vote for a unilateral lift of the arms embargo against Bosnia's Muslims, which would likely necessitate a U.S. military role in withdrawing UN peacekeepers. Thus, for the first time in the three-year war, the maintenance of the status quo seemed destined to draw U.S. troops into the Balkan theater. Second, journalists, activists, former administration officials, and others who had likewise badgered administration officials on and off throughout the war erupted in unison, making life unbearable for those in the White

House defending American nonintervention. Third, disgusted by America's partial engagement, European leaders began publicly slamming the administration for its pusillanimity and hypocrisy. The Serb seizure of Srebrenica and the ongoing war in Bosnia gave rise to a crisis of American leadership.

Congressional Pressure

In early January 1995, nearly three years into the war, and two years after he had teamed with Senator Biden to try to get the Pentagon to arm the Muslims, Dole had introduced a bill to the U.S. Senate calling for the lifting of the arms embargo. He had spoken about it quite combatively throughout the spring of 1995. Even before the events of the summer, Dole had won the support of many Democrats on Capitol Hill who saw the bill as a way to voice their dissatisfaction with Clinton's Bosnia policy. Tired of the administration's delays, Dole was determined to bring the bill up for a vote in July.[48]

That it was Bob Dole who cared about Bosnia presented President Clinton with a problem. On the surface, Dole did not seem a particularly formidable presidential candidate. He had run twice before, both times when Yugoslavia was still a single country, and had fared abysmally. But now the combination of Dole's own war experience, his apparently nonpartisan commitment to the Balkans, and the ghastly images of Srebrenica's petrified refugees gave his voice a heightened authority. With the UN mission in Bosnia collapsing, the American political establishment seemed ready to listen. Dole's bid to lift the embargo against the Muslims did not just represent another clash between the executive and the legislature over foreign policy. It was a clash between a presidential incumbent and his challenger. Clinton did not want to appear weak in front of American voters.

Clinton made other arguments. Just as the Reagan White House had argued during Galbraith's sanctions crusade against Iraq, Clinton insisted that foreign policy should not be made on Capitol Hill. But his real fear was that Dole's initiative would force him to send U.S. troops to Bosnia. The president had publicly promised to deploy U.S. ground forces only if there was "a genuine peace with no shooting and no fighting" or in the "highly unlikely" event that British and French peacekeepers attempted to withdraw and were "stranded and could not get out of a particular place in Bosnia."[49] European governments had made it clear that they would withdraw if the U.S. Congress ever lifted the embargo. Thus, if Dole's initiative passed, it would nearly guarantee that Clinton would have to follow through on the commitment he had made to his NATO allies to help extract their blue helmets. Clinton had been avoiding sending U.S. ground forces to the Balkans from his first day in the White House. He was certainly going to do all he could to avoid a humiliating extraction mission on the eve of his bid for reelection.

Clinton was haunted by the secret NATO withdrawal plan, known as operation 40–104. It committed the United States to deploying some 25,000 troops as part of a 60,000-troop NATO extraction force. As one senior administration official told the *New York Times* on July 8, three days before Srebrenica's fall, "If you were to ask the President and his senior advisers what their greatest fear in Bosnia is, they would give the same answer: [Operation] 40–104."[50] This fear had caused Clinton to begin arguing ahead of Srebrenica's collapse that the United States needed to "bust its rear" to get a peace deal settled. Otherwise, he feared, a U.S. deployment would be "dropped in during the middle of the campaign."[51]

In drawing attention to Bosnia's plight, Dole's motives were not only humanitarian. Although the Senate majority leader knew he was not going to win many presidential votes because of Bosnia per se, he came to the same conclusion that Clinton had reached in 1992 when he began sniping at President Bush over the issue. He saw that the president's policy toward Bosnia revealed larger defects. But if Dole might pick up a stray political point or two, his long track record of concern for the suffering of people in the Balkans indicated that the prime reason he hounded Clinton about his Bosnia policy was that he wanted to see it changed.[52] And he was not alone.

As Dole campaigned for ending the embargo, he put to use the same acerbic streak that American voters would complain about the following year when they reelected Clinton. On July 10, the eve of the Serb seizure of Srebrenica, Dole dramatized the perils of the status quo in an angry speech on the Hill. He said that the notion that UN peacekeepers could be relied upon to protect the Bosnian Muslims required a game of "multilateral make-believe":

> In order to believe that the United States and European approach in Bosnia is working, one simply has to play a game I call "let's pretend." The rules are simple. It goes like this:
> Pretend that the U.N. forces are delivering humanitarian aid to those in need;

Pretend that the U.N. forces control Sarajevo airport;

Pretend that the U.N. forces are protecting safe havens such as Sarajevo and Srebrenica and that no Bosnians are dying from artillery assaults and shelling;

Pretend that there is a credible threat of serious NATO air strikes;

Pretend that the no-fly zone is being enforced;

Pretend that Serbian President Milosevic is not supporting Bosnian Serb forces; . . .

Pretend that U.N. forces can stay in Bosnia forever and that we will never have to contemplate U.N. withdrawal.[53]

Noting that several UN observation posts had been overrun and Serb tanks were within a mile of the town of Srebrenica, Dole argued that despite the UN presence, "Bosnians are still being slaughtered, safe areas are under siege, and the United Nations continues to accommodate Serb . . . brutal aggression and genocide."[54]

That evening, as Serb gunners inched toward Srebrenica's downtown, Clinton and his national security team dined with the congressional leaders of both parties at the White House in an effort to persuade them of the dangers of lifting the embargo. Dole declined the dinner invitation.

Dole had of course earned his right to speak out about war and suffering fifty years before the fall of Srebrenica. After returning from Europe in a cast from head to toe, he had been forced to relearn walking, eating, and dressing. Although his Armenian American doctor in Chicago had performed masterful reconstructive surgery, Dole had remained unable to use his right arm. The mere acts of buttoning his shirt, donning his laceless shoes, and brushing his teeth became challenges. At the Senate Dole was known for awkwardly toting a pen in his right hand to remind handshakers that they would have to make do with the left. Dole's motto had always been, "There are doers, and there are stewers," and the gritty senator believed that the UN, Europe, and the United States had done nothing but stew over Bosnia.

With the fall of the Srebrenica enclave on July 11, Dole went berserk. For the next three weeks, he focused on virtually nothing besides getting his arms embargo bill, which was cosponsored by Joseph Lieberman (D.–Conn.), through both houses of Congress. He spoke on the Senate floor six times and made endless television appearances, shuttling from one studio to another. Like Lemkin, Dole became a one-man lobby. All the arguments that the Clinton team had been making to defend the embargo had proven hollow with the Serb conquest and UN humiliation. On the day of Mladic's victory, Dole declared:

> The main argument made by the administration in opposition to withdrawing the U.N. forces and lifting the arms embargo on Bosnia was that such action would result in the enclaves falling and would lead to a humanitarian disaster. Well, that disaster has occurred today—on the U.N.'s watch, with NATO planes overhead. . . . Mr. President, . . . what will it take for the administration and others to declare this U.N. mission a failure? Will all six safe areas have to be overrun first?[55]

Clinton defenders, too, took to the airwaves, complaining that Dole's bill would force the withdrawal of UN peacekeepers and thus create a void that American troops would have to fill. Dole said the stakes were sufficiently high in Bosnia that, if it came to that, he would support carefully planned U.S. military involvement. He also rewrote the legislation so that the lifting of the embargo would follow and not itself force a UN exodus. Yet administration officials continued to charge him with taking measures that would irresponsibly "Americanize" the Bosnian war. Dole methodically rebutted each of their claims. On *This Week with David Brinkley,* for instance, he pointed out that it was President Clinton who was Americanizing the problem:

> My view is President Clinton [has] already made two promises to send American troops. If there's peace, he'll send 25,000 to keep the peace. He'll send 25,000 to help extricate the French and the British and the Dutch and others who have forces on the ground. That would be Americanization. We're talking about lifting the embargo with no American involvement—it would seem to me a big difference. . . . The Serbs have been the aggressors. We've known it. We've done nothing for 2 1/2 years, and that's why Congress—not Bob Dole—that's why Congress, Democrats and Republicans, say, "Enough is enough."[56]

The Clinton administration went into overdrive to quash what White House spokesman McCurry called the "nutty" Dole-Lieberman initiative. John Shalikashvili, Colin Powell's successor as the chairman of the Joint

Chiefs of Staff, and Secretary Christopher visited Capitol Hill in order to press senators to delay their vote. In response to the administration's complaints about Dole's timing, the Kansas senator said he had been told that all along. "It is always a bad time," he said. "We have waited and waited and waited, hoping something good might happen. But nothing good has happened."[57]

On July 19, 1995, Clinton telephoned Dole to ask him to postpone the vote until after the allied leaders had met in London. The president insisted the meeting would yield a more assertive Western policy. Dole reluctantly agreed. But when Dole heard the London declaration write off Srebrenica, Zepa, and Bihac, he condemned what he called "another dazzling display of ducking the problem" and rejected further delay.[58] "Today there are reports of more NATO military planning," Dole said on July 24. "But planning was never the problem. Executing those plans was and still is the problem. This debate has never been about policy options, but about political will."[59] Dole, and not the president, had become America's spokesman about the outrages inflicted by the Serbs.[60]

Dole had always been a master of the barb, but the sardonic senator was also skilled at going it alone, an approach that was not well suited to rallying enough votes on Capitol Hill to override Clinton's inevitable veto. It was not that Dole was unliked. Despite a faltering beginning in the Senate in which a Republican colleague had described him as "so unpopular, he couldn't sell beer on a troop ship," his twenty-seven years on Capitol Hill had earned him wide respect.[61] But if Dole had become an effective Senate majority leader, he was not always good at asking for help, whether with his coat buttons or with legislation. Once, when Dole had been scheduled to appear on *Face the Nation,* an aide realized that the senator had gotten lost somewhere in the studio. After searching the premises, he finally found Dole standing alone facing a heavy set of double doors. Dole could not open the doors himself and did not dream of asking for assistance. Instead the senator looked up and noted, "Got some doors here."[62]

When it came to the arms embargo issue, though, Dole's stubbornness proved more virtue than vice. He did not take to the Senate floor to wax in grandiloquent, romantic prose about honor, liberty, or the right of self-defense. Instead, he let the television images of thousands of frantic Muslim refugees do the convincing. He earned by repetition what he forfeited in style. In his characteristically choppy, guileless manner, he delivered on a nearly daily basis a simple set of arguments about the administration's failed policy and its consequences both for the Muslims of Bosnia and for the United States.

Dole was not without help. In February 1994 a handful of the State Department dissenters, including Marshall Harris and Steve Walker, who had resigned, and Jim Hooper and John Menzies, who had remained, had met with George Soros, a Hungarian Jew who had come to the United States as a teenager, made his fortune, and recently begun devoting some of his earnings to humanitarian causes. Soros called the meeting because he felt that those who opposed the Clinton policy were protesting in a diffuse manner. They needed to combine their efforts. Soros's chief advisers were Aryeh Neier, who had left Human Rights Watch and become president of Soros's philanthropic organization, and Morton Abramowitz, the career diplomat who had departed the State Department in 1992 and become president of the Carnegie Endowment for International Peace, where he began pushing for U.S. military intervention in Bosnia. With Soros's backing, the group formed a new organization, the Action Council on Peace in the Balkans. The council would build a concerted grassroots and elite lobby for intervention in Bosnia. Hooper remembers, "It had long become clear that lobbying from the inside was not going to work. The only way we would change the policy would be to change the climate outside the building." Between its founding in 1994 and the fall of Srebrenica, the group had published press releases and op-eds, built a formidable, bipartisan letterhead of notables, and helped gather a number of Jewish and other grassroots groups together in an Action Committee to Save Bosnia.

When Dole launched his crusade to lift the embargo in July 1995, the council offered its support. Harris, unemployed since Congressman McCloskey's defeat, was hired to codirect the council with fellow State Department resignee Steve Walker. Harris thus found himself back on Capitol Hill, this time in his new role as a lobbyist. "This was not a pleasant experience," Harris remembers. "Going up to people and asking, 'I know you don't want to, but would you do this?' It was quite awkward, awful really." In addition to generalized lobbying, the council commissioned military analyses in order to combat Pentagon claims that neither using NATO airpower nor lifting the embargo would affect the situation on the ground. "Suddenly, we had military people on our side, saying, 'Yes, it can be done,'" remembers Baratta, Dole's chief foreign policy adviser. "They spelled out in detail which weapons would be effective against Serb hardware, and how the Muslims could supply themselves."

Administration officials fought back, mustering a familiar set of arguments they hoped would quash enthusiasm for the Dole–Lieberman bill.
UN peacekeepers and, soon, U.S. soldiers would be jeopardized, they
argued. Lifting the embargo would be futile because the Muslims would
not know how to use the weapons, and it was unclear who would supply
them. And worst of all, the measure would have perverse consequences
because, as Undersecretary of State Peter Tarnoff noted, despite Dole's
claims that the situation could not get any worse, "That senator is wrong. It
can get a lot worse."[63] But the limits of the imagination now came in
handy. It was impossible to conceive of a worse predicament for Bosnia's
Muslims. The futility, perversity, and jeopardy arguments that held sway for
so long were no longer persuasive. The consequences of America' nonintervention had become too visible and too dire.

On July 26, 1995, the Senate voted 69–29 to require the United States
to stop enforcing the arms embargo. The bill authorized a breaking of the
arms ban only after the United Nations troops had departed Bosnia or
twelve weeks after the Muslim-led Bosnian government requested their
withdrawal. President Clinton could also request unlimited thirty-day
waivers. Still, it was the most stinging repudiation of U.S. policy yet.
Virtually all the Senate's Republicans (forty-eight senators) and almost half
the Senate Democrats (twenty-one senators) voted for the bill. Dole
declared after the vote, "This is not just a vote about Bosnia. It's a vote
about America. It's a vote about what we stand for. About our humanity
and our principles."[64]

For the Democrats who broke ranks with President Clinton and joined
Republicans in serving up a challenge to the president's foreign policy,
Srebrenica had been the key. "For me the turning point was the attack on
Srebrenica, that weekend with all the missing people," said Senator Dianne
Feinstein of California, who had previously opposed lifting the embargo.
"One image punched through to me: that young woman hanging from a
tree. That to me said it all."[65]

At a news conference with President Kim Young-sam of South Korea
the day after the vote, Clinton attempted to deny he had a leadership problem, shifting the blame for the Senate vote to the United Nations and former president George Bush. "You can't go about the world saying you're
going to do something and then not do it," Clinton said, reproaching the
United Nations for failing to call for NATO air strikes. He said his leadership was not at fault. "This distribution of responsibility all grew out of a

decision made prior to my Presidency—which I am not criticizing, I say again—to try to say: 'O.K., here's a problem in Europe. The Europeans ought to take the lead.'"⁶⁶ While publicly Clinton was dodging responsibility, privately the president of the United States was in a panic.

Media/NGO Pressure

With the fall of Srebrenica, the Clinton administration began to experience a hint of what life might be like under siege. Op-ed writers, human rights activists, former diplomats, and journalists had spoken out quite forcefully throughout the war in opposition to Clinton's policy, but nothing ignited their fury quite like the fall of the so-called safe area. The events of mid-July provoked a rare degree of unanimity on the editorial pages in the United States, and those in Paris and London as well. Indeed, as Charles Trueheart of the *Washington Post* pointed out, "Such is the outrage at western impotence, and at the particular failures of leaders, that sometimes the atrocities of the combatants in Bosnia are given short shrift."⁶⁷

In the *Washington Post* and *New York Times* alone, the list of critics in the week after the fall of the enclave included Anthony Lewis, William Safire, Jim Hoagland, George Will, Margaret Thatcher, Zbigniew Brzezinski, Brent Scowcroft, Charles Gati, Robert Kagan, Charles Krauthammer, Anna Husarska, and George Soros. Lewis, a longtime critic, wrote that the fall "calls into question the future of the North Atlantic Alliance" and wrote that it pointed to "the vacuum of leadership in the White House." Richard Cohen of the *Washington Post* described Clinton's "big-mouth, no-stick" administration. Safire wrote that Clinton's "failure of nerve" had turned "a superpower into a subpower."⁶⁸ In the pages of the *New Republic,* Zbigniew Brzezinski, the last national security adviser to a Democratic president, offered a presidential speech that he said could be given "if the post of Leader of the Free World were not currently vacant." The *New Republic* devoted an entire issue to the fall of Srebrenica. The magazine's inimitable literary editor Leon Wieseltier wrote:

> The United States seems to be taking a sabbatical from historical seriousness, blinding itself to genocide and its consequences, fleeing the moral and practical imperatives of its own power. . . . You Americanize the war or you Americanize the genocide. Since the

United States is the only power in the world that can stop the ethnic cleansing, the United States is responsible if the ethnic cleansing continues. Well, not exactly the United States. The American president is an accomplice to genocide. Not so the American people. The president of the United States does not have the right to make the people of the United States seem as indecent as he is. He has the power, but he does not have the right.[69]

Even onetime noninterventionists changed their tune. President Bush's former national security adviser, Brent Scowcroft, who had so opposed using force during 1992, said something different was now at stake: "Now we have a new element involved, and that is just a total collapse of confidence in both the capability and the will of the West, and we cannot afford to let that happen." When asked whether it was worth some American casualties to stop the Serbs, Scowcroft did not hesitate. "Yes. Yes," he said.[70]

The determined press corps was merciless with the State Department and White House spokesmen Nicholas Burns and Mike McCurry. In the week after the safe area's demise, they pounded Clinton's defenders with spirited soliloquies and snide rebukes. Nearly every question posed was preceded by a long summation of U.S. moral failure. Just a few samples of the reporters' questions follow.

On July 12, a reporter to Burns:

> You speak of the U.N. as if it's some distant operation on the moon. I mean, the State Department does. Doesn't—number one—the U.S. have the authority to ask NATO to carry out bombing raids that the president of the United States proposed when he was running for office but dropped when he got elected? Number two, don't you have the moral authority in the United Nations? Why are you going around polling the Europeans before you decide what your position is?

On the 14th, to McCurry: "Is anybody at the White House the least bit ashamed of what's happened to the Bosnians in Srebrenica who trusted U.N. and U.S. policy?"

On the 14th, to Burns:

> Nick, you can filibuster all you want and spew out as many words as you want and talk about despicable and brutal, but the truth is words don't

matter in this case anymore, and they haven't for a long time. So the question is, what action, if any, is the international community willing to take in order to do something about the situation which you, yourself, have gone on repeatedly describing in, you know, horrible terms?

On the 14th, to Burns: "You say that you're very considerate about the stability of the alliance and everything. But what happens to the NATO alliance if this genocide continues? Isn't it totally discredited as an organ which can prevent these things from happening in the heart of Europe?"

On the 17th to Burns:

> With all of the meetings you were describing earlier . . . the United
> States is sort of asking questions and waiting for somebody else to
> answer. . . . Doesn't the United States have to take some kind of a
> leadership role in figuring out how to do it and—and, you know, let
> the others ask you questions? Why aren't you giving out some
> answers and, in fact, taking the lead on this?

On the 18th, to McCurry: "A lot of people in this country seem to think your policy is nutty and a charade. . . . So my point is, are you going to continue this alleged policy of neutrality when people are being slaughtered?"[71]

Many journalists had developed a personal interest in Bosnia when the Bush administration had backtracked over the August 1992 camp revelations. Now, three years later, their anger seeped into their reporting. ABC news anchor Peter Jennings had just completed his third hour-long documentary on the West's failure in Bosnia. He had been just blocks from the Sarajevo market in February 1994 when sixty-eight Bosnians had been massacred. He was disgusted. "Once again Bosnian civilians are forced to flee their homes in terror," Jennings said, introducing a story that led the news, "while the Western European nations and the United States do nothing about it."[72]

The Holocaust was invoked almost immediately after the UN collapse. The State Department press correspondents made the argument that foreign service officers Hooper, Fox, Johnson, Harris, and Western had long made: The United States was *again* allowing genocide to proceed. One reporter asked, "You realize the historical precedent for that, when, of course, the State Department also didn't act 60 years ago?" Another reporter accused the administration of a "business as usual" response, which was exactly "how the United States government reacted in 1939 to a totally parallel situation."[73]

William Safire lamented the triumph of "Nazi-style ethnic cleansing" and said that in the face of the "central moral-military challenge of his Presidency," Clinton will be remembered as a man who "feared, flinched and failed."[74] Charles Gati, a former State Department official and Holocaust survivor, scolded the Clinton administration in the July 13 *Washington Post*:

> President Clinton, please go to see the people of Srebrenica. Tell them "never again" was meant for domestic consumption. . . . Secretary Perry, please go to see the people of Srebrenica. Tell them our defense budget will increase, and we'll make sure our military remains second to none. We are, and will be, ready to fight two regional wars at the same time. But tell them that you can't tell them which two wars we're waiting to fight—it's top secret—but neither of the two is for Srebrenica. Surely the people of Srebrenica will understand that our generals want another bomber, not another quagmire. Sorry, our vital interests are not at stake. . . . Wherever they may be and however many of them are still alive, the people of Srebrenica will appreciate such a candid exposition.[75]

House Speaker Newt Gingrich echoed Dole's charges in the Senate, calling Bosnia "the worst humiliation for the western democracies since the 1930s."[76] French president Chirac commented endlessly on the crisis, likening the world's reaction to the fall of Srebrenica to British and French appeasement of Hitler in Munich. Appearing on *Nightline,* Holbrooke, an in-house bombing advocate, called it "the greatest collective failure of the West since the 1930s." Soros repeated the appeasement charge and said the Serbs had manipulated the UN "much as Nazi Germany used Kapos in the concentration camps."[77] Anthony Lewis scorned the notion that the Europeans could leave their troops in Bosnia and attempt to negotiate a peace. "You can't do business with Hitler. So the world learned when Neville Chamberlain boasted that cringing to Adolf Hitler at Munich in 1938 had brought 'peace in our time.' To Hitler, diplomacy was just an interlude on the way to military victory."[78] The same was true, Lewis and others insisted, with the Serbs.

In response to White House claims that NATO military action might "reignite the war" and jeopardize the cruelly misnamed "safe areas," George Will asked how one could "reignite a conflagration" and reminded readers: "This fatuity calls to mind the 1944 letter in which the U.S. assistant secretary of war, John J. McCloy, said that one reason for not bombing Auschwitz and railroad lines leading to it was that doing so 'might provoke even more vindictive action by the Germans.' Wouldn't have wanted to anger the operators of the crematoriums."[79]

National Public Radio's Scott Simon worried that the Holocaust comparisons, though apt, may have given onlookers additional excuses to do nothing. The Holocaust and the Cambodian and Rwandan genocides had set too high (or low) a standard for American concern or action. "We can watch the murder, rape and plunder of Bosnia's Muslims, but then reassure ourselves that the numbers don't compare yet with the efficient cruelty of Auschwitz or the acres of skulls that made a grisly mosaic across the killing fields of Cambodia," Simon said on *Weekend Edition:*

> Intelligent and informed people have learned to reason themselves out of action. We know the news now well enough to observe that more people have been slaughtered more quickly in Rwanda than in Bosnia. Or even that Sarajevo, a city besieged by war, can suffer as many sniper deaths over a weekend as the number of gun shot [sic] deaths in New York or other American cities beset by crime. No war crime short of Hitler seems to impress us. How close do such atrocities have to resemble the Holocaust for reasonable people to feel that there is only so much genocide they will accept?[80]

For the first time in their history, a number of human rights groups overcame their opposition to using force and called for military intervention to stop the Serb genocide. Two weeks in advance of the fall of the safe area, Holly Burkhalter, advocacy director at Human Rights Watch, had urged her organization to ask the UN to bus the Muslims out of Srebrenica. It was clear the enclave could not be defended by so few peacekeepers. Her colleagues, defenders of the Muslim cause, had declined, saying it was "the UN's job" to defend Srebrenica's civilians. On July 20, with the safe area overrun, Burkhalter published an op-ed in the *Washington Post* entitled "What We Can Do to Stop This Genocide." She noted that the Bosnian Serb effort to eliminate the non-Serb population "in whole or in part" constituted a "textbook case of genocide" that the United States was legally obligated to stop. "Every American who has visited the Holocaust Museum leaves thinking, 'I wish we could have helped before so many died.'" Burkhalter wrote. "This time we can." She appealed to Clinton to call for U.S. army volunteers to join the Europeans protecting the remaining safe areas, to turn over U.S. intelligence to the UN war crimes tribunal, and more immediately, to do everything possible to locate the missing men. "The detention sites should be identified and opened and those people still alive within them released," Burkhalter urged.[81]

A coalition of twenty-seven organizations, most of which had not previously supported the use of military force anywhere, issued a press release demanding military intervention: "Force must be used to stop genocide, not simply to retreat from it. American leadership, in particular, is required. . . . Nothing else has worked." Among the signatories were the American Jewish Committee, the American Nurses Association, the Anti-Defamation League, the American-Arab Anti-Discrimination Committee, Refugees International, World Vision, Physicians for Human Rights, and Human Rights Watch.[82] "You cannot imagine what a big deal this was for some of these groups," Burkhalter recalls. "I mean, never in history had many of us argued for military force. Even the Quakers signed on." Human Rights Watch director Kenneth Roth used the opportunity to go before the HRW board and urge it to settle upon a standard of killing that would trigger calls for military intervention in the future. After heated debate, Human Rights Watch decided that henceforth anytime that "genocide or mass slaughter" could be diagnosed around the world, the group would have to put aside its mistrust of military power and recommend armed intervention. In the Cambodia era, human rights groups had assumed that the U.S. government could do no right. Now, two decades later, after Rwanda and Srebrenica, many were urging the United States to do right *with bombs.*

European Pressure

A third influence on the administration fell into the class of what even strict constructionists of the U.S. national interest might categorize as "vital": U.S. relations with its European allies had decayed to their lowest point since NATO was founded after World War II.

Before July, when the Clinton administration had rejected a complete partition of Bosnia, the Europeans had muttered under their breaths about American meddling. After the fall of Srebrenica, they aired their displeasure publicly. Chirac had been inaugurated as French president on May 17. When he called for the United States and France to team up to reconquer Srebrenica, Clinton was caught off-guard. Chirac's proposal made it difficult for the United States to continue blaming its European allies for inaction. This time Clinton was the one who appeared to be declining a European proposal for military confrontation. Holbrooke remembers, "Chirac basically said, 'If you're not getting in, we're getting out.' This was a dramatic change in the dynamic."

Senior officials in London, Paris, and Bonn described their mounting exasperation with Washington's refusal to live up to its traditional role as leader of the Atlantic alliance. Chirac was asked whether America's reluctance to send troops into Bosnia was undermining U.S. leadership. The *Washington Post* quoted his response: "There is no leader of the Atlantic alliance." Similar frustrations were voiced in London as well. "I don't remember a time where there was so much scorn for American policy," Lawrence Freedman, professor of war studies at Kings College, University of London, told the *Post*. "You don't find anyone here who thinks the U.S. is acting properly. We're told that what we're doing isn't good enough, but there's no attempt to help us."[83] The Europeans were fed up with what Harold Nicolson described in his account of President Woodrow Wilson's failure at Versailles in 1919: "America, eternally protected by the Atlantic, desired to satisfy her self-righteousness while disengaging her responsibility."[84]

The humiliation associated with the fall of Srebrenica ate at Clinton. The occurrence of such savagery in the heart of Europe made him look weak. For the first time, he believed that events in Bosnia might impede other coveted aims. One of Clinton's senior advisers remembers, "This issue had become a cancer on our foreign policy and on his administration's leadership. It had become clear that continued failure in Bosnia was going to spill over and damage the rest of our domestic and foreign policy." Clinton saw that the United States had to make its own decisions. Passivity in the face of Bosnian Serb aggression was no longer a viable policy option.

In these turbulent July days, Clinton often sounded more moved by the damage the fall of Srebrenica was doing to his presidency than by its effect on the lives of defenseless Muslims. On the evening of July 14, the president, who was on the White House putting green, received a briefing from Sandy Berger and Nancy Soderberg, his numbers two and three on the National Security Council. He recognized that he was finally in danger of paying a political price for nonintervention. In a forty-five-minute rant strewn with profanities, Clinton said, "This can't continue. . . . We have to seize control of this. . . . I'm getting creamed!"[85]

At the July 18 meeting where Vice President Gore alluded to the young woman who had hanged herself, Clinton said he backed the use of robust airpower, declaring, "The United States can't be a punching bag in the world anymore."[86] The discussion, though influenced by an awareness of genocide, was rooted in politics first and foremost. Srebrenica was gone; Zepa would soon follow. Clinton had to stop the cycle of humiliation.

U.S. inaction reflected so poorly on the president that even Dick Morris, Clinton's pollster, lobbied for bombing. Morris later recalled that "Bosnia had become a metaphor for Clintonian weakness." He was surprised by Clinton's attitude. "I found that every time I discussed Bosnia with the president, we ran into this word *can't* over and over again," Morris remembered. "'What do you mean *can't?*' I said in one meeting. 'You're the commander in chief; where does *can't* come from?'"[87]

Endgame

With the Clinton presidency implicated, the Bosnian war had to be stopped. Back in June, National Security Adviser Lake had urged Clinton's cabinet members to decide what they wanted a reconstituted Bosnia to look like and work backward. Lake had been trying to get the foreign policy team to think strategically so they did not get perpetually bogged down in crisis management. On July 17 Lake finally unveiled his "endgame strategy" at a breakfast meeting of the foreign policy team. The United States would take over the diplomatic show and back its diplomacy by threatening to bomb the Serbs and lift the embargo.[88] President Clinton took the unusual step of dropping in on the meeting. Clinton said he opposed the status quo. "The policy is doing enormous damage to the United States and our standing in the world. We look weak," he said, predicting it would only get worse. "The only time we've ever made progress is when we geared up NATO to pose a real threat to the Serbs."[89]

Time was short. On July 26, 1995, the U.S. Senate had passed the Dole-Lieberman bill to end U.S. compliance with the embargo. On August 1 the House of Representatives followed suit, authorizing the lift by a veto-proof margin. The Serbs had begun amassing troops around the safe area of

Bihac. Clinton and Lake agreed the time had come to inform the Europeans of the new U.S. policy. They were able to use Dole's embargo legislation as leverage in order to "lay out the marching orders." In a marked contrast with earlier periods in the war and with their complete neglect of the Rwanda genocide, the president's national security advisers met twenty-one times between July 17 and Lake's August 8 departure for Europe. The president joined them in meetings on August 2, 7, and 8.[90] With the clock ticking, they recognized it was time for a "full-court press." Unlike Secretary Christopher's May 1993 trip, in which he offered a tepid sales pitch on behalf of Clinton's "lift and strike" policy, Lake laid out a version of that policy by saying to the Europeans, in effect, "This is what we're prepared to do if there is no settlement. This is what we intend to do. We hope you'll come with us."[91]

Many on the Clinton team were still nervous about of the use of force. Memories of the Vietnam War made Lake and the U.S. military planners especially fearful of open-ended commitments. But senior U.S. officials were emboldened by a new development in the Balkans. Croatia, which had been occupied by rebel Serbs since its war of independence in 1991, had launched an offensive aimed at reconquering lost territory and expelling members of its Serb minority. At the time Lake was unveiling America's "endgame," the Croatian army was sweeping through Serb-held territory in Croatia and western Bosnia. Croatia's success showed that the so-called Serb juggernaut was more of a paper tiger, a vital piece of news for those who had deferred for years to alarmist Pentagon warnings of steep U.S. casualties. It also showed, crucially, that Serbian president Slobidan Milosevic was prepeared to stand back and allow Serbs in neighboring Croatia and Bosnia to be overrun. If NATO intervened, it would face only the Bosnian Serbs, not the Yugoslav National Army.

A number of Western negotiators were secretly relieved that the Serbs had taken Srebrenica and Zepa because the loss of the two Muslim enclaves had tidied the map of Bosnia by eliminating two nettlesome noncontiguous patches of territory. A peace deal seemed easier to reach and, once reached, easier to enforce. And Western diplomats had at last come to the slow realization that they were negotiating not with gentlemen but with evil. Military force was the only answer.

The full-court press produced an immediate turnover. At the July conference of Western leaders, the United States had secured a commitment to bomb the Serbs if they attacked the Gorazde safe area. In the coming weeks Lake, Holbrooke, and others pressed successfully to extend NATO's protective umbrella to three other safe areas—Bihac, Tuzla, and Sarajevo. One of the "keys" that needed to be turned before air strikes could be launched was removed from the hands of the gun-shy civilian head of the UN mission, Akashi, and placed in the hands of UN force commander Janvier, which at least left two generals in charge. More important, Washington and its European allies understood that the next time NATO bombed, it could not launch only pinpricks and it could not allow Serb hostage-taking to diminish allied resolve. UN peacekeepers were withdrawn from Serb territory in late August, where they were achieving almost nothing besides serving as potential hostages.

On August 14, 1995, Secretary Christopher had given Assistant Secretary Holbrooke command over U.S. diplomacy on Bosnia. On August 19 Holbrooke's five-man negotiating team drove over Mount Igman into Sarajevo. The Sarajevo airport had been shut down by Serb shelling, and the Serbs had refused to guarantee the safety of international flights. As a result, the U.S. delegation had no choice but to drive its bulky vehicles along the perilous mountain road that had been widened unsatisfactorily to accommodate Bosnian truck drivers bringing goods into the city. A UN armored personnel carrier transporting part of the U.S. delegation slipped off the road and tumbled down the mountain. Three of Holbrooke's colleagues and friends, Nelson Drew, Robert Frasure, and Joseph Kruzel, were killed. This was the first time American officials had died in the Balkan wars. Holbrooke brought the bodies back to the United States, flying part of the way with his knees wedged up against one of the coffins. The tragedy further energized the new diplomatic effort and heightened U.S. determination to end the war. "For the first time in the entire conflict, we took deaths," Holbrooke says. "And these were the deaths of three treasured senior public servants and friends. Everyone was torn apart. Suddenly, the war had come home."

On August 28, 1995, a shell landed near the very same Sarajevo market where sixty-eight people had been killed in February 1994. This time the Serb attack killed thirty-seven and wounded eighty-eight. From Paris, Holbrooke called Washington, frantic. Clinton, Gore, Christopher, Perry, and Lake were all away on vacation. Deputy Secretary of State Strobe Talbott asked Holbrooke what he wanted to recommend to Christopher and Clinton. "Call us the negotiation team for bombing," Holbrooke said. "We've got to bomb."

And at last NATO did. Beginning on August 30, 1995, and continuing consistently for the next three weeks, NATO planes flew 3,400 sorties and 750 attack missions against fifty-six targets. They avoided aged and rusty Serb tanks and concentrated on ammunition bunkers, surface-to-air missile sites, and communications centers. They called the mission Operation Deliberate Force, as if to announce up front that what might have been called "Operation Halfhearted Force" was a thing of the past. The Bosnian Serb army was sent into a tailspin, and Muslim and Croat soldiers succeeded in retaking some 20 percent of the country that had been seized and cleansed in 1992. When Lake got word that the planes were raining bombs upon the Serb positions, he phoned the president, who was in Wyoming.

"Whoooppeee!" Clinton whispered, confirming, as Congressman Frank McCloskey had told him the year before, that bombing the Serb military did make him feel good.[92]

Backed by the newly credible threat of military force, the United States was easily able to convince the Serbs to stop shelling civilians. In November 1995, the Clinton administration brokered a peace accord in Dayton, Ohio. The agreement left Serbs, 31 percent of the population, with 49 percent of the land. Croats, who made up 17 percent of the population, received 25 percent, and the Muslims, who constituted 44 percent, were allocated just 25 percent. Three ethnically "pure" slivers of territory were almost all that were left of Bosnia. The three groups were kept together in a single country, but under an extremely weak central government. More than 200,000 people had been killed since the war began in April 1992. One out of two people had lost their homes. In December 1995, speaking from the Oval Office, President Clinton movingly invoked the massacres in Srebrenica and the recent killings in the Sarajevo marketplace to justify the deployment of 20,000 U.S. troops to Bosnia.

Although the war was over, Clinton had a small problem. Ever since his administration had abandoned its lift-and-strike policy proposal in May 1993, senior officials had been arguing that Bosnia constituted "a problem from hell." They had said that intervention would be futile or would imperil U.S. interests. It would thus be difficult for those same officials now to retract their earlier rhetoric and convince the American people of the sudden worthiness of contributing troops to enforce the Dayton peace. Entering an election year, the Republican leadership on Capitol Hill was poised to strike.

Several of Clinton's Republican challengers did try to score points, telling the public that Bosnia was not worth a single American life. But

Clinton's presidential challenger, Senator Dole, closed ranks behind the commander in chief. In the late fall, Dole teamed up with Senator John McCain, the Arizona Republican and fellow war hero. The pair publicly backed the president's decision to deploy U.S. troops to Bosnia. Dole and McCain knew that their Republican colleagues would be upset by their refusal to attack Clinton. Dole's campaign managers in New Hampshire told him, "You already got problems. You don't need this!" Dole tried to head off some of the intra-party criticism by calling a meeting with a dozen angry Republican senators. McCain remembered the session. "The rhetoric was intense and emotional: 'Don't put our boys in harm's way.' 'Body bags.' All that," McCain said. "They were just pounding us. . . . I was getting more and more depressed." When the meeting finally ended and the Republican critics filed out into the hall, the Arizona senator despaired. But as McCain walked out with Dole, who had said almost nothing, the majority leader cheerily observed, "Makin' progress!" As bad as it had been, Dole had expected it to be much worse.[93] In the end Dole helped convert twenty-eight Republicans to Clinton's cause. The Senate approved the deployment of U.S. troops to Bosnia by 60 votes in favor, 39 opposed.

Clinton knew significant casualties would harm his prospects in November. "The conventional political wisdom," he said, was that there was "no upside and tons of downside" to the U.S. deployment. But he was willing to risk it: "You have to ask yourself which decision would you rather defend ten years from now when you're not in office." Clinton said. "I would rather explain why we tried" than why "NATO's alliance was destroyed, and the influence of the United States was compromised for ten years."[94] For the first time, Clinton saw the costs of noninvolvement as greater than the risks of involvement.

President Clinton defeated Senator Dole handily in 1996. A year later, in November 1997, Clinton appointed his former challenger chairman of the International Commission on Missing Persons, which had been established to locate some of the 40,000 still missing from the wars in the former Yugoslavia, including the more than 7,000 who disappeared from Srebrenica. The Balkan commission funded the collection of forensic data, DNA identification, and the de-mining of grave sites. Upon accepting the chairmanship, Dole delivered some brief remarks. "Some may question and some do question why we're involved in Bosnia in the first place," Dole said. "I think that's a very easy answer: because we happen to be the leader of the world."[95]

A KLA soldier presents a wallet containing photos of his relatives and one of President Clinton, Summer 1999.

Chapter 12

Kosovo: A Dog and a Fight

The Road to Confrontation

In the aftermath of NATO's bombing and troop deployment, Bosnia remained fairly peaceful. Many foreigners complained about the lingering hostility among Muslims, Croats, and Serbs and the refusal of the nationalist authorities to allow refugees to return to their homes. But however fragile and unsatisfying the terms and the implementation of the Dayton peace agreement, U.S. leadership had brought the savage war in Bosnia to an end. As 60,000 NATO troops patrolled the war-torn country, they oversaw the demining of former confrontation lines, helped demobilize soldiers and train new army and police forces, escorted families back to burned-down villages, and created an overall sense of security and the stirrings of normalcy.

But NATO forces went only part of the way. Since its creation in 1993, the UN war crimes tribunal at The Hague had compiled a long list of suspects. When Serbian president Slobodan Milosevic signed the Dayton accords on behalf of his Bosnian Serb accomplices, he had urged U.S. officials to defer deciding whether suspected war criminals could hold high office in Bosnia. "In the house of a man just hanged," he said, "don't talk about rope."[1] Western leaders had listened. The wording of the Dayton agreement was deliberately vague, and Washington, fearing casualties and "another Somalia," refused to order arrests. Indeed, soon after NATO forces were deployed, Commander Admiral Leighton Smith appeared on Bosnian Serb television and publicly denied that his troops had the authority to round up suspects. Smith did not provide his troops with the names or photographs of indictees for whom they should be on the lookout. U.S. military officers said they would make arrests only if ordered to do so directly by the president. They were not going to be hung out to dry, as they felt they had been in Somalia. For the first two years of the "peace," therefore, nationalist thugs in the Balkans continued to run wild.

Only one voice within the Pentagon regularly dissented: that of Wesley C. Clark. Clark, a decorated Vietnam vet and former Rhodes scholar, had been the J-5, or director for strategy and planning on the Joint Chiefs, during the Rwanda genocide and for much of the Bosnian war. He had been with Holbrooke in August 1995 when the UN APC had crashed and killed their three colleagues. And he had served as military liaison to the Dayton peace talks and watched Milosevic up close. He urged that war criminals be arrested immediately, while the parties were still smarting from NATO bombing. Not for the last time, Clark was ignored. Instead of ordering arrests, U.S. and European diplomats continued to rely upon Milosevic to stabilize the situation. Although they deemed the Serbian dictator responsible for genocide in Bosnia, Western policymakers treated him as an indispensable diplomatic partner. Their first stop was always Belgrade.

Serbia's citizenry held their president in less esteem. The wars orchestrated and funded by Milosevic and fought by Serbs in Croatia and Bosnia had left Serbia ravaged. Five years of militarization, exacerbated by the West's stringent economic sanctions, had sent unemployment and inflation soaring and the people's quality of life tumbling. In 1996 and 1997 Serbia's restive population staged massive demonstrations. Brainwashed by years of Serbian propaganda that held that Serbs were the victims of genocide, the protesters made no mention of Serbia's war crimes. Rather, they demanded an end to Milosevic's corrupt rule and his oppression at home. Milosevic responded by tightening control. He muzzled dissent. He authorized political assassinations. He shut down independent media stations. He stole elections his party could not win. And he began brutalizing ethnic Albanians in the southern Serbian province of Kosovo.

Serbs had a possessive relationship with the impoverished Kosovo province. Kosovo had long been immortalized as the site of the 1389 battle on the Field of Blackbirds, in which the Turks had defeated the Orthodox

Christian Serbs, ushering in five centuries of Ottoman rule.[2] In the second half of the twentieth century, Serbs and Albanians competed for land, jobs, and political privileges in the province. Because of an explosive Albanian birthrate and a Serb exodus, 1.7 million Albanians had come to compose 90 percent of Kosovo's overall population. By the 1980s, feeling outnumbered, Kosovo Serbs had begun complaining of persecution. They received moral support from nationalists in the Serbian Academy of Sciences and Arts. In an inflammatory public memorandum in 1986, the Serbian intellectuals charged Kosovo Albanians with masterminding "the physical, political, legal and cultural genocide of the Serbian population in Kosovo."[3] The following year, Milosevic, then an undistinguished Communist apparatchik, traveled to Kosovo and stoked anti-Albanian sentiment and Serb fervor. He proclaimed before an angry Serb mob that "no one should dare to beat you!"[4] In 1989 Milosevic enhanced his nationalist credentials by stripping Kosovo of the autonomy that had been granted it by Yugoslav dictator Marshal Tito. Albanians were fired from their jobs, schools were closed, and the Serb police presence expanded.

In 1995, when NATO bombing forced the Serbs to negotiate a settlement for Bosnia, Kosovo's Albanians had hoped that the United States and its allies would pressure Serbia into restoring the province's autonomy. Instead, Western negotiators at Dayton affirmed Serbia's territorial integrity and did not broach the subject of Kosovo. This embittered many Kosovo Albanians and paved the way for the rise of a shadowy band of Albanian fighters who called themselves the Kosovo Liberation Army (KLA).[5] The KLA pledged to protect the Albanian people in their homes and win independence for the province. The KLA succeeded in raising money from Albanian émigrés and smuggling arms from its anarchic neighbor, Albania, but it failed at first to attract many recruits in Kosovo. The tide turned in March 1998, when the KLA gunned down several Serbian policemen and Milosevic struck back so violently that popular support for the KLA soared. Serbian forces swept into the region of Drenica and murdered some fifty-eight relatives of KLA strongman Adem Jashari, including women and children. With every KLA attack on a Serbian official, Serbian reprisals intensified, as Serb gunmen torched whole villages suspected of housing KLA loyalists. In the following year, some 3,000 Albanians were killed and some 300,000 others were expelled from their homes, their property burned and their livelihoods extinguished. Television cameras captured civilians chilled by winter snowfalls and terror.

By the late 1990s, Western observers were familiar with Kosovo. Even back in 1992, when the Bush administration had insisted it had "no dog" in the Bosnia fight, it had expressed concern for Kosovo's fate. In what became known as President Bush's "Christmas warning," acting Secretary of State Eagleburger had advised Milosevic that in the event of a Serbian attack on Kosovo, the United States would be "prepared to employ military force against the Serbs in Kosovo and in Serbia proper."[6] In April 1993 President Clinton's otherwise gun-shy secretary of state Warren Christopher distinguished Kosovo from Bosnia on the grounds that deterioration in Kosovo would likely "bring into the fray other countries in the region—Albania, Greece, Turkey." The United States, he said, feared conflict there would "as happened before, [broaden] into a world war."[7] Kosovo was always thought to be "different" from Bosnia because of its potential to unleash violence throughout the rest of the Balkans.

As Serb police and militia committed more and more atrocities in 1998, informed Western journalists and human rights groups descended on the region. The atrocities of the 1990s had taught many American opinionmakers that they could not simultaneously demand both an end to genocide and a policy of nonintervention. Diplomacy without the meaningful threat of military force had too often failed to deter abuse. The Clinton administration came under pressure to respond militarily.

In October 1998 U.S. trouble-shooter Richard Holbrooke again negotiated a deal with Milosevic. In exchange for avoiding NATO air strikes, Milosevic agreed to pull back some of his forces from Kosovo and allow the deployment of 2,000 unarmed, international verifiers. But Serb forces ignored their presence. On January 15, 1999, after pounding the small town of Racak with artillery fire for three days, Serb paramilitary and police units rounded up and executed forty-five Albanian civilians, including three women, a twelve-year-old boy, and several elderly men. The Serb forces left the bodies of those executed facedown in an icy ravine. Within twenty-four hours, Ambassador William Walker, the head of the Kosovo Verification Mission, arrived at the crime scene. Walker, who had first encountered atrocities while serving as an American diplomat in Central America, debriefed villagers and hiked up a nearby hill, where he saw the first body. "It was covered with a blanket, and when it was pulled back, I saw there was no head on the corpse—just an incredibly bloody mess on the neck," Walker told a reporter. He examined three more bodies. On each a bullet hole was visible beneath gray or white hair. Walker roared

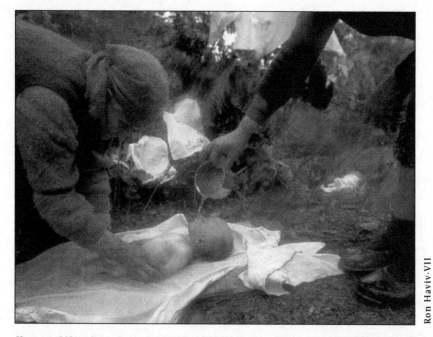

Ron Haviv-VII

Kosovo Albanians forced out of their homes prepare to bury a five-week-old infant who died of exposure in the mountains of Kosovo, Fall 1998.

into the television camera that the Serbs had committed a "crime against humanity."[8]

Senior officials in the Clinton administration were revolted and enraged. Madeleine Albright, the longtime crusader for intervention, had succeeded Christopher as secretary of state. She and the rest of the Clinton team remembered Srebrenica, were still coming to grips with guilt over the Rwanda genocide, and were looking to make amends. They feared that Racak was just the beginning of a campaign of mini-Srebrenicas. Indeed, a rumor circulated that the Serb forces' motto of the day was, "A massacre a day helps keep NATO away." U.S. officials were accompanied by far more aggressive European diplomats than they had known in the mid-1990s. Prime Minister Tony Blair of Britain and his foreign minister, Robin Cook, were intent on stopping Milosevic. In February 1999 the United States and its European allies convened a conference at the French château of Rambouillet, outside Paris, and presented a take-it-or-leave-it proposal. Belgrade was required to remove most of its troops from Kosovo, grant significant autonomy to the Albanians, and allow 25,000 armed peacekeepers (4,000 of them American) to be deployed in Serbia. If the Serbs refused,

NATO would bomb. The Serbs were accustomed to hollow NATO threats. They were not about to surrender control over a province of great historical and symbolic importance. Serb negotiators refused even to entertain the deal.

Beginning on March 24, 1999, NATO jets under the command of General Clark, supreme allied commander for Europe, began bombing Serbia. Allied leaders said they would continue bombing until Milosevic accepted the autonomy compromise. It was the first time in history that the United States or its European allies had intervened to head off a potential genocide.[9]

Response

Values and Interests

The NATO action was not purely humanitarian. Serbia's atrocities had of course provoked NATO action, but Operation Allied Force would probably not have been launched without the perceived threat to more traditional U.S. interests. However real the human suffering of Albanians, the threat to American credibility was also a crucial factor in convincing President Clinton to take action. In a sequence reminiscent of the summer of 1995 in Bosnia, the intensification of Serb violence and the now redundant, duplicitous antics of Milosevic had begun making Clinton, his cabinet, and indeed NATO, which was often invoked in American threats, look silly. It had become humiliating for the alliance to try and fail to deter Serbia, a country of 11 million, which lay within sneezing distance of Hungary, one of NATO's newest members. Western leaders were again, to use Clinton's phrase, "getting creamed."

In addition, after a decade of unrest and with the ascent of the KLA in Kosovo, it was clear that the problem—for Albanians, but also for the United States and Europe—would not go away. Ongoing Serb-Albanian fighting seemed likely to destabilize the fragile ethnic balance in neighboring Macedonia, which was one-quarter Albanian and could not endure the arrival of more Albanians displaced from Kosovo. The Serb crackdown was imperiling the fragile peace in Bosnia, which by then the United States had spent more than $10 billion supporting. Washington was not anxious to see its neighborhood investment squandered. Perhaps most significant, after six years in office, the Clinton administration had built up an institutional memory of its dealings with this particular regime. Because Milosevic was a "repeat offender" and had run circles around the allies hundreds of times the previous decade, U.S. diplomats broke from their traditional tendency to see peace "just around the corner." In short, when NATO began bombing, the Clinton administration was acting with its head as well as its heart.

President Clinton spoke from the Oval Office the night the NATO air campaign began. This time he was the one to invoke the Holocaust. "What if someone had listened to Winston Churchill and stood up to Adolf Hitler earlier?" the president asked. "Just imagine if leaders back then had acted wisely and early enough, how many lives could have been saved, how many Americans would not have had to die?"[10] Clinton adopted the tactics of so many earlier advocates of intervention inside and outside the U.S. government who had been dismissed as soft and emotional.

But Clinton believed he had to demonstrate the peril to American interests as well. "Do our interests in Kosovo justify the dangers to our armed forces?" he asked. "I thought long and hard about that question. I am convinced that the dangers of acting are far outweighed by the dangers of not acting—dangers to defenseless people and to our national interests." Serb-Albanian fighting could drag U.S. allies in the region into a wider conflict. "We have an interest in avoiding an even crueler and costlier war," he said. "Our children need and deserve a peaceful, stable free Europe." The Holocaust, American self-interest, and European stability—Clinton needed and pleaded them all. American public support was essential to what was mostly an American war.[11] The president also assured constituents that the war would not become another Vietnam or Somalia. "I do not intend to put our troops in Kosovo to fight a war," Clinton said.[12] NATO would have to win the war from the air.

From the moment NATO began bombing, Serbian regular military units teamed up with police and militia to do something unprecedented and unexpected: They expelled virtually the entire Albanian population at gunpoint. In a carefully coordinated campaign, armed Serbs launched Operation Horseshoe. Practiced at ethnic cleansing from their days in Bosnia, Yugoslav National Army units surrounded Kosovo towns and villages and used massive artillery barrages to frighten the local inhabitants into flight. In many areas the Serb police separated the women, children, and old men from the men of fighting age. The Serbs executed some of the men in order to eliminate resistance and to demonstrate the costs of remaining in Kosovo. They systematically shredded the Albanians' identification papers, birth certificates, and property deeds, and they looted everything in sight. The Serbs crammed whole families into railroad cars and forced others to walk. The villagers trudged along in silence, refusing to look back as their homes were set ablaze. The Serbs who did the dirty work carried long knives and automatic weapons. Some donned red berets. Many wore woolen ski masks, as if the existence of the UN war crimes tribunal had made them conscious for the first time that they might later be identified and punished. But the Serb gunmen's new attention to covering up their role in war crimes did not make them shy from committing them.

All told, Milosevic's forces drove more than 1.3 million Kosovars from their homes, some 740,000 of whom flooded into neighboring Macedonia and Albania. It was the largest, boldest single act of ethnic cleansing of the decade, and it occurred *while* the United States and its allies were intervening to prevent further atrocity.

Because refugees crossed the border quickly, their stories were quickly relayed around the world. If refugees from previous horrors needed weeks or even years to gain the trust of Western reporters, the hardened correspondents in Kosovo had finally learned after nearly a decade of Balkan atrocities to shift the burden of proof to the alleged perpetrators. Better to trust the unconfirmable and later be proven wrong than the reverse. Christiane Amanpour of CNN was one of many veteran reporters of the Bosnian carnage who reappeared in the Balkans to cover the single largest European exodus in a half century. One Albanian, Mehmet Krashnishi, told her a typical story. He said that the day after the NATO operation began, Serb troops arrived and separated the men from the women: "To the women they said, 'You may go to the border,' and they put us men in the two big rooms. They said, 'Now NATO can save you,' and then they started to shoot. And when they finished shooting us they covered us with straw and corn and set it on fire. We were one hundred and twelve people. I survived with one other man." Like so many survivors, Krashnishi had played dead and fled when the Serbs went to find more fuel for their pyre. He bore burns on his face, and his hands were wrapped in thick white bandages.[13]

The NATO jets had little success deterring the Serbs' cleansing operation. They flew at 15,000 feet so as to elude feisty Serbian air defenses. Pilots were no match for paramilitaries. Weather and visibility were poor early on, impeding NATO's use of laser-guided missiles. Serb troops built fake bridges, camouflaged precious equipment, and used decoys such as inflatable rubber tanks to lure NATO into wasting expensive cruise missiles. One senior U.S. aviator, Brigadier General Daniel Leaf, who flew his first combat missions under fire in his F–16, recalled the feeling of helplessness that NATO pilots experienced: "I could actually see them burning houses. It was extraordinary and horrifying."[14] Serb forces lay low, mingling with the ethnic Albanian population they were terrorizing in order to deter NATO air attacks. There was no telling whether the Serbs would ever give in to NATO demands or whether the fragile allied coalition could be held together to sustain support for NATO's first major mission.

The decision to bomb Serbia marked a radically assertive break from past American responses to atrocity. Still, the intervention replicated many of the familiar patterns. The United States and its allies again fought the "last war," expecting the Serbs to respond to NATO bombing in Kosovo the way they had to NATO bombing in 1995 in Bosnia. Western officials and Albanian victims again engaged in wishful thinking, failing to imagine evil and presuming rational actors, even as they demonized Milosevic as a Balkan Hitler. NATO again carried out its intervention subject to the very constraint that had precluded intervention of any kind in Bosnia and Rwanda: fear of U.S. casualties. And although the bombing campaign paid sizable dividends for the majority of ethnic Albanians, its execution and aftermath have been used to confirm the futility, perversity, and jeopardy of acting to stop atrocity. The positive results of the intervention have received far less attention.

Fighting the Last War—Wishful Thinking

The NATO intervention was initially executed casually. NATO enjoyed 35-to-1 superiority in military manpower over Serbia and a 300-to-1 edge in defense spending.[15] Senior U.S. officials believed that if they simply sent Serbian president Milosevic a signal of allied seriousness, he would scamper to the negotiating table, pen in hand. In 1995 Milosevic had given in to allied demands over Bosnia after a two-week burst of NATO bombing. Remembering the Serbs' paltry resistance and quick concessions, Pentagon officials and Clinton cabinet members predicted NATO would need to bomb for a week at most.

Another assumption colored NATO thinking. Since Milosevic had signed away parts of Bosnia so blithely at Dayton in 1995, policymakers had begun speaking of the Serbian leader as a rational actor whose primary interest lay not in creating Greater Serbia but in tending to "Greater Slobo." On this theory the Serbian president would have been happy to sacrifice Serbs in Kosovo, as he had Serbs in Croatia and Bosnia, if it enabled him to keep power (perhaps by bringing about an easing in international economic sanctions), but he needed the cover of NATO bombing to do so. Thus, most Western observers expected that a light batch of bombing would be all that was needed. NATO launched its intervention with just one-third of the planes eventually dispatched.

In addition to failing to foresee sustained Serb resistance, the allied planners failed to predict that Milosevic would respond to bombing by retaliating so violently and audaciously against the Albanian population in Kosovo. Here again administration officials were not alone. Members of Congress, human rights monitors, and journalists, too, miscalculated. Incredibly, of the 120 Kosovo-related questions asked by reporters at State Department briefings in the three days preceding the bombing, only one concerned the fate of the Kosovar Albanians. Of the nineteen op-eds and editorials in the *Washington Post* and *New York Times* in the two weeks before the bombing, the possibility of a bloody crackdown inside Kosovo was mentioned in just three one-line references.[16]

The omens of bad things to come were certainly present. It was public knowledge that Kosovo was part of Serbia and that some 40,000 Serb army, police, and paramilitary troops backed by 300 tanks occupied it. Nebojsa Pavkovic, commander of Yugoslavia's Third Army Corps, was quoted in the *Washington Post* a few days before NATO intervened: "If attacked from outside, Yugoslavia will deal with the remaining terrorists in Kosovo." "Terrorists," as had been established in Bosnia, was official parlance for all men (armed and unarmed) above the age of sixteen. Still, few Western observers leaped to the conclusion that if bombed, Milosevic would rid Kosovo of its entire Albanian population. They again fell prey to likening the circumstances on the ground in Kosovo to those in Bosnia. In fact the two situations bore little but the neighborhood in common. In Kosovo the Albanians were trapped under Serbia's control. KLA rebels held scattered hillsides, but Serbian regular soldiers and police controlled all of Kosovo's towns and main roads. By contrast, by the time NATO began its massive bombing campaign in Bosnia in 1995, virtually no Croats or

Muslims were left in Serb-held territory. They had already been expelled. Thus, the Serbs could not respond to NATO's late-summer 1995 bombing by killing or deporting them. The country was ethnically tidy in a way that Kosovo was not (yet).

NATO planners were also unable to imagine gratuitous evil on the scale Milosevic had planned. Notwithstanding the perpetration of hundreds of thousands of crimes by Serbs under his control in Bosnia, U.S. officials and citizens still strained to believe that Milosevic would himself order a systematic campaign of destruction. In the American psyche, serial killers remained bug-eyed like Charles Manson or prone to leave their bloody paw prints at the scene of the crime like the late Serbian paramilitary warlord Zeljko "Arkan" Raznjatovic. They simply did not look—or talk—like Slobodan Milosevic, a man who dined out on his charms and maintained a deceptive distance from his crime scenes. At the Dayton peace talks in November 1995, with his sense of humor and charisma, Milosevic had endeared himself to many. He quickly learned the first names of the waitresses at Packy's Sports Bar, a frequent hangout. He sang "Tenderly" with the pianist at the local officer's club.[17] And U.S. negotiators deemed him "brilliant" and "sophisticated," adjectives they did not apply to his Muslim and Croat counterparts. Modern-day mass murderers come well disguised. As Clinton's first-term National Security Adviser Lake notes, "There are very few Genghis Khans around who like to play polo with the heads of their enemies."

During the NATO bombing campaign, Milosevic kept up appearances, playing to the Western gallery. On April 30, 1999, in an interview with Arnaud de Borchgrave of United Press International, he denied that his forces were torching Albanian villages. "Individual houses, yes," Milosevic said. "But not whole villages as we saw on TV in Vietnam, when American forces torched villages suspected of hiding Viet Cong." He criticized the Rambouillet peace conference, quoting a man he admired. "Henry Kissinger has said Rambouillet was a mechanism for the permanent creation of problems and confrontation," Milosevic said. "President Clinton should have listened to this wise geopolitical expert rather than some of his own less knowledgeable advisers."[18]

If anybody should have been able to see through Milosevic's disguise it was General Clark, who directed the NATO operation. From his time at the Dayton peace talks, Clark was well acquainted with the spuriousness of Milosevic's charm, the prevalence of his lies, and the hardness of his heart.

Milosevic had even taunted Clark that he would need just five days to deport all of Kosovo's Albanians.[19] Still, even General Clark's team calculated that the bombing would achieve its aims quickly and the Serbs would expel no more than 200,000 Albanians.

The imminent victims of Milosevic's mercurial wrath also misjudged. The Kosovo Albanian leadership had been urging bombing for months, and U.S. officials assumed they knew what they were doing. Baton Haxiu, an editor at the independent Kosovo daily newspaper *Koha Ditore* ("Daily Times"), wore a T-shirt with a logo that captured the Albanian mood: a Nike swoosh and the motto, "NATO AIR—JUST DO IT." Blerim Shala, editor of the weekly news magazine *Zeri* ("Voice") and a member of the Kosovo delegation at Rambouillet, returned to his homeland from France aware of the risks that lay ahead. "You must understand that the value of individual life in Kosovo before the bombing was zero. The Serbs were the owners of our lives," he says. "When you reach that bottom line, you don't care about the consequences. . . . In the mind of ordinary Albanians, it was better to die than to live under Serbia." Given the choice, virtually every Albanian in Kosovo would have preferred to take his or her chances with NATO bombing over business as usual under Milosevic. One of the few *New York Times* editorials that mentioned the possibility of Serb retaliation against Albanians appeared on March 24, the day NATO began its attack; it noted "that is the risk the Albanians are willing to take."[20]

The Constraint: "No Casualties"

At the start of the air war, the allies' political and military planners hoped that the Serb leadership would quickly agree to grant autonomy to Kosovo's 2 million ethnic Albanians. But when the bombing gave the Serbs a pretext to intensify their killings and expulsions, General Clark attempted to shift Washington's focus away from simply avoiding NATO casualties and to defeating the Serbs and reversing their cleansing operation. Clark tried to accelerate the NATO operation, to plan for a ground invasion, and to deploy Apache helicopters that could fly far closer to the ground and target Serb paramilitaries. But he was rebuffed. NATO was thus almost useless at inhibiting the ethnic cleansing in Kosovo, which was why it had intervened in the first place. "You can't stop human rights violations from a distance," German general Klaus Naumann, former chairman of NATO's military committee, later said. "You must be ready to commit ground troops, or the whole thing is a sham."[21] Critics chided Clinton's "no-ground-troops" mantra, saying that the refusal to risk U.S. soldiers amounted to a new principle of "*combatant immunity.*" Clark argued that it impeded NATO's effectiveness and endangered the lives of Serbian and Albanian civilians.

Clark received no backing from either Defense Secretary William Cohen or the Joint Chiefs of Staff. Cohen, a former Republican senator from Maine, had replaced Defense Secretary William Perry at the start of Clinton's second term. He had not traversed the learning curve of other senior officials who had seen Clinton's presidency damaged by its early impotence on Bosnia. Indeed, while in the Senate, Cohen had asked whether those who urged humanitarian intervention had the necessary staying power. "And the hearts that beat so loudly and enthusiastically to do something, to intervene in areas where there is not an immediate threat to our vital interests," Cohen said, "when those hearts that had beaten so loudly see the coffins, then they switch, and they say, 'What are we doing there?'"[22] Neither Cohen nor the senior U.S. military brass brought Clark, their ground commander, into high-level discussions. They were suspicious of his hawkishness and his back channels to a White House they did not trust. Clark in turn was exasperated by their remoteness and their refusal to give him the tools he needed to succeed. In one exchange with the Joint Chiefs of Staff in Washington, Clark was reminded that since the United States had to be ready to fight simultaneous wars in Korea and the Gulf, it could not overextend itself in the Balkans. "Surely," Clark snapped, "you're not saying that we're going to give up and lose in the only fight we have going, in order to be ready for two other wars that are not threatening?"[23]

Supporters of the NATO mission thought that the U.S. determination to avoid casualties might well doom the operation. On April 8, 1999, Holly Burkhalter, then with Physicians for Human Rights, read an opinion essay on National Public Radio in which she urged President Clinton to deploy ground troops to stop what she feared was genocide. "Milosevic and his forces are clearly destroying at least a part of this ethnic group by forcibly driving almost half of its population out of Kosovo, by targeted killings of community leaders, by the execution of Kosovar men, and boys, and the whole-scale demolition of homes, villages, and cultural and religious sites," Burkhalter said. "If President Clinton avoids taking the painful action necessary to expel Serb forces from Kosovo, he will be remembered as the President on whose watch three genocides unfolded."[24]

Burkhalter and other progressive critics were joined by conservative voices that argued, in effect, "Now that we're in, let's win." Soon after the operation began, Henry Kissinger wrote in *Newsweek,* "NATO cannot survive if it now abandons the campaign without achieving its objective of ending the massacres."[25] The following month he lamented the "generation gap" that was undermining the campaign. "The formative experiences of the Clinton administration's key personnel were either in the trenches of the Vietnam protest movement or in presidential campaigns—or both," Kissinger wrote. "Suspicious of the role of power in foreign policy, they use it ineffectively and without conviction."[26] Senator John McCain, the Arizona Republican, declared, "What shall we do now? Win, by all means necessary."[27]

Gradually, as senior American and European policymakers began to sense that defeat was a distinct possibility, NATO intensified its attacks and did begin playing to win. Instead of crumbling, as many feared it would do under strain, the heterogeneous alliance strengthened its resolve. In phase one NATO jets had struck Serb antiaircraft defenses and command bunkers. On March 29, 1999, NATO entered phase two, increasing the number of planes from 400 to 1,000 and broadening its list of targets to include Yugoslavia's infrastructure below the forty-fourth parallel, far south of Belgrade. On April 3, day eleven of the war, NATO moved into phase three, which permitted attacks on targets in Belgrade. In early April NATO announced it would send to Albania the 5,000-man Task Force Hawk, including twenty-four Apache helicopters. This was one gesture designed to hint that a NATO ground invasion might follow. President Clinton and his cabinet were still ruling out deploying U.S. ground troops, but Clark did his best with head fakes and feints to lure Milosevic into believing that a ground war was still a distant threat. Although Washington had finally agreed to send Clark the Apaches, the same kind of Pentagon foot-dragging that had delayed the dispatch of U.S. APCs during the Rwanda genocide postponed the delivery of the helicopters until late April. And despite Clark's endless badgering, he never received White House permission to use them.

The more determined the allies became, the more they took the war to the Serbian people. On April 23, at the NATO summit, NATO leaders agreed to target the personal property and businesses of Milosevic and his closest associates and to strike targets that would affect millions of civilians by disrupting transportation, water, and electricity. Some forty days into the war, on May 3, 1999, NATO planes began dropping individually parachut-

©Gilles Peress/Magnum

Kosovo Albanians in flight.

ed dispensers the size of tennis-ball cans, or "rubber duckies," onto Yugoslav power grids, where they released spools of carbon graphite thread and caused instant power outages.[28] NATO's attacks on civilian infrastructure turned the war into what Veton Surroi, the editor of *Koha Ditore,* calls the "espresso machine war." "The Serbs would only quit when the war affected Milosevic and his cronies at home personally," Surroi says, "when the shortage of electricity meant they couldn't get their daily espresso."

Because the operation was a "humanitarian intervention," NATO planners were especially sensitive about avoiding violations of international humanitarian law. The Geneva conventions prohibited the bombing of dual civilian-military sites if the "incidental loss of civilian life . . . would be excessive in relation to the concrete and direct military advantage" of the strike. American and European lawyers had almost as much to say about the conduct of the operation as their political superiors. Lawyers from the Pentagon's Judge Advocate General's Office tested each potential target against the laws of war, which greatly restricted what ended up on Clark's target list.

Despite NATO's incremental approach, the intense legal scrutiny, and the unprecedented precision of the new weaponry, some missiles strayed, and even those that stayed on target provoked controversy. NATO jets struck an Albanian refugee column, a Serb passenger train, and other civilian convoys. Perhaps most notorious, on May 7, 1999, relying on an old map, U.S. B-2 bombers hit the Chinese embassy, killing three Chinese citizens and injuring at least twenty others. General Clark received a deluge of mocking faxes to his European command headquarters. "Dear Gen. Clark," the faxes began, "We've moved. Our new address is _____."[29] In targeting dual-use infrastructure in Serbia proper, NATO bombers hit bridges, power plants, communication facilities, television stations, and political party headquarters. The attacks were justified as essential to disrupting Serbian command and control, but critics complained that the same missile that took out the Yugoslav Third Army's generator also shut down the neighborhood hospital. The same bomb that robbed Milosevic of the satellite he needed to broadcast nightly lies on television also deprived Serbian civilians of the right to view the news. NATO's desire to avoid risks to its pilots appeared to increase the civilian toll of war.[30]

Victory?

On May 24, 1999, two months into NATO's campaign, the UN war crimes tribunal for the former Yugoslavia, which had been set up originally to respond to atrocities committed in Croatia and Bosnia, indicted Serbian President Slobodan Milosevic for crimes against humanity and war crimes committed in the previous two months in Kosovo. It was the first time a head of state had been charged during an armed conflict with violations of international law. Already there were few signs the Serbs would throw in the towel, and many in the Clinton administration feared that the indictment would make Milosevic even more defiant and prone to cling to power. According to UN Chief Prosecutor Louise Arbour, senior U.S. officials attempted to block the indictment.

Afraid that NATO might lose its first war, British prime minister Tony Blair began lobbying President Clinton to prepare for a ground invasion. U.S. officials grudgingly began mumbling that they had not taken any option "off the table." General Clark was finally instructed to develop a preliminary plan. Known as the "Wes plan," it called for an attack into a hostile environment from the south by 175,000 NATO troops. Neither the Joint Chiefs nor Defense Secretary Cohen liked the plan, and they communicated their unease to President Clinton. Still, on June 2, 1999, National Security Adviser Sandy Berger met with several Washington foreign policy insiders and made four points. Point one was, "We're going to win." Point four was, "All options are on the table." When he was asked whether that included U.S. ground troops, Berger said, "Go back to point one."[31]

Back in Serbia, dissent was growing. Serb units began to mutiny and to desert. They did not want to die for Kosovo, and they certainly did not want to die for Milosevic. Milosevic's cronies began pressing him to protect their business interests, even if that meant abandoning Kosovo. And Russian president Boris Yeltsin, whom Milosevic trusted for support, dispatched his envoy, former Russian prime minister Viktor Chernomyrdin, with the instruction: "I don't care what you have to do, just end it. It's ruining everything."[32] Yeltsin ranked Russia's ties with the West above any overromanticized Serb-Russian brotherhood. Suddenly, Milosevic faced pressure from disgruntled soldiers, their families, his own associates, and Russia. He was also afraid that if NATO indeed staged a ground invasion, he would be arrested for war crimes.

On June 3, 1999, Milosevic surrendered. On June 9, after seventy-eight days of bombing, the Serbian dictator signed an agreement that forced Serbian troops and police to leave Kosovo and permitted 50,000 NATO peacekeepers to enter it. Although Kosovo would officially remain part of Serbia, with Serbian forces gone, Albanians would finally be able to govern themselves. More than 1 million ethnic Albanians returned to what was left of their homes and slowly began rebuilding their lives, assured for perhaps the first time that they were no longer vulnerable to Belgrade's whims. After 34,000 sorties, only two NATO planes had been shot down. No U.S. or allied forces had been killed. General Clark had managed to overcome White House fear of casualties, Pentagon hostility toward him and his mission, discord among NATO allies, and a severely restricted target list. The man attacked for his strategic judgment and his political instincts won NATO's first war.

In the summer of 1999, just after NATO troops were deployed to aid the transition to autonomy, I toured Kosovo and met a fourteen-year-old Albanian girl with the fair-skinned features of Sidbela Zimic of Sarajevo. Her name was Drita Hyseyni, and she had just survived a massacre in which her parents, grandparents, and brothers had all been killed before her eyes. Although Drita herself absorbed five bullets in the mass execution, she managed to escape the crime scene, dragging her own bloodied body, as well as that of her younger sister, out of the house that the Serb paramilitaries had just set aflame.

Listening to Drita's gruesome story, I was tempted to view her experience as a consequence of NATO bombing. After all, as bad as life was for Albanians under Serb rule before the intervention, it had not come to this. The Serbs had killed some 3,000 Albanians before NATO intervened, but they had left the majority of Albanians alone in their homes. To the naked eye, it seemed that NATO had intervened to fix a leaky faucet but had ended up flooding the house. Drita remembered the taunt of the gunmen as they mowed down her mother and father: "Where's NATO now, *shiptar?*" they chanted, as they unloaded their machine guns into the wilting Hyseyni clan. "Bill Clinton can't save you."[33]

But Drita had a different view. Her scarred face lit up when she recalled the moment she first heard NATO planes overhead. "I knew then, with NATO in the air, we would win," she said. "And we did." Hard as it was to see Kosovo as victorious when the price had been entire families, the Kosovo Albanian survivors treated these sacrifices as the price of freedom. "You must understand," she said firmly, "we were going to be killed anyway. It was only a matter of time. We knew it was better to die with a fight. NATO fought and now we, at least, are free."

Aftermath

The Critiques

A victorious President Clinton traveled to Kosovo in the aftermath of the Serbs' surrender. He spoke with a group of Albanians gathered in a sports pavilion near the main American base in southern Kosovo and summed up the NATO triumph: "Mr. Milosevic wanted to keep control of Kosovo by getting rid of all of you, and we said, 'no.'" The Albanians jammed into the stadium cheered wildly, chanting "Clin-ton! Clin-ton!" The president continued, "Now he has lost his grip on Kosovo and you have returned. No more days hiding in cellars, no more nights freezing in mountains and forests."[34]

The verdict on whether the NATO war was a success and whether such humanitarian interventions should be repeated is mixed at best. Assessments have varied depending on who has been asked and *when*. Clinton administration officials defended both the execution and the effects of NATO's seventy-eight-day bombing campaign, but many others were unpersuaded. Throughout the twentieth century, U.S. officials had frequently argued against intervening to stop genocide, citing futility, perversity, or jeopardy. And when the United States finally intervened in Kosovo to curb Serbia's human rights abuses against Albanians, critics outside the U.S. government made these same arguments. When the United States and its NATO allies finally intervened to prevent genocide, support proved thin. Many bystanders argued that the form the intervention took and the atrocities it provoked confirmed the reasons they had long cited for looking away.

Perversity

The first line of criticism of the NATO operation was that whatever its aspirations to restore NATO credibility and to aid the Kosovo Albanians, Operation Allied Force had actually yielded perverse results. It had damaged NATO and caused the Albanians more suffering. Conservative critics found fault with the premise of using precious U.S. military resources to rescue distant foreigners. They said "social work" should not be NATO's business. The Serbs had symbolically humiliated the Western powers by hanging on so long, and NATO "readiness" had been practically undermined by the expenditure of so many ballistic resources in a country of no vital import.

Progressive critics charged that the United States had revealed the shallowness of its humanitarian commitments by choosing to fly at 15,000 feet. Political theorist Michael Walzer was one who wrote that there was a moral contradiction between NATO's willingness to kill Serb soldiers and inflict collateral damage and its unwillingness to send American soldiers to battle. "This is not a possible moral position," he argued. "You can't kill unless you are prepared to die."[35] Those who questioned the sincerity of NATO's humanitarian aims began looking for ulterior motives. Some argued that the mission had been launched in order to justify a continued role for the U.S. military so as to keep military bases afloat in the United States and to keep Boeing booming. Fringe elements that had not spent much time in the Balkans insisted that NATO was trying to secure yet more markets for American companies or to stuff capitalism down the throats of socialist stalwarts. "The truth is that neither Clinton nor Blair gives a damn about the Kosovar Albanians," said British leftist playwright Harold Pinter. "This action has been yet another blatant and brutal asser- tion of U.S. power using NATO as its missile. It sets out to consolidate one thing—American domination of Europe."[36] Since the intervention took place in the immediate aftermath of Clinton's impeachment scandal, many chuckled that this was the president's way of "wagging the dog," or, in Henry IV's words, busying "giddy minds with foreign quarrels."[37] Others shrugged and muttered that no matter what the deeper reasons for American involvement, if *this* was what humanitarian intervention looked like, they wanted no part of it. They concluded that their earlier mistrust of governments was warranted. When the objectives were humanitarian, states would devote only miserly means.

In February 2000 Human Rights Watch, an organization that had frac- tured over whether to call for military force during the Bosnian war, issued a report that was highly critical of NATO's intervention in Kosovo. On the basis of interviews, press reports, a three-week field mission to Serbia in August 1999, and the scrutiny of bomb damage assessments and autopsy reports, the group concluded that some 500 Serbian and Albanian civilians had been killed during NATO's Kosovo operation. One-third of the inci- dents and more than half of the deaths resulted from attacks on question- able targets such as Serbian radio and television headquarters. The group recommended restrictions on daylight attacks, prohibitions on the use of cluster bombs in populated areas, greater care in attacking mobile targets, and more scrupulous target selection.[38]

The same month the American Association of Jurists and a group of Western and Russian law experts submitted a special report to the UN war crimes tribunal at The Hague claiming the NATO bombing campaign violated international law by recklessly killing civilians. Although the UN court's prosecution office eventually dismissed the charges, it did conduct a preliminary investigation that made NATO officers nervous about future humanitarian interventions and about the danger posed by international courts. This was precisely the kind of foreign scrutiny of U.S. military activ- ity that U.S. Senate opponents of ratification of the genocide convention had hoped to avoid.

NATO Secretary-General George Robertson issued a statement in response to the Human Rights Watch report in which he credited NATO's "extraordinary efforts" to avoid civilian deaths but acknowledged that casualties had regrettably occurred. He urged observers to be careful not to draw false equivalency. "I regret that NATO's action caused even a single civilian death, but these unintended incidents in no way compare to the systematic, unspeakable violence inflicted on civilians by Milosevic's troops and paramilitary forces," Robertson said.[39] In the minds of many skeptics, however, the two sets of violations merged together.

Futility

A second criticism of the intervention was that the violence committed by Albanians in the aftermath of NATO's victory only confirmed there were "no good guys." The alleged symmetry of the parties was said to confirm the futility of trying to do a net service to humanity. For a decade prior to NATO's March 1999 intervention, the Kosovo Albanians had been fired from their jobs, strip-searched, barred from schools, and generally spat upon by armed and unarmed Serbs alike. Just ahead of, and during, the NATO bombing campaign, Albanians watched summary executions, beatings, rapes, and the torching of hundreds of towns. Ninety percent of the Kosovo populace was forcibly displaced from their homes during Serbia's Operation Horseshoe. Yet when Milosevic surrendered, many idealistic foreigners had fully expected that the Albanians would return home, turn the other cheek, and behave responsibly. As Surroi of *Koha Ditore* explained, "Morality was your investment here, so you expect morality as your payback."[40]

But when NATO helped bring about a role reversal and empowered Albanians to realize their rights and control their own destinies, many Albanian returnees behaved brutally. In the year after the NATO victory, while some 50,000 NATO troops patrolled Kosovo, Albanian extremists expelled more than 100,000 Serbs from their homes in Kosovo and killed some 1,500. Prominent Albanian media outlets published the names of those they called Serb "war criminals." Those branded were often gunned down. The Albanian authorities, usually KLA officers who had simply left their uniforms (but rarely their guns) at home, looked away from, actively encouraged, or took part in looting, beatings, and murders. The actual number of Albanian perpetrators of violent acts was quite small, but the general mood among Albanians amounted to "serves them right after what *they* did." Serbs were at last getting their comeuppance. Collective guilt of the sort that Lemkin and others attributed to the German people during the Holocaust was all the rage. Those Serbs who remained in Kosovo ended up mostly clustered in the northern part of the province in a kind of militant ethnic ghetto.

At the same speech in November 1999 where President Clinton drew hearty applause from Albanians for his proclamations about the NATO victory, he broached the tricky subject of Albanian coexistence with Serbs. "You can never forget the injustice that was done to you," he said, as the Albanians clapped with delight. "No one can force you to forgive what was done to you," Clinton continued, again earning thundering acclaim. "But you must try," he concluded, drawing only a sullen silence from the raucous crowd.

History does not offer many examples of the victims of mass violence taking power from their former oppressors, in large measure because outside powers like the United States have been so reluctant to intervene on behalf of targeted minorities. Unless another country acts for self-interested reasons, as was the case when Vietnam invaded Cambodia in 1979, or armed members of the victim group manage to fight back and win, as Tutsi rebels did in Rwanda in 1994, the perpetrators of genocide have usually retained power. Yet the fact that victims have rarely taken over from victimizers has not stopped U.S. policymakers from justifying inaction by claiming an equivalence among all parties to the conflict. "We can't make these people like one another," they said. Although "all sides" rarely acted the same when these statements were made, U.S. government officials frequently cautioned that if the victims (Kurd, Tutsi, or Bosnian Muslim) had acquired the capacity and the power, they, too, would turn against those belonging to the perpetrator group. The logic of these claims was that no matter how attractive the prospect of rescue might seem in the short term, it would make no difference in the long term. The people the United States saved and empowered today would sooner or later torment those they had dislodged. Thus, as we have seen, those who believed in the futility of intervention asked, in effect, "Why bother?"

This futility justification for nonintervention is historically untestable. Holocaust survivor Primo Levi addressed this tendency to equate the perpetrator's behavior and the victim's capacity in *The Drowned and the Saved*:

> I do not know, and it does not much interest me to know, whether in my depths there lurks a murderer, but I do know that I was a guiltless victim and I was not a murderer. I know that the murderers existed . . . and that to confuse them with their victims is a moral disease of an aesthetic affectation or a sinister sign of complicity; above all, it is a precious service rendered (intentionally or not) to the negators of truth.[41]

Levi did not deny that victims could commit evil acts. He conceded that the tendency to be vengeful in the aftermath of terrible suffering was very real—and very understandable. But Levi questioned the assumption that such retribution was inevitable. He also doubted the possibility of equivalence after genocide.

It is somewhat ironic that it was Kosovo that ended up eliciting the first American anti-atrocity intervention of the century. It may have been the least likely, of all the potentially enforceable "peaces," to breed reconciliation. Indeed, there was no original conciliation to *redo*. Albanians and Serbs had cohabitated in the province for generations, but unlike in Bosnia and Rwanda, where an ethnic map once showed intermingled blots and colors reminiscent of a Jackson Pollock painting, the two groups in Kosovo had rarely mixed. Intermarriage was virtually unheard of. This history did not mean that Albanians and Serbs could not live side by side; it just meant that they were unlikely to do so for some time.

But international agencies and Western governments and publics wanted quick, cheap results. After Serbia's surrender, the United Nations set up a civil administration in which foreigners decided local tax rates, television news content, school curriculum, and jail sentences. But police were the most crucial ingredient in a province where the legal system had vanished with the overnight departure of Serbian officialdom. UN police were deployed at a snail's pace, and donors proved parsimonious. German General Klaus Reinhardt, the commander of the NATO-led Kosovo force, noted that the UN budget for Kosovo for the first year was $64 million, "a quarter of that which NATO spent in *one day* of the bombing."[42]

Thousands of foreign aid workers, who became known as "humanitarian imperialists," set up shop in Kosovo. But they lacked the resources and the ideological comfort level to dictate the pace and parameters of Kosovo's development. Instead, they tried to leverage their resources to influence local political decisions and to use their money to build local capacity. Because the locals did not yet fully control their own destiny—Kosovo Albanians were left with "substantial autonomy and self-government" but not independence—the people frequently blamed the outsiders for woes of their own making. Nonetheless, after two years of transitional UN rule, when Kosovo Albanian voters went to the polls in October 2000 to elect their own government, they revealed their moderate leanings. Instead of choosing the hard-line KLA to run the country, as many expected, they elected Ibrahim Rugova, a pacifist philosopher who had led the struggle for Albanian autonomy long before the KLA was even formed.

But outside critics ignored this encouraging sign. Kosovo's tarnished, bloody peace simply ratified the bystanders' earlier, self-justificatory notions that parties that portrayed themselves as "victims" would readily transform themselves into abusers once they were allowed to govern. As a result of Albanian repression, American critics were able to charge NATO with producing two bouts of ethnic cleansing. Allied bombing unleashed the Serb expulsion of 1.3 million Albanians from March to June 1999, and it enabled Albanians to expel 100,000 Kosovo Serbs thereafter.[43] The sui generis ethnic dynamic among Serbs and Albanians was lost on many foreigners. When American skeptics read about violence in the province, they groaned and concluded, "They're at it again." Many of those looking to justify their prior inaction in the face of atrocities in Bosnia began pointing to Kosovo as proof that when "the parties" did not want to live together, there was nothing that foreign, bomb- or checkbook-wielding do-gooders could do about it.

Perfidy

A third criticism of the intervention was that as it was going on interested governments and refugees inflated the extremity of the violence. Critics charged that U.S. officials lied and refugees exaggerated the atrocities, calling them "genocide" and making up huge numbers of murders. They were allegedly doing so in order to stir up support for the bombing.

The "exaggeration" controversy is rooted in the inescapable difficulty of accurately gauging the scale of atrocities while they are being committed.[44] When Madeleine Albright became secretary of state in 1996, she created an Office of War Crimes Analysis at the State Department on the logic that the best way to be sure the bureaucracy would focus on atrocities was to make it the full-time task of one group of U.S. officials. During NATO's intervention in Serbia in 1999, lawyers in this office worked with officials in the intelligence community to analyze and publicize Serb war crimes as soon as they were discovered. The Clinton administration revealed a deeper commitment to learning about the welfare of missing civilians and refugees than it or any other foreign policy team had done before. Much had changed since 1975, when Cambodian refugees poured into Thailand and found few foreigners awaiting them. When Milosevic deported the Albanian population, the head of the State Department's new war crimes unit, Ambassador David Scheffer, an international lawyer who had served as Albright's deputy at the UN during the Srebrenica and Rwanda genocides, immediately flew to Macedonia, where the refugees were arriving. Scheffer conducted fifteen hours of interviews at the border crossing in Blace, Macedonia, speaking with more than 200 refugees. Scheffer's findings, combined with those of the major human rights groups and journalists, were so disturbing that U.S. officials began debating whether or not the wholesale deportation of the Albanians constituted genocide.

This was the State Department's third "g-word" controversy in six years. In crises past, those who opposed U.S. intervention had tended to oppose use of the term. In this case many *supporters* of the NATO campaign argued against labeling Milosevic's atrocities genocide. An American humanitarian intervention was warranted by the brutality of Serb ethnic cleansing and crimes against humanity. Why not leave it at that? As one State Department official who fought the application of the term later recalled, "My view was, 'Why do we need to put the genocide label on it?' People are being killed. Women are being sexually violated and stabbed to death." As he put it, "Let's just look at the facts. The facts necessitate action. This was a systematic attack against a civilian population. That is enough. Everyone is caught up in the 'Is it or isn't it?' We don't need that debate."

Nonetheless, the debate occurred, and Scheffer prevailed. After a century of avoiding the term "genocide," the State Department authorized its tentative use just ten days into the conflict between NATO and Serbia. At that time U.S. officials feared the Serbs were separating the Albanian men from the rest of the refugees in order to execute them. The Srebrenica precedent chilled those who saw the first refugee convoys crossing into Albania and Macedonia made up mainly of women and children. "What we see unfolding in Kosovo," Scheffer said at a press briefing, "are war crimes, ethnic cleansing, crimes against humanity. And these are occurring on such a systematic and widespread basis that we have to conclude that we're witnessing what might be described as *indicators of genocide* unfolding in Kosovo."[45] Scheffer knew that an authoritative diagnosis of genocide would be impossible to make during the Serb campaign of terror. Nonetheless, he did what Lemkin had long ago urged. Serb expulsions and killings were so widespread and well planned that Scheffer used the phrase "indicators of genocide" to capture what the refugees were describing and what human rights investigators were surmising. He did not deliver a formal finding of genocide but raised the specter of genocide. President Clinton himself also used the term on June 25, 1999, citing fears of "deliberate, systematic efforts at genocide."[46] This was a first for a U.S. president.

Although Scheffer issued a relatively tentative and—according to the genocide convention—accurate finding of "indicators of genocide," editorialists, nongovernmental advocates, and others criticized the Clinton team for using the term. They saw that hundreds of thousands of Albanians were being expelled but not murdered. Since most equated genocide with full-scale extermination, they accused the United States of exaggerating the Serb terror in order to justify both the NATO bombing mission and the civilian casualties caused by it. Certainly, some of the frustration with the administration was warranted. It was not a coincidence that having avoided the g-word regarding Bosnia and Rwanda when it wanted to avoid acting, the Clinton administration applied the label proactively only in the one intervention for which it was trying to mobilize support. In this case, a finding of "genocide" would not shame the United States; it would enhance its moral authority. Still, a straight reading of the genocide convention did capture the kind of ethnically based displacements and murders under way. Milosevic was destroying the Kosovo Albanian populace.

U.S. officials were also faulted for their supposedly exaggerated estimates of the number of Albanians killed. In fact, records reveal that most were cautious about suggesting figures. At a State Department press conference on April 9, 1999, reporters pressed Scheffer for a numerical estimate of Albanian deaths. "I think it would be very problematic to speculate at this time on a number," Scheffer said. "I fear [any estimate] would be too low if I did speculate. I think we have to wait to find what the death count is."[47] On April 19, State Department spokesman James Rubin declared, "There are still 100,000 men that we are unable to account for, simply based on the number of men that ought to have accompanied women and children into Macedonia and Albania." Rubin reminded reporters of Serb behavior in the recent past. "Based on past practice," he said, "it is chilling to think where those 100,000 men are. We don't know."[48] Rubin was right. Nobody could then know.

Rubin's formulation became the model for other U.S. officials. Most noted that military-aged men were being systematically separated from refugee columns. They reported concrete cases of mass executions and individual murders, estimated at 4,600. But although they may have assumed the worst, they did not leap publicly to conclusions. They distinguished the number of those Albanians they believed were already murdered and those who were simply unaccounted for. On May 7, 1999, for example, Defense Department spokesman Kenneth Bacon also said:

> 100,000 military-age men are missing. We reckon that over 4,600 have been killed in mass executions in over 70 locations. . . . This could well be a conservative estimate of the number who have been killed in mass executions. Some may have been used to dig graves. Some may have . . . been . . . forced to support the Serb military in various ways. We have reports that some have been used as human shields. Some may have died in the hills or working. We just don't know, and that's one of the mysteries that won't be resolved until this conflict is over.

As reporters continued to grill him, Bacon seemed to lose patience. Sounding like Claiborne Pell during the 1988 Kurdish crisis, he reminded his audience of the obvious: "The fact that they're missing means that we can't interview them and find out exactly what's happened to them."[49] A few days later Secretary Albright told Americans that there would necessarily be many open questions until independent investigators gained full access. "Only when fighting has ended and the people of Kosovo can safely return home will we know the full extent of the evil that has been unleashed in Kosovo," she said. "But the fact that we do not know everything does not mean we know nothing. And the fact that we are unable to prevent this tragedy does not mean we should ignore it now."[50] Albright was breaking from past U.S. practice by relaying what she thought to be the morbid truth even though she knew it would likely increase the pressure for the United States to intervene with ground troops.

In the year following Milosevic's surrender, investigators began digging up mass graves in Kosovo. In September 1999 a Spanish forensic team claimed that it had uncovered war crimes' victims, but far fewer than it had expected. The chief inspector in a Spanish unit, Juan Lopez Palafox, declared, "We were told we were going to the worst part of Kosovo, that we should be prepared to perform more than two thousand autopsies and that we should have to work till the end of November. The result is very different. We uncovered 187 corpses and we are already back." Spanish investigators brought new expectations to their reporting in Kosovo. "In former Yugoslavia," Lopez Palafox continued, "there were crimes, some of which were undoubtedly horrific, but nevertheless related to the war. In Rwanda we saw the bodies of 450 women and children, heaped up inside a church, and all of their skulls had been split open."[51] The Rwanda genocide had set a whole new, modern standard for genocide. Body counts were compared, and the Kosovo tally was said not to measure up.

In November the UN war crimes prosecutors announced that some 4,000 buried bodies had been found. Journalists took this "low" figure as proof the U.S. government had lied. "The numbers are significant, but nowhere near what U.S. officials had indicated during the fighting," CNN's Wolf Blitzer said. "That's 7,000 short of the 11,000 that had been reported to the U.N. after the war." Blitzer's report made no mention of the more than 300 sites that had not been probed at all or of the Serbs' notorious tampering with evidence. Instead, he quoted a former Bush administration official who described the governmental "temptation to take poetic license with the data."[52]

The truth of what Serb forces did to Albanians between March 24, 1999, and June 10, 1999, is of course still emerging. As of November 2000, the UN war crimes tribunal at The Hague confirmed the 4,000 bodies or parts exhumed from more than 500 sites.[53] Officials stressed that not all of those executed or beaten to death in Kosovo had been buried in mass graves at all. Many were dumped into roadside ditches, wells, and vegetable gardens. Some Albanian victims who were initially piled into pits for burial were removed. Bulldozers arrived to cover the Serbs' tracks by scattering body parts in multiple sites or by incinerating the bodies in bonfires or factories. In the village of Izbica, for instance, Albanian villagers buried some 143 bodies after a Serb massacre before they fled in early April. Spy satellite images confirmed the existence of 143 graves. But by the time tribunal investigators arrived in June 1999, the only sign of vanquished life that remained were earthmovers' caterpillar tracks, which crisscrossed the area. The bodies had vanished.

Careful scrutiny of American and refugee claims reveals that U.S. government predictions and refugee descriptions proved remarkably accurate. Despite the frantic dash most refugees made to the border and the terror of the experience, Human Rights Watch has confirmed some 90 percent of what its investigators were told. The UN prosecutor at The Hague also found that four out of five Kosovar refugee reports of the number of bodies in the graves were precise.

The bodies keep turning up. In 2001 some 427 dead Albanians from Kosovo were exhumed in five mass graves that had been hidden in Serbia proper. An additional three mass grave sites, containing more than 1,000 bodies, were found in a Belgrade suburb and awaited exhumation. Each of the newly discovered sites lies near Yugoslav army or police barracks.[54]

Some of the wildest rumors that circulated during Serbia's deportation operation have been confirmed. While NATO was still bombing, essayist Christopher Hitchens received a letter from a former student in Serbia that a friend of his, a truck driver, had been ordered by the Yugoslav army to pick up Albanian corpses in his refrigerated vehicle and drive them into Serbia. Hitchens, a staunch backer of NATO's intervention, did not publicize the letter because even he deemed it "weird and fanciful." He was leery of wartime "rumors."[55] But in July 2001 Zivadin Djordjevic came forward to confirm the rumors. Djordjevic was a fifty-six-year-old diver in Serbia who made his living plunging into the Danube River to rescue vehicles and drowning victims. In April 1999 he was asked to examine a white Mercedes freezer truck found bobbing in the Danube near the town of Kladovo, 150 miles east of Belgrade. Believing it was just another unlucky vehicle, Djordjevic donned his wet suit and swam up to the back door of the truck. When he opened it, he discovered a ghastly cargo of men, women, and children. He first saw what he said was "a half-naked, beautiful, black-haired woman with great white teeth." Then he discerned two boys "no older than 8 years old." The tangled corpses slid into his arms. As he wrestled one back into the truck, another would slither out. "It was the first and only time in my life I have been confronted with such horror," the diver later said.[56]

Two days after NATO began bombing in 1999, we now know, Milosevic ordered his interior minister, Vlajko Stojilkovic, to "clear up" the evidence of war crimes in Kosovo. Stojilkovic used all available refrigeration trucks to remove corpses from execution sites in Kosovo and to destroy or rebury them in Serbia. According to witnesses, some of the corpses were incinerated at furnaces in Bor, Serbia, and Trepca, Kosovo. Milosevic's government thus not only permitted, encouraged, and ordered its security forces to murder the Albanians, but it also tried to cover up the crimes. The UN tribunal has received reports that some 11,334 Albanians are buried in 529 sites in Kosovo alone.[57]

As high as the death toll turned out, it was far lower than if NATO had not acted at all. After years of avoiding confrontation, the United States and its allies likely saved hundreds of thousands of lives. In addition, although prospective and retrospective critics of U.S. intervention have long cited the negative side effects likely to result, the NATO campaign ushered in some very positive unintended consequences. Indicted by the UN war crimes tribunal for Serbia's atrocities in Operation Horseshoe and defeated in battle, President Milosevic became even more vulnerable at home. The Serbian people realized that a Milosevic regime meant corruption, oppression, death, and a future of international isolation and economic desolation. When a Serbian economics professor, Vojislav Kostunica, ran against Milosevic on a platform of change in Serbia's September 2000 election, Milosevic was roundly defeated. When Milosevic attempted to contest the results, the country's miners, workers, police, and soldiers joined with Belgrade's intellectuals and students to end his deadly thirteen-year reign. In March 2001 the Kostunica government arrested Milosevic and in June 2001, in return for some $40 million in urgently needed U.S. aid, Belgrade delivered him to The Hague. The political turnover finally enabled Serbia's citizenry to begin reckoning with Serbian war crimes, a prerequisite to any long-term stability in the region.

The man who probably contributed more than any other single individual to Milosevic's battlefield defeat was General Wesley Clark. The

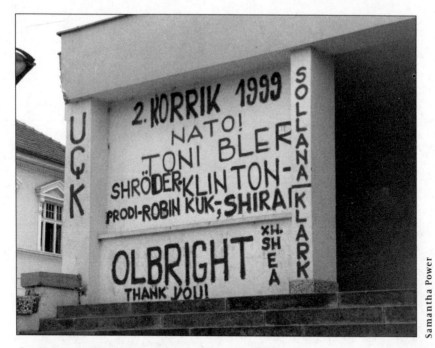

Samantha Power

Graffiti tributes to Western leaders scrawled in Pristina by Kosovo Albanians
after Serbia's surrender.

NATO bombing campaign succeeded in removing brutal Serb police units
from Kosovo, in ensuring the return of 1.3 million Kosovo Albanians, and
in securing for Albanians the right of self-governance. Yet in Washington
Clark was a pariah. In July 1999 he was curtly informed that he would be
replaced as supreme allied commander for Europe. This forced his retirement and ended thirty-four years of distinguished military service.
Favoring humanitarian intervention had never been a great career move.

Former Serbian president Slobodan Milosevic escorted by a UN security guard into the courtroom at The Hague, July 2000.

Chapter 13

Lemkin's Courtroom Legacy

Courtroom Dramas

When Serbian president Slobodan Milosevic arrived at the International War Crimes Tribunal at The Hague, he was the thirty-ninth Yugoslav war crimes suspect to end up behind UN bars. He was initially indicted only for crimes against humanity carried out in Kosovo, but the UN prosecution later broadened the indictment to charge him with genocide in Bosnia. His wife and political accomplice, Mirjana Markovic, condemned the tribunal as a "concentration camp with gas chambers for Serbs." In his initial courtroom appearance, Milosevic lashed out at the "false tribunal" and refused to accept legal counsel. When asked if he wanted to hear his fifty-one-page indictment read to him, he snorted, "That's your problem."[1] At a subsequent session he elaborated: "Don't bother me and make me listen for hours on end to the reading of a text written at the intellectual level of a 7-year-old child, or rather, let me correct myself, a retarded 7-year-old."[2]

But if Milosevic retained a tough pose, times had changed. As he geared up for a long courtroom scene against NATO and the "illegitimate" tribunal, the presiding judge, Richard May, interrupted him. Irritated by the defendant's insouciance, Judge May simply turned off Milosevic's microphone and adjourned the session. "This is not the time for speeches," May said. The once mighty Serbian strongman was escorted from the trial chamber back to his ten-by-seventeen-foot cell. In August 2001, desperate for attention, Milosevic broke the tribunal rules, making a prohibited phone call to Fox News. On the air he repeated his charges against the "illegal" court and said of his role in the Balkan wars, "I'm proud of everything I did."[3] The tribunal reprimanded him and threatened to revoke his phone privileges. The man who ran circles around Western negotiators for nearly a decade was told another transgression would cost him his monthly phone card and seven-minute allotment of daily phone calls.

The Hague detention center, once a deserted emblem of Western half-heartedness, had become the bustling home to many of Milosevic's former partners, subordinates, and foes. Bosnian Serb general Radislav Krstic, commander of the Drina Corps that had carried out the assault on Srebrenica, had also ended up in the Dutch prison facility. U.S. troops swooped up Krstic in eastern Bosnia in December 1998.[4] The arrest was unusual, as the U.S. troops enforcing Bosnia's 1995 Dayton peace agreement had largely abstained from making raids. On the eve of the U.S. deployment, Clinton pollster Dick Morris asked Americans which tasks U.S. soldiers should be performing in Bosnia. The results daunted the president. "The arrest of war criminals was the one they most opposed using American troops for," said Morris. "I think probably because of the heritage of Somalia, hunting for the bad guy." Morris believed that the Bosnian war criminals were never "well enough known for them to be hated." He estimated that Bosnian Serb political leader Radovan Karadzic had 20 percent name recognition as against close to 100 percent for Saddam Hussein: "I don't think that the public ever really got that Karadzic was a son of a bitch. Because he wasn't a head of state, just a general, I think most people didn't know the name."[5] Karadzic was not in fact a general but a self-styled "president."

Washington was so nervous about casualties that NATO commander U.S. admiral Leighton Smith had given troops clear instructions: "Do not provoke"; "live and let live." Although the U.S. base was twelve miles away from the headquarters of Bosnian Serb General Ratko Mladic, the most wanted man in Bosnia, the United States allowed the cocksure general to go right on working. Anxious to avoid inflaming the rage of the now notoriously trigger-happy Mladic, U.S. forces had announced their visits to his army headquarters ahead of time.

But by late 1998, Serb unity had crumbled and NATO had changed its arrest policy. U.S. intelligence officers knew that Krstic was not as dangerous as Mladic (which Krstic himself would argue at length in the Dutch courtroom). And because the UN had kept his indictment secret, he was caught off guard by the sudden confrontation.[6]

Krstic was the highest-ranking military official to be tried in an international courtroom since 1945. On March 13, 2000, a little less than five years after the fateful Srebrenica onslaught, the Serb general found himself pinned into a defendant's box. He had lost his right leg in a wartime mine accident, and as he listened to the opening address of an American prosecutor, Mark Harmon, Krstic rubbed the stump. "This is a case about the triumph of evil," Harmon said:

> A story about how officers and soldiers of the Bosnian Serb army, well-educated men, men who professed to be professional soldiers, who professed to have faith in the Almighty and who professed to represent the ideals of a proud and distinguished Serbian past, organized, planned and willingly participated in genocide or stood silent in the face of it.[7]

Harmon laid out the painstaking, sophisticated planning necessary to kill as many men and boys as quickly as forces under Mladic and Krstic had managed. "Consider, for a moment, what was required to conduct this massive killing operation," Harmon told the tribunal:

- Issuing, transmitting, and disseminating orders to all units that participated in or assisted with the movement, killing, burial and reburial of the victims;
- Assembling a sufficient number of buses and trucks to transport the thousands of Muslim victims to detention centers near the execution sites;
- Obtaining sufficient fuel for these vehicles, at a time when fuel was precious because of the fuel embargo . . .
- Identifying and securing adequate detention facilities near the execution sites in order to hold the prisoners before killing them . . .
- Obtaining sufficient numbers of blindfolds and ligatures for these prisoners . . .
- Organizing the killing squads;
- Requisitioning and transporting heavy equipment necessary to dig large mass graves;

- Burying the thousands of victims who had been executed at
  diverse locations (and later to do the same in reburying);
- Preparing and coordinating propaganda from the Drina Corps
  and all levels of [Serb] military and government . . . to rebut the
  well-founded claims that atrocities had taken place.[8]

At issue in the case was not only Krstic's individual responsibility but
also the unsettled question of whether Serb forces had committed genocide in Bosnia.

Although the Bosnian atrocities had stirred vivid reminders of the
Holocaust, the genocide question remained contested years after the war's
end. It was clear that the Bosnian Serbs, backed by Milosevic in Serbia, had
used the 1992–1995 war to purge all Muslims from the territory under
their control and had killed tens of thousands of civilians. Yet they did not
murder each and every Muslim they got their hands on, as the Nazis and
the Rwandan Hutu had done. If the Holocaust and Rwanda were clear-
cut genocides, Bosnia presented the judges with the challenge of deciding
how broad a definition of genocide to adopt. Because only Muslim men of
fighting age were systematically executed around Srebrenica, whereas
women and children were by and large deported, the Krstic defense team
argued that the Serbs did not commit genocide.

If Lemkin had given the crime of genocide its name back in 1944, it had
taken the creation of the UN criminal tribunal at The Hague for perpetrators at last to be punished for genocide and for the meaning of the term to
be sharpened. The intervening half century had not been kind to the term.
"Genocide" had been used to connote innumerable practices, including
segregation, desegregation, slavery, birth control and abortions, sterilization, the closing of synagogues in the Soviet Union, and even suburbaniza-
tion. Misuse and abuse of language is unavoidable. But one consequence of
the nonexistence of a functional international body to dismiss absurd
genocide claims and weigh the more difficult ones was that the real victims
of genocide had found it difficult to distinguish themselves from the victims of crimes against humanity, social marginalization, or persecution.

In the sixteen-month Krstic trial, the UN bench heard from 128 witnesses and viewed 1,093 exhibits, including photographs from grave sites
showing skulls with blindfolds and bony wrists tied together with wires
and strings. In August 2001, the trial chamber announced its decision.
Krstic hobbled into the courtroom dressed in a dark navy suit, white shirt,

and yellow and black tie. Presiding judge Almiro Rodrigues began by describing the stakes of the case:

> At issue is not only extermination of the Bosnian Muslim men of fighting age alone. At issue is the deliberate decision to kill the men, a decision taken with complete awareness of the impact the murders would inevitably have on the entire group. By deciding to kill all the men of Srebrenica of fighting age, a decision was taken to make it impossible for the Bosnian Muslim people of Srebrenica to survive.

"Stated otherwise," Rodrigues said, "what was ethnic cleansing became genocide."[9] The UN court found that the genocide convention required physical and biological destruction but did not require a plan to exterminate all the members of a group. "In July 1995," the judge said, addressing Krstic's personal responsibility, "you agreed to evil . . . . You are guilty of having agreed to the plan to conduct mass executions of all the men of fighting age. You are therefore guilty of genocide, General Krstic." Since the Nuremberg judges had ignored Lemkin's appeals and excluded genocide from their verdicts, this marked the first ever genocide conviction in Europe. Krstic, fifty-three, was sentenced to serve forty-six years in prison, the court's harshest sentence to date.

Background: The Path to Enforcement

If Lemkin could have followed legal developments at The Hague, he would have been gratified. The creation of the International War Crimes Tribunal for the Former Yugoslavia in 1993 in turn helped spark the establishment in 1994 of a UN court to try those who ordered or committed the Rwanda genocide. It has also fueled efforts to bring to justice the Khmer Rouge perpetrators in Cambodia and to punish Saddam Hussein for his atrocities. These developments helped mobilize states to support the creation of a long-sought International Criminal Court. Prosecutors trying to prove genocide today spend their days perusing Lemkin's papers in an effort to glean the Polish lawyer's "original intent."

Lemkin had always argued that it was only a matter of time before the world's leaders would see both the moral value and the utility of punishing the perpetrators of genocide. When he had fought to get the genocide convention placed on the books, he was never so naive as to believe passage was a sufficient condition for enforcement. He was simply convinced that it was a necessary one. The convention would first enable the court of public opinion to condemn the crime; national courts would then follow by prosecuting genocide suspects who turned up in their midst; and eventually, years later, when the world was "ready," an international criminal body would punish the successors to Talaat and Hitler. These international war crimes trials would punish and incapacitate guilty perpetrators, deter future genocide, establish a historical record of events, and by pinpointing individual responsibility, allow ethnic or religious groups to coexist even after horrific atrocities.

But in 1959, the year of Lemkin's death, the legal routes to enforcement promised only dead ends.[10] Why, in the 1990s, did the world suddenly begin punishing genocide, when the genocide convention had been violated so flagrantly and ignored so unblinkingly since the Holocaust? And what, if anything, have the new courts achieved?

Iraq

The first postwar wave of enthusiasm for international war crimes trials came in 1990 after Saddam Hussein invaded Kuwait. Margaret Thatcher first mooted the idea of prosecuting the Iraqi dictator for war crimes because he seized Western hostages. The British prime minister said in a September 1990 television interview, "If anything happened to those hostages then sooner or later when any hostilities were over we could do what we did at Nuremberg and prosecute the requisite people for their totally uncivilized and brutal behavior. . . . They cannot say: 'We were under orders.' That was the message of Nuremberg."[11] President Bush endorsed Thatcher's recommendation in mid-October. He warned, "Remember, when Hitler's war ended, there were the Nuremberg Trials."[12] On October 28, 1990, Bush elaborated:

> Saddam Hussein plundered a peaceful neighbor, held innocents hostage, and gassed his own people. And all . . . of those crimes are punishable under the principles adopted by the allies in 1945 and unanimously affirmed by the United Nations in 1950. Two weeks ago, I made mention [of] the Nuremberg trials. Saddam Hussein must

know the stakes are high, the cause is just, and today, more than ever, the determination is real.[13]

The idea picked up steam in April 1991 after the Gulf War had been won, when reports circulated that Hussein had again begun killing Kurdish civilians. On the prodding of a number of European foreign ministers, international lawyers recommended either the creation of a criminal court or the filing of genocide charges under the genocide convention before the International Court of Justice. German foreign minister Hans-Dietrich Genscher became the leading spokesman for prosecuting Hussein, raising the idea repeatedly in public speeches throughout 1991.[14] Despite this burst of enthusiasm and the meticulous documentation of the Anfal campaign supplied by Human Rights Watch, neither the United Nations nor the individual member states followed up. Only with the crimes committed in the former Yugoslavia did a war crimes tribunal actually come into existence.

The Former Yugoslavia

Mirko Klarin, a leading Yugoslav reporter, may have been the first to urge that the international community prosecute Balkan war criminals. On May 16, 1991, even before the wars in Slovenia and Croatia had begun, and a full year before the Bosnian conflict, Klarin presciently wrote a spirited appeal in the Yugoslav daily *Borba* ("Struggle") entitled "Nuremberg Now!" Klarin derided the Yugoslav political leaders who said they would deal with crimes against humanity and war crimes after the conflict subsided. It was these very leaders, Klarin insisted, who were inciting ethnic violence and stirring the hate that would cause atrocities. "Would it not be better," he asked, "if our big and small leaders were made to sit in the dock instead of at the negotiating table?" He proposed that "impartial foreign experts in the international laws of war" sit on a tribunal—"no matter how small and modest"—to try those leaders responsible for the crimes against peace and crimes against humanity that had already been committed. "There is no reason to leave the Yugoslav mini-Nuremberg for when 'this is all over,'" Klarin wrote. "It would be much more cost-effective to do it *before*, or rather, *instead of*."[15]

But Klarin was ignored. And the wars in Slovenia, Croatia, and Bosnia followed. With the Bosnia carnage carried out in full view of the international media, Western leaders frequently responded to the outrages by warning that perpetrators of atrocity and war crimes would be held "individually responsible." Human Rights Watch, which was systematically recording evidence of the crimes, began calling for the establishment of a court in July 1992. Because the concentration camps were exposed a few days later, the appeal resonated. On August 13, 1992, the United States, under pressure from elite opinion-makers, joined a Security Council request for states and international humanitarian organizations to submit "substantiated information" concerning war crimes.[16] It was around this time that candidate Clinton helped shame President Bush into compiling all available evidence on the concentration camps. The Holocaust, Clinton said, had taught us the costs of silence in the face of genocide. He urged, "We must discover who is responsible for these actions and take steps to bring them to justice for these crimes against humanity."[17] Senior European diplomats again proposed the creation of an international tribunal. German foreign minister Klaus Kinkel picked up where Genscher, his predecessor, had left off. At the EU-UN conference held in London in late August 1992, he delivered a speech in which he declared, "What is happening here is genocide. The community of nations will pursue all crimes no matter who has committed them."[18] But "pursuit" and "responsibility" were vague terms. Although a state could use the International Court of Justice to charge another state with genocide, no forum yet existed to try *individuals* for atrocities.

In October 1992 momentum picked up. On the recommendation of Tadeusz Mazowiecki, the UN Human Rights Commission's special rapporteur for the former Yugoslavia who later resigned over Srebrenica, the allies called for the creation of an impartial commission of experts to assess the information gathered.[19] The United States lobbied quite deliberately for use of the term "commission." With an eye to stirring associations with the Holocaust, American international lawyers thought the name would link the new effort to the Allied War Crimes Commission, the ineffective World War II body run by Herbert Pell that nonetheless served as a precursor to the Nuremberg tribunal.[20]

In December 1992, as the Bush administration prepared to leave office, acting Secretary of State Eagleburger gave the UN commission a big boost by naming names in Geneva. But whatever its newfound rhetorical support from the United States, the commission lacked the financial and political backing, the personnel, and the security it needed to conduct independent, timely investigations into atrocities. Indeed the commission's name seemed aptly chosen, as it looked destined to duplicate the failure of

Pell's commission. Britain and France were at the time more sympathetic to Belgrade than were Germany or the United States. Prime Minister John Major and President François Mitterrand tried to curb the independence of the commission, as they believed holding killers accountable would interfere with their search for a negotiated settlement. Pursuing justice, they said, would delay peace.[21]

But others insisted that there could be no long-term peace in the Balkans without justice. Spurred on by the leadership of Cherif Bassiouni, a professor of international law and a relentless crusader for international justice, the UN commission plowed ahead and gathered a bounty of refugee testimony and other evidence of atrocity. In February 1993 the commission's five lawyers presented an interim report to the UN secretary-general in which they defined "ethnic cleansing," the term that was then being used as a kind of euphemistic halfway house between crimes against humanity and genocide. The commissioners found that ethnic cleansing—"rendering an area wholly homogenous by using force or intimidation to remove persons of given groups"—had been carried out "by means of murder, torture, arbitrary arrest and detention, extra-judicial executions, rape and sexual assault, confinement of civilians in ghetto areas, forcible removal, displacement and deportations of civilians, deliberate military attacks or threats of attacks on civilians and civilian areas, and wanton destruction of property." They said such crimes constituted crimes against humanity and might well be considered genocide under the convention. They also formally raised the possibility of setting up a UN tribunal to try these crimes. In February 1993 the members of the Security Council, under pressure from human rights organizations and a restless public and no longer paralyzed by the Cold War veto, voted to establish a UN court in The Hague.

We will never know whether a different war in a different place at a different time would eventually have triggered a similar process. But one factor behind the creation of the UN war crimes tribunal for the former Yugoslavia was the coincidence of imagery between the Bosnian war and the Holocaust. Those who lobbied on behalf of prosecuting Bosnia's perpetrators—such as the State Department's Jon Western, Congressman Frank McCloskey, UN ambassador Madeleine Albright, and countless others—were both motivated and aided by memories of Nuremberg. The visual link that people made between their memories of Hitler's death camps and their glimpses of Serb-run concentration camps in Bosnia sparked cries for justice. As public pressure mounted for American and

European leaders to "do something" to stop the Bosnian carnage, creating a court to punish perpetrators seemed a low-cost, low-risk way for Western states to signal that despite their opposition to military intervention, they were not indifferent to Bosnia's suffering.

If the memory of Nuremberg helped sweeten allied and UN officials on the idea of a court in 1992 and 1993, Nuremberg would also provide the foundation for the Hague court's jurisprudence. Its importance in aiding German de-Nazification and reintegration in Europe was widely hailed as an indicator of how the former Yugoslavia, too, could and would move forward after its wars. Even the physical contours of the courtroom in The Hague were modeled on those of Nuremberg's Palace of Justice. And the white bibs worn by the 1990s prosecutors and defense lawyers seemed deliberately chosen to harken back to the UN tribunal's functional parent.

Rwanda

It was a year after the Hague tribunal came into existence that Rwandan Hutu militants and their foot soldiers butchered some 800,000 of their Tutsi and moderate Hutu compatriots. With a UN court in place to hear charges related to the killing of some 200,000 Bosnians, it would have been politically prickly and manifestly racist to allow impunity for the planners of the Rwandan slaughter, the most clear-cut case of genocide since the Holocaust. The Security Council thus passed a resolution establishing a tribunal to prosecute Rwanda's perpetrators. In order to set up a tribunal under its jurisdiction, the Security Council had to show a "threat to international peace and security" so as to override the UN charter's ban on interference in a state's domestic affairs. This had been manageable for the former Yugoslavia because Serbia had effectively invaded Bosnia, its internationally recognized neighbor. Rwanda was tougher because the massacres there had taken place internally. Nonetheless, the Security Council found that the spillover of Rwandan refugees into neighboring countries meant that as in the former Yugoslavia, the atrocities in Rwanda, too, constituted threats to international order. Atrocities within a state were thus found to trump the UN charter's traditional ban on violating state sovereignty.

The Security Council voted 14–1 to set up the court, which would be seated in Arusha, Tanzania, the scene of the once-promising peace process between the Hutu and Tutsi leaders.[22] Rwanda, run mainly by Tutsi rebels and survivors of the genocide, was the one country that voted against it.

Rwandan officials believed the killers should receive the death penalty, but UN rules forbade it. Rwandan leader Paul Kagame said in the aftermath of the arrest of the genocide's ringleader, Théoneste Bagosora: "Belgium lost ten men here compared to one million we have lost at the hands of this man. And the tribunal can only give [Bagosora] a life sentence, while we are sentencing smaller figures to death. He should be tried in front of the aggrieved country, and if found guilty, he should hang."[23] Fearing judges from certain states (like France and Belgium) would be biased, the Rwandan government also opposed holding trials outside Rwanda. The peeved Rwandan representative on the Security Council said a "tribunal as ineffective as this would only appease the conscience of the international community rather than respond to the expectations of the Rwandan people."[24] The results have been mixed.

In 1998, in the first genocide case ever before an international criminal tribunal, Pierre Prosper, a thirty-five-year-old African American prosecutor from Los Angeles, attempted to convince the court that sexual violence against women could be carried out with an intent that amounted to genocide. Prosper set out to prove that Jean-Paul Akayesu, the Hutu mayor of Rwanda's Taba commune, attempted to destroy the Tutsi by raping the women. Downplaying the letter of the genocide convention, Prosper returned to its spirit. He introduced the court to Lemkin and offered a kind of legislative history, arguing, as so many U.S. Supreme Court justices have done with regard to the U.S. Constitution, that the genocide convention was a "living document." He pointed out the importance of interpreting the law broadly since humanity might yet stoop to lower depths. It was, in lawyerspeak, a case of first instance. "For me, the question of whether Akayesu committed genocide turned on the word 'destroy.' What did 'destroy' mean?" Prosper recalls. "The fact that the delegates fifty years before had overlooked 'destroy' was my hook to bring back Lemkin. If I could give that word meaning, I knew I could bring the convention to life."

Prosper prepared draft upon draft of the definition of the word "destroy." In the end he settled upon one that equated "destruction" with attacks on the "very foundation" of the group, the "debilitation" of a group to such an extent that the remaining members could no longer contribute in a meaningful way to society. Prosper echoed Lemkin when he insisted, "Complete annihilation or intended annihilation of a group . . . need not occur." He argued that destruction could take place if people were killed but also if the intellectual class of a group were eliminated or if the women were systematically raped. Prosper believed that a group could physically exist, or escape extermination, but be left so marginalized or so irrelevant to society that it was, in effect, destroyed.

On September 2, 1998, the UN tribunal for Rwanda accepted Prosper's rationale and issued its first ever courtroom verdict. The systematic rape of Tutsi women in Rwanda's Taba commune was found to constitute the genocidal act of "causing serious bodily or mental harm to members of the group." As Taba's former mayor winced slightly, UN judge Laity Kama proclaimed: "The accused, Jean-Paul Akayesu, you are declared guilty of genocide."

The Rwanda court's business was only just beginning. In the same remote Tanzanian town of Arusha where Akayesu was convicted, the once mighty Colonel Bagosora was whiling away his time in a detention facility, awaiting his day in court. The man who had made a mockery of Dallaire's good offices, who had shirked the phone calls of U.S. Deputy Assistant Secretary Bushnell, and who had masterminded the killing of some 800,000 Rwandans, had been apprehended in March 1996. As he had awaited transfer to the UN tribunal, Bagosora prepared a rambling twenty-eight-page defense in which he took the opportunity to express his antipathy for the Tutsi, who had only been partially eliminated: "There never was a Tutsi people, neither in Rwanda nor in Burundi nor anywhere else," the Rwandan colonel wrote. "They are immigrants who should moderate their greedy and arrogant behavior."[25] As of November 2001, Bagosora was one of fifty-three defendants in UN custody in Arusha; eight had been convicted of genocide. If they had not been apprehended, they would likely still be plotting the murder of Rwandan Tutsi.

Cambodia

When trials began for perpetrators from the former Yugoslavia and Rwanda, eyes quickly turned to other countries that had suffered catastrophic violence. It was not long before Western governments, the UN, and Cambodian NGOs began urging that a similar mechanism be put into place to try the aging leaders of the Khmer Rouge.

Cambodia advocates had been lobbying for accountability for some time. Throughout the 1980s, Ben Kiernan, a Khmer-speaking Yale historian who had documented KR atrocities, and Gregory Stanton, an anthropologist and lawyer, had attempted to convince Australian diplomats to file genocide charges at the International Court of Justice against the Khmer Rouge, which still occupied Cambodia's seat at the United Nations. But despite this effort, and one launched in parallel by David Hawk, a human rights activist, neither Australia nor any other state had been willing to take up the task. Kiernan and Stanton had then formed an umbrella organization known as the Campaign to Oppose the Return of the Khmer Rouge (CORKR), which attempted to streamline the efforts of nongovernmental groups trying to promote justice

Beginning in 1990, the coalition, operating out of the Methodist building on Capitol Hill in Washington, expanded. It took its efforts to the international level but also began targeting particular congressional districts for op-ed pieces and petitions. Virginia Senator Chuck Robb and New York Congressman Stephen Solarz convened hearings on Capitol Hill that legitimized the cause. Peter Cleveland, a staffer in Senator Robb's office, consulted with Kiernan and drafted the first U.S. legislation calling for the eventual prosecution of the Khmer Rouge. In early 1994 the Clinton administration assigned Charles Twining, who was by then the ambassador-designate to Cambodia, to work with lawmakers and NGOs to aid Cambodia's justice efforts. Craig Etcheson, the executive director of CORKR, was stunned by the turnaround in the U.S. government's attitude. He recalls: "Previously the State Department had said there would not be any international tribunal, and they wanted to know what I was smoking and where they could get some. But almost overnight they went from being utterly opposed to all kinds of different bureaus becoming engaged."

In 1994 the U.S. Congress passed the Cambodian Genocide Justice Act. The bill set aside $500,000 to collect data on KR crimes against humanity and genocide and to encourage the establishment of a national or international tribunal for the prosecution of perpetrators. More important, it made support for a tribunal official U.S. policy, a marked departure from more than a decade of diplomatically backing the KR.[26] Kiernan won the open-bid competition for the funds and set up the Cambodia Genocide Program at Yale. In 1995 he hired Youk Chhang, a Cambodian, to help run the program's field office, the Documentation Center of Cambodia, which began assembling evidence of the atrocities in order to establish a historical record and to create political pressure for trials. Stanton, who had recently begun working at the State Department, helped convince the human rights bureau there to provide an additional $1 million to fund the documentation effort.

Documentation Center director Youk Chhang's life might be divided into three phases. During the "genocide years," between 1975 and 1979, he

not only lost his sister and his father but, as an eager fifteen-year-old, he
cheered on the killing of a man and woman who committed the pernicious
crime of falling in love without official permission. He is haunted by the
memory of heckling the young couple as they were beaten with bamboo
blows to the back of the neck and buried alive. During his "American
years," he moved from a refugee camp in Thailand to Dallas, Texas, where he
began work for the city government and developed an obsession with
America's fallen icon John F. Kennedy. The current phase, if he has his way,
will constitute the "justice years."

Long before trials were considered a realistic possibility for Cambodia,
the Documentation Center did extraordinary work, identifying some
20,000 mass graves and burial pits throughout the country. Etcheson
believes the graves contain at least 1.1 million victims of execution. The
center gathered evidence of criminality in the form of official party propaganda, correspondence between KR officers, minutes from KR meetings,
"confessions" from victims, and notebooks and personal records kept by
KR officials. The documents provide a picture of cadre activity at the
region, district, and village levels. The KR, like the Nazis before them and
the Iraqis after, were packrats.[27] In prosecuting the Nazi henchmen at
Nuremberg, Justice Robert Jackson assembled more than 5 million pages
of documentation; Chhang suspects that by the time the trials begin in
Cambodia, he will be able to supply prosecutors with a similarly sizable
bundle. Each KR official, in the interest of demonstrating his loyalty and
staying in the good books of his superiors, documented his every movement. "I think they reported back not just every day, but every hour of
every day," marvels Chhang. "They recorded every detail on paper."

The documents show that the KR leaders demanded regular secret
reports on torture and execution. A September 25, 1976, report back to
Nuon Chea, the KR second in command, itemizes the torture carried out
against one prisoner, Man San, at Tuol Sleng. First, according to the report,
the KR interrogators "tortured him with about 20 to 30 wire lashes" and
then moved to a rattan whip. The torturers warned that the prisoner's family
would be killed if he did not confess. "Do you realize that your wife and
child are here?" Man San was asked. "Do you know the state of their health?"
At 10 p.m., when his torturers prepared to move to their "bare hands," he
confessed. Man San was promptly executed, as were his wife and child.[28]

Chhang insists that although Pol Pot's horrors are widely known in the
West, the details contained in these documents will surprise the more than

half of Cambodia's citizens born after Pol Pot's reign. "To this day most Cambodians know about what Pol Pot did more through an American movie, *The Killing Fields,* than through anything learned at home," says Chhang. "They must know more. They want to know more."

But establishing the truth was only one purpose behind the documentation. Chhang will be satisfied only if the senior KR officials implicated in the dense paper trail end up behind bars. None of the KR leaders has ever admitted responsibility for atrocities. In a final interview with the *Far Eastern Economic Review* before he died in 1998, Pol Pot claimed most of the deaths in Cambodia were the responsibility of "Vietnamese agents." He denied any knowledge of the gruesome torture facility at Tuol Sleng. "I was at the top," Pol Pot explained. "I made only big decisions on big issues. I want to tell you—Tuol Sleng was a Vietnamese exhibition. A journalist wrote that. People talk about Tuol Sleng, Tuol Sleng, Tuol Sleng. . . . When I first heard about Tuol Sleng it was on the Voice of America."[29] After Pol Pot's death, people who served beneath him conveniently blamed him for any "excesses." Meas Muth, a wanted KR military leader, said, "The low ranks had to respect the orders. It was like under Hitler. Hitler asked Goering to kill the Jews. If Goering did not do it, he would have been killed."[30] The KR's Nuon Chea dismissed the documentary evidence as "fabrications." Laughing, he asked, "Do I look like a killer?" [31]

Prime Minister Hun Sen first proposed an international court in June 1997. He had just defeated the KR militarily, and with the two ad hoc tribunals plodding along for Yugoslavia and Rwanda and some 2 million deaths as yet unanswered for in Cambodia, hunger for justice was widespread. But after requesting UN help, Hun Sen later resisted international attempts to create a court modeled on the UN Yugoslav and Rwandan tribunals. Judicial independence was not something he wanted Cambodians to begin demanding for themsleves. A former KR cadre himself, Hun Sen wanted to control the legal process. He cited the importance of protecting Cambodia's sovereignty. After so many years of being trampled by foreign meddlers, he said, his country could not allow itself to be treated like the "guard dog outside the courthouse." The Cambodian premier was also uneasy about working with the United Nations, which he blamed for isolating his regime and legitimating the Khmer Rouge throughout the 1980s.[32]

Hun Sen got much of what he demanded. The UN agreed that a new mixed Cambodian-international tribunal would be seated in Cambodia and not, as was first proposed, in The Hague or the Philippines. Cambodia would retain the authority to limit the number and rank of indictees. Cambodian police had arrested "Duch," the man who ran the notorious Tuol Sleng prison and effectively headed the secret police, and Ta Mok, a top political and military leader who exercised absolute control over the KR's southwest zone. But Hun Sen had proven himself unwilling to round up Khieu Samphan, the former head of state, or Ieng Sary, the former foreign minister. The two men lived undisturbed in the northwest province of Pailin, tilling their gardens and enjoying the company of their grandchildren. Even more significant in ensuring Hun Sen's domination over the court, although foreigners would participate, the majority of judges and prosecutors would be Cambodian. Despite all of these concessions by UN negotiators, Hun Sen eventually decided that even this tame court would intrude too much on his power. The mixed tribunal idea was scrapped, and Hun Sen said Cambodia would carry out its own genocide trials—trials that he would inevitably try to control.

Iraq

The Iraqi case has proven even more challenging to international lawyers and justice advocates. In 1997, three years after Human Rights Watch made its unsuccessful bid to see Iraq charged at the ICJ, a governmental and non-governmental coalition at the British House of Commons launched what it called the INDICT campaign. The INDICT coalition appealed to the UN Security Council to set up yet another ad hoc court modeled on those for Yugoslavia and Rwanda. INDICT urged that this court try members of Saddam Hussein's Ba'athist regime not only for the "genocidal Anfal campaign against the Kurds" but also for Iraq's invasion of Iran and Kuwait, its repression and execution of Iraqi citizens, and other crimes. In the Iraqi case, unlike in Cambodia, Rwanda, and eventually Serbia, the same regime that committed the genocide remained in power. Still, advocates hoped to establish an institution whose indictments would at least prevent Iraqi officials from traveling for fear of arrest. Victims could await the day when a successor to Hussein saw fit to turn over suspected Iraqi war criminals to an international body. The Clinton administration and the U.S. Congress were supportive of the initiative. In October 1998 Clinton signed into law the Iraq Liberation Act, section 6 of which called for the establishment of an international tribunal for Iraq. But no concrete steps have yet been taken to establish such a court.

The International Criminal Court (ICC)

In the midst of all this activity to prosecute past perpetrators of atrocities in specific national cases, a far more ambitious campaign was under way around the world. One by one, in a fashion reminiscent of the process that had followed the genocide convention's passage, UN member states had begun submitting their ratifications to the 1998 Rome Treaty, the statute creating a permanent International Criminal Court (ICC) that would try *future* perpetrators of war crimes, crimes against humanity, and genocide. The international tribunal will be formed when sixty countries ratify the treaty. By November 2001, forty-three had done so, nearly one-third of which were Western European states. The court was thought likely to come into existence by the end of 2002. Despite America's pivotal support for the ad hoc tribunals and the Cambodia mixed court, the United States opposed the creation of the ICC on the grounds that rogue prosecutors would use it to harass U.S. soldiers. International lawyers and diplomats modified the court's statute to address U.S. concerns, giving the court jurisdiction only as a last resort. The ICC would step in only if U.S. courts were "unable or unwilling." But neither the Clinton nor the successor Bush administration deemed the benefits to the United States worth any potential infringement on U.S. sovereignty.

The Record

A Giant Without Arms and Legs

Before one rushes to support the International Criminal Court, it is worth asking how the Yugoslav and Rwandan UN courts have fared. Since their creation, both have been slammed as "fig leaves" for international apathy. If the Nuremberg court was criticized for being a tool of state power ("victors' justice"), states seemed all too un-invested in the outcomes of the Hague and Arusha tribunals. The United States and Europe did not initially give the courts the kind of national backing they needed to succeed. Like the UN peacekeepers on the ground in Rwanda and Srebrenica, UN lawyers at the ad hoc tribunals were disappointed by the seeming indifference of the UN member states. They concluded that the major powers were less intent on actually punishing Balkan or Rwandan sinners than they were determined to get the crises out of the headlines. Indeed, while the war in

Bosnia progressed from 1993 until the Dayton agreement was signed in November 1995, the Security Council treated the court at The Hague as a nuisance, not as a diplomatic tool. The first president of the tribunal, Antonio Cassese, appeared before the General Assembly around the time of the Dayton agreement and declared, "Our tribunal is like a giant who has no arms and legs. To walk and work he needs artificial limbs. These artificial limbs are the state authorities."[33] U.S. authorities needed to deliver telephone intercepts and satellite snapshots of fields of unarmed men under Serb supervision that turned into piles of freshly turned earth.

But for the first two years of the UN court's life, the intelligence was not forthcoming. Cassese clawed for money and personnel, which, with nothing to show for the early money invested, was tough to justify. Every penny had to be raised and therefore pinched. Tribunal investigators had trouble getting access to witnesses and grave sites. Arrests were flukes. The courts got custody of only those suspects who strayed into enemy territory or bumped into jarred survivors while abroad.

With the deployment of some 60,000 NATO troops in Bosnia from late 1995 on, many hoped that the Hague process would come to bear a keener resemblance to Nuremberg. But NATO's initial policy of arresting only those war crimes suspects its forces happened to encounter created a surreal situation on the ground: Western reporters could visit alleged culprits as they lounged in local cafes. Unarmed curiosity-seekers could visit the indictees in apartment buildings where their names were emblazoned above their doorbells. And torture survivors watching local television could spot their former assailants at rock concerts sitting alongside state dignitaries. All the while, NATO soldiers steered clear. During the first eighteen months of the NATO deployment, NATO did not arrest a single indictee. Balkan war crimes suspects not only lived freely but also continued to occupy positions of authority, obstructing refugee returns and using the media to continue to demonize their former battlefield foes. "Force protection," or avoiding casualties, often seemed NATO's top priority.

But this policy of nonconfrontation was not cost-free for U.S. policymakers. Human rights groups, op-ed writers, and legislators did not disappear with the signing of the Dayton accords. They hounded the Clinton administration for its "craven" refusal to make arrests. In July 1997 Human Rights Watch, Amnesty International, the International Helsinki Federation, and the Coalition for International Justice, another nongovernmental group funded by philanthropist George Soros, published a full list of the indictees. In their joint Arrest Now! campaign, the human rights advocates listed the suspects' home and work addresses, as well as the places they liked to drink coffee, take walks, or work out. They also included information on the number and nationality of NATO forces nearby. U.S. and NATO officials were humiliated.

Senator Jesse Helms (R.–N.C.), the chairman of the Senate Foreign Relations Committee, compounded the embarrassment by sending a mocking letter to Secretary Albright after the State Department issued a $5 million reward for information leading to the arrest of the leading Serb culprits. "I have the information that you are looking for," Helms wrote:

> Mr. Milosevic and Mr. Mladic both are residing in Belgrade. Mr. Milosevic recently laid a wreath at the Grave of the Unknown Soldier on Mount Avala (to mark the first anniversary of the NATO bombing of Serbia). His address is: Presidential Palace, 15 Uzicka Street, Dedinje district, Belgrade.
>
> Mr. Mladic is apparently unaware that he should be in hiding—he took a leisurely afternoon stroll down Knez Mihailova Street on Friday, March 24, waving at Belgraders as he walked along, and was spotted just this weekend at the Belgrade stadium taking in a soccer match.
>
> Mr. Karadzic remains in the Pale area of Bosnia—living in the midst of thousands of NATO peacekeepers—where he has been seen regularly in public in recent months.
>
> Reward payment should be made to Rev. Franklin Graham's *Samaritan's Purse*, a well-known and highly respected charitable organization in North Carolina (Franklin is Billy Graham's son).
>
> Kindest regards.
>
> Sincerely,
>
> Jesse Helms[34]

A change in NATO policy was catalyzed by this negative publicity, by the internal advocacy of U.S. officials like Madeleine Albright, by the election of the liberal internationalist Tony Blair as British prime minister, and by the recognition that NATO troops would never be able to leave the Balkans if war criminals continued to run the local show.

In July 1997, on Blair's initiative, NATO made its first arrest. British troops snatched a pair of Serb concentration camp guards near their former stomping ground in Prijedor, northern Bosnia, fatally shooting one. The

Serbs staged a few scattered protests, but they blew mainly hot air. With the myth of Serb solidarity again exposed, the major powers began sending a steady trickle of culprits to The Hague. The roll call in the detention unit swelled. In addition, Bosnia's local authorities began themselves detaining the suspects, hoping to earn foreign aid or to score political points at home in the process. Because NATO's threat of arrests had at last been made credible by actual round-ups, some suspects turned themselves in, preferring life in a European prison to life on the run.

Each time the UN court at The Hague seemed on the verge of sagging into extinction, it received an injection of cash, criminals, or credibility. In 1996, when it needed to gain custody of a war crimes suspect in order to stage a trial, Dusan Tadic, a Bosnian Serb camp guard, strolled into a German bar, where he was recognized by one of his victims. In the summer of 1997, when the tribunal was inundated by shrill complaints about Serb killers waltzing through NATO checkpoints, British troops staged their Prijedor raid. In the fall of 1997, when the court was criticized as biased against Serbs, Western diplomats squeezed Croatia to turn over Bosnian Croat commander Tihomir Blaskic and ten more Croat suspects. In 1999, after six years of escaping indictment, Serbian president Milosevic presided over the commission of atrocities in Kosovo, a province in his own republic. This enabled the Hague prosecutor to establish a much clearer chain of command and to indict him publicly with crimes against humanity and war crimes, the first step in the two-year process that eventually landed him in UN custody.

The Hague court has grown beyond anybody's expectation. The very same institution that had a budget of $11 million in 1994, spent more than $96 million in 2000. The detention center initially housed only the relatively low-ranking Tadic; by November 2001 it held forty-eight inmates. And the one-person staff that originally consisted of only deputy prosecutor Graham Blewitt topped 1,000 in 2001, including some 300 on the prosecutor's staff. A court that once occupied a few rooms of the Dorint Insurance building was bursting at the seams of the sprawling complex and on the verge of annexing additional neighborhood property. With three functional courtrooms, a visitor to the Krstic trial could also hear the concentration camp guards from Omarska testifying in their own defense or listen to the wrenching reminiscences of an elderly Muslim woman testifying about the massacre of her family. After a slow start, the Clinton administration played a key role in helping the institution grow. During Clinton's second term, the United States provided the tribunal with more financial support than any other country, as well as senior personnel. Most significant, the United States turned over technical and photographic intelligence that greatly facilitated trials like that of General Krstic. Of course, Clinton also left office while the Bosnian war's three leading men, Mladic, Karadzic, and Milosevic, remained at large.

When it came to rounding up top suspects, the UN court for Rwanda was more successful than its better-publicized and better-resourced counterpart at The Hague. In Bosnia, because the gains of ethnic cleansing were preserved in the Dayton deal, suspected war criminals were able to take shelter, and even prosper, in territory that after the war continued to be controlled by their ethnic group. In Rwanda, by contrast, the ethnic Tutsi who began governing the country after the genocide threatened to arrest and execute killers who dared return. Most of the genocide suspects thus fled to neighboring African countries, where they were apprehended and extradited to the UN court in Arusha. The fifty-three held in custody at the Arusha detention center included many of the highest-ranking officials of the Hutu-controlled government and key planners and inciters of the genocide, including not only ringleader Colonel Bagosora, but the prime minister, the director of Radio Mille Collines, and the leaders of the various machete-wielding militias.

Despite its impressive record of locking up the once-fearsome *génocidaire,* however, the court has struggled. Early on, lawyers and judges were hampered by intermittent phone service, the absence of internet access, and scant research support, so that the prosecution staff often could not communicate with investigators in the field. But even after the logistic headaches eased, the court was plagued by corruption, nepotism, and mismanagement. Squirreled away in east-central Africa in a jumping-off spot for safaris and trips to nearby Mount Kilimanjaro, many staff members lazed about Arusha on cushy UN salaries. The court was so dysfunctional that a few of the early court reporters were found unable to type.

Although some of the corrupt early employees were fired, the tribunal still had not gained its stride by late 2001. International observers continued to fault the snail's pace of the proceedings. Repeated delays exasperated Rwanda's survivors. In addition, human rights advocates began noting the severe due process ramifications to locking up defendants for years on end without trial.

In 1999 the State Department issued a $5 million ransom for information leading to the apprehension of Yugoslavia's three leading war crimes suspects. U.S. forces in the Balkans were not ordered to arrest the indictees.

Department of State, Rewards for Justice Program

Courting Attention

Despite the presence of high-powered defendants in UN custody, none of the early trials had the effect on survivors that the 1961 trial of Adolf Eichmann, the Nazi official in charge of Jewish deportations, for instance, had on Israelis. Citizens in Rwanda and Bosnia paid almost no attention to the court proceedings. Israelis recall the days when they huddled around their radios to hear for the first time the details of Nazi horrors, whereas Bosnians and Rwandans just shrug when the courts are mentioned. They are deemed irrelevant to their daily lives. Ignorance is rife.

For their first six years of existence, the tribunals themselves did virtually nothing to reach out to the countries on whose behalf they were doing justice. The courts thus missed opportunities to deter, to legitimate victim claims, and to establish individual (as opposed to collective) guilt. Although almost every Bosnian had a television set, the trials at The Hague were not broadcast live back to the region. Indeed, shockingly, the UN Press Office did not translate its press releases into Serbo-Croatian until February 2000. Only a few of the indictments were available online. Judges and lawyers

accustomed to working within national judicial systems that needed no
promotion had spent their careers assiduously shying away from the press;
they had no experience attracting attention, as they needed to do if they
were to engage Bosnians or Rwandans with the proceedings. As one senior
lawyer in the court registry at The Hague put it:

> In Western countries courts automatically have a certain respect. They
> are recognized in the community. People understand their role; they
> are covered in the press; citizens may serve in juries. They simply don't
> need to promote themselves. But if you are doing what we are doing,
> hundreds of miles away, in a different language under a different sys-
> tem, you have to do things that courts don't ordinarily do. . . . If you
> just sit here and hear cases, you simply won't get the job done.

The trials also moved so slowly that local interest was hard to sustain.
Conducting complex investigations in foreign lands through interpreters
years after the crimes and without much pertinent international legal
precedent was no easy chore. Courtroom participants had to adjust to the
hybrid nature of the law itself. The tribunals' statute took its adversarial
nature and rules of evidence from the Anglo-American tradition, but, as in
continental Europe, it denied trial by jury, allowed hearsay, and permitted
the questioning of defendants. As precedents were set and the tribunals
began to establish a jurisprudential, historical record of the war, the trial
pace began to quicken somewhat.

But the slowness could not be blamed on the novelty and complexity of
the process alone. Tribunal courtooms in the The Hague and Arusha were
more often vacant than full. Judges allowed innumerable breaks in the proceedings and rarely challenged the relevancy of the counsels' frequently
rambling lines of inquiry. Defense counsel earned in excess of $110 per
hour, an unremarkable rate in the United States and Western Europe but a
monthly wage, or windfall, for Balkan or African lawyers. The incentive
structure thus invited prolix posturing, as defense lawyers stalled trials in
order to be able to bill more hours.

In late 1999 the Hague tribunal finally launched an outreach program
designed to help the trials reach citizens of the former Yugoslavia. This
small office of five was set up to conduct educational seminars, arrange visits for courtroom personnel to the Balkans, and attempt to generate local
media coverage. Although it was a tall order to win (or open) the minds of

AP/Wide World Photos

Indicted by the UN war crimes tribunal for war crimes and genocide in 1995, Bosnian Serb army commander General Ratko Mladic remained at large as of December 2001. Mladic here relaxes in March 1996 at one of his command posts.

a skeptical Bosnian audience, the new outreach office made a few early inroads. With its help, Mirko Klarin, the same independent journalist who in 1991 had recommended the establishment of an international war crimes tribunal and who had covered the Hague court's proceedings since they began, prepared fifteen-minute weekly television summaries of the tribunal's activities. Only Bosnia's independent television networks picked them up, but this at least meant some viewership. One more daring proposal was to stage actual portions of the UN trials on Balkan soil. Some groaned at the mammoth security risks of hauling defendants, lawyers, and judges to a volatile region. Others argued that the money could be better spent on investigations or that the gimmicky nature of a road trip would necessarily make the proceedings seem more like show trials than trials. The greatest boon to interest in the tribunals will be the Milosevic trial, which will start in 2002.

Radio is Rwanda's media outlet of choice. But although the UN tribunal prosecuted well-known, high-level suspects right from the start, few Rwandans listened to the proceedings. In 2000, Internews, an entrepreneurial American NGO, prepared a documentary in the Rwandan language on the UN trials in Arusha. New York producer Mandy Jacobson arranged town-hall-style screening sessions throughout Rwanda. The Rwandans who gathered had never before seen trial footage and gasped at the sight of their tormentors in the dock.

Truth-Telling

For all of the imperfections of the two courts, one reason many tribunal staff were converted to the idea of moving portions of trials to the Balkans and Rwanda was that they thought the proceedings were increasingly delivering messages essential to reconciliation. For the first time, the perpetrators of genocide and crimes against humanity were being forced to appear before a court of law, where their self-serving arguments could be formally challenged. If Serbia's Slobodan Milosevic and Rwanda's Théoneste Bagosora once insisted that "uncontrolled elements" were carrying out the killings, the prosecutors at the Yugoslav and Rwanda tribunals had the opportunity to dismantle these claims, showing that these men were very much in control. The evidence proved that what were once called "failed states" were in fact all too successful in implementing their designs.

In order to achieve their truth-telling aims, prosecutors presented damning visual and oral evidence, including documentary paper trails and hundreds of witness interviews. The very same defendants who claimed to be "out of the loop" were proven repeatedly to be central to it. The lawyers spelled out the elaborate command and control arrangements within each of the factions, demonstrating that military and political leaders were in close contact with the forces committing atrocities.

In the Srebrenica trial, for example, General Krstic said that General Mladic, the true villain, had already dispatched him to Zepa when Mladic began killing the men around Srebrenica.[35] Krstic said this alternative assignment was "no accident" because General Mladic would never have had the nerve to order the murder of so many men in his presence. Yet the prosecution presented evidence that placed Krstic at the scene of the crime and that recorded his directives. They showed Bosnian Serb leader Karadzic later hailing Krstic as a "great commander" and decorating him for his heroics in "planning and implementing the Srebrenica operation."[36]

In both the Yugoslav and the Rwanda tribunals, the self-serving defendants have aided the prosecutors. In the hopes of securing lighter sentences, the suspects have frequently turned on one another. This has facilitated the prosecution of several perpetrators and enabled the courts to establish certain "facts" by broad consensus. Krstic, as mentioned, implicated General Mladic and five more junior officers, describing them as "mad" and responsible for "anything that might have gone on."[37]

The trials have also belied a second claim made by the perpetrators (and, incidentally, by Western policymakers)—that the "ethnic" violence simply exploded spontaneously. Mounds of detailed evidence have demonstrated sophisticated planning and organization behind the bloodiest operations. Elaborate requisitioning of men, vehicles, ammunition, and remote locations were indispensable to most large-scale massacres. The Rwanda trials have shown how lists of Tutsi victims were prepared and systematically distributed down the chain of command, from the state level, to the regional level, to the prefectures, to the communes, and then to the individual hamlets, or cellules. That perpetrators and planners were so few in number and so identifiable indicated that they also could have been stopped.

In the case of the Yugoslav tribunal, although perpetrators clearly committed their crimes on ethnic grounds, the climate in the detention center that houses war crimes suspects has revealed the limits to much of the ethnic passion in the Balkans. The ruddy-faced, chain-smoking Irishman named Tim McFadden who runs the UN prison configured the facility to mandate mixing among prisoners of all ethnicities. None of the prison floors are segregated by nationality. Those dedicated to killing members of rival ethnic groups have thus been forced to watch television, take English or pottery classes, or lift weights with their onetime foes. The inmates have not become security risks to the guards or to one another. Ironically, as the trials have progressed and indictees of the same ethnic group have begun implicating one another in an effort to mitigate their own sentences, severe *intra*-ethnic security risks have arisen. McFadden is now concocting schemes to separate members of the same ethnic group who once conspired.

The trials at the ad hoc tribunals have also affirmed the ghastly claims of survivors, refugees, and Western journalists. The courts were set up, as the Nuremberg court was before them, to verify "incredible events by credible evidence."[38] So far they have given some acknowledgment to victims who were once taunted that their suffering would go unnoticed, unremembered, and above all unredressed. Although the crimes under discussion were eventually documented by journalists in Western countries, the local media in the Balkans and Rwanda usually dismissed the reports as "Western lies." Thus, many citizens still refuse to accept the nature or scale of the crimes committed in their name.

During the Krstic trial, again, a former Bosnian Serb soldier took the stand on behalf of the defense and said, "As a human being, I cannot believe." A former officer in the Drina Corps agreed, noting, "I do not wish or want to believe." He claimed that the "Muslim media" had wildly exaggerated the number of men killed, calling the figure of more than 7,000 murdered Muslims "incredible." It would have been noticed, he said, if "7,000 sparrows had been killed, let alone people."[39]

But the prosecution team presented vivid color photos of mass graves and the clothed skeletons within them. They screened satellite photos of the men gathered in fields awaiting execution. They ran Bosnian Serb television footage of the Serbs hauling men from the woods into buses and firing antiaircraft guns into the forests where the Muslims were scrambling for their lives. A lower-level Bosnian Serb soldier testified that the execution squads fired "over and over . . . until their fingers hurt." And perhaps most damning, the prosecution played intercepted telephone conversations between senior Serb officials. After weeks of denying his own role, General Krstic could only sit stunned and motionless when the prosecution played a recording from July 15, 1995, in which a Serb colonel and Krstic discussed the murder and disposal of their Muslim captives. The colonel asks whether he can have more troops because "there are still 3,500 parcels that I have to distribute." "Parcels" was code for Muslim men and "distribute" code for murder. "Fuck it," Krstic is heard saying, "I'll see what I can do."[40]

Krstic grew visibly agitated in the courtroom as the recording was played, but he recovered quickly, denying his own involvement. Still, it was significant that Krstic's legal team never contested that more than 7,000 men had been murdered. When Krstic was cross-examined as to why he did not report these crimes, he claimed he had "intended" to do so but "feared for my security and that of my family."[41] "Not in my wildest dreams was I able to take steps," Krstic said, confirming the savage event and the cover-up.[42] Serbs had been the original aggressors in the wars in Slovenia,

Croatia, Bosnia, and Kosovo, but their local leaders had emphasized only their suffering. Gradually, thanks in part to The Hague's refusal to go away, Serbia's population began to face the atrocities carried out in their name. Many even recognized that because the UN tribunal was establishing individual responsibility, it could do a great deal to rehabilitate Serbia in the eyes of the rest of the world.

It was not just the perpetrators or the ordinary Serb civilians who needed to hear evidence of what had occurred. It was also, alas, the victims, many of whom still clung to hope. In November 2000, a Muslim woman testified about the fall of Srebrenica and the disappearance of her husband and two sons. Before stepping off the stand, she asked the judges if she could herself pose a question to General Krstic. One of her sons was thirteen when Serb soldiers pulled him away from her outside the Dutch UN base. "I plead that you ask Mr. Krstic if there is any hope," she said to the judge, as she choked on her grief. "At least for that child which they took alive from my hands. I dream about him. He speaks to me. Does Mr. Krstic know if he is somewhere, alive?" Krstic sat frozen, his head down.[43]

Chapter 14

Conclusion

Over the course of the last century, the United States has made modest progress in its responses to genocide. The persistence and proliferation of dissenters within the U.S. government and human rights advocates outside it have made a policy of silence in the face of genocide more difficult to sustain. As Serbian president Slobodan Milosevic learned, state sovereignty no longer necessarily shields a perpetrator of genocide from either military intervention or courtroom punishment.

But such advances have been eclipsed by America's toleration of unspeakable atrocities, often committed in clear view. The personalities and geopolitical constraints influencing U.S. decision-making have shifted with time, but the United States has consistently refused to take risks in order to suppress genocide. The United States is not alone. The states bordering genocidal societies and the European powers have looked away as well. Despite broad public consensus that genocide should "never again" be allowed, and a good deal of triumphalism about the ascent of liberal democratic values, the last decade of the twentieth century was one of the most deadly in the grimmest century on record. Rwandan Hutus in 1994 could freely, joyfully, and systematically slaughter 8,000 Tutsi a day for 100 days without any foreign interference. Genocide occurred *after* the Cold War; *after* the growth of human rights groups; *after* the advent of technology that allowed for instant communication; *after* the erection of the Holocaust Museum on the Mall in Washington, D.C.

Perversely, America's public awareness of the Holocaust often seemed to set the bar for concern so high that we were able to tell ourselves that contemporary genocides were not measuring up. As the writer David Rieff noted, "never again" might best be defined as "Never again would Germans kill Jews in Europe in the 1940s."[1] Either by averting their eyes or attending to more pressing conventional strategic and political concerns, U.S. leaders who have denounced the Holocaust have themselves repeatedly allowed genocide.

What is most shocking about America's reaction to Turkey's killing of Armenians, the Holocaust, Pol Pot's reign of terror, Iraq's slaughter of the Kurds, Bosnian Serbs' mass murder of Muslims, and the Hutu elimination of Tutsi is not that the United States refused to deploy U.S. ground forces to combat the atrocities. For much of the century, even the most ardent interventionists did not lobby for U.S. ground invasions. What is most shocking is that U.S. policymakers did almost nothing to deter the crime. Because America's "vital national interests" were not considered imperiled by mere genocide, senior U.S. officials did not give genocide the moral attention it warranted. Instead of undertaking steps along a continuum of intervention—from condemning the perpetrators or cutting off U.S aid to bombing or rallying a multinational invasion force—U.S. officials tended to trust in negotiation, cling to diplomatic niceties and "neutrality," and ship humanitarian aid.

Indeed, on occasion the United States directly or indirectly aided those committing genocide. It orchestrated the vote in the UN Credentials Committee to favor the Khmer Rouge. It sided with and supplied U.S. agricultural and manufacturing credits to Iraq while Saddam Hussein was attempting to wipe out the country's Kurds. Along with its European allies, it maintained an arms embargo against the Bosnian Muslims even after it was clear that the arms ban prevented the Muslims from defending themselves. It used its clout on the UN Security Council to mandate the withdrawal of UN peacekeepers from Rwanda and block efforts to re-deploy there. To the people of Bosnia and Rwanda, the United States and its Security Council allies held out the promise of protection—a promise that that they were not prepared to keep.

The key question, after a century of false promise, is: Why does the United States stand so idly by?

Knowledge

The most common response is, "We didn't know." This is not true. To be sure, the information emanating from countries victimized by genocide was imperfect. Embassy personnel were withdrawn, intelligence assets on the ground were scarce, editors were typically reluctant to assign their reporters to places where neither U.S. interests nor American readers were engaged, and journalists who attempted to report the atrocities were limited in their mobility. As a result, refugee claims were difficult to confirm and body counts notoriously hard to establish. Because genocide is usually veiled under the cover of war, some U.S. officials at first had genuine difficulty distinguishing deliberate atrocities against civilians from conventional conflict.

But although U.S. officials did not know all there was to know about the nature and scale of the violence, they knew a remarkable amount. From Henry Morgenthau Sr., the well-connected U.S. ambassador in Constantinople in 1915, to Jon Western, the junior intelligence analyst on Bosnia in 1993, U.S. officials have pumped a steady stream of information up the chain to senior decision-makers—both early warnings ahead of genocide and vivid documentation during it. Much of the best intelligence appeared in the morning papers. Back in 1915, when communications were primitive, the *New York Times* managed to publish 145 stories about the Turkish massacre of Armenians. Nearly eighty years later, the same paper reported just four days after the beginning of the Rwanda genocide that "tens of thousands" of Rwandans had already been murdered. It devoted more column inches to the horrors of Bosnia between 1992 and 1995 than it did to any other single foreign story.

In an age of instant information, U.S. officials have gone from claiming that they "didn't know" to suggesting—as President Clinton did in his 1998 Rwanda apology—that they "didn't fully appreciate." This, too, is misleading. It is true that the atrocities that were known remained abstract and remote, rarely acquiring the status of knee-buckling knowledge among ordinary Americans. Because the savagery of genocide so defies our everyday experience, many of us failed to wrap our minds around it. We gradually came to accept the depravity of the Holocaust, but then slotted it in our consciousness as "history"; we resisted acknowledging that genocide was occurring in the present. Survivors and witnesses had trouble making the unbelievable believable. Bystanders were thus able to retreat to the "twilight between knowing and not knowing."

But this is not an alibi. We are responsible for our incredulity. The stories that emerge from genocidal societies are by definition incredible. That was the lesson the Holocaust should have taught us. In case after case of genocide, accounts that sounded far-fetched and that could not be independently verified repeatedly proved true. With so much wishful thinking debunked, we should long ago have shifted the burden of proof away from the refugees and to the skeptics, who should be required to offer persuasive reasons for disputing eyewitness claims. A bias toward belief would do less harm than a bias toward disbelief.

U.S. officials have been reluctant to imagine the unimaginable because of the implications. Indeed, instead of aggressively hunting for deeper knowledge or publicizing what was already known, they have taken shelter in the fog of plausible deniability. They have used the search for certainty as an excuse for paralysis and postponement. In most of the cases of genocide documented in this book, U.S. officials who "did not know" or "did not fully appreciate" chose not to.

Influence

A second response to the question of why the United States did so little is that it could not have done much to stop the horrors. Although Albert Hirschman's categories (futility, perversity, jeopardy) helped classify the main U.S. justifications for inaction, they do not help us determine what the United States *could* have achieved, or at what cost. The only way to ascertain the consequences of U.S. diplomatic, economic, or military measures would have been to undertake them. We do know, however, that the perpetrators of genocide were quick studies who were remarkably attuned both to the tactics of their murderous predecessors and to the world's response. From their brutal forerunners, they learned lessons in everything from dehumanizing their victims and deploying euphemisms to constructing concentration camps and lying about and covering up their crimes. And from the outside world they learned the lesson of impunity.

If anything testifies to the U.S. capacity for influence, it is the extent to which the perpetrators kept an eye trained on Washington and other Western capitals as they decided how to proceed. Talaat Pasha frequently observed that no one had prevented Sultan Abdul Hamid from murdering Armenians. Hitler was emboldened by the fact that absolutely nobody "remembered the Armenians." Saddam Hussein, noting the international community's relaxed response to his chemical weapons attacks against Iran and his bulldozing of Kurdish villages, rightly assumed he would not be punished for using poison gases against his own people. Rwandan gunmen deliberately targeted Belgian peacekeepers at the start of their genocide because they knew from the U.S. reaction to the deaths of eighteen U.S. soldiers in Somalia that the murder of Western troops would likely precipitate their withdrawal. The Bosnian Serbs publicly celebrated the Mogadishu casualties, knowing that they would never have to do battle with U.S. ground forces. Milosevic saw that he got away with the brutal suppression of an independence movement in Croatia and reasoned he would pay no price for committing genocide in Bosnia and Kosovo. Because so many individual perpetrators were killing for the first time and deciding daily how far they would go, the United States and its allies missed critical opportunities to try to deter them. When they ignored genocide around the world, U.S. officials certainly did not intend to give the perpetrators the go-ahead. But since at least some killers thought they were doing the world a favor by "cleansing" the "undesirables," they likely interpreted silence as consent or even support.

Although it is impossible to prove the outcome of actions never tried, the best testament to what the United States might have achieved is what the United States *did* achieve. For all the talk of the likely futility of U.S. involvement, in the rare instances that the United States did act, it made a difference. After Secretary of State George Shultz's condemnations and Senator Claiborne Pell's abortive sanctions effort in 1988, Saddam Hussein did not again use gas against the Kurds. After the appeals of Turkey and the personal encounter of Secretary of State James Baker with Kurdish refugees, the United States joined its allies in creating a safe haven in northern Iraq, enabling more than a million Kurds to return to their homes. A Rwandan hotel owner credits a U.S. diplomat's mere phone calls with helping convince militias not to attack the Tutsi inhabitants of his hotel during the genocide. NATO bombing in Bosnia, when it finally came, rapidly brought that three-and-a-half-year war to a close. NATO bombing in Kosovo in 1999 liberated 1.7 million Albanians from tyrannical Serb rule. And a handful of NATO arrests in the former Yugoslavia has caused dozens of suspected war criminals to turn themselves in. One cannot assume that every measure contemplated by U.S. officials would have been effective, but there is no doubt that even these small or belated steps saved hundreds of thousands of lives. If the United States had made genocide prevention a priority, it could have saved countless more.

Will

The real reason the United States did not do what it could and should have done to stop genocide was not a lack of knowledge or influence but a lack of will. Simply put, American leaders did not act because they did not want to. They believed that genocide was wrong, but they were not prepared to invest the military, financial, diplomatic, or domestic political capital needed to stop it. The U.S. policies crafted in response to each case of genocide examined in this book were not the accidental products of neglect. They were concrete choices made by this country's most influential decisionmakers after unspoken *and* explicit weighing of costs and benefits.

In each case, U.S. policymakers in the executive branch (usually with the passive backing of most members of Congress) had two objectives. First, they wanted to avoid engagement in conflicts that posed little threat to American interests, narrowly defined. And second, they hoped to contain the political costs and avoid the moral stigma associated with allowing genocide. By and large, they achieved both aims. In order to contain the political fallout, U.S. officials overemphasized the ambiguity of the facts. They played up the likely futility, perversity, and jeopardy of any proposed intervention. They steadfastly avoided use of the word "genocide," which they believed carried with it a legal and moral (and thus political) imperative to act. And they took solace in the normal operations of the foreign policy bureaucracy, which permitted an illusion of continual deliberation, complex activity, and intense concern. One of the most important conclusions I have reached, therefore, is that the U.S. record is not one of failure. It is one of success. Troubling though it is to acknowledge, U.S. officials worked the system and the system worked.

To understand why the United States did not do more to stem genocide, it is not enough, of course, to focus on the actions of presidents or their foreign policy teams. In a democracy even an administration disinclined to act can be pressured into doing so. This pressure can come from inside or outside. Bureaucrats within the system who grasp the stakes can patiently lobby or brazenly agitate in the hope of forcing their bosses to entertain a full range of options. Unfortunately, although every genocide generated some activism within the U.S. foreign policy establishment, civil and foreign servants typically heeded what they took to be presidential indifference and public apathy. They assumed U.S. policy was immutable, that their concerns were already understood by their superiors, and that speaking (or walking) out would only reduce their capacity to improve the policy. Bosnia was the sole genocide of the twentieth century that generated a wave of resignations from the U.S. government. It is probably not coincidental that this was the one case where the protests of the foreign servants were bolstered daily by sustained public and press protest outside Foggy Bottom.

The executive branch has also felt no pressure from the second possible source: the home front. American leaders have been able to persist in turning away because genocide in distant lands has not captivated senators, congressional caucuses, Washington lobbyists, elite opinion shapers, grassroots groups, or individual citizens. The battle to stop genocide has thus been repeatedly lost in the realm of domestic politics. Although isolated voices have protested the slaughter, Americans outside the executive branch were largely mute when it mattered. As a result of this society-wide silence, officials at all levels of government calculated that the political costs of getting involved in stopping genocide far exceeded the costs of remaining uninvolved. The exceptions that have proven the rule were the ratification of the genocide convention after Reagan's Bitburg debacle and the NATO air campaign in Bosnia after Senate majority leader Bob Dole united with elite and grassroots activists to make President Clinton feel he was "getting creamed" for allowing Serb atrocities.

With foreign policy crises all over the world affecting more traditional U.S. interests, genocide has never secured top-level attention on its own merits. It takes political pressure to put genocide on the map in Washington. When Alison Des Forges of Human Rights Watch met with National Security Adviser Anthony Lake two weeks into the Rwanda genocide, he informed her that the phones were not ringing. "Make more noise!" he urged. Because so little noise has been made about genocide, U.S. decisionmakers have opposed U.S. intervention, telling themselves that they were doing all they could—and, most important, all they should—in light of competing American interests and a highly circumscribed understanding of what was domestically "possible" for the United States to do.

In the end, however, the inertia of the governed can not be disentangled from the indifference of the government. American leaders have both a circular and a deliberate relationship to public opinion. It is circular because their constituencies are rarely if ever aroused by foreign crises, even genocidal ones, in the absence of political leadership, and yet at the same time U.S. officials continually cite the absence of public support as grounds for inaction. The relationship is deliberate because American leadership has not been absent in such circumstances: It has been present but devoted mainly to minimizing public outrage.

Accountability

One mechanism for altering the calculus of U.S. leaders would be to make them publicly or professionally accountable for inaction. U.S. officials fear repercussions for their sins of commission—for decisions they make and policies they shape that go wrong. But none fear they will pay a price for their sins of omission. If everyone within the government is motivated to avoid "another Somalia" or "another Vietnam," few think twice about playing a role in allowing "another Rwanda."

Other countries and institutions whose personnel were actually present when genocide was committed have undertaken at least some introspection. The Netherlands, France, and the UN have staged inquiries into their responsibility for the fall of Srebrenica and the massacres that followed. But when the UN's investigators approached the U.S. mission in New York for assistance, their phone calls were not returned. In the end the UN team was forbidden from making any independent contact with U.S. government employees. The investigators were granted access to a group of hand-picked junior and midlevel officials who revealed next to nothing about what U.S. officials knew during the Srebrenica massacres.

The French, the Belgians, the UN, and the OAU have staged investigations on their roles in the Rwanda genocide. But in the United States, when some disgruntled members of the Congressional Black Caucus attempted to stage hearings on the part the U.S. played (or failed to play), they were rebuffed. Two officials in the Clinton administration, one at the National Security Council, the other at the State Department, conducted internal studies on the administration's response to the Rwanda slaughter. But they examined only the paper trail and did not publicly disclose their findings. The United States needs congressional inquiries with the power to subpoena documents and to summon U.S. officials of all ranks in the executive *and* legislative branches. Without meaningful disclosure, public awareness, and official shame, it is hard to imagine the U.S. response improving the next time around.

Even nongovernmental attempts at accountability might make a difference. In September 2001, the *Atlantic Monthly* published the results of my three-year investigation into the Clinton administration's response to the genocide in Rwanda. A few weeks later, according to officials on the National Security Council, a memo made its way to the desk of President George W. Bush on the subject of genocide prevention. The memo summarized the findings of the *Atlantic* article and warned of the likely outbreak of ethnic violence in Burundi. During the presidential campaign the previous year, Bush had said stopping genocide was not America's business. "I don't like genocide and I don't like ethnic cleansing," Bush had told Sam Donaldson of ABC, "but I would not send our troops."² After being elected and being presented with an account of the Clinton administration's failure, however, Bush wrote in firm letters in the margin of the memo: "NOT ON MY WATCH." While he was commander in chief, he was saying, genocide would not recur.

Bush's note certainly constituted a welcome statement of intent, but the president was in fact falling back into line with the other American presidents who pledged "never again." In order to put the sentiment into action, he would have to make meaningful public and bureaucratic commitments to stop genocide. He and his top foreign policy aides would need to issue an explicit presidential decision directive, rally support in their speeches, and demand the preparation of "off-the-shelf" contingency military planning. Otherwise, it is highly unlikely that U.S. officials or citizens would behave differently the next time ethnic chauvinists begin systematically wiping out a minority group. In any event, on September 11, 2001, just days after the president jotted his marginalia, Islamic terrorists turned four American civilian airliners into human fuel bombs, murdering more than 3,000 civilians, shattering the nation's sense of invulnerability, and causing the president to focus U.S. resources on a long-term "war on terrorism."

The Future

The September 11 attack on the United States will of course alter U.S. foreign policy. The attack might enhance the empathy of Americans inside and outside government toward peoples victimized by genocide. The fanatics who target the United States resemble the perpetrators of genocide in their espousal of collective responsibility of the most savage kind. They target civilians not because of anything they do personally but because of who they are. To earn a death sentence, it was enough in the twentieth century to be an Armenian, a Jew, or a Tutsi. On September 11, it was enough to be an American. In 1994 Rwanda, a country of just 8 million, experienced the numerical equivalent of more than two World Trade Center attacks every single day for 100 days. On an American scale this would mean 23 million people murdered in three months. When, on September 12, 2001, the United States turned for help to its friends around the world, Americans were gratified by the overwhelming response. When the Tutsi cried out, by contrast, every country in the world turned away.

Even if Americans become better able to imagine slaughter and identify with its victims, the U.S. government is likely to view genocide prevention as an undertaking it can not afford as it sets out to better protect Americans. Many are now arguing, understandably, that fighting terrorism means husbanding the country's resources and avoiding humanitarian intervention, which is said to harm U.S. "readiness." The Kosovo intervention and the Milosevic trial, once thought to mark important precedents, may come to represent high-water marks in genocide prevention and punishment.

This would be a tragic and ultimately self-defeating mistake. The United States should stop genocide for two reasons. The first and most compelling reason is moral. When innocent life is being taken on such a scale and the United States has the power to stop the killing at reasonable risk, it has a duty to act. It is this belief that motivates most of those who seek intervention. But history has shown that the suffering of victims has rarely been sufficient to get the United States to intervene.

Thus, even those driven by a sense of America's moral responsibility have tried to make the case by appealing to the second reason: enlightened self-interest. They warned that allowing genocide undermined regional and international stability, created militarized refugees, and signaled dictators that hate and murder were permissible tools of statecraft. Because these threats to U.S. interests were long-term dangers and not immediately apparent, however, they rarely swayed top U.S. policymakers. Genocide did undermine regional stability, but the destabilized areas tended to lie outside the U.S. sphere of concern. Refugees were militarized, but they tended not to wash up on America's shores. Dictators everywhere were signaled, but how they treated their own citizens was seen to have little impact on American military or economic security. Thus humanitarian intervention came about only on the rare occasions when the shorter term political interests of U.S. policymakers were at stake.

If it was difficult before September 11 to get U.S. decision-makers to see the long-term costs of allowing genocide, it will be even harder today when U.S. security needs are so acute and visible. But security for Americans at home and abroad is contingent on international stability, and there is perhaps no greater source of havoc than a group of well-armed extremists bent on wiping out a people on ethnic, national, or religious grounds.

Western governments have generally tried to contain genocide by appeasing its architects. But the sad record of the last century shows that the walls the United States tries to build around genocidal societies almost inevitably shatter. States that murder and torment their own citizens target citizens elsewhere. Their appetites become insatiable. Hitler began by persecuting his own people and then waged war on the rest of Europe and, in time, the United States. Saddam Hussein wiped out rural Kurdish life and then turned on Kuwait, sending his genocidal henchman Ali Hassan al-Majid to govern the newly occupied country. The United States now has reason to fear that the poisonous potions Hussein tried out on the Kurds will be used next on Americans. Milosevic took his wars from Slovenia and Croatia to Bosnia and then Kosovo. The United States and its European allies are continuing to pay for their earlier neglect of the Balkans by having to grapple with mounting violence in Macedonia that threatens the stability of southeastern Europe.

Citizens victimized by genocide or abandoned by the international community do not make good neighbors, as their thirst for vengeance, their irredentism, and their acceptance of violence as a means of generating change can turn them into future threats. In Bosnia, where the United States and Europe maintained an arms embargo against the Muslims, extremist Islamic fighters and proselytizers eventually turned up to offer succor. Some secular Muslim citizens became radicalized by the partnership, and the failed state of Bosnia became a haven for Islamic terrorists shunned elsewhere in the world. It appears that one of the organizations that infiltrated Bosnia in its hour of need and used it as a training base was Saudi terrorist mastermind Osama bin Laden's al-Qaeda.[3]

The United States should not frame its policy options in terms of doing nothing or unilaterally sending in the marines. America's leadership will be indispensable in encouraging U.S. allies and regional and international institutions to step up their commitments and capacities. Given the immensity of the harm caused by genocide, its prevention is a burden that must be shared. At the same time, the United States should do certain things in every case. It must respond to genocide with a sense of urgency, publicly identifying and threatening the perpetrators with prosecution, demanding the expulsion of representatives of genocidal regimes from international institutions such as the United Nations, closing the perpetrators' embassies in the United States, and calling upon countries aligned with the perpetrators to ask them to use their influence. When the dynamics on the ground warrant it, the United States should establish economic sanctions, freeze foreign assets, and use U.S. technical resources to deprive the killers of their means of propagating hate. With its allies, it should set up safe areas to house refugees and civilians, and protect them with well-armed and robustly mandated peacekeepers, airpower, or both. Given the affront genocide represents to America's most cherished values and to its interests, the United States must also be prepared to risk the lives of its soldiers in the service of stopping this monstrous crime.

For most of the second half of the twentieth century, the existence of the genocide convention appeared to achieve little. The United States did not ratify the treaty for forty years. Those countries that did ratify it never invoked it to stop or punish genocide. And instead of finally making U.S. policymakers more inclined to stop genocide, the belated U.S. ratification seemed only to make them more reluctant to use the "g-word." Still, Raphael Lemkin's coinage has done more good than harm. The international tribunals for the former Yugoslavia and Rwanda and the future International Criminal Court may not have come into existence without the convention's passage. The punishment that these courts dole out may help deter genocide in the long term. In addition, thanks to the existence of the convention and Lemkin's proselytizing around it, the word "genocide," which was not even named until 1948, has acquired a potent moral stigma. The vows of U.S. policymakers to never again allow the crime and the lengths to which they have gone, while allowing genocide, to deny its occurrence is in itself testament to the stigma. Hope for the convention's enforcement lies in this opprobrium and in the determination of those who helped push the United States to live up to its promise.

Few of those who attempted to get the leaden machinery of the U.S. government to respond to genocide began as crusaders or even messengers. Most experienced some moment of recognition that improved their vision and moved them out of a state of denial. Often they were transformed by firsthand exposure to a crime scene—Lemkin and Dallaire, certainly, but also Morgenthau, Karski, Becker, Twining, Quinn, Galbraith, Dole, McCloskey, Holbrooke, and hundreds of unnamed others. They saw something that haunted them, that turned the daily press accounts into vibrant cries from the grave, cries that broke through the cordon sanitaire that deflects unwelcome news.

During World War II, Arthur Koestler described those frustrated few who spoke up in the newspapers and public meetings against Nazi atrocities as "Screamers." The Screamers succeeded in reaching listeners for a moment, Koestler wrote, only to watch them shake themselves "like puppies who have got their fur wet" and return to the blissful place of ignorance and uninvolvement. "You can convince them for an hour," Koestler noted, but then "their mental half-defense begins to work and in a week the shrug of incredulity has returned like a reflex temporarily weakened by shock."[4]

Most of those who protested U.S. policy initially believed that if they could only succeed in conveying the horrors to those who had not borne witness, the community of listeners (local, national, international) would act. They possessed faith in the institutions to which they had offered allegiance. Lemkin, the immigrant, believed in the United States. There was no doubt in his mind that this country would adopt his crusade and ratify and enforce the genocide convention. William Proxmire, the quixotic senator, believed the convention had not been ratified because of some quirk in the legislative process. When he pledged to give a speech a day in the Senate, he thought Senate backlogs would mean a yearlong campaign at most. Although Peter Galbraith was aware of the potency of special interests on Capitol Hill, he believed that there were certain lines that U.S. lawmakers would not see crossed. Romeo Dallaire believed in the promise and nobility of the United Nations, which would never abandon citizens it had promised to protect. And the State Department protesters believed in the department. They were prepared to utilize the dissent channel, to speak out in the open forum, and to send heartfelt memos to the secretary of state. They believed that "never again" *would* the United States allow men and women to be herded into concentration camps in Europe where they would be starved, raped, and murdered.

All of the latter-day Screamers treated silence as if it were a further crime against humanity. They invoked the Holocaust analogy because they thought it would help them link a current crisis with a past tragedy and a current decision to abstain with a past decision to appease. Most of them saw opportunity and alternative where others felt trapped by inevitability and "reality," a reality they did not probe and therefore ultimately would not alter. They knew that it was individuals who would have to make a difference, which was not the same as believing that they would. They were usually branded "emotional," "irrational," "soft," or "naive." Many of them saw their careers destroyed by the stands they took. Some crumbled. A few, like Dallaire, may never recover.

Because of the way the stories turned out, and indeed because of the way genocide *keeps* turning out, it is easy to view these individuals as overly credulous or politically obtuse. But how many of us who look back at the genocides of the twentieth century, including the Holocaust, do not believe that these people were right? How many of us do not believe that the presidents, senators, bureaucrats, journalists, and ordinary citizens who did nothing, choosing to look away rather than to face hard choices and wrenching moral dilemmas, were wrong? And how can something so clear in retrospect become so muddled at the time by rationalizations, institutional constraints, and a lack of imagination? How can it be that those who fight on behalf of these principles are the ones deemed unreasonable?

George Bernard Shaw once wrote, "The reasonable man adapts himself to the world. The unreasonable one persists in trying to adapt the world to himself. Therefore, all progress depends on the unreasonable man." After a century of doing so little to prevent, suppress, and punish genocide, Americans must join and thereby legitimate the ranks of the unreasonable.

Notes

Preface

1. "Statement by President Clinton Regarding Proposals to Deal with Situation in Bosnia," Federal News Service, February 9, 1994.
2. Warren Christopher on *Face the Nation,* CBS, March 28, 1993.
3. "President's Commission on the Holocaust: Remarks on Receiving the Final Report of the Commission," September 27, 1979, *Public Papers of the Presidents of the United States: Jimmy Carter, 1979* (Washington, D.C.: GPO, 1979), p. 1773.
4. "Remarks at the International Convention of B'nai B'rith," September 6, 1984, *Public Papers of the Presidents of the United States: Ronald Reagan, 1987* (Washington, D.C.: GPO, 1987), p. 1244.
5. "Remarks of President George Bush at the Simon Wiesenthal Dinner, Century Plaza Hotel, Los Angeles, California," Federal News Service, June 16, 1991.
6. Clifford Krauss, "U.S. Backs Away from Charge of Atrocities in Bosnia Camps," *New York Times,* August 5, 1992, p. A12.
7. "Remarks at the Dedication of the U.S. Holocaust Memorial Museum," April 22, 1993, *Public Papers of the Presidents of the United States: William J. Clinton, 1993* (Washington, D.C.: GPO, 1994), p. 479.
8. See Leslie Gelb and Richard Betts, *The Irony of Vietnam: The System Worked* (Washington, D.C.: Brookings Institution, 1979).

Chapter 1, "Race Murder"

1. Edward Alexander, *A Crime of Vengeance: An Armenian Struggle for Justice* (New York: Free Press, 1991), p. 10; Jacques Derogy, *Resistance and Revenge: The Armenian Assassination of the Turkish Leaders Responsible for the 1915 Massacres and Deportations,* trans. A. M. Berrett (New Brunswick, N.J.: Transaction, 1990), pp. xix–xxi.
2. Estimates of the number of Armenians who died in 1915–1916 vary widely. Some Turkish historians claim just 200,000 Armenians were killed, mainly in the legitimate suppression of rebellion. See, for example, Stanford J. Shaw and Ezel Kural Shaw, *History of the Ottoman Empire and Modern Turkey,* vol. 2 (Cambridge: Cambridge University Press, 1977), pp. 315–316. Armenian sources often place the figure at more than 1.5 million; see Ronald Grigar Suny, *Looking Toward Ararat: Armenia in Modern History* (Bloomington: Indiana University Press, 1993), p. 114; Robert F. Melson, *Revolution and Genocide: On the Origins of the Armenian Genocide and the Holocaust* (Chicago: University of Chicago Press, 1992), p. 147. British historian Martin Gilbert estimates that some 600,000 Armenians were killed in massacres committed in Anatolia and an additional 400,000 died as a result of the brutalities and starvation inflicted upon them during the forced deportations from

Anatolia into the deserts of Syria and Mesopotamia; some 200,000 Armenians were forcibly converted to Islam. See Martin Gilbert, *The First World War: A Complete History* (New York: Henry Holt, 1994), p. 167.

3. "Says Turks Advise Christians to Flee," *New York Times,* January 11, 1915, p. 2.

4. "A People Killed Twice," *Guardian Weekend,* January 27, 2001, p. 35.

5. State Department translation of law of deportation presented by the Turkish governor of Trebinzond to U.S. consul Oscar Heizer, June 28, 1915, reproduced in the appendix to Leslie A. Davis, *The Slaughterhouse Province: An American Diplomat's Report on the Armenian Genocide, 1915–1917,* ed. Susan K. Blair (New Rochelle, N.Y.: A. D. Caratzas, 1989).

6. Russia was home to around 1.7 million Armenians before the war; some 2 million Armenians lived under harsh Ottoman rule. When the Young Turks seized power in Turkey in 1908, the Armenians lobbying for constitutional reform won some early concessions, but periodic massacres continued and the ethnic chauvinism of the ruling triumvirate led to a burst of "Turkification." Turkey aligned with Germany and Austria in World War I, allowing Germany to control the Dardanelles, Russia's lone warm-water lifeline, and causing Russia to declare war on Turkey in 1914.

7. Alexander, *A Crime of Vengeance,* pp. 69–70.

8. "Armenian Atrocities Scouted by Bernstorff. Calls Reports 'Pure Inventions'— Says the Catholics Wrote Under Pressure," *New York Times,* September 28, 1915, p. 2; "Armenians' Own Fault Bernstorff Now Says. They Brought Reprisals on Themselves by Trying to Stir up Rebellion Against Turkey," *New York Times,* September 29, 1915, p. 1. Count Johann Heinrich von Bernstorff was the German ambassador to the United States.

9. The Friends of Armenia, the Anglo-Armenian Association, and the British Armenia Committee secured meetings with senior British policymakers. Just beginning his scholarly career, British historian Arnold Toynbee joined the British Armenia Committee's propaganda subcommittee and published a pamphlet in 1915 that accused the Ottomans of planning "nothing less than the extermination of the whole Christian population within the Ottoman frontiers." Arnold Toynbee, *Armenian Atrocities: The Murder of a Nation* (London: Hodder & Stoughton, 1915), p. 27. See also Arnold Toynbee, "A Summary of Armenian History up to and Including the Year 1915," in Arnold Toynbee, ed., *The Treatment of Armenians in the Ottoman Empire, 1915–16: Documents Presented to Viscount Grey of Fallodon, Secretary of State for Foreign Affairs, by Viscount Bryce, with a Preface by Viscount Bryce* (London: Sir Joseph Causton and Sons, 1916).

10. Sir Edward Grey to Sir Francis Bertie, British ambassador to France, May 11, 1915, cited in Gary Jonathan Bass, *Stay the Hand of Vengeance: The Politics of War Crimes Tribunals* (Princeton: Princeton University Press, 2000), pp. 115, 348–349.

11. "Allies to Punish Turks Who Murder," *New York Times,* May 24, 1915, p. 1. The concept of crimes against humanity had its roots in the Roman concept of offenses against *jus gentium,* or the laws of all nations. Most Europeans identified with the Armenians' suffering because they were fellow Christians. But when the Russians suggested condemning "crimes against Christianity," it seemed too parochial, and the phrase "crimes against humanity and civilization" was chosen instead.

12. Jay Winter, "Under Cover of War: Genocide in the Context of Total War," paper presented at the National Holocaust Museum, Washington, D.C., September 28, 2000.

13. Henry Morgenthau, *Ambassador Morgenthau's Story* (Reading, England: Taderon Press, 2000), p. 217. Ambassador Morgenthau was the father of Henry Morgenthau Jr., who subsequently authored the famous pastoralization plan (or "potato patch" solution) that would have suppressed German industry after World War II.

14. Henry Morgenthau to Secretary of State Robert Lansing, July 10, 1915, cited in Bass, *Stay the Hand of Vengeance,* p. 346.

15. Morgenthau, *Ambassador Morgenthau's Story,* p. 218.

16. Ibid., p. 222.

17. Ibid., pp. 220, 223.

18. Ibid., p. 227.

19. Ibid., p. 225.

20. Henry Morgenthau to Secretary of State Robert Lansing, August 11, 1915, cited in Bass, *Stay the Hand of Vengeance,* p. 346.

21. Morgenthau, *Ambassador Morgenthau's Story,* p. 218.

22. "Turks Are Evicting Native Christians," *New York Times,* July 12, 1915, p. 4.

23. "Bryce Asks US to Aid Armenia. Says That All Christians in Trebizond, Numbering 10,000, Were Drowned," *New York Times,* September 21, 1915, p. 3.

24. "800,000 Armenians Counted Destroyed," *New York Times,* October 7, 1915, p. 3.

25. "Million Armenians Killed or in Exile," *New York Times,* December 15, 1915, p. 3.

26. "500,000 Armenians Said to Have Perished. Washington Asked to Stop Slaughter of Christians by Turks and Kurds," *New York Times,* September 24, 1915, p. 2; "Says Extinction Menaces Armenia; Dr. Gabriel Tells of More Than 450,000 Killed in Recent Massacres," *New York Times,* September 25, 1915, p. 3.

27. "Armenian Officials Murdered by Turks. Confirmation from Cairo of the Wholesale Atrocities That von Bernstorff Belittles," *New York Times,* September 30, 1915, p. 2. Leopold's crimes were mammoth, but unlike Abdul Hamid's, they were not aimed at wiping out one particular ethnic group. Any and every African slave was vulnerable. When a village failed to meet its rubber quota, Belgian soldiers or rubber company "sentries" often murdered whole communities or chopped the hands off the slaves, leaving them powerless to care for themselves or their families. Piles of severed hands and full skeletons littered Leopold's vast empire. The local people who fled ahead of the Europeans' arrival found their villages burned down when they returned. Exhausted, malnourished laborers were vulnerable to disease, which spread rapidly. All told, according to Jan Vansina, a historian and anthropologist at the University of Wisconsin, the Congo population was cut "by at least half" between 1880 and 1920. Some 10 million people died as a result of Leopold's presence. Cited in Adam Hochschild, *King Leopold's Ghost: A Story of Greed, Terror, and Heroism in Colonial Africa* (Boston: Houghton Mifflin, 1998), pp. 225–234.

28. "Pleas for Armenia by Germany Futile," *New York Times,* October 10, 1915, sec. 2, p. 19.

29. "Turkish Official Denies Atrocities," *New York Times,* October 15, 1915, p. 4.

30. George R. Montgomery, "Why Talaat Pasha's Assassin Was Acquitted," *Current History,* July 1921, p. 554.

31. Henry Morgenthau III, *Mostly Morgenthaus: A Family History* (New York: Ticknor & Fields, 1991), p. 170.

32. "Armenian Women Put up at Auction; Refugee Tells of the Fate of Those in Turkish Hands," *New York Times,* September 29, 1915, p. 3. The Committee on Ar-

menian Atrocities later became the Near East Relief Committee and subsequently the Near East Foundation.

33. Theodore Roosevelt to Samuel Dutton, November 24, 1915, in Theodore Roosevelt, *Fear God and Take Your Own Part* (New York: George H. Doran, 1916), p. 377. Peter Balakian, author of *Black Dog of Fate: A Memoir* (New York: Basic Books, 1997), steered me to Roosevelt's writings on the atrocities with his paper "From Ezra Pound to Theodore Roosevelt: An American Intellectual and Cultural Response to the Armenian Genocide," essay presented at the National Holocaust Museum, Washington, D.C., September 28, 2000.

34. Roosevelt, *Fear God,* pp. 381–382.

35. Balakian, "From Ezra Pound," citing Theodore Roosevelt, *The Letters of Theodore Roosevelt,* vol. 8: *The Days of Armageddon,* ed. Elting E. Morison (Cambridge, Mass.: Harvard University Press, 1954), pp. 1316–1318.

36. "Would Send Here 550,000 Armenians; Morgenthau Urges Scheme to Save Them from the Turks—Offers to Raise $1,000,000," *New York Times,* September 14, 1915, p. 2.

37. "Turkey Bars Red Cross," *New York Times,* October 19, 1915, p. 4.

38. "Appeals for Armenians," *New York Times,* February 18, 1916, p. 2.

39. Morgenthau, *Ambassador Morgenthau's Story,* pp. 13–14.

40. "Government Sends Plea for Armenia," *New York Times,* October 5, 1915.

41. Lansing was aware of the savagery of that deportation, as he added, "It was not to my mind the deportation which was objectionable but the horrible brutality which attended its execution." Secretary of State Robert Lansing to President Woodrow Wilson, November 21, 1916, in *Papers Relating to the Foreign Relations of the United States: The Lansing Papers, 1914–1920,* vol. 1 (Washington, D.C.: GPO, 1939), p. 42.

42. Morgenthau, *Ambassador Morgenthau's Story,* p. 385.

43. Woodrow Wilson, *The Public Papers of Woodrow Wilson,* vol. 5, ed. Stannard Baker and William E. Dodd (New York: Harper and Brothers, 1927), pp. 135–136.

44. Michael Marrus, *The Nuremberg War Crimes Trials, 1945–1946* (New York: Bedford, 1997), pp. 8–10. A few years earlier, President Wilson's adviser Edward House had noted that Lansing was inclined to allow sovereignty to shield all forms of state behavior. "He believes that almost any form of atrocity is permissible provided a nation's safety is involved," House wrote. Christopher Simpson, *The Splendid Blond Beast: Money, Law and Genocide in the Twentieth Century* (New York: Grove, 1993), p. 23.

45. Bass, *Stay the Hand of Vengeance,* p. 103.

46. Ibid., pp. 125–129.

47. Talaat Pasha, "Posthumous Memoirs of Talaat Pasha," trans. M. Zekeria, *Current History,* November 1921, pp. 287–295.

48. Near the close of the twentieth century, the Serb perpetrators of genocide in Bosnia would also evade international sanction by seizing European peacekeepers as hostages in order to stave off NATO air strikes.

49. Bass, *Stay the Hand of Vengeance,* p. 144.

Chapter 2, "A Crime Without a Name"

1. Robert Merrill Bartlett, *They Stand Invincible: Men Who Are Reshaping Our World* (New York: Thomas Y. Crowell, 1959), pp. 96–97. Lemkin's papers and recollections are scattered in a number of institutions. The New York Public Library has

screened four boxes onto microfilm. Larger collections of Lemkin's personal papers are housed at the American Jewish Historical Society at the Center for Jewish History in New York City and the Jacob Rader Marcus Center of the American Jewish Archives located at the Cincinnati, Ohio, campus of Hebrew Union Campus–Jewish Institute of Religion. Rabbi Steven L. Jacobs of the University of Alabama has the most complete collection of Lemkin's files and correspondence and is currently organizing the material for publication. Jacobs has edited a previously unpublished manuscript by Lemkin: Steven L. Jacobs, ed., *Raphael Lemkin's Thoughts on Genocide: Not Guilty* (Lewiston, N.Y.: Edwin Mellen Press, 1992). In 1984, James Martin and the Institute of Historical Review (an organization dedicated to Holocaust denial) published a nominal biography of Lemkin, entitled *The Man Who Invented Genocide*, which was an extended anti-Semitic rant. Jim Fussell, a scholar based in Washington, D.C., is preparing the first full-length biography.

2. Raphael Lemkin, "Totally Unofficial: The Autobiography of Raphael Lemkin," ch. 1. Lemkin's unpublished and incomplete autobiography, which was found among his papers after his death and is now in Jacobs's collection, is haphazardly paginated.

3. George R. Montgomery, "Why Talaat's Assassin Was Acquitted," *Current History*, July 1921, pp. 551–555. Tehlirian lived out his days in California.

4. Several years later, in 1926, Lemkin learned that Scholom Schwarzbart, a Jewish tailor orphaned in a pogrom in Ukraine in 1918, shot the Ukrainian minister of war Semion Petliure in Paris. As in the Tehlirian case, the jury found it difficult to acquit or condemn the bereaved assassin. They declared him "insane" and then freed him. After the Schwarzbart trial, Lemkin wrote an article describing the man's act as a "beautiful crime" and deploring the absence of a law banning the destruction of national, racial, and religious groups.

5. Lemkin Papers, New York Public Library, reel 2.

6. "Acts Constituting a General (Transnational) Danger Considered as Offences Against the Law of Nations," fifth conference of the International Bureau for Unification of Criminal Law, under the auspices of the Fifth Committee of the League of Nations, October 14, 1933, trans. James T. Fussell. Available at http://www.preventgenocide.org/lemkin/madrid1933-english.htm. He formulated his proposal as follows: Whosoever, out of hatred towards a racial, religious or social collectivity, or with a view to the extermination thereof, undertakes a punishable action against the life, bodily integrity, liberty, dignity or economic existence of a person belonging to such a collectivity, is liable, for the crime of barbarity, to a penalty of . . . unless his deed falls within a more severe provision of the given code. Whosoever, either out of hatred towards a racial, religious or social collectivity, or with a view to the extermination thereof, destroys its cultural or artistic works will be liable for the crime of vandalism, to a penalty of . . . unless his deed falls within a more severe provision of the given code. The above crimes will be prosecuted and punished irrespective of the place where the crime was committed and of the nationality of the offender, according to the law of the country where the offender was apprehended.

7. Lemkin, "Autobiography," ch. 1.

8. Eastern Poland had been the scene of fighting among armies and nationalities for centuries. The Swedish and Napoleonic armies, the Russians, the Lithuanians, the Ukrainians, and, earlier, the Mongols and the Tartars had contested the hills and rivers. In *Neighbors* (Princeton: Princeton University Press, 2001), Polish historian Jan Gross gives a wrenching account of the massacre by Poles of some 1,600

Jewish men, women, and children in July 1941 in the small town of Jedwabne, also in the Bialystok region.

9. Raphael Lemkin, "The Evolution of the Genocide Convention," p. 1, reel 2, Lemkin Papers, New York Public Library.

10. In subsequent speaking engagements and lobbying, Lemkin claimed explicitly that he had presented his paper in person at the Madrid conference. William Korey's *Epitaph for Raphael Lemkin* (New York: Jacob Blaustein Institute for the Advancement of Human Rights, 2001) corrected the record, showing that Lemkin had not in fact traveled to Madrid.

11. Korey cites *Proceedings of the Forty-fourth Annual Session of the North Carolina Bar Association* (Durham, N.C.: Christian Printing, 1942), pp. 107–116, made available to him by James Fussell, who is working on a biography of Lemkin.

12. Lemkin, "Autobiography," ch. 1.

13. Korey, *Epitaph for Raphael Lemkin,* p. 12.

14. "The Evolution of the Genocide Convention," reel 2, Lemkin Papers, New York Public Library.

15. Lemkin, "Autobiography," ch. 1.

16. August 22, 1939, meeting with military chiefs in Obersalzburg; emphasis added. In a confidential June 1931 interview with Richard Breitling, editor of the right-wing German daily newspaper *Leipziger Neueste Nachrichten,* Hitler spoke of the "great resettlement policy" he had planned and offered a litany of historical models. "Think of the biblical deportations and the massacres of the Middle Ages and remember the extermination of the Armenians. One eventually reaches the conclusion that masses of men are mere biological plasticine." Quoted in Louis Paul Lochner, *What About Germany?* (New York: Dodd, Mead, 1942), pp. 1–4. See also Kevork B. Bardakjian, *Hitler and the Armenian Genocide* (Cambridge, Mass.: Zoryan Institute, 1985), p. 28. The historic "forgetting" of atrocities was a phenomenon noted by many a brutal regime. While signing death warrants, Stalin remarked: "Who's going to remember all this riff-raff in ten or twenty years' time? No one. Who remembers now the names of the boyars Ivan the Terrible got rid of? No one." Quoted in Jonathan Glover, *Humanity: A Moral History of the Twentieth Century* (New Haven: Yale University Press, 2000).

17. Jacques Derogy, *Resistance and Revenge: The Armenian Assassination of the Turkish Leaders Responsible for the 1915 Massacres and Deportations,* trans. A. M. Berrett (New Brunswick, N.J.: Transaction, 1990), p. 195.

18. Lemkin, "Autobiography," ch. 3, p. 39. Lemkin clearly falls into the "intentionalist" camp in thinking Hitler planned the Holocaust well ahead of its execution. "Functionalist" historians believe that Hitler did not decide upon the Final Solution until the war, in response to a variety of wartime stimuli.

19. Ibid., ch. 3, pp. 39–40.

20. Ibid., p. 44.

21. Bartlett, *They Stand Invincible,* p. 100; Lemkin, "Autobiography," ch. 4, p. 50.

22. Lemkin, "Autobiography," ch. 4, p. 57.

23. Ibid., p. 65. As Lemkin piled up languages, he liked to quote Victor Hugo, who said, "As many languages as you know, as many times you are a human being."

24. Ibid., pp. 66, 69.

25. Ibid., ch. 6, p. 96.

26. Ibid., p. 105.

27. Ibid., ch. 7, p. 2.

28. Ibid., p. 3.

29. Ibid., p. 5.

30. Ibid.

31. Ibid., ch. 7, p. 7.

32. In Winston S. Churchill, *The Churchill War Papers: The Ever-Widening War*, vol. 3: 1941, ed. Martin Gilbert (New York: W. W. Norton, 2000), pp. 1099–1106. Churchill delivered the speech live on August 24, 1941, soon after meeting with President Roosevelt to discuss the Atlantic Charter. Although the United States had not yet entered the war, Churchill said the meeting symbolized "the marshalling of the good forces of the world against the evil forces." He appealed to conquered European peoples to hang on in resistance. "Have faith, have hope," Churchill said, "deliverance is sure." Predicting that Hitler would eventually turn on the United States, he assured listeners that the United States "still retains the power to marshal her gigantic strength and, in saving herself, render an incomparable service to mankind." The line that Lemkin found so memorable was not meant to refer to the extermination of Europe's Jewry (which Churchill did not mention) but to the Germans' "methodical, merciless butchery" of the Russians.

Chapter 3, The Crime *With* a Name

1. Martin Gilbert, *Auschwitz and the Allies* (New York: Holt, Rinehart and Winston, 1981), p. 40.

2. David S. Wyman, *The Abandonment of the Jews: America and the Holocaust, 1941–1945* (New York: New Press, 1998), p. 21. The ascription of collective guilt was common in those days. Earl Warren, later chief justice of the Supreme Court and then California attorney general, testified at a congressional hearing after Pearl Harbor that "every Japanese should be considered in the light of a potential fifth columnist." Some 150,000 Japanese Americans were "relocated," or interned in detention camps during the war. See Greg Robinson, *By Order of the President: FDR and the Internment of Japanese Americans* (Cambridge, Mass.: Harvard University Press, 2001).

3. Gilbert, *Auschwitz and the Allies*, p. 44.

4. E. Thomas Wood and Stanislaw M. Jankowski, *Karski: How One Man Tried to Stop the Holocaust* (New York: John Wiley, 1994), p. 150; emphasis added.

5. Ibid., pp. 150–151.

6. Ibid., p. 119. See also Claude Lanzmann, *Shoah: An Oral History of the Holocaust* (New York: Pantheon Books, 1985), pp. 167–175; Michael T. Kaufman, "Jan Karski Dies at 86; Warned West About Holocaust," *New York Times*, July 15, 2000, p. C15.

7. Jan Karski, *Story of a Secret State* (Boston: Houghton Mifflin, 1944), p. 336.

8. Wood and Jankowski, *Karski*, pp. 151–152.

9. Exchange quoted in William Shawcross, *The Quality of Mercy: Cambodia, Holocaust and Modern Conscience* (New York: Simon & Schuster, 1984), p. 47.

10. Michael Ignatieff, "Raphael Lemkin and the Moral Imagination," lecture at the U.S. Holocaust Memorial Museum, Washington, D.C., December 13, 2000.

11. German Reich Ministry for National Enlightenment and Propaganda, *The Secret Conferences of Dr. Goebbels* (New York: E. P. Dutton, 1970), p. 309.

12. International Committee of the Red Cross, *Report of the International Committee of the Red Cross on Its Activities During the Second World War, September 1, 1939–June 30, 1947*, vol. 1 (Geneva: International Committee of the Red Cross, 1948), p. 21; Walter Laqueur, *The Terrible Secret: Suppression of the Truth About Hitler's "Final Solution"* (New York: Owl Books, 1980), p. 60.

13. See the Bibliography for an extensive list of sources on the subject.

14. Laqueur, *Terrible Secret*, p. 67.

15. Walter Laqueur has shrewdly noted that the placement of these articles sig-naled the *New York Times'* ambivalence about their accuracy. "The editors quite obviously did not know what to make of them," Laqueur wrote. "If it was true that a million people had been killed this clearly should have been front page news. . . . If it was not true, the story should not have been published at all." They compromised, assuming that the reports contained some truth and some exagger-ation and should be relegated to a less than prominent spot. Ibid., p. 74.

16. Albert Müller, *Neue Zürcher Zeitung,* May 5, 1979, quoted in ibid., p. 89.

17. Hershel Johnson to Secretary of State Cordell Hull, April 5, 1943, quoted in Laqueur, *Terrible Secret,* p. 98.

18. Laqueur, *Terrible Secret,* p. 201.

19. W. A. Visser't Hooft, Protestant theologian and first general secretary of the World Council of Churches, spent the war years in Switzerland and used this phrase in his *Memoirs* (London: SCM Press, 1973), p. 166. He wrote that anti-Semitism was less a reason for the world's indifference than "that people could find no place in their consciousness for such an unimaginable horror and that they did not have the imagination, together with the courage, to face it."

20. Karski could rely on nothing but his own words: "I have no proofs, no photo-graphs," he said. "All I can say is that I saw it, and it is the truth." Jan Karski, "Pol-ish Death Camp," *Collier's,* October 14, 1944, pp. 18–19. Karski's story was accom-panied not by a photograph but by a drawing of anonymous, horrified faces. For a discussion of the use of generalized visual images that appeared without captions or specific references, see Barbie Zelizer, *Remembering to Forget: Holocaust Memory Through the Camera's Eye* (Chicago: University of Chicago Press, 1998).

21. These overstatements came on the heels of exaggerations in the British press of Boer crimes committed against British citizens and of course William Ran-dolph Hearst's inflammatory yellow journalism geared toward securing American entry into war against Spain in 1898. See also Raphael Lemkin, "Totally Unoffi-cial: The Autobiography of Raphael Lemkin," ch. 7, p. 2, for Lemkin's description of the reaction of his colleagues in the U.S. government and their tendency to use the Belgian atrocities as a rationale for disbelief.

22. The story of the corpse conversion factory was made up by a British brigadier general. One reporter recalled his hunt for actual proof of atrocities: "I couldn't find any atrocities. . . . I offered sums of money for photographs of children whose hands had been cut off or who had been wounded or injured in other ways. I never found a first-hand Belgian atrocity story; and when I ran down the second-hand stories, they all petered out." See John Taylor, *War Photography: Realism in the British Press* (London: Routledge, 1991), p. 79; Philip Knightley, *The First Casualty: From the Crimea to Vietnam: The War Correspondent as Hero, Propagandist and Myth Maker* (New York: Harcourt Brace Jovanovich, 1975) pp. 105–106.

23. Vernon McKenzie, "Atrocities in World War II—What Can We Believe?" *Jour-nalism Quarterly,* September 1942, p. 268; cited in Deborah L. Lipstadt, *Beyond Be-lief: The American Press and the Coming of the Holocaust, 1933–1945* (New York: Free Press, 1986), pp. 9, 27. Only in 2001 did John Horne and Alan Kramer publish *German Atrocities 1914: A History of Denial* (New Haven: Yale University Press, 2001). They document a brutal German campaign that led to the deaths of some 6,500 Belgian and French civilians and challenge the assumption held for most of the twentieth century that the World War I atrocity reports were hyped.

24. Estimates of the total number of persons who successfully escaped Nazi perse-cution by fleeing to the United States between 1938 and 1945 hover around

250,000—a number that includes refugees and immigrants who fell under a quota system established in the 1924 Immigration Act that admitted 150,000 immigrants annually (with some 27,000 allocated from Germany and Austria). Remarkably, under 50 percent of the entire annual immigration quota was used in any one year from 1938 to 1940. By the end of the war, the total number of quota immigrants dropped below 10 percent of the maximum limit per year. See U.S. Department of Labor, Immigration and Naturalization Service, *Annual Report of the Immigration and Naturalization Service* (Washington, D.C.: GPO, 1943, 1944, and 1945); and David S. Wyman, *Paper Walls: America and the Refugee Crisis, 1938–1941* (New York: Pantheon Books, 1985). Public pressure to do something about the refugee situation in Europe and the United States had led to the 1943 Bermuda conference, which was attended by Allied diplomats and other government officials. But the conference weakly recommended shipping small numbers of refugees to European colonial possessions, requesting cooperation and transportation from neutral countries, and strengthening the impotent Intergovernmental Committee on Refugees created at the Evian conference in 1938. According to Wyman, only one of these plans was actually implemented: A full year after the conference, a camp was finally established near Casablanca to house some 3,000 of the refugees who had managed to reach Spain. Ultimately, however, the camp became home to just 630 refugees. As Rabbi Israel Goldstein observed, "The job of the Bermuda Conference apparently was not to rescue victims of Nazi terror, but to rescue our State Department and the British Foreign Office." See David S. Wyman, ed., *America and the Holocaust,* vol. 3: *The Mock Rescue Conference: Bermuda* (New York: Garland, 1990), pp. v, vi. One of the three official U.S. representatives at the conference, Senator Scott Lucas (D.–Ill.), warned that attempts by Jewish organizations to save European Jewry would lead to the deaths of 100,000 U.S. soldiers, which would in turn yield a dangerous anti-Semitic backlash in the United States. See the Simon Wiesenthal Center Web page, available at http://www.motlc.wiesenthal.com/text/x15/xm1522.html.
25. Laqueur, *Terrible Secret,* p. 96, quoting a letter from Goldberg to Laqueur.
26. "Pole's Suicide Note Pleads for Jews," *New York Times,* June 4, 1943, p. 4. A monument to Szmul Zygielbojm, whose pseudonym was Artur, was unveiled in Warsaw on July 22, 1997, on the fifty-fifth anniversary of the start of the deportation of Warsaw Jews. In 1998 the letter was installed in the permanent collection of the United States Holocaust Memorial Museum in Washington, D.C. Karski spoke at a ceremony marking the event.
27. "Jews' Last Stand Felled 1,000 Nazis," *New York Times,* May 22, 1943, p. 7. More than 10,000 Jews were killed in the Warsaw ghetto uprising. The 56,000 Jews who survived were taken to the Treblinka death camp.
28. The *New York Times* did not again mention Zygielbojm until Jan Karski died in July 2000. Karski's wife, Pola Nirenska, herself a Holocaust survivor whose family had been wiped out in the Holocaust, had thrown herself from the balcony of their Bethesda, Maryland, apartment in 1992 at the age of eighty-one. A dancer, her last piece, presented in Washington in 1990, was inspired by Holocaust victims and called, "In Memory of Those I Loved . . . Who Are No More." See Michael T. Kaufman, "Jan Karski Dies at 86; Warned West About Holocaust," *New York Times,* July 15, 2000, p. C15.
29. Raphael Lemkin, *Axis Rule in Occupied Europe: Laws of Occupation, Analysis of Government, Proposals for Redress* (Washington, D.C.: Carnegie Endowment for International Peace, Division of International Law, 1944). The first part of the book dealt with the different aspects of Nazi rule: the German administration of the occupied lands and their usurpation of sovereignty; the role and function of the German po-

lice and the secret police, the Gestapo; the introduction of discriminatory German law into the occupied territories; the organization of the courts; the disposal of property; the administration of finance; the exploitation of labor through slavery and depopulation; the extremely inhumane treatment of Jews; and the destruction of national and ethnic groups.

30. Melchior Palyi, review of *Axis Rule over Occupied Europe,* by Raphael Lemkin, *American Journal of Sociology* 51, 5 (March 1946): 496–497. Palyi was a Hungarian-born, laissez-faire, anti-Keynesian economist who taught at a number of universities in Germany and the United States.

31. Arthur K. Kuhn, review of *Axis Rule over Occupied Europe,* by Raphael Lemkin, *American Journal of International Law* 39, 2 (April 1945): ix, 360–362.

32. Linden A. Mander, review of *Axis Rule over Occupied Europe,* by Raphael Lemkin, *American Historical Review* 51, 1 (October 1945): 117–120.

33. Daniel Jonah Goldhagen, *Hitler's Willing Executioners: Ordinary Germans and the Holocaust* (New York: Knopf, 1996).

34. Lemkin, *Axis Rule,* pp. xiv, xxiii.

35. Otto D. Tolischus, "Twentieth-Century Moloch: The Nazi-Inspired Totalitarian State, Devourer of Progress—and of Itself," *New York Times Book Review,* January 21, 1945, pp. 1, 24.

36. Raphael Lemkin, "Genocide," *American Scholar* 15, 2 (1946): 227–230. Waldemar Kaempffert, "Genocide Is the New Name for the Crime Fastened on the Nazi Leaders," *New York Times,* October 20, 1946, p. E13, contains a discussion of the other possible terms that Lemkin might have chosen. Lemkin presumably fed this material to the journalist.

37. "Introduction to Part I, The New Word," in "History of Genocide," ch. 1, sec. 5; reel 3, Lemkin Papers, New York Public Library.

38. "Introduction to Part I, The New Word," ch. 1, sec. 6 ("Words as Moral Judgements"), p. 4.

39. Jean Améry, *Jenseits von Schuld und Sühne: Bewältigungsversuche einer Überwältigten* (Beyond Guilt and Atonement: Attempts to Overcome by One Who Has Been Overcome) (Munich: Szczesny Verlag, 1996), p. 59, translated and quoted in Lawrence L. Langer, *The Age of Atrocity: Death in Modern Literature* (Boston: Beacon Press, 1978), p. 51. See also George Steiner, *Language and Silence: Essays on Language, Literature, and the Inhuman* (New Haven: Yale University Press, 1998).

40. Lemkin, *Axis Rule,* p. 79; emphasis added.

41. Ibid.

42. Raphael Lemkin, "The Importance of the Convention," p. 1, reel 2, Lemkin Papers, New York Public Library.

43. *Proceedings of the Forty-fourth Annual Session of the North Carolina Bar Association,* p. 112, cited in William Korey, *An Epitaph for Raphael Lemkin* (New York: Jacob Blaustein Institute for the Advancement of Human Rights, 2001), p. 11.

44. Genocide was incorporated into the French *Encyclopédie Larousse* in 1953 after approval from the French Academy. The *Oxford English Dictionary* first listed "genocide" as an entry in the "Addenda and Corrigenda" section of the 1955 update to the third edition. Hebrew, Yiddish, and Serbo-Croatian all borrow "genocide" without much modification. Though the word did gain great fame around the world, many languages translated the term, contrary to Lemkin's designs, as "mass killing." Polish uses *ludobójstwo,* meaning "people-killing." Armenian uses *tseghasbanutiun,* or "killing of a race." Khmer uses *prolai puch sah,* or "to destroy the race." German uses *Völkermord,* or "murder of a nation." The Rwandan language, Kinyarwandan, uses *n'itsembabwoko,* or "massacring an ethnic group."

45. "History of Genocide," part 1, p. 7.
46. The Roosevelt administration had been very slow to comment on the fate of the Jews. On March 24, 1944, Roosevelt finally condemned the "systematic murder of the Jews" that went on "unabated every hour." He warned that all those in Germany and in satellite countries who knowingly took part in the deportation of Jews were "equally guilty with the executioners" and would share the punishment. On November 8, 1944, General Dwight D. Eisenhower, acting on the advice of the War Refugee Board, threatened "heavy punishment." "Germans!" he declared, "Do not obey any orders . . . urging you to molest, harm or persecute [those in concentration camps], no matter what their religion or nationality may be." "Eisenhower Warns Reich on Prisoners," *New York Times,* November 8, 1944, p. 21.
47. "Genocide," *Washington Post,* December 3, 1944, p. B4.
48. In a book on the history of genocide that was never published, Lemkin rattled off a vast number of factoids concerning those writers he hoped to emulate. He demonstrated a dazzling grasp of literature, science, politics, and the diverse roots and authorship of various terms. I later discovered that Lemkin had lifted verbatim virtually every one of his panoramic literary references, as well as many entire paragraphs, from Bruno Migliorini, *The Contribution of the Individual to Language: Taylorian Lecture, 1952* (Oxford: Clarendon Press, 1952). Lemkin included them without attribution in what he hoped would be his masterpiece. He was not above plagiarizing if it served his cause.

Chapter 4, Lemkin's Law

1. Jurists like Hans Kelsen challenged the "theology of the state" and declared the cult of deference to sovereignty a false necessity. Sovereignty could be redefined. "We can derive from the concept of sovereignty," Kelsen wrote in *Peace Through Law,* "nothing else than what we have purportedly put into its definition." Hans Kelsen, *Peace Through Law* (Chapel Hill, N.C., 1944), pp. 41–42.
2. Raphael Lemkin, *Axis Rule in Occupied Europe: Laws of Occupation, Analysis of Government, Proposals for Redress* (Washington, D.C.: Carnegie Endowment for International Peace, Division of International Law, 1944), p. 31, n. 25. See Ingo Müller, *Hitler's Justice: The Courts of the Third Reich,* trans. Deborah Schneider (Cambridge, Mass.: Harvard University Press, 1991).
3. Mark Mazower, *Dark Continent: Europe's Twentieth Century* (New York: Knopf, 1998), p. 197.
4. Letter to the editor, *New York Times,* November 8, 1946.
5. Robert Merrill Bartlett, *They Stand Invincible: Men Who Are Reshaping Our World* (New York: Thomas Y. Crowell, 1959), p. 102.
6. Critics, of course, railed against the Nuremberg court for its ex post facto lawmaking. They said the ban on crimes against humanity was introduced after the crimes had been committed. Tribunal defenders pointed to customary law and argued that perpetrators of these horrid acts could not have thought they were acting within legal bounds when they exterminated unarmed civilians. They also argued that most nations had pledged to outlaw aggression in 1925 in the Kellogg-Briand Pact. Requiring the link to aggression also technically immunized Allied soldiers against prosecution for war crimes and crimes against humanity, since the Nazis, and not the Allies, were the original invaders. But this was not a

motivation for the jurisdictional decision, as the subject of Allied wartime transgressions was rarely raised at the time.

7. Bartlett, *They Stand Invincible,* p. 102. Lemkin learned that the main part of the town where his parents lived had been burned down, and the population of some 20,000 people had been crowded into a ghetto near the railway station. In his autobiography Lemkin wrote, "This happened more than a year prior to moving my parents, together with others, to _____, to be gassed." It seems Lemkin never learned where his parents were murdered. Raphael Lemkin, "Totally Unofficial: The Autobiography of Raphael Lemkin," ch. 6, p. 105.

8. British prosecutor Hartley Shawcross also used the term several times in his summation. Waldemar Kaempffert, "Genocide Is the New Name for the Crime Fastened on the Nazi Leaders," *New York Times,* October 20, 1946, p. E13.

9. William Korey, *An Epitaph for Raphael Lemkin* (New York: Jacob Blaustein Institute for the Advancement of Human Rights, 2001), p. 25.

10. Herbert Yahraes, "He Gave a Name to the World's Most Horrible Crime," *Collier's,* March 3, 1951, p. 56.

11. Lassa Oppenheim, *International Law,* 7th ed., vol. 1, ed. Hersch Lauterpacht (London: Longmans, 1948), p. 583, declared that it was "generally recognized that a state is entitled to treat its own citizens at its discretion and that the manner in which it treats them is not a matter in which international law, as such, concerns itself." When it came to humanitarian intervention, "by virtue of its personal and territorial supremacy, a state can treat its own nationals according to discretion."

12. "Anti-Genocide Gains Termed Significant," *New York Times,* December 20, 1947, p. 8.

13. Raphael Lemkin, "The Importance of the Convention," p. 2, reel 2, Lemkin Papers, New York Public Library.

14. The organization used a converted indoor skating rink at Flushing Meadow (twenty minutes away) for General Assembly sessions. This was the UN's last stop before moving into permanent headquarters at Turtle Bay.

15. Kathleen Teltsch, "The Early Years," in *A Global Affair: An Inside Look at the United Nations*, ed. Amy Janello and Brennon Jones, p. 12.

16. A. M. Rosenthal, "A Man Called Lemkin," *New York Times,* October 18, 1988, p. A31.

17. Bartlett, *They Stand Invincible,* p. 103. One night his insomnia paid off. In August 1948, as he strolled around Lake Leman in Geneva in the early hours of the morning, Lemkin bumped into the Canadian ambassador, David Wilgress, who also could not sleep. Lemkin seized his chance, charming the Canadian, a history buff, with stories about the Athenians' atrocities in Mytilene, the Mongols' genocide, and the slaughter of the Armenians. Lemkin's new friend introduced him to Herbert Evatt, who was the president of the General Assembly. With Evatt's support, Lemkin said he no longer felt like a "petitioner" but more like a "full-fledged partner." Lemkin, "Autobiography," ch. 10, pp. 13, 15.

18. White proceeded: "If [the UN planners] put on their spectacles and look down their noses and come up with the same old bunny, we shall very likely all hang separately—nation against nation, power against power, defense against defense, people (reluctantly) against people (reluctantly). If they manage to bring the United Nations out of the bag, full blown, with constitutional authority and a federal structure having popular meaning, popular backing, and an over-all authority greater than the authority of any one member or any combination of members, we might well be started on a new road." E. B. White, "Notes and Comment," *New Yorker,* February 24, 1945, p. 17.

19. In the early years of the UN, all of the major newspapers and wire services posted between a half dozen and a dozen correspondents at UN headquarters. This is a far cry from today, when many media do not staff the UN and when those that do post only one or, in the case of the wires, two reporters.

20. Raphael Lemkin, "Genocide," *American Scholar* 15, 2 (1946): 228.

21. Lemkin, "Autobiography," ch. 9, p. 8.

22. Ibid., p. 14.

23. "Genocide Under the Law of Nations," *New York Times,* January 5, 1947, p. E11.

24. Korey, *An Epitaph for Raphael Lemkin,* p. 29.

25. This draft called for the establishment of an "International Office for the administration of all matters" related to the genocide convention, which would gather data on the causes of genocide and make recommendations for alleviating the crime. Each contracting office would also set up national offices linked to the head office in order to gather the names of the perpetrators, details on their genocidal techniques, and recommendations for punishment and prevention. These offices were far more threatening to state sovereignty than a mere law and were thus dropped from later drafts. Ibid., pp. 30–31.

26. Raphael Lemkin, "The Evolution of the Genocide Convention," p. 7, reel 2, Lemkin Papers, New York Public Library.

27. Rosenthal, "A Man Called Lemkin."

28. Lemkin, "The Evolution of the Genocide Convention," p. 5.

29. In 1948 the Economic and Social Council (ECOSOC) of the United Nations appointed an Ad Hoc Committee on Genocide composed of representatives from China, France, Lebanon, Poland, the United States, the Soviet Union, and Venezuela. This committee unanimously adopted a draft, which the council transmitted to the General Assembly in August 1948. The General Assembly in turn referred the report to the assembly's Sixth Committee, which devoted fifty-one meetings in two months to discussing and amending the convention.

30. See Lemkin, "Autobiography," ch. 10, pp. 5–8.

31. Ibid., p. 22.

32. General Assembly president Evatt, Lemkin's friend, allowed him to handpick the chairman of the Legal Committee. In order to avoid delay, Lemkin also rallied a number of delegations to support the idea of avoiding the standard UN practice of requiring passage first in a subcommittee. In this instance the Legal Committee alone would prepare the final draft. It had two early drafts to work from—one that had been prepared by the Secretariat with Lemkin's participation in 1947 and the other prepared by the Special Committee of ECOSOC in May 1948 with Lemkin's behind-the-scenes influence.

33. Lemkin, "Autobiography," ch. 11, p. 27.

34. Although the law moved ahead, Lemkin was dismayed to learn that a pair of clauses were being inserted that limited the initial duration of the law to ten years if sixteen states stepped forward to denounce it and allowed for revisions to the text after a certain number of years. Lemkin was too exhausted and too desperate to fight these additions but later said that he "felt like a babysitter who takes a nap at the wrong time." Opponents had put "blows and knives" into the newborn baby so that it would later die. As it happened, these provisions were never invoked, but Lemkin could not know that at the time. His fear that the convention would perish heightened his paranoia in the years ahead. Lemkin, "Autobiography," ch. 11, p. 58; ch. 13, p. 36.

35. "Genocide and the UN," *Washington Post,* November 9, 1946, p. 8.

36. The United Nations was then composed of fifty-eight member states (twenty-one from the Americas, sixteen from Europe, fourteen from Asia, four from Africa, three from Oceania).

37. Lemkin, "Autobiography," ch. 12, p. 59.

38. "U.N. Votes Accord Banning Genocide," *New York Times,* December 10, 1948, p. 12.

39. John Hohenberg, "The Crusade That Changed the UN," *Saturday Review,* November 9, 1968, p. 87.

40. Rosenthal, "A Man Called Lemkin."

41. Teltsch, "Library Show Recalls Man Behind Treaty on Genocide."

42. Lemkin, "Autobiography," ch. 1.

43. Ibid., ch. 12, p. 61.

Chapter 5, "A Most Lethal Pair of Foes"

1. Reel 4, Lemkin Papers, New York Public Library.

2. Because several countries had ratified the convention nearly simultaneously, there were actually twenty-one "ratifications without reservation": Australia, Cambodia, Costa Rica, Ecuador, El Salvador, Ethiopia, France, Guatemala, Haiti, Iceland, Israel, Jordan, Liberia, Monaco, Norway, Panama, Republic of Korea, Saudi Arabia, Sri Lanka, Turkey, and Yugoslavia. Bulgaria and the Philippines also ratified the Genocide Convention by mid-October 1950, but with reservations. The genocide convention formally entered into force on January 12, 1951. "Pact on Genocide Effected by U.N.," *New York Times,* October 15, 1950, p. 23.

3. Steven Schnur, "Unofficial Man: The Rise and Fall of Raphael Lemkin," *Reform Judaism,* Fall 1982, p. 11. In the *New York Times* the day after the convention was ratified, Lemkin was pictured in a photo beside a short story from UN headquarters at Lake Success. The grainy photo, which was captioned "UN Representatives Ratify Pact Against Genocide," depicts Lemkin in a conspicuous light-colored suit in the back row. In front of him are the dark-suited representatives of the latest four ratifiers, Korea, Haiti, France, and Costa Rica, as well as the president of the General Assembly, Nasrollah Entezam of Iran. Alongside him are Ivan Kerno, the assistant secretary-general for legal affairs; Trygve Lie, the secretary-general; and Fernando Fournier of Costa Rica. Others in the photo are identified by their titles; Lemkin, staring at the camera blankly, is described simply as "chief proponent of the pact." "U.N. Representatives Ratifying Pact Against Genocide," *New York Times,* October 17, 1950, p. 18.

4. Senate Committee on Foreign Relations, *The Genocide Convention: Hearings Before the Senate Subcommittee on the International Convention on the Prevention and Punishment of the Crime of Genocide,* 81st Cong., 2nd sess., 1950, p. 15.

5. Ibid., pp. 204–205.

6. Lemkin, "The Truth About the Genocide Convention," p. 2, reel 3, Lemkin Papers, New York Public Library.

7. A pair of UN studies of the convention later attempted to clarify the meaning of its text. In 1978 N. Ruhashyankiko's *Study on the Question of the Prevention and Punishment of the Crime of Genocide,* UN Doc. E/CN.4/Sub.2/416 (1978), pp. 14–15, reflected on the Sixth Committee debate and found it "sufficient that an act of genocide should have as its purpose the partial destruction of a group. . . . It was not necessary to kill all the members of a group in order to commit genocide." The UN Subcommission on Prevention of Discrimination and Protection of Minorities, *Re-*

vised and Updated Report on the Question of Prevention and Punishment of the Crime of Genocide (the Whitaker Report), UN Doc. E/CN.4/Sub.2/1985/6 (1985), p. 18, found that the phrase "in part" "would seem to imply a reasonably significant number, relative to the total of the group as a whole, or else a significant section of a group such as its leadership." Concerned that too broad an interpretation might devalue the "gravity of the concept of genocide," the special rapporteur recommended consideration of proportionate scale and total numbers. "Other attacks and killings do, of course, remain heinous crimes," he noted, "even if they fall outside the definition of genocide."

8. See Ward Churchill, *A Little Matter of Genocide: Holocaust and Denial in the Americas, 1492 to the Present* (San Francisco: City Light Books, 1997).

9. In fact, the Chinese representative had intended the "mental harm" provision to cover "genocide by narcotics," which the Japanese occupiers had used as a weapon against the Chinese in World War II, permanently impairing their mental facilities and destroying their will to resist. UN, Report of the Ad Hoc Committee on Genocide, Economic, and Social Council, Official Records: third year, seventh sess., suppl. no. 6, April 5–May 10, 1948, p. 15; Sixth Committee, pp. 177, 179. As Adrian Fisher, the State Department legal adviser, testified in 1950, the mental harm provision would apply to violent acts aimed at doing permanent injury to a victim's mental faculties. It would not apply to "embarrassment or hurt feelings, or even the sense of outrage that comes from such action as racial discrimination or segregation, however horrible those may be." Senate Committee on Foreign Relations, *The Genocide Convention,* pp. 263–264.

10. Raphael Lemkin to Gertrude Samuels, June 6, 1950, reel 1, Lemkin Papers, New York Public Library.

11. Hearings on the Genocide Convention, p. 132.

12. LeBlanc, *The United States and the Genocide Convention* (Durham, N.C.: Duke University Press, 1991), p. 20. The transcripts of the executive sessions of the Senate Foreign Relations Committee are not made available to the public for twenty-five years. See *Executive Sessions of the Senate Foreign Relations Committee, Historical Series,* 1976, p. 645.

13. Those who opposed including political groups also claimed that unlike ethnic or national groups, political groups were not sufficiently "cohesive" or recognizable. Of course religious groups, which *were* covered, also lacked ready identifiers. In addition, religious preference was as mutable as political affiliation.

14. Lemkin had hoped to ban cultural genocide, as he had long been convinced that the destruction of language, libraries, churches, and traditions was both a savage wrong in its own right and often a prelude to murder. He liked to say, "First they burn books and then they start burning bodies." But he gave up the battle to punish the destruction of language, monuments, archives, and other cultural foundations when he realized that time was running out in the General Assembly session. The Legal Committee was not supportive, and he could not afford to see the vote postponed until the following year because there was no guarantee the next president of the General Assembly (after Evatt) would support the law. He consoled himself that he could try to get the UN to adopt an additional protocol later. In the words of Joel Wolfsohn of the American Jewish Committee, Lemkin was "willing to throw anything and everything overboard in order to save a ship." William Korey, *An Epitaph for Raphael Lemkin* (New York: Jacob Blaustein Institute for the Advancement of Human Rights, 2001), p. 39, quoting a letter given to him by James Fussell.

15. Duane Tananbaum, *The Bricker Amendment Controversy: A Test of Eisenhower's Political Leadership* (Ithaca, N.Y.: Cornell University Press, 1988), p. 31, citing John Bricker Papers at the Ohio Historical Society.

16. Eisenhower was frustrated at having to fight off the isolationists within his own party, and he blamed Bricker. He told his press secretary, James Hagerty, that "if it's true that when you die the things that bothered you most are engraved on your skull, I am sure I'll have there the mud and dirt of France during [the] invasion and the name of Senator Bricker." Ibid., p. 151, citing *Foreign Relations of the United States, 1952–1954,* vol. 1, pp. 1843–1846. In the face of sustained pressure by the administration, Eisenhower Republicans defected to join liberal Democrats in handily defeating Bricker's version of the measure 50-42 (two-thirds being required in this case). But a watered-down Democratic alternative (the George resolution) lost by just one vote (60-31) in February 1954. Ibid., pp. 167–180.

17. Letter to Thelma Stevens, reel 1, Lemkin Papers, New York Public Library.

18. Reel 1, Lemkin Papers, New York Public Library.

19. See Jessica Tuchman Mathews, "Power Shift," *Foreign Affairs,* January/February 1997, pp. 50–66.

20. Other organizations included the World Alliance for International Friendship Through Religion, the International League for the Rights of Man, the Women's International League for Peace and Freedom, the Congress of Industrial Organizations (CIO), the National Conference for Christians and Jews, the American Friends' Service Committee, the National Catholic Welfare Conference, and the General Federation of Women's Clubs.

21. Even during World War II, when one might have expected attention to be drawn to Hitler's Final Solution, Hollywood had avoided the subject. Of the more than 500 narrative films made on war-related themes between 1940 and 1945, for instance, virtually none focused upon the persecution or extermination of Jews. The dearth of coverage is all the more striking when we note that American Jews played major roles in writing, directing, financing, and acting in Hollywood. Yet at the time the power of Harry Cohn, Louis B. Mayer, and others did not incline them to emphasize Jewish themes. Many famous Jewish actors, including Kirk Douglas, Tony Curtis, John Garfield, and Edward G. Robinson changed their names so as not to sound Jewish. See Ilan Avisar, *Screening the Holocaust: Cinema's Images of the Unimaginable* (Bloomington: Indiana University Press, 1988), pp. 96–97. Avisar notes that Charlie Chaplin's *Great Dictator* (1940) was an exception for its attention to the plight of Jews. Avisar cites Lewis Jacobs, "World War II and the American Film," *Cinema Journal* 1 (Winter 1967–1968): 21.

22. Jeffrey Shandler, *While America Watches: Televising the Holocaust* (Oxford: Oxford University Press, 1999), pp. 30, 34. See also David Margolick, "Television and the Holocaust: An Odd Couple," *New York Times,* January 31, 1999, pp. A31–A32.

23. Lawrence Langer wrote, "There is little horror in the stage version; there is very little in the *Diary* itself. . . . They permit the imagination to cope with the idea of the Holocaust without forcing a confrontation with its grim details." See Lawrence Langer, "The Americanization of the Holocaust on Stage and Screen," in Langer, *Admitting the Holocaust: Collected Essays* (Oxford: Oxford University Press, 1995).

24. "How 'Cheerful' Is 'Anne Frank'?" *Variety,* April 1, 1959, p. 2, quoted in Tim Cole, *Selling the Holocaust* (New York: Routledge, 1999), p. 34.

25. Cynthia Ozick, "Who Owns Anne Frank?" *New Yorker,* October 6, 1997, pp. 76–87.

26. *Judgment at Nuremberg* included edited footage taken by Allied forces entering Germany and liberating concentration camps. The Allies' documentary, *Nazi Concentration Camps,* was first presented as evidence by the prosecution during the Nuremberg trials. See Lawrence Douglas, "Film as Witness: Screening 'Nazi Concentration Camps' Before the Nuremberg Tribunal," *Yale Law Journal,* November 1995, pp. 449–481. Americans first saw images of the camps and their survivors in the spring of 1945, when motion picture companies, with General Eisenhower's encouragement, produced newsreels using similar documentary footage. Shandler, *While America Watches,* p. 10.

27. Shandler, *While America Watches,* pp. 77–78. Hilberg's *Destruction of the European Jews,* rejected by successive publishers, was published in 1961 after being subsidized by a survivor family. See Leon A Jick, "The Holocaust: Its Use–Abuse Within the American Public," *Yad Vashem Studies* 14 (1981): 307.

28. Irving Spiegel, "Shrine Honors Hitler's Victims," *New York Times,* May 30, 1959, p. A5. The article quotes an inscription on a newly dedicated shrine in Jerusalem, in memory of those who died in the "Nazi holocaust in the years from 1933–1945" ("Holocaust" was not yet capitalized). The word "Holocaust" derives from the Greek *holokauston;* it is a translation of the Hebrew *churban,* which means a burnt offering to God and appears in the Old Testament (1 Sam. 7:9). Scholars disagree as to how and when the word first crept into the American lexicon. Some scholars credit Elie Wiesel's *Night* (1959) with popularizing "Holocaust" as a proper noun. Hilberg did not use the term in *The Destruction of the European Jews* (1961). Jick, "The Holocaust," p. 309.

29. Gerd Korman, "The Holocaust in American Historical Writing," *Societas,* Summer 1972, p. 261; Jick, "The Holocaust," p. 314. Notably, it was not until 1979 that the U.S. Department of Justice formed its Office of Special Investigations to detect, denaturalize, and deport Nazi war crimes suspects living in the United States.

30. As Wiesel himself remembered, "The big publishers hesitated, debated, and ultimately sent their regrets." One reason they gave was that American readers "seemed to prefer optimistic books"; Elie Wiesel, *All Rivers Run to the Sea: Memoirs* (New York: Knopf, 1996), p. 325. Primo Levi recalled that several big publishing houses refused his manuscript, and the small house that accepted it published a mere 2,500 copies and went bankrupt soon thereafter. In Levi's notes to the Italian edition of *Survival in Auschwitz,* he described the book's falling into oblivion. "In that harsh period after the war," Levi wrote, "people had little desire to be reminded of the painful times that were hardly over." Ruth K. Angress, "Primo Levi in English," *Simon Wiesenthal Center Annual,* vol. 3 (Chappaqua, N.Y.: Rossel Books, 1986), p. 319.

31. The Universal Declaration of Human Rights passed 48–0 with 8 abstentions, from Byelorussia, Czechoslovakia, Poland, Ukraine, the USSR, Yugoslavia, South Africa, and Saudi Arabia. Lemkin was wrong in believing the coverage overwhelmingly favored the declaration. In 1948, for instance, the *New York Times* published eighty-seven articles on the declaration and fifty-eight on the genocide convention. But Lemkin resented articles on the convention that appeared under headings such as "Two U.N. Achievements."

32. For a detailed account of the drafting of the declaration, see Mary Ann Glendon, *A World Made New: Eleanor Roosevelt and the Universal Declaration of Human Rights* (New York: Random House, 2001).

33. See Josef L. Kunz, "The United Nations Convention on Genocide," *American Journal of International Law* 43, 4 (October 1949): 738–746.

34. This campaign to create binding human rights conventions was eventually caught up in Cold War politics. Two separate covenants were introduced—one on civil and political rights and one on economic and social—but neither was opened for signature until 1966 and neither went into effect until 1976. The nonbinding Universal Declaration of Human Rights (UDHR) has probably been more influential than either of these two international laws.

35. Lemkin, "The U.N. Is Killing Its Own Child," pp. 1–2, reel 2, Lemkin Papers, New York Public Library.

36. Lemkin also lobbied forcefully against a proposal put forth by Francis Biddle to draft a code of international criminal law, or a "Code of Offenses Against the Peace and Security of Mankind," which deemed aggressive war the "supreme crime." Lemkin was afraid this emphasis on aggression would replicate Nuremberg's mistaken neglect of genocide, which for him was the only "supreme crime." See "Text of Biddle's Report on Nuremberg and Truman's Reply," *New York Times,* November 13, 1946, p. 14. Although the draft code of offenses included the definition of "genocide," it omitted the term itself.

37. Lemkin, "Memo on Genocide Convention" (1953), reel 2, Lemkin Papers, New York Public Library. Lemkin appears to have drafted the memo on somebody else's behalf.

38. Raphael Lemkin to Senator H. Alexander Smith, June 12, 1952, forwarded to Assistant Secretary of State John D. Hickerson; Assistant Secretary of State John D. Hickerson to Raphael Lemkin, June 26, 1952; reel 2, Lemkin Papers, New York Public Library.

39. Eleanor Roosevelt became a favorite target. In December 1951 she forever earned Lemkin's disdain when a reporter asked her to comment on the charges lodged by East European expatriate and exile groups in the United States that the Soviet Union was committing genocide. Roosevelt replied casually: "How could you prove it? I'm not sure you can prove that. Unless you can prove it, there's no use bringing it up." Lemkin had worked closely with nongovernmental groups derived from the formerly independent Soviet states and hoped to develop an indictment against the Soviet Union. It was difficult to gather evidence of atrocities carried out behind the iron curtain, but he was sure he had mustered enough proof to bring the weight of public opinion down upon the Soviets. Although Roosevelt had been a frequent critic of Soviet human rights abuses, Lemkin heard her skepticism as a familiar form of denial. The former first lady might as well have been dismissing his cause in Madrid in 1933. "The U.N. Review: U.N. Keeps Hope Alive for Missing Korea P.O.W.s; Trygve Lie Urges Effort to Bar New War," *New York Herald Tribune,* December 30, 1951, p. 12.

40. Glendon, *A World Made New,* p. 60, citing "Verbatim Record," June 12, 1947, Drafting Committee Meeting, Charles Malik Papers, Manuscript Division, Library of Congress.

41. Lemkin, "The Truth About the Genocide Convention," p. 13.

42. "The Crime of Genocide," *New York Times,* October 20, 1957, sec. 4, p. 10.

43. Steven Schnur, "Unofficial Man: The Rise and Fall of Raphael Lemkin," *Reform Judaism,* Fall 1982, p. 45. One letter from an unidentified Clara Hoover does appear in his correspondence. She wrote that she was shattered by Lemkin's "indifference" to her, his long disappearances, and his short-tempered returns. "You say that you *are* an unhappy man," Hoover wrote to him in 1959. "I am, *also.* The best way to overcome unhappiness is to make someone else happy. You can do this very easily. . . . Don't add me to your list of hates and enemies. Is there no room in your

heart for forgiveness?" Clara Hoover to Raphael Lemkin, reel 1, Lemkin Papers, New York Public Library.

44. "28 Are Nominated for Nobel Peace Prize, Including Truman, Churchill and Marshall," *New York Times,* February 28, 1950, p. 21; "Nobel Peace Group Lists 9 Americans," *New York Times,* February 24, 1951, p. 15; and Steven Jacobs, "The Papers of Raphael Lemkin: A First Look," *Journal of Genocide Research* 1, 1 (1999): 108. Lemkin appears to have been actively involved in the nomination drive in 1958 and 1959, urging various acquaintances around the world to send letters to the Nobel committee on his behalf and even personally drafting their nomination letters.

45. Richard J. Walsh to Raphael Lemkin, February 16, 1955, reel 1, Lemkin Papers, New York Public Library. Walsh did suggest that Lemkin contact John Hersey to see if he might be interested in writing a biography of Lemkin, an idea Lemkin himself had apparently earlier proposed. Walsh wrote that although he did not know Hersey personally, "I am certain that it will be much better to have you approach him directly, using your well-known ability to impress your point of view upon various persons."

46. Letters from publishers, reel 1, Lemkin Papers, New York Public Library.

47. Schnur, "Unofficial Man," p. 45.

48. A. M. Rosenthal, "A Man Called Lemkin," *New York Times,* October 18, 1988, p. A31. Lemkin is buried at Mt. Hebron Cemetery in Queens, New York. His tombstone reads: "Dr. Raphael Lemkin (1900–1959) Father of the Genocide Convention."

49. By 1967, fifty-one countries had adopted the convention outright and seventeen more had adopted it with reservations.

50. Jay G. Sykes, *Proxmire* (Washington, D.C.: R. B. Luce, 1972), p. 35. Wisconsin had been home to the country's first graduated income and inheritance taxes, the first child labor law, and the first unemployment compensation law.

51. Ibid., p. 72.

52. Ibid., p. 90.

53. "Pledge to Plead Daily for Ratification of Genocide Treaty," *Congressional Record,* 90th Cong., 1st sess., 1967, 113, pt. 1:266.

54. William Proxmire, *The Fleecing of America* (Boston: Houghton Mifflin, 1980), pp. 6–7.

55. Proxmire later credited Jacob Javits (R.–N.Y.) with keeping the issue on the "front burner" in the Senate Foreign Relations Committee for most of his twenty-four years in the Senate. "Jacob Javits: A Superb Senator," *Congressional Record,* 99th Cong., 2nd sess., 1986, 132, pt. 27:4123.

56. "International Convention on the Prevention and Punishment of the Crime of Genocide," *Congressional Record*–Senate, 99th Cong., 2nd sess., 1986, 132 S 1355, pt. 2:2331.

57. Ibid., 90th Cong., 2nd sess., 1968, 114, pt. 21:27918.

58. Dan Jacobs, *The Brutality of Nations* (New York: Knopf, 1987).

59. "Dissent from U.S. Policy Toward East Pakistan," U.S. Consul General, Dacca, to Secretary of State Henry Kissinger, April 6, 1971; quoted in Lawrence Lifschultz, *Bangladesh: The Unfinished Revolution* (London: Zed Press, 1979), pp. 158–159.

60. *Congressional Record,* 92nd Cong., 2nd sess.,1972, 118, pt. 12:15091.

61. See René Lemarchand, *Burundi: Ethnic Conflict and Genocide* (Washington, D.C.: Woodrow Wilson Center Press, 1996).

62. Confidential cable from Deputy Chief of Mission Michael Hoyt in Bujumbura to the State Department and embassies, May 29, 1972, obtained by Hoyt through the Freedom of Information Act. Hoyt has gathered the embassy cables from this period and plans to analyze them in a forthcoming book, *The Burundi Cables: The American Embassy and the 1972 Genocide.* In the first edition of *"A Problem from Hell,"* I erroneously wrote that Melady "downplayed the atrocities." Hoyt noted the inaccuracy and sent me more than 200 pages' worth of declassified cables from his collection. Melady was in fact quite straightforward in his descriptions of the carnage, but he argued against diplomatic intervention on the grounds that it would be counterproductive.

63. See Roger Morris, *Uncertain Greatness: Henry Kissinger and American Foreign Policy* (New York: Harper & Row, 1977), p. 267. In the fall of 1972, a $100,000 U.S. aid program to Burundi was suspended, but it was quickly restored after a $4 billion nickel deposit was discovered there and agents of Kennecott, Bethlehem Steel, and American Metals Climax began lobbying the State Department to improve its ties so it could influence the nickel's "final disposition."

64. Secret cable from U.S. ambassador Thomas Melady to the State Department and embassies, May 1, 1972.

65. Confidential cable from Secretary of State William Rogers to the U.S. Embassy in Bujumbura, June 20, 1972.

66. Michael Bowen, Gary Freeman, and Kay Miller, *Passing By: The United States and Genocide in Burundi, 1972* (New York: Carnegie Endowment for International Peace, 1973).

67. Confidential cable from Ambassador Thomas Melady to the State Department and embassies, May 15, 1972.

68. Confidential cable from Ambassador Thomas Melady to the State Department and embassies, May 20, 1972.

69. *Congressional Record,* 92nd Cong., 2nd sess., 1972, 118, pt. 16:20593.

70. Ibid., 90th Cong., 1st sess.1967, 113, pt. 1:876.

71. Ibid., pt. 1: 1197.

72. Ibid., 95th Cong., 1st sess., 1977, 123, pt. 2: 2601.

73. Ibid., 90th Cong., 1st sess., 1967, 113, pt. 3:3680.

Chapter 6, Cambodia

1. "Khmer Rouge Troops Enter Phnom Penh," *Washington Post,* April 15, 1975, p. A1.

2. Sydney H. Schanberg, *The Death and Life of Dith Pran* (New York: Penguin, 1985), p. 26. The new regime established what it called the Republic of Democratic Kampuchea.

3. David Chandler, *Voices from S–21: Terror and History in Pol Pot's Secret Prison* (Berkeley: University of California Press, 1999), p. 32, citing John Bryan Starr and Nancy Dyer, eds., *Post Liberation Works of Mao Zedong: Bibliography and Index* (Berkeley: Center for Chinese Studies, 1976), p. 173.

4. William Shawcross, *Sideshow: Kissinger, Nixon and the Destruction of Cambodia,* rev. ed. (New York: Simon & Schuster, 1987), p. 362.

5. François Ponchaud, *Cambodia, Year Zero* (New York: Penguin, 1978), pp. 11, 13.

6. According to official U.S. and South Vietnamese sources, some 4,954 South Vietnamese soldiers, 58,373 North Vietnamese soldiers, and 14,300 civilians were also killed. Cited in Don Oberdorfer, *Tet!* (New York: Doubleday, 1971), p. v.

7. On March 16, 1968, Lieutenant William Calley led the American "Charlie Company" into the village of My Lai, Vietnam. Calley had told his men the night before that the villagers were all enemy supporters and the children all future Vietcong. Although not one villager fired on the U.S. troops, the Americans burnt down all the houses, scalped or disembowled villagers, and raped women and girls or, if they were pregnant, slashed open their stomachs. The Americans machine-gunned and bayoneted villagers by the dozen. Four hours after the Charlie Company arrived, 500 Vietnamese lay dead. Michael Bilton and Kevin Sim, *Four Hours in My Lai* (New York: Viking, 1992), p. 21.

8. Shawcross, *Sideshow,* pp. 19–27; Walter Isaacson, *Kissinger: A Biography* (New York: Simon & Schuster, 1992), p. 176.

9. Tad Szulc, *The Illusion of Peace: Foreign Policy in the Nixon Years* (New York: Viking Press, 1978), p. 54.

10. "Transcript of President's Address to the Nation on Military Action in Cambodia," *New York Times,* May 1, 1970, p. 2. Nixon publicly explained escalation in Cambodia at the same time the United States was de-escalating from Vietnam: "If those North Vietnamese weren't in Cambodia, they'd be over killing Americans. That investment of $250 million in small arms to aid to Cambodia so that they can defend themselves against a foreign aggressor—this is no civil war, it has no aspect of a civil war—the dollars we send to Cambodia saves American lives and enables us to bring Americans home *[sic]*." "The President's News Conference of December 10, 1970," *The Nixon Presidential Press Conferences* (New York: Earl M. Coleman Enterprises, 1978), p. 138.

11. Isaacson, *Kissinger,* p. 638.

12. The $1.85 billion figure represents the sum of all U.S. military and economic aid to the Lon Nol regime over the course of its tenure; Shawcross, *Sideshow,* p. 350; "The President's News Conference of November 12, 1971," *The Nixon Presidential Press Conferences* (New York: Earl M. Coleman Enterprises, 1978), p. 224.

13. Elizabeth Becker, *When the War Was Over: Cambodia and the Khmer Rouge Revolution* (New York: Public Affairs, 1998), p. 99. Pol Pot studied at the Phnom Penh Technical College, specializing in carpentry. He went to Paris in August 1949 to study electronics but failed his exams at the university and in 1953 returned to Phnom Penh, where he earned a reputation as a left-wing journalist. One of thirty-four dissidents challenged publicly by Sihanouk in 1963, he took to the bush.

14. James Pringle, "Sihanouk Adapts to 'Austere Life,'" *Washington Post,* July 18, 1973, p. A18.

15. *New York Times* correspondent Henry Kamm recalls encountering the First Battalion of Commandos of the Teaching Profession, a ragtag band of 474 schoolteachers who carried arms they had never fired. Each received eight rounds of ammunition and was shipped to the front. Henry Kamm, *Cambodia: Report from a Stricken Land* (New York: Arcade, 1998), pp. 66–67.

16. Ben Kiernan, "The American Bombardment of Kampuchea, 1969–1973," *Vietnam Generation* 1, 1 (Winter 1989): 4–41. In the last six months of the bombing, the United States dropped 250,000 tons (compared to the 160,000 tons that fell on Japan during all of World War II); Isaacson, *Kissinger,* p. 636. Kissinger has never publicly acknowledged any American wrongdoing in Cambodia. In 1991 he said, "Journalists keep saying 'bombing Cambodia.' We were bombing four Vietnamese divisions that were killing 500 Americans a week"; quoted in Ben Kiernan, *The Pol Pot Regime: Race, Power, and Genocide in Cambodia Under the Khmer Rouge, 1975–79* (New Haven: Yale University Press, 1996), p. 24.

17. Although precise figures are unknown, according to Kiernan, the evidence of survivors from many parts of Cambodia suggests that U.S. bombing caused "at least tens of thousands, probably in the range of 50,000 to 150,000 deaths"; Kiernan, "The American Bombardment of Kampuchea," p. 32.

18. Jamie Frederic Metzl, *Western Responses to Human Rights Abuses in Cambodia, 1975–80* (New York: St. Martin's Press, 1996), p. 6.

19. Kiernan, "The American Bombardment of Kampuchea," pp. 21–22, quoting an interview with journalist Bruce Palling and Catholic missionary François Ponchaud in Paris, January 1982.

20. "Ousted Cambodian Premier Speaks Out," *New York Times,* March 24, 1973, p. 3.

21. Kenneth Quinn, "The Khmer Krahom Program to Create a Communist Society in Southern Cambodia," February 20, 1974.

22. Elizabeth Becker, "Who Are the Khmer Rouge?" *Washington Post,* March 10, 1974, p. B1.

23. In November 1974 Becker's colleague James Fenton reported for the *Washington Post* from just inside the Vietnamese border. Some 40,000 Cambodians had gathered there after fleeing KR-controlled territory. Fenton relayed refugee claims that KR areas were "undergoing a rapid forced transformation affecting every detail of life, from marriage laws to the Cambodian language itself." "Reconstruction," Fenton wrote, was one of the new words introduced to denote the treatment that awaited any man who violated KR laws by commencing an illicit love affair. James Fenton, "Cambodia: Communism Alters Lifestyle," *Washington Post,* November 24, 1974, p. K1.

24. Elizabeth Becker, "Cambodians Fear Rebel Drive for Seat at U.N.," *Washington Post,* April 23, 1974, p. A18.

25. Sylvana Foa, "Sihanouk Recalled Fondly in Cambodia," *Washington Post,* August 14, 1973, p. A6.

26. Metzl, *Western Responses,* p. 9.

27. Officially, according to Becker, half a million died on the Lon Nol side of the war, whereas 600,000 were said to have died in KR zones; Becker, *When the War Was Over,* p. 170. A CIA demographic report on Cambodia estimates 600,000–700,000 "war-related deaths" during the civil war between the KR and the Lon Nol government. National Foreign Assessment Center, CIA, *Kampuchea: A Demographic Catastrophe* (Washington, D.C.: Document Expediting [DOCEX]. Project, Exchange and Gift Division, Library of Congress, 1980), p. 2.

28. Ponchaud, *Year Zero,* p. 2.

29. Jacques Leslie, "Phnom Penh Civilians Fatalistic; Rockets Fail as a Political Strategy," *Los Angeles Times,* March 30, 1975, sec. 1, p. 10.

30. Sydney H. Schanberg, "The Enigmatic Cambodian Insurgents: Reds Appear to Dominate Diverse Bloc," *New York Times,* March 13, 1975, p. A1.

31. Schanberg was evacuated on one of the last two convoys on April 30, but his erstwhile assistant, Dith Pran, was left behind to face the wrath of the KR. In a story recounted in the 1984 Oscar-winning *Killing Fields,* directed by Roland Joffe, Schanberg, who was racked by guilt for failing to save Pran, spent much of the next three years trying to locate his colleague and friend. When the pair were miraculously reunited on the Thai border in 1980, Schanberg asked for forgiveness for being unable to shelter Pran at the French embassy. Pran responded, "No, no," gripping Schanberg's hand. "It's not like that. Nothing to forgive. We both made a decision. We both agree to stay, no one pushed the other. You tried all you could to keep me, but it didn't work. Not your fault. We stayed because we did not

believe in a blood bath. We were fools; we believed there would be reconciliation. But who could have believed the Khmer Rouge would be so brutal?" Schanberg, *The Death and Life of Dith Pran,* p. 61.

32. Metzl, *Western Responses,* p. 11.

33. Ibid., p. 11, citing "Cambodia Fact Sheets," National Security Council, Sven Kramer to Bill Kendall, March 17, 1975, box 5, Vietnam (1) file, Gerald Ford Library, Ann Arbor, Michigan.

34. *Congressional Record,* 94th Cong., 1st sess., 1975, 121, pt. 7:8796.

35. Sydney H. Schanberg, "Indochina Without Americans: For Most, a Better Life," *New York Times,* April 13, 1975, sec. 4, p. 1.

36. Hearings Before the Committee on International Relations, House of Representatives, 94th Cong., 1st sess., 1975, p. 298.

37. Ibid., pp. 299–300. In her written submission, Abzug urged, "Secretary Kissinger should turn his talents to this area"; see p. 302.

38. *Congressional Record,* 94th Cong., 1st sess., 1975, 121, pt. 6:7902.

39. "Cambodian Aid: Administration's Choice," *Washington Post,* March 17, 1975. As the bloodbath debate intensified, the debate became its own story. Two weeks before Phnom Penh finally fell to the Khmer Rouge, the *New York Times* ran an op-ed piece entitled "The Cambodian Bloodbath Debate" in which journalist Donald Kirk pointed out that "the dialogue resembles a shouting match in which one man accuses the other of lying, and neither has the final evidence to prove his point." Donald Kirk, "The Cambodian Bloodbath Debate," *New York Times,* April 5, 1975, p. 29.

40. Jean-Jacques Cazaux, "Gathering of the Conquered: Lon Nol's Brother Led Surrender in Phnom Penh," *Washington Post,* May 9, 1975, p. A22.

41. Lewis M. Simons, "Khmer Rouge: Victors' Incongruities Begin with Sihanouk," *Washington Post,* April 18, 1975, p. A14.

42. Tom Mathews, Harry Rolnick, and Lloyd Norman, "We Beat the Americans," *Newsweek,* May 5, 1975, p. 34.

43. French embassy officials segregated occupants. Some 800 Westerners who gathered were allowed inside the embassy's four buildings, whereas the 500 or so Cambodians and other Asians were forced to camp out on the grass outside the compound. Schanberg, *The Death and Life of Dith Pran,* p. 28.

44. Kim Willenson and Paul Brinkley-Rogers, "Cambodia's 'Purification,'" *Newsweek,* May 19, 1975, pp. 30–36; Jean-Jacques Cazaux and Claude Juvenal, "Khmer Rouge Acts to 'Purify' Nation," *Washington Post,* May 9, 1975, pp. A1, A16.

45. Sydney H. Schanberg, "Cambodia Reds Are Uprooting Millions as They Impose a 'Peasant Revolution,'" *New York Times,* May 9, 1975, p. A1; emphasis added.

46. Ibid., pp. A1, A15.

47. Cazaux and Juvenal, "Khmer Rouge Acts to 'Purify' Nation."

48. Schanberg, "Cambodia Reds Are Uprooting Millions."

49. Jack Anderson and Les Whitten, "Cambodia: Most Brutal Dictatorship," *Washington Post,* July 21, 1977, p. D15.

50. House Committee on International Relations, *The Vietnam-Cambodia Emergency, 1975, Part I—Vietnam Evacuation and Humanitarian Assistance: Hearings Before the Committee on International Relations on H.R. 5960 (To Clarify Restrictions on the Availability of Funds for the Use of United States Armed Forces in Indochina) and H.R. 5961 (To Authorize Additional Economic Assistance for South Vietnam),* 94th Cong., 1st sess., April 18, 1975, p. 152.

51. Schanberg, "Cambodia Reds Are Uprooting Millions."

52. "'Blood Bath' in Cambodia," *Newsweek,* May 12, 1975, p. 27. "Cambodian Ex-Officers, Wives Reported Slain by Khmer Rouge," *Washington Post,* May 6, 1975, p. A14.

53. Jack Anderson and Les Whitten, "Reports Hint 'Blood Debt' Being Paid," *Washington Post,* May 12, 1975, p. C25. The two columnists consistently spoke out about the KR atrocities, but they also admitted their uncertainty. In a June 4, 1975, column they wrote that the KR "may be guilty of genocide against their own people" and they noted that some 3 million Cambodians had been driven from their homes. But they also conceded that intercepted reports had been "sporadic and fragmentary." "There isn't even hard evidence," their sources told them, "that the killings run to the 80 figure" that Ford cited in early May. Jack Anderson and Les Whitten, "What Befell 3 Million Cambodians?" *Washington Post,* June 4, 1975, p. F11.

54. "Kissinger Sees Atrocity in Events in Cambodia," *New York Times,* May 14, 1975, p. 5.

55. Willenson and Brinkley-Rogers, "Cambodia's 'Purification.'"

56. Nuon Chea to a Danish journalist, quoted in Laura Summers, "The CPK: Secret Vanguard of Pol Pot's Revolution," *Journal of Communist Studies* 3, 1 (March 1987): 11, cited in Chandler, *Voices from S–21,* p. 16.

57. "Winner Seen in Struggle for Top Cambodian Post," *Washington Post,* September 26, 1977, p. A21.

58. Lewis Simons, "Cambodian Leader Moves to Counter Image of Brutality," *Washington Post,* September 30, 1977, p. A20.

59. Ponchaud, *Year Zero,* p. 50.

60. Shawcross, *Sideshow,* p. 56.

61. Metzl, *Western Responses,* p. 31. U.S. interest in Cambodia was piqued in May 1975 by the threat to *American* lives posed by the *Mayaguez* affair. On May 12 the Cambodian navy seized the USS *Mayaguez* sixty miles off the Cambodian coast and accused the crew of spying. Two days later, 250 U.S. marines in eleven helicopters attacked Koh Tang Island, where they believed the U.S. crew was being held. U.S. bombers also targeted a nearby Cambodian airfield, destroying seventeen planes and the Cambodian oil refinery. Press coverage of this event drowned out the atrocity reports during the month of May. The attack was initially seen as a daring display of American nerve, a crucial testament to American resolve, and a means of restoring U.S. credibility in the region. It showed, in Kissinger's words, that there remained "limits beyond which the United States cannot be pushed." In the end, because the attack left thirty-eight American soldiers dead (initially only two deaths were reported) and three U.S. helicopters destroyed, the Ford administration was criticized for mishandling the affair. Peter Goldman, Thomas M. DeFrank, Henry W. Hubbard, and Bruce von Voorst, "Ford's Rescue Operation," *Newsweek,* May 26, 1975. pp. 16–18. See also Milton R. Benjamin, et al., "Victory at Sea," *Newsweek,* May 26, 1975, pp. 18–27, and Ralph Wetterhahn, *The Last Battle: The* Mayaguez *Incident and the End of the Vietnam War* (New York: Carroll & Graf, 2001).

62. Metzl, *Western Responses,* pp. 51, 91.

63. William C. Adams and Michael Joblove, "The Unnewsworthy Holocaust: TV News and Terror in Cambodia," in William C. Adams, ed., *Television Coverage of International Affairs* (Norwood, N.J.: Ablex, 1982), p. 224.

64. "Cambodia's Crime. . . ," *New York Times,* July 9, 1975, p. A36.

65. See Adams and Joblove, "The Unnewsworthy Holocaust," pp. 217–226.

66. "Cambodia Executions Confirmed," *Washington Post,* November 2, 1975, p. A11.

67. In the first few months of KR rule, hundreds of refugees who had managed to slip into Thailand made the decision to return to Cambodia, expecting hard work and Communist indoctrination but desperate to be reunited with their families. Few were ever heard from again.

68. Bruce Palling, "Refugees: Life Harsh in Cambodia," *Washington Post,* July 13, 1975, p. A1.

69. Dan Morgan, "Deaths in Cambodia Laid to U.S. Policy," *Washington Post,* September 31, 1975, p. A14, quoting the nonprofit Indochina Resource Center's report "The Politics of Food: Starvation and Agricultural Revolution in Cambodia."

70. Metzl, *Western Responses,* p. 56; Noam Chomsky and Edward S. Herman, "Distortions at Fourth Hand," *Nation,* June 25, 1977, pp. 789–794.

71. Amnesty International, *Amnesty International: Annual Report, 1974/75* (London: Amnesty International Publications, 1975), p. 86.

72. Amnesty International, *Amnesty International: Report, 1975/76* (London: Amnesty International Publications, 1976), pp. 137–138.

73. Asia Research Department to National Sections Coordination Groups on East and South-East Asia, Amnesty International, ASA/23/01/77, March 3, 1977; cited in Metzl, *Western Responses,* pp. 63–64.

74. Ibid., pp. 82–83. The International Committee of Jurists similarly demanded irrefutable evidence before it publicly censured the KR.

75. Ben Kiernan, "Cambodia and the News, 1975/1976," *Melbourne Journal of Politics,* December 1976/January 1977, p. 6; quoted in Metzl, *Western Responses,* p. 53.

76. Lewis Simons, "Disease, Hunger Ravage Cambodia as Birthrate Falls," *Washington Post,* July 22, 1977, p. A16. Simons quotes a European diplomat who did not contest KR brutality but who said, "It now seems that perhaps no more than 200,000 were executed. From what we know of the size of the Khmer Rouge armed force [then estimated at about 80,000] the mechanics for executions on a more massive scale are just not there."

77. Shawcross, *Sideshow,* p. 47.

78. Estimates of the number of Cambodians gathered at the Thai border varied. By July 1975 there were some 7,000; that number doubled over the next few years, but most Cambodians were trapped inside the country.

79. Becker, *When the War Was Over,* p. 141.

80. Seath K. Teng, "The End of Childhood," in Dith Pran, comp., and Kim DePaul, ed., *Children of Cambodia's Killing Fields: Memoirs by Survivors* (New Haven: Yale University Press, 1997), pp. 157–158.

81. In mid-1976, after the early purge of the civilian and military officials affiliated with Lon Nol, the KR, in Becker's words, "shifted their attention from eliminating or transforming the bourgeoisie to eliminating the bourgeois tendencies in the Party." Becker, *When the War Was Over,* p. 274.

82. Savuth Penn, "The Dark Years of My Life," in Dith Pran, comp., and Kim DePaul, ed., *Children of Cambodia's Killing Fields: Memoirs by Survivors* (New Haven: Yale University Press, 1997), pp. 44–46.

83. Chandler, *Voices from S–21,* p. 76, citing David Ashley's translation of the July 25, 1997, trial of Pol Pot at Anlong Veng.

84. Joan D. Criddle and Teeda Butt Mam, *To Destroy You Is No Loss: The Odyssey of a Cambodian Family* (New York: Atlantic Monthly Press, 1987), pp. 90–105.

85. Chandler, *Voices from S–21,* p. 44, citing Henri Locard, *Le Petit livre rouge de Pol Pot, ou les paroles de l'Angkar* (Paris: L'Harmattan, 1996), p. 175.

86. "Cambodia's Crime," *New York Times,* July 9, 1975, p. 36.

87. H. D. S. Greenway, "The New Cambodia: A Harsh, Joyless Land," *Washington Post,* February 2, 1976, pp. A1, A12.

88. François Ponchaud, "Le Cambodge neuf mois après: I.—Un travail gigantesque," *Le Monde,* February 17, 1976, pp. 1, 4; and François Ponchaud, "Le Cambodge neuf mois après: II.—Un nouveau type d'homme," *Le Monde,* February 18, 1976, p. 2.

89. "Pickaxe Executions by Khmer Rouge Alleged," *Times* (London), April 23, 1976, p. 7; and "Un Réfugié affirme avoir participé 'à l'exécution de cinq mille personnes,'" *Le Monde,* April 23, 1976, p. 3.

90. "The Khmer Rouge: Rampant Terror," *Time,* April 19, 1976, p. 65.

91. Ann Mariano, "Forced Cambodia Labor Depicted," *Washington Post,* April 8, 1977, p. A12. It was March 1978 before a "delegation" of Yugoslav journalists became the first to enter Cambodia; David A. Andelman, "Yugoslavs, After Rare Tour, Tell of a Primitive Cambodia," *New York Times,* March 24, 1978, p. A2. Even then they had to ask the KR leader, "Who are you, comrade Pol Pot?" Kiernan, *The Pol Pot Regime,* p. 9. "Although restricted by the conventions of Communist fraternalism . . . in their dispatches," one Yugoslav journalist confided to *New York Times* correspondent Henry Kamm that the group was "appalled by much of what they saw" in Cambodia; Henry Kamm, "Cambodian Refugees Depict Growing Fear and Hunger," *New York Times,* May 13, 1978, p. A1.

92. Becker, *When the War Was Over,* p. 375.

93. In 1976 Twining sent cables documenting in detail the population transfers, individual refugee accounts of execution, the effects of disease, and the structure of the KR regime.

94. See Metzl, *Western Responses,* p. 62, citing Secretary of State to Embassies, June 8, 1976. The secretary had "spoken out publicly" only in April 1975, just after the takeover.

95. *Congressional Record,* 95th Cong., 2nd sess., 1978, 124, pt. 25:33873.

96. Ibid., pt. 26:34655.

97. Social Committee of the United Nations Economic and Social Council, 62nd Session, Summary Record of the 811th Meeting, May 4, 1977 (E/AC.7/SR.811, May 6, 1977), p. 7; cited in Metzl, *Western Responses,* pp. 87–88.

98. The UN Commission on Human Rights was savagely politicized and ineffective. Ugandan dictator Idi Amin, for instance, had deflected discussion or critique of his regime at the commission for four years because he headed the Organization for African Unity. The forum had deteriorated into a stage for denouncing only Israel, South Africa, and Western colonizers.

99. David Hawk, "Pol Pot's Cambodia: Was It Genocide?" *Toward the understanding and prevention of genocide: Proceeding of the International Conference on the Holocaust and Genocide,* ed. Israel W. Charny (Boulder, Co.: Westview Press, 1984), p. 52.

100. *Human Rights in Cambodia,* Hearing Before the Subcommittee on International Organizations of the Committee on International Relations, House of Representatives, 95th Congress, 1st session, July 26, 1977, p. 15.

101. Letter from Ieng Sary to UN Commission on Human Rights, Geneva, April 1978.

102. Shawcross, *Sideshow,* pp. 61–62.

103. George McArthur, "China Reportedly Ships Arms to Cambodia," *Los Angeles Times,* March 3, 1978, sec. 1, p. 24; Henry Kamm, "Indochina Fighting Breaks out Again," *New York Times,* May 18, 1978, p. A9; Bates Gill and J. N. Mak, eds., *Arms, Transparency and Security in South-East Asia,* Stockholm International Peace Research Institute research report no. 13 (New York: Oxford University Press, 1997), p. 103.

104. Zbigniew Brzezinski, *Power and Principle: Memoirs of the National Security Adviser, 1977–1981* (New York: Farrar, Straus, and Giroux, 1985), p. 199.

105. "Human Rights Violations in Cambodia," p. 18618.

106. *Human Rights in Cambodia,* Hearing Before the Subcommittee on International Organizations of the Committee on International Relations, House of Representatives, 95th Congress, 1st session, May 3, 1977, pp. 19, 35.

107. The first five of these columns were written by both Jack Anderson and Les Whitten from June 1975 to the end of 1977. Jack Anderson wrote another ten columns on Cambodia during the course of 1978.

108. Jack Anderson and Les Whitten, "Cambodia: Most Brutal Dictatorship," *Washington Post,* July 21, 1977, p. D15.

109. Jack Anderson and Les Whitten, "Human Rights Effort Losing Its Zeal," *Washington Post,* November 30, 1977, p. B15.

110. Jack Anderson, "In Cambodia, Obliterating a Culture," *Washington Post,* May 2, 1978, p. B12.

111. Jack Anderson, "Cambodia: A Modern-Day Holocaust," *Washington Post,* May 3, 1978, p. E10.

112. "Out of the Silence," *Economist,* September 10, 1977, p. 131.

113. William Safire, "Silence Is Guilt," *New York Times,* April 24, 1978, p. A23.

114. "The Cambodian Holocaust," *Congressional Record,* 95th Cong., 2nd sess., 1978, 124, pt. 10:13508. See also Representative Stephen Solarz (D.–N.Y.), "The Human Rights Problem in Cambodia," *Congressional Record,* 95th Cong., 2nd sess., 1978, 124, pt. 12:16020; Representative James Mattox (D.–Tex.), "Cambodia: The Worst Human Rights Violator," *Congressional Record,* 95th Cong., 2nd sess., 1978, 124, pt. 11:15131; Senator George McGovern (D.–S. Dak.), "A Question of Conscience and Civilization," *Congressional Record,* 95th Cong., 2nd sess., 1978, 124, pt. 21:27755–27757.

115. *Congressional Record,* 95th Cong., 2nd sess., 1978, 124, pt. 27:35961.

116. *Human Rights in Cambodia,* July 26, 1977, pp. 2, 23.

117. Ibid., pp. 15–16.

118. Jack Anderson, "In Cambodia, Obliterating a Culture," *Washington Post,* May 2, 1978, p. B12.

119. Adams and Joblove, "The Unnewsworthy Holocaust," p. 221. The first description was used on NBC news on July 8, 1975; the later two figures were given on CBS news on August 21, 1978, and NBC news on September 21, 1978.

120. Smith Hempstone, "The Need to Bear Witness to Cambodia's Holocaust," *Washington Post,* May 7, 1978, p. C5.

121. "Human Rights Violations in Cambodia," April 21, 1978, *Public Papers of the Presidents of the United States: Jimmy Carter, 1978,* vol. 2 (Washington, D.C.: GPO, 1979), pp. 767–768.

122. Amnesty International, *Amnesty International: Report, 1978* (London: Amnesty International Publications, 1978), p. 169.

123. It is worth noting that the organization's capacity had greatly expanded in the previous three years. Between 1975 and 1978, expenditures grew to about $1.13 million (about $3.2 million in 1999 dollars), nearly a 225 percent real increase compared to 1975.

124. Amnesty International, *Allegations of Human Rights Violations in Democratic Kampuchea,* statement submitted to UN Subcommission on Prevention of Discrimination and Protection of Minorities, August 1978.

125. U.S. submission to UNCHR, July 6, 1978; cited in Metzl, *Western Responses,* p. 85.

126. George McGovern, "America in Vietnam," in Patrick J. Hearden, ed., *Vietnam: Four American Perspectives* (West Lafayette, Ind.: Purdue University Press, 1990), p. 24.

127. Senate Foreign Relations Committee, *Hearing on the Current Situation in Indochina,* 95th Cong., 2nd sess., 1978, p. 24.

128. Ibid., p. 23.

129. Ibid., p. 29.

130. William F. Buckley Jr., "Cambodia—Our Sinful Sloth," *Los Angeles Times,* September 16, 1977, sec. 2, p. 7.

131. Senate Foreign Relations Committee, *Hearing on the Current Situation in Indochina,* 95th Cong. Sess., 1978, pp. 25–26.

132. Ibid., pp. 26 and 33.

133. Ibid., p. 30.

134. Don Oberdorfer, "McGovern and Cambodia: 'Old Shock Technique,'" *Washington Post,* August 26, 1978, p. A8.

135. McGovern enlisted as a nineteen-year-old after the bombing of Pearl Harbor but says he believed even then that Hitler was the one to stop: "I was always startled after the war to hear people saying they didn't know about Hitler's crimes when I distinctly remembered reading about them before Pearl Harbor. There were reports at least prominent enough to catch the eye of a South Dakota high school student." McGovern went on to fly thirty-five bombing missions in Europe and win the Distinguished Flying Cross.

136. *Facts on File,* September 1, 1978, p. 659.

137. Oberdorfer, "McGovern and Cambodia: 'Old Shock Technique.'"

138. Robert Kaiser, "Press U.N. on Cambodia, 80 Senators Urge Vance," *Washington Post,* October 13, 1978, p. A10.

139. Senators to Secretary of State Cyrus Vance, October 12, 1978. The U.S. report included excerpts from interviews with Cambodian refugees at the Thai border, extracts from twelve earlier reports from the U.S. embassy in Bangkok, Carter's statement to Oslo, Christopher's January statements, transcripts of the congressional hearings and two House resolutions condemning Cambodia, and full copies of Ponchaud's *Year Zero* and Barron's *Murder of a Gentle Land: The Untold Story of a Communist Genocide in Cambodia* (New York: Reader's Digest Press, 1977). The full case—997 pages in all—was formally presented to the Subcommission on the Prevention of Discrimination and Protection of Minorities of the UNCHR (E/CN.4/Sub.2/414, 14 August 1978); cited in Metzl, *Western Responses,* pp. 115–118.

140. John Sharkey, "Vietnam, Cambodia Exchange Bitter Charges," *Washington Post,* January 1, 1978, p. A8; David Binder, "Vietnam Holds Cambodian Region After Bitter Fight, U.S. Aides Say," *New York Times,* January 4, 1978, pp. A1, A6.

141. Elizabeth Becker, "Cambodia Offers to Open Borders to Westerners," *Washington Post,* October 14, 2001, p. A1.

142. In one stop-off they encountered child factory workers whom Becker quickly recognized were the very same children that had been filmed in a documentary prepared earlier by the Yugoslav journalists.

143. Becker, *When the War Was Over,* p. 406.

144. Ibid., p. 409.

145. Ibid., p. 426.

146. This effort had faltered largely because the United States was not quite ready to reconcile but also because of Hanoi's insistence on enormous war reparations and its failure to account for American soldiers who remained missing in action.

147. U.S. embassy, Bangkok, to Secretary of State Cyrus Vance, August 18, 1978; cited in Metzl, *Western Responses,* pp. 123–124.

148. Becker, *When the War Was Over,* p. 394.

149. The number of deaths is impossible to verify because the last nationwide census had been conducted in Cambodia in 1962. Yale historian Ben Kiernan has estimated 1.7 million deaths; Craig Etcheson of the Cambodian Documentation Center believes that more than 2 million died during KR rule, more than half of whom were likely executed. By August 2001, the center had identified more than 1.1 million victims of execution, and nearly a quarter of Cambodia's subdistricts had not yet been surveyed.

150. The *s* stands for *sala,* or "hall," and 21 was the code number for *santebal, a* Khmer term for "security police." Chandler, *Voices from S–21,* p. 3.

151. This included one who was spared because he maintained the prison's electrical generating equipment, another who painted Pol Pot's portraits, and a third who sculpted his bust.

152. Hurst Hannum, "International Law and Cambodian Genocide: The Sounds of Silence," *Human Rights Quarterly,* vol. 11, no. 1 (Feb. 1989), p. 91.

153. The instructions still hang at the Tuol Sleng Museum, Phnom Penh, Cambodia.

154. Ibid., p. 130.

155. "Pro-Vietnam Journalist Cites Cambodian Torture," *Washington Post,* May 11, 1979, p. A23. Some of the reporting in the spring and summer of 1979 qualified atrocity reports—either mentioning that the source of the information was Vietnam or Communist-sympathizing journalists or that there seemed to be few eyewitnesses to the reported atrocities. See, for example, Henry Kamm, "Chinese Invasion Overshadows Cambodia's Plight," *New York Times,* March 4, 1979, p. 11; "Cambodia Situation Unclear," *New York Times,* March 27, 1979, p. A3; "Vietnam Reports Discovery of Cambodian Mass Graves," *New York Times,* April 3, 1979, p. A5; and "Vietnam Says the Pol Pot Forces Beat 26,000 Prisoners to Death," *New York Times,* July 27, 1979, p. A2. As Western reporters were allowed back into Cambodia by the Vietnamese-backed government, the atrocity reports became more authoritative. See James Matlack, "Cambodia: Desolate and Devastated," *Washington Post,* October 25, 1979, p. A1.

156. Don Oberdorfer, "U.S. Accuses Hanoi, Calls for Withdrawal," *Washington Post,* January 8, 1979, pp. A1, A18.

157. See James Dunn, "Genocide in East Timor," in Samuel Totten, William S. Parsons, Israel W. Charny, eds., *A Century of Genocide: Eyewitness Accounts and Critical Views* (New York: Garland, 1997), pp. 264–290; Henry Kamm, "The Silent Suffering of East Timor," *New York Times,* February 15, 1981, sec. 6, p. 35.

158. British media disclosed that British Special Air Services (SAS) commandos had secretly trained Thai-based guerrillas, including the KR, to oppose the Vietnamese-backed government since the mid-1980s. See Simon O'Dwyer-Russell, "SAS Training Jungle Fighters," *Sunday Telegraph,* September 24, 1989, p. 14, and Robert Karniol, "UK Trained Cambodian Guerrillas," *Jane's Defence Weekly,* September 30, 1989, p. 629. Although U.S. involvement may not have been as direct as that of the British, the United States did fund purchases of materiel, including weapons, ostensibly for the KR's non-Communist allies through several ASEAN member

countries. See Paul Quinn-Judge, "Asia Allies Want Open U.S. Aid for Kampuchea Guerrillas," *Christian Science Monitor,* October 12, 1984, p. 11; Elaine Sciolino, "Sihanouk Hints at U.S. Military Aid," *New York Times,* October 14, 1988, p. A3; and Elaine Sciolino, "Tainted Cambodia Aid: New Details," *New York Times,* November 1, 1988, p. A3. The United States technically limited its aid to the non-Communist forces in Cambodia, but the KR's dominance over their coalition partners made the KR the likely beneficiaries. Sydney Schanberg, "Needed: A Public Outcry on Cambodia," *Newsday* (Nassau and Suffolk edition), May 18, 1990, p. 90.

159. According to Richard Holbrooke, assistant secretary of state for East Asian and Pacific Affairs, the Soviets' military shipments to Vietnam more than quadrupled from 1978 to 1979 in support of the Vietnamese occupation; Senate Foreign Relations Committee, Subcommittee on Asian and Pacific Affairs, March 24, 1980. They supplied some $2 billion in weapons to Hanoi in 1979 and 1980 and about $750 million per year thereafter, in addition to some $1 billion annually in economic aid. Nayan Chanda, *Brother Enemy: The War After the War* (New York: Harcourt Brace Jovanovich, 1986), p. 397.

160. Becker, *When the War Was Over,* p. 440.

161. John Burgess, "Khmer Rouge, Fighting to Regain Power, Admit 'Mistakes,'" *Washington Post,* August 10, 1980, p. A21.

162. Daniel Burstein, "A Visit with the Khmer Rouge," *Washington Post,* March 9, 1980, p. C1.

163. John Burgess, "Cambodian Thanks U.S. for Help at U.N.," *Washington Post,* August 8, 1980, p. A1.

164. Elizabeth Becker, "Sihanouk Seeks Backing for Neutral Cambodia," *Washington Post,* February 23, 1980, p. A21.

165. Along with the United States, China, Belgium, Ecuador, Pakistan, and Senegal voted to continue to recognize the KR government, whereas the Soviet Union, Congo, and Panama voted against approving its credentials. Benin, Congo, Guinea-Bissau, India, Madagascar, São Tomé and Principe, and Sierra Leone submitted an "amendment" to the draft resolution that would have kept the Cambodian seat at the UN empty, but the General Assembly chose not to vote on the measure.

166. The Cambodian ambassador to the UN was not Ieng Sary but Thiounn Prasith, who lives to this day in Westchester County, despite countless efforts by Cambodia activists to have him deported.

167. Debate of the General Assembly, 34th sess., 3rd plenary meeting, September 18, 1979.

168. Ibid., p. 50.

169. John Burgess, "Cambodian Thanks U.S. for Help at U.N.," *Washington Post,* August 8, 1980, p. A1.

170. "No Thanks," *Washington Post,* August 11, 1980, p. A18.

171. "Hold-Your-Nose Diplomacy," *Washington Post,* September 17, 1980, p. A18.

172. Jack Anderson, "Pol Pot or Not?" *Washington Post,* September 14, 1980, p. C7.

173. Don Oberdorfer, "U.S. to Support Pol Pot Regime for U.N. Seat," *Washington Post,* September 16, 1980, p. A1.

174. Some of the individuals whose opposition to the KR might have led one to believe they would back Vietnam in fact urged support for the four-party coalition that included the Khmer Rouge. Representative Stephen Solarz was one of them. In the mid-1980s he initiated congressional efforts to aid the non-Communist resistance. "The last thing I wanted to see was the return of the

Khmer Rouge, but the next to last thing I wanted to see was Cambodia dominated by Vietnam," he says. Solarz believed the debate at the Credentials Committee, however symbolic, was an overblown tribute to the guilty consciences that many felt about KR terror. "The debate at the UN was its own *sideshow*. Whether the seat was filled or it remained empty, it had zero to do with the Khmer Rouge. It had more to do with a statement of morality. I thought the breast-beating was irrelevant. I mean, where were these people when Pol Pot was executing his wicked will?"

175. Elaine Sciolino, "Tainted Cambodia Aid: New Details," *New York Times,* November 1, 1988, p. A3.

176. The combination of Western isolation and Vietnamese mismanagement led to a famine. It is extremely difficult to compile meaningful population statistics in Cambodia, but one recent demographic analysis puts the death toll due to the famine at 300,000; see Patrick Heuveline, "The Demographic Analysis of Mortality Crises: The Case of Cambodia, 1970–1979," in Holly E. Reed and Charles B. Keely, eds., *Forced Migration and Mortality* (Washington, D.C.: National Academy Press, 2001), pp. 102–129. Others have argued that widespread famine did not occur; see Judith Banister and E. Paige Johnson, "After the Nightmare: The Population of Cambodia," in Ben Kiernan, ed., *Genocide and Democracy in Cambodia: The Khmer Rouge, the United Nations and the International Community* (New Haven: Yale University Southeast Asia Studies, 1993), pp. 65–139, and Ben Kiernan, "Review Essay: William Shawcross, Declining Cambodia," *Bulletin of Concerned Asian Scholars,* January-March 1986, pp. 56–63.

177. Report to the Economic and Social Council, July 2, 1985, 4/SUB, 2/1985/6.

178. Becker, *When the War Was Over,* pp. 503–504.

179. United Nations, Treaty Series, "United States of America, Democratic Republic of Viet-Nam, Provisional Revolutionary Government of the Republic of South Viet-Nam and Republic of Viet-Nam: Protocol to the Agreement on Ending the War and Restoring Peace in Viet-Nam Concerning the Return of Captured Military Personnel and Foreign Civilians and Captured and Detained Vietnamese Civilian Personnel. Signed at Paris on 27 January 1973," *Treaties and International Agreements Registerd or Filed or Reported with the Secretariat of the United Nations,* p. 203, No. 13296 (1974).

Chapter 7, Speaking Loudly and Looking for a Stick

1. December 1968 remarks quoted in William Korey, "The Genocide Treaty: Unratified 35 Years," *New York Times,* June 23, 1984, sec. 1, p. 23.

2. *Spotlight,* May 14, 1979. See Charles R. Allen Jr., "The Genocide Convention: America's Shame," *Reform Judaism* 10, 4 (Summer 1982): 12.

3. Ibid.

4. *Congressional Record.* 99th Cong., 2nd sess., 1986, 132, pt. 15:S1355.

5. Ibid.

6. Kathleen Teltsch, "Library Show Recalls Man Behind Treaty on Genocide," *New York Times,* December 4, 1983, sec. 1, p. 62.

7. Korey, "The Genocide Treaty"; William Korey, "Lemkin and Trifka: Memory and Justice," *Christian Science Monitor,* August 30, 1984, p. 11.

8. *Congressional Record,* 99th Cong., 1st sess., 1985, 131, pt. 46:S4386.

9. Ibid., pt. 78:S7961.

10. Ibid., pt. 48:S4520. Proxmire got the House statistic from a speech given by Representative Stephen Solarz the previous week.

11. Ibid., 99th Cong., 2nd sess., 1986, 132, pt. 6:S392.

12. Ibid., pt. 14:S1252.

13. "Soviet Hypocrisy," *New York Times,* May 5, 1954, p. 30.

14. Ibid.

15. *Congressional Record,* 99th Cong. 2nd sess., 1986, pt. 14:S1252.

16. Ibid.

17. "U.S. Urges Ratification of Genocide Convention," Department of State, *Bulletin,* November 1984, p. 66. "Remarks at the International Convention of B'nai B'rith," September 6, 1984, *Public Papers of the Presidents of the United States: Ronald Reagan, 1984,* vol. 2 (Washington, D.C.: GPO, 1987), pp. 1242–1246.

18. Bernard Gwertzman, "Reagan Will Submit 1948 Genocide Pact for Senate Approval," *New York Times,* September 6, 1984, p. A1.

19. Bernard Weinraub, "Reagan's German Trip: Furor over Remembrance," *New York Times,* April 18, 1985, p. A1.

20. David Hoffman, "Reagan Defends Plan to Visit German Military Cemetary," *Washington Post,* April 13, 1985, p. A1.

21. Jay Matthews and Helen Dewar, "Wiesenthal Rejects Trip to Bitburg; White House Seeks Holocaust Survivors to Join President," *Washington Post,* April 27, 1985, p. A1.

22. Hoffman, "Reagan Defends Plan."

23. "Transcript of Remarks by Reagan and Wiesel at White House Ceremony," *New York Times,* April 20, 1985, sec. 1, p. 4.

24. David Hoffman, "Honoring Wiesel, Reagan Confronts the Holocaust; Bergen-Belsen Put on Trip Itinerary," *Washington Post,* April 20, 1985, p. A1.

25. David Hoffman, "German Soldiers Called 'Victims'; Reagan Defends Itinerary," *Washington Post,* April 18, 1985, p. A1.

26. The United States attached two reservations, five understandings, and a declaration. The second reservation held that the genocide convention could not authorize any legislation or action by the United States if it were prohibited by the U.S. Constitution. This provision has become a standard accompaniment to U.S. ratifications of international human rights treaties. It is problematic because it leaves the executive branch again free to decide, if a case of genocide arises, whether or not compliance with the treaty in the case at hand violates some provision of the U.S. Constitution, which it will interpret. Future presidents can thus reopen some of the very debates that had stalled ratification in the first place for nearly forty years. With this pair of reservations, the U.S. Senate made it clear that it did not see the law as meaningfully "binding." The Senate understanding held that the words "intent to destroy, in whole or in part" should be interpreted as the intent to destroy "in whole or in *substantial part*" the group concerned. In its 1988 implementing legislation, the Senate would define "substantial part" as "a part of a group of such numerical significance that the destruction or loss of that part would cause the destruction of the group as a viable entity within the nation of which such a group is a part." The Senate understood the words "mental harm" as the "permanent impairment of mental facilities through drugs, torture, or similar techniques." The Senate also "understood" that it would not participate in any future international criminal tribunal without ratifying a separate treaty to that effect.

27. *Congressional Record,* 99th Cong., 1st sess., 1985, 131, pt. 103:S10203.

28. Ibid. An amendment offered by Senator Chris Dodd (D.–Conn.) to modify the effect of the ICJ reservation was defeated 8–9.

29. *Congressional Record*, 99th Cong., 2nd sess., 1986, 132, pt. 15:S1355.

30. Ibid., pt. 16:S1441.

31. Ibid., pt. 15:S1355.

32. Ibid., 100th Cong., 2nd sess., 1988, 134, pt. 8:S552.

33. "Remarks by President Ronald Reagan on the Occasion of Signing the Genocide Convention Implementation Act of 1987," Federal News Service, November 4, 1988.

34. *Congressional Record*, 100th Cong., 2nd sess. 1988, 134, pt. 149:S16798.

Chapter 8, Iraq

1. Middle East Watch, *Genocide in Iraq: The Anfal Campaign Against the Kurds* (New York: Human Rights Watch, 1993), pp. 4–5, 56.

2. Kurds are divided not merely by party but by language and geography: Sorani speakers of the Patriotic Union of Kurdistan (PUK) are located east of the Greater Zab River; Kurmanji speakers of the Kurdish Democratic Party (KDP) are found near the Turkish border to the river's north and west. On September 17, 1998, at the prodding of the Clinton administration, Barzani and Talabani signed the Washington agreement, in which the KDP and PUK affirmed Iraqi territorial integrity, committed themselves to improving the administration of the three northern provinces, and condemned in-fighting among them, pledging "to refrain from resorting to violence to settle differences or seeking outside intervention against each other"; Barton Gellman, "Kurdish Rivals Cement U.S.-Brokered Pact; Leaders of Northern Iraq Rebels Set Aside Bitter Feud, Agree to Share Power and Resources," *Washington Post*, September 18, 1998, p. A26.

3. See the Pike Committee Report, reprinted as "The Select Committee's Investigative Record," *Village Voice,* February 16, 1976, p. 85.

4. Middle East Watch, *Genocide in Iraq,* p. 35.

5. Ibid., pp. 37–38. See also Ismet Sheriff Vanly, "Kurdistan in Iraq," in Gerard Chaliand, ed., *A People Without a Country: The Kurds and Kurdistan* (New York: Olive Branch Press, 1993), pp. 185–188; David Hirst, "Rebels Without Recourse," *The Guardian,* December 7, 1976, p. 4; Shiloah Center for Middle Eastern and African Studies, Tel Aviv University, *Middle East Contemporary Survey*, vol. 1, 1976–1977 (New York: Holmes & Meier, 1978), pp. 410–411; vol. 2, 1977–1978 (New York: Holmes & Meier, 1979), p. 521; and vol. 3, 1978–1979 (New York: Holmes & Meier, 1980), pp. 568–570.

6. Middle East Watch, *Human Rights in Iraq* (New Haven: Yale University Press, 1990), pp. 103–104.

7. The Export-Import Bank discontinued a short-term loan program when Iraqi borrowers failed to meet repayment schedules, but in 1987, under pressure from the Reagan administration, it resumed short-term lending guarantees, setting up a $200 million revolving fund for the purchase of U.S. products.

8. See, for example, a 1985 Amnesty International report documenting the execution of some 300 civilians in one town; Amnesty International's January 1988 press release, "Iraqi Security Forces' Use of Rat Poison, or Thallium, Against Political Opponents"; Elaine Sciolino, "The Big Brother: Iraq Under Saddam Hussein," *New York Times,* February 3, 1985, sec. 6, p.16.

9. Middle East Watch, *Genocide in Iraq,* p. 41, quoting *Al-Iraq,* September 13, 1983.

10. The Nixon administration ordered a moratorium on chemical weapons production in 1969 in the wake of public outcry at the use of napalm and Agent Orange in Vietnam. Yet after several years of lobbying by Reagan administration officials, the Pentagon secured funding for new chemical weapons production in 1985 in order to modernize and replace aging stockpiles. At that time it was generally estimated that the United States possessed approximately 30,000 tons of chemical weapons (with some estimates as high as 35,000–45,000 tons), the vast majority of which were declared obsolete by the Department of Defense. See Michael Weisskopf, "Reagan Seeks to End Chemical-Weapons Ban; Superior Soviet Nerve-Gas Stocks Cited," *Washington Post,* March 1, 1985, p. A6; Bill Keller, "U.S. Preparing New Production of Nerve Gases," *New York Times,* August 11, 1985, sec. 1, p. 1; and Steven R. Bowman, "IB94029: Chemical Weapons Convention: Issues for Congress," *Congressional Research Service Issue Brief,* September 20, 2000. The Geneva Protocol of 1925 bans "the use in war of asphyxiating, poisonous or other gases." It does not ban the production or stockpiling of chemical weapons. In April 1997 the U.S. Senate did ratify the Chemical Weapons Convention (CWC). Complementing the Geneva Protocol of 1925, the CWC does ban the production and stockpiling of chemical weapons and commits signatories to dismantling chemical weapons and their production facilities by 2007, unless the parties agree to extend the deadline. U.S. implementation has been delayed by debates over disposal methods. A recent independent analysis was pessimistic that the United States would complete its chemical weapons disposal by the 2007 deadline. As of May 2001, according to the U.S. Army's "Program Manager for Chemical Demilitarization" website, over 24,000 tons of chemical weapons remain to be disposed of out of the original national stockpile.

11. Anthony H. Cordesman, *Weapons of Mass Destruction in the Middle East* (London: Brassey's, 1991), p. 89; W. Seth Carus, "The Genie Unleashed: Iraq's Chemical and Biological Weapons Program," Washington Institute for Near East Policy paper no. 14, p. 3.

12. Attributed to Lt. Gen. Mahid Abd Al-Roshid, Commander of the Iraqi Army's Seventh Corps, circa 1985. CIA, "Iraq's Chemical Warfare Program: More Self-Reliant, More Deadly." A Research Paper, August 1990, p. 3.

13. Cordesman, *Weapons of Mass Destruction in the Middle East,* p. 92.

14. Statement read by the Department of State spokesman John Hughes, March 5, 1984, cited by the Department of State, *Bulletin,* April 1984, p. 64.

15. George P. Shultz, *Turmoil and Triumph: My Years as Secretary of State* (New York: Charles Scribner's Sons, 1993), p. 239.

16. The 1987 Senate Foreign Relations Committee report attached this resolution. The UN sent fact-finding teams to the Gulf in 1984, 1985, 1986, 1987, and 1988, and each time they concluded that Iraq had used chemical weapons. By September 1988 the teams had made seven separate findings of Iraqi use. Yet the United States extended diplomatic relations with Iraq only months after the first finding in 1984. In July 1988 Iraq finally admitted use but claimed that Iran began the practice and that it was only self-defense. "We believe that every nation has a right to protect itself from invasion. The means might be controversial—there are differences to this matter from different angles," Iraqi foreign minister Tariq Aziz said. "Sometimes such weapons were used in the bloody war, by both sides. It was a very complicated, bloody conflict." Serge Schmemann, "Iraq Acknowledges Its Use of Gas but Says Iran Introduced It in War," *New York Times,* July 2, 1988, p. A3. In August 1988 the UN Security Council passed a resolution sponsored by the

UK, West Germany, Italy, and Japan—and not by the United States—condemning chemical weapons use in the Iran-Iraq war and for the first time stating that "appropriate and effective measures" would be taken if the weapons were used again.

17. David Segal, "The Iran-Iraq War: A Military Analysis," *Foreign Affairs,* Summer 1988, p. 956. Even as late as 1988, this article presented the choice as one "between the possible adverse effects of offending world opinion and the certain adverse effects of being overrun by Iranian soldiers."

18. The UN fact-finding experts found chemical weapons use in 1984 and 1985 but did not single out Iraq by name. In 1986, 1987, and 1988, they explicitly blamed Iraq. The fact-finders began to lose faith. In their report of May 6, 1987, they wrote: "We all firmly believe that, at the specialist level, we have done all we can to identify the types of chemicals and chemical weapons being used in the Iran-Iraq conflict. If, in the future, a further mission is requested, then we will of course all be ready to respond. However, we now feel that technically there is little more that we can do that is likely to assist the United Nations in its efforts to prevent the use of chemical weapons in the present conflict. In our view, *only the concerted efforts at the political level can be effective.*" Report of the Secretary General to the UN Security Council, S/18852, May 8, 1987, pp. 13–19, 25–31; emphasis added.

19. It had just emerged that Reagan's national security adviser, Robert McFarlane, had traveled to Teheran on an Irish passport, carrying a Bible inscribed by President Reagan to the ayatollah. The McFarlane story would prove to be only a hint of the mischief under way in the White House, where with the aid of NSC staffer Oliver North, the Reagan administration had sold arms to the Iranians through an intermediary and then diverted the profits to Nicaragua's anti-Communist *contra* resistance.

20. Middle East Watch, *Human Rights in Iraq,* p. 133.

21. Ibid., pp. 16–17, citing the *Sun* (London), September 8, 1981.

22. Senate Committee on Foreign Relations, *War in the Persian Gulf: The U.S. Takes Sides,* 100th Cong., 1st sess., 1987, S. Prt. 100–160, p. 19.

23. Haywood Rankin, "Travels with Galbraith—Death in Basra, Destruction in Kurdistan," U.S. government memorandum, September 27, 1987, p. 16.

24. Ibid., p. 3.

25. Ibid., p. 6. The Iranian authorities extended this revelry even to foreigners, sending a telegram of congratulations to the family of a German journalist who was killed at the front.

26. Senate Committee on Foreign Relations, *War in the Persian Gulf,* p. 15.

27. U.S. Department of State, *Country Reports on Human Rights Practices for 1987,* report submitted to the House Committee on Foreign Affairs and the Senate Committee on Foreign Relations, 100th Cong., 2nd sess., 1987, p. 1172.

28. "Iraqis Repulse 'Karabala X,'" confidential cable from the U.S. embassy in Baghdad to Secretary of State George Shultz, April 27, 1987, p. 2; reproduced as 00423 in National Security Archive, ed., *Iraqgate: Saddam Hussein, U.S. Policy and the Prelude to the Persian Gulf War (1980–1994)* (Alexandria, Va.: Chadwyck-Healey, 1995).

29. "The Internal Situation in Iraq," cable from the Joint Chiefs of Staff to the Defense Intelligence Agency, August 4, 1987, p. 2; reproduced as 00453 in National Security Archive, ed., *Iraqgate.*

30. Loren Jenkins, "Iranians Detail Charges of Gas Warfare," *Washington Post,* May 11, 1987, p. A1.

31. Alan Cowell, "Iraqis Are Facing a Growing War from Within," *New York Times,* September 22, 1987, p. A6.

32. Meeting with Northern Bureau members and directors of the Ba'ath Party headquarters in the northern governorates; tape is dated May 26, 1988, but Middle East Watch believes the context indicates it was in fact recorded in 1987. Middle East Watch, *Genocide in Iraq,* p. 349.

33. Even after an Iraqi warplane fired a missile into the USS *Stark* in the Persian Gulf in 1987, killing thirty-seven American sailors, the Reagan administration accepted Baghdad's claim that it was a "mistake."

34. Middle East Watch, *Genocide in Iraq,* p. 105.

35. Interview with Sirwa, a Kurd living in England, in Sheri Laizer, *Martyrs, Traitors and Patriots: Kurdistan After the Gulf War* (London: Zed Books, 1996).

36. Kanan Makiya, *Cruelty and Silence: War, Tyranny, Uprising, and the Arab World* (New York: W. W. Norton, 1993), p. 137.

37. Ibid., pp. 137–138.

38. Patrick E. Tyler, "Kurdish Guerrillas Pose Growing Threat to Iraq; Rival Factions Unify, Gain Iran's Backing," *Washington Post,* February 19, 1988, p. A15.

39. "Iran Says It Has Iraqi Border City," *Washington Post,* March 18, 1998, p. A19.

40. Patrick E. Tyler, "Poison Gas Attack Kills Hundreds; Iran Accuses Iraq of Atrocity in Kurdish Region Near Border," *Washington Post,* March 24, 1988, p. A1.

41. Ibid.; emphasis added.

42. Theodore Stanger, "Massacre in Halabja," *Newsweek,* April 4, 1988, p. 38; emphasis added.

43. Russell Watson and John Barry, "Letting a Genie out of a Bottle," *Newsweek,* September 19, 1988, p. 30.

44. David B. Ottaway, "U.S. Decries Iraqi Use of Chemical Weapons: 'Grave Violation' of International Law Cited," *Washington Post,* March 24, 1988, p. A37.

45. Jim Hoagland, "Atrocity du Jour," *Washington Post,* March 26, 1988, p. A2.

46. The Halabja victims' blue lips were thought to be attributable to cyanide gas, which U.S. intelligence did not believe Iraq possessed. Public health experts say that other gases could have caused the discoloring as well. The vehemence of some Americans that the evidence was not definitive has persisted to this day. For example, Stephen C. Pelletiere, a former U.S. intelligence officer, and two colleagues carried out a study for the U.S. Army War College in which they argued "both sides" used chemical weapons in Halabja; Stephen C. Pelletiere, Douglas V. Johnson II, and Leif R. Rosenberger, *Iraqi Power and U.S. Security in the Middle East* (Carlisle Barracks, Pa.: Strategic Studies Institute, U.S. Army War College, 1990). In a more recent book Pelletiere wrote: "On May 23, in fighting over the town, gas was used by both sides. As a result scores of Iraqi Kurdish civilians were killed. It is now fairly certain that Iranian gas killed the Kurds"; Stephen C. Pelletiere, *The Iran-Iraq War: Chaos in a Vacuum* (New York: Praeger, 1992), pp. 136–137.

47. David Ottaway, "U.S. Decries Iraqi Use of Chemical Weapons; 'Grave Violations' of International Law Cited," *Washington Post,* March 24, 1988, p. A37.

48. David Ottaway, "In Mideast, Warfare with a New Nature," *Washington Post,* April 5, 1988, p. A1.

49. "The Gulf: The Battle, the War," *Washington Post,* April 20, 1988, p. A20.

50. "Baghdad's Repressive Measures Against the Kurds," cable from the Joint Chiefs of Staff to the Defense Intelligence Agency, April 19, 1988, p. 2; reproduced as 00555 in National Security Archive, ed., *Iraqgate.*

51. Middle East Watch, *Genocide and Iraq,* p. 232.

52. Ibid., p. 245.

53. Ibid., p. 17.
54. Makiya, *Cruelty and Silence,* p. 187.
55. Ibid., pp. 193–194.
56. Ibid., p. 195.
57. Middle East Watch, *Genocide and Iraq,* pp. 252–258; Makiya, *Cruelty and Silence,* pp. 176–199.
58. In a brief item, the *New York Times* picked up the claim; "Iraq Says It Routed Iranians and Kurds in Fight in Northeast," *New York Times,* April 3, 1988, section 1, p. 14.
59. Elaine Sciolino, "Kurdish Chief Gains Support in U.S. Visit," *New York Times,* June 22, 1988, p. A3. In fact, Talabani's alliance with Iran had predated Hussein's latest campaign of destruction.
60. State Department briefing, Federal News Service, June 15, 1988.
61. Senate Resolution 408, "Condemnation of the Use of Chemical Weapons by Iraq," *Congressional Record,* 100th Cong., 2nd sess., 1988, 134, pt. 95:S8533.
62. Elaine Sciolino, "How the U.S. Cast off Neutrality in Gulf War," *New York Times,* April 24, 1988, sec. 4, p. 2.
63. Robert Pear, "Khomeini Accepts 'Poison' of Ending War with Iraq; U.N. Sending Mission," *New York Times,* July 21, 1988, p. A1.
64. Estimates of the total number of lives lost during the Iran-Iraq war range from 450,000 to 730,000 on the Iranian side and from 150,000 to 340,000 on the Iraqi side. Anthony H. Cordesman and Abraham R. Wagner, *The Lessons of Modern War,* vol. 2: *The Iran-Iraq War* (Boulder, Colo.: Westview Press, 1990), p. 3.
65. Alan Cowell, "A Gulf Truce Leaves Rebels in a Quandary," *New York Times,* August 28, 1988, sec. 1, p. 15; Elaine Sciolino, "Iraqis Reported to Mount Drive Against Kurds," *New York Times,* September 1, 1988, p. A1.
66. Kenneth Roth, Executive Director, Human Rights Watch memo to officials in one European foreign ministry, Washington, D.C., on "Proposed ICJ Action Against Iraq on Basis of Genocide Convention," September 30, 1994, p. 6.
67. "More Chemical Attacks Reported," *New York Times,* August 28, 1988, sec. 1, p. 15.
68. See text of S.2763, *Congressional Record,* 100th Cong., 2nd sess., 1988, 134, pt. 123:S12137–S12138.
69. Muhyeddin Abdula, one of the Kurdish nationals who staged the strike, told the *New York Times,* "We could have done other things, maybe hijack an airplane, but we don't think that is nice"; Clyde F. Farnsworth and Irvin Molotsky, "Washington Talk; Briefing; To Hijack or Fast?" *New York Times,* September 19, 1988, p. A18.
70. Senate Committee on Foreign Relations, *Chemical Weapons Use in Kurdistan: Iraq's Final Offensive,* 100th Cong., 2nd sess., 1988, S. Prt. 100–148:40.
71. Morton Abramowitz, "Swan Song for Iraq's Kurds?" top secret cable from Assistant Secretary of State for Intelligence and Research Morton Abramowitz to Secretary of State George Shultz, September 2, 1988, pp. 2–3; reproduced as 00625 in National Security Archive, ed., *Iraqgate.*
72. "Iraqi Attacks on Kurds," secret cable from Secretary of State George Shultz to the U.S. embassy in Baghdad, September 3, 1988, p. 3; reproduced as 00626 in National Security Archive, ed., *Iraqgate.*
73. "Iraqi Attacks on Kurds," secret cable from the U.S. embassy in Baghdad to Secretary of State George Shultz, September 4, 1988, section 2, pp. 1–2, and section 1, pp. 2–3; reproduced as 00627 in National Security Archive, ed., *Iraqgate.* Internal cable traffic from early September onward takes the following facts as given:

"After ceasefire Iraq began major campaign to crush Kurdish rebellion by depopulating countryside, including [chemical weapons] use, mass deportations/executions." See "Your Treaty with Iraqi Minister of State for Foreign Affairs Saadoun Hammadi, Thursday, September 8, 1988 at 4:15 P.M.," secret briefing memorandum from Assistant Secretary of State for Near Eastern and South Asian Affairs Richard Murphy to Secretary of State George Shultz, September 7, 1988, p. 3; reproduced as 00628 in National Security Archive, ed., *Iraqgate*.

74. State Department briefing, Federal News Service, September 6, 1988. State Department spokespersons Oakley and Redman said they had no information on August 25, August 31, September 1, September 2, September 6, and September 7. Redman's briefing was picked up also in the *Washington Post:* David B. Ottaway, "U.S. Concern Is Expressed to Baghdad; Confirmation Lacking on Chemical Attacks," *Washington Post,* September 7, 1988, p. A24.

75. Jonathan C. Randal, "Refugees Travel Deeper into Turkey to Escape Iraqi Troops," *Washington Post,* September 5, 1988, p. A19; Alan Cowell, "Fleeing Assault by Iraqis, Kurds Tell of Poison Gas and Lives Lost," *New York Times,* September 5, 1988, p. A1.

76. Clyde Haberman, "Kurds' Symptoms: Gas or Poor Diet?" *New York Times,* September 12, 1988, p. A1.

77. Theodore Stanger, "'A Recipe for Disaster,'" *Newsweek,* September 26, 1988, p. 38.

78. Clyde Haberman, "What Drove the Kurds out of Iraq?" *New York Times,* September 13, 1988, p. A6.

79. State Department briefing, Federal News Service, September 8, 1988.

80. Ibid., September 9, 1988.

81. Julie Johnson, "U.S. Asserts Iraq Used Poison Gas Against the Kurds," *New York Times,* September 9, 1988, p. A1.

82. "Secretary's Meeting with Iraqi Minister of State for Foreign Affairs Saadoun Hammadi," secret cable from Secretary of State George Shultz to the U.S. embassy in Baghdad, September 9, 1988, p. 6; reproduced as 00633 in National Security Archive, ed., *Iraqgate*.

83. Patrick E. Tyler, "Iraqi Official Says Kurds Fleeing Army Operation; Envoy Denies Use of Chemical Weapons," *Washington Post,* September 4, 1988, p. A33.

84. Morton Abramowitz, "Iraq's Use of Chemical Weapons on the Kurds," secret information memorandum from Assistant Secretary of State for Intelligence and Research Morton Abramowitz to Undersecretary of State for Political Affairs Michael Armacost, September 17, 1988, p. 2; reproduced as 00648 in National Security Archive, ed., *Iraqgate*.

85. Patrick E. Tyler, "Iraq Denies Using Chemical Weapons on Kurds," *Washington Post,* September 16, 1988, p. A19.

86. Jim Hoagland, "Iraq Is One Place Where Sanctions Might Work," *Washington Post,* September 15, 1988, p. A25.

87. Peter Galbraith, "The Tragedy of Iraqi Kurdistan: The Destruction of a People and Culture," remarks to the international conference, "The Kurds: Human Rights and Cultural Identity," Paris, October 14, 1989.

88. Middle East Watch, *Human Rights in Iraq,* p. 123, citing a letter from Nizar Hamdoon to Edward J. Van Kloberg III, August 22, 1985, as well as a disclosure statement, December 28, 1987, filed at the Department of Justice.

89. Julie Johnson, "U.S. Adamant in Charge Against Iraq," *New York Times,* September 10, 1988, p. A4.

90. Patrick E. Tyler, "Kurds Disappoint Iraqi PR Effort," *Washington Post,* September 18, 1988, p. A30.

91. Middle East Watch, *Human Rights in Iraq,* p. 109.

92. "Iraqi CW Use: Ambassador's Meeting with Hamdun," secret cable from the U.S. embassy in Baghdad to Secretary of State George Shultz, September 10, 1988, sec. 1, p. 3, and sec. 2, pp. 2, 3; reproduced as 00634 in National Security Archive, ed., *Iraqgate.*

93. Senate Committee on Foreign Relations, *Chemical Weapons Use in Kurdistan: Iraq's Final Offensive,* pp. 14–26.

94. Abramowitz, "Iraq's Use of Chemical Weapons on the Kurds."

95. *Congressional Record,* 100th Cong., 2nd sess., 1988, 134, pt. 122:S12035.

96. Ibid., pt. 123:S12136.

97. Senator Claiborne Pell, press conference, September 21, 1988, announcing the release of Galbraith's report for the Senate Foreign Relations Committee.

98. *Legislation to Impose Sanctions Against Iraqi Chemical Use, Markup Before the Committee on Foreign Affairs,* House of Representatives, 100th Cong., 2nd sess., 1988, 134, p. 15.

99. *Congressional Record,* 100th Cong., 2nd sess., 1988, 134, pt. 123:S12136.

100. William Safire, "Stop the Iraqi Murder of the Kurds," *New York Times,* September 5, 1988, p. A21.

101. Ibid.

102. "Murder Within Sovereign Borders," *New York Times,* September 5, 1988, p. A20.

103. Jim Hoagland, "Make No Mistake—This Is Genocide," *Washington Post,* September 8, 1988, p. A21.

104. Jim Hoagland, "A 'Furlough' for Iraq," *Washington Post,* October 12, 1988, p. A19; emphasis added.

105. "Too Tough on Iraq?" *Washington Post,* September 20, 1988, p. A20.

106. Pamela Fessler, "Congress and Iraq: A Chronology of a Decade's Debate over Relations," *Congressional Quarterly,* April 27, 1991, p. 1071.

107. "Overview of US-Iraq Relations and Political Pressure Points," secret internal paper drafted by the Bureau of Near Eastern Affairs/North Gulf Affairs, September 9, 1988, p. 2; reproduced as 00632 in National Security Archive, ed., *Iraqgate.*

108. Responding to assurances from the administration that Iraq was sincere in its pledge to forswear future use, Senator Pell asked, "Can we really be expected to overlook the gassing of thousands of people on the basis of an assurance that is itself predicated on a lie?" *Congressional Record,* 100th Cong., 2nd sess., 1988, 134, pt. 144:S15574.

109. State Department briefing, Federal News Service, September 20, 1988.

110. *Legislation to Impose Sanctions Against Iraqi Chemical Use,* p. 19.

111. Ibid., p. 20.

112. James A. Baker III with Thomas M. DeFrank, *The Politics of Diplomacy: Revolution, War and Peace, 1989–1992* (New York: G. P. Putnam's Sons, 1995), p. 273.

113. See, for example, "Kurdistan Resistance Forces at Peril," cable from the Defense Intelligence Agency, October 24, 1988; reproduced as 00683 in National Security Archive, ed., *Iraqgate.*

114. "Overview of U.S.-Iraq Relations and Political Pressure Points," p. 1.

115. "U.S. Policy Towards Iraq and CW Use," secret action memorandum from Assistant Secretary of State for Near Eastern and South Asian Affairs Richard

Murphy to Undersecretary of State for Political Affairs Michael Armacost, September 19, 1988, pp. 1–2, 5; reproduced as 00650 in National Security Archive, ed., *Iraqgate*.

116. "Overview of US-Iraq Relations and Political Pressure Points," p. 3.

117. "After U.S. Actions, Saddam Changes His Tone," confidential cable from the U.S. embassy in Baghdad to Secretary of State George Shultz, September 12, 1988, p. 2; reproduced as 00635 in National Security Archive, ed., *Iraqgate*.

118. Milton Viorst, "Poison Gas and 'Genocide': The Shaky Case Against Iraq," *Washington Post,* October 5, 1988, p. A25.

119. "U.S. Policy Towards Iraq and CW Use," pp. 1–2, 5.

120. George Shultz, remarks to board of directors of the General Federation of Women's Clubs, State Department, September 9, 1988.

121. Marlin Fitzwater, press conference, Waldorf-Astoria Hotel, New York, September 26, 1988. In the event, the conference was held in Paris in January 1989, and far from censuring Iraq, the closing declaration simply reaffirmed "the importance and continuing validity" of the 1925 protocol. The Kurds themselves were barred from attending the conference, which was open only to states. And the United States ignored Human Rights Watch's request that it raise the matter of amending the 1925 protocol so that it explicitly barred states from using chemical weapons against their own citizens. Middle East Watch, *Human Rights in Iraq,* pp. 112–113.

122. Patrick E. Tyler, "The Kurds: It's Not Genocide," *Washington Post,* September 25, 1988, p. A20.

123. Simande Siaband [Mehrdad Izady], "Mountains, My Home: An Analysis of the Kurdish Psychological Landscape," *Kurdish Times* 2 (Summer 1988): 7, 9, cited in Michael M. Gunter, *The Kurds of Iraq: Tragedy and Hope* (New York: St. Martin's, 1992), p. 35.

124. "Export-Import Financing for Iraq," confidential action memorandum from Assistant Secretary of State for Near Eastern and South Asian Affairs Murphy, Principal Deputy Assistant Secretary of State for Economic and Business Affairs Larson, and Assistant Secretary of State for Humanitarian Affairs Schifter to Secretary of State Shultz, December 12, 1988, p. 5; reproduced as 00739 in National Security Archive, ed., *Iraqgate*.

125. *Developments in the Middle East, October 1988,* Hearing Before the Subcommittee on Europe and the Middle East of the Committee on Foreign Affairs, House of Representatives, 100th Cong., 2nd sess., October 13, 1988, pp. 31 and 43. Opponents of the bill on Capitol Hill were also careful not to appear to condone Iraqi behavior. The statement of Agricultural Committee chairman E. "Kika" de la Garza (D.–Tex.) is telling. He noted that Iraq was a "large and growing market for U.S. agricultural exports. . . . In light of the difficulties that our nation's farmers have faced over the past few years, I am deeply concerned over any possible loss of a major market for U.S. agricultural commodities. At the same time, I in no way wish to condone the use of chemical weapons by Iraq or any other country." *Congressional Record,* 100th Cong., 2nd sess., 1988, 134, pt. 133:H8343.

126. And the influence of lobbies has only increased. Long past are the days when Congressman John Steven McGroarty of California would write a constituent (in 1934): "One of the countless drawbacks of being in Congress is that I am compelled to receive impertinent letters from a jackass like you in which you say I promised to have the Sierra Madre mountains reforested and I have been in Congress two months and haven't done it. Will you please take two running jumps and

go to hell." John F. Kennedy, *Profiles in Courage* (New York: Harper, 1956), p. 10.
127. Walter Lippmann, *The Public Philosophy* (Boston: Little, Brown, 1955), p. 27.
128. Kennedy, *Profiles in Courage,* p. 122.
129. See Galbraith, *Iraq Sanctions Legislation,* p. 14. He argued that because the oil imported from Iraq was subject to an import levy, the sanctions would reduce treasury revenues, thus rendering the sanctions bill a revenue bill. In fact, since oil imports from Iraq would have been replaced by those from other countries, net import fees would not have been affected. If Rostenkowski's claim had been carried to its logical conclusion, virtually no legislation could have originated in the Senate. Laws requiring warning labels on alcohol, for instance, would have reduced pregnant women's liquor intake and thus lowered distilled spirits excise tax revenues.
130. Physicians for Human Rights Press Release, October 22, 1998, "Medical Team Finds Evidence of Iraqi Use of Chemical Weapons on Kurds." On January 10, 1989, Dr. Howard Hu, one of the PHR team members, testified before Congress about the trip. And in February 1989, PHR published "Winds of Death: Iraq's Use of Poison Gas Against Its Kurdish Population," a lengthy, detailed report on its medical mission.
131. *Congressional Record,* 100th Cong., 2nd sess., 1988, 134, pt. 151:S17203.
132. See, for example, Gordon M. Burck and Charles C. Flowerree, *International Handbook on Chemical Weapons Proliferation* (New York: Greenwood Press, 1991), pp. 101–114.
133. Elaine Sciolino, "U.S. Retaliates for Iraqi Expulsion of Diplomat by Replying in Kind," *New York Times,* November 18, 1988, p. A15.
134. Middle East Watch, *Human Rights in Iraq,* p. 110.
135. Middle East Watch, *Genocide in Iraq,* p. 299.
136. Ibid., pp. 306–307.
137. Letter no. 14951, dated November 23, 1988, from the Security Secretariat for the Autonomous Region to the Security Bureau for Sulaymaniyah, citing instructions of the Northern Bureau Command. Cited in Middle East Watch, *Genocide in Iraq,* pp. 300–301.
138. Statements from a November 8, 1988, meeting relayed to *Amn* (the internal Iraq security force) chiefs in the autonomous regions in a set of instructions from the region's security director, dated November 21, 1988, and marked "secret and confidential." Cited in Middle East Watch, *Genocide in Iraq,* p. 321.
139. Middle East Watch, *Genocide in Iraq,* pp. 323–324.
140. Cited in ibid., pp. 352–353.
141. "Guidelines for U.S.–Iraq Policy," secret State Department internal paper, January 20, 1989, p. 2; reproduced as 00761 in National Security Archive, ed., *Iraqgate.*
142. Baker and DeFrank, *The Politics of Diplomacy,* p. 263.
143. Ibid.
144. "Guidelines for U.S.–Iraq Policy," p. 6.
145. Middle East Watch, *Human Rights in Iraq,* p. 113. The resolution was defeated 13-17. See United Nations Economic and Social Council, Commission on Human Rights, Official Records, supplement no. 2, *Report on the 45th Session (30 January–10 March 1989),* E/1989/20, E/CN.4/1989/86, p. 178.
146. Pamela Fessler, "Congress' Record on Saddam: Decade of Talk, Not Action," *Congressional Quarterly,* April 27, 1991, p. 1074.
147. See Alan Cowell, "Iraq Chief, Boasting of Poison Gas, Warns of Disaster If Israelis Strike," *New York Times,* April 3, 1990, p. A1; Patrick E. Tyler, "Iraqi Warns of

Using Poison Gas; Leader Says Attacker Faces Devastation; U.S. Decries Remarks," *Washington Post,* April 3, 1990, p. A1.

148. The five-member delegation, which met with Hussein on April 12, 1990, included Dole, Simpson, Ohio Democrat Howard Metzenbaum, Idaho Republican James McClure, and Alaska Republican Frank Murkowski. Although they handed Hussein a letter at the start of the meeting that stated their "deep concerns" about his military buildup and threats to use chemical weapons against Israel, the meeting was more fawning than demanding. After the invasion of Kuwait, the Iraqis released a transcript of the meeting that the senators did not dispute. According to the transcript, Metzenbaum said, "I am now aware that you are a strong and intelligent man and that you want peace." Simpson stated, "I believe that your problems lie with the Western media and not with the U.S. government. . . . The press is spoiled and conceited. All these journalists consider themselves brilliant political scientists. They do not want to see anything succeeding or achieving its objectives. My advice is that you allow those bastards to come here and see things for themselves." Douglas Waller, "Glass House," *The New Republic,* November 5, 1990, p. 14. See also Pamela Fessler, "Haunted by a Meeting with Saddam," *Congressional Quarterly,* April 27, 1991, p. 1077.

149. Pamela Fessler, "Congress' Record on Saddam: Decade of Talk, Not Action," *Congressional Quarterly,* April 27, 1991, p. 1075.

150. *Congressional Record,* 101st Cong., 2nd sess., 1990, 136, pt. 99:S10904.

151. Ibid., pt. 99:S10908.

152. Amnesty International, *Iraq: Children, Innocent Victims of Political Repression* (New York: Amnesty International, 1989); *Congressional Record,* 101st Cong., 2nd sess., 1990, 136, pt. 98:S10832.

153. In the course of rejecting Saddam Hussein's conditional offer of withdrawal from Kuwait, President Bush repeated this statement at least twice during the course of the day, once before the American Academy for Advancement of Science in Washington, D.C., and again before employees at the Raytheon missile systems plant in Andover, Massachusetts. White House briefing, Federal News Service, February 15, 1991.

154. During the March fighting the United States intervened only once, when Iraq used fixed-wing jets to attack the Kurds, which violated the terms of the March 5 cease-fire accord. American fighter planes shot down two Iraqi bombers that had attacked Kirkuk. The situation was little better in the south, where Iraqi soldiers who managed to escape from their units said their commanders had promised 250 Iraqi dinars in return for each woman or child killed and up to 5,000 dinars for any adult man eliminated. Often loudspeakers would announce safe passage out of the towns on designated routes and then helicopter gunships would strafe those routes. Mosques, cemeteries, libraries, and all the emblems of Shiite life were targeted. Bob Drogin, "Iraq: Saddam Hussein Offers Soldiers Bounty for Killing Babies—Shiites Face Retribution," *Guardian,* March 29, 1991, p. 22.

155. *Congressional Record,* 102nd Cong., 1st sess., 1991, 137, pt. 56:S4647.

156. An additional 800,000 had fled to Iran, and some 700,000 were en route there.

157. Thomas L. Friedman, "Baker Sees and Hears Kurds' Pain in a Brief Visit at Turkish Border," *New York Times,* April 9, 1991, p. A1.

158. William Safire, "Follow the Kurds," *New York Times,* March 28, 1991, p. A25.

159. William Safire, "Bush's Moral Crisis," *New York Times,* April 1, 1991, p. A17.

160. "A Quagmire After All," *Newsweek,* April 29, 1991, p. 23.

161. Ibid.

162. The operation represented a stepping up of previous allied relief efforts. U.S. Air Force transport planes began dropping food and other relief to the Kurdish refugees on April 7, 1991. The last of the U.S. troops in northern Iraq left in July. Security was henceforth provided by a mobile strike force stationed in Turkey and allied planes overhead.

163. Handwritten internal memo from the "Person in Charge of Political Affairs," *Amn* (Erbil), October 18, 1990; cited in Middle East Watch, *Genocide in Iraq,* p. 343.

164. See Christine Gosden, "Halabja 11 Years Later; More Deaths, Little Progress," *Washington Post,* March 10, 1999, p. A23; Christine Gosden and Mike Amitay, "Lessons from Halabja," *Washington Post,* August 20, 1999, p. A35; Christine Gosden, "Why I Went, What I Saw," *Washington Post,* March 11, 1998, p. A19.

165. Gosden, "Why I Went, What I Saw."

166. Middle East Watch, *Genocide in Iraq,* p. 30.

167. Judith Miller, "Iraq Accused," *New York Times Magazine,* January 3, 1993, p. 13.

168. Ibid., p. 32.

169. Middle East Watch, *Genocide in Iraq,* p. 345.

170. Columbia University law professor Lori Damrosch's June 4, 1993, memo to Middle East Watch Director Andrew Whitley, "Kurdish Genocide Case—Legal Memorandum for Governments."

Chapter 9, Bosnia

1. Carole Rogel, *The Breakup of Yugoslavia and the War in Bosnia* (Westport, Conn.: Greenwood Press, 1998), p. 31.

2. See Ed Vulliamy, *Seasons in Hell: Understanding Bosnia's War* (New York: St. Martin's Press, 1994); Roy Gutman, *Witness to Genocide: The 1993 Pulitzer Prize–Winning Dispatches on the "Ethnic Cleansing" of Bosnia* (New York: Macmillan, 1993); and Rezak Hukanovic, *Tenth Circle of Hell: A Memoir of Life in the Death Camps of Bosnia* (New York: Basic Books, 1996). The best account of the political machinations at work behind the terror is Laura Silber and Allan Little's *Yugoslavia: Death of a Nation* (New York: Penguin, 1997).

3. Claude Lanzmann, *Shoah: An Oral History of the Holocaust* (New York: Pantheon, 1985), p. 139.

4. Anna Husarska, "City of Fear," *New Republic,* September 21, 1992, p. 18. In 1992 Serbs expelled and murdered Muslim and Croat citizens alike. Because the Croat and Serb authorities eventually teamed up to destroy Bosnia, however, my focus in this chapter is on the Serb destruction of Bosnia's Muslims. There were of course tens of thousands of Croats and Serbs who remained loyal to the Muslim-led Bosnian government throughout the war. Many exposed themselves to far greater danger by remaining in Bosnian territory and refusing to take shelter with ethnic nationalists in Serb- or Croat-held land.

5. Richard Ben Cramer, *Bob Dole* (New York: Vintage, 1995), pp. 60–62.

6. Bob Dole, "Odd Men Out," *Congressional Record,* 101st Cong., 2nd sess., 1990, 136, pt. 87: S9475.

7. Bob Dole, "Yugoslavia," *Congressional Record,* 101st Cong., 2nd sess., 1990, 136, pt. 117: S13488.

8. Bob Dole, "Get Smart About Foreign Aid," *Washington Post,* March 18, 1991, p. A11.

9. Dole, "Yugoslavia."

10. Helsinki Watch, *War Crimes in Bosnia-Hercegovina,* vol. 1 (New York: Human Rights Watch, 1992), p. 2.

11. Ibid., p. 17.

12. Ibid., p. 2.

13. Boris Johnson and Michael Montgomery, "Yugoslav Ceasefire; Agreed EC Ultimatium: Fighting Must Stop 'if you want to enter Europe of the 20th Century,'" *Daily Telegraph,* June 29, 1991, p. 1.

14. James A. Baker III with Thomas M. DeFrank, *The Politics of Diplomacy: Revolution, War and Peace, 1989–1992* (New York: G. P. Putnam's Sons, 1995), p. 637.

15. Warren Zimmermann, *Origins of a Catastrophe: Yugoslavia and Its Destroyers— the Last Ambassador Tells What Happened and Why* (New York: Times Books, 1996), p. 24.

16. Graham Stewart, *Burying Caesar: Churchill, Chamberlain, and the Battle for the Tory Party* (London: Weidenfeld and Nicolson, 1999), p. 300.

17. Zimmerman, *Origins of a Catastrophe,* p. 22.

18. "After the War: The White House; Excerpts from Bush's News Conference on Postwar Plans," *New York Times,* March 2, 1991, p. A5.

19. "Excerpts from Address of Weinberger," *New York Times,* November 29, 1984, p. A5. The doctrine was of course erratically applied, as, for instance, when the Reagan administration intervened in Latin America, sponsoring and training anti-Communist forces.

20. Colin Powell, *My American Journey* (New York: Random House, 1995), pp. 148–49, 576–77.

21. "Deterring Serbian Aggression in Bosnia-Herzegovina," confidential action memorandum from Thomas M. T. Niles and Eugene McAllister to Deputy Secretary of State Lawrence Eagleburger, April 20, 1992.

22. "Ethnic Cleansing," *Newsweek,* August 17, 1992, p. 19.

23. "Bosnia-Herzegovina: Stabilization," confidential information memorandum from Thomas M. T. Niles to Deputy Secretary of State Lawrence Eagleburger, April 14, 1992.

24. Ibid.

25. Laura Blumenfeld, "A Sense of Resignation: The Bosnia Dissenters; Three Young Men Cut Short Their Careers on Principle," *Washington Post,* August 28, 1993, p. F1.

26. Stephen A. Holmes, "State Dept. Balkan Aides Explain Why They Quit," *New York Times,* August 26, 1993, p. A12.

27. Russell Johnston, *The Yugoslav Conflict: Chronology of Events from 30th May 1991–8th November 1993* (Paris: Defence Committee of the Western European Union, 1993).

28. Confidential cable from Ambassador Warren Zimmerman to Secretary of State James Baker, May 12, 1992. Milosevic's father committed suicide in 1962; his mother did so in 1973.

29. In 1896 the Spanish general Valeriano Weyler instituted martial law over portions of Cuba and relocated all noncombatants in certain areas to concentration camps. He destroyed the emptied villages. Anyone caught outside the camps was considered a rebel. At the time it was estimated that as many as 400,000 to 500,000 were killed in the camps, but more recent calculations suggest that a quarter of the original estimate may be more accurate. Generals Frederick Roberts and Horatio Kitchener organized concentration camps in South Africa in connection with similar scorched-earth tactics against the Boers. In an effort to

neutralize the Boers' guerrilla tactics and to create a better-defined military front, the British began destroying Boer farms and relocating the inhabitants into camps. Disease ran rampant in these camps. Official estimates of the number of people who died in the camps have ranged between 18,000 and 28,000. See S. B. Spies, *Methods of Barbarism: Roberts and Kitchener and Civilians in Boer Republics* (Cape Town: Human & Rousseau, 1977), p. 148; Thomas Packenham, *The Boer War* (New York: Random House, 1993), p. 287.

30. Mark Danner, "America and the Bosnia Genocide," *New York Review of Books,* December 4, 1997, p. 64.

31. Vulliamy, *Seasons in Hell,* p. 201.

32. Roy Gutman, "Prisoners of Serbia's War," *Newsday,* July 19, 1992, p. 7.

33. Roy Gutman, "Like Auschwitz," *Newsday,* July 21, 1992.

34. Roy Gutman, "If Only They Could Flee," *Newsday,* July 26, 1992; Roy Gutman, "There Is No Food, There Is No Air," *Newsday,* July 19, 1992, p. 39.

35. State Department briefing, Federal News Service, August 3, 1992; emphasis added.

36. *Developments in Yugoslavia and Europe—August 1992,* Hearing before the Subcommittee on Europe and the Middle East of the Committee on Foreign Affairs, House of Representatives, 102nd Cong., 2nd sess., August 4, 1992, p. 5.

37. Don Oberdorfer, "State Dept. Backtracks on Atrocity Reports; Calls for Action on Serb Camps Rise," *Washington Post,* August 5, 1992, p. A1.

38. Warren Strobel, *Late-Breaking Foreign Policy* (Washington, D.C.: U.S. Institute for Peace, 1997), p. 150.

39. *Developments in Yugoslavia and Europe—August 1992,* p. 14.

40. R. W. Apple Jr., "State Dept. Asks War Crimes Inquiry into Bosnia Camps," *New York Times,* August 6, 1992, p. A1; State Department briefing, Federal News Service, August 5, 1992.

41. Judy Keen, "Bush Blames 'Sleaze' for Lag in Polls," *USA Today,* August 5, 1992, p. A1.

42. Timothy Clifford, "Clinton, Gore Slam Foreign Failures," *Newsday,* August 6, 1992, p. 17.

43. Clifford Krauss, "U.S. Backs Away from Charge of Atrocities in Bosnia Camps," *New York Times,* August 5, 1992, p. A12.

44. "Clinton-Gore on the Road Again," *Inside Politics,* CNN, August 5, 1992.

45. Krauss, "U.S. Backs Away from Charge of Atrocities."

46. Nigel Baker, "Sending in the Troops," *RTNDA Communicator,* February 1996, p. 25, quoted in Susan Moeller, *Compassion Fatigue: How the Media Sell Disease, Famine, War, and Death* (New York: Routledge, 1999), p. 267.

47. Richard Sobel, *The Impact of Public Opinion on U.S. Foreign Policy Since Vietnam: Constraining the Colossus* (Oxford: Oxford University Press, 2001), p. 183.

48. "Rescue Bosnia," *The New Republic,* August 17 and 24, 1992, p. 7.

49. Jon Western, "Warring Ideas: Explaining U.S. Military Intervention in Regional Conflicts," Ph.D. diss., Columbia University, 2000, p. 300; *Network Evening News Abstracts,* Television News Archives, Vanderbilt University.

50. Joel Brand, Karen Breslav, and Rod Nordland, "Life and Death in the Camps," *Newsweek,* August 17, 1992, p. 22.

51. Cited in Moeller, *Compassion Fatigue,* p. 269.

52. "Europe's Trail of Tears," *U.S. News and World Report,* July 27, 1992, p. 41.

53. "Atrocity in Bosnia," *Washington Post,* August 3, 1992, p. A18.

54. "Milosevic Isn't Hitler, But . . . ," *New York Times,* August 4, 1992, p. A18; "What Goes on in Bosnia's Camps?" *Chicago Tribune,* August 6, 1992, sec. 1, p. 24.

55. "Stop the Death Camps: An Open Letter to World Leaders," *New York Times*, August 5, 1992, p. A14.

56. "Atrocity and Outrage," *Time*, August 17, 1992.

57. Anthony Lewis, "Yesterday's Man," *New York Times*, August 3, 1992, p. A19.

58. Ruth Marcus and Barton Gelman, "Bush Pushes for Access to Serb Camps But Is Wary of Getting Bogged Down," *Washington Post*, August 8, 1992, p. A15. White House briefing, Federal News Service, August 7, 1992.

59. Richard Holbrooke, *To End a War* (New York: Random House, 1998), p. 36.

60. Ibid., p. 39.

61. Ibid., p. 42.

62. Only in October 1992 was the U.S. intelligence community tasked to compile evidence of crimes against humanity. They had previously collected imagery but only to guard against the possibility that U.S. military forces might be deployed to the region. They had inquired about the number of Serb troops deployed, the details of their force disposition, and their standard order of battle doctrine. If an image did not help answer these kinds of questions, it was catalogued and filed away.

63. Sobel, *Impact of Public Opinion*, p. 185.

64. House Foreign Affairs Committee, Hearing of the Europe and Middle East Subcommittee, *Developments in Yugoslavia*, August 4, 1992.

65. Transcript of news conference by President George Bush, "Situation in Bosnia-Hercegovina, from Kennebunkport, Maine," Federal News Service, August 8, 1992.

66. Western, "Warring Ideas," p. 304.

67. Interview, *Newsmaker Saturday*, CNN, August 1, 1992.

68. White House briefing, Federal News Service, August 6, 1992.

69. U.S. Department of State *Dispatch Supplement*, September 1992, p. 14.

70. Mark Danner, "Clinton, the UN, and the Bosnian Disaster," *New York Review of Books*, December 18, 1997, p. 66, quoting "Method to the Madness," decision brief, Center for Security Policy, Washington, D.C., October 2, 1992, p. 3.

71. "News Conference with President Bush," Federal News Service, August 7, 1992.

72. Barton Gellman, "Defense Planners Making Case Against Intervention in Yugoslavia," *Washington Post*, June 13, 1992, p. A16; Eric Schmitt, "Conflict in the Balkans: Bush Calls Allies on a Joint Effort to Help Sarajevo," *New York Times*, June 29, 1992, p. A6.

73. Hearing of the Senate Armed Services Committee, "Situation in Bosnia and Appropriate US and Western Responses," Federal News Service, August 11, 1992.

74. Western, "Warring Ideas," p. 287.

75. After the U.S. intervention in Somalia went sour in 1993 and eighteen U.S. soldiers were killed in a Mogadishu firefight, the bogey became known as "Vietmalia."

76. Laura Silber and Bruce Clark, "US Threatens Serbs with Tougher Bombing Action: Attacks on Bihac Continue Despite NATO Raid on Airfield," *Financial Times* (London), November 23, 1994, p. 28.

77. Roger Cohen, "NATO and the U.N. Quarrel in Bosnia as Serbs Press On," *New York Times*, November 27, 1994, sec. 1, p. 1.

78. John Burns, "Nationalist Says Serbs' Rejection of Pact Means the End of Bosnia," *New York Times*, May 17, 1993, p. A1.

79. Michael Gordon, "Powell Delivers a Resounding No on Using Limited Force in Bosnia," *New York Times*, September 28, 1992, p. A1. The *New York Times* editorial board responded that "the war in Bosnia is not a fair fight and it is not war. It

is slaughter.... President Bush should tell General Powell what President Lincoln once told General McClellan: 'If you don't want to use the army, I should like to borrow it for a while.'" *New York Times,* "At Least Slow the Slaughter," October 4, 1992, p. A16.

80. Colin L. Powell, "Why Generals Get Nervous," *New York Times,* October 8, 1992, p. A35.

81. Zimmermann, *Origins of a Catastrophe,* p. 170.

82. The three networks mentioned Somalia in only fifteen news stories prior to Bush's decision to involve the United States in the airlift. See Strobel, *Late-Breaking Foreign Policy,* p. 132.

83. Western, "Warring Ideas," p. 309, citing data from *Network Evening News Abstract,* Television News Archives, Vanderbilt University.

84. Don Oberdorfer, "U.S. Aide Resigns over Balkan Policy; Administration's Handling of Civil War Decried as 'Ineffective,'" *Washington Post,* August 26, 1992, p. A1.

85. Mary Battiata, "War of the Worlds," *Washington Post Magazine,* June 30, 1996, p. 8.

86. White House briefing, Federal News Service, August 6, 1992.

87. Steven Kull and I. M. Destler, *Misreading the Public: The Myth of a New Isolationism* (Washington, D.C.: Brookings Institution, 1999), p. 95.

88. UN Security Council Resolution 780, October 6, 1992.

89. Lawrence Eagleburger, statement at the International Conference on the former Yugoslavia, Geneva, Switzerland, December 16, 1992. See also Elaine Sciolino, "US Names Figures It Wants Charged with War Crimes," *New York Times,* December 17, 1992, p. A1.

90. It also included Borislav Herak, a Bosnian Serb who confessed to killing more than 230 civilians; Drago Prcac, who ran Omarska; and Adem Delic, commander of the Croatian-run Celibici camp.

91. Sciolino, "US Names Figures."

92. Richard Johnson, "The Pinstripe Approach to Genocide," in Stjepan G. Mestrovic, ed., *The Conceit of Innocence: Losing the Conscience of the West in the War Against Bosnia* (College Station, Tx.: Texas A&M University Press, 1997), pp. 66, 67.

93. UN General Assembly Resolution A/47/121 of December 18, 1992; passed 102 for (including the United States), none against, and 57 abstentions. The portion that accuses Serbian and Montenegrin forces of genocide is buried in a paragraph in the preamble.

94. Patricia Diaz Dennis, assistant secretary of state for human rights and humanitarian affairs, special State Department briefing on report to Congress on human rights practices for 1992, Federal News Service, January 19, 1993.

95. Sobel, *Impact of Public Opinion,* p. 185.

96. Anthony Lake and Roger Morris, "The Human Reality of Realpolitik," *Foreign Policy* 4 (Fall 1971): 158.

97. Holbrooke, *To End a War,* p. 50.

98. Marshall Harris, "Clinton's Debacle in Bosnia," in Mestrovic, ed., *The Conceit of Innocence,* p. 241.

99. Ibid.

100. U.S. Department of State press release, Secretary of State Warren Christopher's press conference and statement, "New Steps Toward Conflict Resolution in the Former Yugoslavia," February 10, 1993, U.S. Department of State Bureau of Public Affairs, Washington, D.C.

101. Quoted in John Darnton, "Does the World Still Recognize a Holocaust?" *New York Times,* April 25, 1993, sec. 4, p. 1. Wiesel told me that he had little choice but to ad-lib because the speech he had prepared for the opening ceremony had been soaked by a heavy downpour and rendered illegible.

102. White House briefing, Federal News Service, April 23, 1993.

103. Hearing of the Foreign Operations Subcommittee of the Senate Appropriations Committee, Federal News Service, March 30, 1993.

104. They also wondered whether they could have done more to protect loved ones and felt guilt over being spared. Of the 650 men, women, and children who were delivered to Auschwitz from Italy with Primo Levi, Levi was one of only three to survive. In 1986, before his apparent suicide, he wrote that his shame of survival "nestled deeply like a woodworm; although unseen from the outside it gnaws and rasps." In his last book Levi wrote that, "You cannot exclude it. It is no more than a supposition, indeed the shadow of a suspicion: that each man is his brother's Cain, that each one of us . . . has usurged his neighbor's place and lived in his stead." *The Drowned and the Saved* (New York: Summit Books, 1986), pp. 81–82.

105. Hearing of the International Operations Subcommittee of the House Foreign Affairs Committee, Federal News Service, April 1, 1993.

106. The cosigners were Marshall Harris, Janet Bogue, Eric Rubin, Gordana Earp, Jon Benton, Jim Moriarty, Brady Kiesling, Ellen Conway, Scott Thompson, Drew Mann, John Menzies, and Mirta Alvarez. See Michael R. Gordon, "12 in State Department Ask Military Move Against the Serbs," *New York Times,* April 23, 1993, p. A1. Jim Hooper, John Fox, and Richard Johnson did not sign the letter because they were not technically working on the region. Johnson was in fact on a one-year assignment in Congressman McCloskey's office on Capitol Hill.

107. Margaret Thatcher in a BBC Television interview, April 13, 1993, as cited in Marion Finlay, "Thatcher Sparks Row over Bosnia," *Toronto Star,* April 14, 1993. William Safire, "Clinton Abdicates as Leader," *New York Times,* July 27, 1995, p. A23.

108. Joseph R. Biden Jr., *To Stand Against Agression: Milosevic, The Bosnian Republic, and the Conscience of the West,* report prepared for the Senate Committee on Foreign Relations, 103rd. Cong., 1st sess., 1993, Committee Print 103–33, p. 3.

109. Robert Kaplan, *Balkan Ghosts: A Journey Through History* (New York: St. Martin's Press, 1993).

110. Bob Dole, "Bosnia: It's Not Too Late; a Plan for Military and Diplomatic Action," *Washington Post,* August 1, 1993, p. C7.

111. Hearing of the Senate Armed Services Committee on U.S. Involvement in Bosnia, Federal News Service, June 7, 1995.

112. Charles Krauthammer, "War and Public Opinion," *Washington Post,* January 11, 1991, p. A21.

113. Richard Morin, "Two Ways of Reading the Public's Lips on Gulf Policy; Differently Phrased Questions Seem at First Glance to Yield Contradictory Results," *Washington Post,* January 14, 1991, p. A9.

114. Paul Taylor and Richard Morin, "Poll Finds Americans Back U.S. Response, but Warily," *Washington Post,* August 10, 1990, p. A1.

115. Ronald Brownstein, "The Times Poll; Americans More Wary About Prospect of War," *Los Angeles Times,* November 16, 1990, p. A1. Poll numbers are notoriously unreliable, as most Americans prefer to answer, "No, but" or "Yes, if." Nonetheless, they can give a hint of the public mood.

116. During the Vietnam and Korea conflicts, opposition to the war increased by 15 percentage points once the casualty toll hit 1,000 and by another 15 points once it reached 10,000.

117. Ronald Brownstein, "The Times Poll; Americans Back Bush Decision Overwhelmingly," *Los Angeles Times,* January 19, 1991, p. A1. Support for the Korean war was never higher than 66 percent, whereas support for the Vietnam conflict peaked in August 1965 and fell consistently as casualties mounted. By 1973 only 29 percent of Americans supported the war. Richard Morin, "Backing for War, Bush Role Grows with Ground Attack," *Washington Post,* February 26, 1991, p. A6.

118. Elizabeth Drew, *On the Edge: The Clinton Presidency* (New York: Simon and Schuster, 1994), p. 153.

119. Interview with Warren Christopher, *Face the Nation,* CBS, March 28, 1993.

120. Interview with Warren Christopher, *Nightline,* ABC, May 25, 1993.

121. Dick Morris, *Behind the Oval Office: Winning the Presidency in the Nineties* (New York: Random House, 1997), p. 253.

122. Johnson, "The Pinstripe Approach," p. 70.

123. Anna Husarska, "Tough on Crime, Murky on Genocide," *Los Angeles Times,* February 16, 1994.

124. Hearing of the House Foreign Affairs Committee, Federal News Service, May 18, 1993.

125. Johnson, "The Pinstripe Approach," p. 72. In June 1993 the United States did join an appeal by the UN World Conference on Human Rights to the UN Security Council to take "necessary measures to end the genocide in Bosnia and Herzegovina."

126. "An Officer and Nerve Shock," *Times* (London), July 31, 1917, p. 8.

127. John Gannan, CIA deputy director for intelligence, "Ethnic Cleansing and Atrocities in Bosnia," statement before a Joint Hearing of the Senate Foreign Relations Committee and Senate Select Committee, Intelligence, Federal News Service, August 7, 1995. The same month the CIA issued this report, Croatia's army seized territory in the country's Krajina border region that had been taken in the 1991 war by Serb forces. In the three-day operation, Croatia forcibly expelled or frightened into fleeing some 200,000 Serbs.

128. State Department briefing, Federal News Service, July 21, 1993.

129. John F. Burns, "Thousands of Shells Hit Sarajevo as Serbian Units' Pincers Close In," *New York Times,* July 24, 1993, p. A1.

130. James C. Thomson Jr., "How Could Vietnam Happen? An Autopsy," *Atlantic Monthly,* April 1968, p. 49; Michael Crozer, *The Bureaucratic Phenomenon* (Chicago: University of Chicago Press, 1964). See Albert O. Hirschman, *Rhetoric of Reaction: Perversity, Futility, Jeopardy* (Cambridge, Mass.: Belknap Press, 1991), p. 115. Thomson himself left the NSC in 1966 in what he called a typical "muddled departure." Because of some combination of frustration and fatigue, it took him time to speak out. In May 1967, while teaching at Harvard University, he wrote a memorable letter to the *New York Times* in which he asserted that men in Washington bore a paramount obligation: "For the greatest power on earth has the power denied to others: the power to take unilateral steps, and to keep taking them; the power to be as ingenious and relentless in the pursuit of peace as we are in the infliction of pain; the power to lose face; the power to admit error; and the power to act with magnanimity." James Thomson, "Alternatives Rejected," *New York Times,* June 4, 1967, p. E13. Thomson's observation would make a fitting epigram for this book.

131. Hirschman described the government official's preexisting attitude of "my country, right or wrong" and his reluctance to leave and thereby abandon his country at the moment it most needs fixing. He wrote that the attitude can become "the wronger, the myer." Bureaucrats often see a choice not between voice and exit but between voice inside the system and voicelessness outside it. See Hirschman, *Rhetoric of Reaction,* pp. 39, 104.

132. Michael Gordon, "A State Dept. Aide on Bosnia Resigns on Partition Issue," *New York Times,* August 5, 1993, pp. A1, A11.

133. News conference, Capitol Hill, Federal News Service, August 5, 1993.

134. Gordon, "A State Dept. Aide on Bosnia Resigns."

135. Steven Walker, resignation letter, Federal News Service, August 23, 1993.

136. Steven A. Holmes, "State Dept. Expert on Croatia Resigns to Protest Policy in Balkans," *New York Times,* August 24, 1993, p. A6. Clinton's press secretary, Dee Dee Myers, likewise said, "I think the president is sympathetic to people who, as a matter of conscience, feel that they have to resign." White House briefing, Federal News Service, August 25, 1993.

137. Drew, *On the Edge,* p. 150.

138. See Mark Bowden, *Black Hawk Down: A Story of Modern War* (New York: Atlantic Monthly Press, 1999).

139. Perry, March 9, 1995, cited in Sobel, *The Impact of Public Opinion,* p. 225.

140. Hearing of the House Foreign Affairs Committee on Foreign Aid Budget for FY94, Federal News Service, May 18, 1993.

141. Hearing of the Europe and Middle East Subcommittee of the House Foreign Affairs Committee, Federal News Service, September 15, 1993.

142. Toby Gati to Secretary of State Warren Christopher, "Legal Analysis," 1993, p. 32. Declassified as attachment to May 18, 1994, memo from Joan Donoghue in the Legal Adviser's Office to a number of the State Department bureaus concerning the occurrence of a possible legal genocide in Rwanda.

143. Ibid., p. 3; emphasis added.

144. Ibid.

145. Johnson, "The Pinstripe Approach," p. 69; Frank McCloskey, "Christopher, Resign," *New York Times,* October 24, 1993, sec. 4, p. 15.

146. Hearing of the House Foreign Affairs Committee on North American Free Trade Agreement (NAFTA), Federal News Service, November 5, 1993.

147. Ibid.

148. McCloskey raised Bosnia at one hearing in 1992, eight in 1993, and six in 1994.

149. Jason Vest, "Battle Cry of the Anti-War Congressman," *Washington Post,* February 19, 1994, p. G1.

150. White House briefing, "Statement by President Clinton Regarding Proposals to Deal with Situation in Bosnia," Federal News Service, February 9, 1994.

151. Dick Kirschten, "How Will Bosnia Play This Fall?" *National Journal,* February 5, 1994, p. 336; and Vest, "Battle Cry of the Anti-War Congressman."

152. Kirschten, "How Will Bosnia Play This Fall?"

153. UN Security Council Resolution 827, May 25, 1993.

154. Michael P. Scharf, *Balkan Justice: The Story Behind the First International War Crimes Trial Since Nuremberg* (Durham, N.C.: Carolina Academic Press, 1997), p. 54.

155. Anna Husarska, "Weak Voices," *New York Times,* July 25, 1995, p. A14.

156. Michael Adler, "Owen Fears Beirut-Style Division of Sarajevo," Agence France-Presse, December 19, 1992.

Chapter 10, Rwanda

1. Memo from Deputy Assistant Secretary of State Prudence Bushnell, through Undersecretary of State for Political Affairs Peter Tarnoff, to Secretary of State Warren Christopher, "Death of Rwanda and Burundi Presidents in Plane Crash Outside Kigali," April 6, 1994. The Rwanda documents were released to Will Ferroggiaro at the National Security Archive under the Freedom of Information Act.
2. Alison Des Forges, "The Method in Rwanda's Madness; Politics, Not Tribalism, Is the Root of the Bloodletting," *Washington Post*, April 17, 1994, p. C2.
3. James Woods, interview, "The Triumph of Evil," *Frontline*, PBS, January 26, 1999, p. 15; available at PBS Online: http://www.pbs.org/wgbh/pages/frontline/shows/evil/interviews/woods.html. The *Interahamwe*, meaning "those who attack together," were Hutu extremist militiamen supported by the National Revolutionary Movement for Development party, which helped orchestrate the slaughter of Tutsi civilians.
4. Cited in Linda Melvern, *A People Betrayed: The Role of the West in Rwanda's Genocide* (London: Zed Books, 2000), p. 71.
5. Alison Des Forges, *Leave None to Tell the Story: Genocide in Rwanda* (New York: Human Rights Watch, 1999), pp. 207–208.
6. Ibid., p. 212.
7. Canadians are extremely supportive of international peacekeeping. Some 80 percent of those polled in 1994 backed Canadian forces' participation in armed UN interventions. A survey published in 1998 placed the figure at 82 percent. National Defense Headquarters, "Canadians on Defense," April 1998.
8. Des Forges, *Leave None to Tell the Story*, pp. 96–179; United Nations, *Report of the Independent Inquiry into the Actions of the United Nations During the 1994 Genocide in Rwanda*, UN Doc. No. A/54/549, December 15, 1999, pp. 3–11, 47–52; Organization of African Unity (OAU), International Panel of Eminent Personalities to Investigate the 1994 Genocide in Rwanda and the Surrounding Events, *Rwanda: The Preventable Genocide* (Organization of African Unity, 2000), chap. 7.
9. IMF Rwanda Briefing Paper, 1992, Article IV, "Consultations and Discussions on a Second Annual Arrangement," May 14, 1992, given to Melvern and cited in *A People Betrayed*, pp. 64–65.
10. Africa Watch, International Federation of Human Rights Leagues, Interafrican Union for Human and Peoples' Rights and the International Center for Human Rights and Democratic Development, *Report of the International Commission of Investigation of Human Rights Violations in Rwanda Since October 1, 1990* (Paris: 1993).
11. United Nations, *Report of the Independent Inquiry*, pp. 3–4. See also report by B. W. Ndiaye, special rapporteur, on his mission to Rwanda, April 8–17, 1993, *Extrajudicial, Summary or Arbitrary Executions*, E/CN.4/1994/7/Add.1 (Geneva: United Nations, 1993).
12. Organization of African Unity, *Rwanda: The Preventable Genocide*, OAU, chap. 9, p. 5.
13. Reprinted and translated in African Rights, *Rwanda: Death, Despair and Defiance* (New York: African Rights, 1995), pp. 42–43. The commandments in fact referred to "Muhutu" and "Mututsi" for the singular and "Bahutu" and "Batutsi" for the plural. I have omitted the prefixes here.
14. OAU, *Rwanda: The Preventable Genocide*, ch. 9, p. 4, citing Federation Internationale des Ligues des Droites de l'Homme, Rwanda Report of March 1993, pp. 24–25.

15. The HRW report by Des Forges, *Leave None to Tell the Story,* includes thirty-two pages of early warnings prior to April 1994. The OAU report found, "If the rest of the world could not contemplate the possibility that they would go that far, it was certainly known that they were prepared to go a great distance indeed"; OAU, *Rwanda: The Preventable Genocide,* ch. 9, p. 3.

16. UN Security Council Resolution 872, October 5, 1993.

17. From 1956 to 1977 the United Nations launched just ten peacekeeping operations; from 1978 to 1987 it staged only one. But in the stormy six years leading up to 1994, the Security Council had authorized twenty missions.

18. Bob Dole, "Peacekeeping and Politics," *New York Times,* January 24, 1994, p. A15. Dole noted that the Security Council, with U.S. assent, had begun, continued, or expanded peacekeeping operations in Mozambique, on the Iraq-Kuwait border, in Somalia, Georgia, Cyprus, El Salvador, Haiti, Rwanda, the former Yugoslavia, and Liberia. In fact, Dole noted, the council had "said no only to Burundi." The Peace Powers Act that he introduced the next day would have banned U.S. troops from serving under foreign command in UN operations. "Our military personnel should be asked to risk their lives only in support of U.S. interests, in operations led by U.S. commanders," Dole wrote. The act also demanded that the White House consult more with Congress before casting Security Council votes for deployments. And it urged that the UN "be put on notice" that the United States would not continue to pay 31.7 percent of peacekeeping costs or subject itself to the "UN's warped accounting methods."

19. "The Clinton Administration's Policy on Reforming Multilateral Peace Operations," Presidential Decision Directive 25, May 3, 1994.

20. Jim Wold, "Clinton Moves to Limit UN Peacekeeping Role," Reuters, May 5 1994. Another Pentagon official described the new policy as "We'll only go where we're not needed"; Woods, *Frontline* interview.

21. Woods, *Frontline* interview.

22. Romeo Dallaire, "The End of Innocence: Rwanda 1994," in Jonathan Moore, ed., *Hard Choices: Moral Dilemmas in Humanitarian Intervention* (Lanham, Md.: Rowman & Littlefield, 1998), pp. 71–86.

23. Philip Gourevitch, *We Wish to Inform You That Tomorrow We Will Be Killed with Our Families: Stories from Rwanda* (New York: Farrar, Straus and Giroux, 1998), pp. 104–107.

24. Iqbal Riza, interview, "The Triumph of Evil," *Frontline,* PBS, January 26, 1999, p. 3; available at PBS Online: http://www.pbs.org/wgbh/pages/frontline/shows/evil/interviews/riza.html.

25. The *New York Times* ran a tiny blurb describing only "violence between the Tutsi and Hutu ethnic groups"; "New Government Is Delayed as Violence Rocks Rwanda," *New York Times,* February 24, 1994, p. A13.

26. United Nations, *Report of the Independent Inquiry,* p. 9.

27. Confidential, priority cable from U.S. embassy in Kigali to State Department, March 24, 1994.

28. In the secretary-general's second report on UNAMIR, issued a week before mass killing began, he wrote, "Continued support for UNAMIR would depend upon the full and prompt implementation of the Arusha peace agreement by the parties. The United Nations presence can be justified only if the parties show the necessary political will to abide by their commitments and to implement the agreement." "Second Progress Report of the Secretary-General on the United Nations Assistance Mission for Rwanda," S/1994/360, March 30, 1994.

29. Des Forges, *Leave None to Tell the Story,* pp. 19, 599; United Nations, *Report of the Independent Inquiry,* p. 27.
30. State Department briefing, Federal News Service, April 8, 1994.
31. *Meet the Press,* NBC, April 10, 1994.
32. *Face the Nation,* CBS, April 10, 1994.
33. Cited in OAU, *Rwanda: The Preventable Genocide,* chap. 10, sec. 15.
34. Des Forges, *Leave None to Tell the Story,* p. 22.
35. Confidential memorandum from Deputy Assistant Secretary of Defense for Middle East/Africa James Woods, through Assistant Secretary of Defense for International Security Affairs Chas Freeman, for Undersecretary of Defense for Policy Frank Wisner, "Talking Points on Rwanda/Burundi," April 11, 1994.
36. *CNN News,* April 7, 1994.
37. *Weekend Edition,* NPR, April 9, 1994.
38. *All Things Considered,* NPR, April 9, 1994.
39. Keith B. Richburg, "Slayings Put Rwanda in Chaos; Clerics, Foreigners Among Casualties; Americans to Leave," *Washington Post,* April 9, 1994, p. A1.
40. Robert McFadden, "Western Troops Arrive in Rwanda to Aid Foreigners," *New York Times,* April 10, 1994, sec. 1, p. A1.
41. Keith B. Richburg, "Westerners Begin Fleeing Rwanda; 170 Americans Leave by Convoy," *Washington Post,* April 10, 1994, p. A1.
42. William Schmidt, "Refugee Missionaries from Rwanda Speak of Their Terror, Grief and Guilt," *New York Times,* April 12, 1994, p. A6.
43. Donatella Lorch, "Strife in Rwanda: Evacuation; American Evacuees Describe Horrors Faced by Rwandans," *New York Times,* April 11, 1994, p. A1.
44. "Tribes Battle for Rwandan Capital; New Massacres Reported," *New York Times,* April 16, 1994, p. A5.
45. Other groups also responded quickly. On April 21 the International Federation of Human Rights declared the killings genocide. Official bodies and states began to follow. The pope first used the word on April 27; on the same day the Czechs and Argentines introduced a draft resolution to the Security Council that pointedly included the term; and Boutros-Ghali declared a "real genocide" on ABC's *Nightline* on May 4, 1994.
46. Julia Preston, "Death Toll in Rwanda Is Said to Top 100,000; U.N. Votes to Pull out Most Peacekeepers," *Washington Post,* April 22, 1994, p. A1.
47. Jennifer Parmelee, "Fade to Blood; Why the International Answer to the Rwandan Atrocities Is Indifference," *Washington Post,* April 24, 1994, p. C3.
48. "Aid Agency Fears Genocide Under Way in Rwanda," Press Association Newsfile, April 28, 1994.
49. Melvern, *A People Betrayed,* p. 177.
50. Confidential memorandum to Ambassador Albright from John S. Boardman, thru Ambassador Walker, "Subject: Your Meeting with Rwandan Patriotic Front (RPF) Representative Claude Dusaidi, Thursday, April 28, 3:00 P.M.," April 28, 1994.
51. On April 8 Dallaire had warned that a ruthless campaign of "ethnic cleansing and terror" was under way. Riza remembered, "There was no reference to an impending genocide.... This term of ethnic killings and ethnic cleansing had been there for a long time and it was adopted, of course, from Bosnia. Ethnic cleansing does not necessarily mean genocide; it means terror to drive people away"; Iqbal Riza, *Frontline* interview, pp. 9–10.
52. Des Forges, *Leave None to Tell the Story,* p. 636.

53. Office of the Secretary of Defense, "Secret Discussion Paper: Rwanda," May 1, 1994; emphasis added.

54. State Department briefing, Federal News Service, April 28, 1994, pp. 1–4.

55. Melvern, *A People Betrayed,* p. 179.

56. Ibid., p. 180.

57. Confidential cable from U.S.-UN to Secretary of State Warren Christopher and embassies, April 27, 1994.

58. United Nations Security Council, "Statement by the President of the Security Council," April 30, 1994, S/PRST/1994/21.

59. Secret memorandum from Assistant Secretary for Intelligence and Research Toby Gati to Assistant Secretary of State for African Affairs George Moose and Legal Adviser Conrad Harper "Rwanda—Geneva Convention Violations," May 18, 1994.

60. Ibid.

61. Confidential cable from Secretary of State Warren Christopher to the U.S. Mission to the UN in Geneva and embassies, "Subject: UN Human Rights Commission: 'Genocide' at Special Session on Rwanda," May 24, 1994.

62. State Department briefing, Federal News Service, June 10, 1994.

63. Michael R. Gordon, "U.S. to Supply 60 Vehicles for U.N. Troops in Rwanda," *New York Times,* June 16, 1994, p. A12.

64. Rita Beamish, "Clinton Shocked at Presidents' Death, Subsequent Violence," Associated Press, April 7, 1994.

65. "Take Care of My Children," *Washington Post,* April 8, 1994, p. A21.

66. Confidential cable from Secretary of State Warren Christopher to the U.S. Mission to the UN, April 15, 1994.

67. UN Security Council Resolution 912, April 21, 1994.

68. OAU, *Rwanda: The Preventable Genocide,* chap. 12, sec. 42.

69. Dallaire, "The End of Innocence," p. 82.

70. Interagency Working Group, "Secret Discussion Paper: Rwanda," May 1, 1994.

71. Ibid.

72. Memo from Undersecretary of Defense for Policy Frank G. Wisner to Deputy National Security Adviser Sandy Berger, "Rwanda: Jamming Civilian Radio Broadcasts," May 5, 1994.

73. Interagency Working Group, "Secret Discussion Paper: Rwanda."

74. "One, Two, Many Rwandas?" *Washington Post,* April 17, 1994, p. C6. The *Washington Post* published a letter from Amnesty International Executive Director William Schulz almost two weeks later, on May 1, 1994, "U.S. Leadership in Rwanda Crisis," p. C6. Schulz's letter expressed shock at the *Post*'s assumption that the United States had no leadership role to play in the Rwandan crisis. "In a disaster of such huge proportions, it is understandable that we may feel impotent and be tempted to cope by withdrawing," Schulz wrote. "We must resist this tendency, however, for it is precisely such isolation and distance that allow us to accept as inevitable the killing of 100,000 people in two weeks." He juxtaposed the paper's spirited editorial support for intervention in Bosnia with its timidity on Rwanda. "As the tragedy unfolds, one has to wonder why the atrocities in Bosnia receive the widespread attention they do while the massacre of tens of thousands in an African country is met with a collective denial of responsibility and a hasty retreat." He urged the United States to "turn its attention to doing whatever it can to alleviate the plight of the equally innocent and defenseless civilian population of Rwanda whose lives are no less worthy of protection." Schulz pressed the

United States to support expanding the UN presence and assisting in the evacuation of at-risk Rwandans.

75. "Cold Choices in Rwanda," *New York Times,* April 23, 1994, p. A24.

76. *Nightline,* ABC, May 4, 1994.

77. Steven Livingstone and Todd Eachus, "Rwanda: U.S. Policy and Television Coverage," in Howard Adelman and Astri Suhrke, eds., *The Path of a Genocide: The Rwanda Crisis from Uganda to Zaire* (New Brunswick, N.J.: Transaction, 1999), p. 209.

78. Paul Richter, "Rwanda Violence Stumps World Leaders; Africa: Though Clinton and Boutros Boutros-Ghali Have Made Guarded Threats, Calls for Action Have Been Eerily Absent," *Los Angeles Times,* April 30, 1994, p. A13.

79. Kevin Merida, "TransAfrica Leader to Fast in Protest; Robinson Labels U.S. Policy on Haitians Discriminatory, Racist," *Washington Post,* April 12, 1994, p. A15.

80. "The Month in Review," *Current History,* September 1994, p. 293.

81. Eleanor Clift and Tom Brazaitis, *War Without Bloodshed: The Art of Politics* (New York: Scribner, 1996), p. 304.

82. Paul Simon, *P.S.: The Autobiography of Paul Simon* (Chicago: Bonus Books, 1999), pp. 340–341.

83. *All Things Considered,* NPR, July 22, 1994.

84. Melvern, *A People Betrayed,* pp. 202–203.

85. Des Forges, *Leave None to Tell the Story,* pp. 624–625.

86. Confidential cable from Deputy Secretary of State Strobe Talbott to the U.S. Mission to the UN, May 13 1994.

87. Holly Burkhalter, "The Question of Genocide: The Clinton Administration," *World Policy Journal,* Winter 1994, p. 50.

88. The RPF was opposed to the deployment both because of its mistrust of France and because the rebels were trying to consolidate their territorial gains in the south and west, where Operation Turquoise was to be launched.

89. On June 22, 1994, the Security Council, under UN Resolution 929, authorized France to deploy a Chapter VII "temporary multinational force" to establish secure humanitarian areas. The duration of the deployment was limited to two months. Around Gisenyi, before the French arrival, the Hutu officials broadcast a message to "Hutu girls," telling them, "Wash yourselves and put on a good dress to welcome our French allies. The Tutsi girls are all dead, so you have your chance." Quoted by Gerard Prunier, *The Rwanda Crisis: History of a Genocide* (New York: Columbia University Press, 1995), p. 292.

90. SWB/France 2 TV, July 14, 1994, quoted in ibid., p. 297.

91. White House briefing, Federal News Service, July 15, 1994.

92. UN Security Council, statement by the president of the Security Council, August 25, 1994, S/PRST/1994/48.

93. "At Last, Rwanda's Pain Registers," *New York Times,* July 23, 1994, p. A18.

94. U.S. Lieutenant General Daniel Schroeder, the U.S. commander of the joint task force on Rwanda, initially seemed poised to be very supportive of Dallaire, his UN counterpart. But after his political masters laid out the rules of the road, Schroeder backed off from his prior commitments. "He wasn't allowed to sustain a single injury, so he essentially stayed out of Rwanda," Dallaire recalls. "It was surreal. You had American NGOs running around Rwanda left and right. Yet U.S. forces couldn't leave their compound."

95. White House briefing, Federal News Service, July 29, 1994.

96. Quoted in Milton Leitenberg, "U.S. and UN Acts Escalate Genocide and Increase Costs in Rwanda" in Helen Fein, ed., *The Prevention of Genocide: Rwanda*

and Yugoslavia Reconsidered (New York: Institute for the Study of Genocide, 1994), pp. 41–42.

97. U.S. Information Agency press conference, Rwanda, Federal News Service, August 24, 1994.

98. Melvern, *A People Betrayed,* pp. 216–217.

99. Secretary-General Kofi Annan at first refused to permit Dallaire to testify. Under public pressure, however, Annan granted a waiver to the general to appear as a witness on matters directly relevant to the case against a Rwandan mayor, Jean Paul Akayesu. The waiver explicitly excluded confidential document and cable traffic between Rwanda and the UN mission in New York. Daphna Shraga, a UN legal affairs officer, said that the trial was "not the appropriate context within which the performance of a peacekeeping operation, the propriety and adequacy of its mandate, its operational activities and the decision-making processes relating thereto, should be assessed"; United Nations, "General Dallaire, Former Commander of UNAMIR, Gives Testimony Before International Criminal Tribunal for Rwanda," Press Release L/2856, February 25, 1988, p. 2.

100. Lara Santoro, "Rwanda Massacres Were Avoidable, General Says," *Christian Science Monitor,* February 27, 1998, p. 7.

101. Dallaire, "The End of Innocence," p. 79.

102. Allan Thompson, "General May Recount Rwanda Horror Again; Tribunal Likely to Recall Canadian," *Toronto Star,* February 27, 1998, p. A1.

103. Ibid.

104. James Bennet, "Clinton Declares U.S., with World, Failed Rwandans," *New York Times,* March 26, 1998, pp. A6, A12.

105. Mike Blanchfield, "General Battles Rwanda 'Demons': After Witnessing the Atrocities of Genocide, Romeo Dallaire Has Had to Endure the Belgian Government's Criticism," *Ottawa Citizen,* December 13, 1998, p. A3.

106. Luke Fisher, "Besieged by Stress: The Horrors of Rwanda Haunt a General," *MacLeans,* October 12, 1998, p. 24.

Chapter 11, Srebrenica

1. The rebellion Mladic mentioned was a Serb uprising crushed by the Turks in 1804. David Rohde, *Endgame: The Betrayal and Fall of Srebrenica, Europe's Worst Massacre Since World War II* (New York: Farrar, Straus and Giroux, 1997), p. 167.

2. Ibid., p. 79.

3. Ibid., p. 369.

4. Confidential cable from U.S. embassy in Sarajevo to Secretary of State Warren Christopher, July 11, 1995; these documents were declassified through the Freedom of Information Act at the request of Bob Silk, a New York lawyer, who filed the request on behalf of the group Students Against Genocide.

5. Rohde, *Endgame,* p. 101.

6. Human Rights Watch, *Bosnia-Hercegovina: The Fall of Srebrenica and the Failure of U.N. Peacekeeping* (New York: Human Rights Watch, 1995), p. 16.

7. Rohde, *Endgame,* p. 132.

8. UN, *Report of the Secretary General Pursuant to General Assembly Resolution 53/35, The Fall of Srebrenica,* November 15, 1999, p. 106, para. 478.

9. "President Clinton's Remarks Before Meeting with Congressional Leaders," U.S. Newswire, July 11, 1995.

10. UN, *Report of the Secretary General,* p. 72, para. 315.

11. Stephen Engelberg and Tim Weiner, "Massacre in Bosnia; Srebrenica: The Days of Slaughter," *New York Times,* October 29, 1995, sec. 1, p. 1.

12. Human Rights Watch, *The Fall of Srebrenica*, p. 20.

13. Engelberg and Weiner, "Massacre in Bosnia."

14. Rohde, *Endgame*, pp. 242, 256, 280.

15. Ibid., p. 194.

16. DPI International Report, Online Newsletter, July 12, 1995, quoted in Human Rights Watch, *The Fall of Srebrenica,* p. 48. This UN propensity for spinning its disasters and debacles was one of the ugliest features of the mission. Akashi's efforts in 1995 were only the latest in a long tradition of packaging failure as success. In 1992, the first year of the war, Lieutenant Colonel Barry Frewer famously informed an open-mouthed press corps that there was no siege of Sarajevo, only "a tactically advantageous position." When the Serbs took territory, burning and looting houses and expelling civilians in their path, UN officials said they were "adjusting" the confrontation line. David Rieff, "Nothing Was Delivered," *New Republic,* May 1, 2000, p. 27. And during previous Serb attacks against safe areas, UN officials repeatedly tried to put a happy face on the shrinking territory under their protection, obfuscating the boundaries of the safe areas and claiming an ever narrower diameter under their authority. Reporters used to joke that Serb attacks led to such predictable efforts by UN officials to shrink the enclaves that the only reliable definition of a "safe area" was the "smallest concentric space into which a bullet cannot pass."

17. UN, *Report of the Secretary General,* p. 87, para. 390.

18. Chris Hedges, "Balkans: 'Srebrenica Is Our Country,' Serbs Boast; Leader Rejects UN Demand to Return Safe Area," *New York Times,* July 13, 1995, p. A6.

19. State Department briefing, Federal News Service, July 12, 1995.

20. Yasushi Akashi to Kofi Annan, July 14, 1995.

21. State Department briefing, Federal News Service, July 12, 1995.

22. Rohde, *Endgame,* p. 225.

23. Bob Woodward, *The Choice* (New York: Simon & Schuster, 1996), pp. 259–260; Chuck Lane, "The Fall of Srebrenica," *The New Republic,* August 16, 1995, pp. 14–18.

24. UN, *Report of the Secretary General,* p. 80, para. 350.

25. Engelberg and Weiner, "Massacre in Bosnia."

26. Michael Dobbs and R. Jeffrey Smith, "New Proof Offered of Serb Atrocities; U.S. Analysts Identify More Mass Graves," *Washington Post,* October 29, 1995, p. A1.

27. State Department briefing, Federal News Service, July 12, 1995.

28. John Pomfret, "Witnesses Allege Abuses by Serbs; Killings, Abductions Cited; Search for Missing to Begin," *Washington Post,* July 16, 1995, p. A1.

29. Rohde, *Endgame,* p. 332.

30. John Pomfret, "'We Count for Nothing'; Srebrenica Refugees Unwelcome in Tuzla," *Washington Post,* July 15, 1995, p. A1.

31. Woodward, *The Choice,* pp. 262–263.

32. Confidential Information Memorandum to Secretary of State Christopher from Assistant Secretary of State for Democracy, Human Rights, and Labor John Shattuck; "Subject: Defense of the Safe Areas in Bosnia," July 19, 1995.

33. Human Rights Watch, *The Fall of Srebrenica,* p. 39. The testimony included here does not correspond precisely to that of the first three Muslim survivors. Detailed transcripts of their testimony is unavailable, but their experiences approximated those quoted by HRW.

34. Ibid., p. 44.
35. Rohde, *Endgame,* p. 265.
36. Ibid., p. 287.
37. Ibid., p. 326. One Dutch hostage, quoted in the Croatian paper *Slobodna Dalmacija* (Independent Dalmatia) on July 25, 1995, reported seeing a truck filled with bodies when the Serbs transported him and other hostages to Bratunac. "We drove next to the truck. There were dead bodies to the left and to the right of it, and the truck itself was filled to the top with corpses," the soldier, Ynse Schellens, said. But he quickly added that the bodies were probably Bosnian Muslim soldiers. Quoted in Human Rights Watch, *The Fall of Srebrenica,* p. 46.
38. Roy Gutman, "An Appeal for Zepa," *Newsday,* July 25, 1995, p. A6.
39. Mazowiecki to Tan Sri Dato' Musa Hitam, chairman of the UNCHR, July 27, 1995.
40. Secretary of State Warren Christopher to the U.S. embassy in Sarajevo, August 16, 1995. Holbrooke, meanwhile, had his own personal line of communication with Tuzla. His twenty-five-year-old son, Anthony, was also helping interview refugees as they crossed from Serb territory into Muslim hands, and he often yelled into the phone that his father should "get his ass in gear." Richard Holbrooke, *To End a War* (New York: Random House, 1998), p. 70.
41. Ambassador Madeleine Albright to Security Council, August 10, 1995.
42. On August 11 a classified cable from the U.S. Mission in Geneva to the State Department updated the secretary on the progress of the Red Cross in locating the missing. The cable ominously reported that "all sites visited to date have either been empty, or occupied by residents from other towns." Yet the cable softened the implications by passing along the ICRC view that some of the missing had been reintegrated into the Bosnian army or returned to their families without reporting to the Red Cross; classified cable from U.S. Mission in Geneva to Secretary of State Warren Christopher, August 11, 1995. The ICRC submitted a formal request to the United States for copies of satellite photographs to aid it with its search after it saw the images of mass graves on CNN.
43. Unclassified memorandum, "BOTTOM LINES: Following are Direct Answers to Possible Issues," undated. See also Dobbs and Smith, "New Proof Offered."
44. White House briefing, Federal News Service, July 14, 1995.
45. State Department briefing, Federal News Service, July 14, 1995.
46. Ibid.
47. Clinton chided the UN for its "crazy" rules of engagement and said, "I never would have put forces on the ground in such a situation," using the conditional tense, which was inappropriate for a head of state who did not put troops on the ground. Woodward, *The Choice,* p. 255.
48. The Senate had in fact voted 58–42 eleven months before to suspend U.S. participation in enforcing the embargo, but implementation had been delayed after Senators George Mitchell (D.–Maine) and Sam Nunn (D.–Ga.) negotiated a compromise agreement.
49. Clinton pollster Dick Morris said his polling showed Americans opposed deploying ground troops to enforce a peace 38-55. Once Clinton began to make an effort to persuade them, however, the numbers jumped to 45-45. Morris also offered a general estimation of the American public's views on U.S. foreign engagement. In one poll he gave those surveyed three options: "to intervene overseas to protect our interests and values and to act as a global police officer; to act as a peacemaker, doing what we can when we can to promote peace without overtax-

ing our resources; to focus primarily on our domestic needs without spending much time at all worrying about the problems of other nations."The unsurprising result, given the loaded wording of the questions, was that 14 percent opted for global cop, 43 percent favored flexible peacemaker, and 37 percent rejected any role at all. Dick Morris, *Behind the Oval Office: Winning the Presidency in the Nineties* (New York: Random House, 1997), pp. 247–256. Polling conducted by Steven Kull and Clay Ramsey shows that Americans are much more supportive of humanitarian interventions and much less casualty-averse than Morris and the foreign policy establishment presume.

50. Elaine Sciolino and Craig R. Whitney, "Costly Pullout in Bosnia Looms Unless U.N. Can Prove Effective," *New York Times,* July 9, 1995, sec. 1, p. 1.

51. George Stephanopoulos, *All Too Human: A Political Education* (Boston: Little, Brown, 1998), p. 383.

52. By the end of the war, Dole's Senate office had published some 150 press releases on the subject of the war in Bosnia.

53. Bob Dole, "Failed Approach in Bosnia," *Congressional Record,* 104th Cong., 1st sess., 1995, 141, pt. 110: S9624.

54. Ibid.

55. Bob Dole, "Thousands of Bosnians Flee," *Congressional Record,* 104th Cong., 1st sess., 1995, 141, pt. 111: S9693.

56. *This Week with David Brinkley,* ABC, July 17, 1995.

57. Bob Dole, "Bosnia," *Congressional Record,* 104th Cong., 1st sess., 141, pt. 116: S10225.

58. Ibid., pt. 119: S10506.

59. Bob Dole, "Bosnian Arms Embargo," *Congressional Record,* 104th Cong., 1st sess., 141, pt. 120: S10537.

60. Columnist William Safire urged, "Public opinion needs rallying with a prime-time TV speech. If [Clinton] cannot do it, the networks should offer national leadership time to Dole, with a grumpy Clinton rebuttal." William Safire, "Clinton Abdicates as Leader," *New York Times,* July 27, 1995, p. A23.

61. In a 1976 vice presidential debate, Dole had blundered badly by bemoaning the "Democrat wars" of the century that he said had killed and wounded 1.6 million Americans, "enough to fill the city of Detroit." By the time of the 1996 election, Dole's Democratic colleagues had come to respect him. Senator Paul Simon said on the floor, "I am supporting Bill Clinton. But I am not going to buy a one-way ticket to Canada if Bob Dole gets elected." Paul Simon, "Senator Dole's Announcement," *Congressional Record,* 104th Cong., 2nd sess., 1996, 142, pt. 68:S5046.

62. Michael Duffy and Nancy Gibbs, "The Soul of Dole," *Time,* August 19, 1996, p. 30.

63. *Nightline,* ABC, July 24, 1995.

64. *Inside Politics,* CNN, July 28, 1995.

65. Elaine Sciolino, "Senate Vote to End Embargo May Prove a Pyrrhic Victory," *New York Times,* July 28, 1995, p. A1.

66. Ibid.

67. Charles Trueheart, "Journalists Take Aim at Policymakers; in Europe and U.S., Media Mirror Mood," *Washington Post,* July 21, 1995, p. A27.

68. Ibid.

69. Leon Wieseltier, "Accomplices to Genocide," *The New Republic,* August 7, 1995, p. 7.

70. *This Week with David Brinkley,* ABC, July 17, 1995.

71. State Department briefing, Federal News Service, July 12, 14, and 17, 1995; White House briefing, Federal News Service, July 14 and 18, 1995.

72. Walter Goodman, "Critic's Notebook; Horror and Despair in the Balkans," *New York Times,* July 25, 1995, p. C18.

73. State Department briefing, Federal News Service, July 12, 1995.

74. William Safire, "The Time Has Come," *New York Times,* July 12, 1995, p. A23.

75. Charles Gati, "Tell It to Srebrenica," *Washington Post,* July 13, 1995, p. A25. Gati, a senior vice president of a money management firm, served on the State Department's policy planning staff from 1993 to 1994.

76. R. W. Apple Jr., "Clinton Is Scrambling to Find Ways to Help UN in Bosnia," *New York Times,* July 14, 1995, p. A1.

77. George Soros, "This Is the Moment of Truth," *Washington Post,* July 16, 1995, p. C7.

78. Anthony Lewis, "Lessons of Disaster," *New York Times,* July 17, 1995, p. A13.

79. George F. Will, "Worthy of Contempt," *Washington Post,* August 3, 1995, p. A31.

80. "A Candid Look at Foreign Policy and Opinion on Bosnia," *Weekend Edition,* NPR, July 15, 1995.

81. Holly Burkhalter, "What We Can Do to Stop This Genocide," *Washington Post,* July 20, 1995, p. A27.

82. Dana Priest, "Coalition Calls for Action in Bosnia; Groups Want More Allied Military Force Used 'to Stop Genocide,'" *Washington Post,* August 1, 1995, p. A14.

83. William Drozdiak, "Allies Set to Prod U.S. into Role in Bosnia," *Washington Post,* July 19, 1995, p. A17.

84. Harold Nicolson, *Peacemaking, 1919* (Gloucester, Mass.: P. Smith, 1984), p. 88.

85. Stephen Engelberg, "How Events Drew U.S. into Balkans," *New York Times,* August 19, 1995, p. A1; Woodward, *The Choice,* pp. 260, 280–281; Thomas W. Lippman and Ann Devroy, "Clinton's Policy Evolution: June Decision Led to Diplomatic Gambles," *Washington Post,* September 11, 1995, p. A1.

86. Woodward, *The Choice,* pp. 261–263.

87. Morris, *Behind the Oval Office,* pp. 252–254.

88. Engelberg, "How Events Drew U.S. into Balkans."

89. Woodward, *The Choice,* pp. 261–262.

90. Lippman and Devroy, "Clinton's Policy Evolution."

91. Woodward, *The Choice,* pp. 265–267.

92. Ibid., p. 270.

93. David Maraniss, "Exploring How Dole Thinks; Clues Lie in His Kansas Roots, War Wound and Senate Service," *Washington Post,* August 4, 1996, p. A1. Dole was never particularly expressive. He had worked with McCain for nearly a decade in the Senate before he told him that while McCain had been held prisoner in Vietnam, Dole had worn a remembrance bracelet, with McCain's name on it.

94. Richard Sobel, *The Impact of Public Opinion on U.S. Foreign Policy Since Vietnam: Constraining the Colossus* (New York: Oxford University Press, 2001), pp. 218–219.

95. Secretary of State Madeleine K. Albright, Bob Dole, and Cyrus Vance, press conference at the Department of State, Washington, D.C., November 7, 1997, as released by the Office of the Spokesman, U.S. Department of State.

Chapter 12, Kosovo

1. Gary J. Bass, "A Look at . . . War Crimes and Punishment; It's a Risky Business," *Washington Post,* November 26, 2000, p. B3.

2. See Tim Judah, *The Serbs: History, Myth, and the Destruction of Yugoslavia* (New Haven: Yale University Press, 1997) and Tim Judah, *Kosovo: War and Revenge* (New Haven: Yale University Press, 2000). In fact, the Serbian kingdom had crumbled several decades before Prince Lazar Hrebeljanovic's demise in this fourteenth-century battle. Serbia did not finally fall to the Turks until 1459.

3. Cited in Laura Silber and Allan Little, *Yugoslavia: Death of a Nation* (New York: Penguin, 1997), pp. 29–35.

4. Silber and Little, *Yugoslavia,* p. 37.

5. Tim Judah, "A History of the Kosovo Liberation Army," in William Joseph Buckley, ed., *Kosovo: Contending Voices on Balkan Interventions* (Grand Rapids, Mich.: William B. Eerdmans, 2000), pp. 108–115.

6. "Hearing of the House International Relations Committee on Kosovo and Possible Deployment of U.S. Troops," Federal News Service, March 10, 1999.

7. Stephen Engelberg, "Weighing Strikes in Bosnia, U.S. Warns of Wider War," *New York Times,* April 25, 1993, p. A20.

8. R. Jeffrey Smith, "This Time, Walker Wasn't Speechless; Memory of El Salvador Spurred Criticism of Serbs," *Washington Post,* January 23, 1999, p. A15.

9. Anticipating Russian and Chinese opposition to the NATO bombing operation, the United States and its European allies did not seek authorization from the UN Security Council. This elicited widespread criticism. UN Secretary-General Kofi Annan later acknowledged the undesirability of seeing the Security Council block action that may have saved hundreds of thousands of lives. Unauthorized actions, he said, would lead the world on a "dangerous path to anarchy." But if the council failed to authorize a humanitarian intervention, it would "betray the very ideals that inspired the founding of the United Nations." "The choice," Annan said, "must not be between Council unity and inaction in the face of genocide—as in the case of Rwanda—on the one hand, *or* Council division and regional action, as in the case of Kosovo, on the other." Kofi Annan, "The Effectiveness of the International Rule of Law in Maintaining International Peace and Security," speech given at The Hague, May 18, 1999, SG/SM/6997.

10. "President Clinton Address to the Nation Regarding NATO Air Strikes Against Serbia," Federal News Service, March 24, 1999.

11. In the 34,000 sorties conducted over seventy-eight days, the United States supplied between 65 and 80 percent of the aircraft and precision ordinance. Michael Ignatieff, *Virtual War: Kosovo and Beyond* (New York: Metropolitan Books, 2000), pp. 92, 206. Anthony Cordesman conducted a study for the Center for Strategic and International Studies, "Lessons and Non-Lessons: Executive Summary," which found that the United States flew more than 60 percent of all sorties, 80 percent of strike sorties, 90 percent of the advanced intelligence and reconnaissance missions, and 90 percent of electronic warfare missions. The United States also fired more than 80 percent of the precision-guided weapons and more than 95 percent of the cruise missiles.

12. Congress later voted to check any decision to commit U.S. ground troops without its go-ahead. Alison Mitchell, "House Votes to Bar Clinton from Sending Ground Troops to Yugoslavia Without Congressional Approval," *New York Times,* April 29, 1999, p. A1.

13. Christiane Amanpour, "Strike on Yugoslavia," CNN, April 3, 1999.

14. Ignatieff, *Virtual War,* p. 105.

15. Ivo Daalder and Michael O'Hanlon, *Winning Ugly: NATO's War to Save Kosovo* (Washington, D.C.: Brookings Institution, 2000), p. 140.

16. Samantha Power, "Misreading Milosevic," *The New Republic,* April 26 and May 3, 1999, p. 24.

17. Richard Holbrooke, *To End a War* (New York: Random House, 1998), p. 231.

18. Arnaud de Borchgrave, "We Are Neither Angels Nor Devils: An Interview with Slobodan Milosevic," United Press International, April 30, 1999.

19. David Halberstam, *War in a Time of Peace: Bush, Clinton, and the Generals* (New York: Scribner, 2001), p. 453.

20. "The Rationale for Air Strikes," *New York Times,* March 24, 1999, p. A26.

21. Carol J. Williams, "Conference Highlights Flaws of NATO's Kosovo Campaign," *Los Angeles Times,* February 6, 2000.

22. Confirmation hearing of former senator William Cohen to be secretary of defense, Senate Armed Services Committee, January 22, 1997.

23. Wesley K. Clark, *Waging Modern War: Bosnia, Kosovo, and the Future of Combat* (New York: Public Affairs, 2001), p. 313.

24. Holly Burkhalter, Statement on Genocide in Kosovo, *All Things Considered,* NPR, April 9, 1999.

25. Henry Kissinger, "Doing Injury to History," *Newsweek,* April 5, 1999, pp. 38–39.

26. Henry Kissinger, "New World Disorder," *Newsweek,* May 31, 1999, p. 41.

27. John McCain, "Now That We're in, We Have to Win," *Time,* April 12, 1999, p. 56.

28. Dana Priest, "Bombing by Committee: France Balked at NATO Targets," *Washington Post,* September 20, 1999, p. A1.

29. Ibid.

30. General Clark feuded constantly with his top air force officer, Lieutenant General Michael C. Short. Clark lobbied for NATO planes to hunt down tanks and artillery terrorizing civilians in Kosovo, whereas Short thought such "tank plinking" would be ineffective. He insisted that the quickest route to bringing Milosevic to heel would be to destroy "strategic" targets, such as Yugoslav ministries and power plants. In one exchange, reported by Dana Priest in the *Washington Post,* Short expressed satisfaction that NATO was at last preparing to strike Serbian special police headquarters. "This is the jewel in the crown," Short said. "To me, the jewel in the crown is when those B-52s rumble across Kosovo," replied Clark. "You and I have known for weeks that we have different jewelers," said Short. "My jeweler outranks yours," said Clark. Dana Priest, "The Battle Inside Headquarters; Tension Grew with Divide over Strategy," *Washington Post,* September 21, 1999, p. A1. See also Clark, *Waging Modern War.*

31. Dana Priest, "A Decisive Battle That Never Was," *Washington Post,* September 19, 1999, p. A1.

32. Judah, *Kosovo: War and Revenge,* p. 274. Russia's role in bringing about the settlement remains cloudy. Just prior to his diplomatic intervention, on May 26, 1999, Viktor Chernomyrdin, Yeltsin's special envoy to the Balkans, had published a bitter op-ed in the *Washington Post* charging that "the United States lost its moral right to be regarded as a leader of the free democratic world when its bombs shattered the ideals of liberty and democracy in Yugoslavia." He had demanded reparations be paid to Yugoslavia and had said he would urge President Boris Yeltsin to freeze U.S.-Russian relations until NATO stopped bombing.

33. "Shiptar" is a derogatory term used by Serbs to describe Albanians.

34. "President Clinton's Remarks at Ferizaj (Urosevac) Area Sports Pavilion, Ferizaj (Urosevac), Kosovo," Federal News Service, November 23, 1999.

35. Michael Walzer, "Kosovo," in William Joseph Buckley, ed., *Kosovo: Contending Voices on Balkan Interventions* (Grand Rapids, Mich.: William B. Eerdmans, 2000), p. 334.

36. *The Guardian,* June 7, 1999.

37. William Shakespeare, *Henry IV, Part II,* 4.5.213.

38. "Human Rights Watch: NATO Killed Yugoslav Civilians," Associated Press, February 6, 2000. See Human Rights Watch, *Civilian Deaths in the NATO Air Campaign* (New York: Human Rights Watch, 2000). See also Amnesty International, *"Collateral Damage" or Unlawful Killings? Violations of War by NATO During Operation Allied Force* (London: Amnesty International, 2000).

39. NATO press release, "Statement by the Secretary General of NATO, Lord Robertson, on the Human Rights Watch Report," February 7, 2000.

40. Michael Ignatieff, "The Reluctant Imperialist," *New York Times Magazine,* August 6, 2000, p. 46.

41. Primo Levi, *The Drowned and the Saved* (New York: Summit Books, 1986), pp. 48–49.

42. Melissa Eddy, "Head of KFOR Troops Blasts NATO Governments Over Lack Of Reconstruction In Kosovo," Associated Press, January 19, 2000.

43. "NATO's Crimes," *Spectator,* March 11, 2000.

44. U.S. credibility was also damaged by NATO's overestimation of the damage it inflicted upon Serb forces and hardware. On May 23, 1999, President Clinton claimed that NATO had destroyed between one-third and one-half of Serb heavy weapons in Kosovo. When the war ended two weeks later, however, the Pentagon and NATO admitted that the real damage was no more than 7–10 percent, which amounted to 800 Serb heavy weapons, including 120 tanks. William Jefferson Clinton, "A Just and Necessary War," *New York Times,* May 23, 1999, sec. 4, p. 17; Cohen, Defense Department news briefing, Federal News Service, June 10, 1999. Once inspectors gained access to the field and found no more than a few dozen charred skeletons of heavy weapons, the estimates sank further. Daalder and O'Hanlon, *Winning Ugly,* pp. 154–155. This drop-off is comparable to the discrepancy between original and final estimates of damage done to Iraqi weaponry during the Gulf War. See Thomas A. Keaney and Elliot A. Cohen, *Gulf War Air Power Survey Summary Report* (Washington, D.C.: Office of the Secretary of the Air Force, 1993), pp. 126–128.

45. Foreign Press Center briefing with David Scheffer, Federal News Service, April 5, 1999; emphasis added.

46. White House briefing, "News Conference with President Bill Clinton," Federal News Service, June 25, 1999.

47. Special State Department briefing, Federal News Service, April 9, 1999.

48. State Department briefing, Federal News Service, April 19, 1999.

49. Defense Department briefing, Federal News Service, May 7, 1999.

50. State Department briefing, "Erasing History," Federal News Service, May 10, 1999.

51. Serge Halimi and Dominique Vidal, "Lessons of War: Media and Disinformation," *Le Monde diplomatique,* March 2000, online.

52. John Bolton, *The World Today with Wolf Blitzer,* CNN, November 10, 1999.

53. UN press briefing by the prosecutor for the UN tribunals for the former Yugoslavia and Rwanda, November 21, 2000. See also Christopher Hitchens, "Body Count in Kosovo," *Nation,* June 11, 2001, and Michael Ignatieff, "Counting Bodies in Kosovo," *New York Times,* November 21, 1999, sec. 1, p. 1.

54. Anthony Lloyd, "Corpses Testify to State-Run Cover-Up of Kosovo Slaughter," *Times* (London), August 20, 2001, p. 1.

55. Hitchens, "Body Count in Kosovo," p. 9.

56. Dusan Stojanovic, "Officials Detail Milosevic Cover-Up Attempt," Associated Press, July 28, 2001.

57. UN Mission in Kosovo press release, Novermber, 10, 1999.

Chapter 13, Lemkin's Courtroom Legacy

1. Robert H. Reid, "Milosevic Refuses to Enter Plea," Associated Press, July 3, 2001.

2. Marlise Simons, "Milosevic Calls Tribunal Unfair, Infantile and a 'Farce,'" *New York Times,* October 31, 2001, p. A6.

3. "Milosevic Reprimanded for TV Call," *CNN Online,* August 24, 2001.

4. The only prior arrest by U.S. soldiers had been made the previous January, when they had seized Goran Jelisic, the self-described "Serb Adolf."

5. Gary Jonathan Bass, *Stay the Hand of Vengeance: The Politics of War Crimes Tribunals* (Princeton: Princeton University Press, 2000), p. 231.

6. Bosnian Serb hard-line president Nikola Poplasen reacted angrily to Krstic's arrest, claiming it had "embittered and upset" Serbs and would undermine implementation of the Dayton agreement. Poplasen's regime had been so uncooperative all along, however, that his relations with NATO could hardly have gotten worse. Steven Erlanger, "Bosnian Serb General Is Arrested by Allied Force in Genocide Case," *New York Times,* December 3, 1998, p. A1.

7. Mark Harmon, opening statement at the trial of Radislav Krstic, March 13, 2000, International Criminal Tribunal for the Former Yugoslavia (ICTY), p. 1.

8. Ibid., pp. 11–12.

9. ICTY press release, "Radislav Krstic Becomes the First Person to Be Convicted of Genocide at the ICTY and Is Sentenced to 46 Years Imprisonment," August 2, 2001.

10. Lemkin had lived to see an International Law Commission (ILC) draw up a statute for the permanent international criminal court mentioned in the genocide convention. Drafted in 1951 on the invitation of the General Assembly, however, this charter only gathered dust for the better part of four decades. In 1989 the assembly requested that the ILC "address the question of establishing an international criminal court." But it was the war in Bosnia and the creation of the two ad hoc tribunals that energized this process.

11. Margaret Thatcher, interview with David Frost, *Frost on Sunday,* TV-am, September 3, 1990.

12. *U.S. Department of State Dispatch* 1, 8 (October 22, 1990), p. 205.

13. Ibid., 1, 11 (November 12, 1990), p. 260.

14. Speech of German Minister of Foreign Affairs Hans-Dietrich Genscher upon receiving an honorary doctorate from the University of Ottawa, September 27, 1991.

15. Mirko Klarin, "Nuremberg Now !", *Borba,* May 16, 1991 (online), cited in ICTY, *The Path to the Hague: Selected Documents on the Origins of the ICTY* (online).

16. UN Security Council Resolution 771, August 13, 1992.

17. Clifford Krauss, "U.S. Backs Away from Charge of Atrocities in Bosnia Camps," *New York Times,* August 5, 1992, p. A12.

18. Speech of German Foreign Minister Klaus Kinkel at London conference, August 26, 1992. Before the UN General Assembly in September 1992, Kinkel again spoke about setting up an international tribunal. French Foreign Minister Roland Dumas also urged the creation of a court, and three ministers from the Conference on Security and Cooperation in Europe (CSCE) were already working on a draft convention for the tribunal when Eagleburger made his speech, naming names.

19. UN Security Council Resolution 780, October 6, 1992.

20. Michael P. Scharf, *Balkan Justice: The Story Behind the First International War Crimes Trial Since Nuremberg* (Durham, N.C.: Carolina Academic Press, 1997), p. 41.

21. Bass, *Stay the Hand of Vengeance,* p. 211.

22. Arusha was deemed near enough to enable ready travel to and from Rwanda but not too near to seem like a politically biased institution that would dispense only victors' (or in this case, victims') justice.

23. Andrew Purvis, "Colonel Apocalypse," *Time International,* June 10, 1996. The UN would try only the ringleaders of genocide, and the Rwandan government would punish those lower-level culprits who acted on their command. This meant that those who followed orders would receive the death penalty, while those who gave them would earn a maximum life sentence, usually served in a European prison.

24. Payam Akhavan, "The International Criminal Tribunal for Rwanda: The Politics and Pragmatics of Punishment," *American Journal of International Law* 90 (1996), pp. 501, 504–508.

25. Purvis, "Colonel Apocalypse."

26. The measure held that "the policy of the United States [is] to support efforts to bring to justice members of the Khmer Rouge for their crimes against humanity." 22 U.S.C. 2656, part D, secs. 571–574, April 30, 1994.

27. The SS files alone had filled six freight cars. Gary Bass, "A Look at . . . War Crimes and Punishment; It's a Risky Business," *Washington Post,* November 26, 2000, p. B3.

28. Elizabeth Becker, "New Links in Khmer Rouge Chain of Death," *New York Times,* July 16, 2001, p. A6.

29. Nate Thayer, "Day of Reckoning," *Far Eastern Economic Review* 160, 44 (October 30, 1997), p. 17.

30. Bou Saroeun, Vong Sokheng, and Christine Chaumea, "Khmer Rouge Deny Killer Role," *Phnom Penh Post* 10/15, July 20–August 2, 2001.

31. Seth Mydans, "As Cambodia Prepares to Try Khmer Rouge Leaders for Massacres, They Deny Guilt," *New York Times,* August 21, 2001, p. A9.

32. Thomas Hammarberg, "How the Khmer Rouge Tribunal Was Agreed: Discussions Between the Cambodian Government and the UN," part 1: March 1997–March 1999; part 2: March 1999–January 2001, published in *Searching for the Truth,* the magazine of the Cambodian Documentation Center, May 2001.

33. Antonio Cassese, Speech Before the UN General Assembly, November 7, 1995, UN Document no. A/50/PV.52.

34. Letter from Jesse Helms to Secretary of State Madeleine Albright, April 3, 2000.

35. Krstic said that Mladic told him he would personally command the units that had arrived, which included a battalion of military police and an interior ministry unit.

36. Institute for War and Peace Reporting (IWPR), "Krstic Accuses Mladic of Srebrenica Attack," *Tribunal Update* 195, October 24, 2000.

37. Ibid.

38. Justice Robert H. Jackson, "Report to the President on Atrocities and War Crimes," United States Department of State *Bulletin*, June 7, 1945.

39. IWPR, "Srebrenica Massacre Denial—Defense Witnesses Refuse to Accept Massacres Took Place," *Tribunal Update* 198, November 15, 2000.

40. *ICTY Transcript: Krstic (IT-98-33)*, June 22, 2000, p. 4462.

41. IWPR, "Krstic 'Feared' Speaking out over Srebrenica," *Tribunal Update* 196, October 31, 2000.

42. Anthony Deutsch, "Accused Serb General Claims Cover Up," Associated Press, October 25, 2000. The Serb public had still not come around to accepting that their soldiers committed the bulk of the atrocities in the Balkan wars. A July 2001 poll in *Politika* found that half the Serbian population admitted that Serbs committed war crimes. But of these, 45 percent still believed other nations had acted more inhumanely and 28 percent thought Serb crimes should be covered up. IWPR, "Regional Report: Serbia's Faltering War Crime Prosecution," *Tribunal Update* 234, September 12, 2001.

43. Marlise Simons, "Trial Reopens Pain of 1995 Bosnian Massacre," *New York Times,* November 7, 2000, p. A3.

Conclusion

1. David Rieff, *Slaughterhouse: Bosnia and the Failure of the West* (New York: Simon & Schuster, 1995), p. 27.

2. *ABC News This Week with Sam Donaldson,* January 23, 2000.

3. The Center for Peace in the Balkans, "Bin Laden's Balkan Connections," September 2001.

4. Arthur Koestler, "The Nightmare That Is Reality," *New York Times Magazine,* January 9, 1944, p. 5.

Bibliography

Turkey

Ahmad, Feroz. *The Young Turks: The Committee of Union and Progress in Turkish Politics, 1908–1914*. Clarendon Press, 1969.

Alexander, Edward. *A Crime of Vengeance: An Armenian Struggle for Justice*. Free Press, 1991.

Ambrosius, Lloyd E. *Woodrow Wilson and the American Diplomatic Tradition: The Treaty Fight in Perspective*. Cambridge University Press, 1987.

Auron, Yair. *The Banality of Indifference: Zionism and the Armenian Genocide*. Transaction, 2000.

Baker, Ray Stannard, and William E. Dodd, eds. *The Public Papers of Woodrow Wilson*. Harper and Brothers Publishers, 1925.

Balakian, Peter. *Black Dog of Fate: A Memoir*. Basic Books, 1997.

Boyajian, Dickran H. *Armenia: The Case for a Forgotten Genocide*. Educational Book Crafters, 1972.

Bryce, James. *The Treatment of the Armenians in the Ottoman Empire, 1915–16*. Gomidas Institute Books, 2000.

Dadrian, Vahakn N. *The History of the Armenian Genocide: Ethnic Conflict from the Balkans to Anatolia to the Caucasus*. Berghahn Books, 1995.

Davis, Leslie A. *The Slaughterhouse Province: An American Diplomat's Report on the Armenian Genocide, 1915–1917*. Ed. Susan K. Blair. A. D. Caratzas, 1989.

Derogy, Jacques. *Resistance and Revenge: The Armenian Assassination of the Turkish Leaders Responsible for the 1915 Massacres and Deportations*. Trans. A. M. Berrett. Transaction, 1990.

Evans, Laurence. *United States Policy and the Partition of Turkey, 1914–1924*. Johns Hopkins University Press, 1965.

Gilbert, Martin. *The First World War: A Complete History*. Henry Holt, 1994.

Horne, John, and Alan Kramer. *German Atrocities, 1914: A History of Denial*. Yale University Press, 2001.

Hovannisian, Richard, ed. *The Armenian Genocide in Perspective*. Transaction, 1986.

_____, ed. *Remembrance and Denial: The Case of the Armenian Genocide*. Wayne State University Press, 1998.

Keegan, John. *The First World War*. Knopf, 1999.

Lewis, Bernard. *The Emergence of Modern Turkey*. Oxford University Press, 1961.

Mazian, Florence. *Why Genocide? The Armenian and Jewish Experiences in Perspective*. Iowa State University Press, 1990.

Melson, Robert F. *Revolution and Genocide: On the Origins of the Armenian Genocide and the Holocaust*. University of Chicago Press, 1992.

Miller, Donald E., and Lorna Touryan Miller. *Survivors: An Oral History of the Armenian Genocide*. University of California Press, 1993.

Morgenthau, Henry. *Ambassador Morgenthau's Story*. Taderon Press, 2000.

Morgenthau, Henry III. *Mostly Morgenthaus: A Family History*. Ticknor & Fields, 1991.

Morison, Elting E., ed. *The Letters of Theodore Roosevelt: The Days of Armageddon, 1914-1919*, vol. 8. Harvard University Press, 1954.

Riggs, Henry H. *Days of Tragedy in Armenia: Personal Experiences in Harpoot, 1915–1917*. Gomidas Institute, 1997.

Roosevelt, Theodore. *Fear God and Take Your Own Part*. George H. Doran, 1916.

Shaw, Stanford J., and Ezel Rural Shaw. *History of the Ottoman Empire and Modern Turkey*, vol. 2. Cambridge University Press, 1977.

Suny, Ronald Grigar. *Looking Toward Ararat: Armenia in Modern History*. Indiana University Press, 1993.

Toynbee, Arnold. *Armenian Atrocities: The Murder of a Nation*. Hodder & Stoughton, 1915.

Werfel, Franz. *The Forty Days of Musa Dagh*. Viking, 1934.

Winter, Jay, and Blaine Baggett. *The Great War and the Shaping of the 20th Century*. Penguin Studio, 1996.

The Holocaust

Arendt, Hannah. *Eichmann in Jerusalem: A Report on the Banality of Evil*. Viking, 1963.

Avisar, Ilan. *Screening the Holocaust: Cinema's Images of the Unimaginable*. Indiana University Press, 1988.

Bartlett, Robert Merrill. *They Stand Invincible: Men Who Are Reshaping Our World*. Thomas Y. Crowell Company, 1959.

Berenbaum, Michael. *The World Must Know: The History of the Holocaust as Told in the United States Holocaust Memorial Museum*. Little, Brown, 1993.

Bierman, John. *Righteous Gentile: The Story of Raul Wallenberg, Missing Hero of the Holocaust*. Viking, 1981.

Block, Gay, and Malka Drucker. *Rescuers: Portraits of Moral Courage in the Holocaust*. Holmes & Meier, 1992.

Breitman, Richard. *Official Secrets: What the Nazis Planned, What the British and Americans Knew*. Hill & Wang, 1998.

Breitman, Richard, and Alan M. Kraut. *American Refugee Policy and European Jewry, 1933–1945*. Indiana University Press, 1987.

Browning, Christopher R. *Ordinary Men: Reserve Police Battalion 101 and the Final Solution in Poland*. HarperCollins, 1992.

Clendinnen, Inga. *Reading the Holocaust*. Cambridge University Press, 1999.

Cole, Tim. *Selling the Holocaust*. Routledge, 1999.

Cole, Wayne S. *Charles A. Lindbergh and the Battle Against American Intervention in World War II*. Harcourt Brace Jovanovich, 1974.

Delbo, Charlotte. *Auschwitz and After*. Yale University Press, 1995.

Favez, Jean-Claude. *The Red Cross and the Holocaust*. Cambridge University Press, 1999.

Feingold, Henry L. *The Politics of Rescue, the Roosevelt Administration and the Holocaust, 1938–1945*. Rutgers University Press, 1970.

Fogelman, Eva. *Conscience and Courage: Rescue of Jews During the Holocaust*. Anchor Books, 1994.

Frank, Anne. *Anne Frank: The Diary of a Young Girl.* Trans. B.M. Mooyart. Double-day, 1993.

Friedlander, Saul, ed. *Probing the Limits of Representation: Nazism and the Final Solu-tion.* Harvard University Press, 1992.

Friedman, Saul S. *No Haven for the Oppressed: United States Policy Toward Jewish Refugees, 1938–1945.* Wayne State University Press, 1973.

Geras, Norman. *The Contract of Mutual Indifference: Political Philosophy After the Holocaust.* Verso, 1998.

German Reich Ministry for National Enlightenment and Propaganda. *The Secret Conferences of Dr. Goebbels; The Nazi Propaganda War, 1939–1943.* E.P. Dutton, 1970.

Gilbert, Martin. *Auschwitz and the Allies.* Holt, Rinehart, and Winston, 1981.

———. *The Second World War.* Fontana/Collins, 1990.

Goldhagen, Daniel Jonah. *Hitler's Willing Executioners: Ordinary Germans and the Holocaust.* Knopf, 1996.

Golub, Jennifer, and Renae Cohen. *What Do Americans Know About the Holocaust?* American Jewish Committee, 1993.

Goodwin, Doris Kearns. *No Ordinary Time.* Simon & Schuster, 1994.

Gross, Jan T. *Neighbors: The Destruction of the Jewish Community in Jedwabne, Poland.* Princeton University Press, 2001.

Hallie, Philip. *Lest Innocent Blood Be Shed: The Story of Le Chambon and How Good-ness Happened There.* Harper & Row, 1979.

Hilberg, Raul. *The Destruction of the European Jews.* Holmes & Meier, 1985.

Horowitz, Gordon J. *In the Shadow of Death: Living Outside the Gates of Mauthausen.* Free Press, 1990.

Insdorf, Annette. *Indelible Shadows: Film and the Holocaust.* Cambridge University Press, 1989.

Jaspers, Karl. *The Question of German Guilt.* Greenwood Press, 1948.

Karski, Jan. *Story of a Secret State.* Houghton Mifflin, 1944.

Katz, Steven T. *The Holocaust in Historical Context.* Vol. 1: *The Holocaust and Mass Death Before the Modern Age.* Oxford University Press, 1994.

Langer, Lawrence L. *Admitting the Holocaust: Collected Essays.* Oxford University Press, 1995.

———. *The Age of Atrocity: Death in Modern Literature.* Beacon Press, 1978.

Lanzmann, Claude. *Shoah: An Oral History of the Holocaust.* Pantheon Books, 1985.

Laqueur, Walter. *The Terrible Secret: An Investigation of the Truth About Hitler's "Final Solution."* Owl Books, 1980.

Laqueur, Walter, and Richard Breitman. *Breaking the Silence.* Simon & Schuster, 1986.

Lemkin, Raphael. *Axis Rule in Occupied Europe: Laws of Occupation, Analysis of Gov-ernment, Proposals for Redress.* Carnegie Endowment for International Peace, Di-vision of International Law, 1944.

Levi, Primo. *The Drowned and the Saved.* Summit Books, 1986.

———. *Survival at Auschwitz: The Nazi Assault on Humanity.* Touchstone, 1996.

Lifton, Robert Jay. *The Nazi Doctors: Medical Killing and the Psychology of Genocide.* Basic Books, 1986.

Linenthal, Edward T. *Preserving Memory: The Struggle to Create America's Holocaust Museum.* Viking, 1995.

Lipstadt, Deborah L. *Beyond Belief: The American Press and the Coming of the Holo-caust, 1933–1945.* Free Press, 1986.

_____. *Denying the Holocaust: The Growing Assault on Truth and Memory.* Maxwell Macmillan International, 1993.

Lochner, Louis Paul. *What About Germany?* Dodd, Mead, 1942.

Lookstein, Haskel. *Were We Our Brothers' Keepers? The Public Response of American Jews to the Holocaust, 1938–1944.* Hartmore House, 1985.

Marrus, Michael R. *The Holocaust in History.* Meridian, 1987.

_____. *The Nuremberg War Crimes Trials, 1945–1946.* Bedford, 1997.

Mazower, Mark. *Dark Continent: Europe's Twentieth Century.* Knopf, 1998.

Meltzer, Milton. *Rescue: The Story of How the Gentiles Saved Jews in the Holocaust.* Harper & Row, 1988.

Miller, Judith. *One by One, by One: Facing the Holocaust.* Simon & Schuster, 1990.

Morse, Arthur D. *While Six Million Died: A Chronicle of American Apathy.* Random House, 1968.

Müller, Ingo. *Hitler's Justice: The Courts of the Third Reich.* Trans. Deborah Schneider. Harvard University Press, 1991.

Novick, Peter. *The Holocaust in American Life.* Houghton Mifflin, 1999.

Oliner, Samuel P., and Pearl M. Oliner. *The Altruistic Personality: Rescuers of Jews in Nazi Europe.* Free Press, 1988.

O'Neill, William L. *A Democracy at War: America's Fight at Home and Abroad in World War II.* Harvard University Press, 1995.

Robinson, Greg. *By Order of the President: FDR and the Internment of Japanese Americans.* Harvard University Press, 2001.

Rosenbaum, Alan S. *Is the Holocaust Unique? Perspectives on Comparative Genocide.* Westview Press, 1996.

Rosenbaum, Ron. *Explaining Hitler: The Search for the Origins of His Evil.* Random House, 1998.

Rosenfeld, Alvin H. *Thinking About the Holocaust: After Half a Century.* Indiana University Press, 1997.

Rubenstein, Richard L. *The Cunning of History: Mass Death and the American Future.* Harper & Row, 1975.

Sereny, Gitta. *Into That Darkness: An Examination of Conscience.* Vintage Books, 1983.

Shandler, Jeffrey. *While America Watches: Televising the Holocaust.* Oxford University Press, 1999.

Simpson, Christopher. *The Splendid Blond Beast: Money, Law and Genocide in the Twentieth Century.* Grove Press, 1993.

Steiner, George. *Language and Silence: Essays on Language, Literature, and the Inhuman.* Yale University Press, 1998.

Visser 't Hooft, and Willem Adolph. *Memoirs.* SCM Press, 1973.

Wiesel, Elie. *All Rivers Run to the Sea: Memoirs.* Knopf, 1996.

Wood, E. Thomas, and Stanislaw M. Jankowski. *Karski: How One Man Tried to Stop the Holocaust.* John Wiley, 1994.

Wyman, David S. *The Abandonment of the Jews: America and the Holocaust, 1941–1945.* New Press, 1998.

_____. *Paper Walls: America and the Refugee Crisis, 1938–1941.* Pantheon Books, 1985.

Wyman, David S., ed. *America and the Holocaust: A Thirteen-Volume Set Documenting the Editor's Book, The Abandonment of the Jews, Vol. 3, The Mock Rescue Conference: Bermuda.* Garland Publishing, Inc., 1990.

Zelizer, Barbara. *Remembering to Forget: Holocaust Memory Through the Camera's Eye.* University of Chicago Press, 1998.

Cambodia

Acharya, Amitav, Pierre Lizée, and Sorpong Peou. *Cambodia: The 1989 Paris Peace Conference, Background Analysis and Documents.* Kraus International Publications, 1991.

Becker, Elizabeth. *When the War Was Over: Cambodia and the Khmer Rouge Revolution.* Public Affairs, 1998.

Bilton, Michael, and Kevin Sim. *Four Hours in My Lai.* Viking, 1992.

Chanda, Nayan. *Brother Enemy: The War After the War.* Harcourt Brace Jovanovich, 1986.

Chandler, David P. *Voices from S-21: Terror and History in Pol Pot's Secret Prison.* University of California Press, 1999.

Fenton, James. *All the Wrong Places: Adrift in the Politics of Asia.* Penguin, 1988.

Haas, Michael. *Genocide by Proxy: Cambodian Pawn on a Superpower Chessboard.* Praeger, 1991.

Hildebrand, George C., and Gareth Porter. *Cambodia: Starvation and Revolution.* Monthly Review Press, 1976.

Jackson, Karl D. *Cambodia, 1975–1978: Rendezvous with Death.* Princeton University Press, 1989.

Kamm, Henry. *Cambodia: Report from a Stricken Land.* Arcade, 1998.

Kiernan, Ben. *How Pol Pot Came to Power: A History of Communism in Kampuchea, 1930–1975.* Verso, 1985.

———. *The Pol Pot Regime: Race, Power, and Genocide in Cambodia Under the Khmer Rouge, 1975–79.* Yale University Press, 1996.

Kiernan, Ben, ed. *Genocide and Democracy in Cambodia: The Khmer Rouge, the United Nations and the International Community.* Yale University Southeast Asia Studies, 1993.

McNamara, Robert S., with Brian Van DeMark. *In Retrospect: The Tragedy and Lessons of Vietnam.* Times Books, 1995.

Metzl, Jamie Frederic. *Western Responses to Human Rights Abuses in Cambodia, 1975–80.* St. Martin's Press, 1996.

National Foreign Assessment Center. *Kampuchea: A Demographic Catastrophe.* Document Expediting (DOCEX) Project, Exchange and Gift Division, Library of Congress, 1980.

Ponchaud, François. *Cambodia, Year Zero.* Penguin, 1978.

Pran, Dith, comp., and Kim DePaul, ed. *Children of Cambodia's Killing Fields: Memoirs by Survivors.* Yale University Press, 1997.

Rodman, Peter W. *More Precious Than Peace: The Cold War and the Struggle for the Third World.* Charles Scribner's Sons, 1994.

Russell, Bertrand. *War Crimes in Vietnam.* Monthly Review Press, 1967.

Schanberg, Sydney H. *The Death and Life of Dith Pran.* Penguin, 1985.

Shawcross, William. *Cambodia's New Deal: A Report.* Carnegie Endowment for International Peace, 1994.

———. *The Quality of Mercy: Cambodia, Holocaust and Modern Conscience.* Simon & Schuster, 1984.

———. *Sideshow: Kissinger, Nixon and the Destruction of Cambodia.* Rev. ed. Simon & Schuster, 1987.

Vann Nath. *A Cambodian Prison Portrait: One Year in the Khmer Rouge's S-21.* White Lotus Press, 1998.

Welaratna, Usha. *Beyond the Killing Fields: Voices of Nine Cambodian Survivors in America.* Stanford University Press, 1993.

Wetterhahn, Ralph. *The Last Battle: The Mayaguez Incident and the End of the Vietnam War.* Carroll & Graf, 2001.

Iraq

Burck, Gordon M., and Charles C. Flowerree. *International Handbook on Chemical Weapons Proliferation.* Greenwood Press, 1991.
Carus, W. Seth. "The Genie Unleashed: Iraq's Chemical and Biological Weapons Program." Policy Papers No. 14. Washington Institute for Near East Policy, 1989.
Chaliand, Gerard, ed. *A People Without a Country: The Kurds and Kurdistan.* Olive Branch Press, 1993.
Cordesman, Anthony H. *Weapons of Mass Destruction in the Middle East.* Brassey's, 1991.
Cordesman, Anthony H., and Abraham R. Wagner. *The Lessons of Modern War.* Vol. 2: *The Iran-Iraq War.* Westview Press, 1990.
Dekker, Ige F., and Harry H. G. Post, eds. *The Gulf War of 1980–1988: The Iran-Iraq War in International Legal Perspective.* Martinus Nijhoff Publishers, 1992.
Eagleton, William. *The Kurdish Republic of 1946.* Oxford University Press, 1963.
Gunter, Michael M. *The Kurds of Iraq: Tragedy and Hope.* St. Martin's Press, 1992.
Hassanpour, Amir. *Nationalism and Language in Kurdistan.* Mellen Research University Press, 1992.
Kreyenbroek, Philip G., and Christine Allison. *Kurdish Culture and Identity.* Zed Books, 1996.
Kreyenbroek, Philip G., and Stefan Sperl, eds. *The Kurds: A Contemporary Overview.* Routledge, 1992.
Laizer, Sheri. *Martyrs, Traitors and Patriots: Kurdistan After the Gulf War.* Zed Books, 1996.
Makiya, Kanan. *Cruelty and Silence: War, Tyranny, Uprising and the Arab World.* W. W. Norton, 1993.
_____. *Republic of Fear: The Politics of Modern Iraq.* University of California Press, 1998.
McDowall, David. *The Kurds.* Minority Rights Group, 1991.
_____. *A Modern History of the Kurds.* I. B. Tauris, 1996.
Meiselas, Susan. *Kurdistan: In the Shadow of History.* Random House, 1997.
Middle East Watch. *Genocide in Iraq: The Anfal Campaign Against the Kurds.* Human Rights Watch, 1993.
_____. *Human Rights in Iraq.* Yale University Press, 1990.
National Security Archive, ed. *Iraqgate: Saddam Hussein, U.S. Policy and the Prelude to the Persian Gulf War (1980–1994).* Chadwyck-Healey, 1995.
Olson, Robert, ed. *The Kurdish Nationalist Movement in the 1990s: Its Impact on Turkey and the Middle East.* University Press of Kentucky, 1996.
Pelletiere, Stephen C. *The Iran-Iraq War: Chaos in a Vacuum.* Praeger, 1992.
Pelletiere, Stephen C., and Douglas V. Johnson II. *Lessons Learned: The Iran-Iraq War.* Strategic Studies Institute, U.S. Army War College, 1991.
Randal, Jonathan C. *After Such Knowledge, What Forgiveness? My Encounters with Kurdistan.* Farrar, Straus and Giroux, 1997.
Shiloah Center for Middle Eastern and African Studies, Tel Aviv University. *Middle East Contemporary Survey.* Vols 1–3. Holmes & Meier, 1978–1980.

U.S. Senate Committee on Foreign Relations. *Chemical Weapons Use in Kurdistan: Iraq's Final Offensive*. 100th Cong., 2nd sess., 1998. S. Prt. 100–148.
———. *War in the Gulf*. 98th Cong., 2nd sess., 1984. S. Prt. 98–225.
———. *War in the Persian Gulf: The U.S. Takes Sides*. 100th Cong., 1st sess., 1987. S. Prt. 100–160.

The Former Yugoslavia

Article 19. *Forging War: The Media in Serbia, Croatia and Bosnia-Herzegovina*. Article 19, 1994.
Banac, Ivo. *The National Question in Yugoslavia: Origins, History, Politics*. Cornell University Press, 1984.
Cohen, Ben, and George Stamkoski, eds. *With No Peace to Keep: United Nations Peacekeeping and the War in the Former Yugoslavia*. Grainpress, 1995.
Cohen, Leonard J. *Broken Bonds: Yugoslavia's Disintegration and Balkan Politics in Transition*. Westview Press, 1995.
Cohen, Roger. *Hearts Grown Brutal: Sagas of Sarajevo*. Random House, 1998.
Cushman, Thomas, and Stjepan G. Mestrovic, eds. *This Time We Knew: Western Responses to Genocide in Bosnia*. New York University Press, 1996.
Daalder, Ivo H. *Getting to Dayton: The Making of America's Bosnia Policy*. Brookings Institution, 2000.
Gjelten, Tom. *Sarajevo Daily: A City and Its Newspaper Under Siege*. HarperCollins, 1995.
Glenny, Misha. *The Fall of Yugoslavia: The Third Balkan War*. Penguin, 1993.
Gutman, Roy. *Witness to Genocide: The 1993 Pulitzer Prize–Winning Dispatches on the "Ethnic Cleansing" of Bosnia*. Macmillan, 1993.
Halberstam, David. *War in a Time of Peace: Bush, Clinton, and the Generals*. Scribner, 2001.
Hall, Brian. *The Impossible Country*. Penguin, 1994.
Haviv, Ron. *Blood and Honey: A Balkan War Journal*. TV Books/Umbrage, 2001.
Helsinki Watch. *War Crimes in Bosnia-Hercegovina*. Vols. 1–2. Human Rights Watch, 1992–1993.
Holbrooke, Richard. *To End a War*. Random House, 1998.
Honig, Jan Willem, and Norbert Both. *Srebrenica: Record of a War Crime*. Penguin, 1997.
Hukanovic, Rezak. *The Tenth Circle of Hell: A Memoir of Life in the Death Camps of Bosnia*. Basic Books, 1996.
Human Rights Watch. *Bosnia-Hercegovina: The Fall of Srebrenica and the Failure of U.N. Peacekeeping*. Human Rights Watch, 1995.
Ignatieff, Michael. *Blood and Belonging*. Farrar, Straus and Giroux, 1994.
———. *The Warrior's Honor: Ethnic War and the Modern Conscience*. Henry Holt, 1998.
International Commission on the Balkans. *Unfinished Peace: Report of the International Commission on the Balkans*. Carnegie Endowment, 1996.
Judah, Tim. *The Serbs: History, Myth, and the Destruction of Yugoslavia*. Yale University Press, 1997.
Kaplan, Robert. *Balkan Ghosts: A Journey Through History*. St. Martin's Press, 1993.
Malcolm, Noel. *Bosnia: A Short History*. New York University Press, 1996.
Mestrovic, Stjepan, ed. *The Conceit of Innocence: Losing the Conscience of the West in the War Against Bosnia*. Texas A&M University Press, 1997.

Mousavizadeh, Nader, ed. *The Black Book of Bosnia: The Consequences of Appeasement*. New Republic–Basic Books, 1996.

Owen, Robert C., ed. *Deliberate Force: A Case Study in Effective Air Campaigning*. Air University Press, 2000.

Peress, Gilles. *Farewell to Bosnia*. Scala, 1994.

Rieff, David. *Slaughterhouse: Bosnia and the Failure of the West*. Simon & Schuster, 1995.

Rogel, Carole. *The Breakup of Yugoslavia and the War in Bosnia*. Greenwood Press, 1998.

Rohde, David. *Endgame: The Betrayal and Fall of Srebrenica, Europe's Worst Massacre Since World War II*. Farrar, Straus and Giroux, 1997.

Silber, Laura, and Allan Little. *Yugoslavia: Death of a Nation*. Penguin, 1997.

Stover, Eric, and Gilles Peress. *The Graves: Srebrenica and Vukovar*. Scalo, 1998.

Sudetic, Chuck. *Blood and Vengeance: One Family's Story of the War in Bosnia*. Norton, 1998.

Thompson, Mark. *A Paper House: The Ending of Yugoslavia*. Pantheon Books, 1992.

United Nations. *Report of the Secretary General Pursuant to General Assembly Resolution 53/35: The Fall of Srebrenica*. UN Doc. No. A/54/549, November 15, 1999.

Vulliamy, Ed. *Seasons in Hell: Understanding Bosnia's War*. St. Martin's Press, 1994.

West, Rebecca. *Black Lamb and Grey Falcon: A Journey Through Yugoslavia*. Viking, 1941.

Western, Jon. "Warring Ideas: Explaining U.S. Military Intervention in Regional Conflicts." Ph.D. diss., Columbia University, 2000.

Zimmermann, Warren. *Origins of a Catastrophe: Yugoslavia and Its Destroyers—the Last Ambassador Tells What Happened and Why*. Times Books, 1996.

Zimmermann, Warren, [et al.] *Bosnia: What Went Wrong? A Foreign Affairs Reader*. Council on Foreign Relations, 1998.

Rwanda

Adelman, Howard, and Astri Suhrke, eds. *The Path of a Genocide: The Rwanda Crisis from Uganda to Zaire*. Transaction, 1999.

African Rights. *Rwanda: Death, Despair, Defiance*. African Rights, 1995.

Barnett, Michael. *Eyewitness to a Genocide: The United Nations and Rwanda*. Cornell University Press, 2002.

Berkeley, Bill. *The Graves Are Not Yet Full: Race, Tribe and Power in the Heart of Africa*. Basic Books, 2001.

Des Forges, Alison. *Leave None to Tell the Story: Genocide in Rwanda*. Human Rights Watch, 1999.

Destexhe, Alain. *Rwanda and Genocide in the Twentieth Century*. New York University Press, 1995.

Feil, Scott R. *Preventing Genocide: How the Early Use of Force Might Have Succeeded in Rwanda*. Carnegie Corporation of New York, 1998.

Gourevitch, Philip. *We Wish to Inform You That Tomorrow We Will Be Killed with Our Families: Stories from Rwanda*. Farrar, Straus and Giroux, 1998.

Human Rights Watch. *The Aftermath of Genocide in Rwanda: Absence of Prosecution, Continued Killings*. Human Rights Watch, 1994.

_____. *Beyond the Rhetoric: Continuing Human Rights Abuses in Rwanda*. Human Rights Watch, 1993.

_____. *Shattered Lives: Sexual Violence During the Rwandan Genocide and Its After-math*. Human Rights Watch, 1996.

Keane, Fergal. *Season of Blood: A Rwanda Journey.* Viking, 1995.

Klinghoffer, Arthur Jay. *The International Dimension of Genocide in Rwanda.* New York University Press, 1998.

Kuperman, Alan J. *The Limits of Humanitarian Intervention: Genocide in Rwanda.* Brookings Institution, 2001.

Lemarchand, René. *Rwanda and Burundi.* Praeger, 1970.

Mamdani, Mahmood. *When Victims Become Killers: Colonialism, Nativism, and the Genocide in Rwanda.* Princeton University Press, 2001.

Melvern, Linda. *A People Betrayed: The Role of the West in Rwanda's Genocide.* Zed Books, 2000.

Moore, Jonathan, ed. *Hard Choices: Moral Dilemmas in Humanitarian Intervention.* Rowman & Littlefield, 1998.

Organization of African Unity, International Panel of Eminent Personalities to Investigate the 1994 Genocide in Rwanda and the Surrounding Events. *Rwanda: The Preventable Genocide.* Organization of African Unity, 2000.

Peress, Gilles. *The Silence.* Scalo, 1995.

Peterson, Scott. *Me Against My Brother: At War in Somalia, Sudan, and Rwanda.* Routledge, 2000.

Prunier, Gerard. *The Rwanda Crisis: History of a Genocide.* Columbia University Press, 1995.

United Nations. *Report of the Independent Inquiry into the Actions of the United Nations During the 1994 Genocide in Rwanda.* UN Doc. No. A/54/549. December 15, 1999.

Uvin, Peter. *Aiding Violence: The Development Enterprise in Rwanda.* Kumarian Press, 1998.

Kosovo

Buckley, William Joseph, ed. *Kosovo: Contending Voices on Balkan Interventions.* William B. Eerdmans, 2000.

Clark, Wesley K. *Waging Modern War: Bosnia, Kosovo, and the Future of Combat.* Public Affairs, 2001.

Daalder, Ivo, and Michael O'Hanlon. *Winning Ugly: NATO's War to Save Kosovo.* Brookings Institution, 2000.

Ignatieff, Michael. *Virtual War: Kosovo and Beyond.* Metropolitan Books, 2000.

Independent International Commission on Kosovo. *The Kosovo Report: Conflict, International Response, Lessons Learned.* Oxford University Press, 2001.

Judah, Tim. *Kosovo: War and Revenge.* Yale University Press, 2000.

Malcolm, Noel. *Kosovo: A Short History.* New York University Press, 1998.

Physicians for Human Rights. *War Crimes in Kosovo: A Population-Based Assessment of Human Rights Violations Against Kosovar Albanians.* Physicians for Human Rights, 1999.

U.S. State Department. *Ethnic Cleansing in Kosovo: An Accounting.* U.S. State Department, 1999.

Vickers, Miranda, and James Pettifer. *Albania: From Anarchy to a Balkan Identity.* New York University Press, 1997.

General History and Politics

Allison, Graham. *The Essence of Decision: Explaining the Cuban Missile Crisis.* Little, Brown, 1971.

Anderson, Benedict. *Imagined Communities: Reflections on the Origin and Spread of Nationalism.* Verso, 1983.

Baker, James A. III, with Thomas M. DeFrank. *The Politics of Diplomacy: Revolution, War and Peace, 1989–1992.* G. P. Putnam's Sons, 1995.

Becker, Ernest. *The Denial of Death.* Free Press, 1973.

Berlin, Isaiah. *The Crooked Timber of Humanity: Chapters in the History of Ideas.* John Murray, 1990.

Beschloss, Michael, and Strobe Talbott. *At the Highest Level: The Inside Story of the End of the Cold War.* Little, Brown, 1993.

Boutros-Ghali, Boutros. *Unvanquished: A U.S.-U.N. Saga.* Random House, 1999.

Bowden, Mark. *Black Hawk Down: A Story of Modern War.* Atlantic Monthly Press, 1999.

Brodsky, Joseph. *Less Than One: Selected Essays.* Farrar, Straus and Giroux, 1986.

Brzezinski, Zbigniew. *Power and Principle: Memoirs of the National Security Adviser, 1977–1981.* Farrar, Straus, and Giroux, 1985.

Bush, George H. W., and Brent Scowcroft. *A World Transformed.* Knopf, 1998.

Christopher, Warren. *Chances of a Lifetime.* Scribner, 2001.

Clinton, W. David. *The Two Faces of National Interest.* Louisiana State University Press, 1994.

Cohen, Stanley. *States of Denial: Knowing About Atrocities and Suffering.* Polity Press, 2001.

Cramer, Richard Ben. *Bob Dole.* Vintage Books, 1995.

_____. *What It Takes: The Way to the White House.* Random House, 1990.

Crozier, Michel. *The Bureaucratic Phenomenon.* University of Chicago Press, 1967.

Damrosch, Lori Fisler. *Enforcing Restraint: Collective Intervention in Internal Conflicts.* Council on Foreign Relations Press, 1993.

Dobbs, Michael. *Madeleine Albright.* Henry Holt, 1999.

Drew, Elizabeth. *On The Edge: The Clinton Presidency.* Simon & Schuster, 1994.

Fishkin, James S. *The Limits of Obligation.* Yale University Press, 1982.

Gamson, William A. *Talking Politics.* Cambridge University Press, 1992.

Gay, Peter. *The Cultivation of Hatred.* Norton, 1993.

Gelb, Leslie, and Richard Betts. *The Irony of Vietnam: The System Worked.* Brookings Institution, 1979.

Gellner, Ernest. *Nations and Nationalism.* Cornell University Press, 1983.

Gilbert, Felix. *To the Farewell Address: Ideas of Early American Foreign Policy.* Princeton University Press, 1961.

Glendon, Mary Ann. *A World Made New: Eleanor Roosevelt and the Universal Declaration of Human Rights.* Random House, 2001.

Goodwin, Richard. *Remembering America.* Little, Brown, 1988.

Haass, Richard. *Intervention: The Use of American Military Force in the Post Cold War World.* Brookings Institution, 1999.

_____. *The Reluctant Sheriff: The United States, After the Cold War.* Council on Foreign Relations Press, 1997.

Halberstam, David. *The Best and the Brightest.* Random House, 1972.

Halperin, Morton H. *Bureaucratic Politics and Foreign Policy.* Brookings Institution, 1974.

Hartz, Louis. *The Liberal Tradition in America: An Interpretation of American Political Thought Since the Revolution.* Harcourt Brace, 1955.

Hearden, Patrick J. *Vietnam: Four American Perspectives: Lectures by George S. McGovern.* Purdue University Press, 1990.

Henkin, Louis. *The Age of Rights.* Columbia University Press, 1990.

Hersh, Seymour M. *The Price of Power: Kissinger in the Nixon White House.* Summit Books, 1983.

Hirsch, John L., and Robert B. Oakley. *Somalia and Operation Restore Hope: Reflections on Peacemaking and Peacekeeping.* United States Institute of Peace Press, 1995.

Hirschman, Albert O. *Exit, Voice, and Loyalty: Responses to Decline in Firms, Organizations and States.* Harvard University Press, 1970.

——————. *The Passions and the Interests: Political Arguments for Capitalism Before Its Triumph.* Princeton University Press, 1977.

——————. *The Rhetoric of Reaction: Perversity, Futility, Jeopardy.* Belknap Press, 1991.

Hobsbawm, Eric. *Nations and Nationalism Since 1780: Programme, Myth, Reality.* Cambridge University Press, 1990.

Hoffmann, Stanley. *Duties Beyond Borders: On the Limits and Possibilities of Ethical International Politics.* Syracuse University Press, 1981.

——————. *The Ethics and Politics of Humanitarian Intervention.* University of Notre Dame Press, 1996.

Humphrey, John P. *Human Rights and the United Nations: A Great Adventure.* Transnational Publishers, 1984.

Isaacson, Walter. *Kissinger: A Biography.* Simon & Schuster, 1992.

Jackall, Robert. *Moral Mazes: The World of Corporate Managers.* Oxford University Press, 1988.

Janello, Amy, and Brennon Jones, eds. *A Global Affair: An Inside Look at the United Nations.* Jones & Janello, 1995.

Johnson, Robert David. *The Peace Progressives and American Foreign Relations.* Harvard University Press, 1995.

Kelsen, Hans. *Peace Through Law.* University of North Carolina Press, 1944.

Kennedy, John F. *Profiles in Courage.* Harper, 1956.

Knightley, Phillip. *The First Casualty: From the Crimea to Vietnam: The War Correspondent as Hero, Propagandist and Myth Maker.* Harcourt Brace Jovanovich, 1975.

Korey, William. *NGOs and the Universal Declaration of Human Rights: "A Curious Grapevine."* St. Martin's Press, 1998.

Krasner, Stephen. *Sovereignty: Organized Hypocrisy.* Princeton University Press, 1999.

Kull, Steven, and I. M. Destler. *Misreading the Public: The Myth of a New Isolationism.* Brookings Institution, 1999.

Lippman, Thomas. *Madeleine Albright and the New American Diplomacy.* Westview Press, 2000.

Lippmann, Walter. *Public Opinion.* Harcourt Brace, 1922.

——————. *The Public Philosophy.* Little, Brown, 1955.

Mansbridge, Jane J., ed. *Beyond Self-Interest.* University of Chicago Press, 1990.

May, Ernest R. *"Lessons" of the Past: The Use and Misuse of History in American Foreign Policy.* Oxford University Press, 1973.

McDougall, Walter. *Promised Land, Crusader State: The American Encounter with the World Since 1776.* Houghton Mifflin, 1997.

Milgram, Stanley. *Obedience to Authority: An Experimental View.* Harper & Row, 1974.

Moeller, Susan. *Compassion Fatigue: How the Media Sell Disease, Famine, War, and Death.* Routledge, 1999.

Morgenthau, Hans J., and Kenneth W. Thompson. *Politics Among Nations: The Struggle for Power and Peace.* 6th ed. Knopf, 1985.

Morris, Dick. *Behind the Oval Office: Winning the Presidency in the Nineties.* Random House, 1997.

Morris, Roger. *Uncertain Greatness: Henry Kissinger and American Foreign Policy.* Harper & Row, 1977.

Muravchik, Joshua. *The Uncertain Crusade: Jimmy Carter and the Dilemmas of Human Rights Policy.* Hamilton Press, 1986.

Neustadt, Richard E., and Ernest R. May. *Thinking in Time: The Uses of History for Decision-Makers.* Free Press, 1986.

Nicolson, Harold George. *Peacemaking 1919.* P. Smith, 1984.

Niebuhr, Reinhold. *Moral Man and Immoral Society: A Study in Ethics and Politics.* Charles Scribner's Sons, 1932.

Powell, Colin, with Joseph E. Persico. *My American Journey.* Random House, 1995.

Public Papers of the Presidents of the United States: Jimmy Carter, 1979. GPO, 1979.

Public Papers of the Presidents of the United States: Ronald Reagan, 1987. GPO, 1987.

Ratcliffe, James M., ed. *The Good Samaritan and the Law.* Anchor Books, 1966.

Reed, Laura W., and Carl Kaysen. *Emerging Norms of Justified Intervention.* American Academy of Arts and Sciences, 1993.

Scarry, Elaine. *The Body in Pain: The Making and Unmaking of the World.* Oxford University Press, 1985.

Sheleff, Leon Shaskolsky. *The Bystander: Behavior, Law, Ethics.* Lexington Books, 1978.

Shklar, Judith. *Legalism: Law, Morals and Political Trials.* Harvard University Press, 1986.

_____. *Ordinary Vices.* Belknap Press of Harvard University Press, 1984.

Shute, Stephen, and Susan Hurley, eds. *On Human Rights: The Oxford Amnesty Lectures 1993.* Basic Books, 1993.

Smith, Tony. *Foreign Attachments: The Power of Ethnic Groups in the Making of American Foreign Policy.* Harvard University Press, 2000.

Sobel, Richard. *The Impact of Public Opinion on U.S. Foreign Policy Since Vietnam: Constraining the Colossus.* Oxford University Press, 2001.

Stephanopoulos, George. *All Too Human: A Political Education.* Little, Brown, 1998.

Stewart, Graham. *Burying Caesar: Churchill, Chamberlain, and the Battle for the Tory Party.* Weidenfeld and Nicolson, 1999.

Strobel, Warren P. *Late-Breaking Foreign Policy: The News Media's Influence on Peace Operations.* United States Institute of Peace Press, 1997.

Sykes, Jay G. *Proxmire.* R. B. Luce, 1972.

Szulc, Tad. *The Illusion of Peace: Foreign Policy in the Nixon Years.* Viking, 1978.

Tananbaum, Duane. *The Bricker Amendment Controversy: A Test of Eisenhower's Political Leadership.* Cornell University Press, 1988.

Taylor, John. *War Photography: Realism in the British Press.* Routledge, 1991.

Walzer, Michael. *The Company of Critics: Social Criticism and Political Commitment in the Twentieth Century.* Basic Books, 1988.

_____. *Just and Unjust Wars: A Moral Argument with Historical Illustrations.* 2nd ed. Basic Books, 1992.

Wills, Garry. *Inventing America: Jefferson's Declaration of Independence.* Doubleday, 1978.

Woodward, Bob. *The Agenda: Inside the Clinton White House*. Simon & Schuster, 1994.

_____. *The Choice*. Simon & Schuster, 1996.

Genocide

Andreopoulos, George J., ed. *Genocide: Conceptual and Historical Dimensions*. University of Pennsylvania Press, 1994.

Arendt, Hannah. *The Origins of Totalitarianism*. Harcourt, Brace, 1951.

Bowen, Michael, Gary Freeman, and Kay Miller. *Passing By: The United States and Genocide in Burundi*. Carnegie Endowment for International Peace, 1973.

Chalk, Frank Robert, and Kurt Jonassohn. *The History and Sociology of Genocide: Analyses and Case Studies*. Yale University Press, 1990.

Chang, Iris. *The Rape of Nanking: The Forgotten Holocaust of World War II*. Basic Books, 1997.

Charny, Israel W., ed. *Genocide: A Critical Bibliographic Review*. Mansell, 1998.

_____. *How Can We Commit the Unthinkable? Genocide: The Human Cancer*. Hearst Books, 1982.

_____, ed. *Toward the Understanding and Prevention of Genocide: Proceedings of the International Conference on the Holocaust and Genocide*. Westview Press, 1984.

Churchill, Ward. *A Little Matter of Genocide: Holocaust and Denial in the Americas, 1492 to the Present*. City Lights Books, 1997.

Conquest, Robert. *The Harvest of Sorrow: Soviet Collectivization and the Terror-Famine*. Oxford University Press, 1986.

Dunn, James. *Timor: A People Betrayed*. ABC Books, 1996.

Fein, Helen. *Accounting for Genocide: National Responses and Jewish Victimization During the Holocaust*. Free Press, 1979.

Hochschild, Adam. *King Leopold's Ghost: A Story of Greed, Terror, and Heroism in Colonial Africa*. Houghton Mifflin, 1998.

Horowitz, Irving Louis. *Taking Lives: Genocide and State Power*. Transaction, 1997.

Jacobs, Dan. *The Brutality of Nations*. Knopf, 1987.

Jonassohn, Kurt, and Karin Solveig Bjornson. *Genocide and Gross Human Rights Violations*. Transaction, 1998.

Korey, William. *An Epitaph for Raphael Lemkin*. Jacob Blaustein Institute for the Advancement of Human Rights, 2001.

Kuper, Leo. *Genocide: Its Political Use in the Twentieth Century*. Yale University Press, 1981.

LeBlanc, Lawrence J. *The United States and the Genocide Convention*. Duke University Press, 1991.

Lemarchand, René. *Burundi: Ethnic Conflict and Genocide*. Woodrow Wilson Center Press, 1996.

_____. *Burundi: Ethnocide as Discourse and Practice*. Woodrow Wilson Center Press, 1994.

Lemkin, Raphael. Personal papers. Microfilm. New York Public Library Collection.

Lifschultz, Lawrence, *Bangladesh, The Unfinished Revolution,* Zed Press, 1979.

Muhith, A. M. A. *American Response to Bangladesh Liberation War*. University Press Limited, 1996.

Nekrich, Aleksandr M. *The Punished Peoples: The Deportation and Fate of Soviet Minorities at the End of the Second World War*. Norton, 1978.

Packenham, Thomas. *The Scramble for Africa: The White Man's Conquest of the Dark Continent from 1876 to 1912.* Random House, 1991.

Rabe, John. *The Good Man of Nanking: The Diaries of John Rabe.* Knopf, 1998.

Rotberg, Robert I., and Thomas G. Weiss. *From Massacres to Genocide: The Media, Public Policy and Humanitarian Crises.* Brookings Institution, 1996.

Rummel, R. J. *Lethal Politics: Soviet Genocide and Mass Murder Since 1917.* Transaction, 1990.

Sartre, Jean-Paul. *On Genocide.* Beacon Press, 1968.

Schabas, William A. *Genocide in International Law: The Crimes of Crimes.* Cambridge University Press, 2000.

Staub, Ervin. *The Roots of Evil: The Origins of Genocide and Other Group Violence.* Cambridge University Press, 1989.

Taylor, John G. *East Timor: The Price of Freedom.* Zed Books, 1999.

Todorov, Tzvetan. *The Conquest of America: The Question of the Other.* Harper & Row, 1984.

_____. *Facing the Extreme: Moral Life in the Concentration Camps.* Metropolitan Books, 1996.

Totten, Samuel, William S. Parsons, and Isreal W. Charny, eds. *A Century of Genocide: Eyewitness Accounts and Critical Views.* Garland, 1997.

Wallimann, Isidor, and Michael N. Dobkowski, eds. *Genocide and the Modern Age: Etiology and Case Studies of Mass Death.* Greenwood Press, 1987.

International Justice

Ball, Howard. *Prosecuting War Crimes and Genocide: The Twentieth Century Experience.* University Press of Kansas, 1999.

Bass, Gary Jonathan. *Stay the Hand of Vengeance: The Politics of War Crimes Tribunals.* Princeton University Press, 2000.

Bassiouni, M. Cherif. *Crimes Against Humanity in International Criminal Law.* M. Nijhoff Publishers and Kluwer Academic Publishers, 1992.

Brackman, Arnold C. *The Other Nuremberg: The Untold Story of the Tokyo War Crimes Trials.* Morrow, 1987.

Cassese, Antonio. *Violence and Law in the Modern Age.* Princeton University Press, 1988.

Fuller, Lon L. *The Morality of Law.* Yale University Press, 1964.

Goldstone, Richard J. *For Humanity: Reflections of a War Crimes Investigator.* Yale University Press, 2000.

Hart, Herbert Lionel Adolphus. *The Concept of Law.* Oxford University Press, 1961.

Hayner, Priscilla B. *Unspeakable Truths: Confronting State Terror and Atrocity.* Routledge, 2001.

Kritz, Neil, ed. *Transitional Justice.* 3 vols. United States Institute of Peace, 1995.

Maguire, Peter H. *Law and War: An American Story.* Columbia University Press, 2000.

Minow, Martha. *Between Vengeance and Forgiveness: Facing History After Genocide and Mass Violence.* Beacon Press, 1998.

Morris, Virginia, and Michael P. Scharf. *An Insider's Guide to the Criminal Tribunal for the Former Yugoslavia: A Documentary History and Analysis.* Transnational Publishers, 1995.

_____. *An Insider's Guide to the Criminal Tribunal for Rwanda.* Transnational Publishers, 1998.

Neier, Aryeh. *War Crimes: Brutality, Genocide, Terror, and the Struggle for Justice.* Times Books, 1998.

Osiel, Mark. *Mass Atrocity, Collective Memory, and the Law.* Transaction, 1997.

Persico, Joseph. *Nuremberg: Infamy on Trial.* Viking, 1994.

Post, Robert, and Carla Hesse, eds. *Human Rights in Political Transitions: Gettysburg to Bosnia.* Zone Books, 1999.

Scharf, Michael P. *Balkan Justice: The Story Behind the First International War Crimes Trial Since Nuremberg.* Carolina Academic Press, 1997.

Sewall, Sarah, and Carl Kaysen, eds. *The United States and the International Criminal Court: National Security and International Law.* Rowman & Littlefield, 2000.

Taylor, Telford. *The Anatomy of the Nuremberg Trials: A Personal Memoir.* Knopf, 1992.

_____. *Nuremberg and Vietnam: An American Tragedy.* Quadrangle, 1970.

Teitel, Ruti G. *Transitional Justice.* Oxford University Press, 2000.

Weschler, Lawrence. *A Miracle, a Universe: Settling Accounts with Torturers.* University of Chicago Press, 1990.

West, Rebecca. *A Train of Powder: Six Reports on the Problem of Guilt and Punishment in Our Time.* Viking, 1955.

Acknowledgments

The list of those who have aided and abetted this project, while they inspired its author, is long.

The book is very much the product of energy and insights generated at the Carr Center for Human Rights Policy at the Kennedy School of Government. Greg Carr's vision produced the Center, and his commitment sustains it. I am grateful to him and to Graham Allison, who brought me on board. Center director Michael Ignatieff offered constant encouragement, even when it meant enduring a distracted executive director. Jill Clarke somehow managed to keep the Center afloat and the trains running early, while ensuring that I never missed an interview. Serge Troie, my brilliant research assistant, dug so deep that he could now write his own multivolume encyclopedia on U.S. responses to genocide. Jeremy Freeman stepped in heroically to supply crucial research support and commentary in the book's hectic, final days. Ingrid Tamm Grudin supplied sage advice through the project's multiple incarnations. Camilla Catenza, Jim Fleming, Jasmine Friedman, Jess Hobart, and the peerless Sarah Sewall have helped build a first-class institution that will produce cutting-edge policy analysis for years to come.

A grant from George Soros's Open Society Institute enabled me to interview hundreds of men and women from Cambodia, Kurdistan, Rwanda, and Bosnia. Many of these survivors were willing to relive their trauma because they thought their stories might play a small role in sparking rescue for others. Their testimony, combined with their resilient faith in the United States, were constant motivators. I am grateful also to the current and former U.S. government officials who opened themselves up, revisiting experiences that most had hoped would remain forgotten. A few appeared as characters in this book, but most are visible only indirectly in the narratives reconstructed or the perspectives conveyed. I have tried to portray the logic behind their decisions and non-decisions fairly. If I have strayed in fact or in tone, I hope that they will step forward and offer their own accounts.

600 ACKNOWLEDGMENTS

More detailed and more international examinations of these cases and new studies of others are needed. An organization that will galvanize future research is the National Security Archive, the invaluable Washington non-profit organization that uses the Freedom of Information Act to secure the declassification of U.S. government documents. When I interned at the Archive as a college sophomore, I had no idea how much I would later benefit from their work. Will Ferroggiaro, director of their Rwanda project, deserves special thanks. Many senior officials in the U.S. government agreed to speak with me only because he granted me access to documents that bore their signatures.

The indefatigable Morton Abramowitz, my first boss, has been a steady compass. It was his advocacy on Bosnia, combined with the prescriptive genius of the late, great Frederick C. Cuny, that convinced me to move to the Balkans to see for myself what might be done. Several years later, as I began my first round of Washington interviews, my cell phone rang. Mort had something urgent he wished to impart. "As you begin interviewing people, you have to guard against two things," he grumbled, "selective memory and absolute dishonesty." I did not know then that he would pop up as a character in so many of the cases, but my reporting has only confirmed that his candor and conviction predated the Bosnia war. Sometime in the final month of my writing, he called again, this time with a question. "In all of your research," he asked, "did any American official ever say to you, without going on about all the constraints they faced, 'Boy, I really blew it!'" As I looked back through dozens of notebooks, I realized that only one had done so: Mort himself. I am honored to have worked with him. I know I have learned from him; I hope it shows.

Four individuals played pivotal roles six years ago in encouraging me to turn an amateur, sweeping survey of U.S. responses to genocide into a book. Miro Weinberger, my trusted friend for whom all things seem possible, pressed me to explain and not merely expose the gap between American promise and practice on genocide. Anthony Lewis, whose columns had helped keep Bosnia "on the map" in the United States even as it vanished from the maps of the Balkans, convinced me nothing like it had been done. Martin Peretz, whose *New Republic* had given me a voice during the Bosnia war and given U.S. policy-makers an appropriately difficult time, helped convince Basic Books to publish it. And Leon Wieseltier, the wisest man in Washington and the most stirring moralist around, offered cherished counsel from start to weary finish.

For their support from near and far, I thank Arthur Applbaum, Murat Armbruster, Amy Bach, Doreen Beinart, Peter Berkowitz, Tom Blanton, Julian Borger, Charlotte Bourke, Steven Bourke, Bina Breitner, Sally Brooks, Robert Brustein, Diane Caldwell, Gillian Caldwell, Jack Caldwell, Casey Cammann, Mark Casey, Lenore Cohen, Roger Cohen, Rebecca Dale, Romeo Dallaire, Owen Dawson, Debra Dickerson, Christine Dionne, Scott Faber, Gregg Farano, Helen Fein, Marshall Ganz, David Gelber, Pumla Gobodo-Madikizela, Oren Harman, Lukas Haynes, Arnold Hiatt, Stanley Hoffman, Hrvoje Hranski, Swanee Hunt, Tom Keenan, Peter Kornbluh, Roy Kreitner, Kate Lowenstein, Victor Luftig, Jane Mansbridge, Pedro Martinez, Taddy McAllister, Erin McBreen, Jamie Metzl, Bob Mnookin, Katie Moore, Elizabeth Neuffer, Luis Ocampo, Frank Pearl, Ann Peretz, Stephen Power, Josh Prager, David Rieff, Ken Roth, Debra Ryan, Maurice Saah, Moshe Safdie, John Schumann, Alexis Sinduhije, Anne-Marie Slaughter, Mary Smart, Alison Smith, Chuck Sudetic, Stacy Sullivan, Doug Stone, Fred Strebeigh, Rebecca Symington, Margaret Talbot, Piotr Wandycz, Liz Wilcox, and Curt Wood.

I am especially indebted to those who took the time to read drafts, saving me from errors and steering me in new directions. Martha Minow taught me how to look at law with an eye to its political underpinnings and moral consequences. Nick Papandreou, the unlucky first reader of the first draft of the book, brought his novelist's eye and crusader's heart to a messy text. A wonderful range of friends and colleagues offered comments: Michael Barnett, Gary Jonathan Bass, Elizabeth Becker, Antonia Chayes, Ben Cohen, Chuck Cohen, Alison des Forges, Craig Etcheson, Kate Galbraith, Arkadi Gerney, Philip Gourevitch, Joost Hilterman, Jonathan Moore, Andy Moravscik, Aryeh Neier, Jennifer Pitts, Jonathan Randal, Frederick Wiseman, and Jay Winter. I am grateful to Mike Kelly, Cullen Murphy, and Yvonne Rolzhausen at the *Atlantic Monthly* for the phenomenal care they devoted to my Rwanda article, and to Ron Haviv, Susan Meiseles, and Gilles Peress who graced the book's pages with their stunning photographs.

Two individuals got *"A Problem from Hell"* into print. Sarah Chalfant at the Wylie Agency took me on as a client when this book was no more than a gleam in an unemployed law-student's eye. She never let the publishing world's bouts of indifference shake her faith in the project's value. Vanessa Mobley, my editor at Basic Books, fought for and promoted the book with a rare combination of zeal and grace. I was blessed to have such a committed, talented duo behind me. Gail Winston and Christine Walsh at HarperCollins trusted that the book could reach a wider audience and gave its message an energized new life in paperback. Jim Fussell delivered an index that has rendered the book and its lessons far more accessible to scholars and casual readers.

And finally, I must thank my dream team. Seven courageous friends—Holly Burkhalter, Sharon Dolovich, Laura Pitter, David Rohde, Elizabeth Rubin, Elliot Thomson, and the aforementioned Miro Weinberger—guided me by listening, by doing, and by being unashamed to don cocktail umbrellas in the rain. Anna Husarska, who shares more than a birthday and a homeland with Raphael Lemkin, taught me how to report war and observe people. Frederick Zollo introduced me to an America I had never seen, stocked my library, insisted this book mattered when it seemed it couldn't, and became the voice inside my head that kept me honest. Michal Safdie offered comfort and passion at the most difficult times. She made her family my family and supplied daily sustenance and beauty. With their boundless generosity, Doris Kearns Goodwin and Dick Goodwin kept me off the disabled list. And with their insights into American politics and faith in America's potential, they reminded me why it was worth hunting for the "better angels." Sayres Rudy gave me his time, his critical mind, his wit, and his unswerving friendship. He left me dazed and the book changed.

And my parents, Vera Delaney and Edmund Bourke: When their twenty-three-year-old daughter told them she wanted to go and cover a war where innocent people were dying, they hoped it was a phase that would soon pass. When it didn't, they reluctantly joined the charge, buying her an inaugural lap-top, neatly storing away a mound of Bosnia clips, and poring over every last word of every last draft of this book. Apart from being my parents, my teachers, and my closest friends, they are quite simply the two most extraordinary individuals I have ever met.

—*Samantha J. Power*

Index

United States
  Armenian massacres, response to, xix, 5,
    13–14
  Balkan atrocities, knowledge of, 264–269
  Bosnia, opposition to intervention in,
    260–263
  Bosnia, backing statehood for, 249
  domestic politics, xviii, 503, 509
  elections: *1992*, 274, 286; *1994*, 359;
    1996, 424, 431
  genocide convention, opposition to,
    65–70;
    Proxmire and, 79–85, 155–161,
    165–169;
    ratification of, 163–169
  Hitler, suppression of truth about,
    34–35
  Holocaust, indifference during,
    128–129
  Iraqi Kurds, response to genocide
    against, 173, 185–186, 190–195,
    203–212
  Marines, witness Rwandan genocide,
    354
  military campaigns abroad, justification
    for, 305–306
  modest progress in response to geno-
    cide, 503
  opposition to ICC, 491
  Pentagon, 122, 330, 332, 342, 366,
    370–373, 379–381, 383, 413, 423,
    426, 438, 444, 451, 456–457, 459
  public opinion, 276, 289, 294, 304–305
  silence, society–wide, xviii, 122, 229,
    373–377, 509
  terrorism and, 511–512
Universal Declaration of Human Rights
  (UDHR), 74
universal jurisdiction, principle of 19–22
UNPROFOR, 281, 304, 396, 403
U.S. State Department. *see also* Albright,
  Baker, Christopher, Kissinger, Lans-
  ing, Muskie, Shultz, Vance
  Dissent Channel, 287, 292, 515
  dissenters, 287, 301, 311–318, 503
  Intelligence and Research (INR),
    209–210, 292, 320–321
  Legal Advisor's Office, 124, 245, 321, 372
  Near Eastern Affairs, Bureau for (NEA),
    209–210, 224–226
  Office of War Crimes Analysis, 467

  Open Forum, 296–298, 410, 515
  Riegner Telegram, 34
Uwilingiyimana, Agathe, 330, 331–332

Van Hollen, Chris, 212–216
Vance, Cyrus, 136, 142, 147, 259–260
"victor's justice," 492
Vieira de Mello, Sergio, 398
Vietnam
  Cambodia, attacks from, 140–142
  Cambodia, mass murders and, 142–145
  Cambodia, occupation of, 148–149
  lessons from, 283–285, 294, 315
  relations with Khmer Rouge, 136–137
  "syndrome," 261
  U.S. policy toward, 146–147
Viorst, Milton, 223–224
Vishinsky, Andrei, 53
Vulliamy, Ed, 271, 275, 277

Walker, Steven, 314–315, 428
Walker, Amb. William, 446–447
Wallace, Vice Pres. Henry, 27–28
Walzer, Michael, 461–462
War Crimes Commission, 80–81, 204, 291,
  482–483
war crimes tribunal; for former Yugoslavia.
  see International Criminal Tribunal
  for the former Yugoslavia; for
  Rwanda. *see* International Criminal
  Tribunal for Rwanda
War Refugee Board (1944), 35, 44
warning. *see also* evidence of genocide
  identity cards, used to target groups,
    350
  informants, warnings of, 343–344
  lists, used to target groups, 144, 249, 333,
    500
  massacres, Croatia, 254–255; early
    Rwandan massacres, 337; Halabja
    massacre, 188–193; Racak (Kosovo),
    446; Srebrenica massacre, 393–398,
    400
  militias, formation and training of, 252,
    337–338
  peacekeepers, held hostage or massacred,
    332, 392, 394–439
  relocation, 87–90, 96, 104–107, 175,
    250, 452–453
  separation of sexes, families, 96,
    177–178, 392, 402, 417

SAMANTHA POWER, currently the U.S. ambassador to the United Nations, served from 2009 to 2013 as the Special Assistant to President Barack Obama and Senior Director for Multilateral Affairs and Human Rights at the National Security Council. She was the founding executive director of the Carr Center for Human Rights Policy at the Harvard Kennedy School and is also the author of *Chasing the Flame: Sergio Viera de Mello and the Fight to Save the World*—the basis for the award-winning HBO documentary, "Sergio"—and the co-editor of *The Unquiet American: Richard Holbrooke in the World*. A former Balkan war correspondent and a recipient of the National Magazine Award and the Pulitzer Prize, Power lives in New York City.